W9-CIC-224

NTC's
Super-Mini
ENGLISH
Dictionary

NTC's
Super-Mini
ENGLISH
Dictionary

McGraw-Hill

Chicago New York San Francisco Lisbon London Madrid Mexico City
Milan New Delhi San Juan Seoul Singapore Sydney Toronto

Library of Congress Cataloging-in-Publication Data

Spears, Richard A.
    NTC's super-mini English dictionary / Richard A. Spears.
        p.   cm.
    ISBN 0-07-138748-X
    1. English language—Dictionaries.   I. Title: Super-mini English
dictionary.   II. Title

    PE1628 .S5828   2002
    423—dc21   2001055891

McGraw-Hill

A Division of The McGraw-Hill Companies

1 2 3 4 5 6 7 8 9 0   TCP/TCP   1 0 9 8 7 6 5 4 3 2

ISBN 0-07-138748-X

This book was set in Minion
Printed and bound by Transcontinental Printing

Cover design by Nick Panos
Interior design by Terry Stone

McGraw-Hill books are available at special quantity discounts to use as
premiums and sales promotions, or for use in corporate training programs.
For more information, please write to the Director of Special Sales,
Professional Publishing, McGraw-Hill, Two Penn Plaza, New York, NY
10121-2298. Or contact your local bookstore.

This book is printed on acid-free paper.

Contents

Introduction

NTC's Super-Mini English Dictionary is for persons who are seeking to improve their ability to speak, read, write, and understand American English. It is a small, portable dictionary that will help with spelling, pronunciation, part of speech, meaning, irregular forms, and the appropriate use of 8,200 senses of 7,600 common words. This dictionary defines words using the smallest possible vocabulary, but when necessary, uses additional words to define difficult concepts. In many cases, more than one definition is given to help in figuring out the meaning of a word or expression.

Many of the entry words in the dictionary have more than one sense. *Please study all the relevant senses* to make sure you have found the right one.

Nominals (*n.*) that do not follow the regular spelling or pronunciation rules in the formation of the plural are marked *irreg.*, and the form of the plural is given in the entry. Verbs (*tv., iv.*) that do not follow the regular rules for the formation of the past tense and past participle are marked *irreg.*, and the proper forms are given in the entry. The comparative and superlative forms of adjectives (*adj.*) and adverbs (*adv.*) are listed when there are forms—as with *red, redder, reddest*—that replace, or that exist in addition to, the comparatives and superlatives formed with *more* and *most*. After many of the definitions, you will find comments, enclosed in parentheses, containing further information about the entry word.

Useful Spelling Rules

The following basic spelling rules equip the learner to create and identify the most important derived and inflected forms of regular English nouns and verbs. Words that have important irregular forms that do not follow these rules are identified in the dictionary.

Regular Verb Forms

Note: Many verbs that have irregular past-tense forms or irregular past participles nevertheless form the present tense and the present participle regularly.

For the third-person singular (the form used with *he, she, it,* and singular nouns) in the present tense:

■ Add *-s* to the bare verb. If the bare verb ends in *y* preceded by a consonant, change *y* to *ie* and then add *-s*. If the bare verb ends in *s, z, x, ch,* or *sh,* add *-es.*

like > Bill likes
cry > the baby cries
walk > Anne walks
buy > the man buys
carry > a truck carries
fix > she fixes
pass > it passes
notify > he notifies
catch > she catches

For the past tense and the past participle:

■ Add *-ed* to the bare verb. If the bare verb ends in *y* preceded by a consonant, change *y* to *i* before adding *-ed*. If the bare verb ends in *e*, just add *-d*.

walk > walked
like > liked
judge > judged
try > tried
carry > carried
measure > measured

For the present participle:

■ Add *-ing* to the bare verb. If the bare verb ends in a single *e* preceded either by a consonant or by *u*, drop the *e* before adding *-ing*. If the bare verb ends in *ie*, change *ie* to *y* before adding *-ing*.

judge > judging
take > taking
ask > asking
carry > carrying
pay > paying
pursue > pursuing
hoe > hoeing
see > seeing
go > going
lie > lying

Doubling of consonants in participles and past-tense forms:

■ When *-ed* or *-ing* is added to a word that ends in a consonant (other than *h*, *w*, *x*, or *y*) preceded by a single vowel, and the final syllable is stressed, then the consonant is normally doubled. Thus *commit* and *control*, which are accented on the last syllable, become *committed* and *controlling*, but *limit* and *cancel*, which are accented on the first syllable, become *limited* and *canceling*. Similarly, *stop* becomes *stopping*, but *look*, in which the consonant is preceded by two vowels, becomes *looking*.

Within the dictionary, forms that do not follow these doubling rules are noted in individual entries. The most typical exceptions to the doubling rules are words with a final *c* that becomes *ck* rather than doubling (e.g., *picnicking*), verbs that are compounds, and verbs with closely related noun senses or more than one pronunciation. Outside the dictionary, learners will encounter other exceptions. Variation also occurs, because sometimes another option is correct, although less familiar in American English than the option given here.

Regular Noun Plurals

To form the plural of a regular noun:

- If the singular form ends in *s*, *z*, *x*, *ch*, or *sh*, add *-es*.

  kiss > kisses
  box > boxes
  match > matches
  dish > dishes
  bus > buses

- If the singular form ends in *y* preceded by a consonant, change *y* to *ie* and then add *-s*.

  baby > babies
  library > libraries
  university > universities
  butterfly > butterflies

- For nouns ending in *o*, the regular plural form may be formed by adding *-es* or by adding *-s*. For some words, both spellings are possible. In this dictionary, each entry for a noun ending in *o* specifies the correct plural form or forms for that word.

  radio > radios
  potato > potatoes
  tornado > tornados or *tornadoes*

■ For all other regular nouns, add -s to the singular form to make the plural.

table > *tables*
boy > *boys*
television > *televisions*
valley > *valleys*

An Important Note on the English Plural

The English plural makes English very difficult for adults to learn. Many English nouns cannot be made plural, unlike their counterparts in other languages. Nothing sounds more "non-English" than *advice*, *information*, or *baggage* with the plural *s* on the end. Among the American English nouns in this dictionary, there are many that the learner should not attempt to make plural—ever! In addition, many of the nouns that can be followed by the plural *s* seem to be plural but really refer to *kinds* or *types* of the noun in question. For example, when the word *margarine* has an *s* on the end, it refers to different kinds, types, or varieties of margarine.

> **margarine** [ˈmɑr dʒə rɪn] *n.* a food made from animal or vegetable fats, used in place of butter; a spread for bread. (Pl only for types and instances.)

Many American English nouns can take the plural *s* while only referring to different kinds, types, instances, or varieties of the noun.

Pronunciation

The symbols of the International Phonetic Alphabet are used to show the pronunciation of the words in this dictionary. The speech represented here is that of educated people, but it is not formal or overly precise. It is more representative of the West and the middle of the country than of the East, South, or upper Midwest.

Pronunciation of American English is variable in different regions of the country, but most native speakers of American English can understand one another quite well.

The goal of the pronunciation scheme is to provide the student with one acceptable model of pronunciation for each entry. Where the numbered senses of an entry are all pronounced the same way, the phonetic representation follows the main entry word. In entries where even one of the numbered senses is pronounced differently from the rest, all the senses are provided with a phonetic representation.

Sounds represented here as [or] are often pronounced as [ɔr] in some parts of the East. Similarly, the sequence [ɛr] is often pronounced [ær] in parts of the East. One heavy stress is marked for most words. The dictionary user should expect to hear variation in the pronunciation of most of the words listed in this or any dictionary, but should remain confident that the model provided here is understood and accepted in all parts of the country.

The chart on the next page shows the symbols used here and what they correspond to in some simple English words.

$[\alpha]$	stop top	$[\Lambda]$	nut shut	$[n]$	new funny	$[\theta]$	thin faith
$[æ]$	sat track	$[\mathord{\vartheta}^\iota]$	bird turtle	$[\eta]$	bring thing	$[u]$	food blue
$[\alpha\upsilon]$	cow now	$[f]$	feel if	$[o]$	coat wrote	$[\upsilon]$	put look
$[\alpha\iota]$	bite my	$[g]$	get frog	$[\mathord{o}\iota]$	spoil boy	$[v]$	save van
$[b]$	beet bubble	$[h]$	hat who	$[\mathord{o}]$	caught yawn	$[w]$	well wind
$[d]$	dead body	$[i]$	feet leak	$[p]$	tip pat	$[\mathtt{m}]$	wheel while
$[\eth]$	that those	$[\iota]$	bit hiss	$[r]$	rat berry	$[z]$	fuzzy zoo
$[d\mathord{\textyogh}]$	jail judge	$[j]$	yellow you	$[s]$	sun fast	$[\mathord{\textyogh}]$	pleasure treasure
$[e]$	date sail	$[k]$	can keep	$[\int]$	fish sure	$[']$	'water ho'tel
$[\varepsilon]$	get set	$[l]$	lawn yellow	$[t]$	top pot		
$[\mathord{\vartheta}]$	above around	$[m]$	family slam	$[t\int]$	cheese pitcher		

xv

Terms, Abbreviations, and Symbols

①, ②, ③, **etc.** a number within a circle refers to the sense number of a word. The circled number by itself refers to a sense within the entry in which the circled number is found.

~ the swung dash stands for the entryhead at the beginning of the entryblock in which the swung dash was found.

acronym a word made from the initial letters of a phrase, such as SCUBA, self-contained underwater breathing apparatus

adj. adjective; adjectival

adv. adverb; adverbial

aux. auxiliary

colloquial of a word or phrase that is more appropriate for speech rather than formal writing

comp comparative

conj. conjunction

cont. contraction

e.g. for example, by way of example

emphasis intensity, force, or special importance as shown by a word

euphemistic of a word or phrase that is better, more pleasing, or more polite than a word or phrase it is used as a replacement for

fig. figurative

interj. interjection

interrog. interrogative

irreg. irregular

iv. intransitive verb

n. noun; nominal

objective of the form of a pronoun that serves as the object of a verb or preposition

part. participle

phr. phrase

pl plural

pp past participle

prep. preposition

pres. present

pron. pronoun

pt past tense

reflexive of a sense of transitive verb that requires an object that refers to the same being as the subject refers to, as in *one must apply oneself*

sg singular

subjective of the form of a pronoun that serves as the subject of a verb

sup superlative

taboo of an offensive word or phrase usually avoided in polite speaking or writing

tv. transitive verb

A

a 1. ['e] *n.* the first in a series; the highest grade. (Capitalized. Note: Use A before words that begin with a consonant sound; use AN before words that begin with a vowel sound.) **2.** ['e, ə] *article* one; any. (See also AN.) **3.** ['e, ə] *prep.* each; every; per. (See also AN.)

abandon [ə 'bæn dən] *tv.* to leave someone or something and not return; to desert someone or something.

abbreviation [ə bri vi 'e ʃən] *n.* a shortened word or phrase that takes the place of a longer word or phrase.

abdomen ['æb də mən] *n.* the part of the body between the chest and the legs and the internal organs within it.

ability [ə 'bɪl ə ti] *n.* the power, capacity, or skill to do something.

able ['e bəl] *adj.* skilled; well qualified; capable. (Adv: *ably.*)

abode [ə 'bod] *n.* the place where one lives.

about [ə 'baʊt] **1.** *prep.* regarding someone or something; concerning someone or something; having to do with someone or something. **2.** *adv.* approximately; nearly. **3.** *adv.* almost; not quite. **4.** ~ **to do** almost ready to do something.

above [ə 'bʌv] **1.** *prep.* over—but not touching—someone or something. **2.** *prep.* greater than something; higher than something; more than something. **3.** *adv.* [written about or presented] previously [in the same written work or on the same page]. **4.** *adv.* in or at a higher place; over. **5.** *adv.* of a greater amount or quantity. **6.** ~ **average** higher or better than the general level of quality. **7.** ~ **par** better than average or normal.

abroad [ə 'brɔd] *adv.* in another country; overseas.

absence ['æb səns] **1.** *n.* the quality of [someone's] not being present. (No pl.) **2.** *n.* a period of time when someone is not present. **3.** *n.* a lack; a deficiency. (No pl.)

absent ['æb sənt] **1.** *adj.* not present at a place; away from a place. **2.** *adj.* not in existence; not evident; not present or visible. **3.** *adj.* [appearing] vague or not interested. (Adv: *absently.*)

absorb [əb 'zɔrb] **1.** *tv.* to soak up a liquid. **2.** *tv.* to learn something; to take in new information; to learn something easily. (Fig. on ①.)

1

absorbent [əb 'zɔr bənt] *adj.* able to soak up liquids. (Adv: *absorbently.*)

abundant [ə 'bʌn dənt] *adj.* full; brimming; in large amounts. (Adv: *abundantly.*)

abuse 1. [ə 'bjuz] *tv.* to harm someone in some way, such as physically or emotionally; to use something in a way that damages it. **2.** [ə 'bjuz] *tv.* to use something badly or improperly. **3.** [ə 'bjus] *n.* unfair or cruel treatment of someone; action that damages something. (No pl form in this sense.) **4.** [ə 'bjus] *n.* improper use. (No pl form in this sense.)

accent ['æk sɛnt] **1.** *n.* the force or stress put on a word or a part of a word during speech. **2.** *n.* a mark written over a letter of the alphabet that gives the letter a special pronunciation or stress. **3.** *n.* a way of speaking a language, and especially of pronouncing a language. **4.** *tv.* to emphasize something, especially to put ① on a word or a part of a word during speech.

accept [æk 'sɛpt] *tv.* to take something that is offered. (Compare this with EXCEPT. The object can be a clause with THAT ⑦.)

acceptable [æk 'sɛp tə bəl] *adj.* worth accepting; satisfactory; good enough. (Adv: *acceptably.*)

accident ['æk sɪ dənt] *n.* an unexpected event, usually involving harm to someone or something.

accidental [æk sɪ 'dɛn təl] *adj.* not on purpose; done or happening by mistake. (Adv: *accidentally.*)

accomplish [ə 'kɑm plɪʃ] *tv.* to finish something; to successfully complete something.

accomplishment [ə 'kɑm plɪʃ mənt] *n.* something that has been completed or achieved; a success.

according to [ə 'kɔrd ɪŋ tu] **1.** as stated by someone; as indicated by something. **2.** in proportion to something.

account [ə 'kaʊnt] **1.** *n.* a report; a description; one's version of what happened in an event. **2.** *n.* a record of income [or money received] and expenses [or money paid out] assigned to a particular person, business, or class of transactions.

accountant [ə 'kaʊnt nt] *n.* someone who is responsible for maintaining financial records or accounts; someone who prepares tax records.

accuracy [ˈæk jə rə si] *n.* correctness; the degree of freedom from errors. (No pl.)

accurate [ˈæk jə rət] *adj.* correct; exact; without error. (Adv: *accurately.*)

accuse [ə ˈkjuz] *tv.* to claim or charge that someone has done something, usually something wrong or illegal.

accustom to [ə ˈkʌs təm tu] to cause someone or something to become familiar with something.

ache [ˈek] 1. *n.* a pain; a soreness. 2. *iv.* to hurt; to be sore.

achieve [ə ˈtʃiv] 1. *tv.* to accomplish what was intended; to gain or get something. 2. *iv.* to advance; to get ahead.

acknowledgment [æk ˈnɑl ɪdʒ mənt] 1. *n.* admission; stating that something is so. (No pl.) 2. *n.* the recognition given to someone for doing something well. 3. *n.* a report of having received something.

acquire [ə ˈkwaɪr] *tv.* to get something; to receive something.

across [ə ˈkrɔs] 1. *prep.* from one side of something to the other side. 2. *prep.* on the other side of something. 3. *adv.* to the other side of something.

act [ˈækt] 1. *n.* a division of a play or musical. 2. *n.* one of many short performances within a longer program. 3. *n.* something that is done; an instance of doing something. 4. *n.* a law. 5. *iv.* to perform in a play, film, TV program, or similar performance. 6. *iv.* to behave in a certain way; to behave as if one is or feels a certain way. 7. ~ **up** [for a thing or a person] to behave badly.

action [ˈæk ʃən] 1. *n.* activity; movement. (Pl only for types and instances.) 2. *n.* the plot of a story; the events that happen in a story. (No pl.)

active [ˈæk tɪv] 1. *adj.* moving; functioning; operating. (Adv: *actively.*) 2. *adj.* lively; moving at a rapid, steady pace; busy. (Adv: *actively.*) 3. *adj.* of or about sentences in which the subject does the action that is expressed in the verb. (The opposite of PASSIVE ②. Adv: *actively.*)

activity [æk ˈtɪv ə ti] *n.* action; movement; doing something.

actor [ˈæk tɚ] *n.* a performer, male or female, in a play, musical, or movie. (See also ACTRESS.)

actress [ˈæk trəs] *n.* a female performer in a play, musical, or movie. (See also ACTOR.)

actual [ˈæk tʃu əl] *adj.* real; existing. (Adv: *actually.*)

3

actually ['æk tʃ(u) ə li] *adv.* in fact; really.

ad ['æd] *n.* an ADVERTISEMENT.

adapt [ə 'dæpt] **1.** *iv.* to change or modify to fit in; to adjust to new conditions. **2.** *tv.* to change or modify something to fit with something else; to adjust something to new conditions.

add ['æd] *tv.* to join something to something else; to include something with something else.

addition [ə 'dɪ ʃən] **1.** *n.* the adding together of two or more numbers. (Pl only for types and instances.) **2.** *n.* putting someone or something into something else. (Pl only for types and instances.)

additional [ə 'dɪʃ ə nəl] *adj.* extra; [something] further; more; added. (Adv: *additionally.*)

address 1. ['æ drɛs, ə 'drɛs] *n.* the street name and number, city, state, and other information telling the location of something, such as a building or house. **2.** [ə 'drɛs] *n.* a formal speech. **3.** [ə 'drɛs] *tv.* to write the street name, number, city, state, and other information on an envelope or package. **4.** [ə 'drɛs] *tv.* to speak directly to a person or a group of people. **5.** [ə 'drɛs] *tv.* to respond to a question; to say something about an issue or problem.

adequate ['æd ə kwɪt] *adj.* just enough but not more than enough; good enough. (Adv: *adequately.*)

adhesive [æd 'hi sɪv] **1.** *adj.* sticky; designed to stick to things. (Adv: *adhesively.*) **2.** *n.* glue; paste. (Pl only for types and instances.)

adj. an abbreviation of ADJECTIVE.

adjective ['æ dʒɛk tɪv] *n.* a word that describes or modifies a noun or nominal.

adjust [ə 'dʒʌst] **1.** *tv.* to change something in a small way in order to try to make it work or fit better. **2.** *iv.* to become used to someone or something; to adapt to someone or something.

adjustable [ə 'dʒʌst ə bəl] *adj.* changeable; able to be changed in small amounts. (Adv: *adjustably.*)

administer [æd 'mɪn ɪs tə·] **1.** *tv.* to manage something. **2.** *tv.* to give or dispense something, such as medicine, medical care, or justice, to someone.

administration [æd mɪn ɪ 'stre ʃən] **1.** *n.* the work of managing and directing. (No pl.) **2.** *n.* the office and staff of a high-ranking elected official, such as a president, governor, or mayor. **3.** *n.* a group of people who manage something.

4

admiration [æd mə 're ʃən] *n.* a feeling of pride, pleasure, and respect for someone or something. (No pl.)

admire [æd 'maɪ&] *tv.* to regard someone or something with pride, pleasure, and respect.

admit [æd 'mɪt] **1.** *tv.* to allow someone or something to enter into someplace. **2.** *tv.* to allow someone to become a member of a club or organization. **3.** *tv.* to say that one has done something one is accused of; to say that something is true. (The object can be a clause with THAT ⑦.)

adolescence [æd ə 'lɛs əns] *n.* the period of time between being a child and being an adult; the teenage years.

adolescent [æd ə 'lɛs ənt] **1.** *n.* a teenager; someone who is older than a child but not yet an adult. **2.** the *adj.* use of ①.

adopt [ə 'dɑpt] **1.** *iv.* to become the parent or parents of a child through legal proceedings. **2.** *tv.* to gain possession of and become responsible for the child of someone else, through the legal system. **3.** *tv.* to acquire a new practice, belief, or habit.

adoption [ə 'dɑp ʃən] **1.** *n.* acquiring and becoming responsible for the child of someone else, through the legal system. (Pl only for types and instances.) **2.** *n.* acquiring a new practice, belief, or habit. (No pl.)

adorable [ə 'dor ə bəl] *adj.* very cute; worthy of being adored. (Adv: *adorably.*)

adore [ə 'dor] *tv.* to admire and be fond of someone or something.

adult [ə 'dʌlt] **1.** *adj.* mature; fully grown; fully developed. **2.** *adj.* showing the behavior of a mature person. **3.** *adj.* intended for persons who are mature. (Often used referring to sex and violence in entertainment.) **4.** *n.* someone or something that is fully grown.

adv. an abbreviation of ADVERB.

advance [æd 'væns] **1.** *n.* a forward motion. **2.** *n.* money that is given to someone ahead of schedule or before it is earned; a loan taken against money that is to be paid at a later time. **3.** *iv.* to progress or move forward; to move to a higher or better level. **4.** *tv.* to move someone or something forward or to a higher level. **5.** *tv.* to give someone money ahead of schedule or before it is earned. **6.** *adj.* prior; before the event. (Prenominal only.)

advantage [æd 'væn tɪdʒ] *n.* something good or useful that will help someone with something; a benefit.

5

adventure [æd 'vɛn tʃɚ] *n.* excitement; challenge. (Pl only for types and instances.)

adverb ['æd vɚb] *n.* a word that modifies or describes a verb, a verb phrase, an adjective, a sentence, or another adverb. (Abbreviated *adv.* here.)

advertise ['æd vɚ taɪz] **1.** *iv.* to make [something] known to the public, especially through signs, television, radio, newspapers, or magazines. **2.** *tv.* to make something known to the public through signs, television, radio, newspapers, magazines, or other means; to publicize something. (The object can be a clause with THAT ⑦.)

advertisement [æd vɚ 'taɪz mənt] *n.* a commercial; a notice about something, displayed to the public.

advice [æd 'vaɪs] *n.* recommendations or suggestions provided to help someone. (Compare this with ADVISE. No pl. Number is expressed with *piece(s)* or *bit(s) of advice*.)

advise [æd 'vaɪz] *tv.* to give [someone] a particular kind of advice; to suggest doing something. (The object can be a clause with THAT ⑦.)

advocate 1. ['æd vo ket] *tv.* to be in favor of something and argue for it. **2.** ['æd və kət] *n.* someone who does ①.

affair [ə 'fer] **1.** *n.* a matter that needs attention; business. **2.** *n.* a temporary, intimate relationship between two people who are not married to each other. **3.** *n.* a party; a social function.

affect [ə 'fɛkt] **1.** *tv.* to influence someone or something; to have an effect on someone or something. (Compare this with EFFECT.) **2.** *tv.* to display or exhibit a kind of behavior, especially by pretending or imitating.

affection [ə 'fɛk ʃən] *n.* love, caring, or fondness. (No pl.)

affirmative [ə 'fɚ mə tɪv] *adj.* meaning *yes.*

afford [ə 'ford] *tv.* to be able to buy something.

afraid [ə 'fred] *adj.* fearful of someone or something; scared of someone or something. (Not prenominal.)

after ['æf tɚ] **1.** *conj.* later in time than when something happens; when something has finished happening. **2.** *prep.* at a later time than something; later in time than something. **3.** *prep.* further along in a sequence or series than someone or something. **4.** *prep.* in the name of someone; in honor of someone; for someone. **5.** *adv.* behind; to the rear; following.

6

afternoon [æf tɚ 'nun] **1.** *n.* the time of day from noon until the evening. **2.** the *adj.* use of ①. **3.** ~s *adv.* every AFTERNOON.

afterward(s) ['æf tɚ wɚd(z)] *adv.* after; following; later.

again [ə 'gɛn] **1.** *adv.* once more; another time. **2.** *adv.* as [something was] before.

against [ə 'gɛnst] **1.** *prep.* in opposition to someone or something; as an opponent of someone or something. **2.** *prep.* in a direction opposite to something. **3.** *prep.* coming toward and meeting someone or something. **4.** *prep.* [leaning or tilting and] in contact with someone or something.

age ['edʒ] **1.** *n.* the amount of time that someone or something has been alive or in existence. (No pl.) **2.** *n.* advanced ①; evidence of much ①; oldness. (No pl.) **3.** *n.* the specific ① of a person, usually given as a number of years; the specific ① of something. **4.** *n.* [for a person] the condition of having a certain ③; the time when a person has a certain ③. (The number comes after *age* and refers to years, unless some other measure is given, such as months, weeks, or days.) **5.** *n.* a period or stage of life. **6.** *n.* a period of history; a generation; an era. **7.** *iv.* to become old; to show increasing ①. **8.** *iv.* [for cheese, wine, whiskey, beef, etc.] to mature; to reach a peak of quality, taste, and strength. **9.** *tv.* to cause someone or something to grow old or appear old.

agent ['e dʒənt] **1.** *n.* someone who represents someone else; someone who sells certain things such as insurance, travel, tickets, land, buildings, etc. **2.** *n.* something that causes someone or something else to do something; something that causes some result to happen. **3.** *n.* a spy.

ago [ə 'go] *adj.* in the past; [time] already gone by. (After a noun that expresses a length of time.)

agony ['æg ə ni] *n.* an intense, deep pain in the mind or the body; a deep suffering. (Pl only for types and instances.)

agree [ə 'gri] **1.** *iv.* [for people] to be in harmony or have the same opinion; [for people] to have no conflict of opinion or desire. **2.** *iv.* [for facts or things] to be consistent or to harmonize. **3.** *iv.* [for a form of a word] to match the form of another word grammatically. **4.** *tv.* to decide together that something is true or should happen; to accept someone's opinion that something is true or should happen. (The object can be a clause with THAT ⑦.) **5.** ~ **to** to consent to something; to approve something. **6.** ~ **(up)on** to agree to the choice of someone or something. **7.** ~ **with** to hold the same opinion as some-

7

one else. **8.** ~ **with** to look good or go well with; to be in accord with.

agreeable [ə ˈgri ə bəl] **1.** *adj.* pleasant; satisfactory. (Adv: *agreeably.*) **2.** *adj.* acceptable.

agreement [ə ˈgri mənt] *n.* a state of agreeing; holding the same opinion as someone else; a state of accepting a proposal.

ahead [ə ˈhɛd] **1.** *adv.* into the future; [preparing] for the future. **2.** *adv.* forward; continuing in the same direction. **3.** *adv.* into an advanced position; into a better position. **4.** ~ **of** at a place in front of or in advance of; earlier than.

aid [ˈed] **1.** *n.* help; assistance; support. (No pl.) **2.** *n.* something that helps someone or something else. **3.** *tv.* to provide someone or something with ①.

aim [ˈem] **1.** *tv.* to point something toward a target or a goal. **2.** *n.* a goal; a purpose; an intention. **3.** *n.* the accurate pointing or directing of something. (No pl.) **4.** ~ **at** to point or direct at.

air [ˈer] **1.** *n.* the mixture of gases that surrounds the earth; the mixture of gases that people normally breathe. (No pl.) **2.** *n.* a mood or atmosphere. (No pl.) **3.** *tv.* to express a view or an opinion in public; to make something known.

air conditioner [ˈer kən dɪ ʃən ɚ] *n.* a machine that cools indoor air.

aircraft [ˈer kræft] *n., irreg.* a machine, such as an airplane or a helicopter, that flies in the air. (Pl: *aircraft.*)

airline [ˈer laɪn] *n.* a company that operates a number of aircraft for passengers or cargo.

airmail [ˈer mel] **1.** *n.* a system for sending international mail by airplane. (No pl.) **2.** *adv.* [sending mail] by ①. **3.** *tv.* to send something by ①.

airplane [ˈer plen] *n.* a heavier-than-air vehicle that flies through the air.

airport [ˈer port] *n.* a place where airplanes land and take off.

aisle [ˈaɪl] *n.* a walkway between rows of seats, as in a theater, or between rows of shelves, as in a supermarket.

alarm [ə ˈlɑrm] **1.** *n.* a warning sound or signal. **2.** *n.* a device that makes a warning sound or signal. **3.** *n.* excitement, anxiety, or shock. (No pl.) **4.** *n.* a clock that has a bell or other signal that is sounded to wake someone up. **5.** *tv.* to frighten or scare someone; to make someone afraid or fearful of danger.

alcohol ['æl kə hɔl] **1.** *n.* a liquid chemical used to make wounds and skin very clean or sterile or to dissolve substances. (Pl only for types and instances.) **2.** *n.* the substance found in beer, wine, and hard liquors that causes someone to be drunk. (Pl only for types and instances.) **3.** *n.* beer, wine, whiskey, spirits; drinks that contain ②. (No pl.)

alert [ə 'lɚt] **1.** *adj.* wary; aware; watchful. (Adv: *alertly*.) **2.** *tv.* to warn someone about something, especially danger.

algebra ['æl dʒə brə] *n.* a branch of mathematics using letters and other symbols to represent numbers or sets of numbers in equations. (No pl.)

alike [ə 'laɪk] **1.** *adj.* similar; the same or almost the same. (Not prenominal.) **2.** *adv.* in the same way. **3.** *adv.* equally; in the same amount or degree.

alive [ə 'laɪv] **1.** *adj.* living; not dead. (Not prenominal.) **2.** *adj.* active, lively, or full of energy. (Fig. on ①. Not prenominal.)

all ['ɔl] **1.** *adj.* each and every one [of the people or things]; the full amount [of something]; the whole extent of [something]. **2.** *adj.* the greatest amount possible [of something]. **3.** *pron.* everything or everyone mentioned earlier in the conversation or writing. (Treated as sg or pl.) **4.** *pron.* everything. (Treated as sg.) **5.** *adv.* completely.

allergy ['æl ɚ dʒi] *n.* a physical response to a substance—an allergen—causing sneezing, itching, a rash, or other symptoms.

alley ['æl i] **1.** *n.* a narrow road or pathway behind or between buildings. **2.** *n.* a place where bowling is done, a *bowling alley*.

alligator ['æl ə get ɚ] *n.* a large reptile of the crocodile family.

allow [ə 'laʊ] *tv.* to make sure that there is a certain amount of time for something to be done.

allowance [ə 'laʊ əns] **1.** *n.* an amount of something, such as money, given to someone. **2.** *n.* an amount of something—time, forgiveness, tolerance—that is provided or allowed for someone or something.

almost ['ɔl most] *adv.* nearly, but not quite.

aloft [ə 'lɔft] **1.** *adj.* in a higher place; in the air. (Not prenominal.) **2.** *adv.* to a higher place; into the air.

alone [ə 'lon] **1.** *adj.* by oneself; having no one else nearby. (Not prenominal.) **2.** *adv.* by oneself; with no help.

along [ə 'lɔŋ] **1.** *prep.* next to something for a distance; in a path next to something. **2.** ~ **with** in addition to; together with.

9

aloof [ə 'luf] *adj.* unfriendly; reserved; unsympathetic. (Adv: *aloofly.*)

aloud [ə 'laʊd] *adv.* audibly; [of speech] spoken so that it can be heard.

alphabet ['æl fə bɛt] *n.* the list of letters—in proper order—used to write a language.

alphabetical [æl fə 'bɛt ɪ kəl] *adj.* arranged in the order of the letters in the alphabet. (Adv: *alphabetically* [...ɪk li].)

alphabetize ['æl fə bə taɪz] *tv.* to place words in the same order as the letters of the alphabet.

already [ɔl 'rɛd i] *adv.* by now; by this point in time; previously. (This is different from *all ready.*)

also ['ɔl so] *adv.* as well; too; in addition.

altar ['ɔl tɚ] *n.* a table used in religious ceremonies. (Compare with ALTER.)

alter ['ɔl tɚ] *tv.* to change something; to make something different. (Compare with ALTAR.)

alteration [ɔl tə 're ʃən] **1.** *n.* change caused intentionally. (No pl form in this sense.) **2.** *n.* the result of a change.

although [ɔl 'ðo] *conj.* even though; despite; in spite of.

altogether ['ɔl tə gɛð ɚ] *adv.* completely. (Different from *all together.*)

aluminum [ə 'lum ə nəm] **1.** *n.* a metal that is lightweight and does not rust easily. (No pl.) **2.** *adj.* made of ①.

always ['ɔl wez] **1.** *adv.* every time; each time. **2.** *adv.* forever; without end.

am ['æm] *iv., irreg.* the first-person present sg form of BE. (Reduced to *'m* in the contraction I'M.)

amaze [ə 'mez] *tv.* to cause wonder in someone; to astound or astonish someone.

ambulance ['æm bjə ləns] *n.* a vehicle for taking sick or injured people to the hospital.

amend [ə 'mɛnd] *tv.* to change something; to modify something (especially laws).

amendment [ə 'mɛnd mənt] *n.* a change made by correcting or adding to something.

America [ə 'mɛr ɪ kə] **1.** *n.* the continents of the New World. **2.** *n.* the United States of America. **3. the ~s** *n.* North and South America. (Treated as pl.)

amid [ə 'mɪd] *prep.* in the midst of; during.

among [ə 'mʌŋ] **1.** *prep.* in the midst of people or things; surrounded by things or people. **2.** *prep.* within a group; within a set of choices. (Use BETWEEN with two people or things. Use AMONG with more than two.)

amount [ə 'maʊnt] **1.** *n.* how much there is of something; the quantity. **2.** *iv.* to be equal to a numerical figure; to total up to something. **3.** ~ **to** to become worthwhile or valuable.

amphibian [æm 'fɪb i ən] *n.* a kind of animal, such as a frog, that lives in water and on land.

ample ['æm pəl] *adj.* large enough; sufficient and adequate. (Adv: *amply*. Comp: *ampler*; sup: *amplest*.)

amputation [æm pjə 'te ʃən] *n.* the removal of all or part of an arm, a leg, a finger, or a toe. (Pl only for types and instances.)

amuse [ə 'mjuz] *tv.* to make someone laugh or smile; to give someone pleasure.

amusement [ə 'mjuz mənt] **1.** *n.* happiness; pleasure; enjoyment. (No pl.) **2.** *n.* something that makes someone happy; entertainment.

an ['æn] **1.** *article* one; any. (Note: Use A before words that begin with a consonant sound; use AN before words that begin with a vowel sound.) **2.** *prep.* each; per. (See note at ①.)

analyses [ə 'næl ə siz] pl of ANALYSIS.

analysis [ə 'næl ə sɪs] **1.** *n.* the process of analyzing or of examining something very closely. (No pl form in this sense.) **2.** *n., irreg.* an in-depth examination of an issue or topic. (Pl: ANALYSES.) **3.** *n.* psychoanalysis. (No pl form in this sense.)

analyze ['æn ə laɪz] *tv.* to examine the details of something.

ancestor ['æn sɛs tə] *n.* a person, usually no longer living, from whom a person descends.

anchor ['æŋ kə] **1.** *n.* a heavy object, attached to a ship or boat, that catches on the sea bottom to keep the ship or boat from drifting away. **2.** *n.* something that holds something else in place. **3.** *n.* a newscaster; a central newscaster who introduces news reports from other people. **4.** *tv.* to keep a ship in place by lowering ① into the water. **5.** *tv.* to secure something; to hold something in place. **6.** *iv.* [for a ship] to remain in a place by dropping ①.

ancient ['en tʃənt] **1.** *adj.* from long ago in history. **2.** *adj.* very old. **3.** *n.* someone who lived long ago.

11

and ['ænd] **1.** *conj.* in addition to; plus; also. **2.** *conj.* then; as a result.

angel ['en dʒəl] **1.** *n.* a heavenly being; a messenger of God. **2.** *n.* a very kind, sweet person. (Fig. on ①.)

anger ['æŋ gɚ] **1.** *n.* strong feelings of annoyance and being upset. (No pl.) **2.** *tv.* to upset someone; to annoy someone very much.

angle ['æŋ gəl] **1.** *n.* a figure formed where two lines or surfaces come together. **2.** *n.* a point of view; a way of looking at an issue or idea. (Informal.) **3.** *tv.* to place two surfaces or lines so that they intersect. **4.** *iv.* to turn, perhaps sharply.

angry ['æŋ gri] *adj.* irate; upset; annoyed. (Adv: *angrily.* Comp: *angrier*; sup: *angriest*.)

anguish ['æŋ gwɪʃ] *n.* mental pain or suffering; grief. (No pl.)

animal ['æn ə məl] **1.** *n.* a living creature that is not a plant. **2.** *adj.* from or containing ①. **3.** *adj.* relating to functions of the body instead of the mind.

ankle ['æŋ kəl] *n.* the joint that connects the foot with the leg.

anklebone ['æŋ kəl bon] *n.* the main bone of the ankle.

anniversary [æn ə 'vɚ sə ri] *n.* the annual commemoration of the date of an event that occurred in the past.

announce [ə 'nɑʊns] **1.** *tv.* to make something known to people. (The object can be a clause with THAT ⑦.) **2.** *tv.* to speak out the name of someone or something that is arriving.

announcement [ə 'nɑʊns mənt] *n.* a declaration; a public statement.

annoy [ə 'nɔɪ] *tv.* to bother or pester someone.

annual ['æn ju əl] *adj.* happening once a year; happening every year; happening yearly. (Adv: *annually.*)

anonymous [ə 'nɑn ə məs] *adj.* unnamed; from an unknown source; created or done without revealing the name or identity of the creator or doer. (Adv: *anonymously.*)

another [ə 'nʌð ɚ] **1.** *pron.* an additional one; a different one. **2.** *adj.* consisting of one more of the same kind; [an] additional [one]. (Prenominal only.)

answer ['æn sɚ] **1.** *n.* a reply; a response to a question; a solution to a problem on a test. **2.** *n.* a response to a situation; a way of solving a problem. **3.** *tv.* to give a response to something, such as a test question or a letter. **4.** *tv.* to reply to someone. (The object can be a clause with THAT ⑦.) **5.** *iv.* to give a reply.

12

ant ['ænt] *n.* a small insect that lives in a colony.

antenna [æn 'tɛn ə] **1.** *n.* a device that collects or receives electro-magnetic signals that have been broadcast, such as for radio or tele-vision. (Pl: *antennas*.) **2.** *n., irreg.* one of the sensitive feelers found in pairs on the heads of insects and some sea creatures. (Pl: ANTENNAE or *antennas*.)

antennae [æn 'tɛn i] a pl of ANTENNA ②.

antic ['æn tɪk] **1.** *n.* a playful or silly act. (Often pl.) **2.** *adj.* silly; play-ful. (Adv: *anticly* or *antically* […ɪk li].)

anticipate [æn 'tɪs ə pet] *tv.* to expect something to happen; to pre-pare for something that is expected to happen. (The object can be a clause with THAT ⑦.)

antique [æn 'tik] **1.** *adj.* old, especially if valuable; belonging to a time long ago. **2.** *n.* an object that was made long ago.

antonym ['æn tə nɪm] *n.* a word that means the opposite of another word.

anxiety [æŋ 'zaɪ ə ti] *n.* nervousness; worry. (Sg or pl with the same meaning. Not countable.)

anxious ['æŋk ʃəs] **1.** *adj.* nervous; worried; troubled, especially with a feeling of dread or concern. (Adv: *anxiously*.) **2.** *adj.* eager to do something; excited about doing something.

any ['ɛn i] **1.** *pron.* whichever one or ones. (To point out one from a group of two, use EITHER.) **2.** *pron.* even the smallest amount or num-ber. (Always in the negative or questions. Use SOME in affirmative statements or commands.) **3.** *adj.* whichever [one or ones]. (To point out one from a group of two, use EITHER.) **4.** *adj.* even the smallest amount or number [of something]. (Always in the negative or ques-tions. Use SOME in affirmative statements or commands.) **5.** *adv.* even the smallest amount.

anybody ['ɛn i bɑd i] **1.** *pron.* some person; any person; anyone; even one person. (Always in the negative or questions. Use SOMEBODY in affirmative statements or commands. No pl.) **2.** *n.* an important per-son. (Used in the negative or questions; use SOMEBODY in affirmative statements or commands. No pl.) **3.** *n.* any random person; whoever; no matter who. (No pl.)

anyhow ['ɛn i hɑʊ] *adv.* in any case; anyway; at any rate.

anymore [æn i 'mɔr] **1.** *adv.* at the present time in contrast to an ear-lier time. (This is different from *any more*. Usually in negative sen-

13

tences.) **2.** *adv.* nowadays; recently. (This is different from *any more*. Common but not standard English when used in affirmative sentences.)

anyone ['ɛn i wən] **1.** *pron.* some person; any person; anybody. (Always in the negative or questions. Use SOMEONE in the affirmative. No pl.) **2.** *n.* just any person; whoever; no matter who. (No pl.)

anyplace ['ɛn i ples] **1.** *adv.* no matter where; in, at, or to a place; wherever. **2.** *adv.* [not] in, at, or to any place; [not] in, at, or to even one place. (Always in the negative or questions. Use SOMEPLACE in the affirmative.)

anything ['ɛn i θɪŋ] **1.** *n.* any thing, object, or event. (No pl.) **2.** *n.* [not] a single thing; [not] even one thing, object, or event. (Always in the negative or questions. Use SOMETHING in the affirmative. No pl.) **3.** *adv.* in any way. (Always in the negative or questions.)

anytime ['ɛn i tɑɪm] *adv.* whenever; at any time; no matter when.

anyway ['ɛn i we] *adv.* in any case; anyhow; nevertheless; at any rate.

anywhere ['ɛn i ʌɛr] **1.** *adv.* anyplace; wherever; in, at, or to any place; in, at, or to an unnamed place; in, at, or to whatever place. **2.** *adv.* [not] somewhere; [not] in, at, or to even one place. (Always in the negative or questions. Use SOMEWHERE in affirmative statements and commands.)

apart [ə 'pɑrt] **1.** *adv.* not together; separately. **2.** *adv.* in pieces; into pieces.

apartment [ə 'pɑrt mənt] *n.* a place to live within a large building; living quarters.

ape ['ep] **1.** *n.* a large monkeylike mammal without a tail. **2.** *tv.* to copy or mock someone or something; to imitate someone or something.

apologize [ə 'pɑl ə dʒɑɪz] *iv.* to make an apology; to say that one is sorry.

apology [ə 'pɑl ə dʒi] *n.* a statement of regret for having done something.

apostrophe [ə 'pɑs trə fi] **1.** *n.* the mark of punctuation (') showing where one or more letters have been omitted. **2.** *n.* the mark of punctuation (') used to show possession in nouns. (In regular sg nouns, add the apostrophe plus an *s*. In regular pl nouns, add the apostrophe after the pl *s*.)

apparatus [æp ə 'ræt əs] *n.* a device; equipment. (No pl form in this sense. Number is expressed with *piece(s) of apparatus*.)

appeal [ə 'pil] **1.** *n.* a plea for help; a request. **2.** *n.* a legal request that a court decision be examined by a higher judge or court. **3.** *n.* attraction; something that draws someone or something closer. (No pl.) **4.** *tv.* to request that a court decision be examined by a higher judge or court. **5.** *iv.* to be attractive to someone.

appear [ə 'pɪr] **1.** *iv.* to become visible; to come into sight. **2.** *iv.* to seem to be a certain way; to look a certain way.

appearance [ə 'pɪr əns] **1.** *n.* the way someone or something looks. (No pl form in this sense.) **2.** *n.* an act of becoming a visible presence; becoming seen.

appendices [ə 'pɛn də siz] a pl of APPENDIX ②.

appendix [ə 'pɛn dɪks] **1.** *n.* a small growth at the end of the large intestine. (Pl: *appendixes.*) **2.** *n., irreg.* a section at the end of a book or document that gives additional information. (Pl: APPENDICES or *appendixes.*)

appetite ['æp ə taɪt] *n.* a desire for something, especially food or drink.

applaud [ə 'plɔd] **1.** *iv.* to clap the hands together to show appreciation or approval. **2.** *tv.* to show appreciation for someone or something by clapping one's hands together.

applause [ə 'plɔz] *n.* a show of approval by clapping one's hands together. (No pl.)

apple ['æp əl] *n.* a firm, round fruit that has red, green, or yellow skin and is white inside.

appliance [ə 'plaɪ əns] *n.* a machine, usually found in the home, with a specific function.

application [æ plə 'ke ʃən] **1.** *n.* applying for something. (No pl form in this sense.) **2.** *n.* an instance of ①. **3.** *n.* a printed form used in applying for something, such as a job. **4.** *n.* spreading something on something else. (No pl form in this sense.) **5.** *n.* a specific use for something.

apply [ə 'plaɪ] **1.** *tv.* to put or spread something on something else. **2.** *tv.* to use something; to make use of something. **3.** *tv.* to cause oneself to work or study hard. (Takes a reflexive object.) **4.** *iv.* to request something that requires approval—such as a loan, a job, or admission to a school—usually in writing or through some other formal process. **5.** *iv.* to be appropriate or relevant to someone or something.

15

appoint [ə 'pɔɪnt] **1.** *tv.* to choose someone for a job or position; to assign someone to a position. **2.** *tv.* to fill a vacant office, position, or job; to determine who will serve in an office, position, or job. **3.** *tv.* to set a time. **4.** ~ **to** to select or assign to serve in a particular role.

appointment [ə 'pɔɪnt mənt] **1.** *n.* choosing someone to fill a position or to take a job. (Pl only for types and instances.) **2.** *n.* an arranged meeting; an agreement to meet at a specific time and place.

appreciate [ə 'pri ʃi et] **1.** *tv.* to be grateful for someone or something; to value someone or something. (The object can be a clause with THAT ⑦.) **2.** *iv.* to increase in value.

appreciation [ə pri ʃi 'e ʃən] **1.** *n.* a feeling of being grateful for someone or something. (No pl.) **2.** *n.* the recognition of the value of something. (No pl.) **3.** *n.* a rise in value; an increase in value. (No pl.)

approach [ə 'protʃ] **1.** *tv.* to go near someone or something; to get closer to someone or something in time or space. **2.** *iv.* [for someone or something] to come closer in time or space. **3.** *n.* a way of solving a problem. **4.** *n.* an entrance; a path to something. **5.** *n.* an instance of [someone or something] coming closer.

appropriate **1.** [ə 'pro pri ɪt] *adj.* correct; suitable; proper. (Adv: *appropriately.*) **2.** [ə 'pro pri et] *tv.* to take something for one's own use; to steal something. **3.** [ə 'pro pri et] *tv.* to set aside money for a specific purpose; to budget funds.

approve [ə 'pruv] **1.** *iv.* to judge [someone or something] to be satisfactory or agreeable. **2.** *tv.* to grant approval of someone or something.

approximate **1.** [ə 'prak sə mət] *adj.* estimated; not exact. (Adv: *approximately.*) **2.** [ə 'prak sə met] *tv.* to estimate something; to guess the amount of something. **3.** [ə 'prak sə met] *tv.* to be similar to someone or something; to appear to be almost the same as someone or something.

apricot ['e prə kat] **1.** *n.* a soft, fuzzy, yellowish fruit that is smaller than a peach and has a large pit. **2.** *adj.* made with ①.

April ['e prəl] Go to MONTH.

apron ['e prən] **1.** *n.* a protective skirt worn over one's clothing; a protective covering for the front of one's clothing. **2.** *n.* the part of a theater stage that is in front of where the curtain hangs.

apt ['æpt] **1.** *adj.* likely to do something; prone to doing something. **2.** *adj.* clever; easily taught. **3.** *adj.* suitable; appropriate; fitting. (Adv: *aptly.*)

aquaria [ə 'kwɛr i ə] a pl of AQUARIUM.

aquarium [ə 'kwɛr i əm] **1.** *n., irreg.* a container for plants and animals that live in the water. (Pl: *aquariums* or AQUARIA.) **2.** *n., irreg.* a public building containing ① for public viewing.

Arabic numeral ['ɛr ə bɪk 'num ə rəl] *n.* the most usual form of number, such as 1, 2, 3, 4, 5. (These forms come from Arabic script.)

arc ['ɑrk] **1.** *n.* a curve; a portion of a circle. **2.** *iv.* to form a curve; to take the shape of a curve.

arch ['ɑrtʃ] **1.** *n.* a curved structure over an opening, usually holding the weight of the wall above it. **2.** *n.* the curved part of the bottom of the foot. **3.** *iv.* to bend in the shape of ①; to curve like ①.

archery ['ɑrtʃ ə ri] *n.* the sport or skill of shooting with a bow and arrow. (No pl.)

architect ['ɑrk ə tɛkt] *n.* someone who designs buildings.

architecture ['ɑrk ɪ tɛk tʃɚ] **1.** *n.* the designing of buildings; the study of building design. (Pl only for types and instances.) **2.** *n.* the particular design of a building. (No pl.)

arctic ['ɑrk tɪk] **1.** *adj.* relating to the ARCTIC. (Sometimes capitalized.) **2.** *adj.* very cold; freezing. (Adv: *arctically* [...ɪk li].)

Arctic *n.* the area around the Arctic Ocean, near the North Pole. (No pl. Treated as sg.)

are ['ɑr] *iv., irreg.* a form of the verb BE used in the second-person sg present and in all three persons in the present-tense pl. (Reduced to *'re* in contractions.)

area ['ɛr i ə] **1.** *n.* a space; a section. **2.** *n.* a measure of a section of a flat surface, determined, for instance, by multiplying the length of the surface by its width. **3.** *n.* a subject; a field of interest or study.

arena [ə 'rin ə] *n.* a large open space surrounded by tiers of seats, where performances and sporting events take place.

aren't ['ɑrnt] *cont.* are not.

aren't I? *cont.* am I not. (Used in the asking of certain questions.)

argue ['ɑr gju] **1.** *iv.* to disagree [with someone] verbally; to quarrel [with someone] verbally. **2.** *tv.* to debate a point or issue by means of an argument. (The object can be a clause with THAT ⑦.)

argument ['ɑr gjə mənt] **1.** *n.* a quarrel, especially if spoken; a dispute. **2.** *n.* a debate or discussion of an issue on which people disagree.

17

arise [ə 'rɑɪz] **1.** *iv., irreg.* to get up; to rise; to stand up. (Pt: AROSE; pp: ARISEN.) **2.** *iv., irreg.* to develop; to happen.

arisen [ə 'rɪz ən] pp of ARISE.

arithmetic 1. [ə 'rɪθ mə tɪk] *n.* the part of mathematics using numbers to add, subtract, multiply, and divide. **2.** [ɛr ɪθ 'mɛt ɪk] the *adj.* use of ①. (Adv: *arithmetically* [...ɪk li].)

arm ['ɑrm] **1.** *n.* one of the upper limbs of a human being. **2.** *n.* one of the two parts of a chair that support the arms of someone who sits in the chair. **3.** *tv.* to equip someone or something with weapons.

armchair ['ɑrm tʃɛr] *n.* a seat, usually cushioned, with supports for the arms.

armed ['ɑrmd] **1.** *adj.* carrying a gun or other weapons. **2.** *adj.* ready for war; prepared for battle.

armistice ['ɑr mɪs tɪs] *n.* a truce.

armpit ['ɑrm pɪt] *n.* the hollow underneath the place where the arm joins the shoulder.

armrest ['ɑrm rɛst] *n.* the part of a chair or seat that supports someone's arm.

arms *n.* guns; weapons.

army ['ɑrm i] *n.* a large group of land-based soldiers.

aroma [ə 'rom ə] *n.* an odor, especially one that is pleasant or agreeable.

arose [ə 'roz] pt of ARISE.

around [ə 'rɑund] **1.** *prep.* enclosing someone or something all about; surrounding someone or something. **2.** *prep.* close to a certain time or location. **3.** *prep.* [traveling or touring] in various places in something; at different locations within something. (With verbs such as *run, walk, go, crawl, travel,* and *drive.*) **4.** *prep.* moving in a curved or circular pathway with relation to someone or something. **5.** *adv.* on every side; on all sides. **6.** *adv.* following a circle or a curve.

arouse [ə 'rɑuz] **1.** *tv.* to wake someone up. **2.** *tv.* to awaken someone's interest, causing curiosity, anger, sexual stimulation, or general interest.

arrange [ə 'rendʒ] **1.** *tv.* to put things in a particular order; to put things in specific locations. **2.** *tv.* to prepare plans for something; to plan details for something. **3.** *tv.* to adapt a piece of music in a particular way.

arrangement [ə 'rendʒ mənt] **1.** *n.* the order or positions in which things have been put or placed. **2.** *n.* a group of flowers arranged in a pleasing way. **3.** *n.* a piece of music that has been altered for a particular purpose.

arrangements [ə 'rendʒ mənts] *n.* plans; provisions for something.

arrest [ə 'rɛst] **1.** *n.* the taking and holding of someone using the authority of the law. **2.** *tv.* to take someone to the police station for breaking a law. **3.** *tv.* to stop something from moving or working; to bring something to an end.

arrival [ə 'raɪ vəl] *n.* the reaching of the place that one is going to; coming to a place.

arrive [ə 'raɪv] *iv.* to reach the place that one is going to.

arrogance ['ɛr ə gəns] *n.* an unpleasant attitude of superiority; excessive pride. (No pl.)

arrogant ['ɛr ə gənt] *adj.* with an unpleasant attitude of superiority; showing arrogance. (Adv: *arrogantly.*)

arrow ['ɛr o] **1.** *n.* a thin, sharply pointed stick that is shot from a bow. **2.** *n.* a pointed symbol, indicating direction or position.

art ['ɑrt] **1.** *n.* the skilled creation of things of beauty or significant interest. (No pl. Typically painting, drawing, sculpture, fiction, poetry, theater, dance, music, film, and photography.) **2.** *n.* the product of ①, such as a painting, drawing, or sculpture. (No pl. Number is expressed with *work(s) of art.*) **3.** *n.* the skill required to do or to make something creative; a creative craft.

article ['ɑr tɪ kəl] **1.** *n.* a small part or section of a written document, especially an official document such as a contract. **2.** *n.* a specific item; a piece of something. **3.** *n.* a word like A, AN, and THE in English. **4.** *n.* a small section of writing in a larger work, as in a newspaper or an encyclopedia.

artificial [ɑr tə 'fɪʃ əl] *adj.* not authentic; not occurring in nature. (Adv: *artificially.*)

artist ['ɑr tɪst] *n.* someone who creates ART ② or practices ART ①.

artistic [ɑr 'tɪs tɪk] *adj.* creatively pleasing; showing creativity. (Adv: *artistically* [...ɪk li].)

arts *n.* areas of activity associated with a kind of art. (Treated as pl.)

artwork ['ɑrt wɜ˞k] **1.** *n.* one or more pieces of art, such as a painting or a sculpture. (No pl.) **2.** *n.* the pictures or illustrations that appear with written text. (No pl.)

19

as [ˈæz] **1.** *conj.* to the same amount or degree; equally; in the same way. **2.** *conj.* while; during; at the same time. **3.** *conj.* in the way that. **4.** *conj.* because; since. **5.** *prep.* in the role or function of something.

as if AND **as though** *conj.* in the same way that it would be if [something were to happen].

as long as AND **so long as 1.** provided that...; on the condition that.... **2.** since...; given the fact that.... **3.** during or throughout the period of time that....

as though Go to AS IF.

ash [ˈæʃ] **1.** *n.* what remains after matter has burned or exploded. (The pl form is used when referring to the individual particles and pieces.) **2.** *n.* a tree of the olive family. **3.** *n.* the wood of ②. (Pl only for types and instances.)

ashamed [əˈʃemd] *adj.* having shame [about something]. (Adv: *ashamedly* [əˈʃem əd li].)

ashore [əˈʃɔr] **1.** *adv.* to or onto the shore [from the water]. **2.** *adv.* on the beach or on land next to water, as opposed to in or on the water.

aside [əˈsɑɪd] **1.** *n.* something said that is not meant to be heard by all present; a remark made by an actor to the audience. **2.** *adv.* to the side; to one side; apart from someone or something. **3.** *adv.* away from oneself; to the side of oneself.

ask [ˈæsk] **1.** *tv.* to put a question to someone. **2.** *tv.* to request information by stating a question. (The object can be a clause with THAT ⑦.) **3.** *tv.* to request that someone do something or give one something. **4.** *tv.* to question someone about someone or something. **5.** *tv.* to invite someone to do something; to suggest that someone do something.

asleep [əˈslip] **1.** *adj.* sleeping; not awake. (Not prenominal.) **2.** *adj.* [of arms, legs, hands, feet] temporarily not feeling anything. (Not prenominal.)

aspersion [æs ˈpɚ ʒən] *n.* a critical or derogatory remark.

asphalt [ˈæs fɔlt] **1.** *n.* a black, tarlike substance used for pavement. (No pl form in this sense.) **2.** *tv.* to cover the surface of something with ①.

aspirin [ˈæs prɪn] **1.** *n.* a medication for relieving pain, used especially for headaches. (No pl.) **2.** a tablet of ①. (Sg or pl with the same meaning.)

20

ate

assail [ə 'sel] **1.** *tv.* to attack someone or something. **2.** *tv.* to criticize someone or something strongly.

assault [ə 'sɔlt] **1.** *tv.* to attack someone. **2.** *tv.* to attack someone sexually. **3.** *n.* an act of attacking someone or something. **4.** the *adj.* use of ③.

assemble [ə 'sɛm bəl] **1.** *tv.* to bring things or people into a collection or group. **2.** *tv.* to put something together; to construct something from its parts. **3.** *iv.* [for a group of people] to come together.

asset ['æ sɛt] **1.** *n.* an item of value; an item of someone's property. **2.** *n.* a useful skill; a useful quality. (Fig. on ①.)

assist [ə 'sɪst] **1.** *tv.* to help someone or something; to help someone with something. **2.** *n.* an act of assistance.

assistance [ə 'sɪs təns] *n.* help; aid; cooperation. (No pl.)

assistant [ə 'sɪs tənt] *n.* someone who helps someone; someone whose job is to help someone.

associate 1. [ə 'so si ət] *n.* a colleague; someone who works with someone else. **2.** [ə 'so si ət] *adj.* [of a job or position] not at the highest level, but typically at a higher level than an assistant. **3.** [ə 'so si et] *iv.* to make social contact with someone.

association [ə so si 'e ʃən] **1.** *n.* a connection or link between two things, people, or thoughts. **2.** *n.* a club, society, or organization; an alliance. **3.** *n.* a friendship; a relationship.

assume [ə 'sum] **1.** *tv.* to believe that something really is as one thinks it is; to suppose something is true. (The object can be a clause with THAT ⑦.) **2.** *tv.* to take control of something; to move into a role of leadership or responsibility for something.

assure [ə 'ʃʊr] *tv.* to promise someone something; to say something encouraging and positive to someone.

asterisk ['æs tə rɪsk] *n.* a starlike symbol (*) that is typically used to highlight something or to direct the reader's attention to a related note.

at [æt] **1.** *prep.* located on a point or in a place. **2.** *prep.* in the direction of someone or something; toward someone or something. **3.** *prep.* engaged in something; being in a certain state or process. **4.** *prep.* toward someone or something. **5.** ~ **last** finally; after a long wait.

ate ['et] pt of EAT.

21

athlete [ˈæθ lɪt] *n.* someone who participates in sports actively, especially a team member.

athletic [æθ ˈlɛt ɪk] **1.** *adj.* strong; active; in good physical condition. (Adv: *athletically* [...ɪk li].) **2.** *adj.* relating to athletes; in or for athletics. (Adv: *athletically* [...ɪk li].)

athletics *n.* active sports; exercise and training for sports. (Treated as sg or pl. Not countable.)

atlas [ˈæt ləs] *n.* a book of maps.

atmosphere [ˈæt məs fɪr] **1.** *n.* the mixture of gases that surrounds a planet, especially the air that surrounds the earth. **2.** *n.* the air that is nearby; the air that one is breathing. (No pl.) **3.** *n.* the mood or feeling in a particular place. (No pl.)

atom [ˈæt əm] *n.* the smallest part of an element that has all the chemical properties of the element.

attach [ə ˈtætʃ] **1.** *tv.* to fasten something to something else. **2.** *tv.* to associate a quality with someone or something; to think of a quality as belonging to someone or something.

attack [ə ˈtæk] **1.** *tv.* to try to harm someone or something, physically or verbally. **2.** *tv.* to begin work on a problem. (Fig. on ①.) **3.** *n.* an act of physical or verbal violence against someone or something. **4.** *n.* a sudden period of sickness or disease.

attempt [ə ˈtɛmpt] **1.** *n.* an effort to do something; a try at doing something. **2.** *tv.* to try to do something.

attend [ə ˈtɛnd] **1.** *tv.* to be present at a place or event; to be present somewhere over a period of time. **2.** *iv.* to deal with someone or something; to manage something.

attendance [ə ˈtɛn dəns] **1.** *n.* someone's presence at a location or event. (No pl.) **2.** *n.* the number of people present; the identity of the people attending something. (No pl.)

attendant [ə ˈtɛn dənt] *n.* someone who assists or helps someone else, especially someone important.

attention [ə ˈtɛn ʃən] *n.* care in doing something; careful and watchful awareness. (No pl.)

attic [ˈæt ɪk] *n.* the room at the top of a house, just under the roof.

attitude [ˈæt ə tud] **1.** *n.* a way of thinking, behaving, and feeling. **2.** *n.* a particular position or angle, especially of an aircraft.

attorney [ə ˈtɚ ni] *n.* a lawyer.

22

attractive [ə ˈtræk tɪv] *adj.* pretty; pleasing to the eye; handsome; creating interest. (Adv: *attractively.*)

auction [ˈɔk ʃən] *n.* a sale where each item is sold to the person offering to pay the highest price.

audience [ˈɔ di əns] **1.** *n.* a group of spectators who watch and listen to someone or something. **2.** *n.* the group of people who see a particular film, TV show, etc. **3.** *n.* a formal interview or meeting with a very important person.

audio [ˈɔ di o] **1.** *n.* broadcast or recorded sound, not video; the part of television that can be heard. (No pl.) **2.** the *adj.* use of ①.

auditorium [ɔ dɪ ˈtor i əm] **1.** *n.* the part of a performance hall where the audience sits. **2.** *n.* a large room or building used for public meetings, lectures, and similar things.

August [ˈɔg əst] Go to MONTH.

aunt [ˈænt] *n.* the sister of one's mother or father; the wife of the brother of one's mother or father; the wife of one's uncle.

authentic [ɔ ˈθen tɪk] *adj.* real; genuine; known to be real or true. (Adv: *authentically* [...ɪk li].)

author [ˈɔ θɚ] **1.** *n.* someone who writes books, poems, plays, articles, or similar compositions. **2.** *tv.* to write something; to compose something.

authorities *n.* members of a group who have the AUTHORITY ① to do something, such as to make rules; the police; the government.

authority [ə ˈθor ə ti] **1.** *n.* the power and right to do something; control and managing in general. (No pl.) **2.** *n.* an expert.

auto [ˈɔt o] *n.* a car; an AUTOMOBILE.

autograph [ˈɔt ə græf] **1.** *n.* someone's signature, especially the signature of a famous person. **2.** the *adj.* use of ①. **3.** *tv.* to sign one's name on something.

automatic [ɔt ə ˈmæt ɪk] **1.** *adj.* [of a machine] acting by itself; not needing outside help to perform a process. (Adv: *automatically* [...ɪk li].) **2.** *adj.* done without thinking; done out of habit or by instinct. (Adv: *automatically* [...ɪk li].)

automobile [ɔt ə mo ˈbil] *n.* a car; a vehicle that can carry a small number of passengers.

autumn [ˈɔt əm] *n.* fall; the season after summer and before winter.

aux. an abbreviation of AUXILIARY VERB.

auxiliary [ɔg 'zɪl jə ri] **1.** *adj.* secondary; supplementary; substitute. **2.** *n.* an AUXILIARY VERB. (Abbreviated *aux.* here.)

auxiliary verb AND **verbal auxiliary** [ɔg 'zɪl jə ri vɚb, 'vɚb əl ɔg 'zɪl jə ri] *n.* a word that is used before a verb to affect its tense, aspect, or mood.

available [ə 'vel ə bəl] *adj.* ready; accessible and not assigned or committed to something else.

avenue ['æv ə nu] **1.** *n.* a wide street in a city, sometimes lined with trees. **2.** *n.* a figurative pathway, representing a route to success.

average ['æv (ə) rɪdʒ] **1.** *n.* an amount obtained by adding several numbers together and then dividing that total by the quantity of numbers that were added. **2.** *n.* something that is usual, typical, or normal. (No pl.) **3.** *tv.* to add several figures and then divide that total by the number of figures that were added. **4.** *adj.* usual; typical; normal; ordinary. (Adv: *averagely.*) **5.** ~ **out** to even out ultimately.

aviation [ev i 'e ʃən] *n.* the flying of aircraft; the management of flying aircraft. (No pl.)

avocado [ɑv ə 'kɑd o] **1.** *n.* a tropical fruit with rough green, black, or purple skin, soft green flesh, and a large pit. (Pl ends in -s.) **2.** *n.* the edible part of ①. (No pl.) **3.** *adj.* made from ②.

avoid [ə 'vɔɪd] **1.** *tv.* to elude contact with someone or something; to manage not to make contact with someone or something. **2.** *tv.* to prevent something from occurring.

await [ə 'wet] *tv.* to expect someone or something to arrive; to wait for the arrival of someone or something.

awake [ə 'wek] **1.** *adj.* not asleep; alert. (Not prenominal.) **2.** *iv., irreg.* to stop sleeping; to wake. (Pt: AWOKE; pp: AWOKEN. See also AWAKEN.) **3.** *tv., irreg.* to make someone or something stop sleeping; to wake someone or something up. (See also AWAKEN.) **4.** *tv., irreg.* to bring back memories of someone or something into one's thoughts.

awaken [ə 'wek ən] **1.** *iv.* to stop sleeping; to wake. (See also AWAKE.) **2.** *tv.* to make someone or something stop sleeping; to wake someone or something up. (See also AWAKE.) **3.** *tv.* to bring back memories of someone or something into one's thoughts; to arouse in someone a new or hidden feeling, interest, talent, awareness, or emotion.

award [ə 'word] **1.** *n.* something given to someone as repayment; something given to someone as a prize. **2.** *tv.* to give something to someone as the result of an official legal decision; to order the payment of money in a court of law. **3.** *tv.* to give a prize to someone; to give someone something as the result of an official decision.

aware [ə 'wɛr] **1.** *adj.* alert; conscious; having control of one's senses. (Not usually prenominal.) **2.** *adj.* knowledgeable; in a state of knowing something. (Takes a clause with THAT ⑦.) **3.** *adj.* conscious of someone or something.

away [ə 'we] **1.** *adj.* at some distance; apart in distance. (Not prenominal.) **2.** *adj.* [of a game] not played on the home team's court or field. **3.** *adv.* at a distance from one position or direction to another; from one state or position to another. **4.** *adv.* without stopping; continuously.

awe ['ɔ] **1.** *n.* a strong feeling of wonder and respect. (No pl.) **2.** *tv.* to fill someone with wonder and respect.

awful ['ɔ fʊl] *adj.* horrible; terrible; very bad. (Adv: AWFULLY.)

awfully ['ɔf (ə) li] **1.** *adv.* terribly; horribly; badly. **2.** *adv.* very; really.

awhile [ə 'ʍɑɪl] *adv.* for a short length of time; for a little bit of time.

awkward ['ɔk wɚd] **1.** *adj.* clumsy; not graceful. (Adv: *awkwardly.*) **2.** *adj.* hard to manage; hard to control; not easily used. (Adv: *awkwardly.*) **3.** *adj.* embarrassing; embarrassed. (Adv: *awkwardly.*)

awning ['ɔ nɪŋ] *n.* a covering, extending over a walkway, door, or window.

awoke [ə 'wok] pt of AWAKE.

awoken [ə 'wok ən] pp of AWAKE.

ax(e) ['æks] *n.* a tool that consists of a heavy metal wedge attached to a handle, used to chop wood. (Pl: AXES.)

axes 1. ['æk sɪz] pl of AXIS. **2.** ['æk sɪz] pl of AX(E).

axis ['æks ɪs] *n., irreg.* an imaginary line that goes through the center point of a sphere or a ball. (Pl: AXES.)

axle ['æk səl] *n.* the rod that connects a pair of wheels.

B

baby ['be bi] 1. *n.* an infant; a newly born child. 2. *tv.* to treat someone or something like ①. 3. the *adj.* use of ①.

babysat ['beb i sæt] pt/pp of BABYSIT.

babysit ['be bi sɪt] 1. *iv., irreg.* to care for someone's children. (Pt/pp: BABYSAT.) 2. *tv., irreg.* to take care of children whose parents are away.

babysitter ['be bi sɪt ɚ] *n.* someone who takes care of children whose parents are away.

back ['bæk] 1. *n.* the part of a body along the spine. 2. *n.* the rear part of something. 3. *n.* the part of a chair that supports ①. 4. *iv.* to move backward out of something. 5. *tv.* to support someone or something with money. 6. *adj.* rear; opposite the front. (Prenominal only.) 7. *adv.* to or toward the rear; backward. 8. *adv.* earlier; in or to the past. 9. ~ **out** to move backward out of something. 10. ~ **out** [for someone] to withdraw from something.

backbone ['bæk bon] *n.* the spine.

background ['bæk graʊnd] 1. *n.* [in a picture] the scene behind the main subject. 2. *n.* the events leading up to something. (No pl.) 3. *n.* the past training, education, and experience of someone.

backrest ['bæk rest] *n.* the vertical part of a chair that supports someone's back.

back-to-back 1. *adj.* adjacent and touching backs. 2. *adj.* following immediately. (Said of things or events. In this case, the events are figuratively back-to-front.)

backup ['bæk əp] 1. *n.* a substitute or replacement for someone or something. 2. *n.* [in computers] a copy of a computer file or document. 3. *adj.* spare; extra.

backward ['bæk wɚd] 1. *adv.* toward the rear; with the back part going first. (Also **backwards**.) 2. *adv.* in a way that is the opposite of the normal way; in a way that reverses the order or direction of something. 3. *adj.* directed toward the back or the starting point. 4. *adj.* in a worse or earlier state; not modern. (Adv: *backwardly*.) 5. *adj.* hesitant or shy. (Adv: *backwardly*.)

backyard ['bæk 'jard] *n.* the lawn or area behind a house.

bacon ['bek ən] *n.* meat from the back and sides of a hog. (Pl only for types and instances.)

bacteria [bæk 'tɪr i ə] *n.* a group of tiny, one-celled organisms. (BAC-TERIA is pl. The sg is *bacterium*.)

bad ['bæd] **1.** *adj., irreg.* wicked; evil; not good. (Adv: *badly*. Comp: WORSE; sup: WORST.) **2.** *adj., irreg.* of poor quality; inferior; worthless; defective; not good. (Adv: *badly*. Comp: WORSE; sup: WORST.) **3.** *adj., irreg.* serious; severe. (Adv: *badly*. Comp: WORSE; sup: WORST.) **4.** *adj., irreg.* harmful; not healthful. (Adv: *badly*. Comp: WORSE; sup: WORST.) **5.** *adj., irreg.* [of a person, a creature, or a part of one's body feeling or appearing] sick, hurt, or unwell. **6.** *adj., irreg.* unpleasant; disagreeable; not nice. (Adv: *badly*. Comp: WORSE; sup: WORST.) **7.** *adj.* [of food] decayed or spoiled. **8.** *adv.* very much. (Colloquial.)

badge ['bædʒ] *n.* a pin or medal worn to show membership in an organization.

badly ['bæd li] **1.** *adv.* in an inferior or defective manner; poorly; not well. **2.** *adv.* unpleasantly; disagreeably; not well. **3.** *adv.* seriously; severely. **4.** *adv.* very much; to a great extent. (Fig. on ③.)

bag ['bæg] **1.** *n.* a sack; a pouchlike container. **2.** *n.* the contents of ①. **3.** *tv.* to put items into ①. **4.** *tv.* to kill wild game.

baggage ['bæg ɪdʒ] *n.* luggage or suitcases. (No pl. Treated as sg. Number is expressed with *piece(s) of baggage*.)

baggy ['bæg i] *adj.* puffy; having extra material that hangs in loose folds. (Adv: *baggily*. Comp: *baggier*; sup: *baggiest*.)

bail out 1. to parachute out of an airplane. **2.** to escape from or abandon something. **3.** to pay bail or bond money to get a person out of jail.

bait ['bet] **1.** *n.* someone or something used as a lure or temptation. (Pl only for types and instances.) **2.** *tv.* to put a worm or some kind of food on a hook in order to attract fish. **3.** *tv.* to put a lure into a trap.

bake ['bek] **1.** *tv.* to cook something using dry heat, usually in an oven. **2.** *tv.* [for the sun or hot, dry weather] to make someone or something very hot. (Fig. on ①.) **3.** *iv.* to cook food by placing it in a hot oven.

baker ['bek ɚ] *n.* someone who bakes foods, usually breads or pastries.

27

bakery ['bek ri] *n.* a store or place where bread products and pastries are prepared and sold.

balance ['bæl əns] **1.** *n.* an even placement of weight; a stable position with weight placed evenly; the ability to stay in such a position. (No pl.) **2.** *n.* a device that compares the weights of two objects. **3.** *n.* an equality in weight, proportion, or value; harmony. (No pl.) **4.** *n.* the amount of money remaining on a bill after part of the bill has been paid; the amount of money remaining in an account after a transaction. **5.** *tv.* to place something in such a way that it is stable. **6.** *tv.* to apply credits and debits to an account to determine the correct amount of money in the account. **7.** *tv.* to make something have symmetry in appearance or character.

balcony ['bæl kə ni] **1.** *n.* a platform that extends outward from a room that is higher than ground level. **2.** *n.* [in a hall or auditorium] an upper level of seats that extends over the main floor.

bald ['bɔld] *adj.* having no hair on the head; without hair. (Comp: *balder*; sup: *baldest*.)

ball ['bɔl] **1.** *n.* a round object; a sphere. **2.** *n.* a toy that is a round object. **3.** *n.* an elegant dance or party.

ballet [bæ 'le] *n.* a form of graceful and precise dance that tells a story without using speech or singing. (Pl only for types and instances.)

balloon [bə 'lun] *n.* a container of rubber, fabric, or some other material that can be filled with air or gas.

ballot ['bæl ət] **1.** *n.* a method of voting involving pieces of paper or machines. **2.** *n.* a piece of paper on which one's vote is marked.

bamboo [bæm 'bu] **1.** *n.* a type of very tall, woody grass typically found in warm countries. (No pl.) **2.** *adj.* made from the stems or wood of ①.

banana [bə 'næn ə] **1.** *n.* a long, tropical fruit with a yellow skin around a soft, white edible pulp. **2.** *adj.* made of or flavored with ①.

band ['bænd] **1.** *n.* a group of musicians, often including singers. **2.** *n.* a tribe; a group of people. **3.** *n.* a flat, thin strip of some material that is used to hold objects together. **4.** *n.* a stripe. **5.** ~ **together** to unite in opposition to someone or something; to unite against someone or something.

bandage ['bæn dɪdʒ] **1.** *n.* a wrapping used to cover and protect a wound against dirt, germs, and infection. **2.** *tv.* to place ① on someone or something.

28

bandit ['bæn dɪt] *n.* a robber, especially one belonging to a band of outlaws.

bandwagon ['bænd wæg ən] **1.** *n.* a wagon or large cart that carries a band, as in a parade or circus. (Old.) **2.** *n.* [in idioms] an imaginary vehicle on which people following a particular trend or fad can ride.

bang ['bæŋ] **1.** *n.* a sudden, loud noise; the sound of an explosion. **2.** *tv.* to hit something against something else, making a loud noise. **3.** *iv.* to hit [something]; to make loud noises by striking something.

bangs *n.* hair that hangs down over the forehead or eyes rather than being combed back. (Treated as pl, but not countable.)

banish ['bæn ɪʃ] **1.** *tv.* to expel someone from a certain place; to forbid someone to return to a certain place. **2.** *tv.* to send or drive something, such as a problem, away. (Fig. on ①.)

bank ['bæŋk] **1.** *n.* a corporation that lends, saves, and protects money. **2.** *n.* the building where money is loaned, saved, and protected. **3.** *n.* a place where certain objects are stored. **4.** *n.* the land along the side of a river, stream, or canal. **5.** *n.* a row or set of objects. **6.** *iv.* to do business with ①. **7.** ~ **on** to count on something; to rely on something.

banker ['bæŋ kɚ] *n.* someone who is an owner of or an important officer in a bank.

banquet ['bæŋ kwɪt] **1.** *n.* a dinner and speeches, usually connected with a celebration or an event. **2.** *n.* a special dinner with a large menu; a feast.

bar ['bɑr] **1.** *n.* a counter or flat surface that someone stands behind to prepare and serve drinks or food to people. **2.** *n.* a counter or flat surface where different kinds of food items are kept, from which people choose whatever they would like to eat. **3.** *n.* a place where people can buy alcoholic drinks. **4.** *n.* a rigid rod of metal, wood, or some other material. **5.** *n.* a rectangular object made of certain kinds of material, such as soap or various metals. **6.** *n.* a measure in a piece of music. **7.** *tv.* to secure a door or window by placing ④ across it.

barbecue AND **barbeque** ['bɑr bə kju] **1.** *n.* an outdoor grill used to cook food. **2.** *n.* a party or meal where people eat food cooked on a grill. **3.** *n.* the food that is prepared on an outdoor grill, especially food cooked with a spicy tomato sauce. **4.** *tv.* to cook food on a grill, often with a spicy tomato sauce. **5.** *iv.* [for food] to cook on an outdoor grill, often with a spicy tomato sauce.

barbeque Go to BARBECUE.

barber ['bɑr bɚ] *n.* someone who cuts or styles hair, especially men's hair.

bare ['ber] **1.** *tv.* to uncover. **2.** *adj.* naked; exposed. (Adv: *barely.* Comp: *barer*; sup: *barest.*) **3.** *adj.* empty. (Adv: *barely.* Comp: *barer*; sup: *barest.*)

barefoot(ed) ['ber fʊt(əd)] **1.** *adv.* without shoes or socks; with nothing on the feet. **2.** *adj.* not wearing shoes or socks; having nothing on the feet.

barely ['ber li] *adv.* hardly; only just; not quite.

bargain ['bɑr gən] **1.** *n.* something that was bought for less money than it would normally cost. **2.** *n.* an agreement. **3.** ~ **for** to expect or anticipate something; to foresee something. **4.** ~ **with** to set the terms of an agreement or a sale with someone.

bark ['bɑrk] **1.** *n.* the outer surface of a tree. (Pl only for types and instances.) **2.** *n.* the sound that is made by a dog. **3.** *iv.* to make the noise of a dog.

barn ['bɑrn] **1.** *n.* a large farm building for keeping livestock and storing supplies and equipment. **2.** *n.* a large building where trucks and buses are kept and serviced.

barnyard ['bɑrn jɑrd] *n.* the fenced area surrounding a barn; a farmyard.

barometer [bə 'rɑm ə tɚ] **1.** *n.* a device that measures the air pressure that is all around us. **2.** *n.* something that indicates possible changes. (Fig. on ①.)

barrel ['ber əl] **1.** *n.* a large, rounded wooden container with a flat top and bottom. **2.** *n.* the contents of ①. **3.** *n.* the standard measurement of oil, equal to 42 U.S. gallons. **4.** *n.* the part of a gun through which the bullets travel.

barren ['ber ən] **1.** *adj.* [of a female] not capable of producing offspring; [of a female] sterile. **2.** *adj.* not capable of supporting plant life.

barricade ['ber ə ked] **1.** *n.* something that blocks the way. **2.** *tv.* to block off a passageway or a pathway.

barrier ['ber i ɚ] **1.** *n.* something that physically separates people or things. **2.** *n.* something that emotionally or spiritually separates people or things. (Fig. on ①.)

base ['bes] **1.** *n.* the bottom, supporting part of something. **2.** *n.* a starting point; the foundation from which other things develop. **3.** *n.*

a center of operations; the main site of a business or organization. **4.** *n.* the center of operations and living quarters of a military unit. **5.** *n.* a chemical that is the opposite of an acid. **6.** *n.* [in baseball] one of the four "points" of the baseball diamond. **7.** *adj.* forming or serving as ① or ②; acting as a foundation.

baseball ['bes bɔl] **1.** *n.* a team sport played with two teams of nine members each. (No pl.) **2.** *n.* the white, leather-covered ball used in ①.

basement ['bes mənt] *n.* a space within the foundations of a building, tall enough to permit a person to stand.

bases 1. ['be siz] pl of BASIS. **2.** ['be sɪz] pl of BASE.

bashful ['bæʃ fʊl] *adj.* easily embarrassed; shy. (Adv: *bashfully.*)

basic ['bes ɪk] **1.** *adj.* fundamental; simple and required. (Adv: *basically* [...ɪk li].) **2.** *adj.* simple. (Adv: *basically* [...ɪk li].)

basin ['be sən] **1.** *n.* a large, shallow bowl or similar structure. **2.** *n.* the contents of ①. **3.** *n.* the area of land that is drained by a river or a system of rivers.

basis ['be sɪs] **1.** *n., irreg.* the foundation of something; the part of something from which other things develop. (Pl: BASES ['be siz].) **2.** *n., irreg.* an agreed-upon standard or status.

basket ['bæs kɪt] **1.** *n.* a container woven of strips of wood, twigs, or similar material. **2.** *n.* the contents of ①. **3.** *n.* [in basketball] the net, and the hoop to which it is attached, that are part of a basketball goal. **4.** *n.* a goal or score in the game of basketball.

basketball ['bæs kɪt bɔl] **1.** *n.* a team sport where points are scored by sending a ball through a BASKET ③. (No pl.) **2.** *n.* a ball used in ①.

bat ['bæt] **1.** *n.* a mouselike mammal that has large wings and usually flies at night. **2.** *n.* a wooden or metal club used in the game of baseball. **3.** *tv.* to hit a ball with ②. **4.** *tv.* to hit something; to slap at something.

batch ['bætʃ] **1.** *n.* a group of things processed at the same time. **2.** *tv.* to group things together.

bath ['bæθ] **1.** *n., irreg.* the washing of someone or something. (Pl: ['bæðz] or ['bæθs].) **2.** *n., irreg.* water for bathing. **3.** *n., irreg.* a bathtub; a tub used for bathing. **4.** *n., irreg.* a bathroom; a room with a bathtub or shower.

bathe ['beð] **1.** *iv.* to take a bath; to wash. (The pres. part. is *bathing* for all senses.) **2.** *tv.* to clean or wash someone; to give someone a bath. **3.** *tv.* to put water on something; to make something wet or moist.

bathrobe ['bæθ rob] *n.* a loose, coatlike garment worn before or after bathing or over pajamas. (See also ROBE.)

bathroom ['bæθ rum] *n.* a room having at least a toilet and a sink, and usually also a bathtub or a shower.

bathtub ['bæθ təb] *n.* a large tub for bathing.

bathwater ['bæθ wɑt ɚ] *n.* water for bathing; the water contained in a bathtub. (No pl.)

batter ['bæt ɚ] **1.** *n.* a mixture—thinner than dough—of flour, eggs, sugar, water, etc., which, when baked, becomes cake, cookies, etc. (No pl form in this sense.) **2.** *n.* a mixture of flour, water, and other ingredients into which meat, fish, or vegetables are dipped and then fried. (No pl form in this sense.) **3.** *n.* [in baseball] a player with a bat who tries to hit balls thrown by a pitcher. **4.** *tv.* to hit someone or something many times; to physically abuse someone or something.

battery ['bæt ɚ ri] **1.** *n.* a cylinder-shaped or square object inserted into flashlights, portable radios, cameras, etc., to provide electrical power. **2.** *n.* beating someone; striking and harming someone. (No pl.) **3.** *n.* a group of many large guns or other weapons. **4.** *n.* a series of tests or examinations.

battle ['bæt əl] **1.** *n.* a fight between two opposing forces during a war. **2.** *n.* a fight or crusade against someone or something. (Fig. on ①.) **3.** *tv.* to fight someone or something.

bawl ['bɔl] *iv.* to cry very loudly; to sob.

bay ['be] **1.** *n.* an opening in the shoreline of an ocean, sea, or lake, capable of sheltering ships. **2.** *iv.* to make a long, deep howl like a dog, wolf, etc.

be ['bi] **1.** *iv., irreg.* to exist in a certain way or as a certain thing; to exist in a certain state or condition. (Present tense: *I am, you are, he is, she is, it is, we are, you are, they are.* Pt: *I was, you were, he was, she was, it was, we were, you were, they were.* Pp: BEEN. Pres. part.: *being.*) **2.** *iv., irreg.* to occur; to happen. **3.** *iv., irreg.* to have a location; to exist at a specific place. **4.** *iv., irreg.* to exist. (Usually with THERE ③.) **5.** *iv., irreg.* to be ① in the process of doing something.

beach ['bitʃ] **1.** *n.* a shore covered with sand, pebbles, or stones. **2.** *tv.* to run or drive something onto the shore.

bead ['bid] **1.** *n.* a small piece of wood, metal, glass, plastic, stone, gemstone, or other material, usually with a hole through it for a string or a thread. **2.** *n.* a droplet of a liquid.

beak ['bik] *n.* the bill of a bird; the hard mouth structure of a bird or a turtle.

beam ['bim] **1.** *n.* a long, flat piece of wood, concrete, or metal. **2.** *n.* a ray of light; a stream of light; a stream of laser energy. **3.** *iv.* to radiate light; to make or give light. **4.** *iv.* to smile brightly; to look very happy.

bean ['bin] *n.* a seed of certain kinds of plants, and sometimes also the pod, used as food.

bear ['ber] **1.** *n.* a powerful, furry animal with a short tail and claws. **2.** *n.* someone who believes that prices on stocks or bonds will fall. **3.** *tv., irreg.* to carry or transport something. (Pt: BORE; pp: BORNE.) **4.** *tv., irreg.* to accept the consequences of something; to take responsibility for something. **5.** *tv., irreg.* to manage to support someone or something; to carry the weight of someone or something. **6.** *tv., irreg.* to produce offspring; to give birth to a child. (When this sense is used in the passive voice and focuses on the child, as in *Jimmy was born in 1996*, the pp is BORN; otherwise, the pp is BORNE.) **7.** *tv., irreg.* [for a plant] to produce or yield something, such as fruit, flowers, or leaves. **8.** ~ **down** to put pressure or weight on someone or something. **9.** ~ **up** to remain brave under a mental or emotional burden.

beard ['bɪrd] *n.* hair that grows on the side of the face, the chin, and the neck, usually of a male.

beast ['bist] **1.** *n.* a monster; a scary creature. **2.** *n.* an animal, especially one with four feet.

beat ['bit] **1.** *n.* the rhythm of poetry or music. **2.** *n.* one unit of a musical measure. **3.** *n.* the area or route that someone, especially a police officer, walks on a regular basis. **4.** *tv., irreg.* to hit someone or something, especially repeatedly. **5.** *tv., irreg.* to mix food ingredients with a kitchen tool. **6.** *tv., irreg.* to win a game against someone or something; to triumph over someone or something in a competition. **7.** *iv., irreg.* to hit against someone or something again and again. **8.** *iv., irreg.* [for a heart] to throb; [for a heart] to pulse over and over. **9.** the pt and a pp of ④. **10.** ~ **up** to strike someone as in BEAT ④; to hit someone repeatedly, typically with the fists. **11.** ~ **up** to mix something, such as an egg, as in ⑤; to damage something.

beaten ['bit n] pp of BEAT.

beautiful ['bju tə fʊl] *adj.* having great beauty; very pretty. (Adv: *beautifully* ['bju tə fli].)

beauty ['bju ti] **1.** *n.* the quality that makes someone or something very pleasing to look at; the quality that makes something very pleasing to hear or to think about. (No pl.) **2.** *n.* someone or something that is beautiful or excellent. **3.** *n.* excellence; suitability; cleverness. (No pl.)

beaver ['bi vɚ] *n., irreg.* a furry, plant-eating animal that dams up streams to form a pond in which it builds its dwelling or lodge. (Pl: *beaver* or *beavers*.)

became [bɪ 'kem] pt of BECOME.

because [bɪ 'kɔz] *conj.* for the reason that.

become [bɪ 'kʌm] **1.** pp of ②. **2.** *iv., irreg.* to come to be something; to grow to be something. (Pt: BECAME; pp: BECOME.) **3.** *iv., irreg.* to turn into something; to change into something. **4.** *tv., irreg.* [for clothing, a haircut, etc.] to look good on someone; to make someone look attractive.

bed ['bɛd] **1.** *n.* a piece of furniture used to sleep on, usually raised and with a mattress, sheets, and blankets. **2.** *n.* a flat base; a foundation; a bottom layer of support. **3.** *n.* the soil at the bottom of a body of water. **4.** *n.* an area of soil where flowers and other plants grow. **5.** ~ **down** to lie down to sleep for a period of time.

bedclothes ['bɛd klo(ð)z] *n.* sheets and a blanket; the cloth coverings for a bed. (Treated as pl, but not countable.)

bedding ['bɛd ɪŋ] *n.* the mattress coverings, sheets, and blankets used on a bed. (No pl.)

bedroom ['bɛd rum] *n.* a room in a dwelling place where someone sleeps.

bedside ['bɛd saɪd] *n.* the side of a bed; the area beside a bed.

bedtime ['bɛd taɪm] *n.* the time when someone usually goes to bed.

bee ['bi] *n.* a small insect that can sting and that makes honey.

beef ['bif] *n.* the meat of a cow, steer, or bull. (No pl.)

beefsteak ['bif stek] *n.* a slice of the flesh of a cow, steer, or bull, eaten as food. (Usually STEAK.)

beehive ['bi haɪv] *n.* a place where bees live, reproduce, and make honey.

beeline ['bi lɑɪn] *n.* the direct line of flight that a bee follows between its home and a food source.

been [bɪn] pp of BE.

beer ['bɪr] 1. *n.* a beverage (containing alcohol) made from grain and flavored with hops. (Pl only for types and instances.) 2. *n.* a glass or can of ①; a serving of ①.

beet ['bit] *n.* a plant with a large, dark red root that is eaten as a vegetable.

beetle ['bit əl] *n.* a small insect whose wings are hard and protect its body.

before [bɪ 'for] 1. *conj.* at an earlier time than; previous to the time when [something happens]. 2. *prep.* earlier than something; previous to something. 3. *prep.* in front of someone or something. 4. *adv.* earlier; previously. 5. *adv.* until this moment in time; in the past.

beg ['bɛg] 1. *iv.* to plead for something; to ask for something very humbly. 2. ~ **off** to make excuses for not doing something.

began [bɪ 'gæn] pt of BEGIN.

beggar ['bɛg ɚ] *n.* someone who asks for charity, especially money or food; a panhandler.

begin [bɪ 'gɪn] 1. *iv., irreg.* [for something] to start [happening]; for someone or something to start [doing something]. (Pt: BEGAN; pp: BEGUN.) 2. *iv., irreg.* to start to do something. 3. *tv., irreg.* to start something; to commence something.

beginner [bɪ 'gɪn ɚ] *n.* someone just learning to do something; an amateur.

beginning [bɪ 'gɪn ɪŋ] 1. *n.* the start; the origin. (No pl form in this sense.) 2. ~**s** *n.* the earliest stage of the origin of someone or something.

begun [bɪ 'gʌn] pp of BEGIN.

behavior [bɪ 'hev jɚ] *n.* the manner in which someone acts or behaves; conduct; manners. (Pl only for types and instances.)

behind [bɪ 'hɑɪnd] 1. *prep.* in or to a place farther back than someone or something else; at the rear of someone or something. 2. *prep.* later than someone or something; coming after someone or something; not current with something. 3. *prep.* serving as the reason for something. 4. *prep.* in support of someone or something. 5. *adv.* toward the back; further back in place or time.

being ['bi ɪŋ] *n.* a living thing; a living creature.

35

belch 1. *n.* an audible release of stomach gas through the mouth. **2.** *n.* a puff of smoke or other vapors released or pushed out. **3.** *iv.* to make ①.

belief [bɪ 'lif] **1.** *n.* something that is thought to be true; an opinion. **2.** *n.* a rule or principle of a religion or faith. (Often pl.)

believe [bɪ 'liv] **1.** *tv.* to accept that someone or something is true or real. (The object can be a clause with THAT ⑦.) **2.** *tv.* to have an opinion about something; to suppose something. (The object is a clause with THAT ⑦.)

bell ['bɛl] **1.** *n.* a cupped metal shell that makes a ringing sound when struck. **2.** *n.* the sound made by ① to mark the start or the finish of a period of time.

belly ['bɛl i] **1.** *n.* the stomach area of the body; a large, and sometimes rounded front part of the body. (Informal.) **2.** *n.* the inside of certain things. **3.** *n.* the underside of certain things.

belong [bɪ 'lɔŋ] *iv.* [for someone or something] to have a proper or appropriate place or typical location.

belongings [bɪ 'lɔŋ ɪŋz] *n.* the things that one owns; one's possessions. (Treated as pl, but not countable.)

below [bɪ 'lo] **1.** *prep.* beneath someone or something; under someone or something; lower than someone or something. **2.** *prep.* lower in status or rank than someone or something. **3.** *adv.* to a lower deck on a ship. **4.** *adv.* later [in a book or other written work]; after or following [on the same page or within the same written work].

belt ['bɛlt] **1.** *n.* a strip of leather or similar material fastened around the waist, to hold up trousers. **2.** *n.* a long, continuous loop of strong, flexible material used in machinery to transfer power. **3.** *n.* a seat belt; a strap in a car that holds people securely in the seat.

bench ['bɛntʃ] **1.** *n.* a seat—often unpadded—for two or more people. **2.** *n.* a place where players on a sports team sit when they are not playing. **3.** *n.* the seat a judge sits on. **4.** *n.* a judge or a group of judges in a court of law.

bend ['bɛnd] **1.** *n.* a curve; a turn. **2.** *iv., irreg.* to become curved or crooked; to go in a direction away from a straight line. (Pt/pp: BENT.) **3.** *iv., irreg.* to change one's mind; to yield. **4.** *tv., irreg.* to cause an object to curve; to change the shape of a flexible object.

beneath [bɪ 'niθ] **1.** *prep.* under someone or something; below someone or something; lower than someone or something. **2.** *prep.* inferior to someone or something; worse than someone or something.

36

benefit ['bɛn ə fɪt] **1.** *n.* an advantage; something that is helpful or has a good effect. **2.** *n.* the sum of money paid to someone under the terms of an insurance or retirement contract. (Often pl.) **3.** *n.* something that one receives—in addition to a salary—for working, such as health insurance, life insurance, etc. **4.** *n.* an event with special entertainment, given to raise money for a worthy cause. **5.** *tv.* to serve to the good of someone or something. **6.** ~ **from** to improve or to profit from something; to be better because of something.

bent ['bɛnt] **1.** pt/pp of BEND. **2.** *adj.* crooked or curved; not straight.

berry ['bɛr i] *n.* the small, juicy fruit of a bush or shrub.

beside [bɪ 'saɪd] *prep.* at, by, or to the side of someone or something; next to someone or something.

besides [bɪ 'saɪdz] **1.** *prep.* in addition to someone or something; as well as someone or something. **2.** *adv.* also; furthermore; in any case; at any rate.

best ['bɛst] **1.** *adj.* the most excellent [thing]. (The sup. form of GOOD. See also BETTER.) **2.** *adv.* most excellently. (The sup. form of WELL. See also BETTER.) **3.** *tv.* to defeat someone; to do [something] much better than someone; to outwit someone.

bet ['bɛt] **1.** *n.* an amount of money gambled on something; a wager. **2.** *tv., irreg.* to make a wager. (Pt/pp: *bet*.) **3.** *tv., irreg.* to predict something; to make a guess that something will happen. (The object is a clause with THAT ⑦.)

betray [bɪ 'tre] **1.** *tv.* to do something that shows that one is not loyal to a person; to be unfaithful to someone or something. **2.** *tv.* to show a sign of something; to reveal something.

better ['bɛt ɚ] **1.** *adj.* of more goodness; of greater benefit. (The comp. form of GOOD. See also BEST.) **2.** *adj.* healthier than before; improved in health; having recovered from an illness; in good health again. (Not prenominal.) **3.** *adv.* with more quality; with greater benefit. (The comp. form of WELL. See also BEST.) **4.** *tv.* to improve oneself; [for something] to improve itself.

between [bɪ 'twin] **1.** *prep.* in the middle of two people or things; with something on both sides. **2.** *prep.* both together; in combination with the two. **3.** *prep.* in comparing two people or things.

beverage ['bɛv rɪdʒ] *n.* a drink other than water.

beware [bɪ 'wɛr] **1.** *tv.* to be cautious with something; to be alert to a problem. (Almost always a command.) **2.** to be cautious of someone or something. (Almost always a command. More common than ①.)

bewildered [bɪ 'wɪl dɚd] *adj.* confused; puzzled; perplexed. (Adv: *bewilderedly.*)

beyond [bi 'jɑnd] **1.** *prep.* farther than someone or something; on the other side of someone or something. **2.** *prep.* past someone's ability to understand or comprehend. **3.** *adv.* past; further; on the other side of someone or something.

bias ['baɪ əs] **1.** *n.* a prejudice. **2.** *tv.* to prejudice someone.

biased ['baɪ əst] *adj.* prejudiced; favoring one over another. (Adv: *biasedly.*)

bib ['bɪb] *n.* a napkin or piece of cloth worn around the neck.

bible ['baɪb əl] **1.** *n.* the holy writings of the Jewish religion; the Hebrew Scriptures. (Capitalized.) **2.** *n.* the holy writings of the Christian religion. (Capitalized.) **3.** *n.* a manual; a guidebook; a book of authority.

biblical ['bɪb lɪ kəl] *adj.* relating to the Bible. (Adv: *biblically* [...ɪk li].)

bicycle ['baɪ sɪ kəl] **1.** *n.* a vehicle with a metal frame and two wheels, operated by foot pedals. **2.** *iv.* to travel by ①.

bid ['bɪd] **1.** *n.* an offer of an amount of money for something for sale, especially at an auction. **2.** *n.* the presentation of the price for one's services, especially in a competition joined by others to do the same work. **3.** *n.* an attempt to seek or take power or control of something. **4.** *tv., irreg.* to offer an amount of money for something, especially at an auction. (Pt/pp: *bid.*)

big ['bɪg] **1.** *adj.* large; great in amount or size. (Comp: *bigger;* sup: *biggest.*) **2.** *adj.* important. (Comp: *bigger;* sup: *biggest.*) **3.** *adj.* adult; grown-up. (Comp: *bigger;* sup: *biggest.*)

bike ['baɪk] **1.** *n.* a bicycle. **2.** *n.* a motorcycle. **3.** *iv.* to ride a bicycle or motorcycle.

bilingual [baɪ 'lɪŋ gwəl] **1.** *adj.* [of a person] able to speak two languages. (Adv: *bilingually.*) **2.** *adj.* referring to two languages. (Adv: *bilingually.*)

bill ['bɪl] **1.** *n.* a written notice of money owed. **2.** *n.* a legal draft of a proposed law. **3.** *n.* a piece of printed money that is different from a coin. **4.** *n.* the hard part of a bird's mouth. **5.** *n.* the visor of a cap; the part of a cap that extends from the head and shields the eyes from the sun. **6.** *tv.* to present a notice of charges to someone or something.

billion [ˈbɪl jən] **1.** *n.* 1,000,000,000; a thousand million of something, usually units of money. (A British *billion* is a million million.) **2.** *adj.* amounting to or equal to 1,000,000,000 of something.

bin [ˈbɪn] *n.* a container or enclosed space used for storage.

bind [ˈbaɪnd] *tv., irreg.* to secure something to something else with a tie or band; to tie something together with something else. (Pt/pp: BOUND.)

binocular [bə ˈnɑk jə lɚ] *adj.* relating to both eyes; involving both eyes.

binoculars *n.* a viewing device made of two small telescopes, side by side. (Treated as a pl. Number is expressed with *pair(s) of binoculars*.)

biology [baɪ ˈɑl ə dʒi] *n.* the scientific study of living animals and plants. (No pl.)

bird [ˈbɚd] *n.* an animal that has feathers and wings.

birth [ˈbɚθ] **1.** *n.* the process of being born. **2.** *n.* the origin of something; the way something has come into being. (Fig. on ①.)

birthday [ˈbɚθ de] *n.* the date on which someone was born; a date of birth.

birthmark [ˈbɚθ mark] *n.* a pigmented mark on the skin, usually red, brown, black, or purple, present from birth.

birthplace [ˈbɚθ ples] *n.* the city and country where someone was born; the place of someone's birth.

biscuit [ˈbɪs kɪt] *n.* a round, flat cake of bread, made with baking powder.

bisect [ˈbaɪ sɛkt] *tv.* to cut something into two equal parts; to split something down the middle.

bit [ˈbɪt] **1.** pt of BITE. **2.** *n.* a small amount of something; a tiny piece of something. **3.** *n.* the mouthpiece on a bridle, used to control a horse. **4.** *n.* the basic unit of information in a computer; a binary digit. **5.** *n.* the end of a drilling tool that bores or cuts holes.

bite [ˈbaɪt] **1.** *n.* a mouthful of food; the amount of food taken in at one time. **2.** *n.* a light meal; a snack; a small amount of food. **3.** *n.* the mark or wound made on the skin when someone is BITTEN as in ④ by an animal or stung by an insect. **4.** *tv., irreg.* to grip or tear something with the teeth; to close the teeth around an object. (Pt: BIT; pp: BITTEN.) **5.** *iv., irreg.* [for a creature] to be able to pierce skin with its teeth; [for a creature] to have a habit of attacking people or other creatures with its teeth.

39

bitten ['bɪt n] pp of BITE.

bitter ['bɪt ɚ] **1.** *adj.* very sharp or harsh in taste; not sweet, salty, or sour. (Adv: *bitterly.*) **2.** *adj.* [of wind or weather] extremely cold. (Adv: *bitterly.*) **3.** *adj.* emotionally painful; distressful. (Adv: *bitterly.*) **4.** *adj.* resentful; hateful. (Adv: *bitterly.*)

bizarre [bɪ 'zɑr] *adj.* very strange; eccentric; weird. (Adv: *bizarrely.*)

black ['blæk] **1.** *adj.* the color of coal; the color of the darkest night; the opposite of white. (Comp: *blacker;* sup: *blackest.*) **2.** *adj.* [of coffee served] without cream or milk. **3.** *adj.* evil; wicked. (Adv: *blackly.* Comp: *blacker;* sup: *blackest.*) **4.** *adj.* [of people, usually of African decent] having dark-colored skin. (Occasionally capitalized.) **5.** *adv.* [of coffee served] without cream or milk. **6.** *n.* someone who is of African descent having dark-colored skin. (Sometimes capitalized.)

blacken ['blæk ən] **1.** *tv.* to make something black; to cause something to become black. **2.** *iv.* to become very dark or black; to turn black.

blackness ['blæk nəs] *n.* the state of being black. (No pl.)

blackout ['blæk ɑut] **1.** *n.* a complete loss of all electricity or power; a situation of complete darkness, especially caused by a loss of electrical power. **2.** *n.* a state of not being conscious.

blade ['bled] **1.** *n.* the flat, sharpened edge of a knife or tool. **2.** *n.* the flat, wide part of an oar or propeller. **3.** *n.* a long, flat leaf of grass or other plant. **4.** *n.* the metal part of an ice skate that makes contact with the ice.

blame ['blem] **1.** *n.* the responsibility for causing something that is bad or wrong. (No pl.) **2.** *tv.* to place the responsibility for doing something wrong on a person. **3.** ~ **for** to hold someone responsible for something; to name someone as the cause of something. **4.** ~ **on** to say that something is someone's fault; to place the guilt for something on someone.

blank ['blæŋk] **1.** *n.* an empty line or a space on a form. **2.** *adj.* without marks; having no writing. (Comp: *blanker;* sup: *blankest.*) **3.** *adj.* [of a facial expression] not showing recognition or response. (Adv: *blankly.* Comp: *blanker;* sup: *blankest.*)

blanket ['blæŋ kɪt] **1.** *n.* a piece of thick fabric, used to keep someone warm. **2.** *n.* a layer of something that covers something else. (Fig. on ①.) **3.** *tv.* [for something as in ②] to cover something.

blare ['blɛr] **1.** *n.* a loud, harsh noise. **2.** *iv.* to make a loud, harsh noise.

blast ['blæst] **1.** *n.* a strong, sudden gust of air; a sudden, heavy wind. **2.** *n.* the noise and violent gust of air created by an explosion. **3.** *n.* an explosion. **4.** *tv.* to blow something up; to explode something. **5.** ~ **off** [for a rocket ship] to take off and head toward a destination.

blaze ['blez] **1.** *n.* a fire; a flame. **2.** *iv.* to burn brightly; to burn with bright flames.

bleach ['blitʃ] **1.** *n.* a substance that removes color or stains. (Pl only for types and instances.) **2.** *iv.* to become white or lighter; to turn white or lighter. **3.** *tv.* to turn something white or lighter; to cause something to become white or lighter.

bled ['blɛd] pt/pp of BLEED.

bleed ['blid] **1.** *iv., irreg.* to lose blood, as from a wound. (Pt/pp: BLED.) **2.** *iv., irreg.* [for color, ink, or dye] to seep or soak into other colors or dyes.

blend ['blɛnd] **1.** *n.* a mixture. **2.** *tv.* to combine something with something else. **3.** *iv.* to mix well or attractively with people or things. **4.** ~ **in** to mix well with someone or something; to combine with someone or something.

bless ['blɛs] **1.** *tv.* to make someone or something holy through a religious ritual. **2.** *tv.* to ask God to place favor on the food that is to be eaten or on people or things.

blessing ['blɛs ɪŋ] **1.** *n.* a prayer calling for God's favor or protection. **2.** *n.* God's favor or good fortune given to someone or something. **3.** *n.* approval.

blew ['blu] pt of BLOW.

blind ['blaɪnd] **1.** *adj.* unable to see; sightless. (Adv: *blindly.* Comp: *blinder;* sup: *blindest.*) **2.** *adj.* [of anger] irrational. (Adv: *blindly.* Comp: *blinder;* sup: *blindest.*) **3.** *tv.* to take away someone's or something's sight permanently or temporarily.

blinds *n.* a kind of window shade made of horizontal, or sometimes vertical, slats that can be tilted to block vision or shut out light. (Treated as pl.)

blink ['blɪŋk] **1.** *n.* a quick closing and opening of the eyes. **2.** *iv.* [for a light] to flash on and off quickly. **3.** *tv.* to close and open one's eyes quickly. **4.** *iv.* [for one's eyelids] to close and open quickly. **5.** *tv.* to turn a light on and off quickly; to flash a light.

bliss ['blɪs] *n.* complete happiness; joy. (No pl.)

41

blister ['blɪs tɚ] **1.** *n.* a bubble of fluid under the skin, formed by a burn or irritation. **2.** *iv.* [for a part of the skin] to raise up and fill with fluid in response to a burn or irritation. **3.** *tv.* to cause ① to form on someone or something.

blizzard ['blɪz ɚd] *n.* a snowstorm with strong winds, heavy snow, and possible thunder and lightning.

block ['blɑk] **1.** *n.* a solid piece of something, such as wood, stone, or ice. **2.** *n.* a large, flat piece of stone or wood on which items are cut, chopped, or split. **3.** *n.* the distance along a street from one intersection to the next. **4.** *n.* a group of seats or tickets for seats that are next to each other, as with the theater, an airline flight, or a sporting event. **5.** *tv.* to be or get in the way of something.

blond ['blɑnd] **1.** *adj.* [of hair] fair or light in color. (Comp: *blonder*; sup: *blondest*.) **2.** *n.* someone with light-colored hair. (BLONDE is sometimes used for females.)

blonde ['blɑnd] *n.* a woman or a girl with light-colored hair. (See also BLOND.)

blood ['blʌd] *n.* a red fluid moving through the bodies of animals. (No pl.)

bloodshed ['blʌd ʃed] *n.* injury or death caused by violence. (No pl.)

bloody *adj.* covered with blood.

bloom ['blum] **1.** *iv.* [for a plant] to produce flowers or blossoms. **2.** *iv.* [for a flower bud] to open.

blossom ['blɑs əm] **1.** *n.* a flower. **2.** *iv.* to produce flowers; to bloom. **3.** *iv.* [for a flower bud] to open.

blot ['blɑt] **1.** *n.* a spot or smeared area of ink. **2.** *tv.* to remove an excess amount of moisture by placing an absorbent paper over it and pressing. **3.** *tv.* to dry or clean something by placing an absorbent paper over it and pressing.

blouse ['blɑʊs] *n.* a woman's shirt.

blow ['blo] **1.** *iv., irreg.* [for wind or air] to be in motion. (Pt: BLEW; pp: BLOWN.) **2.** *iv., irreg.* [for something] to be lifted by or carried in the air or wind. **3.** *iv., irreg.* [for a sound-producing device, such as a horn] to make sound. **4.** *iv., irreg.* [for a fuse] to burn out. **5.** *tv., irreg.* to exhale air or smoke. **6.** *tv., irreg.* to sound a whistle or a horn, trumpet, or similar instrument. **7.** *n.* a hard hit or knock. **8.** ~ **up** to inflate something. **9.** ~ **up** to enlarge a photograph.

blown ['blon] pp of BLOW.

42

blue ['blu] **1.** *n.* the color of a clear sky on a bright day; the color of a deep, clear ocean. (Pl only for types and instances.) **2.** the *adj.* use of ①. (Comp: *bluer;* sup: *bluest.*) **3.** *adj.* sad. (Adv: *bluely.* Comp: *bluer;* sup: *bluest.*)

bluff ['blʌf] **1.** *n.* a steep hill or cliff with a wide front. **2.** *n.* a harmless deception; a trick that will not result in harm. **3.** *tv.* to deceive someone or some creature; to mislead someone or some creature into doing something.

blunder ['blʌn dɚ] **1.** *n.* a stupid mistake; a clumsy error. **2.** *iv.* to make a stupid mistake.

blunt ['blʌnt] **1.** *adj.* without a sharp edge or point. (Adv: *bluntly.* Comp: *blunter;* sup: *bluntest.*) **2.** *adj.* to the point; frank; not subtle. (Adv: *bluntly.* Comp: *blunter;* sup: *bluntest.*) **3.** *tv.* to make something dull; to make something less sharp.

board ['bord] **1.** *n.* a flat, thin piece of wood; a plank. **2.** *n.* a flat piece of wood or other rigid material, used for a specific purpose. **3.** *n.* daily meals [when associated with one's lodging]. (No pl. Treated as sg.) **4.** *n.* a group of people who manage a company or other organization. **5.** *n.* a flat, sturdy piece of material on which a game is played. **6.** *tv.* to get on a ship, bus, train, or plane. **7.** *iv.* to receive meals and living space in exchange for money or work.

boast ['bost] **1.** *n.* a bragging statement. **2.** *iv.* to brag or exaggerate. **3.** *tv.* [for something] to offer or have a particular characteristic.

boat ['bot] *n.* a floating means of transportation, smaller than a ship, that carries people and cargo.

bob ['bab] **1.** *n.* a quick up-and-down movement. **2.** *iv.* to move up and down quickly, as with something floating on water. **3.** *tv.* to cut something, especially hair, short.

body ['bad i] **1.** *n.* the whole physical structure of a living creature or plant. **2.** *n.* a dead human or animal; a corpse. **3.** *n.* the main part of something. **4.** *n.* a collection of people or things taken as a group; a group; a collection. **5.** *n.* a large mass of something; an object.

bodyguard ['bad i gard] *n.* someone who guards and protects someone else.

boil ['bɔɪl] **1.** *n.* a painful sore place surrounding an infection. **2.** *n.* the condition of something that BOILS as in ⑤. (No pl.) **3.** *tv.* to make a liquid so hot that it bubbles and turns into vapor. **4.** *tv.* to cook something by putting it in a liquid that is very hot as in ⑤. **5.** *iv.* [for a liquid] to become so hot that it bubbles and turns into vapor. **6.** *iv.*

43

[for something] to cook in a liquid that is very hot as in ⑤. **7.** ~ **down** [for a liquid] to be condensed to something by BOILING as in ⑥. **8.** ~ **down** [for a complex situation] to be reduced to its essentials. **9.** ~ **out** to remove something from something by BOILING as in ⑤.

boiler ['bɔɪl ɚ] *n.* a large, heated tank that makes hot water or steam.

bold ['bold] **1.** *adj.* confident; sure of oneself; courageous. (Adv: *boldly.* Comp: *bolder;* sup: *boldest.*) **2.** *adj.* without shame; rude; not shy. (Adv: *boldly.* Comp: *bolder;* sup: *boldest.*) **3.** *adj.* [of printing] darker and thicker. (Comp: *bolder;* sup: *boldest.*)

bolt ['bolt] **1.** *n.* a metal pin or rod, with THREADS, used to connect or attach things. **2.** *n.* a rod that fastens a door, window, or gate. **3.** *n.* a flash or streak of lightning. **4.** *n.* a sudden, quick movement; an unexpected, quick movement. **5.** *n.* a roll of cloth. **6.** *tv.* to fasten two or more objects together with ①. **7.** *tv.* to lock a door, gate, or window by sliding a metal ② into place. **8.** *iv.* to run away from someone or something; to move away from someone or something quickly and suddenly.

bomb ['bam] **1.** *n.* an explosive weapon or device. **2.** *tv.* to attack an area by dropping ① on it from planes. **3.** *tv.* to use ① to cause damage or injury to someone or something.

bond ['band] **1.** *n.* a link or something in common that brings together two people or two groups of people. **2.** *n.* something that causes two objects to stick together. **3.** *n.* an agreement in which someone or a company promises, as an investment, to pay back a certain sum of money by a particular date. **4.** *iv.* [for an adhesive or paint] to become firmly attached.

bone ['bon] **1.** *n.* any one of the many parts of an animal's skeleton. **2.** *n.* the hard substance of which ① is made. (No pl.) **3.** *tv.* to remove ① from meat before cooking it.

bonfire ['ban faɪɚ] *n.* a large, controlled outdoor fire.

bonnet ['bab ət] *n.* a cloth hat for women or girls; any hat for women or girls.

bonus ['bon əs] **1.** *n.* something extra. **2.** the *adj.* use of ①.

book ['bʊk] **1.** *n.* a stack of pages, held within a cover. **2.** *n.* a subdivision of a longer written work. **3.** *n.* a set of objects that are held together under a cover. **4.** *tv.* to process a charge against someone who has been arrested for committing a crime. **5.** *tv.* to reserve space in advance for something, such as a play, an airplane flight, a room in a hotel, or a table in a restaurant. **6.** *tv.* to reserve the services of a performer in advance.

bookcase ['bʊk kes] *n.* a set of shelves for books.

bookkeeper ['bʊk kip ɚ] *n.* someone who keeps track of the accounts of a company or an organization.

bookkeeping ['bʊk kip ɪŋ] *n.* the job of keeping track of the accounts of a company or an organization. (No pl.)

booklet ['bʊk lət] *n.* a thin book; a pamphlet.

bookmark ['bʊk mɑrk] *n.* something placed between the pages of a book to keep the reader's place.

books *n.* the records of the money spent and earned by a company or organization. (Treated as pl, but not countable.)

bookshelf ['bʊk ʃɛlf] *n., irreg.* a horizontal board for holding and displaying books, as in a bookcase. (Pl: BOOKSHELVES.)

bookshelves ['bʊk ʃɛlvz] pl of BOOKSHELF.

bookshop ['bʊk ʃɑp] *n.* a store where books are sold.

bookstore ['bʊk stɔr] *n.* a store where books are sold.

boom ['bum] **1.** *n.* a large, echoing noise made when something explodes or crashes. **2.** *n.* a time of strong economic growth. **3.** *n.* a large, horizontal pole or beam used for support or in the lifting of a weight. **4.** *iv.* to make a large, echoing noise like an explosion or a crash.

boost ['bust] **1.** *n.* an upward push; an upward movement. **2.** *tv.* to push someone or something upward from beneath. **3.** *tv.* to increase something; to raise something.

boot ['but] **1.** *n.* a heavy shoe, often waterproof. **2.** *tv.* to kick someone or something. **3.** *tv.* to start a computer, causing it to make a series of checks and set up its operating system. **4.** ~ **out** to force someone to leave something or someplace.

booth ['buθ] **1.** *n., irreg.* a seating area in a restaurant having bench seats with backs, placed on two sides of the table or around the table. (Pl: ['buðz] or ['buθs].) **2.** *n., irreg.* a small, enclosed space, such as the enclosure containing a public telephone. **3.** *n., irreg.* a display table or area—possibly enclosed—at a fair or a market.

border ['bɔr dɚ] **1.** *n.* a decorated area at the edge of something, and the edge itself. **2.** *n.* the dividing line between two countries, states, or other political units. **3.** *tv.* to adjoin or be next to a particular area.

borderline ['bɔr dɚ laɪn] *n.* the line that marks a border—not clearly on either side of the border.

bore ['bɔr] **1.** pt of BEAR. **2.** *tv.* to drill a hole in something. **3.** *tv.* to make someone tired by being dull. **4.** *iv.* to drill; to make a hole. **5.** *n.* someone or something that is boring; someone or something that is dull.

boredom ['bɔr dəm] *n.* a state or condition where one is bored and finds everything dull and uninteresting.

boring ['bɔr ɪŋ] *adj.* dull; not entertaining; causing people to lose interest and perhaps become sleepy. (Adv: *boringly.*)

born ['bɔrn] **1.** a pp of BEAR. **2.** *adj.* possessing a certain quality or character since birth; by birth; natural. (Prenominal only.) **3.** *adj.* having a particular place of birth or national heritage. (Usually in hyphenated combinations.)

borne ['bɔrn] a pp of BEAR.

borrow ['bar o] **1.** *tv.* to ask for, accept, and use something from someone with the intention of returning or replacing it. **2.** *tv.* to take something, such as a custom, trait, or idea, and use it as one's own.

bosom ['bʊz əm] **1.** *n.* the chest of a human. (Formal or literary.) **2.** *n.* the center of feeling in a human. (Literary.) **3.** *n.* the [pair of] breasts of a woman. (No pl form in this sense.)

boss ['bɔs] *n.* someone who is in charge of other people's work or of other workers.

botany ['bat n i] **1.** *n.* the study of plants. (No pl form in this sense.) **2.** *n.* the description of plant life in a certain area. (No pl form in this sense.)

both ['boθ] **1.** *adj.* one and one other; the two [people or things]. (See also EACH and EVERY.) **2.** *pron.* one thing or person and another thing or person; the two things or people.

bother ['bað ɚ] **1.** *n.* something that is time-consuming or annoying to do. **2.** *tv.* to annoy someone or something; to upset someone or something. **3.** *tv.* to interrupt or disturb someone.

bottle ['bat əl] **1.** *n.* a container, usually glass or plastic, with an opening at the end of a short or long neck. **2.** *n.* the contents of ①. **3.** *tv.* to put something in ①, usually for future use or sale. **4.** ~ **up** [for someone] to keep serious emotions within and not express them.

bottleneck ['bat l nɛk] *n.* a narrow or crowded passage, like the neck of a bottle.

46

bottom ['bɑt əm] **1.** *n.* the lowest level of something; the deepest point of something. **2.** *n.* the underside of something; the lowest surface of something. **3.** *n.* land underneath water; the ground under a body of water. **4.** *n.* the part of the body on which one sits; the buttocks. **5.** *adj.* relating to the lowest part of something; relating to the underneath part of something.

bought ['bɔt] pt/pp of BUY.

boulder ['bol dɚ] *n.* a huge stone.

boulevard ['bʊl ə vɑrd] *n.* a wide city street, usually lined with trees.

bounce ['baʊns] **1.** *n.* the return movement of an object when it hits a surface. **2.** *iv.* to spring up or away after hitting a surface. **3.** *tv.* to toss someone upward gently, causing an upward movement as in ②. **4.** *tv.* to cause something to hit against a surface and spring back. **5.** ~ **off** to rebound from something. **6.** ~ **out** to rebound out of or away from something.

bound ['baʊnd] **1.** pt/pp of BIND. **2.** *adj.* tied up; fastened; glued into covers. **3.** *iv.* to jump; to leap forward; to bounce up. **4.** *n.* an upward jump; a forward jump.

boundary ['baʊn dri] *n.* a border; a line that marks the edge of a thing or a place.

bouquet [bo 'ke] *n.* an arrangement of cut flowers; a grouping of cut flowers that can be held in one hand.

bout ['baʊt] **1.** *n.* an attack of a disease. **2.** *n.* a specific contest or event, especially a boxing match.

bow **1.** ['bo] *n.* a pretty knot, usually with two or more large loops. **2.** ['bo] *n.* a weapon that shoots arrows. **3.** ['bo] *n.* a stick with strings of hair stretched from end to end, used to play a stringed instrument, such as a violin. **4.** ['baʊ] *n.* an act of bending the body to show respect or in response to applause. **5.** ['baʊ] *n.* the front part of a ship or a boat. **6.** ['bo] *iv.* to bend into a curve, similar to ②; to form a curve. **7.** ['baʊ] *iv.* to bend the body when greeting or honoring someone. **8.** ['bo] *tv.* to cause something to bend into a curve, like the curve of ②; to cause something straight to form a curve. **9.** ~ **out** ['baʊ aʊt] to withdraw from something.

bowel ['baʊ əl] *n.* the upper or lower intestine; the upper and lower intestine.

bowels *n.* the inner part of something; the inner workings of something.

47

bowl ['bol] **1.** *n.* a deep, rounded dish; a deep, rounded container. **2.** *n.* the contents of ①. **3.** *n.* the part of a pipe that holds the tobacco. **4.** *iv.* to play the game of bowling.

bowling ['bo lɪŋ] *n.* a game where a player rolls a large, hard ball along a narrow wooden floor in order to knock down as many as possible of the ten pins at the other end. (No pl.)

box ['baks] **1.** *n.* a rigid, cube-shaped container, used for storage or delivery. **2.** *n.* the contents of ①. **3.** *n.* a private seating area in a sports stadium, theater, etc. **4.** *n.* an empty square printed on a piece of paper or on a form. **5.** *n.* a square or rectangular container or receptacle designed for any of a number of special functions.

boy ['bɔɪ] *n.* a male human, not yet fully matured.

brace ['bres] **1.** *n.* a support; something that holds something else in place. **2.** *tv.* to prepare oneself for an impact or some other strong force. **3.** *tv.* to prepare oneself for bad news.

bracelet ['bres lɪt] *n.* a piece of jewelry worn around the wrist.

braces *n.* metal wires or bands attached to teeth to straighten them. (Treated as pl, but not countable.)

bracket ['bræk ɪt] **1.** *n.* an L-shaped object attached to a wall to support a shelf. **2.** *n.* a printed character used to set off items or to enclose a set of words. **3.** *tv.* to enclose words in ②, [such as these words].

brag ['bræg] **1.** *iv.* to boast; to say too many good things about oneself. **2.** *tv.* to claim something in a boastful manner. (The object is a clause with THAT ⑦.)

braggart ['bræg ɚt] *n.* someone who brags; someone who boasts.

braid ['bred] **1.** *tv.* to interweave three or more strands of rope or bundles of hair, string, etc., into one ropelike band. **2.** *n.* a ropelike band made of woven strands.

brain ['bren] *n.* the part of the body inside the head that is the center of thinking and feeling and that controls the movement and operation of the body.

brake ['brek] **1.** *n.* a device that slows or stops a machine or vehicle. (Often pl. Compare this with BREAK.) **2.** *tv.* to cause something to stop or slow down. (Pt/pp: *braked*.) **3.** *iv.* to stop or slow down.

branch ['bræntʃ] **1.** *n.* a part of a tree that grows out of the trunk; an armlike part of a tree. **2.** *n.* a small stream or river that joins to a larger river. **3.** *n.* a division of a company; a smaller part of a larger organization or structure. **4.** ~ **off** to separate off from something; to divide away from something. **5.** ~ **out** [for a branch] to grow out of a tree branch or trunk. **6.** ~ **out** [for someone] to expand away from something; to diversify away from narrower interests.

brand ['brænd] **1.** *n.* a trade name; the name of a product by which the product is widely recognized. **2.** *n.* a special kind or type of something. **3.** *n.* a mark burned into the skin of cattle. **4.** *tv.* to mark cattle by burning a unique mark into their skin.

brass ['bræs] **1.** *n.* a metal made from copper and zinc. (Pl only for types and instances.) **2.** *n.* the family of wind instruments made of ① or some other metal, including the trumpet, trombone, and tuba. (Pl only for types and instances.) **3.** the *adj.* use of ① or ②.

brave ['brev] **1.** *tv.* to withstand something; to face something without fear. **2.** *adj.* showing courage; willing to face danger. (Adv: *bravely.* Comp: *braver;* sup: *bravest.*)

bread ['brɛd] **1.** *n.* a type of food made by baking a mixture of flour, water, and other ingredients, often including yeast. (No pl. Treated as sg. Number is expressed with *piece(s), slice(s),* or *loaves of bread.*) **2.** *tv.* to cover food with crumbs or meal before cooking it.

breadth ['brɛdθ] **1.** *n.* width; the measurement of something from side to side. **2.** *n.* extent.

break ['brek] **1.** *n.* a fracture; a place where something—especially a bone—has been broken. (Compare this with BRAKE.) **2.** *n.* a short period of rest from work. **3.** *n.* the period of time between school terms. **4.** *n.* an escape from jail or prison. **5.** *n.* the ending of a relationship with someone or something; the ending of an association with someone or something. **6.** *n.* a stop in a continuous action; an interruption. **7.** *n.* a chance to do something; an opportunity to do something. **8.** *tv., irreg.* to cause something to fall apart; to crush something. (Pt: BROKE; pp: BROKEN.) **9.** *tv., irreg.* to damage something; to make something not work correctly; to make something unusable. **10.** *tv., irreg.* to crack something; to fracture something, especially a bone. **11.** *tv., irreg.* to violate an agreement or promise by failing to do what was promised. **12.** *tv., irreg.* to exchange a large unit of money for the same amount of money in smaller units. **13.** *iv., irreg.* to shatter; to smash; to fall apart. **14.** *iv., irreg.* to fail to operate; to stop functioning properly. **15.** *iv., irreg.* to crack; to fracture. **16.** ~ **in** to burst into a place and violate someone's privacy. **17.** ~ **in** to interrupt someone's conversation. **18.** ~ **into** to enter a closed area by force. **19.** ~ **off** [for a piece of something] to become separated from

49

the whole. **20.** ~ **out** to get out of a confining place or situation; to escape from something or someplace. **21.** ~ **out** [for the skin] to erupt with a specific disease such as measles, chicken pox, rubella, etc. **22.** ~ **up** to break something into smaller pieces.

breakfast ['brɛk fəst] **1.** *n.* the first meal of the day. **2.** *iv.* to eat ① [somewhere or at some time].

breast ['brɛst] **1.** *n.* the chest; the part of the body between the neck and the stomach. **2.** *n.* the edible upper body of a fowl. **3.** *n.* one of the two milk-producing parts on the chest of the human female; a mammary gland.

breath ['brɛθ] **1.** *n.* the air that moves in and out of the body when someone or something inhales or exhales. **2.** *n.* someone's exhaled air, especially if felt or smelled.

breathe ['brið] **1.** *iv.* to suck air into the lungs and push air out of the lungs. **2.** *tv.* to inhale or exhale something; to take something into the lungs or expel something from the lungs or throat.

bred ['brɛd] pt/pp of BREED.

breed ['brid] **1.** *n.* a group of creatures representing a unique or different kind or type; a subgroup of a certain species. **2.** *n.* a kind of something; a class of something. **3.** *iv., irreg.* to reproduce; to mate. (Pt/pp: BRED.) **4.** *tv., irreg.* to cause selected members of some kind of animal to reproduce, often for specific characteristics.

breeze ['briz] **1.** *n.* a light wind; a gentle wind. **2.** ~ **in** to enter a place quickly, in a happy and carefree manner. **3.** ~ **through** to complete some task rapidly and easily. **4.** ~ **through** to travel through a place rapidly.

brew ['bru] **1.** *n.* a liquid drink made by heating various ingredients in water. **2.** *tv.* to make a liquid drink by mixing and heating various ingredients in water. **3.** *tv.* to make beer or ale. **4.** *iv.* to develop; to gather; to form. **5.** *iv.* [for a liquid drink] to develop into its final form.

bribe ['braɪb] **1.** *n.* an offer of something, especially money, in exchange for a favor from someone. **2.** *tv.* to offer someone something, especially money, in exchange for a favor.

brick ['brɪk] **1.** *n.* a rectangular block—used in building things—made of cement or baked clay. **2.** the *adj.* use of ①.

bride ['braɪd] *n.* a woman who is about to be married or has just been married.

bridegroom ['braid grum] *n.* a groom; a man who is about to be married or has just been married.

bridesmaid ['braidz med] *n.* a woman who attends the bride at a wedding.

bridge ['bridʒ] **1.** *n.* a raised way over a river, street, train tracks, etc. **2.** *n.* something that links people or things. (Fig. on ①.) **3.** *n.* the navigation and control center of a ship. **4.** *n.* the upper part of the nose; the part of the nose between the eyes. **5.** *n.* the part of a pair of eyeglasses that rests on the nose. **6.** *n.* a type of card game for four people. (No pl.)

brief ['brif] **1.** *adj.* short in time; to the point. (Adv: *briefly.* Comp: *briefer;* sup: *briefest.*) **2.** *n.* [in law] a document that describes certain facts or information about a legal case. **3.** *tv.* to acquaint someone with certain facts or information.

briefs *n.* short and close-fitting underpants. (Treated as pl. Number can be expressed with *pair(s) of briefs.* Also countable.)

bright ['brait] **1.** *adj.* shiny; full of light; reflecting much light. (Adv: *brightly.* Comp: *brighter;* sup: *brightest.*) **2.** *adj.* smart; intelligent. (Adv: *brightly.* Comp: *brighter;* sup: *brightest.*) **3.** *adj.* vivid; brilliant. (Adv: *brightly.* Comp: *brighter;* sup: *brightest.*)

brilliant ['bril jənt] **1.** *adj.* bright; shiny. (Adv: *brilliantly.*) **2.** *adj.* intelligent; smart; talented. (Adv: *brilliantly.*) **3.** *adj.* excellent. (Adv: *brilliantly.*)

brim ['brim] **1.** *n.* the top edge of something, such as a cup. **2.** *n.* the circular, flat edge of a hat.

bring ['briŋ] **1.** *tv., irreg.* to carry or escort someone or something from a more distant place to a closer place. (Pt/pp: BROUGHT.) **2.** *tv., irreg.* to cause something to happen; to result in something. **3.** *tv., irreg.* to cause something to enter into a different state. **4.** ~ **back** to remind someone of something.

brisk ['brisk] **1.** *adj.* [of movement, actions, activity, or rhythm] quick, rapid, or swift; [of rhythm, music, or activity] lively. (Adv: *briskly.* Comp: *brisker;* sup: *briskest.*) **2.** *adj.* stimulating; chilly. (Adv: *briskly.* Comp: *brisker;* sup: *briskest.*)

bristle ['bris əl] *n.* a short, stiff hair, as on a brush or on the back of a hog.

brittle ['brit əl] *adj.* hard, but easily cracked or broken. (Comp: *brittler;* sup: *brittlest.*)

51

broad ['brɔd] **1.** *adj.* wide; vast; extensive; far-reaching. (Adv: *broadly.* Comp: *broader;* sup: *broadest.*) **2.** *adj.* main; general. (Adv: *broadly.* Comp: *broader;* sup: *broadest.*)

broadcast ['brɔd kæst] **1.** *n.* a television or radio program. **2.** *tv.* to transmit a radio or television signal or program. **3.** *tv.* to make news widely known; to tell something to many people. **4.** *iv.* to transmit or send out radio waves.

broccoli ['brɑk ə li] *n.* a green vegetable that grows in branched stalks ending in clumps of buds. (No pl.)

broil ['brɔil] **1.** *tv.* to cook something by placing it over or under an open flame. **2.** *iv.* [for food] to cook over or under an open flame.

broke ['brok] **1.** pt of BREAK. **2.** *adj.* having no money; completely without money; penniless.

broken ['brok ən] **1.** pp of BREAK. **2.** *adj.* not working; not functioning; not operating; out of order.

bronze ['brɑnz] **1.** *n.* a brownish metal made from copper and tin. (Pl only for types and instances.) **2.** *n.* a third-place medal; an award for coming in third place in a competition. **3.** *adj.* made from ①.

brook ['bruk] *n.* a stream; a creek; a small river.

broom ['brum] *n.* a long-handled brush that is used to sweep floors.

broth ['brɔθ] *n.* the liquid part of soup. (Pl only for types and instances.)

brother ['brʌð ɚ] *n.* a male sibling.

brought ['brɔt] pt/pp of BRING.

brow ['brɑu] *n.* the forehead; the area around the eyebrows.

brown ['brɑun] **1.** *n.* a deep, reddish tan color similar to the color of dirt or wood. (Pl only for types and instances.) **2.** *adj.* of the color of ①. (Comp: *browner;* sup: *brownest.*) **3.** *tv.* to cook something until it turns dark or gets crisp. **4.** *iv.* [for food] to cook until it becomes ②.

browse ['brɑuz] **1.** *iv.* to look at goods casually when shopping. **2.** ~ **through** to examine the contents of something, such as a book.

bruise ['bruz] **1.** *n.* a colored mark on the skin caused by being struck. **2.** *tv.* to cause ① by striking the body.

brunt ['brʌnt] *n.* the main force or impact of an attack.

brush ['brʌʃ] **1.** *n.* a device used for cleaning, combing, or painting—made of hard bristles attached to a handle. **2.** *tv.* to clean something, such as one's teeth, with ①. **3.** *tv.* to arrange or groom hair with ①. **4.** ~ **away** to remove something from something by brushing; to get dirt or crumbs off something by brushing. **5.** ~ **off** to remove something from someone or something by brushing. **6.** ~ **up on** to improve one's knowledge of something or one's ability to do something.

brute ['brut] **1.** *n.* any animal except a human; a beast. **2.** *n.* a bully; someone who is cruel. **3.** *adj.* great [strength]; powerful [force].

bubble ['bʌb əl] **1.** *n.* a thin, spherical film of liquid that encloses a pocket of gas or air. **2.** *n.* a sphere of air within a solid or a liquid. **3.** *iv.* [for moving liquid] to make a sound that includes the popping or collapsing of ① or ②.

buck ['bʌk] **1.** *n.* the male of certain kinds of animals, such as deer and rabbits. **2.** *n.* one American dollar bill; a dollar. (Slang.) **3.** *iv.* [for an animal that is being ridden] to jump in an attempt to throw its rider.

bucket ['bʌk ɪt] **1.** *n.* a pail; an open-topped container with a curved wire handle. **2.** *n.* the contents of ①.

buckle ['bʌk əl] **1.** *n.* a fastener for securing a belt or strap. **2.** *tv.* to fasten a shoe, belt, etc., by using ①. **3.** *tv.* to cause pavement to bend and rise up. **4.** *iv.* [for pavement] to rise, fold, or break due to a force such as an earthquake or because of excessive heat. **5.** *iv.* [for someone's knees] to fold or collapse.

bud ['bʌd] **1.** *n.* the part of a plant that becomes a leaf or a flower. **2.** *n.* a flower that has not opened all the way; a flower whose petals are still wrapped together. **3.** *iv.* [for a plant] to develop and open the parts that become leaves or flowers.

buddy ['bʌd i] **1.** *n.* a friend; a pal. **2.** ~ **up to** to become overly familiar or friendly with someone. **3.** ~ **up with** to join with another person to form a pair that will do something together or share something.

budget ['bʌdʒ ət] **1.** *n.* a financial plan; an estimate of how much money will be earned and spent during a period of time. **2.** *n.* an amount of money allocated for a particular purpose. **3.** *tv.* to provide or reserve an amount of money for a particular purpose. **4.** *adj.* cheap; economical.

buffalo ['bʌf ə lo] *n., irreg.* a type of wild ox native to Asia, Africa, and the Americas. (Pl: *buffalo, buffalos,* or *buffaloes*.)

buffet [bə 'fe] **1.** *n.* a large cabinet for holding utensils for serving and eating as well as tablecloths and napkins. **2.** *n.* a table or counter having bowls of food that diners can serve for themselves. **3.** the *adj.* use of ① or ②.

bug ['bʌg] **1.** *n.* any small insect or creature like an insect; any annoying insect. **2.** *n.* the flu; any minor sickness. (Informal.) **3.** *n.* an electronic device that permits someone to listen in secret to someone's private conversation. **4.** *n.* a problem; something that is wrong with a system, especially in a computer program. **5.** *tv.* to equip a room, telephone, etc., with ③. **6.** *iv.* [for someone's eyes] to open up wide and become very apparent.

build ['bɪld] **1.** *tv., irreg.* to make something from separate pieces; to construct something. (Pt/pp: BUILT.) **2.** *tv., irreg.* to develop something; to establish something a little bit at a time. **3.** *iv., irreg.* [for something] to increase. **4.** *n.* the form of the body; the shape of the body; the muscle structure of the body. **5.** ~ **in** to make someone or something an integral part of an organization or a structure. **6.** ~ **up** to prepare someone for something; to lead a person into a proper state of mind to receive some information.

builder ['bɪld ɚ] *n.* someone who builds buildings for a living.

building ['bɪl dɪŋ] **1.** *n.* a structure where people live, work, or play. **2.** *n.* the business of constructing ①. (No pl.) **3.** the *adj.* use of ① or ②.

built ['bɪlt] pt/pp of BUILD.

bulb ['bʌlb] **1.** *n.* any rounded or globe-shaped object. **2.** *n.* a glass globe, with a special wire inside, that is used to create light from electricity. **3.** *n.* a swelling between the stem and roots of some plants, used for storing food for the plant.

bulk ['bʌlk] **1.** *n.* a great amount; a large amount of something. (No pl.) **2.** *n.* the major portion of something; the largest and most important part. (No pl.) **3.** *adj.* [containing] large [quantities or amounts].

bull ['bʊl] **1.** *n.* the male animal corresponding to a cow, if it is able to breed. **2.** *n.* someone who believes that prices on stocks or bonds will rise. **3.** *adj.* [of certain animals] male.

bulldozer ['bʊl doz ɚ] *n.* a powerful tractor equipped with a strong blade that can push dirt and rocks.

bullet ['bʊl ɪt] *n.* a small piece of lead fired from a gun.

54

bulletin ['bʊl ə tən] **1.** *n.* a special news report; a piece of news; official information. **2.** *n.* a journal or newsletter published by a specific group.

bully ['bʊl i] **1.** *n.* someone, usually a male, who is mean or threatening. **2.** *tv.* to threaten someone; to be mean to someone.

bumblebee ['bʌm bəl bi] *n.* a large, hairy, black and yellow bee.

bump ['bʌmp] **1.** *n.* a lump or swelling in an otherwise flat area. **2.** *n.* a knock; a blow; a hit; a forceful contact. **3.** *tv.* to make forceful contact with someone or something. **4.** *tv.* [for an airline] to cancel someone's airplane reservation without warning. **5.** ~ **into** to have a surprise meeting with someone. **6.** ~ **into** to crash into someone or something.

bumper ['bʌm pɚ] **1.** *n.* a strong, protective metal or fiberglass bar on the front and back of a vehicle. **2.** *n.* any device designed to protect someone or something from an impact. **3.** *adj.* large; abundant; plentiful.

bun ['bʌn] **1.** *n.* a bread product, such as that used to hold cooked hamburger meat or a wiener. **2.** *n.* a sweetened bread roll, sometimes with fruit or other fillings.

bunch ['bʌntʃ] **1.** *n.* a group of things that grow together or are placed together. **2.** *n.* a group of people or things; a large number of things or people.

bundle ['bʌn dəl] **1.** *n.* a group of things gathered together. **2.** *tv.* to include a selection of software with the sale of computer hardware. **3.** ~ **up** to wrap up in protective clothing or bedding as protection against the cold.

bunk ['bʌŋk] **1.** *n.* a narrow bed. **2.** *n.* nonsense. (Informal. No pl form in this sense.) **3.** ~ **down** to lie down to sleep. **4.** ~ **with** to share a bedroom or sleeping area.

bunny ['bʌn i] *n.* a rabbit; a hare.

buoy ['bɔɪ, 'bu i] **1.** *n.* a floating aid to navigation, used to display warnings or directions. **2.** *n.* a floating ring that can support a person in the water.

burden ['bɚd n] **1.** *n.* a heavy load. **2.** *n.* a heavy responsibility that strains a person. (Fig. on ①.) **3.** *tv.* to give someone or something a heavy load.

55

bureau ['bjʊr o] **1.** *n.* a department or agency, especially one relating to government. (From French.) **2.** *n.* a chest of drawers; a piece of furniture that clothes are kept in.

burglar ['bɚglɚ] *n.* a criminal who enters someplace illegally to steal things.

burial ['bɛr i əl] *n.* the burying of something, especially a dead body.

burn ['bɚn] **1.** *n.* the mark caused by a flame or something that is very hot. **2.** *n.* an injury caused to someone who has been harmed by high heat. **3.** *tv., irreg.* to set fire to something; to destroy something by fire. (Pt/pp: usually *burned*, but sometimes BURNT.) **4.** *tv., irreg.* to damage someone or something with too much heat. **5.** *tv., irreg.* to consume a fuel or an energy source. **6.** *tv., irreg.* to sting something; to cause something to have a sharp feeling of heat. **7.** *iv., irreg.* to provide light; to give off light. **8.** *iv., irreg.* [for an injury] to sting. **9.** *iv., irreg.* to be on fire. **10.** *iv., irreg.* [for food] to become scorched from overcooking.

burner ['bɚ nɚ] *n.* a device that makes a controlled flame for cooking or heating.

burnt ['bɚnt] a pt/pp of BURN.

burrow ['bɚ o] **1.** *n.* a hole that an animal digs in the ground for a place to live. **2.** *iv.* [for a small animal] to work its way, digging, into soil, leaves, snow, etc.

burst ['bɚst] **1.** *tv., irreg.* to break something open; to cause something to explode. (Pt/pp: *burst.*) **2.** *iv., irreg.* to explode; to suddenly break open. **3.** *n.* a sudden outbreak; a violent outbreak; a barrage. **4.** *n.* a spurt; a quick, intense event. **5.** ~ **in** to intrude or come in thoughtlessly and suddenly and interrupt someone or something. **6.** ~ **out** [for people] to come out of a place rapidly.

bury ['bɛr i] **1.** *tv.* to put something in the ground, to cover something with dirt or soil. **2.** *tv.* to place a dead person or other creature in the ground. **3.** *tv.* to conceal someone or something; to hide someone or something.

bus ['bʌs] **1.** *n.* an enclosed motor vehicle that carries many passengers. **2.** *n.* [in a computer] a circuit that allows new devices and equipment to be connected to the main computer. **3.** *tv.* to transport someone using ①. **4.** *tv.* to remove dirty dishes from a table after a meal in a restaurant or cafeteria.

bush ['bʊʃ] *n.* a plant with several woody branches.

56

bushel ['bʊʃ əl] **1.** *n.* a unit of measurement of dry goods, especially crops, equal to 64 pints or 32 quarts. **2.** *adj.* holding or containing ①.

bushy ['bʊʃ i] *adj.* [of hair or fur] thick, dense, and shaggy. (Adv: *bushily.* Comp: *bushier;* sup: *bushiest.*)

business ['bɪz nəs] **1.** *n.* a profession; an occupation. **2.** *n.* buying, selling, or trading. (No pl.) **3.** *n.* a corporation; a company. **4.** *n.* affair; concern; a matter of interest. (No pl.)

busy ['bɪz i] **1.** *adj.* working; at work; having things to do. (Adv: *busily.* Comp: *busier;* sup: *busiest.*) **2.** *adj.* [of a telephone connection] in use. (Comp: *busier;* sup: *busiest.*) **3.** *adj.* occupied with something else at the time. (Comp: *busier;* sup: *busiest.*) **4.** *adj.* distracting to look at because of clashing patterns; having too much detail. (Adv: *busily.* Comp: *busier;* sup: *busiest.*) **5.** *tv.* to make work for oneself; to occupy oneself with something.

but ['bʌt, bət] **1.** *conj.* on the contrary; however. **2.** *conj.* except. **3.** *prep.* except someone or something; except for someone or something; other than someone or something; besides someone or something. **4.** *adv.* only; merely; just.

butcher ['bʊtʃ ɚ] **1.** *n.* someone who kills animals that will be used for meat. **2.** *n.* someone who cuts up and sells the meat of animals. **3.** *tv.* to kill and cut up an animal for food. **4.** *tv.* to kill someone or something with great cruelty.

butt ['bʌt] **1.** *n.* the end or base of something. **2.** *n.* the leftover end of a cigar or cigarette. **3.** *n.* part of the body on which one sits; the buttocks. (Informal.) **4.** *n.* someone who is the victim of ridicule or the object of jokes or rudeness. **5.** *tv.* to strike or push hard against someone or something with the head. (Said especially of animals with horns.) **6.** ~ **in** to interrupt someone or something. **7.** ~ **into** to intrude upon something; to break into a conversation.

butter ['bʌt ɚ] **1.** *n.* the fatty part of milk left after it has been stirred and mixed over and over. (Pl only for types and instances.) **2.** *n.* certain foods mashed into a spreadable substance. (Pl only for types and instances.) **3.** *tv.* to put ① on something, usually bread.

butterfly ['bʌt ɚ flaɪ] *n.* an insect with large, brightly colored wings.

buttermilk ['bʌt ɚ mɪlk] *n.* a drink made from milk to which certain kinds of bacteria have been added. (No pl.)

buttocks ['bʌt ʌks] *n.* the part of the human body upon which one sits.

57

button ['bʌt n] **1.** *n.* a small, hard disc, used to fasten clothes or fabric. **2.** *n.* a small disc or similar device that is pressed to close an electrical circuit. **3.** *n.* a badge bearing a message, worn on the clothing. **4.** *tv.* to fasten or close two pieces of fabric together with ①.

buy ['baɪ] **1.** *tv., irreg.* to purchase something; to pay money in exchange for something. (Pt/pp: BOUGHT.) **2.** *tv., irreg.* to acquire something, such as time. (Fig. on ①.) **3.** *tv., irreg.* to believe something. (Informal.) **4.** *n.* something that is offered for sale at a very good price.

buzz ['bʌz] **1.** *n.* the sound that bees make; a rapid humming sound. (Pl only for types and instances.) **2.** *iv.* to make a loud humming sound as bees do. **3.** *n.* a telephone call.

by ['baɪ] **1.** *prep.* near someone or something; next to someone or something; alongside someone or something; beside someone or something. **2.** *prep.* [passing] near someone or something. **3.** *prep.* through the use of someone or something. **4.** *prep.* [done] through the process of doing something. **5.** *prep.* a word used in indicating the dimensions of something, especially the dimensions of a square area. (See also MULTIPLY ①.) **6.** *prep.* before some time; not later than some time. **7.** *prep.* [surpassing someone or something] according to a specific amount. **8.** *prep.* allotted according to something; in units of something. **9.** *adv.* past; beyond.

Bye (-bye) ['baɪ ('baɪ)] *interj.* Good-bye; Farewell.

byte ['baɪt] *n.* a unit of computer data, made up of eight bits.

C

cab [ˈkæb] *n.* a TAXI; a TAXICAB.

cabbage [ˈkæb ɪdʒ] *n.* a large, round vegetable with green or purple leaves. (Not usually pl unless referring to different kinds, types, or varieties. Number is expressed with *head(s) of cabbage.*)

cabin [ˈkæb ən] **1.** *n.* a small house made of wood, especially in a far-away area. **2.** *n.* a private room on a ship. **3.** *n.* the part of an airplane where the passengers sit.

cabinet [ˈkæb (ə) nət] **1.** *n.* a piece of furniture with shelves, used for storing or displaying something; a small storage unit with a door, as found in a kitchen. **2.** *n.* the group of people who advise a president, prime minister, etc.

cable [ˈkeb əl] **1.** *n.* a thick, heavy, strong length of wire or rope. **2.** *n.* a telegram. (These were once sent over a telegraph cable.) **3.** ~ **(television)** *n.* television programming received over a cable. (No pl form in this sense.)

cacti [ˈkæk tɑɪ] a pl of CACTUS.

cactus [ˈkæk təs] *n., irreg.* a desert plant with pulp on the inside and needles on the outside. (Pl: CACTI or *cactuses.*)

café [kæ ˈfe] *n.* a place to buy simple meals; a small restaurant.

cafeteria [kæf ə ˈtɪr i ə] *n.* a restaurant where one can choose from many selections, usually by passing by the items and placing one's choice of food on a tray.

cage [ˈkedʒ] **1.** *n.* an enclosure with bars or wires, where living creatures are kept. **2.** *tv.* to put someone or something in ①.

caged [ˈkedʒd] *adj.* enclosed; not free.

cake [ˈkek] **1.** *n.* a sweet, baked, breadlike food. (Pl only for types and instances.) **2.** *n.* a single, complete unit of ①.

calculate [ˈkæl kjə let] **1.** *iv.* to estimate; to figure out values. **2.** *tv.* to add, subtract, multiply, or divide numbers; to figure out the value of something. (The object can be a clause with THAT ⑦.)

calculator [ˈkæl kjə let ɚ] *n.* a machine that adds, subtracts, multiplies, and divides figures and performs other mathematical functions.

59

calculus ['kæl kjə ləs] *n.* a branch of higher mathematics using special symbols and operations. (No pl.)

calendar ['kæl ən dɚ] **1.** *n.* a system for keeping track of years and the divisions of years. **2.** *n.* a chart or table showing days, weeks, and months. **3.** *n.* a schedule of events; a list of events.

calf ['kæf] **1.** *n., irreg.* a young cow or bull. (Pl: CALVES.) **2.** *n., irreg.* the back of the leg from the knee to the ankle.

call ['kɔl] **1.** *n.* a shout; a cry. **2.** *n.* an instance of someone contacting someone by telephone; a message or a conversation using the telephone; a telephone call; a phone call. **3.** *n.* a decision; a choice. **4.** *tv.* to try to contact someone by telephone; to telephone someone. **5.** *tv.* to demand someone's presence. **6.** *tv.* to name someone or something; to refer to or address someone or something as something. **7.** *tv.* [for an umpire] to make a decision in a ball game. **8.** ~ **up** to call someone, a group, or a company on the telephone. **9.** ~ **off** to cancel something, especially an event that has been planned for a certain date.

caller ['kɔ lɚ] **1.** *n.* someone who makes a telephone call. **2.** *n.* a visitor.

calm ['kɑm] **1.** *adj.* quiet; serene; at peace. (Adv: *calmly.* Comp: *calmer;* sup: *calmest.*) **2.** *n.* a time or feeling of peace and quiet. (No pl.) **3.** ~ **down** to relax; to become less busy or active.

calorie ['kæl ə ri] *n.* a unit of energy supplied by food.

calves ['kævz] pl of CALF.

came ['kem] pt of COME.

camel ['kæm əl] *n.* a large desert animal with one or two fatty humps on its back.

camera ['kæm (ə) rə] **1.** *n.* a device that takes pictures; a device that makes photographs. **2.** *n.* a device that records live action for television or movies.

camp ['kæmp] **1.** *n.* a remote or rural temporary residence, such as for soldiers, pioneers, refugees, people on vacation, etc. **2.** *n.* a remote or rural place where children are sent in the summer. **3.** *n.* a permanent living area for training and retraining members of various military organizations. **4.** *iv.* to take a vacation in a natural setting; to stay outside in a remote or rural area, sleeping in a tent or a camper instead of a hotel.

campaign [kæm 'pen] **1.** *n.* the period of time before an election when the candidates try to persuade people to vote for them. **2.** *n.* a coordinated series of events with a specific goal or purpose.

camper ['kæm pɚ] **1.** *n.* someone who CAMPS ④; someone who takes a vacation in a rural or remote area. **2.** *n.* a special vehicle, designed for camping.

campfire ['kæmp fɑɪɚ] *n.* a fire that campers cook on and sit around at night to keep warm while telling stories and enjoying the outdoors.

campsite ['kæmp sɑɪt] *n.* the area where campers set up their tents.

campus ['kæmp əs] **1.** *n.* the buildings, lawns, and other areas of a school, college, or university. **2.** *n.* the buildings and surrounding areas of a large company. **3.** the *adj.* use of ① or ②.

can ['kæn, kən] **1.** *aux.* a word indicating ability to do something. (See also COULD.) **2.** *aux.* a form indicating permission to do something. (In general use but considered informal. In more formal English, MAY is used for this function. See also COULD.) **3.** *tv.* to preserve food by sealing it in an airtight container. (Pt/pp: *canned.*) **4.** *n.* a container shaped like a tube with a top and a bottom, usually made of metal. **5.** *n.* the contents of ④.

canal [kə 'næl] *n.* a long waterway—usually man-made—that is not a river.

canary [kə 'nɛr i] *n.* a small, yellow bird that sings.

cancel ['kæn səl] **1.** *tv.* to end or stop something that is occurring or planned. **2.** *tv.* to place a mark on a postage stamp, check, ticket, etc., so that it cannot be used again.

cancer ['kæn sɚ] **1.** *n.* a disease characterized by a tumor or tumors growing and spreading throughout the body. (Pl only for types and instances.) **2.** *n.* something evil or horrible that spreads out over an area. (Fig. on ①.)

candidate ['kæn dɪ det] **1.** *n.* someone who is seeking a public office or other job. **2.** *n.* a recommended or possible choice of a thing or person.

candle ['kæn dəl] *n.* an object of wax molded around a string or wick. (The wick burns and gives off light.)

candlestick ['kæn dəl stɪk] *n.* a holder for a candle.

candy ['kæn di] **1.** *n.* a sweet food made with sugar and additional flavors. (Pl only for types and instances. Number is expressed by *piece(s) of candy.*) **2.** *n.* a piece or a serving of ①.

61

cane ['ken] *n.* a stick used as an aid in walking.

canned ['kænd] *adj.* preserved; sealed into a container.

cannon ['kæn ən] *n., irreg.* a large gun. (Pl: *cannon* or *cannons*.)

cannot [kə 'nɑt] *aux.* the negative form of CAN. (See also CAN'T.)

canoe [kə 'nu] **1.** *n.* a small boat that is moved by paddling. **2.** *iv.* to travel by ①.

canopy ['kæn ə pi] *n.* a fabric cover that hangs over something.

can't [kænt] *cont.* cannot.

canvas ['kæn vəs] **1.** *n.* a heavy, sturdy fabric made from cotton or another strong fiber. (Pl only for types and instances.) **2.** *n.* a panel of fabric—usually stretched on a frame—that painters paint on. **3.** *n.* a painting that has been painted on ②.

canyon ['kæn jən] *n.* a deep, narrow valley, often with a river running through it.

cap ['kæp] **1.** *n.* a (round) cover for the head, often with a shade for the eyes. **2.** *n.* the cover or the top of a bottle or small jar; a small lid. **3.** *tv.* to close something with ②; to put ② on something. **4.** *tv.* to limit something at a specific point.

capable ['ke pə bəl] **1.** *adj.* able; having the power or ability to do something. (Adv: *capably*.) **2.** ~ **of** having the ability to do something or the capacity for doing something.

capacity [kə 'pæs ə ti] **1.** *n.* the amount of something that a space or container will hold; the amount of space in something. **2.** *n.* the ability to do something. (No pl.) **3.** *n.* a job, role, or function; a set of responsibilities.

cape ['kep] **1.** *n.* a long, sleeveless garment worn over clothes. **2.** *n.* a piece of land that sticks out into a body of water.

capital ['kæp ɪ təl] **1.** *n.* a city that is the center of a government. (Compare this with CAPITOL.) **2.** *n.* any special or central city, with reference to a certain feature or attribute. **3.** *n.* an uppercase letter of the alphabet. **4.** *n.* money that is invested with the hope that it will earn more money. (No pl.) **5.** *adj.* [of a crime] punishable by death.

capitol ['kæp ɪ təl] *n.* the building where legislators do their work. (Compare this with CAPITAL.)

capsule ['kæp səl] **1.** *n.* a dose of medicine in a gelatin shell that dissolves when swallowed. **2.** *n.* the part of a spaceship where astronauts live and work.

captain [ˈkæp tən] 1. *n.* someone in charge of a ship, boat, or airplane. 2. *n.* an officer in the military or the police. 3. *n.* the leader of a team.

capture [ˈkæp tʃə] 1. *tv.* to catch someone or something; to make someone or something a captive. 2. *tv.* to take something by force; to take control of something. 3. *tv.* to accurately show a feeling or atmosphere through artistic expression.

car [ˈkɑr] 1. *n.* an automobile; a vehicle that can carry a small number of passengers. 2. *n.* one unit of a train. 3. *n.* any of a number of different structures used to carry goods or people.

caramel [ˈkær ə məl, ˈkɑr məl] 1. *n.* a kind of candy made by heating sugar. (Pl only for types and instances.) 2. *adj.* made with or flavored with ①.

carbon [ˈkɑr bən] *n.* a chemical element occurring in nature as coal, graphite, and diamonds. (No pl.)

card [ˈkɑrd] 1. *n.* a stiff, rectangular piece of paper. 2. *n.* a rectangle of stiff paper used in games, such as bridge or poker.

cardboard [ˈkɑrd bord] 1. *n.* a kind of heavy, thick, stiff paper. (Pl only for types and instances.) 2. *adj.* made of ①.

cardinal [ˈkɑrd nəl] 1. *n.* a bird—the males of which are bright red—with a crest on its head. 2. *n.* a high-ranking official of the Roman Catholic Church.

cardinal number AND **cardinal numeral** a number used in counting, such as one, two, three. (Can be shortened to CARDINAL. See also ORDINAL NUMBER.)

cardinal numeral Go to CARDINAL NUMBER.

care [ˈkɛr] 1. *n.* serious attention; focused thought; caution. (No pl.) 2. *n.* the responsibility of providing for, protecting, or medically treating someone. (No pl.) 3. *n.* a worry; a source of anxiety; a concern.

career [kə ˈrɪr] 1. *n.* one's chosen work; what one does to earn money. 2. the *adj.* use of ①.

careful [ˈkɛr fʊl] 1. *adj.* cautious; avoiding danger or damage. (Adv: *carefully.*) 2. *adj.* detailed; thorough. (Adv: *carefully.*)

careless [ˈkɛr ləs] *adj.* without care; clumsy; done without thought. (Adv: *carelessly.*)

carelessness [ˈkɛr ləs nəs] *n.* a lack of concern; a lack of care. (No pl.)

caretaker [ˈkɛr tek ɚ] **1.** *n.* someone who watches over and protects a building or property. **2.** *n.* someone who takes care of someone else.

cargo [ˈkɑr go] *n.* goods being carried by a vehicle; freight. (Pl only for types and instances. Pl: *cargoes* or *cargos*.)

carnival [ˈkɑr nə vəl] *n.* a circus; a traveling amusement show having RIDES ④.

carol [ˈkɛr əl] *n.* a song of joy, especially a Christmas song.

carpenter [ˈkɑr pən tɚ] *n.* someone who builds things with wood.

carpet [ˈkɑr pɪt] **1.** *n.* a rug; a thick floor covering made out of fabric. **2.** *tv.* to cover a floor with ①.

carriage [ˈkɛr ɪdʒ] *n.* a car or vehicle pulled by horses.

carrot [ˈkɛr ət] *n.* a vegetable with a long, thin, edible orange root.

carry [ˈkɛr i] **1.** *tv.* to pick up and take someone or something somewhere. **2.** *tv.* to support the weight of something. **3.** *tv.* to spread a disease or sickness. **4.** *tv.* to win the vote of a state or district. **5.** *tv.* [when adding a column of numbers, if the result is greater than 9] to transfer units of ten to the next column to the left as units of one. **6.** *tv.* [for a store] to have an item available for sale. **7.** *iv.* [for a voice or sound] to travel far. **8.** ~ **off** to take someone or something some distance away. **9.** ~ **on** to cry; to act rowdy. **10.** ~ **out** to complete a deed. **11.** ~ **out** to take something out with one.

cart [ˈkɑrt] **1.** *n.* a vehicle pulled by a horse, mule, dog, etc. **2.** *n.* a large basket on wheels, such as those found in grocery stores and other shops.

carton [ˈkɑrt n̩] **1.** *n.* a cardboard or plastic container or package. **2.** *n.* ① considered as a measurement of something.

cartoon [kɑr ˈtun] **1.** *n.* a drawing or series of drawings that is usually intended to be funny. **2.** *n.* a film in which each frame is a drawing. (Also an *animated cartoon*.)

carve [ˈkɑrv] **1.** *tv.* to cut or sculpt wood, ivory, soap, or some other substance into a shape. **2.** *tv.* to slice or cut up cooked meat for serving at a meal.

case [ˈkes] **1.** *n.* a crate; a box. **2.** *n.* an instance; an occurrence. **3.** *n.* a legal action or lawsuit.

cash [ˈkæʃ] **1.** *n.* money; currency, but not a check or a credit card. (No pl.) **2.** *tv.* to exchange a check for currency. **3.** *tv.* to give money in exchange for a check.

cashier [kæ 'ʃɪr] *n.* someone who handles the paying out and taking in of money, especially at a store or bank.

cassette [kə 'sɛt] **1.** *n.* a plastic case containing a pair of reels of magnetic audiotape or videotape. **2.** ~ **player** a device that plays back sound recorded on a cassette. **3.** ~ **recorder** a device that records sound onto a cassette and plays it back.

cast ['kæst] **1.** *n.* all of the performers in a play, musical, opera, TV show, or movie. **2.** *n.* a protective support for a broken bone, often made from plaster. **3.** *tv., irreg.* to throw something. (Pt/pp: *cast*.) **4.** *tv., irreg.* to throw a fishing lure into the water; to drop a fishing net into the water. **5.** *tv., irreg.* to create a shadow on something. **6.** *tv., irreg.* to move and aim one's eyes or line of sight at someone or something. **7.** *tv., irreg.* to select the performers for a play, film, opera, etc. **8.** *tv., irreg.* to create an object by pouring a soft substance into a mold and letting it harden into the shape of the mold.

castle ['kæs əl] **1.** *n.* a large fortress where a country's king and queen live. **2.** *n.* a game piece in chess, usually shaped like ①.

casual ['kæʒ ju əl] **1.** *adj.* [of someone] relaxed and free; [of an event] not formal. (Adv: *casually*.) **2.** *adj.* done without thought or planning. (Adv: *casually*.)

cat ['kæt] **1.** *n.* one of a member of the family of mammals that includes ②, lions, leopards, tigers, jaguars, and lynxes. **2.** *n.* a small mammal, with claws, sharp teeth, and whiskers, often kept as a pet.

catalog AND **catalogue** ['kæt ə lɔg] **1.** *n.* a book or list containing descriptions of things, often of things that are for sale. **2. (card) catalog** *n.* the files of cards listing the books and publications in a library and their locations within the library—or the equivalent information stored in computer files. **3.** *tv.* to arrange or categorize items on a list or in ① or ②.

catch ['kætʃ] **1.** *tv., irreg.* to seize and hold someone or something. (Pt/pp: CAUGHT.) **2.** *tv., irreg.* to find someone in the act of doing something. **3.** *tv., irreg.* to get a disease caused by bacteria or viruses. **4.** *tv., irreg.* to reach or make contact with someone or something just in time. **5.** *tv., irreg.* to experience something through one of the senses; to understand someone or something. **6.** *tv., irreg.* [for something] to snare or entangle someone or something. **7.** *n.* a game or pastime where people throw and receive a ball back and forth. **8.** *n.* an act of grasping or receiving something as in ①. **9.** *n.* a fastener; a locking or latching device.

catcher ['kætʃ ɚ] *n.* [in baseball] the player who is behind the batter.

65

caterpillar ['kæt ə pɪl ɚ] *n.* the creature, somewhat like a worm, that is the young form of a butterfly or a moth.

cathedral [kə 'θi drəl] *n.* a large, important church, especially a major, ancient church.

catholic ['kæθ (ə) lɪk] **1.** *adj.* universal; wide ranging. (Adv: *catholically* […ɪk li].) **2.** *adj.* of or about the Roman Catholic Church or religion. (Capitalized.) **3.** *n.* a member of the Roman Catholic Church. (Capitalized.)

Catholicism [kə 'θɑl ə sɪz əm] *n.* the religion and teachings of the Roman Catholic Church. (No pl.)

catsup Go to KETCHUP.

cattle ['kæt əl] *n.* cows and bulls in general. (No pl. Treated as pl, but not countable. Number is expressed with *head of cattle*, as in *10 head of cattle.*)

Caucasian [kɔ 'ke ʒən] **1.** *adj.* [of a person, usually of European descent] having light-colored skin; WHITE ⑥. (In common, but not technical, use.) **2.** *n.* a CAUCASIAN as in ① person; a person having WHITE ⑥ skin.

caught ['kɔt] pt/pp of CATCH.

cause ['kɔz] **1.** *tv.* to make something happen. **2.** *n.* someone or something that makes something happen; someone or something that produces an effect. **3.** *n.* a philosophy or a charity; a political or social movement.

caution ['kɔʃn] *n.* care; being careful.

cave ['kev] *n.* a natural chamber or tunnel inside a mountain or under the earth.

cavern ['kæv ɚn] *n.* a large cave; a large chamber in a cave.

cavity ['kæv ɪ ti] **1.** *n.* a hole; a hollow, enclosed space. **2.** *n.* a rotten place on a tooth.

cease ['sis] **1.** *tv.* to stop doing something; to quit doing something. **2.** *iv.* to stop; to finish.

ceiling ['si lɪŋ] **1.** *n.* the underside of a roof; a surface that forms the overhead part of a room. **2.** *n.* the upper limit of something, especially of costs. (Fig. on ①.)

celebrate ['sɛl ə bret] **1.** *tv.* to have a festive event or a party on a special day or for a special season. **2.** *tv.* to perform a specific procedure or a ritual. **3.** *tv.* to praise someone or something. **4.** *iv.* to be festive for a certain reason.

celebration [sɛl ə 'bre ʃən] *n.* a festival; a festive event.

celery ['sɛl (ə) ri] *n.* a light-green vegetable with long, crisp stalks and leafy ends. (No pl. Number is expressed with *stick(s)* or *stalk(s) of celery*.)

cell ['sɛl] **1.** *n.* the basic biological unit of living tissue. **2.** *n.* a subdivision of certain things, such as in a beehive or as with zones for portable wireless telephones. **3.** *n.* a cagelike room for keeping prisoners. **4.** *n.* a battery; one of the sections of a battery.

cellar ['sɛl ɚ] *n.* a basement; an underground room.

cello ['tʃɛl o] *n.* a stringed instrument, similar to a violin but larger. (It stands on the floor between the player's knees. Pl ends in *-s*.)

cellular ['sɛl jə lɚ] **1.** the *adj.* form of CELL ① or ②. (Adv: *cellularly*.) **2.** ~ **telephone** a portable telephone using radio-wave transmission within a large area that is divided into smaller cells, allowing the same radio frequency to be used in different cells by different users. (Often shortened to *cell phone*.)

Celsius ['sɛl si əs] **1.** *n.* the metric system of measuring temperature. (No pl form in this sense. Named for the Swedish astronomer Anders Celsius. The same as CENTIGRADE. Abbreviated *C.*) **2.** the *adj.* use of ①. (② follows DEGREES. Abbreviated *C.*)

cement [sɪ 'mɛnt] **1.** *n.* a gluelike substance that joins things together. (Pl only for types and instances.) **2.** *n.* a gray powder made of clay and limestone that hardens when mixed with water. (No pl.) **3.** *tv.* to join two things together.

cemetery ['sɛm ə tɛr i] *n.* a graveyard; a place where dead people are buried.

censor ['sɛn sɚ] **1.** *n.* someone who seeks to remove offensive words and pictures from material seen by the public. **2.** *tv.* to suppress the publication or performance of offensive material.

census ['sɛn səs] **1.** *n.* the process of counting the number of people who live in an area. **2.** *n.* the official number of people who live in an area; a report of what was found in collecting information for ①.

cent ['sɛnt] *n.* a penny; one one-hundredth of a dollar.

center ['sɛn tɚ] **1.** *n.* the point in the middle of a circle or sphere that is the same distance from all points on the circle or on the surface of the sphere; a place that is in the middle of something. **2.** *n.* a major site or focus of an activity. **3.** *adj.* middle. (Prenominal only.) **4.** *tv.* to place someone or something in the middle of something.

67

Centigrade ['sɛnt ə gred] *n.* the metric system of measuring temperature. (No pl. The same as CELSIUS. Abbreviated *C.*)

centimeter ['sɛnt ə mit ɚ] *n.* a measure of length, equal to one one-hundredth of a meter. (An inch is 2.54 centimeters.)

central ['sɛn trəl] **1.** *adj.* near the center. (Adv: *centrally.*) **2.** *adj.* primary; essential. (Adv: *centrally.*)

century ['sɛn tʃə ri] **1.** *n.* one hundred years. **2.** *n.* a block of time that begins every one hundred years, starting sometime close to the birth of Jesus Christ or some other specific event.

ceramic [sə 'ræm ɪk] *adj.* made of hard, baked clay, able to withstand great heat.

ceramics *n.* the making of pottery by shaping clay and baking it until it hardens. (Treated as sg.)

cereal ['sɪr i əl] **1.** *n.* one of a number of plants that provide grain. (Pl only for types and instances.) **2.** *n.* a food product made from grains, usually served at breakfast with milk. (Pl only for types and instances.)

ceremony ['sɛr ə mon i] **1.** *n.* a tradition or ritual associated with a particular event. **2.** *n.* the formal behavior seen in certain religious, social, or political events. (No pl.)

certain ['sɚt n] **1.** *adj.* definite or known, but not stated; particular and specific, but not identified. (Prenominal only.) **2.** *adj.* sure; confident; having no doubt (about something).

certainly ['sɚt n li] **1.** *adv.* definitely; surely; positively. **2.** *adv.* yes, by all means. (An answer to a question.)

certainty ['sɚt n ti] **1.** *n.* the state of being sure or certain. (No pl.) **2.** *n.* something that is known to be true.

certificate [sɚ 'tɪf ə kɪt] **1.** *n.* an official document pledging that the statements written on it are true. **2.** *n.* an official document that shows that someone has achieved a certain kind of training or education.

chain ['tʃen] **1.** *n.* links or rings, especially made of metal, that are joined together in a row. **2.** *n.* a group of stores or businesses with the same name, owned by the same company or person. (A *chain store.*) **3.** *tv.* to bind someone or something with ①.

chair ['tʃɛr] **1.** *n.* a piece of furniture for sitting, sometimes with arms; a piece of furniture for one person to sit on. **2.** *n.* a person who presides over a committee or a meeting. **3.** *n.* the head of a department, especially in a university. **4.** *tv.* to lead or preside over a meeting, department, or committee.

chairman ['tʃɛr mən] *n., irreg.* the head of a department or committee; the person in charge of a meeting. (Either male or female. See also CHAIR. Pl: CHAIRMEN.)

chairmen ['tʃɛr mən] pl of CHAIRMAN.

chalk ['tʃɔk] **1.** *n.* a soft, white limestone. (Pl only for types and instances.) **2.** *n.* a stick of ① used for writing, as on a chalkboard. (No pl. Number is expressed with *piece(s)* or *stick(s) of chalk.*)

challenge ['tʃæl ɪndʒ] **1.** *n.* a dare; an invitation to a competition. **2.** *n.* a difficult task. **3.** *tv.* [for a difficult task] to test someone or something.

chamber ['tʃɛm bɚ] **1.** *n.* a room. **2.** *n.* a division of government, such as the House of Representatives or the Senate of the United States Congress, separately; certain organizations, such as the chamber of commerce of an area. **3.** *n.* a compartment within something; an enclosed space inside the body.

chameleon [kə 'mil (i)jən] **1.** *n.* a lizard that changes the color of its skin to match its surroundings. **2.** *n.* someone who is very changeable.

champ ['tʃæmp] *n.* a champion; a winner.

champagne [ʃæm 'pen] *n.* a sparkling white wine made in the Champagne area of France, or similar wines made elsewhere. (Pl only for types and instances.)

champion ['tʃæmp i ən] **1.** *n.* a winner; someone who has won a contest or competition. **2.** *n.* someone who supports or argues in favor of someone or something; someone who advocates something. **3.** *tv.* to support someone or something; to speak in favor of someone or something.

chance ['tʃæns] **1.** *n.* fate; fortune. (No pl.) **2.** *n.* the probability that something might happen. (No pl.) **3.** *n.* an opportunity. **4.** *tv.* to risk something.

change ['tʃendʒ] **1.** *n.* the process of becoming something different. (Pl only for types and instances.) **2.** *n.* something new or different; something that replaces something else. **3.** *n.* bills or coins of lower value given in exchange for bills or coins of a higher value; the money returned to someone who has paid a sum higher than the price. (No pl. Treated as sg.) **4.** *n.* loose coins. (No pl. Treated as sg.) **5.** *tv.* to replace something. **6.** *tv.* to cause something to become different.

69

7. *tv.* to remove clothing and put on different clothing. **8.** *tv.* to replace a baby's dirty diaper with a clean one. **9.** *iv.* to become different. **10.** *iv.* to take off one set of clothes and put on another.

channel ['tʃæn l] **1.** *n.* a deeper passage through a harbor, where vessels can sail safely; the deepest part of a river or stream. **2.** *n.* the frequencies assigned to a particular television station.

chaos ['ke ɑs] *n.* complete confusion; complete disorder; anarchy. (No pl.)

chapel ['tʃæp əl] *n.* a place of worship that is smaller than a sanctuary.

chapter ['tʃæp tɚ] **1.** *n.* a division within a book; a section of a book. **2.** *n.* a division of an organization or society.

character ['kɛr ɪk tɚ] **1.** *n.* a person in a book, movie, play, television show, etc. **2.** *n.* the nature of someone or something; the essential qualities of someone or something, especially someone's moral qualities. **3.** *n.* high personal quality; integrity; moral goodness. (No pl.) **4.** *n.* an unusual or eccentric person. **5.** *n.* a symbol used in writing, such as a letter, number, or other symbol.

characteristic [kɛr ɪk tə 'rɪs tɪk] **1.** *n.* a single feature; a special quality of someone or something. **2.** *adj.* relating to the features or qualities of something. (Adv: *characteristically* [...ɪk li].)

charcoal ['tʃɑr kol] *n.* a carbon-based fuel made by burning wood partially. (Pl only for types and instances.)

charge ['tʃɑrdʒ] **1.** *n.* the cost of something; the amount of money needed to pay for something. (Often pl.) **2.** *n.* control [of someone or something]. (No pl.) **3.** *n.* someone or something that must be watched over. **4.** *n.* an accusation; a statement that someone has done something criminal. **5.** *n.* a sudden, moving attack. **6.** *n.* the amount of electrical energy stored in a battery or a particle of matter. **7.** *n.* the explosive material used in one explosion. **8.** *tv.* to present a claim of a sum of money for goods or services. **9.** *tv.* to place ① on an account instead of paying cash. **10.** *tv.* to rush toward and attack someone or something. **11.** *tv.* to provide a battery with energy; to send electricity through something, such as a circuit. **12.** *tv.* to ask for pay at a certain rate.

charity ['tʃɛr ɪ ti] **1.** *n.* love, kindness, and generosity shown toward other people. (No pl.) **2.** *n.* an organization that helps people in need.

charm ['tʃɑrm] **1.** *n.* a pleasing, attractive personality trait. (Pl only for types and instances.) **2.** *n.* a small toy or trinket worn on a necklace or bracelet. **3.** *n.* something that has magical powers. **4.** *tv.* to influence someone by using ①.

chart ['tʃɑrt] **1.** *n.* a statistical table; a graph, table, or diagram. **2.** *n.* a map, especially a map for navigation on water. **3.** *tv.* to plan one's route on a map. **4.** *tv.* to arrange a set of figures or statistics on ①.

chase ['tʃes] **1.** *n.* an act of running after someone or something. **2.** *tv.* to run after someone or something.

chat ['tʃæt] **1.** *iv.* to talk; to have a friendly talk. **2.** *n.* a pleasant conversation; a friendly talk.

chatter ['tʃæt ɚ] **1.** *iv.* to talk about unimportant things. **2.** *iv.* [for one's teeth] to click together because of fear or coldness. **3.** *n.* unimportant talk. (No pl.)

cheap ['tʃip] **1.** *adj.* inexpensive; not costing a lot of money. (Adv: *cheaply.* Comp: *cheaper;* sup: *cheapest.*) **2.** *adj.* poorly made; of poor quality; of poor value. (Adv: *cheaply.* Comp: *cheaper;* sup: *cheapest.*)

cheat ['tʃit] **1.** *tv.* to deceive someone in a game or in commerce, as a means of gaining money or some other advantage. **2.** *iv.* to succeed by doing something that is not fair or honest. **3.** *n.* someone who CHEATS as in ① or ②; someone who does not play fairly.

check ['tʃɛk] **1.** *n.* a written order to a bank to pay an amount of money to someone or something. **2.** *n.* the mark (✓). **3.** *n.* the bill for a meal in a restaurant. **4.** *n.* something that stops or restrains someone or something. **5.** *n.* a brief look at someone or something; an inspection of someone or something. **6.** *tv.* to examine something; to look at something closely but quickly. **7.** *tv.* to put one's belongings into the care of someone and receive a receipt for the property. **8.** *tv.* to restrain someone or something; to stop someone or something.

checkup ['tʃɛk əp] *n.* a physical examination done by a physician; a mechanical inspection done by a mechanic.

cheek ['tʃik] *n.* the part of the face below the eye.

cheekbone ['tʃik bon] *n.* the bone just below the eye.

cheer ['tʃir] **1.** *n.* an encouraging yell; some applause and shouting meant to encourage someone. **2.** *n.* happiness; a good state of mind. (No pl.) **3.** *iv.* to yell and shout in support of someone or something; to yell in encouragement. **4.** *tv.* to encourage someone by shouts of support. **5.** ~ **up** [for a sad person] to become happy.

71

cheerful [ˈtʃɪr fʊl] **1.** *adj.* in good spirits; full of cheer; happy. (Adv: *cheerfully.*) **2.** *adj.* pleasant; [of something] bright and pleasing. (Adv: *cheerfully.*)

cheery [ˈtʃɪr i] **1.** *adj.* full of cheer; showing cheer. (Adv: *cheerily.* Comp: *cheerier*; sup: *cheeriest.*) **2.** *adj.* bright and cheerful; causing cheer. (Adv: *cheerily.* Comp: *cheerier*; sup: *cheeriest.*)

cheese [ˈtʃiz] **1.** *n.* a food made from the solid parts of processed milk. (Pl only for types and instances.) **2.** the *adj.* use of ①.

chef [ˈʃɛf] **1.** *n.* a professional cook. **2.** *n.* any cook; whoever is doing the cooking.

chemical [ˈkɛm ɪ kəl] **1.** *n.* an element or a mixture of basic elements. **2.** the *adj.* use of ①. (Adv: *chemically* [...ɪk li].)

chemist [ˈkɛm ɪst] *n.* a scientist whose specialty is the theory and use of substances.

cherish [ˈtʃɛr ɪʃ] **1.** *tv.* to treat someone or something very lovingly; to have great fondness for someone or something. **2.** *tv.* to keep the idea of someone or something in one's mind.

cherry [ˈtʃɛr i] **1.** *n.* a tree that produces small, round, bright red fruits with one pit. **2.** *n.* wood from ①. (Pl only for types and instances.) **3.** *n.* the fruit of ①. **4.** *adj.* made with or flavored with ③. **5.** *adj.* made from ②.

chess [ˈtʃɛs] *n.* a game played by two people on a special board, with 32 pieces. (No pl.)

chest [ˈtʃɛst] **1.** *n.* the upper front part of the body. **2.** *n.* a piece of furniture with drawers, used to store clothes, linen, and other items. (Often *chest of drawers.*) **3.** *n.* a large, wooden storage box.

chew [ˈtʃu] **1.** *tv.* to crush food with the teeth before swallowing it. **2.** *iv.* to bite down with the teeth.

chick [ˈtʃɪk] *n.* a baby chicken or other baby bird.

chicken [ˈtʃɪk ən] **1.** *n.* a bird raised on a farm for meat and eggs; a hen or a rooster. **2.** *n.* the meat of ①. (No pl.) **3.** *adj.* made with or flavored with ②.

chief [ˈtʃif] **1.** *n.* the head of an organization or group; the leader. **2.** *adj.* most important; principal; main. (Adv: *chiefly.*)

child [ˈtʃaɪld] *n., irreg.* a young person; a boy or a girl; someone's son or daughter. (Pl: CHILDREN.)

childhood [ˈtʃaɪld hʊd] *n.* the time period during which one is a child.

children ['tʃɪl drɪn] pl of CHILD.

chill ['tʃɪl] **1.** *n.* a coldness, especially a damp coldness. **2.** *n.* a cold feeling; a lasting cold feeling caused by being in the cold too long. **3.** *n.* a coldness of manner; an unpleasant attitude; an unfriendly attitude. (Fig. on ①. No pl.) **4.** *n.* a sense of severe fright, possibly accompanied by the feeling of ②. **5.** *tv.* to cool something. **6.** *iv.* to become cool or cold.

chilly ['tʃɪl i] *adj.* cold; cool. (Comp: *chillier;* sup: *chilliest.*)

chimney ['tʃɪm ni] *n.* the structure that carries smoke to the outside and above a building.

chimpanzee [tʃɪm 'pæn zi] *n.* an African ape, closely related to humans.

chin ['tʃɪn] *n.* the part of the face below the lower lip.

china ['tʃaɪn ə] *n.* high-quality dishes, cups, and saucers made of fine, thin ceramic material. (No pl.)

chip ['tʃɪp] **1.** *n.* a small piece that has broken off a larger object. **2.** *n.* the dent that is left where a small piece of something has broken off. **3.** *n.* a flat, crunchy, fried or baked snack made of starch. (Usually made from potatoes or corn. Also short for *potato chip.*) **4.** *tv.* to break off a small piece of something. **5.** *tv.* to shape something by picking away or cutting away at it piece by piece. **6.** *iv.* [for something] to lose a small bit, through CHIPPING as in ④.

chisel ['tʃɪz əl] **1.** *n.* a sharp-edged tool for removing pieces from wood or stone. **2.** *tv.* to shape something with ①.

chocolate ['tʃɑk (ə) lət] **1.** *n.* a tasty, sweet food made from roasted cacao beans, usually in the form of candy, syrup, a brewed beverage, or a flavor in cooking. (Pl only for types and instances.) **2.** *n.* a piece of ①. **3.** *adj.* made with or flavored with ①.

choice ['tʃɔɪs] **1.** *n.* a selection from which one can choose. (Pl only for types and instances.) **2.** *n.* the actual selection; someone or something chosen or selected. **3.** *adj.* of very high quality; excellent; best; optimal. (Adv: *choicely.*)

choir ['kwaɪɚ] *n.* a singing group, especially one in a church.

choke ['tʃok] **1.** *n.* the part of an engine that controls the amount of air that goes into the engine. **2.** *tv.* to cut off someone's or some creature's air supply. **3.** *iv.* to react to having one's air supply cut off.

choose ['tʃuz] **1.** *tv., irreg.* to pick or select someone or something from a group. (Pt: CHOSE; pp: CHOSEN.) **2.** *iv., irreg.* to do the process of selection.

choosy ['tʃu zi] *adj.* hard to please; hard to make happy; particular. (Adv: *choosily.* Comp: *choosier;* sup: *choosiest.*)

chop ['tʃɑp] **1.** *n.* a movement with an axe or blade that cuts into something; a blow that cuts into something. **2.** *n.* a slice of meat, including some bone, especially lamb or pork. **3.** *tv.* to cut something by hitting it with something sharp.

chord ['kɔrd] *n.* two or more musical tones played at the same time.

chore ['tʃɔr] *n.* a regular task; a duty.

chorus ['kɔr əs] **1.** *n.* a group of people who sing together; a choir. **2.** *n.* the part of a song that is repeated after each verse. **3.** *n.* words or noises that are said together or at the same time.

chose ['tʃoz] pt of CHOOSE.

chosen ['tʃo zən] pp of CHOOSE.

Christian ['krɪs tʃən] *n.* a member of the CHRISTIAN RELIGION.

Christian religion AND **Christianity** ['krɪs tʃən rɪ 'lɪdʒ ən, krɪs tʃi 'æn ə ti] *n.* a religion whose basis is in the teachings of Jesus Christ.

Christianity [krɪs tʃi 'æn ə ti] Go to CHRISTIAN RELIGION.

Christmas ['krɪs məs] *n.* December 25; the day on which the birth of Christ is celebrated by many Christians.

chrome ['krom] **1.** *n.* chromium or metal plated with chromium. (No pl form in this sense.) **2.** *adj.* covered or plated with chromium.

chromium ['krom i əm] *n.* a brittle metallic element. (No pl form in this sense.)

chromosome ['krom ə som] *n.* one of many very tiny cellular structures containing genes.

chuckle ['tʃʌk əl] **1.** *n.* a soft, happy laugh. **2.** *iv.* to laugh softly and happily.

chum ['tʃʌm] *n.* a good friend; a buddy.

chunk ['tʃʌŋk] *n.* a thick, irregularly shaped piece of something.

church ['tʃɚtʃ] **1.** *n.* a building where Christians gather to worship. **2.** *n.* the worship service celebrated within ①. (No pl.) **3.** *n.* the members of a particular religious organization. **4.** *n.* the institutional organization of a religious body, its policies, and its practices. (No pl.)

cider ['saɪ də] *n.* apple juice; juice pressed from apples. (Pl only for types and instances.)

cigar [sɪ 'gɑr] *n.* a carefully packed roll of dried tobacco leaves, used for smoking.

cigarette [sɪg ə 'rɛt] *n.* a small roll of cut tobacco wrapped in paper, used for smoking.

cinema ['sɪn ə mə] **1.** *n.* the business of making motion pictures; the movies. (No pl form in this sense.) **2.** *n.* a movie theater.

circle ['sɔ kəl] **1.** *n.* a curved line where every point on the line is the same distance from a center point. **2.** *n.* anything shaped like ①; a ring. **3.** *n.* a group of people with related interests. **4.** *tv.* to form a ring around someone or something. **5.** *tv.* to draw a ring around something that is written or printed.

circuit ['sɔ kɪt] **1.** *n.* a complete trip around something. **2.** *n.* the path that the flow of electricity follows.

circular ['sɔ kjə lɚ] **1.** *n.* a printed sheet that is sent to many people. **2.** *adj.* in the shape of a circle; round; ringlike. (Adv: *circularly.*)

circulate ['sɔ kjə let] **1.** *tv.* to send something from person to person; to send something from place to place. **2.** *tv.* to carry something, such as medicine, by way of the circulation of blood. **3.** *iv.* to go around from person to person. **4.** *iv.* [for blood] to flow from the heart through the body and back to the heart.

circulation [sɔk jə 'le ʃən] *n.* the process of circulating.

circus ['sɔ kəs] *n.* a traveling show featuring clowns, acrobats, animals, magicians, and other similar acts.

cite ['saɪt] **1.** *tv.* to use someone or something as a reference to support a claim or statement of fact. **2.** *tv.* to refer to or list a citation. **3.** *tv.* to recognize someone for having done an exceptional deed. **4.** *tv.* to give someone an order to appear in court.

citizen ['sɪt ə zən] *n.* someone who is a legal resident of a specific political region; someone who has full rights of membership in a state or country.

citizenship ['sɪt ə zən ʃɪp] **1.** *n.* the state of being an official citizen. (No pl.) **2.** *n.* the behavior expected of a citizen. (No pl.)

citrus ['sɪ trəs] **1.** *n.* a family of fruit including oranges, tangerines, grapefruit, limes, lemons, etc. (No pl.) **2.** the *adj.* use of ①.

city ['sɪt i] **1.** *n.* a large town; a large residential and business center. **2.** the *adj.* use of ①. **3.** ~ **hall** *n.* the administrative building for a city government. (Sometimes capitalized.)

civil ['sɪv əl] **1.** *adj.* of or about citizens and their government, activities, rights, and responsibilities. **2.** *adj.* polite; courteous; behaving properly. (Adv: *civilly.*) **3.** *adj.* relating to a legal action that does not deal with criminal law.

civilian [sɪ 'vɪl jən] *n.* a citizen who is not in the military.

civilize ['sɪv ə laɪz] *tv.* to make someone or a culture more organized and less primitive.

claim ['klem] **1.** *n.* a document or statement requesting that a payment be made. **2.** *n.* a statement presented as fact; a statement that something is true. **3.** *tv.* to assert one's right to own something. **4.** *tv.* to say a statement as fact; to state that something is true. (The object can be a clause with THAT ⑦.)

clam ['klæm] **1.** *n.* an edible marine animal having a pair of shells that open like a book. **2.** the *adj.* use of ①.

clamp ['klæmp] **1.** *n.* a device that holds things together with pressure. **2.** *tv.* to hold things together with pressure.

clap ['klæp] **1.** *n.* the sound made when one brings one's palms together, as in applause. **2.** *n.* a loud burst of thunder. **3.** *iv.* to make applause.

clarinet [klɛr ə 'nɛt] *n.* a tube-shaped musical instrument of the woodwind family.

clash ['klæʃ] **1.** *n.* a fight; a battle; a skirmish. **2.** ~ **with** to quarrel or fight with someone. **3.** ~ **with** to be in conflict with something else.

clasp ['klæsp] **1.** *n.* a hook or fastener that holds something closed. **2.** *n.* a firm grasp; the holding of something tightly. **3.** *tv.* to take hold of someone or something firmly; to hold someone or something tightly.

class ['klæs] **1.** *n.* a group of similar things. **2.** *n.* someone's social and economic ranking. **3.** *n.* a course that is taught; a subject that is taught. **4.** *n.* a specific session of learning; a period of time spent in instruction. **5.** *n.* all the people in a certain grade or year of schooling. **6.** *n.* a term of address for a group of students in a classroom. (No pl.) **7.** *n.* the ability to behave properly, politely, or elegantly. (No pl.)

classic ['klæs ɪk] **1.** *n.* something, especially art, music, or writing, that is of very high quality and will be or is remembered through history. **2.** *adj.* of high quality; the best; of great and lasting importance; serving as a standard for others of its kind. **3.** *adj.* typical; just as one would anticipate.

classical ['klæs ɪ kəl] **1.** *adj.* of or about ancient Greece and Rome. (Adv: *classically* […ɪk li].) **2.** *adj.* [of music, such as symphonies and operas, dance, and other art forms] serious and requiring a high degree of training and skill.

classmate ['klæs met] *n.* someone in the same class at school.

classroom ['klæs rum] *n.* a room in a school or building where classes are held.

clause ['klɔz] **1.** *n.* a phrase that has a subject and a verb. **2.** *n.* a single provision in a legal document.

claw ['klɔ] **1.** *n.* a sharp, hard, curved nail on the foot of an animal or a bird. **2.** *n.* the pinchers of a lobster, crab, or other shellfish. **3.** *n.* the part of the hammer that is used for removing nails. **4.** *tv.* to scratch or tear someone or something with ①.

clay ['kle] **1.** *n.* a kind of sticky soil, used for pottery. (Pl only for types and instances.) **2.** *adj.* made of or concerning ①.

clean ['klin] **1.** *adj.* tidy; not dirty. (Adv: *cleanly.*) **2.** *adj.* new; fresh; unused. **3.** *adj.* morally pure; not DIRTY ②. (Adv: *cleanly.*) **4.** *adj.* smooth; even; not rough. (Adv: *cleanly.*) **5.** *tv.* to make something ①. **6.** *tv.* to prepare an animal for cooking and eating by removing the parts that cannot be eaten.

cleaner ['klin ɚ] **1.** *n.* soap, bleach, or some other product that cleans. (Pl only for types and instances.) **2.** *n.* someone who cleans clothing and fabric for a living.

cleaners *n.* a business that launders or cleans clothing and other items. (Treated as sg or pl.)

cleanse ['klɛnz] *tv.* to clean something well; to make something more pure.

clear ['klɪr] **1.** *adj.* transparent; allowing light through. (Adv: *clearly.* Comp: *clearer;* sup: *clearest.*) **2.** *adj.* bright; free from clouds or fog. (Adv: *clearly.* Comp: *clearer;* sup: *clearest.*) **3.** *adj.* without marks or blemishes; without defects. (Comp: *clearer;* sup: *clearest.*) **4.** *adj.* easy to understand; making perfect sense. (Adv: *clearly.* Comp: *clearer;* sup: *clearest.*) **5.** *adj.* easy to hear or see. (Adv: *clearly.* Comp: *clearer;* sup: *clearest.*) **6.** *adj.* certain; easy to understand. (Adv: *clearly.* Comp:

77

clearer; sup: *clearest.*) **7.** *adj.* without anything in the way. (Comp: *clearer;* sup: *clearest.*) **8.** *adv.* completely; all the way. **9.** *tv.* to move someone or something so that the way is open. **10.** *tv.* to make an area empty by removing people or things. **11.** *tv.* to chop down trees and remove stones from the land. **12.** *tv.* to remove blame or guilt from someone or something. **13.** *tv.* [for a bank] to send a check successfully through procedures necessary to have the check paid. **14.** *iv.* [for a check] to successfully travel through the procedures necessary to assure payment. **15.** *iv.* [for the sky] to become free of clouds. **16.** ~ **up** [for something] to become more understandable. **17.** ~ **up** [for a disease] to improve or become cured. **18.** ~ **up** [for the sky] to become clearer.

clergy ['klɚ dʒi] *n.* ministers; priests; pastors. (No pl. Number is expressed by the phrase *member(s) of the clergy.*)

clerk ['klɚk] **1.** *n.* an office worker, especially one who keeps track of records, files, and information. **2.** *n.* someone who helps customers with goods and sales; someone who works behind a counter and helps customers.

clever ['klɛv ɚ] *adj.* [of someone or a creature] capable of interesting, creative activities. (Adv: *cleverly.* Comp: *cleverer;* sup: *cleverest.*)

cliché [kli 'she] *n.* an expression that is trite and tiresome and is used too often.

click ['klɪk] **1.** *n.* a short, quick noise; a snapping sound. **2.** *tv.* to make a noise by snapping things together. **3.** *iv.* to snap; to make a snapping noise.

client ['klaɪ ənt] *n.* someone served by a company or by a professional such as a lawyer.

cliff ['klɪf] *n.* a high, steep wall of rock or earth.

climate ['klaɪ mət] **1.** *n.* the typical weather conditions of a certain area. **2.** *n.* the general atmosphere, mood, attitude, or feeling.

climax ['klaɪ mæks] **1.** *n.* the most exciting point in an event; the most intense part of an event; the most dramatic point of a story. **2.** *iv.* to reach the most exciting point in an event.

climb ['klaɪm] **1.** *n.* the process of going up something, especially through much effort or using the hands and feet. **2.** *tv.* to go up something, especially through much effort or using the hands and feet. **3.** *iv.* to go to a higher level.

climber ['klaɪm ɚ] **1.** *n.* someone who hikes or climbs up mountains, cliffs, slopes, etc. **2.** *n.* a plant that grows up something.

clinic ['klɪn ɪk] *n.* a medical office where minor medical problems are treated.

clip ['klɪp] **1.** *n.* a device that holds sheets of paper together; a small device for gripping or holding things together. **2.** *n.* a brief part of a film, book, magazine, or newspaper. **3.** *tv.* to hold things together with ①.

cloak ['klok] **1.** *n.* a long coat without sleeves; an outer garment like a cape. **2.** *tv.* to cover something up; to obscure something.

clock ['klɑk] **1.** *n.* a machine that keeps track of the time of day; a timepiece. **2.** *tv.* to measure the length of time it takes for someone or something to do something; to measure a rate of speed. **3.** ~ **in** to record one's time of arrival, usually by punching a time clock. **4.** ~ **out** to record one's time of departure, usually by punching a time clock.

clockwork ['klɑk wɚk] *n.* the moving parts inside a clock or mechanical device, such as a wind-up toy.

clogged ['klɔgd] *adj.* blocked.

close 1. ['klos] *adj.* near in space or time. (Adv: *closely.* Comp: *closer;* sup: *closest.*) **2.** ['klos] *adj.* near in spirit; dear; intimate; confidential. (Adv: *closely.* Comp: *closer;* sup: *closest.*) **3.** ['klos] *adj.* careful; strict. (Adv: *closely.* Comp: *closer;* sup: *closest.*) **4.** ['klos] *adj.* almost equal; almost the same. (Adv: *closely.* Comp: *closer;* sup: *closest.*) **5.** ['klos] *adv.* near in space or time. **6.** ['kloz] *tv.* to shut something. **7.** ['kloz] *tv.* to bring something to an end; to conclude something. **8.** ['kloz] *tv.* to complete an electrical circuit. **9.** ['kloz] *iv.* to shut. **10.** ['kloz] *iv.* to end; to finish; to bring to an end; to conclude. **11.** ['kloz] *n.* the end; the finish; the conclusion. **12.** ~ **up** [for an opening] to close completely.

closed ['klozd] *adj.* not open; shut.

closet ['klɔz ɪt] **1.** *n.* a small room where clothing and personal objects are kept. **2.** *adj.* secret; hiding; covert.

cloth ['klɔθ] **1.** *n.* woven material; woven fabric. (Pl only for types and instances.) **2.** *n., irreg.* a piece of woven material or fabric. (Pl: [klɔðz].)

clothe ['kloð] *tv.* to put garments on someone or something; to dress someone or something.

clothes ['klo(ð)z] *n.* clothing; garments; something to wear, such as a shirt, a sweater, pants, or socks. (Treated as pl, but not countable.)

clothesline ['kloz laɪn] *n.* a length of rope on which clothes and other laundry can be hung to dry.

clothespin ['kloz pɪn] *n.* a wooden or plastic clip used to attach damp clothes to a clothesline.

clothing ['klo ðɪŋ] *n.* clothes; garments. (No pl. Treated as sg.)

cloud ['klaʊd] **1.** *n.* a large white or gray mass in the sky, made of water vapor. **2.** *n.* a large puff of smoke or dust; a visible mass of gas or particles that is still or moves in the air. **3.** *tv.* to obscure something; to hide something. **4.** ~ **up** [for the sky] to fill with clouds.

cloudy ['klaʊ di] **1.** *adj.* [of sky] having clouds. (Adv: *cloudily.* Comp: *cloudier;* sup: *cloudiest.*) **2.** *adj.* not able to be seen through clearly. (Fig. on ①. Adv: *cloudily.* Comp: *cloudier;* sup: *cloudiest.*)

clown ['klaʊn] **1.** *n.* a performer who wears a funny costume and makeup and tries to make people laugh. **2.** *n.* someone who is always making jokes and trying to make other people laugh.

club ['klʌb] **1.** *n.* a large, thick, blunt wooden stick. **2.** *n.* a nightclub; a place where liquor is served or where people can dance. **3.** *n.* an organization or group of people who meet to pursue a specific activity. **4.** *n.* one of four different symbols found in a deck of playing cards; the symbol (♣). **5.** *n.* the stick with a metal end used to hit a golf ball. (Short for *golf club.*) **6.** *tv.* to beat someone or something with ①.

clue ['klu] *n.* a hint; some information that will help to solve a problem.

clump ['klʌmp] **1.** *n.* a group of something; a mass of something. **2.** *tv.* to group things together; to gather something into ①.

clumsy ['klʌm zi] *adj.* awkward; likely to trip or stumble on something. (Adv: *clumsily.* Comp: *clumsier;* sup: *clumsiest.*)

clutch ['klətʃ] *tv.* to grasp something; to hold onto something.

clutches ['klətʃ əz] *n.* one's grasp; a person's holding onto someone or something.

coach ['kotʃ] **1.** *n.* someone who is in charge of a team; someone who trains players on a team. **2.** *n.* someone who trains someone else. **3.** *n.* an enclosed carriage, typically pulled by horses. **4.** *n.* a railway car where passengers ride in seats. (As opposed to railway cars where people can eat or can lie down to sleep.) **5.** *n.* a cross-country bus; a bus used for touring or carrying people over a long distance. **6.** *n.* the tourist section of an airplane; the cheapest kind of air travel. (No pl.)

80

7. *adv.* [traveling] in or by ⑥. **8.** *tv.* to instruct someone in a sport, skill, or craft.

coal ['kol] **1.** *n.* a black mineral made of carbon, used as fuel. (Pl only for types and instances.) **2.** *n.* a hot, glowing chunk of burning ① or charcoal.

coarse ['kors] **1.** *adj.* having a rough texture; not smooth. (Adv: *coarsely.* Comp: *coarser;* sup: *coarsest.*) **2.** *adj.* vulgar; crude. (Adv: *coarsely.* Comp: *coarser;* sup: *coarsest.*)

coast ['kost] **1.** *n.* land along and beside the sea. **2.** *iv.* to glide without using energy.

coastal ['kos təl] *adj.* along the coast; on the coast. (Adv: *coastally.*)

coat ['kot] **1.** *n.* a heavy item of clothing, worn over one's other clothes during cold weather. **2.** *n.* the fur of an animal; the pelt of an animal. **3.** *n.* a layer of something, such as paint, that covers a surface. **4.** *tv.* to cover the surface of something with a layer of something.

cob ['kab] *n.* the central core of an ear of corn. (Short for CORNCOB.)

cobweb ['kab web] *n.* a spider's web, especially when old and filled with dust.

cocoa ['ko ko] **1.** *n.* a powder made by processing cacao seeds; powdered chocolate. (No pl form in this sense.) **2.** *n.* a drink made by mixing powdered chocolate with milk and sugar. (No pl form in this sense.)

cocoon [kə 'kun] *n.* the protective shell in which a caterpillar wraps itself while it transforms into a butterfly or a moth.

cod ['kad] **1.** *n., irreg.* a kind of edible fish that lives in cold water. (Pl: *cod.*) **2.** *n.* the flesh of ①, eaten as food. (No pl.)

code ['kod] **1.** *n.* a secret writing system; a system of symbols used for communication. **2.** *n.* a set of laws; a set of rules. **3.** *tv.* to translate a message into ①. **4.** *tv.* to mark an object with a special number or symbol.

coffee ['kɔf i] **1.** *n.* the roasted beans of a kind of tree. (Either whole or ground. Pl only for types and instances.) **2.** *n.* a drink made from roasted, ground ①. (No pl.) **3.** ~ **break** *n.* a rest period during which coffee or some other refreshment is enjoyed.

coffeepot ['kɔf i pat] *n.* a pot used to brew and serve coffee.

coffin ['kɔf ən] *n.* a box in which the body of a dead person is placed for burial.

81

coil ['kɔɪl] **1.** *n.* a length of something, such as rope, wound into a stack of circular loops. **2.** *n.* a circular loop. **3.** *tv.* to wrap something around and around into a circle. **4.** *iv.* to form into a circular loop.

coin ['kɔɪn] **1.** *n.* a piece of money made from metal. **2.** *tv.* to press metal into ①; to make money from metal. **3.** *tv.* to invent a new word; to make up a new word.

coke ['kok] **1.** *n.* the substance that is left after gas has been removed from coal, which—when burned—gives off very strong heat. (No pl form in this sense.) **2. Coke** *n.* Coca-Cola™, the protected trade name of a soft drink. **3.** *n.* a generic name for cola drinks. (Never capitalized. Objected to as an infringement of the Coca-Cola™ trade name.) **4.** *n.* cocaine. (Slang. No pl form in this sense.)

cold ['kold] **1.** *n.* a physical state or property of something having relatively less heat. (No pl.) **2.** *n.* weather that is characterized by ①; a lack of warmth in the outside temperature. (No pl.) **3.** *n.* a common illness that causes sneezing, a runny nose, a sore throat, etc. **4.** *adj.* not hot; not having heat. (Comp: *colder;* sup: *coldest.*) **5.** *adj.* [of a living creature] uncomfortable from not having heat. (Adv: *coldly.* Comp: *colder;* sup: *coldest.*) **6.** *adj.* mean; unfriendly; unpleasant. (Adv: *coldly.* Comp: *colder;* sup: *coldest.*)

collapse [kə 'læps] **1.** *n.* an instance of falling down; a loss of the air contained in something. (No pl.) **2.** *n.* the total ruin of something. **3.** *iv.* to fall down; to become ruined. **4.** *iv.* to fail; to break down completely.

collar ['kɑl ɚ] **1.** *n.* the part of a piece of clothing that wraps around the neck. **2.** *n.* a band around the neck of an animal.

collect [kə 'lɛkt] **1.** *tv.* to ask for or to receive money that is owed. **2.** *tv.* to gather items together; to bring items together. **3.** *tv.* to find and take, get, or buy something or a class of things as a hobby. **4.** *adj.* [of a telephone call] charged to the person or number called. **5.** *adv.* charging a telephone call to the person or telephone number called.

collection [kə 'lɛk ʃən] **1.** *n.* the collecting of things. (No pl form in this sense.) **2.** *n.* the donation of money during a church service or some other types of meetings. **3.** *n.* a group of similar objects gathered together. **4.** *n.* a group of people. **5.** *n.* the (amount of) money donated during a church service or in a similar setting.

college ['kɑl ɪdʒ] *n.* a school of higher education; an undergraduate division within a university.

colon ['ko lən] **1.** *n.* the punctuation mark ":" used to introduce a list of things. **2.** *n.* the lower part of the large intestine.

colonial [kə 'lon i əl] **1.** *adj.* of or about a colony. (Adv: *colonially.*) **2.** *adj.* of or about the original thirteen colonies of the United States. (Adv: *colonially.*) **3.** *n.* a person who lives or lived in a colony.

colony ['kɑl ə ni] **1.** *n.* an area that is settled and ruled by a country but is located apart from it. **2.** *n.* the place where a social group of ants or termites lives and breeds.

color ['kʌl ɚ] **1.** *n.* the quality of light that causes people to see the differences among red, orange, yellow, blue, green, purple, etc.; a hue; a tint. **2.** *tv.* to give something ①; to paint or draw with something that has ①. **3.** *tv.* to affect something; to influence something. (Fig. on ②.) **4.** *iv.* to draw with crayons or markers. **5.** *adj.* [of film or video recording] using all the colors, not just black and white.

colt ['kolt] *n.* a young male horse.

column ['kɑl əm] **1.** *n.* a supporting pillar or a thick post. **2.** *n.* a series of words or symbols arranged in a line from top to bottom. **3.** *n.* a newspaper article, especially one written by a columnist.

coma ['ko mə] *n.* a state of complete unconsciousness, often due to illness.

comb ['kom] **1.** *n.* a toothed strip of plastic or something similar, used for arranging hair. **2.** *n.* the red growth on top of the heads of chickens and turkeys. **3.** *tv.* to arrange one's hair with ①. **4.** *tv.* to thoroughly look through an area for something; to search a place for something.

combat 1. ['kɑm bæt] *n.* war; conflict; battle. (No pl.) **2.** ['kɑm bæt] the *adj.* use of ①. **3.** [kəm 'bæt] *tv.* to fight someone or something; to battle someone or something. (Pt/pp: *combated.*)

combination [kɑm bɪ 'ne ʃən] **1.** *n.* the process of combining. (Pl only for types and instances.) **2.** *n.* something that is made by an act of combining. **3.** *n.* the sequence of numbers needed to open a *combination lock* as in ④. **4.** ~ **lock** *n.* a lock that is opened by turning a dial to a secret **COMBINATION** ③ of numbers or by pressing numbered buttons in the proper sequence, instead of with a key.

combine [kəm 'baɪn] **1.** *tv.* to join two or more things together. **2.** *iv.* to unite; to join.

come ['kʌm] **1.** *iv., irreg.* to move toward someone or something; to move toward the location of the person who is speaking. (Pt: CAME; pp: *come.*) **2.** *iv., irreg.* to arrive; to get somewhere. **3.** *iv., irreg.* [for

83

goods that have been purchased] to arrive or be available equipped in a certain way. **4.** ~ **around** to agree in the end; to agree finally. **5.** ~ **around** to return to consciousness. **6.** ~ **back** to return to a place or to an advantageous or favorable state or condition. **7.** ~ **in** to enter. (Often a command or polite request.) **8.** ~ **in** to arrive; [for a shipment of something] to arrive. **9.** ~ **on** to hurry along after someone. (Usually a command.) **10.** ~ **on** [for electricity or some other device] to start operating. **11.** ~ **on** to walk out and appear on stage. **12.** ~ **on** [for a pain] to begin hurting; [for a disease] to attack someone. **13.** ~ **on** to yield; to agree. (Usually a command.) **14.** ~ **on** [for a program] to be broadcast on radio or television. **15.** ~ **out** to exit; to leave the inside of a place. **16.** ~ **out** to result; to succeed; to happen. **17.** ~ **out** to come before the public; to be published; to be made public. **18.** ~ **to** to become conscious; to return to consciousness.

comedy ['kɑm ə di] **1.** *n.* a funny play or movie; the opposite of a tragedy. **2.** *n.* the element of movies or plays that makes people laugh; the opposite of tragedy. (No pl.)

comfort ['kʌm fət] *n.* the quality of relief, ease, satisfaction.

comfortable ['kʌm fət ə bl] *adj.* giving comfort, ease, or rest.

comic ['kɑm ɪk] **1.** *adj.* funny; humorous. (Adv: *comically* [...ɪk li].) **2.** *n.* a pamphlet printed in color on cheap paper where stories are told in colorful drawings. (From *comic book.*) **3.** *n.* someone who tells jokes and funny stories.

comics *n.* the newspaper pages containing cartoons and *comic strips.* (Treated as pl.)

command [kə 'mænd] **1.** *n.* an order; a statement that tells someone what to do; a direction; an instruction. **2.** *tv.* to give an order to someone. **3.** *tv.* to control someone or something. **4.** *tv.* [for someone or someone's character] to deserve and receive respect and attention.

commencement [kə 'mɛns mənt] **1.** *n.* the start of something; the beginning of something. (More formal than START. No pl form in this sense.) **2.** *n.* the graduation ceremony where diplomas are awarded.

comment ['kɑm ɛnt] **1.** *n.* a remark about something; a statement about something. **2.** *tv.* to state an opinion; to make a remark. (The object is a clause with THAT ⑦.)

commercial [kə 'mɚ ʃəl] **1.** *adj.* of or about commerce. (Adv: *commercially.*) **2.** *n.* an advertisement on television or radio. (From *commercial announcement.*)

commit [kə 'mɪt] **1.** *tv.* to do a crime; to do something illegal. **2.** *tv.* to place someone [in a mental institution].

committee [kə 'mɪt i] *n.* a group of people who meet to perform a specific duty, usually as part of a larger organization.

common ['kɑm ən] **1.** *adj.* usual; typical; frequently encountered; widespread. (Adv: *commonly.* Comp: *commoner;* sup: *commonest.*) **2.** *adj.* shared or used by two or more people. (Adv: *commonly.*) **3.** *adj.* without distinction; ordinary. (Adv: *commonly.* Comp: *commoner;* sup: *commonest.*)

commotion [kə 'mo ʃən] *n.* a disturbance; a clamor; a noisy interruption.

communication [kə mjun ɪ 'ke ʃən] **1.** *n.* sending and receiving information. (No pl.) **2.** *n.* an announcement or statement in written or spoken form.

communications *n.* the means or media for communication.

community [kə 'mjun ə ti] **1.** *n.* an area or region where people live and communicate with each other; a neighborhood or town. **2.** *n.* a group of people who have a common interest, occupation, or background. **3.** the *adj.* use of ① or ②.

companion [kəm 'pæn jən] **1.** *n.* someone with whom time is spent. **2.** *n.* something that matches something else; something that is part of a set.

company ['kʌm pə ni] **1.** *n.* a business organization; a business. **2.** *n.* guests; visitors. (No pl. Treated as sg.)

comparative [kəm 'per ə tɪv] **1.** *adj.* of or about studies based on comparison. (Adv: *comparatively.*) **2.** *adj.* of or about a form of an adverb or adjective that typically has an -*er* suffix or is a combination of the adverb or adjective and the word *more.* (Some adverbs and adjectives have irregular COMPARATIVES ④, however.) **3.** *adj.* as compared with others. (Adv: *comparatively.*) **4.** *n.* a form of an adjective or adverb as described in ②. (Abbreviated *comp.* here.)

compare [kəm 'per] *tv.* to determine or show how two things are the same or different.

comparison [kəm 'per ə sən] *n.* showing how things are the same or different. (Pl only for types and instances.)

compass ['kʌm pəs] **1.** *n.* a device that points to the north and indicates direction for the purposes of travel or finding out where one is located. **2.** *n.* a simple device used to draw circles or parts of circles.

85

compete [kəm ˈpit] *iv.* to participate in a game, contest, or rivalry, with the hope of winning; to take part in a game or contest.

competition [kɑm pɪ ˈtɪ ʃən] **1.** *n.* a contest. **2.** *n.* the state that exists between rivals. (No pl.) **3.** *n.* a rival or a group of rivals. (No pl.)

competitive [kəm ˈpɛt ɪ tɪv] **1.** *adj.* eager to compete; aggressive in competition. (*Adv: competitively.*) **2.** *adj.* low in price; [of a low price] able to compete. (*Adv: competitively.*) **3.** *adj.* involving competition. (*Adv: competitively.*)

complain [kəm ˈplen] *iv.* to say that one is unhappy, angry, or annoyed.

complaint [kəm ˈplent] **1.** *n.* a statement expressing annoyance or anger about something. **2.** *n.* a statement that a crime has been committed. **3.** *n.* a sickness; an illness.

complete [kəm ˈplit] **1.** *adj.* entire; whole; with all the necessary parts. (*Adv: completely.*) **2.** *tv.* to finish something; to end something; to do something until it is done. **3.** *tv.* to make something whole; to fill in all the parts of something.

complex 1. [ˈkɑm plɛks] *n.* a set of related buildings. **2.** [ˈkɑm plɛks] *n.* a psychological condition. **3.** [kɑm ˈplɛks, ˈkɑm plɛks] *adj.* difficult; complicated; hard to understand. (*Adv: complexly.*)

compliment [ˈkɑm plɪ mənt] *n.* a statement of praise.

composition [kɑm pə ˈzɪ ʃən] **1.** *n.* the process of putting things together to form one whole thing. (No pl.) **2.** *n.* the arrangement of the parts of something. (No pl.) **3.** *n.* a piece of music, a symphony; a piece of writing, such as an essay or a poem. **4.** *n.* the process of writing a piece of music or an essay, narrative, research paper, etc. (No pl.) **5.** *n.* the things that make up something; the ingredients of something; the parts of something. (No pl.)

comprehend [kɑm prɪ ˈhɛnd] *tv.* to understand something.

comprehension [kɑm prɪ ˈhɛn ʃən] *n.* understanding; the ability to understand someone or something. (No pl form in this sense.)

compromise [ˈkɑm prə maɪz] **1.** *n.* an agreement to settle an argument where both sides yield a little. **2.** *iv.* to come to an agreement by which both sides yield a little. **3.** *tv.* to endanger someone's reputation, position, or morals.

computer [kəm ˈpjut ɚ] **1.** *n.* an electronic machine that processes data at high speeds. **2.** the *adj.* use of ①.

comrade [ˈkɑm ræd] *n.* a friend; a companion.

conceal [kən ˈsil] *tv.* to hide someone or something.

86

concept ['kɑn sɛpt] *n.* a thought; an idea; a notion.

concern [kən 'sən] **1.** *tv.* to matter to someone; to be important to someone; to worry someone. **2.** *tv.* to be about something; to have to do with something; to deal with something. **3.** *n.* a matter of interest; a matter of importance; something that is of interest. **4.** *n.* care; worry; anxiety. (Pl only for types and instances.)

concert ['kɑn sət] **1.** *n.* a musical performance by one or more musicians. **2.** the *adj.* use of ①.

conclude [kən 'klud] **1.** *tv.* to finish something; to come to the end of something. **2.** *tv.* to reach an opinion by thinking about something. (The object is a clause with THAT ⑦.) **3.** *iv.* [for a process or activity] to finish or end.

conclusion [kən 'klu ʒən] **1.** *n.* the end of something. **2.** *n.* the final decision reached by thinking about something.

concrete 1. ['kɑn krit] *n.* a stonelike material made from cement, sand, gravel, and water, used in construction and paving. (No pl.) **2.** ['kɑn krit] *adj.* made from ①. **3.** [kɑn 'krit] *adj.* actual; existing; real; definite; not abstract. (Adv: *concretely*.)

condense [kən 'dɛns] **1.** *tv.* to cause a gas or vapor to become a liquid by cooling it. **2.** *tv.* to make a document or speech shorter. **3.** *tv.* to make a liquid more dense. **4.** *iv.* to change from vapor to liquid.

condition [kən 'dɪ ʃən] **1.** *n.* a state of being; a situation that someone or something is in. (No pl.) **2. conditions** *n.* a group of related states or situations, as with the weather or the state of the economy. **3.** *n.* the state of someone's health. (No pl.) **4.** *n.* something that is necessary before something else can happen. **5.** *tv.* to shape someone's or something's behavior; to train someone or something. **6.** *tv.* to cause someone to become more physically fit.

condo Go to CONDOMINIUM.

condominium AND **condo** [kɑn də 'mɪn i əm, 'kɑn do] **1.** *n.* a building containing dwellings that are owned by different individuals. **2.** *n.* an individually owned apartment in a building where all apartments are similarly owned.

conduct 1. ['kɑn dəkt] *n.* behavior; the way someone behaves. (No pl.) **2.** [kən 'dʌkt] *tv.* to lead someone or something; to guide someone or something. **3.** [kən 'dʌkt] *tv.* to behave [oneself] in a particular manner. (Takes a reflexive object.) **4.** [kən 'dʌkt] *tv.* to provide a path for electricity or heat to travel.

conductor [kən 'dʌk tər] 1. *n.* someone who directs an orchestra, band, choir, or other musical group. 2. *n.* someone who checks tickets and collects fares on a train. 3. *n.* a substance electricity or heat can travel through.

cone ['kon] 1. *n.* a solid form that changes from a circle at one end to a point at the other end. 2. *n.* a crisp, thin, ①-shaped pastry, used for holding ice cream. 3. *n.* the seed-bearing fruit of a pine tree.

conference ['kɑn frəns] *n.* a meeting to discuss a specific topic.

confess [kən 'fɛs] *tv.* to admit something; to state that one has done something wrong. (The object can be a clause with THAT ⑦.)

confession [kən 'fɛ ʃən] *n.* the process or activity of confessing or admitting something. (Pl only for types and instances.)

confidence ['kɑn fɪ dəns] 1. *n.* a strong trust in someone or something; a strong belief in someone or something. (No pl.) 2. *n.* a feeling of assurance; a belief in oneself and one's abilities. (No pl.)

confidential [kɑn fɪ 'dɛn ʃəl] 1. *adj.* secret; kept as secret. (Adv: *confidentially.*) 2. *adj.* [of someone] trusted with secrets.

confine [kən 'faɪn] 1. *tv.* to keep someone or a creature in a small space; to enclose someone or some creature in a small space. 2. *tv.* to restrict or limit conversation or statements to a particular subject.

confirm [kən 'fɚm] 1. *tv.* to check something to make certain it is true, accurate, complete, or still in effect. (The object can be a clause with THAT ⑦.) 2. *tv.* to approve and agree that someone should be officially chosen for office. (The object can be a clause with THAT ⑦.)

confirmed [kən 'fɚmd] 1. *adj.* shown to be true, accurate, complete, or still in effect. 2. *adj.* determined to remain in a particular state.

conflict 1. ['kɑn flɪkt] *n.* disagreement; fighting. (Pl only for types and instances.) 2. [kən 'flɪkt] *iv.* [for things] to differ or disagree.

confuse [kən 'fjuz] *tv.* to puzzle someone; to make someone wonder about something.

confusion [kən 'fju ʒən] 1. *n.* a feeling of being confused or puzzled. (No pl.) 2. *n.* a noisy lack of order. (No pl.)

congratulate [kən 'grætʃ ə let] *tv.* to extend one's good wishes to someone.

congregation [kɑŋ grə 'ge ʃən] *n.* a group of people, especially in a church service.

congress ['kɑŋ grəs] 1. *n.* the group of people elected to make laws. 2. *n.* a meeting of representatives to or members of an organization.

88

3. *n.* the House of Representatives and the Senate of the United States. (Capitalized. No pl.)

conj. an abbreviation of CONJUNCTION.

conjugate ['kɑn dʒə get] *tv.* to tell the forms of a verb in a language.

conjunction [kən 'dʒʌŋk ʃən] *n.* a part of speech that connects words, phrases, and clauses. (Abbreviated *conj.* here.)

connect [kə 'nɛkt] **1.** *tv.* to serve as a link between two things. **2.** *tv.* to join or attach certain electronic devices. **3.** *tv.* to link someone or something through an electronic means. **4.** *tv.* to relate something to something else; to associate one thought with another. **5.** *iv.* to link with something; to link to something.

connection [kə 'nɛk ʃən] **1.** *n.* the physical link among or between things. **2.** *n.* the relationship among or between thoughts. **3.** *n.* the electronic link that connects two people by telephone. **4.** *n.* an airplane flight that one boards at an intermediate stop. **5.** *n.* someone who is a social or business contact.

conquer ['kɑŋ kɚ] **1.** *tv.* to defeat someone in war; to subdue a people, army, or land. **2.** *tv.* to overcome a difficulty.

conquest ['kɑn kwɛst] **1.** *n.* the attempt to subdue, defeat, or conquer a people or a country. (Pl only for types and instances.) **2.** *n.* the object or target of ①. (Fig. on ①.) **3.** *n.* someone who is the target of a romantic or sexual quest.

conscious ['kɑn ʃəs] **1.** *adj.* awake, alert, and aware of immediate surroundings. (Adv: *consciously.*) **2.** *adj.* intentional; intended. (Adv: *consciously.*)

consent [kən 'sɛnt] *n.* permission; approval. (No pl.)

consequence ['kɑn sə kwɛns] **1.** *n.* a result; an outcome. **2.** *n.* importance; something having important significance. (No pl form in this sense.)

conservation [kɑn sɚ 've ʃən] *n.* the practice of conserving, protecting, or preserving something, such as water, the state of the land, or other resources. (No pl.)

consider [kən 'sɪd ɚ] **1.** *tv.* to think carefully about something. (The object can be a clause with THAT ⑦.) **2.** *tv.* to think of someone or something in a certain way. (The object can be a clause with THAT ⑦.) **3.** *tv.* to take something into account. (The object can be a clause with THAT ⑦.)

considerable [kən ˈsɪd ɚ ə bəl] *adj.* rather large; not small or minimal. (Adv: *considerably*.)

considerate [kən ˈsɪd ə rɪt] *adj.* thoughtful of other people. (Adv: *considerately*.)

consideration [kən sɪd ə ˈre ʃən] **1.** *n.* the thought given toward a decision. (No pl form in this sense.) **2.** *n.* something to be kept in mind when making a decision. **3.** *n.* respect for other people's feelings and opinions. (No pl form in this sense.)

consignment [kən ˈsaɪn mənt] *n.* a shipment of goods.

consonant [ˈkɑn sə nənt] **1.** *n.* a speech sound that is made by restricting the flow of sound or air in the vocal tract; a speech sound that is not a vowel. (The word has different meanings depending on whether one is talking about sounds or spelling letters. These are the IPA symbols for the American English consonants: p, t, k, b, d, g, f, h, s, m, n, ŋ, v, z, ʒ, ʃ, θ, ð, l, r, w, j.) **2.** *n.* a letter of an alphabet that represents ①. (These are the individual letters that represent American English consonants: p, t, k, b, d, g, f, h, s, m, n, v, z, l, r, w, j, y, c, q, x.)

constant [ˈkɑn stənt] **1.** *adj.* continuous; continuing without stopping. (Adv: *constantly*.) **2.** *adj.* loyal; faithful; unchanging. (Adv: *constantly*.) **3.** *n.* a figure, quality, or measurement that stays the same.

constellation [kɑn stə ˈle ʃən] *n.* a particular group of stars.

constrict [kən ˈstrɪkt] *tv.* to tighten something; to make something narrower; to make something contract.

construct 1. [kən ˈstrʌkt] *tv.* to build something; to put something together. **2.** [ˈkɑn strʌkt] *n.* a theory; a made-up idea.

construction [kən ˈstrʌk ʃən] **1.** *n.* the process of building. (No pl.) **2.** *n.* the business of building buildings; the business of constructing buildings. (No pl.)

consult [kən ˈsʌlt] **1.** *tv.* to seek advice or information from someone or something. **2.** *iv.* to offer and supply technical business advice as a profession.

consultant [kən ˈsʌl tənt] *n.* someone who consults; someone who is hired by a company to give advice.

consume [kən ˈsum] **1.** *tv.* to eat or drink something. **2.** *tv.* to use something; to use all of something.

consumer [kən ˈsu mɚ] *n.* someone who buys a product or a service.

90

consummate 1. ['kɑn sə mət] *adj.* perfect; total and ideal. (Adv: *consummately.*) **2.** ['kɑn sə met] *tv.* to fulfill something; to complete something; to make something complete.

cont. an abbreviation of CONTRACTION ③.

contact ['kɑn tækt] **1.** *tv.* to communicate with someone; to get in touch with someone. **2.** *tv.* to touch someone or something. **3.** *n.* touching; coming together. (No pl.) **4.** *n.* a person inside an organization through whom one can get needed information or favors. **5.** *n.* a metal part that touches another metal part, closing an electrical circuit.

contagious [kən 'te dʒəs] *adj.* [of a disease] easily passed from person to person. (Adv: *contagiously.*)

contain [kən 'ten] **1.** *tv.* to hold someone or something; to have, hold, or include someone or something as a part of a larger thing. **2.** *tv.* to hold back something; to restrain something; to keep something under control.

container [kən 'te nɚ] *n.* something that contains something.

contamination [kən tæm ə 'ne ʃən] **1.** *n.* making something impure; polluting something. (No pl.) **2.** *n.* a substance that causes ①. (No pl.)

contemplation [kɑn təm 'ple ʃən] *n.* serious thought. (No pl.)

contempt [kən 'tempt] *n.* hatred; loathing. (No pl.)

content 1. [kən 'tent] *adj.* satisfied; pleased. (Adv: *contently.*) **2.** ['kɑn tent] *n.* something that is contained within something, such as the text of a book or the ingredients of food. (No pl.)

contention [kən 'ten ʃən] **1.** *n.* a claim. **2.** *n.* struggling together; competition. (No pl form.)

contents *n.* the ingredients that make up something; everything that is contained within something. (Treated as pl. Sometimes sg.)

contest 1. ['kɑn test] *n.* a competition that will determine a winner. **2.** [kən 'test] *tv.* to challenge something, especially in a court of law.

contestant [kən 'tes tənt] *n.* someone who competes in a contest; a competitor.

context ['kɑn tekst] *n.* the words before and after another word that help determine its meaning.

continent ['kɑn tə nənt] *n.* one of the large landmasses of earth: Africa, Australia, North America, South America, Antarctica, Europe, and Asia.

continental [kɑn tə 'nɛn təl] **1.** *adj.* of or about a continent; contained within a continent. (Adv: *continentally*.) **2.** *adj.* of or about the continent of Europe and the cultures and people found there. (England is sometimes included.)

continual [kən 'tɪn ju əl] *adj.* happening again and again; repeated; over and over. (Compare this with CONTINUOUS. Adv: *continually*.)

continue [kən 'tɪn ju] **1.** *tv.* to make something keep on happening. (Takes a gerund as an object.) **2.** *tv.* to resume something after an interruption. **3.** *tv.* to postpone a trial until a later time. **4.** *iv.* to go on happening; to remain the same way. **5.** *iv.* to resume after being stopped.

continuous [kən 'tɪn ju əs] *adj.* without stopping; without an interruption; ongoing. (See also CONTINUAL. Adv: *continuously*.)

contract 1. ['kɑn trækt] *n.* a legal document that describes an agreement between two or more people or companies. **2.** [kən 'trækt] *tv.* to hire someone under ① for a specific project. **3.** [kən 'trækt] *tv.* to catch a disease. **4.** [kən 'trækt] *iv.* to enter into an agreement with someone; to agree to do something by ①. **5.** [kən 'trækt] *iv.* to shrink; to shorten; to come together; to become narrow.

contraction [kən 'træk ʃən] **1.** *n.* an amount of shrinking. (Pl only for types and instances.) **2.** *n.* the tensing of a muscle, especially of the uterus during childbirth. **3.** *n.* a shortened word, made by replacing a letter or letters with an apostrophe (’); the shortening of one or more spoken words by removing a sound or sounds. (Abbreviated CONT. here.)

contradict [kɑn trə 'dɪkt] *tv.* to say something that is contrary to what someone else has said; to correct or argue with an alleged error of fact.

contradiction [kɑn trə 'dɪk ʃən] *n.* a statement that is the opposite of something that has been said.

contrary 1. ['kɑn trɛr i] *adj.* completely opposite; opposed. (Adv: *contrarily* [kɑn 'trɛr ə li].) **2.** [kɑn 'trɛr i, 'kɑn trɛr i] *adj.* stubborn; refusing to do what is wanted. (Adv: *contrarily* [kɑn 'trɛr ə li].)

contrast 1. ['kɑn træst] *n.* a noticeable difference; an obvious difference. **2.** ['kɑn træst] *n.* noticeable differences between the light and dark parts of an image. (No pl.) **3.** [kən 'træst] *tv.* to compare the differences found in two or more things. **4.** [kən 'træst] *iv.* to be noticeably different.

92

contribute [kən 'trɪb jut] **1.** *tv.* to give money, time, or labor, usually for a good cause. **2.** *iv.* to give [something] to someone or something.

control [kən 'trol] **1.** *n.* authority; the power to direct someone or something. **2.** *n.* a lever or other device used to operate machinery or something like a radio or television set. (Often pl.) **3.** *tv.* to have power over something; to have authority over something; to direct someone or something; to rule someone or something. **4.** *tv.* to exercise the power to restrain, regulate, steer, guide, or command someone or something.

convenient [kən 'vin jənt] **1.** *adj.* suitable. (Adv: *conveniently.*) **2.** *adj.* available; within reach. (Adv: *conveniently.*)

convention [kən 'vɛn ʃən] **1.** *n.* a large meeting; a group of people gathered together for a specific purpose. **2.** *n.* a formal agreement between countries. **3.** *n.* the way things are typically done; the way things are expected to be done.

conventional [kən 'vɛn ʃə nəl] *adj.* usual and typical; basic and standard. (Adv: *conventionally.*)

conversation [kɑn vɚ 'se ʃən] *n.* discussion; talk between people. (Pl only for types and instances.)

convey [kən 've] **1.** *tv.* to take someone or something from one place to another. **2.** *tv.* to express something; to communicate something. (Fig. on ①.)

convince [kən 'vɪns] *tv.* to persuade someone about something; to persuade someone that something is true.

convincing [kən 'vɪn sɪŋ] **1.** *adj.* acting to persuade someone of something. (Adv: *convincingly.*) **2.** *adj.* realistic; like the real thing. (Adv: *convincingly.*)

convulsion [kən 'vʌl ʃən] *n.* an uncontrollable, violent jerking of muscles.

cook ['kʊk] **1.** *n.* someone who prepares food to be eaten. **2.** *tv.* to prepare food for eating by heating it. **3.** *iv.* to prepare food; to work as ①.

cookbook ['kʊk bʊk] *n.* a book that gives detailed instructions on how to prepare different kinds of food; a book of recipes.

cookie ['kʊk i] *n.* a small, sweet cake made of flour, sugar, eggs, and other ingredients.

cool ['kul] **1.** *adj.* between warm and cold; somewhat cold but not very cold. (Adv: *coolly.* Comp: *cooler;* sup: *coolest.*) **2.** *adj.* calm, not

93

excited; relaxed. (Informal. Adv: *coolly.* Comp: *cooler;* sup: *coolest.*) **3.** *adj.* less than friendly; unfriendly; reserved. (Adv: *coolly.* Comp: *cooler;* sup: *coolest.*) **4.** *adj.* admirable; very good. (Informal. Comp: *cooler;* sup: *coolest.*) **5.** *tv.* to make something less warm. **6.** *iv.* to become less warm.

cooperate [ko ˈɑp ə ret] *iv.* to work together with someone to get something done; to unite in order to get something done more easily.

cop [ˈkɑp] *n.* a police officer. (Informal.)

copier [ˈkɑp i ɚ] *n.* a machine that makes copies of documents.

copper [ˈkɑp ɚ] *n.* a soft, reddish tan metallic element. (No pl.)

copulate [ˈkɑp jə let] *iv.* [for two creatures] to join together sexually, usually in order to breed.

copulation [kɑp jə ˈle ʃən] *n.* sexual intercourse; joining together sexually. (Pl only for types and instances.)

copy [ˈkɑp i] **1.** *n.* one item made to look like or work like another item; a duplicate; a replica. **2.** *n.* a single issue of a newspaper, book, or magazine. **3.** *n.* written material that is ready to be edited or rewritten. (No pl.) **4.** *tv.* to make a duplicate of something. **5.** *tv.* to imitate someone's actions. **6.** *tv.* to reproduce written material by writing it by hand. **7.** *tv.* to cheat on a test by writing the answers from someone else's paper.

copyright [ˈkɑp i rɑit] **1.** *n.* the legal right to produce, publish, or sell a book, play, song, movie, or other work of music or literature. **2.** *tv.* to protect one's exclusive right to publish a work of music or literature by registering one's ownership with the government copyright office.

cord [ˈkord] **1.** *n.* a thick string; a thin rope. (Pl only for types and instances.) **2.** *n.* a wire with a protective covering, especially those that connect an electrical appliance to an electrical outlet.

cordless [ˈkord ləs] *adj.* not having or needing an electrical power cord; operated by battery. (Adv: *cordlessly.*)

core [ˈkor] **1.** *n.* the center of something; the heart of something; the important part. **2.** *n.* the hard part of the inside of a fruit, especially of an apple or a pear. **3.** *tv.* to cut ② from a piece of fruit.

cork [ˈkork] **1.** *n.* the light, soft bark of the cork oak tree, used in many products. (Pl only for types and instances.) **2.** *n.* the piece of shaped ① that fits in the neck of a bottle. **3.** *adj.* made of ①. **4.** *tv.* to seal a bottle by putting ② into the neck of the bottle.

corn ['kɔrn] **1.** *n.* a tall cereal plant producing large grains on corn-cobs, sometimes called *maize.* (No pl. Number is expressed with *corn stalk(s).*) **2.** *n.* the soft and tender young grains of ① eaten by humans as a vegetable. (No pl. Number is expressed with *kernel(s) of corn* for the individual grains. *Ear(s) of corn* refers to grains of ① still attached to the CORNCOB they grow on.) **3.** *n.* hard grains of ①, eaten by live-stock or processed into other foods. (No pl. Number is expressed with *ear(s) of corn* or *kernel(s) of corn* as in ②.) **4.** *n.* a hard, painful patch of skin on the foot or toe. **5.** *adj.* made from ③; having ③ as an ingredient.

corncob ['kɔrn kɑb] *n.* the cylinder of fiber that corn grows on.

corner ['kɔr nɚ] **1.** *n.* the point where two lines meet; the line formed where two surfaces meet. **2.** *n.* the space where two walls meet. **3.** *n.* one of the four squared areas nearest to the intersection of two streets. **4.** *tv.* to trap someone or some creature in a place or situa-tion from which it is difficult or impossible to escape.

cornfield ['kɔrn fild] *n.* a field where corn is grown; a field of corn plants.

cornflakes ['kɔrn fleks] *n.* a breakfast cereal of toasted flakes of corn. (Treated as sg or pl.)

corporation [kɔr pə 're ʃən] *n.* a business, firm, or company.

corpse ['kɔrps] *n.* a dead body.

corral [kə 'ræl] **1.** *n.* a fenced area where horses and cattle are kept. **2.** *tv.* to put livestock into ①.

correct [kə 'rɛkt] **1.** *adj.* right; without error; true. (Adv: *correctly.*) **2.** *adj.* proper; acceptable. (Adv: *correctly.*) **3.** *tv.* to mark answers on a test as right or wrong; to point out the mistakes. **4.** *tv.* to fix a mis-take; to change a wrong answer to the right answer; to make some-thing right.

correction [kə 'rɛkt ʃən] *n.* a change that is made when something wrong is replaced with something right.

correspondence [kɔr ə 'spɑn dəns] **1.** ~ **between** the similarity between two things; the likeness of two things; the resemblance of two things. **2.** *n.* letters; records of communication. (No pl form in this sense.)

corridor ['kɔr ə dɚ] **1.** *n.* a hallway; a passage between two rows of rooms. **2.** *n.* a narrow strip of land allowing a city or country to be connected to the sea or to distant parts of the same city or country.

corrupt [kə 'rʌpt] **1.** *adj.* not honest; [of politicians] easily influenced by the payment of money. (Adv: *corruptly*.) **2.** *tv.* to make someone become bad; to make a good person become bad; to make a moral person become immoral. **3.** *tv.* to ruin something in the execution of a process.

cost ['kɔst] **1.** *n.* the price of something; the amount of money that one must pay to buy something. (Pl only for types and instances.) **2.** *n.* a sacrifice; the loss of something in order to achieve something. **3.** *tv., irreg.* to require a specific amount of money for purchase. (Pt/pp: *cost.*) **4.** *tv., irreg.* to cause the loss of something; to sacrifice something. **5.** *tv., irreg.* to require the expenditure of time, work, or energy.

costly ['kɔst li] **1.** *adj.* costing a lot of money; expensive. (Comp: *costlier*; sup: *costliest.*) **2.** *adj.* serious; troublesome; unfortunate. (Comp: *costlier*; sup: *costliest.*)

costume ['kɑs tum] *n.* clothes that are worn when someone is pretending to be someone else or from another time or place; clothes that represent another culture, time period, or person, as used in the theater.

cot ['kɑt] *n.* a narrow bed made of a piece of canvas stretched over a frame, used especially for camping.

cottage ['kɑt ɪdʒ] *n.* a small house, especially a small home in the country; a vacation house.

cotton ['kɑt n] **1.** *n.* a soft white fiber used to make yarn, thread, and fabric. (No pl. Number is expressed with *bale(s) of cotton.*) **2.** *n.* cloth woven of ①. (Pl only for types and instances.) **3.** *n.* the plant that produces ①. (Pl only for types and instances.) **4.** *adj.* made out of ① or ②.

couch ['kaʊtʃ] *n.* a long piece of furniture that two or more people can sit on or that someone can lie down on; a sofa.

cougar ['ku gɚ] *n.* a large, tan, wild cat; a mountain lion.

cough ['kɔf] **1.** *n.* the act or sound of forcing air from the lungs quickly and with force, sending a dry, rough noise through the throat. **2.** *iv.* to force air out of the lungs as in ①.

could ['kʊd] **1.** *aux.* the past form of CAN ①, expressing ability. **2.** *aux.* the past form of CAN ②, expressing permission. **3.** *aux.* a form of CAN ②, used in making polite requests. **4.** *aux.* a form of CAN ①, expressing possibility or an explanation.

couldn't ['kʊd nt] **1.** *cont.* could not; was not able [to do something]. **2.** *cont.* could not?; wouldn't you please?

could've ['kʊd əv] *cont.* could have. (Where HAVE is an auxiliary.)

council ['kaʊn səl] *n.* a group of people who are appointed or elected to make laws for a city, school, church, or other organization. (Compare this with COUNSEL.)

counsel ['kaʊn səl] **1.** *tv.* to advise someone; to give someone advice. (Compare this with COUNCIL.) **2.** *n.* advice; a piece of advice. (No pl.)

counselor ['kaʊn sə lɚ] **1.** *n.* someone who advises people; someone who gives advice. **2.** *n.* someone who is in charge of children at a camp. **3.** *n.* a lawyer. (Also a term of address for a lawyer.)

count ['kaʊnt] **1.** *n.* the total of people or things obtained after one has figured out how many there are. **2.** *tv.* to figure out how many; to determine how many.

countable ['kaʊnt ə bəl] *adj.* able to be counted or enumerated; subject to being counted.

counter ['kaʊn tɚ] **1.** *n.* a flat surface at which customers sit or stand to be served in a fast-food store, bank, or other establishment. **2.** *n.* [in a kitchen] a flat surface where food is prepared. **3.** *n.* a device that is used to count objects or people; a device that keeps track of the number of objects or people.

counterfeit ['kaʊn tɚ fɪt] **1.** *adj.* fake; imitation; not genuine. **2.** *n.* an illegal copy; a fake. **3.** *tv.* to make an illegal copy of something, especially money.

countless ['kaʊnt ləs] *adj.* not capable of being counted; too numerous to be counted. (Adv: *countlessly.*)

country ['kʌn tri] **1.** *n.* a nation, including its land and its people; a political subdivision. **2.** *n.* land without many people or buildings; the opposite of *city.* (No pl.) **3.** the *adj.* use of ① or ②.

county ['kaʊn ti] *n.* a political division of most U.S. states.

couple ['kʌp əl] *n.* two people, usually male and female, who share a romantic interest. (Treated as sg when referring to a unit and pl when referring to the individuals.)

coupon ['ku pɑn, 'kju pɑn] *n.* a printed form that offers a discount for a product or service.

courage ['kɚ ɪdʒ] *n.* bravery; a lack of fear. (No pl.)

courageous [kə 're dʒəs] *adj.* fearless; facing danger in spite of fear. (Adv: *courageously.*)

97

courier [ˈkɚ i ɚ] *n.* a messenger; someone who transports documents or other valuable items.

course [ˈkors] **1.** *n.* the pathway or route of someone or something. **2.** *n.* a sequence of actions. **3.** *n.* a class offered by a school or an instructor. **4.** *n.* one of the parts of a meal in which parts are served separately. **5.** *iv.* [for water] to flow in a river; [for tears] to run down one's face.

court [ˈkort] **1.** *n.* the place where legal matters are decided and the people who are present there, such as a judge and other officials. (Pl only for types and instances.) **2.** *n.* the space where certain games such as basketball and tennis are played.

courteous [ˈkɚ ti əs] *adj.* showing courtesy; polite; well mannered. (Adv: *courteously.*)

courtesy [ˈkɚ tɪs i] **1.** *n.* a state of being polite and showing good manners. (No pl.) **2.** *n.* an act of kindness; a favor; a thoughtful act.

courthouse [ˈkort haʊs] **1.** *n., irreg.* a building containing the rooms where court is held. (Pl: [...haʊ zɚz].) **2.** *n.* the building that houses the government offices—including the county court—of a particular county.

courtroom [ˈkort rum] *n.* a room where a session of court is held.

cousin [ˈkʌz ən] *n.* the child of one's aunt or uncle; the nephew or niece of one's parent.

cove [ˈkov] *n.* a small bay along the coast.

cover [ˈkʌv ɚ] **1.** *n.* the protective top—like a lid—for something. **2.** *n.* the front and back of a book or magazine. **3.** *n.* a blanket. **4.** *n.* something that is hiding a secret; a legal business that is operating as a disguise for an illegal business. **5.** *tv.* to place something on top of something else to protect or hide it; to spread something on top of something else to protect or hide it. **6.** *tv.* to coat the surface of something; to spread over something. **7.** *tv.* to amount to enough money to pay for something. **8.** *tv.* to include something; to discuss or reveal something. **9.** *tv.* to travel a certain distance. **10.** *tv.* to occupy a certain area; to extend over a certain area. **11.** *tv.* to shelter someone or something; to provide shelter for someone or something.

cow [ˈkaʊ] **1.** *n.* an adult female of a kind of very large animal that provides milk and is eaten for meat. **2.** *n.* the female of certain animals, including the elephant.

coward [ˈkaʊ ɚd] *n.* someone who has no courage; someone who runs away from danger.

98

cowardice [ˈkaʊ ɚ dɪs] *n.* lack of courage. (No pl.)

cowboy [ˈkaʊ bɔɪ] *n.* someone, usually a male, who works on a cattle ranch.

coworker [ˈko wɚ kɚ] *n.* a fellow worker; someone with whom one works.

coyote [kaɪ ˈot (i)] *n.* an animal, similar to a large, skinny dog, that lives in western North America.

cozy [ˈko zi] *adj.* snug; warm and comfortable. (Adv: *cozily.* Comp: *cozier;* sup: *coziest.*)

crab [ˈkræb] **1.** *n.* an edible sea creature with a hard shell, four pairs of legs, and one pair of claws. **2.** *n.* the meat of ① eaten as food. (No pl.) **3.** *n.* an unhappy person who complains a lot.

crabby [ˈkræb i] *adj.* unhappy and making complaints. (Adv: *crabbily.* Comp: *crabbier;* sup: *crabbiest.*)

crack [ˈkræk] **1.** *n.* the line that is made in something when it splits or breaks; a narrow opening in something or between two things. **2.** *n.* a short, sharp noise like the noise of a powerful slap. **3.** *n.* a remark that is intended to hurt or make someone feel bad. **4.** *tv.* to break something without separating it into pieces; to fracture something. **5.** *tv.* to strike someone; to hit someone somewhere. **6.** *iv.* [for something] to break without separating into pieces.

cracker [ˈkræk ɚ] *n.* a flat, thin, square, unsweetened biscuit, often salted.

cradle [ˈkred l] **1.** *n.* a small, rocking bed for a baby or a doll. **2.** *n.* the place where something begins; the origin of something. **3.** *tv.* to hold a baby in one's arms while rocking it back and forth; to hold something carefully.

craft [ˈkræft] **1.** *n.* a special skill for creating something; a special talent. **2.** *n., irreg.* a boat, especially a small one. (Pl: *craft.*) **3.** *tv.* to build or create something that requires skill or talent.

craftsman [ˈkræfts mən] *n., irreg.* someone who builds something by hand. (Pl: CRAFTSMEN.)

craftsmen [ˈkræfts mən] pl of CRAFTSMAN.

cram [ˈkræm] **1.** *tv.* to force someone or something into a small space. **2.** *tv.* to fill a space too full; to put too many people or things into a space.

crane ['kren] 1. *n.* a bird with long legs and a long neck—usually feeding on fish, frogs, etc. 2. *n.* a large machine with a movable arm that lifts and moves very heavy things.

crank ['kræŋk] 1. *n.* an arm or lever that transfers rotating motion to a shaft or axle. 2. *tv.* to make something work by turning ①.

crash ['kræʃ] 1. *n.* the loud sound of something hitting something else. 2. *n.* a sudden economic disaster; a time when the stock market falls rapidly. 3. *n.* a vehicle accident; a loud collision of vehicles. 4. *tv.* to cause a loud collision of a vehicle and something else. 5. *iv.* to make a sudden, loud noise. 6. *iv.* [for a computer] to stop working.

crate ['kret] *n.* a rough wooden or plastic shipping box.

crave ['krev] *tv.* to have a very strong desire for something; to want something very badly.

crawl ['krɔl] 1. *iv.* to move on one's hands and knees; to move forward in a horizontal position. 2. *iv.* [for something] to move very slowly. (Fig. on ①.)

crayon ['kre an] *n.* a colored stick of wax, used for drawing on paper or making pictures.

crazy ['krez i] 1. *adj.* insane; mentally ill. (Adv: *crazily.* Comp: *crazier;* sup: *craziest.*) 2. *adj.* stupid; foolish. (Adv: *crazily.* Comp: *crazier;* sup: *craziest.*) 3. *adj.* wild; bizarre. (Adv: *crazily.* Comp: *crazier;* sup: *craziest.*)

cream ['krim] 1. *n.* the fatty part of cow's milk that rises to the top. (No pl.) 2. *n.* a soft, thick substance used to benefit or carry medicine to the skin. 3. *tv.* to mash something to a creamy texture.

creamy ['krim i] *adj.* containing a lot of cream; as smooth as cream. (Adv: *creamily.* Comp: *creamier;* sup: *creamiest.*)

crease ['kris] 1. *n.* a deep fold; a line made in something by folding it and pressing down along the fold. 2. *tv.* to make a line in something, such as paper or fabric, by folding it and pressing down.

create [kri 'et] 1. *tv.* to bring something new into being; to invent something. 2. *tv.* to cause something to happen; to bring about something.

creation [kri 'e ʃən] 1. *n.* bringing something new into being. (No pl.) 2. *n.* the process of bringing the universe into being. (No pl.) 3. *n.* the universe; everything created by God. (No pl. Often capitalized.) 4. *n.* something that is invented; something that is produced or made for this time.

creative [kri 'e tɪv] *adj.* able to think of new ideas or new ways to solve problems; able to develop works of art. (Adv: *creatively.*)

creator [kri 'et ɚ] **1.** *n.* someone who creates something; an inventor. **2. the Creator** *n.* the deity; God. (No pl form in this sense. Treated as sg.)

creature ['kri tʃɚ] *n.* a living animal; a living being.

credible ['krɛd ə bəl] *adj.* believable; worthy of belief; worthy of trust. (Adv: *credibly.*)

credit ['krɛd ɪt] **1.** *n.* an arrangement allowing a person to purchase goods or services now and pay later, or to borrow money now and pay it back later. (No pl.) **2.** *n.* the amount of money in an account; an account balance greater than zero. **3.** *n.* an amount of money that is added to an account. **4.** *n.* recognition given to someone for having done something. (No pl.) **5.** *n.* mention of someone's work on a book, movie, or performance appearing in a list of similar writers, artists, or technicians. **6.** ~ **card** *n.* a plastic card that allows someone to use CREDIT ① extended by a bank.

creek ['krik] *n.* a small, narrow river; a small stream.

creep ['krip] **1.** *iv., irreg.* to move slowly, with the body close to the ground. (Pt/pp: *creeped* or CREPT.) **2.** *iv., irreg.* to grow along a surface; to grow up a wall. **3.** *n.* a very slow movement. (No pl.)

crept ['krɛpt] a pt/pp of CREEP.

crest ['krɛst] **1.** *n.* the top of something; the top of a mountain; the top of a wave; the high point of a flood. **2.** *n.* a tuft of feathers on the head of a bird; a tuft of fur on the head of an animal. **3.** *n.* a particular decoration that a family uses on stationery and other personal objects. (Often alluding to one's ancestors.) **4.** *iv.* [for a flood or a wave] to reach its high point.

crew ['kru] **1.** *n.* a group of people who work together, especially on a ship, a plane, at a theater, etc. **2.** *n.* the people on a team that competes in boat races.

crib ['krɪb] **1.** *n.* a baby's bed that has sides so the baby can't fall out. **2.** *n.* a storage shed for grain.

cricket ['krɪk ɪt] **1.** *n.* a small, long-legged insect, the male of which makes a chirping noise by rubbing his front wings together. **2.** *n.* an outdoor sport played in England with a (flat) bat and a ball. (No pl.)

crime ['krɑɪm] *n.* the breaking of laws in general. (Pl only for types and instances.)

criminal [ˈkrɪm ə nəl] *n.* someone who commits a crime; someone who breaks a law.

crises [ˈkraɪ siz] pl of CRISIS.

crisis [ˈkraɪ sɪs] *n., irreg.* a serious and threatening situation, the resolution of which will determine the future. (Pl: CRISES.)

crisp [ˈkrɪsp] **1.** *adj.* easily broken; easily snapped into parts. (Adv: *crisply.* Comp: *crisper;* sup: *crispest.*) **2.** *adj.* fresh; firm. (Adv: *crisply.* Comp: *crisper;* sup: *crispest.*) **3.** *adj.* [of air] cool and refreshing. (Adv: *crisply.* Comp: *crisper;* sup: *crispest.*)

critic [ˈkrɪt ɪk] **1.** *n.* someone who writes evaluations of artistic works or performances. **2.** *n.* someone who finds fault with people or things.

criticism [ˈkrɪt ə sɪz əm] **1.** *n.* the process of evaluating and presenting statements that analyze and make judgments about something or someone's performance. (No pl.) **2.** *n.* a critical remark or statement. (Usually negative unless specifically positive.)

criticize [ˈkrɪt ə saɪz] **1.** *tv.* to find fault with someone or something. **2.** *iv.* to judge the good and bad points of something. (Usually negative unless specifically positive.)

croak [ˈkrok] **1.** *n.* the noise that a frog makes. **2.** *iv.* to make the characteristic sound of a frog. **3.** *iv.* to make a noise like ①.

crocodile [ˈkrɑk ə daɪl] **1.** *n.* a large, dangerous reptile with many teeth and a powerful tail. **2.** *adj.* made from the skin of ①.

crook [ˈkrʊk] **1.** *n.* a criminal; a thief. **2.** *n.* a bent part of something; a hooked part of something. **3.** *tv.* to bend something; to make a bend or a hook in something. **4.** *iv.* to bend.

crooked [ˈkrʊk əd] **1.** *adj.* bent; not straight; twisted. (Adv: *crookedly.*) **2.** *adj.* not honest; thieving; criminal. (Adv: *crookedly.*)

crop [ˈkrɑp] **1.** *n.* a plant or food product grown and harvested by a farmer. **2.** *tv.* to cut or trim something.

cross [ˈkrɔs] **1.** *n.* a sign or structure in a form similar to an *X.* **2.** *n.* a vertical post with a horizontal post attached to it near the top, which people were hung on as a punishment in ancient times. **3.** *n.* the shape of the Christian symbol on which Jesus died. **4.** *n.* a combination or blend; a hybrid. **5.** *tv.* to move from one side of something to the other; to go across something. **6.** *tv.* to form an intersection with something else. **7.** *tv.* to anger someone; to upset someone. **8.** *tv.* to breed species or varieties of animals in such a way as to give yet a dif-

102

ferent creature. **9.** *iv.* to make an intersection; to form the shape of ②.

crow ['kro] **1.** *n.* a large, black bird. **2.** *iv.* [for a rooster] to make its loud noise.

crowd ['kraʊd] **1.** *n.* a large group of people; a gathering of people. **2.** *iv.* [for many people or creatures] to gather closely together.

crown ['kraʊn] **1.** *n.* the circular metal object worn on the heads of royal persons. **2.** *n.* something that is worn around the head like ①. **3.** *n.* the office or authority of a monarch. (No pl.) **4.** *n.* the top part of something, especially a tooth, a hat, or a mountain. **5.** *tv.* to make someone king or queen.

crude ['krud] **1.** *adj.* in a natural state; not refined; raw. (Adv: *crudely.* Comp: *cruder;* sup: *crudest.*) **2.** *adj.* vulgar; without manners. (Adv: *crudely.* Comp: *cruder;* sup: *crudest.*) **3.** *adj.* not expertly done; rough; awkward. (Adv: *crudely.* Comp: *cruder;* sup: *crudest.*)

cruel ['kru əl] **1.** *adj.* evil; wicked; fond of causing pain. (Adv: *cruelly.* Comp: *crueler;* sup: *cruelest.*) **2.** *adj.* causing pain; causing suffering. (Adv: *cruelly.* Comp: *crueler;* sup: *cruelest.*)

cruelty ['kru əl ti] *n.* harshness; the quality of causing pain and distress. (Pl only for types and instances.)

cruise ['kruz] **1.** *n.* a trip on a boat for pleasure; a vacation on a boat or ship. **2.** *iv.* to travel at a constant speed.

crumb ['krʌm] *n.* a particle of bread or cake.

crumble ['krʌm bəl] **1.** *tv.* to cause something to fall apart into tiny pieces; to break something up into tiny pieces. **2.** *iv.* to fall apart into tiny pieces.

crumple ['krʌm pəl] **1.** *iv.* to collapse as if undergoing the action of ①. **2.** ~ **up** to make random folds in something while crushing it.

crunch ['krʌntʃ] **1.** *n.* the sound of something snapping and breaking, especially of something being chewed. **2.** *n.* the pressure felt when many deadlines happen at the same time.

crunchy ['krʌn tʃi] *adj.* making a breaking noise when chewed. (Adv: *crunchily.* Comp: *crunchier;* sup: *crunchiest.*)

crusade [kru 'sed] **1.** *n.* a fight against something bad; a fight for something good. **2.** *iv.* to fight against something bad; to fight for something good. **3. The ~s** *n.* the religious expeditions of the Christians against the Muslims in the twelfth and thirteenth centuries. (Capitalized. Treated as pl.)

103

crush ['krʌʃ] **1.** *tv.* to squeeze or press on something with great force and collapse it. **2.** *tv.* to break something into small pieces by pressing or pounding. **3.** *tv.* to force juice out of fruit by squeezing it. **4.** *n.* a strong desire for someone; an infatuation with someone.

crust ['krʌst] *n.* the hard outside layer of something, including the earth, a pie, a loaf of bread, etc.

crutch ['krʌtʃ] *n.* a support under the arms that helps a lame person walk.

cry ['kraɪ] **1.** *n.* an expression of pain or anger; a loud expression of emotion. **2.** *n.* a shout; a call. **3.** *n.* a period of weeping. **4.** *iv.* to weep; to sob; to shed tears.

crystal ['krɪs təl] **1.** *n.* a solid chemical compound occurring in a regular shape, such as a square or rectangle. **2.** *n.* a hard, clear substance like glass that contains a lot of lead. (Pl only for types and instances.) **3.** *n.* clear, expensive drinking vessels made of ②. (No pl.) **4.** *n.* the clear cover over the face of a watch. **5.** *adj.* made from ②. **6.** *adj.* clear; transparent.

cub ['kʌb] *n.* one of the young of certain animals, including bears, lions, and foxes.

cube ['kjub] **1.** *n.* a solid object having six square sides all the same size. **2.** *n.* the number that is the result of multiplying some other number by itself two times. **3.** *tv.* to multiply a number by itself two times, that is, number × number × number. **4.** *tv.* to cut up food into little CUBES as in ①.

cucumber ['kju kəm bɚ] *n.* a long, green vegetable, eaten raw in salads or pickled.

cud ['kʌd] *n.* a lump of chewed food that an animal, such as a cow, brings back into its mouth from its stomach in order to chew it some more.

cuddle ['kʌd l] *tv.* to hold someone with love and affection; to hug someone for a while.

cue ['kju] **1.** *n.* a long, narrow stick used to hit balls in billiards and similar games. **2.** *n.* something that is a signal for someone to do or say something; a line that prompts an actor to say the next line or do the next action. **3.** *tv.* to signal something to do or say something; to give someone ②.

cuff ['kʌf] **1.** *n.* the turned-up edge of cloth near the ankles on trousers; the thicker material near the wrists on shirts. **2.** *tv.* to hit someone with one's hand.

cuisine [kwɪ ˈzin] **1.** *n.* a particular way—usually national or cultural—of preparing food. **2.** *n.* food, especially the food of a particular country or region.

cult [ˈkʌlt] **1.** *n.* members of a strange or radical system of worship or admiration. **2.** *adj.* attracting a small number of fans, who seem like ①.

cultivate [ˈkʌl tə vet] **1.** *tv.* to grow plants or crops. **2.** *tv.* to develop an interest (in someone or something); to nurture an interest (in someone or something). (Fig. on ①.)

culture [ˈkʌl tʃɚ] **1.** *n.* the social patterns of the people in a particular domain. **2.** *n.* the artistic and social tastes of a society. (No pl.) **3.** *n.* a growth of bacteria in a container in a laboratory.

cunning [ˈkʌn ɪŋ] **1.** *adj.* clever; sly; tricky. (Adv: *cunningly*.) **2.** *n.* cleverness; slyness. (No pl form in this sense.)

cup [ˈkʌp] **1.** *n.* a drinking container having a loop-shaped handle. **2.** *n.* the contents of ①. **3.** *n.* a standard unit of measurement equal to eight ounces. **4.** *n.* an award; a trophy. (Often shaped like ① or a larger vessel.)

cupboard [ˈkʌb ɚd] *n.* a cabinet lined with shelves, used to store plates, cups, food, or kitchen supplies.

cupcake [ˈkʌp kek] *n.* a small cake, shaped as if it had been cooked in a cup.

curb [ˈkɚb] **1.** *n.* the raised edge or rim of a road. **2.** *n.* a restraint; a control. **3.** *tv.* to restrain something; to control something; to keep something back.

cure [ˈkjʊr] **1.** *n.* a medicine that will make a sick person better; a remedy. **2.** *tv.* to make someone well again; to get rid of a disease or a bad habit. **3.** *tv.* to preserve meat by salting, smoking, or drying it.

curiosity [kjʊr i ˈɑs ə ti] *n.* the quality of wanting to know something; wondering about something.

curious [ˈkjʊr i əs] **1.** *adj.* inquisitive; wanting to learn about something. (Adv: *curiously*.) **2.** *adj.* weird; odd; strange; unusual. (Adv: *curiously*.)

curl [ˈkɚl] **1.** *n.* a group of hairs that are looped or twisted. **2.** *n.* twist; an amount of twisting. (No pl.) **3.** *n.* something that is shaped like a loop or a spiral. **4.** *tv.* to cause a bunch of hairs to twist into loops or coils. **5.** *tv.* to cause something to wind around an object; to wind something around an object. **6.** *iv.* to twist into loops or coils.

105

currency [ˈkɚ ən si] **1.** *n.* the kind of money that is used in a partic-ular country. **2.** *n.* the quality of being in general use. (No pl.)

current [ˈkɚ ənt] **1.** *adj.* up-to-date; recent; of or about the present time. (Adv: *currently.*) **2.** *n.* a moving stream of air or water; a flow. **3.** *n.* the flow of electricity; the rate of the flow of electricity.

curse [ˈkɚs] **1.** *n.* a word or statement asking a powerful being to bring evil or harm to someone or something. **2.** *n.* a word used when say-ing ①. **3.** *tv.* to utter ② against someone or something. (Pt/pp: *cursed* [ˈkɚst].) **4.** *iv.* to utter ②.

curt [ˈkɚt] *adj.* rudely brief; short (with someone or something) in a rude way. (Adv: *curtly.*)

curtain [ˈkɚt n] *n.* a piece of fabric hung as a barrier to sight.

curve [ˈkɚv] **1.** *n.* a smooth bend; a continuously bending line. **2.** *tv.* to make something bend; to bend something into ①. **3.** *iv.* to bend in the shape of ①.

cushion [ˈkʊʃ ən] **1.** *n.* a padded pillow for sitting. **2.** *tv.* to soften something from shock or impact.

custodian [kə ˈstod i ən] **1.** *n.* someone who has custody over some-one else; someone who is in charge of someone or something. **2.** *n.* a janitor; someone who keeps someplace clean and makes small repairs.

custody [ˈkʌs tə di] *n.* care; guardianship.

custom [ˈkʌs təm] **1.** *n.* a tradition; a social tradition; a socially expected practice. **2.** *n.* a habit; a regular practice; a usual event. **3.** *adj.* made to order; specially made for a customer.

customer [ˈkʌs tə mɚ] *n.* someone who buys a product or a service from a person or a business.

customs [ˈkʌs təmz] *n.* a government department authorized to con-trol the importation of goods into a country.

cut [ˈkʌt] **1.** *n.* an opening made in the skin accidentally. **2.** *n.* a reduc-tion in an amount of money; the taking away of funds for something. **3.** *n.* a piece of something that has been CUT as in ④ from something; a piece [of meat]. **4.** *tv., irreg.* to separate something from something else with a sharp object; to sever something from something else. (Pt/pp: *cut.*) **5.** *tv., irreg.* to make an opening in something with a sharp object. **6.** *tv., irreg.* to shorten something with a sharp object; to trim something with a sharp object. **7.** *tv., irreg.* to reduce some-thing; to decrease something. **8.** *tv., irreg.* to dissolve something; to dilute something. **9.** *iv., irreg.* to slice into something. **10.** ~ **down**

106

on to reduce the amount of something or of doing something; to use or buy less of something.

cute ['kjut] *adj.* clever and pretty; simple and attractive. (Adv: *cutely.* Comp: *cuter;* sup: *cutest.*)

cycle ['saɪ kəl] **1.** *n.* one instance of a process that repeats over and over. **2.** *iv.* to ride a bicycle.

cyclist ['saɪ klɪst] *n.* someone who rides a bicycle or motorcycle, especially as a regular activity.

cyclone ['saɪ klon] *n.* a tornado; a strong, violent wind that moves in a circle.

cylinder ['sɪl ən dɚ] **1.** *n.* a tube; a solid or hollow object with a circular top and bottom and long, curved sides. **2.** *n.* the part of a car engine in which a piston moves back and forth.

cymbal ['sɪm bəl] *n.* one of a pair of brass discs that are struck together to make a loud, ringing noise in orchestras and bands.

cynic ['sɪn ɪk] *n.* someone who believes the worst about everything and everybody.

cynical ['sɪn ɪ kəl] *adj.* believing the worst about everything and everybody. (Adv: *cynically* […ɪk li].)

czar AND **tsar** ['zɑr] **1.** *n.* the male leader of Russia; a Russian king. (Until 1917.) **2.** *n.* a leader; someone who is in charge of something. (Fig. on ①.)

D

dad ['dæd] *n.* a father. (Also a term of address.)

daddy ['dæd i] *n.* a familiar nickname for a father. (Capitalized when written as a proper noun.)

daffodil ['dæf ə dɪl] *n.* a kind of flower with large, typically yellow, trumpet-shaped blossoms.

dagger ['dæg ɚ] *n.* a short, sharp knife carried as a weapon.

daily ['de li] **1.** *adj.* done or occurring every day. **2.** *adj.* suitable for a single day. **3.** *adv.* on every day.

dairy ['dɛr i] **1.** *n.* a company that processes milk products. **2.** the *adj.* use of ①.

daisy ['de zi] *n.* a long-stemmed plant bearing circular flowers, typically white with yellow centers.

dam ['dæm] *n.* a solid barrier in a river or stream that holds back the flow of water.

damage ['dæm ɪdʒ] **1.** *n.* harm; an act that causes loss or pain. (No pl.) **2.** *tv.* to harm something.

damages *n.* charges or costs for harm or loss, usually considered to be a punishment.

damn ['dæm] **1.** *adj.* cursed; declared to be bad as in ③. (Prenominal only. A curse word. Use only with caution.) **2.** *interj.* I am angry!; I am frustrated! (A curse word. Use only with caution.) **3.** *tv.* to declare something to be bad.

damp ['dæmp] *adj.* moist; slightly wet. (Adv: *damply.* Comp: *damper;* sup: *dampest.*)

dance ['dæns] **1.** *tv.* to perform a type of movement of the body, usually with music. **2.** *iv.* to move one's body in a rhythm, usually to music, usually with another person. **3.** *n.* the art and study of the movement of the body, in rhythm, especially to music. (No pl.) **4.** *n.* a set series of body movements done to music. **5.** *n.* an act or session of ②. **6.** *n.* a social event where music is played and people DANCE as in ②.

danger ['den dʒɚ] **1.** *n.* the possibility of harm. (No pl.) **2.** *n.* someone or something that could cause harm, injury, or death.

108

dangerous ['den dʒɚ əs] *adj.* risky; having the potential for causing harm. (Adv: *dangerously*.)

dare ['dɛr] **1.** *n.* a challenge; a statement that challenges someone to take a risk. **2.** *aux.* to have enough courage or boldness [to do something]. (Usually used in negative sentences and questions.)

dark ['dɑrk] **1.** *adj.* without light. (Adv: *darkly*. Comp: *darker;* sup: *darkest*.) **2.** *adj.* not light in color; having little brightness or color. (Adv: *darkly*. Comp: *darker;* sup: *darkest*.) **3.** *n.* the absence of light; darkness; nighttime. (No pl.)

darken ['dɑr kən] **1.** *tv.* to make something darker. **2.** *iv.* to become darker.

darkness ['dɑrk nəs] *n.* the quality of having no light. (No pl.)

data ['det ə, 'dæt ə] *n.* information; pieces of information; facts; a set of facts. (The Latin pl of *datum*. Treated as sg or pl in English.)

date ['det] **1.** *n.* the number of the day of a month, often including the name of the month or the name of the month and the year; the name of a month and the year; the year. (① refers to the number of the day of a month; the day of the week is called the DAY.) **2.** *n.* a brown, fleshy fruit with a long pit, grown on certain palm trees. **3.** *n.* a social meeting between two people, typically male and female, who have planned to go somewhere or do something together. **4.** *n.* a person with whom one has a DATE as in ③. **5.** *tv.* to mark something with ①; to show the ① of something. **6.** *tv.* to show or signal that someone or something is out-of-date or old-fashioned. **7.** *tv.* to have DATES as in ③ with a particular person. **8.** *iv.* to go out on DATES as in ③ frequently or habitually.

daughter ['dɔ tɚ] *n.* a female child.

dawn ['dɔn] **1.** *n.* the period of morning when light is first seen in the eastern sky; sunrise. **2.** *n.* the beginning of something. (Fig. on ①.) **3.** *iv.* [for the day] to become bright or light.

day ['de] **1.** *n.* a period of 24 hours, especially from midnight to midnight; one of the seven divisions of the week. (The days of the week, in order, are MONDAY, TUESDAY, WEDNESDAY, THURSDAY, FRIDAY, SATURDAY, SUNDAY.) **2.** *n.* the period of time between sunrise and sunset; the opposite of night. **3.** *n.* the time spent at work; the hours of work. **4.** *n.* a time; a period.

daybreak ['de brek] *n.* dawn; the first light of day. (No pl.)

daylight ['de laɪt] *n.* the light of day. (No pl.)

days *adv.* during the daytime; during each day.

dead ['dɛd] **1.** *adj.* no longer living. **2.** *adj.* not having the electrical energy to work. (Fig. on ①). **3.** *adj.* not active; dull. (Fig. on ①. Comp: *deader;* sup: *deadest.*) **4.** *adv.* completely; exactly; absolutely. **5.** *n.* the time when it is the darkest, coldest, etc. (No pl.) **6. the ~** *n.* dead people; people who have died. (No pl. Treated as pl, but not countable.) **7. ~ end** the end of a route or passage with no way to get elsewhere except to return.

deadline ['dɛd laɪn] *n.* the date when something is due; the time by which something must be finished.

deaf ['dɛf] **1.** *adj.* not able to hear. (Adv: *deafly.* Comp: *deafer;* sup: *deafest.*) **2.** *adj.* unwilling to hear; heedless. (Fig. on ①. Adv: *deafly.* Comp: *deafer;* sup: *deafest.*) **3. the ~** *n.* people who are DEAF ①. (No pl. Treated as pl, but not countable.)

deal ['dil] **1.** *tv., irreg.* to pass out cards in a card game. (Pt/pp: DEALT.) **2.** *tv., irreg.* to deliver something, such as a blow. **3.** *iv., irreg.* to pass out cards in a card game. **4.** *n.* a bargain; an agreement for the purchase of goods or services, especially if at a cost lower than expected.

dealer ['di lɚ] **1.** *n.* someone who passes out cards in a card game. **2.** *n.* someone who is in the business of trade; someone who buys and sells certain products. (Usually a RETAIL merchant.)

dealt ['dɛlt] pt/pp of DEAL.

dean ['din] *n.* the head of a teaching division within a university, a college, or a private school.

dear ['dɪr] **1.** *adj.* loved very much. (Adv: *dearly.* Comp: *dearer;* sup: *dearest.*) **2.** *adj.* a form of address used at the beginning of a letter. **3.** *n.* a treasured person; a person who is loved very much. (Also a term of address.)

death ['dɛθ] **1.** *n.* the state of being dead. (No pl.) **2.** *n.* the act of dying; the end of life.

debate [dɪ 'bet] **1.** *n.* an event where two or more people with different points of view talk about an issue. **2.** *n.* a formal, structured argument where the two sides of an issue are presented in an orderly fashion by opposing speakers. **3.** *n.* formal, structured arguing done as a school activity. (No pl.) **4.** *tv.* to discuss and argue something with someone. **5.** *iv.* [for two people or groups] to speak for the opposite sides of an issue.

debit ['dɛb ɪt] **1.** *n.* a record of an amount that is owed or must be subtracted from the balance in an account. (Compare this with DEBT.)

2. *tv.* to charge an amount of money against someone's account. **3.** *tv.* to charge someone's account for a sum of money.

debt ['dɛt] *n.* the condition of owing something to someone. (Pl only for types and instances.)

decade ['dɛk ed] **1.** *n.* a period of ten years. **2.** *n.* one of the ten equal divisions of a century, such as 1950–1959.

decay [dɪ 'ke] **1.** *n.* rot; the rotting of something. (No pl.) **2.** *iv.* to rot. **3.** *tv.* to cause something to rot.

deceive [dɪ 'siv] *tv.* to make someone believe something that is not true.

December [dɪ 'sɛm bɚ] Go to MONTH.

decent ['di sənt] **1.** *adj.* proper; well behaved; well mannered; modest. (Adv: *decently.*) **2.** *adj.* kind; nice. (Adv: *decently.*) **3.** *adj.* good enough; pretty good; adequate. (Informal. Adv: *decently.*)

deception [dɪ 'sɛp ʃən] *n.* deceiving, cheating, or defrauding. (No pl form in this sense.)

decide [dɪ 'saɪd] **1.** *tv.* to determine the outcome of something. **2.** *tv.* to make a choice; to reach a decision about something. (The object can be a clause with THAT ⑦.) **3.** ~ **on** to choose something; to pick something out.

decimal point ['dɛs (ə) məl pɔɪnt] *n.* a period (.) that separates whole numbers from fractions.

decision [dɪ 'sɪ ʒən] *n.* a choice; a selection; a judgment; a resolution.

deck ['dɛk] **1.** *n.* a set of cards; a pack of cards. **2.** *n.* the floor of a ship. **3.** *n.* a raised wooden patio, attached to the back door of a house.

declare [dɪ 'klɛr] *tv.* to proclaim something; to make something known; to say something publicly. (The object can be a clause with THAT ⑦.)

decline [dɪ 'klaɪn] **1.** *iv.* to move from good to bad; to move from high to low; to move from better to worse. **2.** *iv.* to turn [something] down; to refuse [something]. **3.** *tv.* to list the different case endings of a noun or adjective. (Compare this with CONJUGATE.) **4.** *tv.* to turn something down; to refuse an offer. **5.** *n.* the gradual change from high to low; the loss of power, strength, or health.

decorate ['dɛk ə ret] **1.** *tv.* to put up decorations. **2.** *tv.* to honor a soldier with a medal. **3.** *iv.* to paint a room, put up wallpaper, hang drapes, lay carpet, or add furniture to a room.

111

decoration [dɛk ə 're ʃən] **1.** *n.* an object or things used to make something or a place look pretty. **2.** *n.* an award or honor given to a soldier.

decorative ['dɛk ə rə tɪv] *adj.* pretty; used for decorating. (Adv: *decoratively.*)

decrease 1. ['di kris] *n.* a drop; a fall; a lessening; a reduction. **2.** ['di kris] *n.* the amount that something has been reduced or lessened. **3.** [dɪ 'kris] *iv.* to become less; to become smaller in size or strength. **4.** [dɪ 'kris] *tv.* to cause something to become less; to cause something to become smaller in size or strength.

deduct [dɪ 'dʌkt] **1.** *tv.* to subtract something from a larger amount. **2.** *tv.* to subtract the cost of something from one's taxable income.

deed ['did] **1.** *n.* something that is performed; an act; an action. **2.** *n.* a legal document that officially transfers the ownership of land or buildings to someone. (Compare this with TITLE ④.)

deep ['dip] **1.** *adj.* extending far down from the top or far back from the front. (Adv: *deeply.* Comp: *deeper;* sup: *deepest.*) **2.** *adj.* reaching a certain depth; extending a certain distance down, in, or back. (Follows a measure of depth. Comp: *deeper.*) **3.** *adj.* [of a sound] low-pitched and strong. (Adv: *deeply.* Comp: *deeper;* sup: *deepest.*) **4.** *adj.* [of a color] intense or strong. (Adv: *deeply.* Comp: *deeper;* sup: *deepest.*) **5.** *adj.* intense; strong; extreme. (Adv: *deeply.* Comp: *deeper;* sup: *deepest.*) **6.** *adj.* difficult to understand; past one's understanding. (Comp: *deeper;* sup: *deepest.*)

deer ['dɪr] *n., irreg.* a fast, hoofed animal, the males of which have antlers. (Pl: *deer.*)

defeat [dɪ 'fit] **1.** *tv.* to cause someone to lose; to beat someone in a contest. **2.** *n.* loss [of a contest]; failure to win. (No pl.) **3.** *n.* an instance of winning as in ①. **4.** *n.* a loss of a contest.

defect 1. ['di fɛkt, dɪ 'fɛkt] *n.* a flaw. **2.** [dɪ 'fɛkt] *iv.* to go over to the other side of a conflict; to join up with one's enemies.

defend [dɪ 'fɛnd] *tv.* to fight for someone or something physically or verbally; to protect someone or something.

defendant [dɪ 'fɛn dənt] *n.* someone who is the target of legal action in a court of law.

defense [dɪ 'fɛns] **1.** *n.* protection against someone or something; defending someone or something; preparation to defend against someone or something. (Pl only for types and instances.) **2.** *n.* the skill of a sports team in protecting its goal or in preventing the other

112

team from scoring points. (Pl only for types and instances.) **3.** *n.* the lawyer or lawyers who defend someone in court. (No pl.) **4.** *n.* the way that a lawyer argues a case in favor of a defendant; an argument used to defend oneself. (No pl.)

defensive [dɪ 'fɛn sɪv] *adj.* protective; used for defense. (Adv: *defensively.*)

define [dɪ 'faɪn] *tv.* to explain the meaning of a word or expression.

definite ['dɛf ə nɪt] *adj.* certain; sure. (Adv: *definitely.*)

defy [dɪ 'faɪ] *tv.* to resist authority; to go against a rule or a regulation.

degree [dɪ 'gri] **1.** *n.* a unit of measurement, as used for measuring temperature or angles. **2.** *n.* the extent of something; the level of something. **3.** *n.* a title awarded by a university or college to a student who has met certain requirements. **4.** *n.* a level in the comparison of adjectives or adverbs.

delete [dɪ 'lit] *tv.* to remove something from something, especially from a list or a piece of writing.

delicate ['dɛl ə kɪt] **1.** *adj.* fragile; easily damaged. (Adv: *delicately.*) **2.** *adj.* subtly flavored. (Adv: *delicately.*)

delicious [dɪ 'lɪʃ əs] *adj.* pleasing to the senses, especially taste and smell. (Adv: *deliciously.*)

delight [dɪ 'laɪt] **1.** *n.* pleasure; joy. **2.** *n.* something that is pleasing; something that causes joy. **3.** *tv.* to give someone pleasure; to cause someone joy; to please someone.

delightful [dɪ 'laɪt fʊl] *adj.* causing delight; giving pleasure. (Adv: *delightfully.*)

deliver [dɪ 'lɪv ɚ] **1.** *tv.* to take something [to someone or someplace]. **2.** *tv.* [for a woman] to give birth to a baby. **3.** *tv.* [for a doctor or someone else] to assist a baby in being born. **4.** *tv.* to give a speech; to read something out loud.

delivery [dɪ 'lɪv ə ri] **1.** *n.* the act of taking something to someone. **2.** *n.* something that is taken to someone. **3.** *n.* the process of giving birth. **4.** *n.* the style or manner of speaking; the style used when giving a speech. (No pl.)

deluge ['dɛl judʒ] **1.** *n.* a great flood. **2.** *n.* a violent rainstorm. **3.** *n.* a great abundance of something. (Fig. on ②.) **4.** *tv.* to overwhelm someone with a flood of something.

deluxe [də 'lʌks] *adj.* of very good quality; of great luxury. (Adv: *deluxely.*)

113

demand [dɪ 'mænd] **1.** *n.* an urgent request; a strong order. **2.** *n.* [buyers'] strength of desire for a product or service. (No pl.) **3.** *tv.* to ask urgently for something; [for an authority] to request something firmly. (The object can be a clause with THAT ⑦.) **4.** *tv.* to require something; to need something. (The object can be a clause with THAT ⑦.)

democracy [dɪ 'mɑ krə si] **1.** *n.* the system of government ultimately controlled by the people who are governed. (No pl.) **2.** *n.* a country whose system of government is ①.

demolish [dɪ 'mɑl ɪʃ] *tv.* to destroy something; to tear something down.

demon ['di mən] *n.* an evil spirit; a devil.

demonstrate ['dɛm ən stret] **1.** *tv.* to show how something is done; to show how something works. **2.** *tv.* to show one's emotions; to show one's feelings. **3.** *iv.* to protest by marching, chanting, or rallying in public.

den ['dɛn] **1.** *n.* the lair or home of a wild animal. **2.** *n.* a center of bad or illegal activities. **3.** *n.* a room in a house used for studying or working.

denial [dɪ 'nɑɪ əl] *n.* insisting that something does not exist or is not true; denying that something exists or is true. (Pl only for types and instances.)

dense ['dɛns] *adj.* thick; tightly packed together. (Adv: *densely.* Comp: *denser;* sup: *densest.*)

dent ['dɛnt] **1.** *n.* a shallow hollow in a surface; an indentation; a place where a small part of a surface has been pressed down or pressed inward. **2.** *tv.* to make a small hollow in something.

dental ['dɛn təl] *adj.* of or about the teeth or their care. (Adv: *dentally.*)

dentist ['dɛn tɪst] *n.* a health-care professional who specializes in the care of the teeth.

deny [dɪ 'nɑɪ] **1.** *tv.* to declare that something is not true. (The object can be a clause with THAT ⑦.) **2.** *tv.* to refuse to grant someone or something permission to do something; to refuse to allow someone or something to have something.

depart [dɪ 'pɑrt] **1.** *iv.* to go away; to start a journey by leaving a place. **2.** *tv.* to go away from a place; to leave a state or status.

department [dɪ 'pɑrt mənt] **1.** *n.* a unit within an organization. **2.** the *adj.* use of ①. **3.** ~ **store** *n.* a large store where merchandise is sold in various departments.

dependent [dɪ 'pɛn dənt] **1.** *adj.* relying on someone else for support or care. (Adv: *dependently.*) **2.** *n.* someone who relies on someone else for support. **3.** *n.* someone who can be listed on a wage earner's income-tax form as ② and thereby reduce the wage earner's taxes.

deposit [dɪ 'pɑz ɪt] **1.** *n.* an amount of money paid toward a product or service. **2.** *n.* an amount of money paid as security on a rented dwelling. **3.** *n.* something that is put down; something that is laid down. **4.** *n.* money that is put in a monetary account. **5.** *tv.* to place money in a monetary account. **6.** *tv.* to put something down in a specific place.

depository [dɪ 'pɑz ɪ tor i] **1.** *n.* a place where things are kept safe; a place where things are deposited and kept safe. **2.** *n.* a warehouse.

depression [dɪ 'prɛ ʃən] **1.** *n.* a part of a surface that is lower than the rest of the surface. **2.** *n.* a time of general economic weakness; a time of high unemployment and weak demand for goods and services. (When capitalized, it refers to the (U.S.) Great Depression, which lasted from October 29, 1929, until the late 1930s.) **3.** *n.* a state of mind where someone is hopelessly sad.

depth ['dɛpθ] *n.* the distance from top to bottom or front to back. (Pl only for types and instances.)

derogatory [dɪ 'rɑg ə tor i] *adj.* showing contempt; rude; very negative and critical. (Adv: *derogatorily* [dɪ rɑg ə 'tor ə li].)

descend [dɪ 'sɛnd] **1.** *tv.* to move from a higher part to a lower part on or along something; to climb down something. **2.** *iv.* to go down; to go from a high place to a lower place; to move downward. **3.** *iv.* to come from an earlier time.

descendant [dɪ 'sɛn dənt] *n.* someone's child, grandchild, great-grandchild, and so on.

describe [dɪ 'skrɑɪb] *tv.* to tell about someone or something in written or spoken words.

description [dɪ 'skrɪp ʃən] *n.* a statement that describes someone or something.

desert 1. ['dɛz ət] *n.* an area of land with little rainfall and little or no human population. (Compare this with DESSERT.) **2.** ['dɛz ət] the *adj.* use of ①. **3.** [dɪ 'zət] *tv.* to abandon someone or something; to go away and leave someone or something behind. **4.** [dɪ 'zət] *tv.* to leave

115

a place and make it empty. **5.** [dɪ 'zɚt] *iv.* to be absent from military duty without permission.

deserve [dɪ 'zɚv] *tv.* to be worthy of something; to merit something.

design [dɪ 'zaɪn] **1.** *n.* a plan showing how something will be made; the way something is arranged; the layout of something. **2.** *n.* a (visual) pattern; drawings or markings. **3.** *tv.* to make the plans for building or decorating something. **4.** *tv.* to plan and execute an arrangement of pictures, images, diagrams, lines, circles, etc.

designer [dɪ 'zaɪ nɚ] *n.* someone who makes designs; someone who plans how buildings, clothing, rooms, or works of graphic art will look.

desire [dɪ 'zaɪɚ] **1.** *n.* a strong wish for something; a request for something. **2.** *n.* someone or something that is wished for. **3.** *tv.* to want something very much.

desk ['dɛsk] *n.* a piece of furniture with a flat top—often with drawers on the lower part.

desolate ['dɛs ə lɪt] *adj.* barren; without people. (Adv: *desolately.*)

desperate ['dɛs pə rɪt] *adj.* willing to try anything because nothing has worked. (Adv: *desperately.*)

dessert [dɪ 'zɚt] *n.* a special, often sweet, food served at the end of a meal. (Compare this with DESERT.)

destiny ['dɛs tə ni] *n.* the force that determines future events. (Pl only for types and instances.)

destroy [dɪ 'strɔɪ] *tv.* to make someone or something completely useless; to do away with someone or something.

destruction [dɪ 'strʌk ʃən] **1.** *n.* ruining or destroying something. (No pl.) **2.** *n.* ruins; the result of destroying. (No pl.)

detail 1. ['di tel, dɪ 'tel] *n.* a small fact about something. **2.** ['di tel] *n.* a drawing that shows all of the fine or small parts of something. **3.** [dɪ 'tel] *tv.* to give all the facts of a story or issue.

detain [dɪ 'ten] **1.** *tv.* to delay someone or something; to keep someone or something from leaving. **2.** *tv.* [for the police] to keep or hold someone.

detect [dɪ 'tɛkt] *tv.* to become aware of something; to discover something.

detective [dɪ 'tɛk tɪv] *n.* a police officer or other licensed person who searches for information about crimes.

detention [dɪ 'ten ʃən] *n.* keeping someone from leaving; holding someone in a place such as a jail or a classroom. (Pl only for types and instances.)

determine [dɪ 'tɚ mɪn] *tv.* to figure something out. (The object can be a clause with THAT ⑦.)

determined [dɪ 'tɚ mɪnd] *adj.* intending to do something; driven to do something; having the will to do something. (Adv: *determinedly*.)

deterrent [dɪ 'tɚ ənt] *n.* something that keeps someone or something from doing something; something that encourages someone or something not to do something.

detest [dɪ 'tɛst] *tv.* to hate someone or something very much. (The object can be a clause with THAT ⑦.)

detour ['di tu ɚ] **1.** *n.* a route that turns away from the regular route and is taken to avoid someone or something. **2.** *iv.* to use ①; to travel the long way around something.

develop [dɪ 'vɛl əp] **1.** *tv.* to create something and attempt to cause it to flourish. **2.** *tv.* [in photography] to cause images to appear on film through chemical processes. **3.** *tv.* [for someone or some creature] to begin to show signs of something or experience something. **4.** *tv.* to build houses, buildings, and stores on empty land. **5.** *iv.* to grow and mature. **6.** *iv.* to grow and prosper; to strengthen; to mature.

device [dɪ 'vaɪs] *n.* a tool or machine meant to be used for a specific purpose.

devil ['dɛv əl] **1.** *n.* an evil spirit; a demon. **2.** *n.* Satan; the supreme spirit of evil. (Sometimes capitalized.) **3.** *n.* someone who is mischievous.

devout [dɪ 'vaʊt] **1.** *adj.* actively religious. (Adv: *devoutly*.) **2.** *adj.* sincere; deeply committed to someone or something. (Fig. on ①. Adv: *devoutly*.) **3. the ~** *n.* religious people. (No pl. Treated as pl, but not countable.)

dew ['du] *n.* tiny drops of water that have fallen from cooling, moist air. (Pl only for types and instances.)

diabetes [daɪ ə 'bit ɪs] *n.* a disease where there is too much sugar in the blood and urine. (Treated as sg.)

diagonal [daɪ 'æg ə nəl] **1.** *adj.* at an angle, but not perpendicular. (Adv: *diagonally*.) **2.** *n.* a line that goes from one corner of a four-sided figure to the opposite corner.

diagram [ˈdaɪ ə græm] **1.** *n.* a drawing that helps explain something. **2.** *tv.* to make a drawing to help explain something. **3.** *tv.* to make a drawing that shows the relationships between the parts of a sentence.

dial [ˈdaɪl] **1.** *n.* on an older telephone, the wheel—with holes for one's finger—that is turned in order to make a telephone call. **2.** *n.* the part of a watch or a clock that has the numbers on it; the face of a watch or clock. **3.** *tv.* to place a telephone call to someone or to some number, either by rotating ① of a telephone or by pushing the buttons of a telephone. **4.** *iv.* to operate a telephone by turning ① or pushing buttons. **5.** ~ **tone** *n.* the sound heard when one picks up a telephone receiver, indicating that a telephone call can be made.

dialect [ˈdaɪ ə lɛkt] *n.* a variety of a language.

dialogue AND **dialog** [ˈdaɪ ə lɔg] **1.** *n.* speech between two or more people. (No pl.) **2.** *n.* a discussion between two or more people who express differences of opinion.

diameter [daɪ ˈæm ɪ tɚ] *n.* the length of a straight line within a circle and going through the center of the circle.

diamond [ˈdaɪ (ə) mənd] **1.** *n.* a figure with four sides of equal length that is viewed as standing on one of its points. **2.** *n.* a playing card that has one or more shapes like (♦) on it. **3.** *n.* a clear gem formed from carbon. **4.** *n.* [in baseball] the space defined by the four bases.

diaper [ˈdaɪ (ə) pɚ] **1.** *n.* a piece of cloth or other fiber that a baby wears between its legs before the baby has learned to use a toilet. **2.** *tv.* to put ① on a baby.

diary [ˈdaɪ (ə) ri] *n.* a journal; a book in which one records the events in one's life.

dice [ˈdaɪs] **1.** pl of DIE ③. **2.** *tv.* to chop a food up into tiny cubes.

dictate [ˈdɪk tet] **1.** ~**s** *n.* directions; orders that must be obeyed. **2.** *tv.* to determine the outcome of some process. **3.** *tv.* to speak a message that is recorded in shorthand or electronically for later transcription. **4.** *iv.* to say something that is being recorded for later transcription.

dictation [dɪk ˈte ʃən] **1.** *n.* speaking something aloud for someone to write down or type, as for students to write down as a classroom exercise or for a secretary to type on a typewriter or computer. (The speech is sometimes recorded and then transcribed later. No pl form in this sense.) **2.** *n.* the words that are spoken, recorded, or transcribed as in ①. (No pl form in this sense.)

dictionary [ˈdɪk ʃə nɛr i] *n.* a book that explains the meanings of words.

did [dɪd] pt of DO.

didn't ['dɪd nt] *cont.* did not.

die ['daɪ] **1.** *iv.* to stop living; to become dead. (Pres. part.: DYING.) **2.** *iv.* [for a machine] to stop working. (Fig. on ①.) **3.** *n., irreg.* a small cube that has a different number of spots on each side. (Pl: DICE. Usually pl.) **4.** ~ **away;** ~ **down** to fade away. **5.** ~ **back** [for vegetation] to DIE as in ① part of the way back to the roots. **6.** ~ **out** [for a species or family] to perish totally because of the failure to produce offspring. **7.** ~ **out** [for an idea, practice, style, etc.] to fade away through time.

diet ['daɪ ɪt] **1.** *n.* the food that a person or an animal usually and typically eats. **2.** *n.* a controlled or prescribed selection of foods. **3.** *iv.* to control one's choice of foods for the purpose of losing weight.

differ ['dɪf ɚ] **1.** ~ **from** to be different from something else. **2.** ~ **with** to disagree with someone.

difference ['dɪf rəns] **1.** *n.* a way that two people or things are not alike. (Pl only for types and instances.) **2.** *n.* the amount remaining when one amount is subtracted from another. (No pl.)

different ['dɪf rənt] *adj.* not the same. (Adv: *differently.*)

difficult ['dɪf ə kəlt] *adj.* hard to do; hard to understand. (Adv: *difficultly.*)

difficulty ['dɪf ə kəl ti] *n.* the quality of being hard to do or understand. (Pl only for types and instances.)

dig ['dɪg] *tv., irreg.* to make a hole in something by removing part of it, as with removing soil with a shovel. (Pt/pp: DUG.)

digest **1.** ['daɪ dʒɛst] *n.* a short version of a long piece of writing; a summary or a collection of summaries. **2.** [dɪ 'dʒɛst] *tv.* to dissolve food in the stomach so that it can be changed into a form that the body can use. **3.** [dɪ 'dʒɛst] *tv.* to take thoughts into the mind; to think about something very deeply and make it part of one's thinking. (Fig. on ②.)

digestion [dɪ 'dʒɛs tʃən] *n.* the process of breaking down food in the stomach so that it can be changed into a form that will give nourishment to the rest of the body. (No pl.)

digit ['dɪdʒ ɪt] **1.** *n.* a number from 0 through 9. **2.** *n.* a finger or a toe.

digital ['dɪdʒ ɪ təl] **1.** *adj.* [of a clock or watch] using numbers rather than hands. (Adv: *digitally.*) **2.** *adj.* of or about storing, retrieving, and working with information that is stored electronically using the digits 0 and 1. (Adv: *digitally*.)

dignified ['dɪg nə faɪd] *adj.* noble; showing decorum. (Adv: *dignifiedly*.)

dignity ['dɪg nə ti] *n.* self-respect; personal worth. (No pl.)

dilemma [dɪ 'lɛm ə] *n.* a difficult choice between two options.

dilute [dɪ 'lut] **1.** *tv.* to weaken something by the addition of a fluid. **2.** *tv.* to make something weaker; to make something less severe. (Fig. on ①.)

dim ['dɪm] **1.** *adj.* barely lit; not bright. (Adv: *dimly*. Comp: *dimmer*; sup: *dimmest*.) **2.** *adj.* vague; unclear in the mind; hard to remember. (Adv: *dimly*. Comp: *dimmer*; sup: *dimmest*.)

dime ['daɪm] *n.* a coin worth 10 U.S. cents.

dimension [dɪ 'mɛn ʃən] *n.* the measurement of something in one direction; the length, the width, or the depth of something.

diminish [dɪ 'mɪn ɪʃ] **1.** *tv.* to cause something to become smaller; to cause something to become less important; to reduce something. **2.** *iv.* to become smaller; to become less important; to decrease.

dine ['daɪn] *iv.* to eat a meal, especially to eat dinner.

dingy ['dɪn dʒi] *adj.* old-looking; dirty; faded; drab; discolored. (Adv: *dingily*. Comp: *dingier*; sup: *dingiest*.)

dining room ['daɪn ɪŋ rum] *n.* in a house, building, or apartment, the room where meals are served.

dinner ['dɪn ɚ] **1.** *n.* the main meal of the day; either a large midday meal or a large evening meal. **2.** *n.* a formal event where an evening meal is served.

dinosaur ['daɪ nə sor] *n.* a large, prehistoric reptile that is now extinct.

dip ['dɪp] **1.** *n.* a sharp slope downward. **2.** *n.* a quick plunge into water or other liquid; a quick swim in water. **3.** *n.* a creamy mixture of foods or a thick sauce that is eaten with crackers, potato chips, or vegetables. (Pl only for types and instances.) **4.** *tv.* to lower and raise something quickly.

diploma [dɪ 'plom ə] *n.* a certificate of graduation from a school or college.

diplomacy [dɪ 'plo mə si] **1.** *n.* tact; skill used in dealing with people. (No pl.) **2.** *n.* the business of maintaining good relationships between countries. (No pl.)

120

direct [dɪ 'rɛkt] **1.** *adj.* going from one place to another place without leaving the path; going the straightest or shortest way. (Adv: *directly.*) **2.** *adj.* exact; to the point; forthright. (Adv: *directly.*) **3.** *tv.* to guide someone or something; to be in charge of someone or something. **4.** *tv.* to establish and oversee the design and execution of a play or a film, particularly overseeing the actors' performances; to instruct actors how to perform in a particular play, opera, film, etc. **5.** ~ **object** *n.* a noun, pronoun, or phrase that receives the action of a *transitive verb*; a noun, pronoun, or phrase on which the verb operates.

direction [dɪ 'rɛk ʃən] **1.** *n.* the guidance or control of something. (No pl.) **2.** *n.* the path taken by something that moves; movement. **3.** *n.* the way that someone or something faces, such as to the north, south, east, or west.

directions **1.** *n.* instructions. **2.** *n.* a statement of how to get to a place.

director [dɪ 'rɛk tɚ] **1.** *n.* someone who leads a group of musicians as they perform; a conductor; someone who DIRECTS ④ actors, films, plays, etc. **2.** *n.* someone who is in charge of an institution, company, school, or department.

directory [dɪ 'rɛk tə ri] **1.** *n.* a list of names arranged in the order of the alphabet, usually including addresses and telephone numbers. **2.** *n.* any list that shows where to find someone or something.

dirt ['dɚt] **1.** *n.* soil; earth. (No pl.) **2.** *n.* dust, grime, mud; filth. (No pl.)

dirty ['dɚ ti] **1.** *adj.* not clean. (Adv: *dirtily.* Comp: *dirtier;* sup: *dirtiest.*) **2.** *adj.* of or about sex or excrement in a crude way. (Adv: *dirtily.* Comp: *dirtier;* sup: *dirtiest.*) **3.** *tv.* to cause something to become unclean.

disable [dɪs 'e bəl] *tv.* to make something not work; to make someone or something powerless.

disagree [dɪs ə 'gri] *iv.* not to agree with someone; to have an opinion different from someone else's opinion.

disagreeable [dɪs ə 'gri ə bəl] *adj.* not pleasant; unpleasant. (Adv: *disagreeably.*)

disagreement [dɪs ə 'gri mənt] *n.* a difference in opinion; a failure to agree. (Pl only for types and instances.)

disappear [dɪs ə 'piɚ] **1.** *iv.* to vanish; to cease to appear; to go out of sight. **2.** *iv.* to cease to exist in a place; to be no longer in a place.

121

disappoint [dɪs ə 'pɔɪnt] *tv.* to fail to please someone; to make someone unhappy by not doing something that was expected or desired; to make someone unhappy by not being or happening as expected or desired.

disapproval [dɪs ə 'pruv əl] *n.* rejection; the failure to give approval to someone or something; unfavorable opinion. (No pl.)

disc Go to DISK.

discharge 1. ['dɪs tʃɑrdʒ] *n.* the sound of an explosion; the firing of a gun. **2.** ['dɪs tʃɑrdʒ] *n.* the release of someone or something, especially when this requires official approval. **3.** ['dɪs tʃɑrdʒ] *n.* the carrying out of one's duties; the performance of one's duties. (No pl.) **4.** ['dɪs tʃɑrdʒ] *n.* giving something off; releasing something. **5.** ['dɪs tʃɑrdʒ] *n.* something that is given off; something that is let out. **6.** [dɪs 'tʃɑrdʒ] *tv.* to fire a gun; to cause an explosion. **7.** [dɪs 'tʃɑrdʒ] *tv.* to dismiss someone from employment. **8.** [dɪs 'tʃɑrdʒ] *tv.* to let something out; to pour something out. **9.** [dɪs 'tʃɑrdʒ] *tv.* to do one's duty; to keep a promise; to repay a debt.

discipline ['dɪs ə plɪn] **1.** *n.* controlled behavior achieved as the result of training; order. (Pl only for types and instances.) **2.** *n.* a field or branch of learning. **3.** *tv.* to punish someone. **4.** *tv.* to train someone or something to behave properly; to train someone or something to be obedient.

discomfort [dɪs 'kʌm fɚt] **1.** *n.* an uncomfortable feeling. (Pl only for types and instances.) **2.** *n.* something that causes an uncomfortable feeling.

discount 1. ['dɪs kaʊnt] *n.* an amount subtracted from the price of a product or service; a savings in price. **2.** ['dɪs kaʊnt] *tv.* to subtract an amount from the cost of a product or service. **3.** [dɪs 'kaʊnt] *tv.* to disregard someone or something; to disregard what someone says or does; to not believe something.

discourage [dɪ 'skɚ ɪdʒ] **1.** *tv.* to cause someone to feel dejected; to take away someone's interest or excitement in something. **2.** *tv.* to try to talk someone out of doing something; to try to persuade someone not to do something.

discover [dɪ 'skʌv ɚ] *tv.* to find something for the first time; to become aware of something for the first time; to find out for the first time how something functions or happens. (The object can be a clause with THAT ⑦.)

122

discovery [dɪ 'skʌv ə ri] **1.** *n.* an instance of discovering something. **2.** *n.* someone or something that has been discovered; something not known of before.

discreet [dɪ 'skrit] *adj.* very cautious, so as not to draw anyone's attention; keeping something a secret; able to keep a secret. (Adv: *discreetly.*)

discuss [dɪ 'skʌs] *tv.* to talk about something; to have a conversation about something.

discussion [dɪ 'skʌ ʃən] *n.* a conversation, often with more than two people.

disease [dɪ 'ziz] *n.* an illness; a sickness.

disgrace [dɪs 'gres] **1.** *n.* shame; the loss of honor. (Pl only for types and instances.) **2.** *tv.* to bring shame upon someone.

disguise [dɪs 'gaɪz] **1.** *n.* something that conceals who someone really is; something that conceals what something really is. **2.** *tv.* to change the appearance of a thing or a person to make identification difficult.

disgust [dɪs 'gʌst] **1.** *n.* a strong feeling of dislike; a loathing for someone or something. (No pl.) **2.** *tv.* to revolt someone; to offend someone.

disgusting [dɪs 'kʌs tɪŋ] *adj.* causing disgust; offensive; sickening. (Adv: *disgustingly.*)

dish ['dɪʃ] **1.** *n.* a plate; a flat, circular object used to serve food or to eat from. **2.** *n.* a particular food that is served at a meal.

dishonest [dɪs 'ɑn ɪst] *adj.* not honest. (Adv: *dishonestly.*)

dishwater ['dɪʃ wɑt ɚ] *n.* the water that dishes are to be washed in; water that dishes have been washed in. (No pl.)

disillusioned [dɪs ə 'lu ʒənd] *adj.* freed from illusion.

disk AND **disc** ['dɪsk] **1.** *n.* a thin, flat, and circular object. **2.** ~ **drive** *n.* a device inside a computer, used for reading and storing digital information on a spinning disk. (Can be shortened to DRIVE.)

diskette [dɪ 'skɛt] *n.* a device—usually held in a square of plastic—for storing digital computer information. (Can be shortened to DISK.)

dismal ['dɪz məl] *adj.* dull and filled with gloom. (Adv: *dismally.*)

dismiss [dɪs 'mɪs] **1.** *tv.* to allow people to leave; to send people away. **2.** *tv.* to end someone's employment. **3.** *tv.* to refuse to consider something; to refuse to listen to someone or something.

disobey [dɪs ə 'be] *tv.* to ignore someone's direct orders.

123

display [dɪ ˈsple] **1.** *tv.* to show something; to exhibit something. **2.** *n.* something that is shown; something that is exhibited.

dispute [dɪ ˈspjut] **1.** *n.* a disagreement; a debate; a fight. **2.** *tv.* to question something; to doubt something is true; to disagree with something.

dissolve [dɪ ˈzɑlv] **1.** *tv.* to melt a solid, such as sugar, into a liquid. **2.** *tv.* to break up a union or a bond; to end an association. **3.** *iv.* [for a solid] to become mixed in a liquid.

distance [ˈdɪs təns] *n.* the length of the space between two things.

distant [ˈdɪs tənt] **1.** *adj.* far away; not near in space or time. (Adv: *distantly.*) **2.** *adj.* not very friendly; aloof. (Adv: *distantly.*)

distinct [dɪ ˈstɪŋkt] **1.** *adj.* different; separate; able to be seen as unique. (Adv: *distinctly.*) **2.** *adj.* obvious; easy to notice. (Adv: *distinctly.*)

distress [dɪ ˈstrɛs] **1.** *n.* grief; anxiety. (No pl.) **2.** *tv.* to trouble someone; to cause someone to feel anxiety, discomfort, or suffering.

distribute [dɪ ˈstrɪb jut] *tv.* to give or sell something [to someone]; to divide something among several people.

district [ˈdɪs trɪkt] *n.* an area; a region; a part of a country, state, county, or city.

distrust [dɪs ˈtrʌst] **1.** *n.* a lack of trust. (No pl.) **2.** *tv.* not to trust someone or something; not to put one's trust in someone or something.

disturb [dɪ ˈstɚb] **1.** *tv.* to bother or annoy someone or something; to interrupt someone or something. **2.** *tv.* to change, handle, or move something.

disturbance [dɪ ˈstɚb əns] *n.* a bother; an annoyance.

ditch [ˈdɪtʃ] **1.** *n.* a long, low, narrow deep place in the ground, where water can flow. **2.** *tv.* to land an airplane in the water and abandon it. **3.** *tv.* to abandon or get rid of someone or something.

dive [ˈdaɪv] **1.** *n.* a jump into something, especially water, usually with one's hands or head first. **2.** *n.* an underwater swim, as with scuba diving; time spent underwater. **3.** *n.* a plunge; a quick movement down. **4.** *iv., irreg.* to jump into deep water, entering smoothly, leading with the feet or with the hands raised above the head. (Pt: *dived* or *dove*; pp: *dived.*) **5.** *iv., irreg.* to spend time underwater, as with scuba diving. **6.** *iv., irreg.* to go down quickly; to plunge down. **7.** *iv., irreg.* to move away and hide quickly.

124

diver ['daɪ vɚ] **1.** *n.* someone who dives into water, especially in a contest with other divers. **2.** *n.* someone who swims underwater, as with scuba diving.

divert [dɪ 'vɚt] **1.** *tv.* to cause someone or something to change direction. **2.** *tv.* to embezzle money; to intercept money that belongs to someone else. **3.** *tv.* to distract or gain the interest of someone or some creature.

divide [dɪ 'vaɪd] **1.** *tv.* to split something into smaller portions. **2.** *iv.* to separate; to split up.

dividend ['dɪv ə dɛnd] **1.** *n.* a number that is divided by another number. **2.** *n.* a part of the profit of a company given to the shareholders of the company. **3.** *n.* a benefit; something that is gained from doing something.

divine [dɪ 'vaɪn] **1.** *adj.* of or about God; holy; sacred. (Adv: *divinely.*) **2.** *adj.* fabulous; excellent; wonderful. (Fig. on ①. Adv: *divinely.*)

division [dɪ 'vɪ ʒən] **1.** *n.* the process of dividing one number by another number. (No pl.) **2.** *n.* a split; a dividing line. **3.** *n.* a major part of a very large company. **4.** *n.* dividing into portions. (Pl only for types and instances.)

divisor [dɪ 'vaɪ zɚ] *n.* a number that is divided into another number.

divorce [dɪ 'vɔrs] **1.** *n.* the legal ending of a marriage. (Pl only for types and instances.) **2.** *tv.* to end one's marriage to someone. **3.** *tv.* to grant ① to a husband and wife.

dizzy ['dɪz i] **1.** *adj.* feeling like everything is spinning around; not steady. (Adv: *dizzily.* Comp: *dizzier;* sup: *dizziest.*) **2.** *adj.* confusing; hectic. (Informal. Adv: *dizzily.* Comp: *dizzier;* sup: *dizziest.*)

do ['du] **1.** *tv.* to perform an action; to finish an action; to end an action. (Pt: DID; pp: DONE. See also DOES.) **2.** *tv.* to solve something; to find an answer. **3.** *tv.* to cover a distance; to go at a certain speed. **4.** *iv.* to be OK; to suit one's needs. **5.** *iv.* to get along; to function or exist. (Used to ask if someone is feeling all right, to inquire of someone's health.) **6.** *aux.* a question word in the pres. and pt. (In the future tense, *will* is used.) **7.** *aux.* a form used to make negative constructions. **8.** *aux.* a form used to emphasize a verb. **9.** *aux.* a particle used to repeat a verb that has already been said or written.

dock ['dɑk] **1.** *n.* a pier; a platform built for moving things and people on and off boats and ships. **2.** *n.* a platform for loading and unloading goods. **3.** *tv.* to bring a ship or boat up to ①. **4.** *iv.* [for a boat or ship] to arrive at ①; [for a boat or ship] to tie up to ①.

125

doctor ['dɑk tɚ] **1.** *n.* someone who has received the highest degree from a university. (Abbreviated *Dr.*) **2.** *n.* someone who is licensed to practice medicine; a medical ①. (Abbreviated *Dr.* when used as a title.)

document ['dɑk jə mənt] **1.** *n.* a piece of paper or an electronic file with information (usually writing or printing) on it; a text. **2.** *tv.* to make and keep written records about something. **3.** *tv.* to list the evidence that will support what one has written. **4.** *tv.* to record something in detail over time.

dodge ['dɑdʒ] **1.** *tv.* to get out of the way of someone or something. **2.** *tv.* to avoid something; to evade something. (Fig. on ①.)

doe ['do] *n.* a female of certain animals, such as the deer.

does ['dʌz] *aux.* the third-person present sg of DO.

doesn't ['dʌz ənt] *cont.* does not.

dog ['dɔg] **1.** *n.* a common pet found in many homes and sometimes used in hunting. **2.** *tv.* to follow someone closely; to pursue someone eagerly.

doghouse ['dɔg haʊs] *n., irreg.* a small outdoor shelter for a dog to sleep in. (Pl: [...haʊ zəz].)

doldrums ['dol drəmz] **1.** *n.* an area of light winds, at sea, north of the equator. (Treated as pl.) **2.** *n.* inactivity; gloominess; boredom. (Treated as pl.)

doll ['dɑl] **1.** *n.* a figure of a human or animal, often a baby, used as a toy. **2.** *n.* an attractive or cute male or female of any age. (Informal.)

dollar ['dɑl ɚ] *n.* the main unit of money in the United States; 100 cents; $1. (The dollar is also the name of the main unit of money in several other countries, but each is worth a value different from that of the U.S. dollar.)

domain [do 'men] **1.** *n.* the area where someone or something is typically found. **2.** *n.* the area under the control of a ruler.

dome ['dom] *n.* a rounded roof; the top of a building shaped like an upside-down bowl.

domestic [də 'mɛs tɪk] **1.** *adj.* of or about the home; of, about, or within the family. (Adv: *domestically* [...ɪk li].) **2.** *adj.* not imported; not foreign. (Adv: *domestically* [...ɪk li].) **3.** *adj.* tame; not wild. (Adv: *domestically* [...ɪk li].)

126

dominate ['dɑm ə net] *tv.* to control someone or something; to be the most important person or thing among certain other people or things.

donate ['do net] *tv.* to give something to a charity or other organization.

done ['dʌn] **1.** pp of DO. **2.** *adj.* completed; finished. (Not compared. Not prenominal.) **3.** *adj.* [of food] having been cooked fully or enough. (Can be compared.)

donkey ['dɑŋ ki] *n.* an animal that has four feet and hooves, is smaller than a horse, and is used to carry people or things.

don't ['dont] *cont.* do not.

donut Go to DOUGHNUT.

doom ['dum] **1.** *n.* a horrible fate; a death that cannot be avoided. (No pl.) **2.** *tv.* to cause someone or something to fail; to cause something to be ruined or destroyed. **3.** *tv.* [for something] to condemn someone to an unpleasant future.

door ['dor] **1.** *n.* a movable panel of wood, glass, or metal that fits into an opening through which someone or something may pass. **2.** *n.* the opening into which ① fits. **3.** *n.* the (figurative) route or pathway to something, such as opportunity. (Fig. on ②.)

doorstep ['dor stɛp] *n.* a step just outside a door.

doorway ['dor we] *n.* the opening in a wall through which a person can walk to enter or exit a room; the opening into which a door fits.

dorm ['dorm] *n.* a DORMITORY; a building in which students live on a college campus.

dormitory ['dorm ɪ tor i] **1.** *n.* a building or room containing beds for a number of people, especially on a college campus. (Abbreviated as DORM.) **2.** *n.* a room housing sleeping facilities for a number of people.

dose ['dos] **1.** *n.* the amount of medicine that is to be taken at one time. **2.** *tv.* to give someone or something a specific amount of medicine.

dot ['dɑt] *n.* a small spot; a small, round mark.

double ['dʌb əl] **1.** *adj.* having twice the amount as something else. (Adv: *doubly*.) **2.** *tv.* to cause something to become twice the amount that it previously was. **3.** *iv.* to become twice the amount that something was previously.

127

doubt ['daʊt] **1.** *n.* lack of belief; a state of not being certain. (No pl.) **2.** *n.* a feeling of disbelief about something; a feeling of not being certain about something. (Often pl.) **3.** *tv.* not to believe or trust something; to be uncertain about something; to consider something unlikely.

dough ['do] *n.* a soft mixture of flour, water, and possibly other ingredients. (Pl only for types and instances.)

doughnut AND **donut** ['do nət] *n.* a small, deep-fried cake shaped in a ring.

dove 1. ['dov] a pt of DIVE. **2.** ['dʌv] *n.* a gray or white bird, a little smaller than a pigeon. (Often thought of as a symbol of peace.)

down ['daʊn] **1.** *adj.* aimed toward a lower place or level; associated with a place or area that is lower than where one is at the moment. **2.** *adj.* sad; unhappy. **3.** *adj.* finished; completed. (Not prenominal.) **4.** *adv.* from a higher place to a lower place; in a direction from a higher place to a lower place. **5.** *adv.* from an earlier time to a later time. **6.** *adv.* [moving] toward the south; [moving] to a place that corresponds to south on a map. **7.** *adv.* onto paper; into writing. **8.** *adv.* as an advance payment against the purchase price. **9.** *adv.* toward having less energy, strength, production, volume, or intensity. **10.** *adv.* over [to someplace]; in a specific direction. (Informal.) **11.** *prep.* on or along something to a lower place. **12.** *prep.* to the end of something; along the length of something. **13.** *tv.* to make someone fall to the ground; to knock someone over. (Informal.) **14.** *tv.* to eat or swallow something very quickly and without much chewing. **15.** *n.* soft feathers, used inside pillows, quilts, etc. (No pl.)

downpour ['daʊn pɔr] *n.* a very heavy rainfall.

downtown ['daʊn 'taʊn] **1.** *adv.* [moving] toward the center of a town or city; [moving] into the center of a town or city. **2.** *adv.* at the center of a town or city. **3.** *adj.* in the center of a town or city; in the business district of a town or city. **4.** *n.* the center of a town or city; the business district of a town or city. (No pl.)

downward ['daʊn wɚd] *adj.* moving or directed toward a lower position; moving toward a lower level. (Adv: *downwardly.*)

downward(s) *adv.* toward a lower position; toward a lower level.

doze ['doz] **1.** *n.* a nap; a small amount of sleep. **2.** *iv.* to take a nap; to sleep for a short period of time.

dozen ['dʌz ən] **1.** *n.* a set of twelve things. **2.** *adj.* twelve; a set or total of twelve.

128

drab ['dræb] *adj.* dull; gray; boring; not exciting. (Adv: *drably.* Comp: *drabber*; sup: *drabbest.*)

draft ['dræft] **1.** *n.* a current of air—usually cold—inside an enclosed space. **2.** *n.* a roughly drawn plan; an early version of a document before the final copy is written. **3.** *tv.* to force someone to serve in the military. **4.** *tv.* to choose someone to do a job or a task. (Fig. on ③.)

drag ['dræg] **1.** *tv.* to pull someone or something along on the ground. **2.** *tv.* to force someone or something to come along. **3.** *tv.* [for someone or something] to touch the ground while being moved.

drain ['dren] **1.** *n.* a pipe or ditch that takes liquids away from an area. **2.** *n.* something that takes away something else a little bit at a time; something that slowly takes something else away. **3.** *tv.* to draw liquid away from a place. **4.** *tv.* to empty a container of a liquid. **5.** *tv.* to take something away slowly, a bit at a time. (Fig. on ④.) **6.** *tv.* to drink all the contents of a glass or container. **7.** *tv.* to empty something by drinking all the liquid from it. (Informal.) **8.** *tv.* to remove someone's energy, endurance, or other quality. **9.** *iv.* [for something] to lose liquid slowly.

drainage ['dren ɪdʒ] **1.** *n.* removing liquid from something or someplace. (No pl.) **2.** *n.* the ability of an area to drain properly. (No pl.)

drama ['drɑm ə] **1.** *n.* the study of plays and the theater. (No pl.) **2.** *n.* a serious play or movie; a play or movie that is not a comedy. **3.** *n.* emotional, exciting, or thrilling events. (No pl. Treated as sg.)

drank ['dræŋk] pt of DRINK.

drape ['drep] **1.** *n.* a heavy curtain. (Often pl.) **2.** *n.* the particular way that fabric hangs. (No pl.) **3.** *tv.* to cover someone or something with fabric that hangs down in a decorative way.

drapery ['drep ri] *n.* pleated fabric panels that hang in front of windows. (Sometimes pl with the same meaning.)

draw ['drɔ] **1.** *n.* an attraction; a reason people go to a particular place. **2.** *iv., irreg.* to make pictures using pen, pencil, crayon, etc. (Pt: DREW; pp: DRAWN.) **3.** *tv., irreg.* to make a picture of something with a pen, pencil, crayon, marker, etc. **4.** *tv., irreg.* to attract someone or something. **5.** *tv., irreg.* to take a breath; to take in air. **6. a ~** *n.* a tie; a game where both teams have the same score.

drawer ['drɔr] *n.* a storage box or compartment that slides in and out of a desk, dresser, etc.

drawing ['drɔ ɪŋ] **1.** *n.* making pictures with a pen, pencil, crayon, etc. (No pl form in this sense.) **2.** *n.* a picture that is drawn; a sketch.

129

drawn ['drɔn] pp of DRAW.

dread ['drɛd] **1.** *n.* strong fear that something [bad] might happen or fear of something that is going to happen. (No pl.) **2.** *tv.* to approach something in the future with fear, wishing that it would not happen.

dreadful ['drɛd fʊl] *adj.* horrible; terrible. (Adv: *dreadfully.*)

dream ['drim] **1.** *iv., irreg.* to have thoughts and images while one sleeps. (Pt/pp: *dreamed* or DREAMT.) **2.** *tv., irreg.* to see something in one's DREAMS as in ③. (The object can be a clause with THAT ⑦.) **3.** *n.* the thoughts and images one has while sleeping. **4.** *n.* a desire; a wish.

dreamt ['drɛmt] a pt/pp of DREAM.

drench ['drɛntʃ] *tv.* to cover someone or something with liquid—water unless some other liquid is mentioned.

dress ['drɛs] **1.** *n.* an item of women's clothing covering an area from the shoulders to somewhere along the legs. **2.** *n.* clothing in general. (No pl.) **3.** *adj.* [of clothing, shoes, etc.] formal. (Prenominal only.) **4.** *tv.* to put clothes on someone. **5.** *tv.* to bandage a wound or cut. **6.** *tv.* to prepare an animal's body for cooking or for market. **7.** *iv.* to put clothes on oneself as in ④.

dresser ['drɛs ɚ] *n.* a piece of furniture with several drawers that clothes are kept in; a chest of drawers.

dressing-down a scolding.

drew ['dru] pt of DRAW.

drift ['drɪft] **1.** *n.* a mass of snow or sand that is moved by the wind. **2.** *n.* a gradual movement toward someone or something, especially in air or water. (No pl.) **3.** *iv.* to move toward something or away from something gradually; to move gradually in some direction. **4.** *iv.* [for someone] to move from place to place without a purpose or established plan.

drill ['drɪl] **1.** *n.* a machine that is used to make a hole in something. **2.** *n.* a classroom practice exercise. **3.** *n.* an event where people practice what they would do in a real emergency. **4.** *tv.* to make a hole in something with ①. **5.** *tv.* to train people by having them practice. **6.** *iv.* to make holes with ①.

drink ['drɪŋk] **1.** *tv., irreg.* to swallow a liquid. (Pt: DRANK; pp: DRUNK.) **2.** *iv., irreg.* to use or consume [alcohol]. **3.** *n.* a liquid meant to be swallowed. **4.** *n.* a container filled with a liquid that is meant to be swallowed. **5.** *n.* a kind of ③ that contains alcohol.

drip ['drɪp] **1.** *n.* the action of liquid falling one drop at a time. **2.** *n.* the sound of a liquid falling one drop at a time. **3.** *tv.* to cause something to fall one drop at a time. **4.** *iv.* to fall one drop at a time; to leak; to release one drop at a time.

drive ['draɪv] **1.** *tv., irreg.* to cause a car or other vehicle to move, and to direct its movement. (Pt: DROVE; pp: DRIVEN.) **2.** *tv., irreg.* to take someone in a vehicle to someplace. **3.** *tv., irreg.* to ram or force something into or through something else. **4.** *iv., irreg.* to ride in and steer or direct [a vehicle]. **5.** *n.* a trip in a car or other vehicle; the act of traveling as in ④. **6.** *n.* the energy and desire to do something. (No pl.) **7.** *n.* a place to guide or park a car between a road and a house or garage. **8.** *n.* an electronic device inside a computer, used for storing and reading computer files and programs. (Short for *disk drive.*)

driven ['drɪv ən] pp of DRIVE.

driver ['draɪ vɚ] *n.* someone who drives a car or other vehicle.

driveway ['draɪv we] *n.* a short length of road from the street to a house or garage.

droop ['drup] *iv.* to sag; to wilt; to hang down.

drop ['drɑp] **1.** *n.* a small ball of liquid; a small amount of liquid. **2.** *n.* a sudden fall; a sudden downward movement. **3.** *n.* the length of a fall; the distance between something and the ground. **4.** *tv.* to let someone or something fall, either by accident or on purpose. **5.** *tv.* to leave something out; to omit something. **6.** *tv.* to stop something; to end something; to stop talking about something. **7.** *iv.* to fall; to go lower; to sink. **8.** ~ **out of** [for someone] to resign from or cease being a member of something; [for someone] to leave school.

drought ['draʊt] *n.* a long period of time without any rain; a long dry period; a lack of rain.

drove ['drov] pt of DRIVE.

drown ['draʊn] **1.** *tv.* to kill someone or something by suffocating the person or thing underwater. **2.** *tv.* to flood an area with a liquid. **3.** *iv.* to die underwater as in ①.

drowsy ['draʊ zi] *adj.* tired; sleepy. (Adv: *drowsily.* Comp: *drowsier*; sup: *drowsiest*.)

drug ['drʌg] **1.** *n.* a medicine. **2.** *n.* a substance used illegally for the pleasure it creates. **3.** *tv.* to give someone ①.

druggist ['drʌg ɪst] *n.* someone who is licensed to package and sell medicine.

131

drugstore ['drʌg stor] *n.* a place where medicine is sold, along with makeup, toothpaste, and many other items.

drum ['drʌm] **1.** *n.* a musical instrument, usually shaped like a cylinder, with a flexible cover stretched over one or both ends. **2.** *n.* a container shaped like ①.

drummer ['drʌm ɚ] *n.* someone who plays a drum or a number of them.

drumstick ['drʌm stɪk] **1.** *n.* the stick or mallet used to play a drum. **2.** *n.* the leg of a chicken or a turkey when served as food. (Fig. on ①.)

drunk ['drʌŋk] **1.** pp of DRINK. **2.** *n.* a person who has taken too much alcohol. **3.** *adj.* concerning a person who has taken too much alcohol. (Also **drunken**. Comp: *drunker*; sup: *drunkest*.)

drunken ['drʌŋk ən] DRUNK ③.

dry ['draɪ] **1.** *adj.* not wet; not moist; without water. (Adv: *dryly*. Comp: *drier*; sup: *driest*.) **2.** *adj.* not allowing alcohol to be sold; without alcohol. **3.** *adj.* boring; not interesting. (Adv: *dryly*. Comp: *drier*; sup: *driest*.) **4.** *tv.* to cause something to be ①; to remove all the moisture from something. **5.** *iv.* to become ①; to completely lose moisture. **6.** ~ **out** [for someone or something wet] to become dry. **7.** ~ **out** to recover from too much alcohol and the effects of drunkenness.

dryer ['draɪ ɚ] *n.* a machine that dries clothes.

dual ['du əl] *adj.* having two parts; having two purposes. (Adv: *dually*.)

duck ['dʌk] **1.** *n.* a kind of fowl that lives near water, has a bill, and has webbed feet for swimming. **2.** *n.* the meat of ①. (No pl.) **3.** *n.* a sturdy kind of cotton cloth. (Pl only for types and instances.) **4.** *iv.* to stoop down so that one doesn't get hit by something; to dip one's head so one doesn't bump it into something. **5.** *iv.* to avoid being seen by moving quickly somewhere. **6.** *tv.* to dip one's head down so that it is not hit against something.

due ['du] **1.** *adj.* owing; having to be paid. (Not prenominal.) **2.** *adv.* directly; in the exact direction; straight.

duel ['du əl] **1.** *n.* a formal battle between two men, once fought with guns or swords, to settle a quarrel of honor. **2.** *tv.* [for two men] to fight each other in a formalistic battle to avenge an insult to one of them. **3.** *iv.* [for two men] to fight a battle of honor according to a formal code.

132

dues *n.* a sum of money owed by each member of an organization. (Treated as pl. Rarely countable.)

duet [du 'ɛt] *n.* music to be performed by two people.

dug ['dʌg] pt/pp of DIG.

dull ['dʌl] **1.** *adj.* not sharp; blunt. (Adv: *dully.* Comp: *duller;* sup: *dullest.*) **2.** *adj.* not exciting; boring. (Adv: *dully.* Comp: *duller;* sup: *dullest.*) **3.** *adj.* not shiny. (Adv: *dully.* Comp: *duller;* sup: *dullest.*) **4.** *adj.* not smart; somewhat stupid. (Adv: *dully.* Comp: *duller;* sup: *dullest.*) **5.** *tv.* to make something less sharp. **6.** *tv.* to lessen physical or emotional pain.

dumb ['dʌm] **1.** *adj.* stupid; foolish; not smart. (Adv: *dumbly.* Comp: *dumber;* sup: *dumbest.*) **2.** *adj.* [of animals] not able to speak. (Can be offensive when applied to humans. Adv: *dumbly.* Comp: *dumber;* sup: *dumbest.*)

dummy ['dʌm i] **1.** *n.* something that takes the place of the real thing; a substitute. **2.** *n.* a mannequin; a store display model having a human form. **3.** *n.* a large doll with a movable mouth used by a ventriloquist in performances. **4.** *n.* someone who acts stupid. (Derogatory.)

dump ['dʌmp] **1.** *n.* a place where trash is taken. **2.** *tv.* to unload something into a pile; to empty something into a pile.

dunce ['dʌns] *n.* a stupid-acting person; someone who learns things slowly.

dung ['dʌŋ] *n.* feces, especially from animals. (No pl.)

dunk ['dʌŋk] *tv.* to push someone or something underwater for a few moments.

duration [dɚ 'e ʃən] *n.* the amount of time that something lasts. (No pl form.)

during ['dɚ ɪŋ] **1.** *prep.* throughout an event that lasts a period of time; all through a period of time. **2.** *prep.* at some point in a period of time; at some time within a period of time.

dusk ['dʌsk] *n.* the period of the day after the sun sets but before it is completely dark; twilight.

dust ['dʌst] **1.** *n.* a fine powder of dried earth. (No pl.) **2.** *n.* a fine powder, especially particles that settle from the air and coat indoor surfaces. (No pl.) **3.** *tv.* to clean a surface or a place by removing ②. **4.** *tv.* to cover something with ① or ②. **5.** *tv.* to spray crops with an insect killer or a weed killer. (Referred originally to powdered chem-

133

icals.) **6.** *iv.* to remove ② from something or from a place as a part of cleaning.

dusty [ˈdʌs ti] **1.** *adj.* covered with dust; full of dust. (Adv: *dustily.* Comp: *dustier;* sup: *dustiest.*) **2.** *adj.* like dust; [of a color] somewhat gray, as if mixed with dust. (Comp: *dustier;* sup: *dustiest.*)

duty [ˈdu ti] **1.** *n.* a task; an obligation; a responsibility. **2.** *n.* a tax placed on products from another country.

dwarf [ˈdworf] **1.** *n., irreg.* someone or something that is smaller than normal or typical. (Pl: DWARVES or *dwarfs.*) **2.** *adj.* smaller than expected; smaller than normally found. (Prenominal only.) **3.** *tv.* [for someone or something large] to make someone or something appear even smaller in a comparison.

dwarves [ˈdworvz] a pl of DWARF.

dwell [ˈdwel] **1.** *iv., irreg.* to live someplace; to live in a place. (Pt/pp: *dwelled* or DWELT.) **2.** ~ **on** to linger on something; to keep thinking about an idea.

dwelling [ˈdwel ɪŋ] *n.* a residence; a place where someone lives.

dwelt [ˈdwelt] a pt/pp of DWELL.

dwindle [ˈdwɪnd l] *iv.* to decrease piece by piece; to get smaller gradually.

dye [ˈdaɪ] **1.** *n.* a liquid that is used to color fabric or hair. **2.** *tv.* to color something by placing it in ①; to color something with ①. (Pres. part.: *dyeing.*)

dying [ˈdaɪ ɪŋ] **1.** the pres. part. of DIE. **2.** *adj.* in the process of becoming dead.

dynamite [ˈdaɪ nə maɪt] **1.** *n.* a chemical that is meant to explode, usually ammonium nitrate. (Pl only for types and instances.) **2.** *n.* someone or something that causes a great shock or surprise; someone or something exciting that attracts a lot of attention or interest. (Fig. on ①. Informal.) **3.** *tv.* to destroy something by an explosion with ①.

E

each [ˈitʃ] **1.** *adj.* every [one]. **2.** *pron.* every one [of those mentioned before]; every individual person or thing [of those mentioned before]. **3.** *adv.* for every one.

eager [ˈi gɚ] *adj.* acting very willing and ready to do something. (Adv: *eagerly.*)

eagle [ˈi gəl] *n.* a strong bird of prey of the hawk family, having excellent vision.

ear [ˈɪr] **1.** *n.* the organ of hearing, one of which is located on either side of the head. **2.** *n.* the external, visible part of the organ of hearing. **3.** *n.* a CORNCOB and the corn growing on it.

earache [ˈɪr ek] *n.* a pain in the inner part of the ear.

eardrum [ˈɪr drəm] *n.* a very thin bit of tissue inside the ear that vibrates when struck by sound waves.

early [ˈɚ li] **1.** *adj.* happening toward the first part of something; happening toward the beginning of something. (Comp: *earlier;* sup: *earliest.*) **2.** *adj.* arriving before the expected time. (Comp: *earlier;* sup: *earliest.*) **3.** *adj.* ancient; happening long ago in time. (Comp: *earlier;* sup: *earliest.*) **4.** *adv.* during or toward the first part of something. (Comp: *earlier;* sup: *earliest.*) **5.** *adv.* before the expected time. (Comp: *earlier;* sup: *earliest.*)

earn [ˈɚn] **1.** *tv.* to gain a sum of money or something else of value, especially by working. **2.** *tv.* to merit something; to deserve something. (Fig. on ①.)

earnest [ˈɚ nəst] *adj.* very serious; wishing to do [something] very well. (Adv: *earnestly.*)

earring [ˈɪr rɪŋ] *n.* a piece of jewelry worn on the ear.

earth [ˈɚθ] **1.** *n.* the planet we live on; the third planet from the sun. (Often capitalized. No pl.) **2.** *n.* soil; land. (No pl.) **3.** *n.* the surface of ①. (No pl.)

earthly [ˈɚθ li] *adj.* of or on the earth; of a part of life on earth rather than in heaven.

earthquake AND **quake** [ˈɚθ kwek, ˈkwek] *n.* a violent shaking of the ground by natural forces.

135

earthworm [ˈəθ wəm] *n.* a worm that lives in the soil.

ease [ˈiz] **1.** *tv.* to make something less hard to do; to make something easier. **2.** *tv.* to make something become less strong or have less pain. **3.** *tv.* to move something [somewhere] gently and carefully. **4.** *iv.* to become less hard or less difficult. **5.** *n.* freedom from problems or bother; peaceful rest. (No pl.)

easel [ˈiz əl] *n.* a stand that holds an artist's canvas.

east [ˈist] **1.** *n.* the direction to the right of someone or something facing north; the direction where the sun appears to rise. (No pl.) **2.** *n.* the eastern region of a country. (Capitalized when referring to a specific region of the United States.) **3.** *adj.* in ①; from ①; toward ①; of or about ①. (Prenominal only.) **4.** *adv.* at, facing, or toward ①.

easy [ˈi zi] **1.** *adj.* simple; not hard; not difficult. (Adv: *easily*. Comp: *easier*; sup: *easiest*.) **2.** *adv.* without stress; without worry; relaxed. Comp: *easier*; sup: *easiest*.)

eat [ˈit] **1.** *tv., irreg.* to put food in one's mouth, chew, and swallow it. (Pt: ATE; pp: EATEN.) **2.** *tv., irreg.* to create a hole by chewing or wearing something away. **3.** *iv., irreg.* to take food into the body. **4.** ~ **up** to eat everything; to eat eagerly.

eaten [ˈit n] pp of EAT.

echo [ˈɛk o] **1.** *n.* a sound that is heard twice because the sound waves have bounced off a surface and returned. (Pl ends in -es.) **2.** *iv.* [for a sound] to reflect back. **3.** *tv.* to reflect sound; to repeat a sound. **4.** *tv.* to repeat something that someone has said.

eclipse [ɪ ˈklɪps] **1.** *n.* the darkening of a celestial body when another body passes between it and the star that gives it light. **2.** *tv.* to block the light from the sun or the moon. **3.** *tv.* to surpass someone; to make someone become less important than oneself. (Fig. on ②.)

economic [ɛk ə ˈnɑm ɪk] **1.** *adj.* of or about ECONOMICS. (Adv: *economically* […ɪk li].) **2.** *adj.* saving money; using money wisely. (Also **economical**. Adv: *economically* […ɪk li].)

economics 1. *n.* financial matters or issues. (Usually treated as sg.) **2.** *n.* the study of the production and use of goods and services in a society. (Treated as sg.)

edge [ˈɛdʒ] **1.** *n.* the rim of something; the outer border of something. **2.** *n.* the cutting part of a cutting tool or instrument. **3.** *n.* an advantage. (No pl.) **4.** *tv.* to provide something with a border.

edgewise [ˈɛdʒ waɪz] *adv.* leading with an edge; with the edge going first.

edible [ˈɛd ə bəl] *adj.* able to be eaten. (Adv: *edibly.*)

edit [ˈɛd ɪt] *tv.* to prepare text, video, or audio for publication or production.

edition [ɪ ˈdɪ ʃən] *n.* the copies of one book made in one printing or series of printings until the text is changed or revised.

editor [ˈɛd ɪ tɚ] **1.** *n.* someone who prepares text for publication; someone who prepares film, video, or audio for production. **2.** *n.* someone who works for a newspaper, a magazine, or a book publisher, arranging for new material, editing, and production.

educate [ˈɛdʒ ə ket] *tv.* to teach someone something; to instruct someone how to do something.

education [ɛdʒ ə ˈke ʃən] **1.** *n.* the teaching of knowledge and skills; a system for teaching knowledge and skills. (No pl.) **2.** *n.* the learning or knowledge that is obtained by studying or being taught. (No pl.)

eel [ˈil] **1.** *n.* a long, snakelike fish not having fins. **2.** *n.* the edible flesh of ①. (No pl.)

effect [ɪ ˈfɛkt] **1.** *n.* a result; something that happens because of something else. (Compare this with AFFECT.) **2.** *tv.* to cause a result; to produce a result.

effective [ɪ ˈfɛk tɪv] *adj.* good at producing or causing results. (Adv: *effectively.*)

efficient [ɪ ˈfɪ ʃənt] *adj.* organized; using time, energy, and money without waste. (Adv: *efficiently.*)

effigy [ˈɛf ə dʒi] *n.* a crude representation of a disliked person, usually made for ridicule or mocking.

effort [ˈɛf ɚt] *n.* the use of physical or mental energy to do hard work.

egg [ˈɛg] **1.** *n.* the female reproductive cell. **2.** *n.* a round object, containing ①, covered with a shell, produced by a female bird or reptile and often used for food. **3.** *n.* the edible part of ②. **4.** *n.* some amount of ③. (No pl. Treated as sg.)

eggshell [ˈɛg ʃɛl] *n.* the hard, protective outside layer of a bird's egg.

ego [ˈi go] **1.** *n.* one's sense of oneself and one's value. (Pl ends in -*s.*) **2.** *n.* an overly large sense of self-esteem; a view of oneself that makes one seem far more important than one really is. (Pl ends in -*s.*)

137

eight ['et] 8. (See FOUR for more information.)

eighteen ['et tin] 18. (See FOUR for more information.)

eighteenth [et 'tinθ] 18th. (See FOURTH for more information.)

eighth ['etθ] 8th. (See FOURTH for more information.)

eightieth ['et i əθ] 80th. (See FOURTH for more information.)

eighty ['et i] 80. (See FORTY for further information.)

either ['i ðɚ] 1. *adj.* one or the other [choosing between two people or things]; no matter which [of two]. 2. *adj.* both; each of two; one and the other. 3. *pron.* one person or thing, or the other person or thing; one person or thing from a choice of two people or things. (Treated as sg.) 4. *adv.* as well; in addition; also. (Only in negative constructions. Use TOO in the affirmative.)

either....or *conj.* one or the other from a choice of two things.

elaborate 1. [ɪ 'læb (ə) rɪt] *adj.* having many details; complex. (Adv: *elaborately*.) 2. [ɪ 'læb ə ret] *iv.* to explain [something], using many details.

elastic [ə 'læs tɪk] 1. *adj.* [of something that is] able to return to its original shape after being stretched. (Adv: *elastically* [...ɪk li].) 2. *n.* [in clothing] a band of fabric and rubber that can stretch.

elbow ['ɛl bo] 1. *n.* the joint where the arm bends in the middle. 2. *n.* a pipe that is bent, curved, or shaped like the angle of ①.

elder ['ɛld ɚ] 1. *n.* someone who is considered to be among the older members of a group or society. 2. *n.* the leader of certain churches, ethnic groups, or communities. 3. *adj.* older. (Used especially with kinship terms.)

elect [ɪ 'lɛkt] *tv.* [for a group of voters] to choose someone by voting.

election [ɪ 'lɛk ʃən] *n.* the process of voting to choose between two or more options.

electric [ɪ 'lɛk trɪk] 1. *adj.* carrying electricity; of or about electricity. (Also *electrical.* Adv: *electrically* [...ɪk li].) 2. *adj.* producing electricity. (Adv: *electrically* [...ɪk li].) 3. *adj.* powered by electricity. (Adv: *electrically* [...ɪk li].) 4. *adj.* exciting; full of excitement; thrilling. (Adv: *electrically* [...ɪk li].)

electrical [ɪ 'lɛk trɪ kəl] *adj.* electric; producing or carrying electricity; of or about electricity. (Adv: *electrically* [...ɪk li].)

138

electricity [ɪ lɛk ˈtrɪs ə ti] *n.* a source of power that comes from batteries, electric companies, and natural occurrences like friction and lightning. (No pl.)

electromagnetic [ɛ lɛk tro mæg ˈnɛt ɪk] *adj.* concerning electric and magnetic waves, especially as used in broadcasting. (Adv: *electromagnetically* […ɪk li].)

electron [ɪ ˈlɛk trɑn] *n.* a negatively charged particle, smaller than an atom.

electronic [ɪ lɛk ˈtrɑn ɪk] *adj.* of or about modern electrical circuits as found in radios and television sets. (Adv: *electronically* […ɪk li].)

electronics *n.* the study and design of the electrical circuits used in computers, radios, televisions, etc. (Treated as sg.)

elegance [ˈɛl ə gəns] *n.* fine style, grace, and beauty. (No pl.)

elegant [ˈɛl ə gənt] *adj.* beautiful; having or showing good taste. (Adv: *elegantly*.)

element [ˈɛl ə mənt] **1.** *n.* one of several kinds of basic matter that cannot be broken down further into other kinds of basic matter. **2.** *n.* a piece of a larger theme.

elementary [ɛl ə ˈmɛn tri] *adj.* basic; introductory.

elephant [ˈɛl ə fənt] *n.* a large land mammal of Africa and Asia, with tough gray skin, large ears, and a long trunk.

elevator [ˈɛl ə ve tɚ] *n.* a moving cage or chamber that carries people and things from floor to floor in a building with more than one story.

eleven [ɪ ˈlɛv ən] 11. (See FOUR for more information.)

eleventh [ɪ ˈlɛv ənθ] 11th. (See FOURTH for more information.)

elf [ˈɛlf] *n., irreg.* a small humanlike creature—full of mischief—of fairy tales and myths. (Pl: ELVES.)

elk [ˈɛlk] **1.** *n., irreg.* [in North America] a large deer, the males of which have large, spreading horns. (Pl: *elk* or *elks*.) **2.** *n., irreg.* [in Europe] a moose.

elm [ˈɛlm] **1.** *n.* a large tree that loses its leaves each fall and is planted to make shade. **2.** *n.* wood from ①. (Pl only for types and instances.) **3.** *adj.* made of ②.

else [ˈɛls] **1.** *adj.* otherwise; apart from someone or something; instead. **2.** *adj.* in addition to someone or something; as well.

elsewhere [ˈɛls ʍɛr] *adv.* in some other place.

elude [ɪ ˈlud] **1.** *tv.* to evade or avoid capture, often by being clever. **2.** *tv.* [for a concept] to be hard to remember or understand.

elusive [ɪ ˈlu sɪv] *adj.* [of someone or something that is] hard to find or hard to catch. (Adv: *elusively*.)

elves [ˈɛlvz] pl of ELF.

embarrass [ɛm ˈbɛr əs] *tv.* to make someone feel ashamed or uncomfortable by making something visible or known in public.

embrace [ɛm ˈbres] **1.** *tv.* to hug someone closely; to take someone into one's arms. **2.** *tv.* to accept something, such as a belief, tenet, or policy. **3.** *iv.* for two people to hug one another.

emerge [ɪ ˈmɚdʒ] **1.** *iv.* to come out from someplace; to come into view from someplace. **2.** *iv.* to become apparent.

emergency [ɪ ˈmɚ dʒən si] **1.** *n.* a time when urgent action is needed; a dangerous situation that must be taken care of at once. **2.** the *adj.* use of ①. **3.** ~ **room** *n.* the place in a hospital where injuries and sudden illnesses are cared for.

emotion [ɪ ˈmo ʃən] **1.** *n.* feeling—other than with the physical senses—or a show of feeling. (No pl.) **2.** *n.* a feeling, such as sadness, joy, anxiety, etc.

emperor [ˈɛmp ɚ rɚ] *n.* someone, especially a male, who rules an EMPIRE.

emphases [ˈɛm fə siz] pl of EMPHASIS.

emphasis [ˈɛm fə sɪs] **1.** *n.* importance that is placed on or given to something. (No pl.) **2.** *n., irreg.* something that has received or should receive ①. (Pl: EMPHASES.) **3.** *n.* increased loudness or (voice) stress given to particular syllables, words, or phrases. (No pl.)

emphasize [ˈɛm fə saɪz] **1.** *tv.* to place special importance on something. **2.** *tv.* to stress something, especially a syllable, word, or phrase.

empire [ˈɛm paɪr] *n.* a group of countries ruled by an EMPEROR or EMPRESS.

employ [ɛm ˈplɔɪ] **1.** *tv.* to hire someone to do work for pay. **2.** *tv.* to use something for a particular purpose.

employable [ɛm ˈplɔɪ ə bəl] *adj.* suitable for employment. (Adv: *employably*.)

employee [ɛm ˈplɔɪ i] *n.* someone who works for a company or a person for pay.

employer [ɛm ˈplɔɪ ɚ] *n.* a person or company that employs people.

employment [ɛm 'plɔɪ mənt] **1.** *n.* the condition of holding a job. (No pl.) **2.** *n.* the work that one does; one's job. (No pl.)

empress ['ɛm prəs] *n.* a woman who rules an EMPIRE.

empty ['ɛmp ti] **1.** *adj.* having nothing or no one within; vacant. (Comp: *emptier;* sup: *emptiest.*) **2.** *adj.* without meaning; without purpose; senseless. (Fig. on ①. Adv: *emptily.* Comp: *emptier;* sup: *emptiest.*) **3.** *tv.* to cause something to be ① by removing all the contents. **4.** *iv.* [for something] to become ①.

enable [ɛn 'e bəl] *tv.* to give someone or something the capability of doing something.

enact [ɛn 'ækt] **1.** *tv.* to make a bill into a law; to pass a law. **2.** *tv.* to perform a part in a play or a movie; to act something out.

enamel [ɪ 'næm əl] **1.** *n.* a paint that dries to make a hard protective glaze or coat. (No pl form in this sense.) **2.** *n.* a hard surface coating, usually made of porcelain. (No pl form in this sense.) **3.** *n.* the hard outer layer of teeth. (No pl form in this sense.) **4.** *tv.* to cover something with ①.

enclose [ɛn 'kloz] **1.** *tv.* to put something in an envelope, box, etc. **2.** *tv.* to close something in on all sides; to put walls up around something.

enclosed [ɛn 'klozd] **1.** *adj.* included in an envelope or a package. **2.** *adj.* shut in on all sides; surrounded; having walls around on all sides.

encore ['ɑŋ kor] **1.** *n.* the performance of an additional piece of music, or a repeat of a piece of music, after the end of a concert, at the demand of the audience. **2.** *adj.* repeated.

encounter [ɛn 'kɑʊn tɚ] **1.** *tv.* to meet someone or something by chance. **2.** *n.* a meeting, especially by chance.

encourage [ɛn 'kɚ ɪdʒ] *tv.* to give someone the courage or confidence to do something.

encouragement [ɛn 'kɚ ɪdʒ mənt] *n.* words or actions that encourage someone. (No pl.)

encyclopedia [ɛn sɑɪ klə 'pid i ə] *n.* a collection of books that provides detailed information on many subjects.

end ['ɛnd] **1.** *n.* the final stopping point of a continuing process. (No pl.) **2.** *n.* the last part of something. **3.** *n.* death. (A euphemism.) **4.** *n.* a purpose; an intended outcome; a result. **5.** *iv.* to stop; to finish; to

141

exist no longer. **6.** *tv.* to stop something; to finish something. **7.** ~ **up** to come to an end.

endeavor [ɛn 'dɛv ɚ] **1.** *n.* an attempt to do something; a struggle to do something. **2.** ~ **to do** to try to do something; to try very hard to do something.

endless ['ɛnd ləs] *adj.* without end; continuous; without stopping. (Adv: *endlessly.*)

endurance [ɛn 'dur əns] *n.* the ability to keep going; the ability to endure. (No pl.)

endure [ɛn 'dur] **1.** *tv.* to withstand something; to put up with something; to tolerate something. **2.** *iv.* to last; to keep going.

enemy ['ɛn ə mi] **1.** *n.* an opponent of someone or something; someone who fights against someone or something. **2.** *n.* a country that another country fights against during a war; an army that another army fights against during a war.

energy ['ɛn ɚ dʒi] *n.* the power needed to do something; the force that powers people or machines. (No pl.)

engage [ɛn 'gedʒ] **1.** *tv.* to take up someone's time; to keep someone busy. **2.** *tv.* to obtain the services of someone. **3.** *tv.* to rent something or a place. **4.** *iv.* [for mechanical parts] to move into operating position with one another.

engine ['ɛn dʒən] **1.** *n.* a machine that uses power from gas, electricity, water pressure, steam, etc., to create power or motion. **2.** *n.* a powered train car that pulls or pushes the other train cars; a locomotive.

engineer [ɛn dʒə 'nɪr] **1.** *n.* someone who drives a locomotive. **2.** *n.* someone who has training in a branch of engineering. **3.** *tv.* [for ②] to do the designing and planning of something, such as a building, bridge, computer, automobile, etc.

England ['ɪŋ glənd] *n.* the island country northwest of the rest of Europe.

English ['ɪŋ glɪʃ] **1. the** ~ *n.* the citizens of England, considered as a group. (No pl form in this sense. Treated as pl.) **2.** *n.* the primary language spoken by the people of the United States of America, England and the rest of the United Kingdom, Canada, Australia, and New Zealand, as well as one of the official languages of South Africa and India. (No pl form in this sense.) **3.** *adj.* of or about the English people and their culture.

enjoy [ɛn 'dʒɔɪ] *tv.* to have something that is good; to feel fortunate to have something; to take pleasure in something.

enjoyment [ɛn 'dʒɔɪ mənt] *n.* joy; pleasure; happiness. (Pl only for types and instances.)

enlarge [ɛn 'lɑrdʒ] **1.** *tv.* to make something larger; to make something bigger. **2.** *iv.* to become larger; to become bigger.

enormous [ɪ 'nɔr məs] *adj.* huge; large; very big. (Adv: *enormously.*)

enough [ɪ 'nʌf] **1.** *adj.* as much as is needed; as much as is necessary; adequate. **2.** *pron.* a necessary amount; an adequate amount. **3.** *adv.* to an adequate degree. (Follows an adjective or a verb.)

enroll AND **enrol** [ɛn 'rol] *tv.* to sign someone up for a club, school, or other group.

ensure [ɛn 'ʃʊr] *tv.* to make sure that something happens; to make something certain to happen. (Compare this with INSURE.)

enter ['ɛn tɚ] **1.** *tv.* to go into a place; to come into a place. **2.** *tv.* to join something; to begin a career or course of study. **3.** *tv.* to write down something in a journal, log, or record book. **4.** *tv.* to type data or other information into a computer. **5.** *n.* the key labeled *enter* on a computer keyboard.

entertain [ɛn tɚ 'ten] **1.** *tv.* to amuse someone; to provide an audience with amusement. **2.** *tv.* to provide guests or associates with food, amusement, and hospitality. **3.** *tv.* to consider something; to think about something.

entertainment [ɛn tɚ 'ten mənt] *n.* amusement; an entertaining performance. (A pl form is rare.)

enthusiasm [ɛn 'θuz ɪ æz əm] *n.* excited interest; zeal. (No pl form in this sense.)

enthusiastic [ɛn θuz ɪ 'æs tɪk] *adj.* full of enthusiasm; excited; interested. (Adv: *enthusiastically* [...ɪk li].)

entire [ɛn 'taɪɚ] *adj.* whole; including everyone or everything. (Adv: *entirely.*)

entirety [ɛn 'taɪr ə ti] *n.* a state of completeness.

entrance 1. ['ɛn trəns] *n.* the right to go into a place; the right to enter a place. (No pl.) **2.** ['ɛn trəns] *n.* an instance of entering. **3.** ['ɛn trəns] *n.* the way into a room or place; the door to a room or other place. **4.** [ɛn 'træns] *tv.* to charm someone.

entry ['ɛn tri] **1.** *n.* going into a place or a room. **2.** *n.* an entrance; the way into a room or a place. **3.** *n.* a piece of information or data that

143

is put into a computer, journal, database, dictionary, encyclopedia, or record book, or is put on a list.

envelop [ɛn 'vɛl əp] *tv.* to wrap around someone or something; to completely cover someone or something.

envelope ['ɛn və lop] *n.* a paper cover that letters and documents are placed in for mailing.

envious ['ɛn vi əs] *adj.* feeling envy; wanting something that someone else has. (Adv: *enviously.*)

environment [ɛn 'vaɪ ən mənt] *n.* the state and nature of the immediate area.

envy ['ɛn vi] **1.** *n.* a negative, greedy feeling toward someone who has someone or something that one wants. (No pl.) **2.** *tv.* to have a negative feeling toward someone who has someone or something that one wants.

epidemic [ɛp ə 'dɛm ɪk] **1.** *n.* a disease that spreads very rapidly from person to person. **2.** the *adj.* use of ①. (Adv: *epidemically* […ɪk li].) **3.** *adj.* spreading rapidly, as ①. (Fig. on ②. Adv: *epidemically* […ɪk li].)

equal ['i kwəl] **1.** *adj.* the same as someone or something; in the same amount or degree. (Adv: *equally.*) **2.** *tv.* to be the same as someone or something else; to have the same amount or degree of something as someone or something else. **3.** *n.* a person who is on the same level as someone else—in social standing, ability, rank, etc.

equality [ɪ 'kwɑl ə ti] *n.* the condition of having the same amount or degree of something as someone or something else. (No pl.)

equalize ['i kwə laɪz] *tv.* to cause something to equal something else.

equation [ɪ 'kwe ʒən] *n.* a statement showing that two amounts are equal.

equator [ɪ 'kwet ɚ] *n.* the imaginary line around the middle of the earth (or any planet) halfway between the north and south poles.

equip with [ɪ 'kwɪp wɪθ] **1.** to provide someone with the necessary supplies. **2.** to provide something with accessories or attachments.

equipment [ɪ 'kwɪp mənt] *n.* things that are furnished or supplied, especially the tools and supplies needed to do a job. (No pl. Number is expressed with *piece(s) of equipment.*)

equivalent [ɪ 'kwɪv ə lənt] *adj.* same; equal in level or degree. (Adv: *equivalently.*)

144

erase [ɪ 'res] **1.** *tv.* to remove something written or drawn in pencil, ink, or chalk by rubbing it with an eraser. **2.** *tv.* to wipe something clean by removing the writing—especially chalk or pencil writing—on it. **3.** *tv.* to remove something completely. (Fig. on ①.)

eraser [ɪ 'res ɚ] *n.* a small rubber object that erases pencil markings; a rectangular block of felt that rubs out chalk markings.

erect [ɪ 'rɛkt] **1.** *adj.* standing straight up in a vertical position. (Adv: *erectly.*) **2.** *adj.* upright; straight up. **3.** *tv.* to build something. **4.** *tv.* to cause something to stand in a vertical position.

erode [ɪ 'rod] **1.** *tv.* to wear something away gradually; to rub something away gradually. **2.** *iv.* to become worn away; to become rubbed away.

erosion [ɪ 'ro ʒən] **1.** *n.* the gradual destruction of rock or land by the action of wind and water. (No pl form in this sense.) **2.** *n.* the breaking down or diminishing of something gradually. (No pl form in this sense. Fig. on ①.)

err [ɛr, ɚ] *iv.* to make a mistake; to be wrong.

errand ['ɛr ənd] *n.* a short trip to do something useful or helpful.

error ['ɛr ɚ] **1.** *n.* a mistake; something that is wrong. **2.** *n.* a bad play by someone on a baseball team.

erupt [ɪ 'rʌpt] **1.** *iv.* [for a volcano] to explode. **2.** *iv.* [for anger, violence, arguments, etc.] to be released suddenly.

eruption [ɪ 'rʌp ʃən] **1.** *n.* an explosion of a volcano; a flowing out of material from a volcano. **2.** *n.* a bursting forth of anger, violence, fighting, etc.

escalator ['ɛs kə le tɚ] *n.* a moving staircase that carries people to a higher or lower floor of a building.

escape [ɛ 'skep] **1.** *n.* fleeing a dangerous place, an enclosed place, or a bad situation. (Pl only for types and instances.) **2.** *iv.* to become free; to get away. **3.** *iv.* to leak from a container. **4.** *iv.* to elude being caught; to avoid being caught. **5.** *tv.* to (seem to) avoid being seen, heard, remembered, etc.

escort **1.** ['ɛ skort] *n.* someone who accompanies someone else as a companion. **2.** [ɛ 'skort] *tv.* to accompany someone else; to guide someone; to lead someone; to guard someone.

especially [ɛ 'spɛʃ ə li] *adv.* mainly; primarily; particularly.

essay ['ɛs e] *n.* a written work about a specific topic.

145

essence [ˈɛs əns] **1.** *n.* the most important part of something; the important features that make up someone or something. **2.** *n.* a perfume or similar substance.

essential [ɪ ˈsɛn ʃəl] **1.** *adj.* necessary; needed. (Adv: *essentially.*) **2.** *adj.* basic; constituting the nature or foundation of something. (Adv: *essentially.*) **3.** ~**s** *n.* the basic and necessary elements.

establish [ɛ ˈstæb lɪʃ] **1.** *tv.* to start an organization; to found an organization. **2.** *tv.* to start something, such as a policy or plan. **3.** *tv.* to place oneself or itself as something or in a specific role. (Takes a reflexive object.) **4.** *tv.* to prove something; to determine the truth of something. (The object can be a clause with THAT ⑦.)

establishment [ɛ ˈstæb lɪʃ mənt] **1.** *n.* establishing something. (No pl.) **2.** *n.* a company or organization.

estate [ɛ ˈstet] **1.** *n.* everything that someone owns; the property of someone who has just died. **2.** *n.* a house and related buildings set on a large piece of property.

esteem [ɛ ˈstim] *n.* opinion or regard, favorable unless indicated otherwise. (No pl.)

estimate 1. [ˈɛst ə mət] *n.* a statement that shows about how much someone will charge to do a certain amount of work; an approximate calculation of an amount of money, intended to represent the final cost fairly closely. **2.** *n.* [ˈɛst ə mət] *n.* a guess or projection. **3.** [ˈɛst ə met] *tv.* to calculate how much something will cost; to determine an approximate amount of money. (The object can be a clause with THAT ⑦.) **4.** [ˈɛst ə met] *tv.* to guess or project an outcome.

estimation [ɛst ə ˈme ʃən] *n.* one's opinion or judgment. (No pl.)

et cetera [ˈɛt ˈsɛt ə rə] and other similar things; and so forth; and other things like those just named. (Abbreviated as ETC.)

etc. an abbreviation of ET CETERA.

eternal [ɪ ˈtɚ nəl] *adj.* without ending; existing forever. (Adv: *eternally.*)

eternity [ɪ ˈtɚ nə ti] *n.* time without beginning or end. (No pl.)

ethic [ˈɛθ ɪk] *n.* the body of morals governing a person or a group. (No pl.)

ethics 1. *n.* standards of right and wrong within a society. (Treated as pl, but not countable.) **2.** *n.* the study of the standards of right and wrong; the study of morals. (Treated as sg.)

146

ethnic ['ɛθ nɪk] *adj.* of or about a particular variety, group, or sub-group of people, such as divisions according to race, language, country, etc. (Adv: *ethnically* [...ɪk li].)

euphemism ['ju fə mɪz əm] *n.* a word or phrase that replaces a less polite or more harsh word or expression.

Europe ['jʊ əp] *n.* the countries located to the north of the Mediterranean Sea.

evade [ɪ 'ved] *tv.* to avoid doing something; to avoid the consequences of something.

evaluate [ɪ 'væl ju et] *tv.* to study and make a judgment about the value of someone or something.

evaluation [ɪ væl ju 'e ʃən] **1.** *n.* studying the worth, value, or status of something. (Pl only for types and instances.) **2.** *n.* a judgment or statement about the status or quality of someone or something.

eve ['iv] *n.* the night or day before an important day.

even ['i vən] **1.** *adj.* smooth; not rough; level; on the same level; uniform. (Adv: *evenly.*) **2.** *adj.* [of a number] able to be divided by 2 with nothing left over. (Adv: *evenly.*) **3.** *adj.* equal. (Adv: *evenly.*) **4.** *adv.* still [more]; yet [more]. (Used to make a comparison stronger.) **5.** *adv.* more than expected; in a way that would not be expected. **6.** *tv.* to smooth something out; to make something smooth; to make something level.

evening ['iv nɪŋ] **1.** *n.* the last part of the day; the period of the day after the afternoon and before the night. **2.** the *adj.* use of ①.

evenings *adv.* every evening; happening every evening.

event [ə 'vɛnt] *n.* something that happens; an occurrence.

eventual [ə 'vɛn tʃu əl] *adj.* at some time in the future. (Adv: *eventually.*)

eventually [ə 'vɛn tʃu ə li] *adv.* ultimately; at some later time.

ever ['ɛv ɚ] **1.** *adv.* at any time. (Used especially in negative sentences, questions, and sentences with *if*, and after comparatives with *than*, after superlatives, or after *as*.) **2.** *adv.* always; forever.

every ['ɛv ri] **1.** *adj.* all; each. (For two people or things, use BOTH.) **2.** *adj.* per; once during each unit. **3.** *adj.* all possible.

everybody ['ɛv ri bɑd i] *pron.* every person; everyone.

everyday ['ɛv ri de] **1.** *adj.* happening every day. (Prenominal only.) **2.** *adj.* common; ordinary; not special. (Compare this with *every day* (adv.), meaning "each day.")

everyone ['ɛv ri wən] *pron.* every person; all; everybody. (Treated as sg.)

everything ['ɛv ri θɪŋ] **1.** *pron.* each thing. **2.** *pron.* the only thing that is important; the only goal or value.

everywhere ['ɛv ri ʍɛr] *adv.* in all places; in every location; at every point.

evidence ['ɛv ə dəns] *n.* something that proves a claim or statement. (No pl.)

evil ['i vəl] **1.** *adj.* very bad; capable of doing very bad things. (Adv: *evilly.*) **2.** *n.* badness. (Pl only for types and instances.)

evolution [ɛv ə 'lu ʃən] **1.** *n.* the changes of something from an early stage to a more advanced stage. (No pl.) **2.** *n.* the scientific theory that all living creatures developed from simpler forms of life over millions of years. (No pl.)

exact [ɪg 'zækt] *adj.* without mistakes; precise; completely correct. (Adv: *exactly.*)

exactly [ɪg 'zækt li] **1.** *adv.* precisely; accurately; only as requested or ordered. **2.** *interj.* That is quite right!

exaggerate [ɪg 'zædʒ ə ret] **1.** *tv.* to make something seem larger or more severe than it really is. **2.** *iv.* to claim that something is more or less than it really is.

exam [ɪg 'zæm] *n.* an EXAMINATION.

examination [ɪg zæm ɪ 'ne ʃən] **1.** *n.* examining, studying, or observing someone or something. (Pl only for types and instances.) **2.** *n.* a test; a series of questions given to test someone's knowledge of a certain topic.

examine [ɪg 'zæm ɪn] **1.** *tv.* to look at someone or something very closely. **2.** *tv.* to make a medical study of the state of someone's body.

example [ɪg 'zæm pəl] **1.** *n.* something that clarifies what one is talking about; a sample of what is being talked about. **2.** *n.* someone or something that should be imitated; a model.

exceed [ɛk 'sid] **1.** *tv.* to go beyond the limits of something; to surpass the upper boundary of something. **2.** *tv.* to surpass something.

excel [ɛk 'sɛl] *iv.* to do very well at something; to be outstanding at something.

excellence [ˈɛk sə ləns] *n.* a superior quality; the best quality possible; an extremely good quality. (No pl.)

excellent [ˈɛk sə lənt] *adj.* superior; extremely good; outstanding; of very high quality. (Adv: *excellently.*)

except [ɛk ˈsɛpt] *tv.* to exclude someone or something; to omit someone or something. (Compare this with ACCEPT.)

excess 1. [ˈɛk sɛs] *n.* the amount that is over a certain limit or boundary; the part of something that is too much. (No pl.) **2.** [ˈɛk sɛs] *adj.* extra; beyond the proper limit; beyond what is needed.

excesses [ɛk ˈsɛs əs] *n.* spending for expensive things; wasting money by spending it on things that cost a lot of money.

excessive [ɛk ˈsɛs ɪv] *adj.* extra; beyond the proper limit; beyond what is needed; too much. (Adv: *excessively.*)

exchange [ɛks ˈtʃendʒ] **1.** *tv.* to trade something for something else; to trade someone for someone else. **2.** *n.* an instance of giving someone something for something else; an instance of trading something for something else. **3.** *n.* a conversation; a short dialogue. **4.** *n.* a place where things, such as stocks, are bought and sold. **5.** *n.* a particular part of the telephone switching system, represented in the United States by the first three digits of a local telephone number.

excite [ɛk ˈsaɪt] *tv.* to interest or stimulate someone or something.

excited [ɛk ˈsaɪt ɪd] *adj.* aroused; stimulated; caused to be very interested. (Adv: *excitedly.*)

excitement [ɛk ˈsaɪt mənt] *n.* the feeling of great interest, eagerness, and stimulation. (A pl form is rare and is not countable.)

exciting [ɛk ˈsaɪ tɪŋ] *adj.* causing excitement; very interesting; stimulating. (Adv: *excitingly.*)

exclaim [ɛk ˈsklem] *tv.* to shout something; to say something with strong feeling. (The object is a clause with THAT ⑦.)

exclamation [ɛk sklə ˈme ʃən] *n.* a loud statement; a statement made with strong feeling or emotion.

excrement [ˈɛk skrə mənt] *n.* feces; solid waste from the bowels. (No pl.)

excuse 1. [ɛk ˈskjus] *n.* a reason that attempts to explain or justify something that is wrong. **2.** [ɛk ˈskjuz] *tv.* to forgive someone for bad manners; to pardon someone. **3.** [ɛk ˈskjuz] *tv.* to give someone permission to leave. **4.** ~ **oneself** to make polite apologies or explanations before leaving a place.

149

excused [ɛk 'skjuzd] *adj.* pardoned; condoned, forgiven.

execute ['ɛks ə kjut] **1.** *tv.* to do something as ordered; to carry out something; to perform an act. **2.** *tv.* to kill someone as a punishment; to punish someone with death. **3.** *tv.* to make a document effective as of a certain date by signing it.

execution [ɛks ə 'kju ʃən] **1.** *n.* the doing of something; the carrying out of an order. (No pl.) **2.** *n.* the killing of someone as a punishment.

executive [ɛg 'zɛk jə tɪv] **1.** *n.* someone who manages an organization in business or government. **2.** *adj.* in the manner of ①; firm and authoritative. **3.** *adj.* of or about the branch of government that manages, but not the branches that make laws and run the courts.

exempt [ɛg 'zɛmpt] **1.** *tv.* to free someone from a duty or obligation. **2.** *adj.* free from a duty or obligation.

exercise ['ɛk sə saɪz] **1.** *n.* active use of the muscles of the body. (No pl form in this sense.) **2.** *n.* a specific act of ①. **3.** *n.* a question or problem designed to train someone in problem solving. **4.** *n.* an activity designed to train someone for a military task. **5.** *tv.* to actively use one or more muscles or areas of the body. **6.** *tv.* to actively use something, such as a power, right, privilege, or option. **7.** *iv.* to be physically active in order to strengthen the heart and muscles or to lose weight.

exhale [ɛks 'hel] **1.** *iv.* to breathe out; to push air out from the lungs. **2.** *tv.* to breathe air or smoke out of the body.

exhaust [ɛg 'zɔst] **1.** *n.* steam, gas, or vapor that is the waste product of burning. (No pl.) **2.** *tv.* to use up all of someone's or something's resources or energy. **3.** *tv.* to cause someone to become very tired.

exhausted [ɛg 'zɔs təd] **1.** *adj.* very tired. **2.** *adj.* [of a supply] used up.

exhibit [ɛg 'zɪb ət] **1.** *tv.* to show signs of something; to indicate something. **2.** *tv.* to display one's works of art in a public place. **3.** *n.* a show of one's artwork, as in an exhibition. **4.** *n.* a piece of evidence used in a court trial.

exhibition [ɛk sə 'bɪʃ ən] *n.* the public display of something, usually works of art.

exile ['ɛg zaɪl] **1.** *n.* forcing one out of one's home country. (No pl form in this sense.) **2.** *n.* someone who has been banished. **3.** *tv.* to banish someone; to force one from one's homeland.

exist [ɛg 'zɪst] **1.** *iv.* to be; to be in reality. **2.** *iv.* to last through time; to continue to be. **3.** *iv.* to manage to live with only the minimum of physical needs met.

existence [ɛg 'zɪs təns] **1.** *n.* being; the condition of actually being or existing. (No pl.) **2.** *n.* living; continuing to be; a way of living. (No pl.)

exit ['ɛg zɪt] **1.** *n.* the way out, especially from a place or room. **2.** *n.* the roadway leading off a highway. **3.** *n.* leaving someplace, especially a stage. **4.** *iv.* to leave [a place, such as a stage or a highway]. **5.** *tv.* to leave a place.

expand [ɛk 'spænd] **1.** *tv.* to enlarge something; to make something wider or longer; to cause something to grow bigger. **2.** *iv.* to enlarge; to make wider or longer; to swell up; to grow bigger. **3.** ~ **on** to explain something by using more details.

expect [ɛk 'spɛkt] *tv.* to anticipate the arrival of something; to anticipate the birth of a baby; to anticipate that something will happen. (The object can be a clause with THAT ⑦.)

expedition [ɛk spɪ 'dɪ ʃən] *n.* a trip; a journey; a specific course of travel to a certain place.

expel [ɛk 'spɛl] **1.** *tv.* to force someone or something out of a place. **2.** *tv.* to order that someone not attend a school, usually because of bad behavior or bad grades; to end someone's membership in an organization.

expend [ɛk 'spɛnd] *tv.* to spend something, such as time or energy; to use something up.

expense [ɛk 'spɛns] *n.* the amount of money that a product or service costs; an item of cost, as in a budget.

expensive [ɛk 'spɛn sɪv] *adj.* costing a lot of money; high-priced; costly. (Adv: *expensively*.)

experience [ɛk 'spɪr i əns] **1.** *n.* knowledge gained from remembering past events and the results of one's actions during those events; skills gained from living one's life. (No pl.) **2.** *n.* something that happens to someone; an event that gives someone ①. **3.** *tv.* to learn about something by being involved in it when it happens; to feel or encounter something.

experiment [ɛk 'spɛr ə mənt] **1.** *n.* a test that is carried out to prove an idea or theory or show that it is wrong. **2.** *iv.* to try something in order to find out about it.

151

expert ['ɛk spɚt] **1.** *n.* someone who is an authority on something; someone who knows a lot about a certain topic. **2.** *adj.* having a lot of knowledge or skill. (Adv: *expertly.*)

expire [ɛk 'spaɪr] **1.** *iv.* to end; to terminate; to be valid no longer. **2.** *iv.* to die. (Euphemistic.)

explain [ɛk 'splen] **1.** *tv.* to make something easier to understand; to talk in detail about something; to make something clear. **2.** *tv.* to give an excuse for something. (The object can be a clause with THAT ⑦.)

explanation [ɛk splə 'ne ʃən] *n.* information that makes something easier to understand; a description. (Pl only for types and instances.)

explode [ɛk 'splod] **1.** *iv.* to blow up, as with a bomb; to burst. **2.** *iv.* to get very angry. (Fig. on ①.) **3.** *tv.* to cause something to EXPLODE as in ①.

explore [ɛk 'splor] **1.** *tv.* to study and examine a place that has not been examined before. **2.** *tv.* to examine or consider a plan or idea carefully. (Fig. on ①.)

explosion [ɛk 'splo ʒən] *n.* a loud, violent burst; an act of exploding; the blowing up of something.

explosive [ɛk 'splo sɪv] **1.** *adj.* likely to explode; capable of exploding. (Adv: *explosively.*) **2.** *adj.* dangerous; having the potential for leading to violence or disorder. (Fig. on ①. Adv: *explosively.*) **3.** *n.* something that is used to blow something up, such as dynamite; a material that will explode.

export 1. ['ɛk sport] *n.* a product that is shipped to another country; a product that is sold to another country. **2.** ['ɛk sport] the *adj.* use of ①. **3.** [ɛk 'sport] *tv.* to ship a product to another country for sale; to sell a product in another country.

expose [ɛk 'spoz] **1.** *tv.* to cause something to be open to public knowledge; to remove something from hiding; to make something known. **2.** *tv.* to unmask someone; to cause someone's faults or wrongdoing to be revealed. **3.** *tv.* to allow photographic film to be touched by light rays.

exposure [ɛk 'spo ʒɚ] **1.** *n.* showing something to the public; showing something that was hidden. (Pl only for types and instances.) **2.** *n.* attention given to someone or something by newspapers, television, magazines, etc. (No pl.) **3.** *n.* a section of film [used in photography] that will produce a single image.

express [ɛk 'sprɛs] **1.** *tv.* [for someone] to put a thought or idea into words; to speak about an idea. **2.** *tv.* [for someone] to convey a feel-

152

ing or emotion through words, signs, gestures, or writing. **3.** *tv.* [for something] to indicate something; to show something. **4.** *adj.* [of transportation] traveling without stopping or with fewer stops. **5.** *adj.* of or about a rapid means of shipment or delivery.

expression [ɛk 'sprɛ ʃən] **1.** *n.* the look on one's face that indicates how one feels. **2.** *n.* the process of expressing oneself in some way. **3.** *n.* a phrase or clause that is used to express an idea; an idiom.

expressway [ɛk 'sprɛs we] *n.* a highway that does not intersect with any roads, but has ramps that allow one to get on and off at junctions.

extend [ɛk 'stɛnd] **1.** *tv.* to stretch something, making it longer. **2.** *tv.* to make something last longer in time. (Fig. on ①.) **3.** *tv.* to present an offer; to utter an offer or a wish. **4.** *iv.* to increase in length. **5.** *iv.* to spread out in all directions. **6.** *iv.* to continue in space or time.

extension [ɛk 'stɛn ʃən] **1.** *n.* something that is added to something to make it longer or larger; an additional part. **2.** *n.* extra time given beyond a deadline. **3.** *n.* an electric cord that acts to extend the distance between an electric receptacle and the device that needs to be plugged in. (Short for *extension cord*.)

extent [ɛk 'stɛnt] *n.* the distance or degree to which something extends or reaches; the degree to which something is covered or accounted for.

exterior [ɛk 'stɪr i ɚ] **1.** *n.* the outside of something. **2.** the *adj.* use of ①.

external [ɛk 'stɚ nəl] **1.** *adj.* outside; outer. (Adv: *externally*.) **2.** *adj.* coming from the outside; being affected by someone or something on the outside. (Adv: *externally*.)

extinct [ɛk 'stɪŋkt] **1.** *adj.* [of a plant or animal species that is] no longer in existence. **2.** *adj.* [of a volcano] no longer capable of erupting.

extra ['ɛk strə] **1.** *adj.* more or greater than is expected; more or greater than usual; additional. **2.** *adv.* more than usual; additionally. **3.** *n.* an actor who is hired to be part of the background or part of a crowd.

extreme [ɛk 'strim] **1.** *adj.* to the greatest degree; to the furthest point possible in any direction; furthest. (Adv: *extremely*.) **2.** *n.* one of two things that are as far apart from each other as possible. **3.** *n.* the greatest degree of a measure of something.

eye ['ɑɪ] **1.** *n.* one of the two organs of sight; an EYEBALL. **2.** *n.* the ring of color on someone's eye; the iris. **3.** *tv.* to glance at or look at some-

153

one or something; to watch someone or something. (The pres. part. is *eying* or *eyeing*.)

eyeball ['aɪ bɔl] *n.* the round part of the eye that sits in the socket. (The same as EYE ①.)

eyebrow ['aɪ braʊ] *n.* the curved ridge of hair on one's forehead, just above the eye.

eyeful ['aɪ fʊl] the full vision of a shocking or surprising sight.

eyeglasses ['aɪ glæs əz] *n.* two lenses held together by a frame and worn in front of the eyes to improve vision. (Treated as pl. Usually shortened to GLASSES.)

eyelash ['aɪ læʃ] *n.* one of the many small, thin hairs that grow on the edge of the eyelid.

eyelid ['aɪ lɪd] *n.* the fold of skin that moves over the eye.

eyesight ['aɪ saɪt] *n.* vision; the ability to see. (No pl form in this sense.)

eyewitness ['aɪ 'wɪt nəs] *n.* someone who sees an event happen; someone who sees an accident or crime take place.

F

F Go to FAHRENHEIT.

fable ['fe bəl] **1.** *n.* a story that teaches a lesson, often using animals as the characters of the story. **2.** *n.* a lie; a story about an event that did not really happen.

fabric ['fæb rɪk] *n.* material or cloth made by weaving threads together. (Pl only for types and instances.)

fabricate ['fæb rɪ ket] **1.** *tv.* to build something. **2.** *tv.* to make up a story or a lie; to invent an excuse. (Fig. on ①.)

face ['fes] **1.** *n.* the front part of the head from the hair to the chin. **2.** *n.* a look; an expression; the way someone's ① looks. **3.** *n.* the front part or surface of something. **4.** *tv.* to look at someone or something or toward a particular direction. **5.** *tv.* to deal with someone or something. **6.** *tv.* to cover the front part of something or the edges of something with a decoration.

facilities *n.* a bathroom; a restroom. (Euphemistic. Treated as pl, but not countable.)

facility [fə 'sɪl ə ti] *n.* something—especially a building or equipment—built, provided, or established for a specific purpose; a building or site used by a company for its business, especially for a factory or offices. (Often pl.)

fact ['fækt] *n.* something that is true; something that really happened.

factor ['fæk tɚ] *n.* one of a number of elements that contribute to a result.

factory ['fæk tə ri] *n.* a building where products are made, usually with machines.

faculty ['fæk əl ti] **1.** *n.* the teachers at a school, college, or university, as a group. **2.** *n.* a skill; an ability, especially a mental ability. **3.** the *adj.* use of ①.

fad ['fæd] *n.* a very popular thing that everyone does or has for a short period of time.

fade ['fed] **1.** *iv.* to lose color; to become pale; to become less bright. **2.** *iv.* to become weak; to lose energy. (Fig. on ①.) **3.** *tv.* to cause something to lose color or become pale as in ①.

Fahrenheit [ˈfɛr ən haɪt] **1.** *n.* a system of measuring temperature that is not metric. (No pl. From Gabriel Fahrenheit, a German physicist who invented the Fahrenheit scale.) **2.** the *adj.* use of ①. (Follows DEGREE(S). Abbreviated *F.*)

fail [ˈfel] **1.** *tv.* not to succeed at something, especially a course or an examination in school. **2.** *tv.* to give a student a grade that means failure. **3.** *tv.* not to help someone; to let someone down. **4.** *iv.* [for part of a person's body] to become weak; [for something] to stop working; [for something] not to succeed. **5.** *iv.* [for a business] not to succeed. **6.** *iv.* not to succeed in a task that one has tried to do; not to pass a school course.

failing [ˈfel ɪŋ] **1.** *n.* a fault; a weakness of character. **2.** *prep.* lacking something; without something.

failure [ˈfel jɚ] **1.** *n.* failing; not succeeding. (Pl only for types and instances.) **2.** *n.* someone whose life has had almost no success.

faint [ˈfent] **1.** *adj.* barely noticeable; dim; not clear. (Adv: *faintly.* Comp: *fainter;* sup: *faintest.*) **2.** *adj.* [of someone] temporarily weak or dizzy; [of someone] about to pass out. (Adv: *faintly.* Comp: *fainter;* sup: *faintest.*) **3.** *iv.* to pass out; to lose consciousness.

fair [ˈfɛr] **1.** *n.* a yearly event held in a town, state, or county. **2.** *adj.* just; honest; giving good judgments; not favoring one thing or person over another. (Adv: *fairly.* Comp: *fairer;* sup: *fairest.*) **3.** *adj.* [of skin or hair] very light in color. (Adv: *fairly.* Comp: *fairer;* sup: *fairest.*) **4.** *adj.* [of someone] having light hair or skin as in ③. (Comp: *fairer;* sup: *fairest.*) **5.** *adj.* considerable; ample. (Adv: *fairly.*) **6.** *adj.* not too bad; pretty good; adequate. (Adv: *fairly.* Comp: *fairer;* sup: *fairest.*)

fairy [ˈfɛr i] *n.* a small mythical being that looks human, does magic, and sometimes has wings.

faith [ˈfeθ] **1.** *n.* a strong belief in something that cannot be proved; a strong belief in someone or in a god. (No pl.) **2.** *n.* a particular religion. **3.** *n.* loyalty; trust. (No pl.)

faithful [ˈfeθ fʊl] *adj.* loyal.

fake [ˈfek] **1.** *tv.* to make a copy of something with the purpose of deceiving someone. **2.** *tv.* to pretend to do something or have something in order to deceive someone. **3.** *n.* something that is made to take the place of an original in order to deceive someone. **4.** *n.* someone who is a fraud. **5.** *adj.* false; not genuine; made in order to deceive someone.

fall ['fɔl] **1.** *iv., irreg.* to drop to a lower level from a higher level. (Pt: FELL; pp: FALLEN.) **2.** *iv., irreg.* to lose power; to be defeated. (Fig. on ①.) **3.** *iv., irreg.* [for vision] to aim downward. **4.** *iv., irreg.* to go from a standing position to a lying position in one quick movement; to collapse. **5.** *iv., irreg.* [for an event] to happen on a particular day of the week or in a particular month of the year. **6.** *n.* the autumn; the season between summer and winter. **7.** *n.* suddenly going from a standing position to a lying position. **8.** *n.* a decrease; a drop; a lowering. **9.** *n.* the collapse of a political unit; a defeat, especially when at war. **10.** ~ **apart** to break into pieces; to disassemble. (Both literal and figurative uses.) **11.** ~ **down** to drop or topple.

fallen ['fɔl ən] pp OF FALL.

fallow ['fæl o] *adj.* [of land] not farmed for a period of time, usually in order to help replenish the soil with nutrients.

falls *n.* a waterfall. (Treated as pl.)

false ['fɔls] **1.** *adj.* not true; wrong; incorrect. (Adv: *falsely.* Comp: *falser;* sup: *falsest.*) **2.** *adj.* not loyal; not faithful. (Adv: *falsely.* Comp: *falser;* sup: *falsest.*) **3.** *adj.* not real; artificial; fake. (Comp: *falser;* sup: *falsest.*)

fame ['fem] *n.* the quality of being very well known. (No pl.)

familiar [fə 'mɪl jɚ] **1.** *adj.* known; well known; common. (Adv: *familiarly.*) **2.** *adj.* friendly; overly friendly. (Adv: *familiarly.*)

family ['fæm (ə) li] **1.** *n.* a group of people related to each other. **2.** *n.* a mother, father, and one child or more; a parent and one child or more. **3.** *n.* a group of things that are related in some way or share common features, such as animals, plants, languages, etc. **4.** the *adj.* use of ①, ②, or ③.

famine ['fæm ən] *n.* a period of time when there is little or no food.

famous ['fe məs] *adj.* very well known.

fan ['fæn] **1.** *n.* someone who admires someone or something very much. (A shortening of FANATIC.) **2.** *n.* a device or machine used to move air in order to cool someone or something. **3.** *tv.* to move air onto something.

fanatic [fə 'næt ɪk] *n.* someone who is too eager about and devoted to someone or something.

fancy ['fæn si] **1.** *adj.* elegant; stylish; nicely decorated. (Adv: *fancily.* Comp: *fancier;* sup: *fanciest.*) **2.** *n.* the imagination; the ability to cre-

157

ate imaginative ideas or images. **3.** *n.* something that is imagined; a notion.

fang ['fæŋ] *n.* a long, sharp tooth.

fantasy ['fæn tə si] *n.* interesting thoughts and visions in the mind, somewhat like a dream. (Pl only for types and instances.)

far ['far] **1.** *adj., irreg.* more distant; not as close as something else. (Comp: FARTHER or FURTHER; sup: FARTHEST or FURTHEST.) **2.** *adv., irreg.* at or to a distant time or place; a long way away in time or space. (Comp: FARTHER or FURTHER; sup: FARTHEST or FURTHEST.) **3.** *adv.* much; many; a lot. (Used before a comp. such as *more, less,* or *longer.*)

fare ['fɛr] **1.** *n.* the amount of money required to ride a bus, train, plane, subway, taxi, etc. **2.** *n.* the food that is served at a meal. (No pl.)

farewell [fɛr 'wɛl] **1.** *n.* an act of leaving and saying good-bye. **2.** the *adj.* use of ①. **3.** *interj.* good-bye.

farm ['farm] **1.** *n.* a parcel of land used to grow crops or to raise animals. **2.** *tv.* to work on the land to make it grow plants, especially food; to plow land. **3.** *iv.* to grow crops and raise animals as a living. **4.** the *adj.* use of ①.

farmer ['far mɚ] *n.* someone who grows crops and raises animals on a farm.

farsighted ['far saɪt ɪd] **1.** *adj.* able to see things that are farther away better than things that are close. (Adv: *farsightedly.*) **2.** *adj.* wisely looking into the future. (Adv: *farsightedly.*)

fart ['fart] **1.** *iv.* to release gas from the bowels through the anus. (Potentially offensive. The topic and the word are not heard in polite company. Use with caution.) **2.** *n.* the sound or odor of the release of gas from the bowels. **3.** *n.* a stupid and annoying person.

farther ['far ðɚ] **1.** *adj.* more distant in space or time. (One of the comp. forms of FAR, along with FURTHER.) **2.** *adv.* more distant in space or time. (One of the comp. forms of FAR, along with FURTHER.)

farthest ['far ðəst] *adj.* the most distant in space or time. (One of the sup. forms of FAR, along with FURTHEST.)

fashion ['fæ ʃən] **1.** *n.* the current, typical styles of dress or behavior within a society. (Pl only for types and instances.) **2.** *n.* the manner or way in which something is done; a method. (No pl.) **3.** *tv.* to form or shape something; to form something by hand.

fast ['fæst] **1.** *adv.* quickly; rapidly. (Comp: *faster*; sup: *fastest*.) **2.** *adv.* tight(ly); without moving; securely. **3.** *adj.* quick; rapid; speedy; not slow. (Comp: *faster*; sup: *fastest*.) **4.** *adj.* [of a clock or watch] showing a time that is later than the real time. (Comp: *faster*; sup: *fastest*.) **5.** *iv.* to go without food. **6.** *n.* a period of time when someone does not eat, for religious, health, or political reasons.

fasten ['fæs ən] **1.** *tv.* to tie, lock, or hook something closed. **2.** *tv.* to attach something to someone or something.

fastener ['fæs ən ɚ] *n.* a device that secures or fastens something shut.

fastidious [fæ 'stɪd i əs] **1.** *adj.* hard to please; choosing carefully. (Adv: *fastidiously*.) **2.** *adj.* preferring cleanliness and orderliness. (Adv: *fastidiously*.)

fat ['fæt] **1.** *n.* animal tissue filled with oil. (Pl only for types and instances.) **2.** *n.* loose flesh filled with ①. (No pl.) **3.** *adj.* overweight; having too much ②. (Adv: *fatly*. Comp: *fatter*; sup: *fattest*.)

fatal ['fet əl] *adj.* causing death; resulting in death. (Adv: *fatally*.)

fate ['fet] **1.** *n.* a force that is said to control what happens. (Pl only for types and instances.) **2.** *n.* the destiny of someone or something; what will happen to someone or something. **3.** *tv.* [for ①] to determine what happens to someone or something. (Usually passive.)

father ['fɑ ðɚ] **1.** *n.* the male parent of a child. (Also a term of address. Capitalized when written as a proper noun.) **2.** *n.* the inventor of something; the founder of something; the leader of something. (Fig. on ①.) **3.** *tv.* [for a male creature] to fertilize an egg, which will lead to the development of a child.

fatigue [fə 'tig] **1.** *n.* a state of being very tired from too much mental or physical work. (No pl.) **2.** *tv.* to tire someone or something; to make someone or something tired.

fatten ['fæt n] **1.** *tv.* to cause someone or something to grow larger. **2.** *tv.* to increase the size or value of an offer. (Fig. on ①.)

fatty ['fæt i] *adj.* full of or containing fat. (Comp: *fattier*; sup: *fattiest*.)

faucet ['fɔs ɪt] *n.* a device that controls the flow of water or some other liquid from a pipe or container; a tap.

fault ['fɔlt] **1.** *n.* a personal shortcoming; a flaw in someone's personality. **2.** *n.* the responsibility for causing something bad to happen. (No pl.) **3.** *n.* a crack in the surface of the earth.

faulty ['fɔl ti] *adj.* flawed; incorrect; having an error or mistake. (Adv: *faultily*. Comp: *faultier*; sup: *faultiest*.)

159

favor ['fe vɚ] 1. *n.* a state of being valuable or worthy in someone else's view. (No pl.) 2. *n.* an act of kindness; something nice that is done for someone else. 3. *tv.* to prefer someone or something; to like someone or something at the expense of someone or something else. 4. *tv.* to support someone or something; to support an issue, a plan, a theory, an option, etc. 5. *tv.* to expect someone or something to win.

favorable ['fev ɚ rə bəl] 1. *adj.* approving; supporting. (Adv: *favorably.*) 2. *adj.* beneficial; being to one's advantage; advantageous; helpful. (Adv: *favorably.*)

favorite ['fev (ə) rɪt] 1. *adj.* preferred over every other choice; liked better than everything or everyone else. 2. *n.* someone or something that is preferred over every other choice; someone or something that is liked better than everyone or everything else.

fax ['fæks] 1. *n.* a machine that sends an exact copy of a piece of paper to another machine, over telephone lines. 2. *n.* something that has been sent or received by way of ①. 3. the *adj.* use of ① or ②. 4. *tv.* to send a document to someone by using ①.

fear ['fɪr] 1. *n.* the feeling of being afraid; the feeling of being in danger. (Pl only for types and instances.) 2. *n.* a specific source of ① and the feeling caused by that source. 3. *tv.* to be afraid of someone or something. 4. *tv.* to feel that something unpleasant is the case or may happen. (Often used as a polite way of expressing regret that one must say something unpleasant. The object is a clause with THAT ⑦.)

fearless ['fɪr ləs] *adj.* without fear; brave; courageous. (Adv: *fearlessly.*)

feast ['fist] 1. *n.* a large meal, especially one for a special occasion; a banquet. 2. *iv.* to eat a lot of food, often in the company of others, especially as part of a celebration.

feat ['fit] *n.* a remarkable accomplishment; an act or deed that shows skill or talent.

feather ['fɛð ɚ] *n.* one of many hard stems bearing soft fibers that cover the body of a bird.

feature ['fi tʃɚ] 1. *n.* an important aspect of something; a quality of something that stands out. 2. *n.* a part of the face. 3. *n.* a special article in a newspaper; an important news story. 4. *tv.* to present or focus on an important element of something. 5. *tv.* to present someone special as an actor in a movie, play, or television show.

February ['fɛb ru ɛr ɪ] Go to MONTH.

feces ['fi siz] *n.* excrement; animal waste. (From Latin. Treated as pl, but not countable.)

160

fed ['fɛd] pt/pp of FEED.

federal ['fɛd (ə) rəl] **1.** *adj.* of or about the organization of a group of states. (Adv: *federally*.) **2.** *adj.* of or about the United States government. (Adv: *federally*.)

federation [fɛd ə 're ʃən] **1.** *n.* the formation of a governmental body by smaller governments that join together while still governing their own internal affairs. (No pl form in this sense.) **2.** *n.* a government formed by smaller governments that join together while each governs its own internal affairs. **3.** *n.* a league or union of people or nations.

fee ['fi] *n.* money that is paid in exchange for a service or privilege.

feeble ['fi bəl] *adj.* weak; frail; lacking force; lacking strength. (Adv: *feebly*. Comp: *feebler*; sup: *feeblest*.)

feed ['fid] **1.** *tv., irreg.* to nourish someone or something with food; to give food to someone or something. (Pt/pp: FED.) **2.** *tv., irreg.* to supply something without stopping; to provide something without stopping. (Fig. on ①.) **3.** *n.* food that is given to animals, especially on a farm. (Pl only for types and instances.)

feel ['fil] **1.** *tv., irreg.* to touch someone or something. (Pt/pp: FELT.) **2.** *tv., irreg.* to experience or sense being touched by someone or something. **3.** *tv., irreg.* to receive information by touching. **4.** *tv., irreg.* to experience an emotion; to experience something in one's mind. (The object can be a clause with THAT ⑦.) **5.** *tv., irreg.* to consider something; to have an opinion about something. (The object is a clause with THAT ⑦.) **6.** *iv., irreg.* to experience [an emotion]; to experience [something in one's mind]. **7.** *n.* a kind of shape or texture that is sensed by touching. (No pl.)

feeler ['fi lɚ] **1.** *n.* an antenna; a part of the body of an insect or shellfish that is used for touching or sensing. **2.** *n.* an inquiry or suggestion that is made to determine what other people are thinking or feeling.

feeling ['fi lɪŋ] **1.** *n.* sensation produced by touching something or by being touched by something; the ability to feel things. (No pl.) **2.** *n.* a sensation that is a response to touch, pressure, heat, cold, or pain. **3.** *n.* an emotion. **4.** *n.* an idea based on what one feels or suspects.

feelings ['fi lɪŋz] *n.* an emotion; the ability to feel emotions.

feet ['fit] pl of FOOT.

fell ['fɛl] pt of FALL.

fellow ['fɛl o] 1. *n.* a man; a male. 2. *n.* a position of rank or status at a school or university, usually without teaching responsibilities. (For either sex.) 3. *adj.* similar; alike; sharing a common interest or occupation. (For either sex. Prenominal only.)

fellowship ['fɛl o ʃɪp] 1. *n.* a group; a social organization. (Not restricted to males.) 2. *n.* friendly discussion and activity with other people; friendship. (No pl.) 3. *n.* money that is given to an advanced student to pay for schooling.

felt ['fɛlt] 1. pt/pp of FEEL. 2. *n.* a thick cloth made of pressed fibers. (Pl only for types and instances.) 3. *adj.* made of ②.

female ['fi mel] 1. *adj.* of or about women or girls; of or about animals of the sex that can bear young or lay eggs. 2. *n.* a woman; a girl; an animal of the sex that bears young or lays eggs.

feminine ['fɛm ə nɪn] 1. *adj.* of or about the characteristics of women; of or about the qualities of women. (Adv: *femininely.*) 2. *adj.* of or about the one of the three grammatical genders that is neither masculine nor neuter.

fence ['fɛns] *n.* a barrier that encloses a space to keep people or things from coming into or leaving that space.

fender ['fɛn dɚ] *n.* a part of a vehicle's body that forms a protective shield over a wheel.

ferryboat ['fɛr i ˌbot] *n.* a boat that takes cars and people across a river or a lake.

fertile ['fɚt əl] 1. *adj.* able to reproduce or develop new life easily. (Adv: *fertilely.*) 2. *adj.* [of soil] rich in (plant) food that helps reproduction and growth. (Adv: *fertilely.*) 3. *adj.* creative; able to produce good ideas. (Fig. on ①. Adv: *fertilely.*)

fertilize ['fɚ tə ˌlaɪz] 1. *tv.* to provide nutrients to the land so that crops will grow well. 2. *tv.* [for a male reproductive cell] to join with a female reproductive cell; [for a male's sperm] to join with a female's ovum (egg). 3. *tv.* to cause a male reproductive cell to join with a female reproductive cell, as in ②.

fervor ['fɚ vɚ] *n.* passion; excitement; strong emotion. (No pl.)

festival ['fɛs tə vəl] *n.* a public celebration, especially in honor of a certain occasion.

festive ['fɛs tɪv] *adj.* merry; exciting; like a celebration; joyous. (Adv: *festively.*)

fetch ['fɛtʃ] **1.** *tv.* to bring something to someone; to go somewhere and get something for someone. **2.** *tv.* [for something] to bring in a certain amount of money when sold.

fever ['fi vɚ] *n.* a state of sickness where the temperature of the body rises above normal.

feverish ['fi vɚ ɪʃ] **1.** *adj.* having a higher body temperature than normal. (Adv: *feverishly.*) **2.** *adj.* excited and fast; restless. (Fig. on ①. Adv: *feverishly.*)

few ['fju] **1.** *adj.* not many; a smaller number than expected. (Used with items that can be counted. Compare this with LITTLE. Used without *a.* Comp: *fewer*; sup: *fewest.*) **2. a ~** *n.* a small number [of those items previously mentioned]. (Treated as pl. Use *a little* for things that cannot be counted.)

fiber ['faɪ bɚ] **1.** *n.* one of many threads, strands, or rigid cellular structures that form many plant, animal, and artificial substances. **2.** *n.* edible plant FIBERS as in ①. (Pl only for types and instances.)

fiction ['fɪk ʃən] **1.** *n.* literature that is written about imaginary events and not about real events. (No pl.) **2.** *n.* information that is not true but instead has been created by someone. (Pl only for types and instances.)

fiddle ['fɪd l] **1.** *n.* a violin. (Informal.) **2.** *iv.* to play ①.

field ['fild] **1.** *n.* a large area of land used for a specific purpose, such as growing crops, raising cattle, playing certain sports, fighting a battle, landing airplanes, etc. **2.** *n.* an area of knowledge; an area of study.

fierce ['fɪrs] *adj.* violent; cruel; untamed; wild. (Adv: *fiercely.* Comp: *fiercer*; sup: *fiercest.*)

fiery ['faɪɚ i] **1.** *adj.* burning; flaming. (Comp: *fierier*; sup: *fieriest.*) **2.** *adj.* very emotional; passionate; full of passion. (Fig. on ①. Comp: *fierier*; sup: *fieriest.*)

fifteen ['fɪf 'tin] 15. Go to FOUR.

fifteenth ['fɪf 'tinθ] 15th. Go to FOURTH.

fifth ['fɪfθ] **1.** 5th. Go to FOURTH. **2.** *n.* 20 percent of a full gallon of liquor.

fiftieth ['fɪf ti əθ] 50th. Go to FOURTH.

fifty ['fɪf ti] 50. Go to FORTY.

fig ['fɪg] *n.* a soft, sweet fruit with many seeds.

163

fight ['faɪt] **1.** *n.* a struggle; a battle. **2.** *tv., irreg.* to battle someone; to make combat against someone. (Pt/pp: FOUGHT.) **3.** *iv., irreg.* to do battle; to argue.

figure ['fɪɡ jɚ] **1.** *n.* a human body; the form of a human body. **2.** *n.* a person, usually well known or important. **3.** *n.* a digit; one of the numbers from 0 to 9. **4.** *n.* a total; a sum; an amount. **5.** *n.* a chart or diagram in a book that explains information in the text. **6.** *tv.* to consider something; to believe something. (The object is a clause with THAT ⑦.)

file ['faɪl] **1.** *n.* a metal tool that is scraped over rough surfaces to make them smooth and even. **2.** *n.* a folder or other container used for holding and storing papers in an organized way. **3.** *n.* the papers within ②; the information contained in ②. **4.** *n.* a computer file; a unit of data or information in digital form, such as is stored on a floppy disk or disk drive. **5.** *tv.* to smooth something with ①. **6.** *tv.* to organize papers by putting them into the appropriate ②; to put a piece of paper in the appropriate ②. **7.** *iv.* to move in a line, going into or out of a place.

fill ['fɪl] **1.** *tv.* to provide what is requested; to supply a product when it is requested; to meet someone's demand for something. **2.** *iv.* to become full.

filling ['fɪl ɪŋ] **1.** a repaired cavity in a tooth. **2.** a substance put inside a pie or pastry.

film ['fɪlm] **1.** *n.* the material that photographs or movies are recorded on. (Pl only for types and instances.) **2.** *n.* a movie; a motion picture. **3.** *n.* a thin layer of something; a coating. **4.** *tv.* to record someone or something on ① in a particular place or manner.

filter ['fɪl tɚ] **1.** *n.* a device that strains fluids or gases to separate solids from them; a device that cleans a fluid or gas that passes through it. **2.** *tv.* to pass a substance through ①.

filth ['fɪlθ] *n.* grime; dirt that is difficult to clean off. (No pl.)

filthy ['fɪl θi] the *adj.* form of FILTH.

fin ['fɪn] **1.** *n.* a flat organ—like a small fan—on a fish that allows it to control its movement in the water. **2.** *n.* one of a pair of rubber or plastic shoes with flat projections, used by divers to move themselves through the water.

final ['faɪ nəl] **1.** *adj.* last; at the end; ultimate. (Adv: *finally.*) **2.** *n.* the last examination in a school course. (Often pl, referring to the last examinations in all of one's courses for the term or semester.)

164

finally ['fɑɪn ə li] *adv.* at last, after much asking, waiting, or delay.

financial [fə 'næn ʃəl] *adj.* of or about business matters dealing with money. (Adv: *financially*.)

find ['fɑɪnd] **1.** *tv., irreg.* to discover or locate someone or something that one was looking for. (Pt/pp: FOUND.) **2.** *tv., irreg.* to recover something; to discover something. **3.** *tv., irreg.* to decide that someone or something has a certain quality; to consider someone or something to be a certain way. (The object can be a clause with THAT ⑦.)

fine ['fɑɪn] **1.** *n.* an amount of money that must be paid as a punishment; a penalty. **2.** *adj.* acceptable or suitable; very good; excellent. (Adv: *finely*. Comp: *finer*; sup: *finest*.) **3.** *adj.* of high quality; very delicate and of high quality. (Adv: *finely*. Comp: *finer*; sup: *finest*.) **4.** *adj.* not coarse; consisting of small particles; in the form of a powder. (Adv: *finely*. Comp: *finer*; sup: *finest*.) **5.** *adj.* very thin; very small. (Adv: *finely*. Comp: *finer*; sup: *finest*.) **6.** *adv.* well; nicely; excellently. **7.** *tv.* to charge someone or something an amount of money as a punishment or penalty.

finger ['fɪŋ gɚ] *n.* one of the five extensions or digits at the end of the hand.

fingernail ['fɪŋ gɚ nel] *n.* the hard, flat covering at the end of each finger.

fingerprint ['fɪŋ gɚ prɪnt] *n.* the light, oily mark left by the ridges on the skin of one's fingers.

fingertip ['fɪŋ gɚ tɪp] *n.* the end of a finger.

finish ['fɪn ɪʃ] **1.** *tv.* to bring something to an end; to complete or conclude something. **2.** *tv.* to use all of something; to eat or drink all of something. **3.** *tv.* to cover something made out of wood with a protective coat of varnish, paint, or something similar. **4.** *iv.* [for someone] to reach the end of doing something. **5.** *n.* the end; the conclusion; the final part of something. **6.** *n.* a protective coating of paint, varnish, lacquer, or stain on a wooden surface; a protective coating on any surface.

fire ['fɑɪɚ] **1.** *n.* heat, flames, and light made by burning something. (Pl only for types and instances.) **2.** *n.* an area of burning with ①. **3.** *n.* passion; strong emotion; fervor. (Fig. on ①. No pl.) **4.** *n.* the shooting of weapons; the noise made by shooting guns. (No pl.) **5.** *tv.* to get rid of an employee; to end someone's employment.

firecracker ['fɑɪɚ kræk ɚ] *n.* a small device that explodes when set afire, making a lot of noise.

165

firefighter ['faɪə faɪt ə˞] n. someone who is trained to put out fires and rescue people.

fireplace ['faɪə ples] n. a place in a house or building where a fire can be built to provide heat.

fireproof ['faɪə pruf] 1. adj. not able to catch fire; hard to burn. 2. tv. to make something so it is able to resist to fire.

fireworks ['faɪə wə˞ks] n. explosives that make loud noises and beautiful displays of light and smoke when lit. (Treated as pl. Rarely sg.)

firm ['fə˞m] 1. adj. solid; hard. (Adv: firmly. Comp: firmer; sup: firmest.) 2. adj. not easily moved; steady. (Adv: firmly. Comp: firmer; sup: firmest.) 3. adj. final and not to be changed. (Adv: firmly. Comp: firmer; sup: firmest.) 4. n. a company; a business.

first ['fə˞st] 1. adj. before everything or everyone else; at the beginning. (The ordinal number for ONE. Adv: firstly.) 2. adv. before anything else; before another event. 3. adv. never having happened before. 4. n. someone or something that is the ① thing or person. (No pl.)

firsthand ['fə˞st 'hænd] 1. adj. direct; coming from the source directly; witnessed. 2. adv. directly; from the source.

fish ['fɪʃ] 1. n., irreg. any of various animals without legs that live underwater and typically have fins and scales. (Pl: fish unless referring to a number of species.) 2. n. the meat of ① used as food. (No pl.) 3. iv. to try to catch ①.

fishbowl ['fɪʃ bol] n. a container that fish are kept in; a small aquarium.

fisherman ['fɪʃ ə˞ mən] n., irreg. someone who catches fish for a living; a man who fishes. (Pl: FISHERMEN.)

fishermen ['fɪʃ ə˞ mən] pl of FISHERMAN.

fishhook ['fɪʃ hʊk] n. a sharp hook used to catch fish.

fist ['fɪst] n. the hand with the fingers closed tightly.

fit ['fɪt] 1. iv., irreg. to be the right size for something. (Pt/pp: fit or fitted.) 2. tv., irreg. to suit someone or something; to be matched to someone or something. 3. tv., irreg. [for something] to be the right size for someone or something. 4. tv., irreg. to make something match something else in some way. 5. adj. suitable; having the things that are needed. (Adv: fitly. Comp: fitter; sup: fittest.) 6. adj. healthy; in good condition. (Comp: fitter; sup: fittest.) 7. n. the way that something FITS as in ①.

five ['fɑɪv] **1.** 5. (See FOUR for more information.) **2.** *n.* a BILL ③ or NOTE ③ worth 5 dollars.

fix ['fɪks] **1.** *tv.* to repair something; to make something work again. **2.** *tv.* to make something firm; to place something firmly into something. **3.** *tv.* to prepare food or drink. **4.** *tv.* to choose a date and time; to determine a date, time, or place.

fixings ['fɪks ɪŋz] *n.* all the condiments that accompany a certain kind of food.

flag ['flæg] **1.** *n.* a piece of cloth of a certain color pattern that represents a country, state, city, school, or organization, or is used as a signal. **2.** *iv.* to become tired; to weaken.

flagpole ['flæg pol] *n.* a pole on which a flag is mounted or attached.

flake ['flek] *n.* a loose piece of something; a bit of something; a thin, light piece of something.

flame ['flem] **1.** *n.* a tongue of fire; a segment of yellow, white, blue, or red light that shoots out from a fire. **2.** *n.* an angry e-mail message. **3.** *tv.* to criticize someone sharply in a message on the Internet. (Slang.)

flammable ['flæm ə bəl] *adj.* INFLAMMABLE; likely to catch fire; easily set on fire. (Adv: *flammably.*)

flap ['flæp] **1.** *n.* a cover, placed over an opening, that is hinged or attached at one end. **2.** *iv.* to move back and forth, as with the movement of birds' wings. **3.** *tv.* to move something back and forth, as with the movement of birds' wings.

flare ['flɛr] **1.** *n.* a bright flame. **2.** *n.* something that provides a bright light, used as a signal or as a warning of danger.

flash ['flæʃ] **1.** *n.* a quick, strong burst of light. **2.** *iv.* to give off a burst of light for a brief moment. **3.** *tv.* to make something give off a burst of light for a brief moment.

flashlight ['flæʃ lɑɪt] *n.* a small, portable light that typically uses batteries for power.

flat ['flæt] **1.** *adj.* [of a surface] level, even, and smooth. (Adv: *flatly.* Comp: *flatter;* sup: *flattest.*) **2.** *adj.* having lost air; not filled with air. (Adv: *flatly.* Comp: *flatter;* sup: *flattest.*) **3.** *adj.* stable; not moving higher or lower. (Comp: *flatter;* sup: *flattest.*) **4.** *adj.* dull; not exciting. (Adv: *flatly.* Comp: *flatter;* sup: *flattest.*) **5.** *adj.* [sounding a musical sound] lower in pitch than what something is supposed to be. (Adv: *flatly.* Comp: *flatter;* sup: *flattest.*) **6.** *n.* an apartment. **7.** *n.* a note that is one-half step lower in pitch than a natural note. **8.** *n.* a tire with no air in it.

flatter ['flæt ɚ] **1.** *tv.* to attempt to influence someone with praise, possibly insincere praise. **2.** *tv.* to cause someone to feel pleased or honored. **3.** *tv.* [for an article of clothing] to make a person look good.

flavor ['fle vɚ] **1.** *n.* a specific taste; the way something tastes. **2.** *n.* something that is added to a food to give it a specific taste. **3.** *n.* a special quality or characteristic.

flaw ['flɔ] *n.* a fault; a defect; an indication of damage.

flea ['fli] *n.* a tiny insect that lives on an animal's skin, sucking blood and eating dead skin.

fled ['flɛd] pt/pp of FLEE.

flee ['fli] **1.** *tv., irreg.* to escape from danger. (Pt/pp: FLED.) **2.** *iv., irreg.* to run quickly away from something or toward something.

flesh ['flɛʃ] **1.** *n.* the soft part of the body covered by skin; meat. (No pl.) **2.** *n.* the soft part of a fruit or vegetable that can be eaten. (No pl.)

flew ['flu] pt of FLY.

flexible ['flɛk sə bəl] **1.** *adj.* able to bend easily; not rigid. (Adv: *flexibly.*) **2.** *adj.* able to be changed; able to serve a number of purposes. (Fig. on ①. Adv: *flexibly.*)

flicker ['flɪk ɚ] **1.** *n.* a light or flame that is not steady; a light or flame that wavers. **2.** *n.* a short burst of energy or excitement that dies out quickly. (Fig. on ①.) **3.** *iv.* to burn unsteadily; to burn as a flame.

flight ['flaɪt] **1.** *n.* flying; flying through the air. (Pl only for types and instances.) **2.** *n.* running away from someone or something; an escape from danger. (No pl.) **3.** *n.* a set of stairs.

flimsy ['flɪm zi] *adj.* likely to fall apart; not very durable; poorly made. (Adv: *flimsily.* Comp: *flimsier;* sup: *flimsiest.*)

fling ['flɪŋ] *tv., irreg.* to throw; to toss, especially to get rid of something. (Pt/pp: FLUNG.)

flint ['flɪnt] *n.* a kind of hard stone that makes sparks when struck. (No pl form in this sense.)

flip ['flɪp] **1.** *n.* a throw that tosses something into the air; a tossing action that moves something. **2.** *n.* a kind of jump where one turns one's body in the air. **3.** *tv.* to cause something to turn about or spin through the air.

flirt ['flɚt] *n.* someone who tries to attract someone's attention romantically or sexually.

float ['flot] **1.** *iv.* to remain on top of water or a liquid; to stay above water. **2.** *iv.* to hover; to remain in the air. (Fig. on ①.) **3.** *tv.* to release something so it can move as in ①.

flood ['flʌd] **1.** *n.* a large amount of water lying on land that is normally dry. **2.** *n.* a powerful surge of water moving over the land. **3.** *n.* a large amount of something. (Fig. on ②.) **4.** *tv.* to cover an area with water; to cover something with water. **5.** *iv.* to spill or overflow with great volumes of water; to become covered with a great amount of water.

floor ['flor] **1.** *n.* the surface of a room that is walked on; the inside bottom surface of a room. **2.** *n.* one level of a building; a story.

flop ['flɑp] **1.** *tv.* to cause something flat to fall heavily somewhere. **2.** *iv.* [for someone or something] to fall heavily into or onto something. **3.** *iv.* to fail. (Informal.) **4.** *n.* a failure.

florist ['flor ɪst] *n.* someone who arranges and sells flowers for a living.

flour ['flɑʊ ɚ] *n.* a powder made from grinding wheat, corn, or other grain, used in cooking. (Compare this with FLOWER. Pl only for types and instances.)

flow ['flo] **1.** *n.* the movement of running water; the movement of a fluid. (No pl.) **2.** *n.* the even and ordered movement of things in a series. (No pl. Fig. on ①.) **3.** *iv.* to move like running water; to move smoothly along a route. **4.** *iv.* to move easily and in an orderly fashion.

flower ['flɑʊ ɚ] **1.** *n.* a plant that produces blossoms. **2.** *n.* a blossom; the brightly colored petals of a plant. **3.** *iv.* to bloom; [for a plant] to produce ②.

flown ['flon] pp of FLY.

fluent ['flu ənt] *adj.* able to speak, read, write, or understand a language as well as a native speaker of that language. (Adv: *fluently.*)

fluff ['flʌf] **1.** *n.* soft, light fiber, such as wool, cotton, or hair. (No pl form in this sense.) **2.** *n.* a mass or tuft of ①. **3.** *n.* something that is not important and without much meaning. (Fig. on ①. No pl form in this sense.) **4.** ~ **up** to puff up a pillow; to make something fluffy.

fluffy ['flʌf i] *adj.* soft, light, and airy. (Adv: *fluffily.* Comp: *fluffier;* sup: *fluffiest.*)

fluid ['flu ɪd] **1.** *n.* a liquid or a gas; a substance that can flow. (Technically, a gas is a fluid.) **2.** *adj.* moving freely; flowing freely as with a liquid or a gas. (Adv: *fluidly*.)

flung ['flʌŋ] pt/pp of FLING.

flunk ['flʌŋk] **1.** *tv.* to give a student a failing grade; [for a teacher] to make a judgment that prevents a student from going on to a higher grade. **2.** *tv.* [for a student] to fail to pass a test or to fail to qualify for promotion. **3.** *iv.* to fail to pass [a test]; to fail [to be promoted to the next academic level].

flush ['flʌʃ] **1.** *n.* an act of releasing water to cleanse a toilet bowl. **2.** *tv.* to clean something, especially a toilet bowl, with a stream of water.

flute ['flut] *n.* a musical instrument that is shaped like a long, thin pipe.

flutter ['flʌt ɚ] **1.** *iv.* [for birds, moths, butterflies, etc.] to fly though the air, moving their wings. **2.** ~ **around;** ~ **about** to move back and forth quickly. (Fig. on ①.) **3.** *iv.* to beat irregularly; to pulse irregularly. **4.** *n.* a quick but gentle movement, as with the movement of a bird's wings.

fly ['flaɪ] **1.** *tv., irreg.* to "drive" an airplane; to guide something that moves through the air. (Pt: FLEW; pp: FLOWN.) **2.** *tv., irreg.* to raise or otherwise display a flag. **3.** *iv., irreg.* to move through the air; to move in the air. **4.** *iv., irreg.* to travel by airplane. **5.** *iv., irreg.* [for time] to pass quickly. (Fig. on ③.) **6.** *n.* a small insect; a bug; a mosquito. **7.** *n.* the flap of material that covers a zipper in trousers.

foam ['fom] *n.* a mass of small bubbles; froth. (Pl only for types and instances.)

foci ['fo saɪ] a pl of FOCUS.

focus ['fok əs] **1.** *n.* the position or setting of a lens that provides the clearest image. (No pl.) **2.** *n., irreg.* the center of attention; the center of interest. (Fig. on ①. Pl: *focuses* or FOCI.) **3.** *tv.* to adjust a lens, or the eyes, so that the image that passes through them is sharp and clear.

foe ['fo] *n.* the enemy in general; an enemy.

fog ['fɔg] *n.* water vapor suspended in the air; a heavy mist. (No pl.)

foggy ['fɔg i] *adj.* covered or filled with fog; [of weather] having much fog. (Adv: *foggily*. Comp: *foggier*; sup: *foggiest*.)

foil ['fɔɪl] **1.** *n.* a very thin, light sheet of metal, usually aluminum, used to wrap food or as a decoration. (Pl only for types and instances.) **2.** *tv.* to spoil someone's plans; to prevent something from happening.

fold ['fold] **1.** *tv.* to bend something so that part of it lies on top of the rest of it; to double something over onto itself. **2.** ~ **up** [for something] to close by FOLDING as in ①. **3.** ~ **up** [for a business] to cease operating.

folder ['fol dɚ] *n.* a holder made of heavy paper used for filing, organizing, or storing papers.

foliage ['fo li ɪdʒ] *n.* leaves. (No pl form in this sense.)

folk ['fok] **1.** *n.* a group of people. (No pl. Treated as pl. See also FOLKS.) **2.** *adj.* of or about the common people; traditional.

folklore ['fok lor] *n.* traditions, stories, customs, and beliefs that are passed down from generation to generation within a culture. (No pl.)

folks *n.* people in general, often relatives. (Treated as pl. Informal.)

follow ['fɑl o] **1.** *tv.* to come after someone or something in space or time. **2.** *tv.* to pursue someone or something; to go after someone or something. **3.** *tv.* to obey a set of rules or instructions. **4.** *tv.* to understand a person is who leading one through an explanation; to understand an explanation as someone explains it. **5.** *tv.* to study or pay attention to or have a continuing interest in something, such as a sport. **6.** *iv.* [for something] to happen as a logical or typical result of something.

folly ['fɑl i] **1.** *n.* stupid behavior; foolishness. (No pl form in this sense.) **2.** *n.* a silly thing to do.

fond ['fɑnd] *adj.* loving; tender. (Adv: *fondly.* Comp: *fonder;* sup: *fondest.*)

food ['fud] *n.* something that is eaten by animals and plants. (Pl only for types and instances.)

fool ['ful] **1.** *n.* an idiot; a stupid person; someone who has no common sense. **2.** *tv.* to trick someone; to play a joke on someone. **3.** ~ **around** to waste time doing something unnecessary or doing something amateurishly.

foolish ['ful ɪʃ] *adj.* silly; lacking sense; stupid; ridiculous. (Adv: *foolishly.*)

foolproof ['ful pruf] *adj.* not capable of failing; so simple that a fool could use it without problems.

foot ['fʊt] **1.** *n., irreg.* the end of a leg; the part of a human or animal body that touches the ground and supports the body. (Pl: FEET.) **2.** *n.*

the bottom or lower end of a bed, mountain, cliff, ladder, hill, page, etc. (No pl.) **3.** *n., irreg.* a unit of measurement equal to 12 inches or just over 30 centimeters.

football ['fʊt bɔl] **1.** *n.* a sport played between two teams of eleven players each, on a field having a goal on each end, using ②. (No pl. Compare this with SOCCER.) **2.** *n.* the leather, oval ball used in ①. **3.** the *adj.* use of ① or ②.

foothold ['fʊt hold] *n.* a space for one's foot that helps one climb up or down something. (Pl: *footholds.*)

footnote ['fʊt not] **1.** *n.* a note at the bottom of a page that clarifies or provides a source for something that appears higher on the page. **2.** *tv.* to provide ① for a piece of information.

footpath ['fʊt pæθ] *n., irreg.* a path that is made for walking. (Pl: ['fʊt pæðz].)

footprint ['fʊt prɪnt] **1.** *n.* the mark made by pressing a foot in soft earth or snow. **2.** *n.* the mark made by tracking dirt from a muddy area onto a clean floor.

footstep ['fʊt stɛp] **1.** *n.* a step made while walking. **2.** *n.* the sound made by a person's step.

for [for] **1.** *prep.* meant to be used by someone or something; meant to belong to someone; meant to be given to someone. (Indicates who or what will benefit.) **2.** *prep.* meant to be used in doing something; with a function or purpose connected with something. **3.** *prep.* instead of someone or something; in place of someone or something. **4.** *prep.* in favor of someone or something; in support of someone or something. **5.** *prep.* in search of someone or something. (Indicates the target of the search.) **6.** *prep.* in a certain amount; by the exchange of a certain amount. **7.** *prep.* during something; throughout a period of time. **8.** *conj.* because; since; as. (Formal.)

forbade AND **forbad** [for 'bed, for 'bæd] pt of FORBID.

forbid [for 'bɪd] **1.** *tv., irreg.* to prohibit something. (Pt: FORBADE or FORBADE; pp: FORBIDDEN.) **2.** *tv., irreg.* to state that someone must not do something; to prohibit someone from doing something.

forbidden [for 'bɪd n] **1.** pp of FORBID. **2.** *adj.* prohibited; banned; not allowed.

force ['fors] **1.** *n.* power; physical strength. (Pl only for types and instances.) **2.** *n.* military strength. (No pl.) **3.** *n.* an influence; someone or something that is an influence. **4.** *n.* a group of soldiers, police officers, etc. **5.** *tv.* to push or move something using ①. **6.** *tv.* to make someone do something, especially by the use of ①.

forearm 1. ['for arm] *n.* the lower part of the arm, between the elbow and the wrist. **2.** ~ **against** [for 'arm...] to prepare oneself for something before it happens. (Takes a reflexive object.)

forefront ['for frənt] in the place of greatest activity and visibility.

forehead ['for hɛd] *n.* the part of the face between the eyebrows and the hair.

foreign ['for ɪn] *adj.* not native to one's country; of or about a country other than one's own. (Adv: *foreignly.*)

foreigner ['for ən ɚ] *n.* someone who comes from another country; someone who was born in another country.

foremost ['for most] **1.** *adj.* first; most important. **2.** *adv.* first; most importantly.

foresaw [for 'sɔ] pt of FORESEE.

foresee [for 'si] *tv., irreg.* to be aware of something before it happens; to imagine or predict that something will happen. (Pt: FORESAW; pp: FORESEEN. The object can be a clause with THAT ⑦.)

foreseen [for 'sin] pp of FORESEE.

forest ['for əst] *n.* a large area of land covered with trees.

forever [for 'ɛv ɚ] *adv.* always; with no beginning and no end; throughout all time.

foreword ['for wɚd] *n.* the introduction to a book or speech; a preface. (Compare with FORWARD.)

forfeit ['for fɪt] *tv.* to give up something; to lose something as a punishment.

forgave [for 'gev] pt of FORGIVE.

forget [for 'gɛt] **1.** *tv., irreg.* to lose a piece of information from one's memory. (Pt: FORGOT; pp: FORGOT or FORGOTTEN. The object can be a clause with THAT ⑦.) **2.** *tv., irreg.* to leave someone or something behind; not to take someone or something with oneself.

forgive [for 'gɪv] **1.** *tv., irreg.* to pardon someone for an error or wrongdoing. (Pt: FORGAVE; pp: FORGIVEN.) **2.** *tv., irreg.* to cancel payment of a debt; to relieve someone of a debt before it is paid back.

forgiven [for 'gɪv ən] pp of FORGIVE.

forgot [for 'gɑt] pt of FORGET; a pp of FORGET.

forgotten [for 'gɑt n] a pp of FORGET.

fork ['fork] **1.** *n.* an eating tool with a handle and two, three, or four spikes, used to gather and hold food when eating. **2.** *n.* the place where something splits into two branches. **3.** *n.* one of the two branches that something splits into. **4.** *iv.* to split into two branches.

form ['form] **1.** *n.* a shape; the shape of someone or something; the way someone or something is shaped. **2.** *n.* a kind; a sort; a type. **3.** *n.* a document that has blank spaces on it that need to be filled with information. **4.** *n.* a word or part of a word. **5.** *iv.* to come into being; to be created. **6.** *tv.* to develop something; to develop into something; to cause something to come into being. **7.** *tv.* to make up something; to be a part of something.

formal ['form əl] **1.** *adj.* according to custom; according to rules. (Adv: *formally.*) **2.** *adj.* [of behavior, language use, clothes, etc.] serious and proper; [of a person or situation] having serious and proper behavior, dress, etc. (Adv: *formally.* See also INFORMAL.) **3.** *adj.* [of clothing] of the highest level or style prescribed by the rules of manners. (Adv: *formally.*) **4.** *adj.* [of an event] where fancy clothing as in ③ is expected or required. (Adv: *formally.*) **5.** *n.* a woman's (usually long) gown suitable for an event that is ④.

format ['for mæt] **1.** *n.* the way events are ordered or arranged; the way things are placed on a page. **2.** *tv.* to arrange something to look a certain way, as with the order and arrangement in the pages of a book or other document. (Pt/pp: *formatted.* Pres. part.: *formatting.*) **3.** *tv.* to make a computer disk ready to accept information. (Pt/pp: *formatted.* Pres. part.: *formatting.*)

former ['for mɚ] **1.** *adj.* past; previous. (Prenominal only. Adv: *formerly.*) **2. the ~** *n.* the first of two things mentioned. (No pl. Treated as sg or pl, but not countable.)

formula ['form jə lə] **1.** *n., irreg.* a series of symbols that show the chemical ingredients of a substance. (Pl: *formulas* or FORMULAE.) **2.** *n., irreg.* a mathematical rule that is expressed with numbers or symbols. (Pl: *formulas* or FORMULAE.) **3.** *n.* a pattern or a standard set of parts or actions. (Fig. on ②.) **4.** *n.* animal milk or another milk substitute for feeding babies. (No pl.)

formulae ['form jə laɪ] a pl of FORMULA.

forsake [for 'sek] *tv., irreg.* to abandon someone or something; to give someone or something up. (Pt: FORSOOK; pp: FORSAKEN.)

forsaken [for 'sek ən] pp of FORSAKE.

174

forsook [for 'sʊk] pt of FORSAKE.

fort ['fɔrt] **1.** *n.* a structure or building used for defense that can withstand enemy attack; a number of strong buildings behind a barrier. **2.** *n.* a permanent military base.

forth ['fɔrθ] *adv.* forward; onward; outward.

forties *n.* the decade beginning in 1940; the 1940s. (Similar definitions for *twenties, thirties, fifties, sixties, seventies, eighties, nineties*.)

fortieth ['fɔr ti əθ] 40th. Go to FOURTH.

fortress ['fɔr trɪs] *n.* a very strong building built to resist attacks. (See also FORT.)

fortunate ['fɔr tʃə nɪt] **1.** *adj.* lucky; bringing good results; representing good fortune. (Adv: *fortunately.*) **2.** *adj.* having had good luck. (Adv: *fortunately.*)

fortune ['fɔr tʃən] **1.** *n.* good luck; success. (No pl.) **2.** *n.* everything that will happen to someone in the future. **3.** *n.* a lot of money and property that someone owns.

forty ['fɔr ti] **1.** *n.* the cardinal number 40; the number between 39 and 41. (No pl. Similar definitions for TWENTY, THIRTY, FIFTY, SIXTY, SEVENTY, EIGHTY, NINETY.) **2.** *adj.* 40; consisting of 40 things; having 40 things. (Similar definitions for TWENTY, THIRTY, FIFTY, SIXTY, SEVENTY, EIGHTY, NINETY.) **3.** *pron.* 40 people or things already mentioned or able to be determined by context. (Similar definitions for TWENTY, THIRTY, FIFTY, SIXTY, SEVENTY, EIGHTY, NINETY.)

forum ['fɔr əm] *n.* a meeting where someone can discuss something; a place where someone can talk about something, especially items of public interest.

forward ['fɔr wərd] **1.** *adv.* ahead; toward the front; into the future. (Also **forwards.**) **2.** *adj.* [moving] toward the front; [looking] into the future. **3.** *tv.* to have mail sent onward to a new address when one moves.

fought ['fɔt] pt/pp of FIGHT.

foul ['faʊl] **1.** *adj.* dirty; nasty and rotten. (Adv: *foully.* Comp: *fouler;* sup: *foulest.*) **2.** *adj.* nasty; rude and unpleasant. (Adv: *foully.* Comp: *fouler;* sup: *foulest.*) **3.** *adj.* evil; really bad. (Fig. on ①. Adv: *foully.* Comp: *fouler;* sup: *foulest.*) **4.** *adj.* [of a ball] going outside the proper playing area. (Sports.) **5.** *adj.* [of weather] bad. (Adv: *foully.* Comp: *fouler;* sup: *foulest.*) **6.** *tv.* to make something dirty. **7.** *n.* an action in a game that is against the rules. **8.** *n.* [in baseball] a ball that is hit

175

outside the proper playing area. **9.** ~ **up** to make an error. (Informal.)

found ['faʊnd] **1.** pt/pp of FIND. **2.** tv. to establish an organization; to provide money or support to help start an organization. (Pt/pp: *founded*.)

foundation [faʊn 'de ʃən] **1.** *n.* the base of a building. (Rarely pl.) **2.** *n.* the base of a custom or tradition; a basis. (Fig. on ①.) **3.** *n.* an institution that gives out money or grants to special causes.

fountain ['faʊnt n] **1.** *n.* a stream of water that sprays up into the air. **2.** *n.* a structure—designed and built by humans—that sprays a stream of water into the air.

four ['for] **1.** *n.* the cardinal number 4; the number between 3 and 5. (No pl. The ordinal form is FOURTH. Similar definitions for ONE, TWO, THREE, FIVE, SIX, SEVEN, EIGHT, NINE, TEN, ELEVEN, TWELVE, THIRTEEN, FOURTEEN, FIFTEEN, SIXTEEN, SEVENTEEN, EIGHTEEN, NINETEEN.) **2.** *adj.* 4; consisting of 4 things; having 4 things. (The ordinal form is FOURTH. This covers other terms as in ①.) **3.** *pron.* 4 people or things already mentioned or able to be determined by context. (The ordinal form is FOURTH. This covers other terms as in ①.)

fourteen ['for 'tin] 14. Go to FOUR.

fourteenth ['for 'tinθ] **1.** *n.* one of 14 equal parts. **2.** *adj.* of the 14th item in a series of things; of the item between the 13th and 15th in a series; between the 13th and 15th. **3.** *pron.* the 14th item in a series of people or things already mentioned or able to be determined by context.

fourth ['forθ] **1.** *n.* 4th; one of 4 equal parts; a quarter; a half of a half. (Similar definitions for THIRD, FIFTH, SIXTH, SEVENTH, EIGHTH, NINTH, TENTH, ELEVENTH, TWELFTH, THIRTEENTH, FOURTEENTH, FIFTEENTH, SIXTEENTH, SEVENTEENTH, EIGHTEENTH, NINETEENTH, TWENTIETH, THIRTIETH, FORTIETH, FIFTIETH, SIXTIETH, SEVENTIETH, EIGHTIETH, NINETIETH, [ONE] HUNDREDTH, [ONE] THOUSANDTH, [ONE] MILLIONTH, [ONE] BILLIONTH, and [ONE] TRILLIONTH. See also FIRST, SECOND.) **2.** *n.* the 4th item in a series of people or things already mentioned or able to be determined by context. (This covers other terms as in ①. See also FIRST, SECOND.) **3.** *adj.* of the 4th item in a series of things; of the item between the 3rd and 5th in a series. (This covers other terms as in ①. See also FIRST, SECOND.) **4.** *adv.* in the 4th position or rank. (This covers other terms as in ①. See also FIRST, SECOND.)

176

fowl ['faʊl] **1.** *n., irreg.* one of a number of various kinds of birds of limited flight, kept for their eggs or meat, such as the chicken, duck, turkey, etc. (Pl: *fowl* or *fowls*.) **2.** *n.* the meat of ①. (No pl.)

fox ['fɑks] **1.** *n.* a wild animal related to the dog, having a bushy tail. **2.** *n.* the fur or pelt of ①. (No pl.) **3.** *adj.* made of ②.

fraction ['fræk ʃən] **1.** *n.* a part of a whole number. **2.** *n.* a small piece or portion of something. (No pl.)

fracture ['fræk tʃɚ] **1.** *n.* a break or crack, especially a break in a bone. **2.** *tv.* to break something by creating a crack in it. **3.** *iv.* to break; to crack.

fragile ['frædʒ əl] *adj.* easily broken; delicate. (Adv: *fragilely*.)

fragment ['fræg mənt] **1.** *n.* a small piece of something. **2.** *iv.* to break into pieces or sections. **3.** *tv.* to break something into pieces or sections.

fragrance ['fre grəns] *n.* a smell or scent that is pleasant.

fragrant ['fre grənt] *adj.* smelling good; having a nice smell. (Adv: *fragrantly*.)

frail ['frel] *adj.* thin and weak; not strong; easily hurt. (Adv: *frailly*.)

frame ['frem] **1.** *n.* a structure that provides support for something. **2.** *n.* a firm border that something, such as a door, a window, or a picture, is set into. **3.** *n.* the shape or form of a human body; the structure of the body. **4.** *tv.* to place something in ②; to build ② for something. **5.** *tv.* to cause someone to appear guilty of a crime by manipulating evidence or lying.

frank ['fræŋk] *adj.* straightforward; truthful; honest; [of someone] speaking the truth even if it "hurts." (Adv: *frankly*. Comp: *franker*; sup: *frankest*.)

frankfurter ['fræŋk fɚ tɚ] *n.* a meat-filled sausage named for Frankfurt, Germany; a hot dog.

frantic ['fræn tɪk] *adj.* very excited; wild with emotion. (Adv: *frantically* [...ɪk li].)

fraud ['frɔd] **1.** *n.* cheating; something done to deceive someone. (No pl.) **2.** *n.* a false or deceiving thing or act. **3.** *n.* someone who pretends to be someone or something else.

fray ['fre] **1.** *tv.* to cause a rope or string to unravel; to separate the threads that make up string or rope. **2.** *iv.* to unravel; to become worn at the edges. **3.** *n.* an argument; a brawl.

177

freak ['frik] **1.** *n.* someone or something that is not normally developed. (Not polite for humans.) **2.** *adj.* very unusual. (Prenominal only.)

freckle ['frɛk əl] **1.** *n.* one of many small dark dots on the skin. **2.** *iv.* to become covered with ①, usually because of exposure to the sun.

free ['fri] **1.** *adj.* independent; not someone's slave; not ruled by a bad ruler. (Adv: *freely.* Comp: *freer;* sup: *freest.*) **2.** *adj.* costing no money; without cost. **3.** *adj.* not limited; not restricted; not bound by rules. (Adv: *freely.* Comp: *freer;* sup: *freest.*) **4.** *adj.* not busy; available. (Comp: *freer;* sup: *freest.*) **5.** *adj.* generous; lavish; giving. (Adv: *freely.* Comp: *freer;* sup: *freest.*) **6.** *adj.* having an open path; having nothing in one's way. **7.** *adv.* without cost; without having to pay money. **8.** *tv.* to release someone or something.

freedom ['fri dəm] **1.** *n.* liberty; a state where one is free from constraint. (No pl.) **2.** *n.* a right.

freeze ['friz] **1.** *iv., irreg.* to become solid as the temperature gets colder. (Pt: FROZE; pp: FROZEN.) **2.** *iv., irreg.* [for someone or some creature] to become very cold in cold weather. **3.** *iv., irreg.* to become completely still; to stop all movement. (Fig. on ①.) **4.** *tv., irreg.* to turn something into ice; to cause something to harden as the temperature gets colder. **5.** *tv., irreg.* to place food in a freezer so that it stays fresh; to preserve something at an extremely low temperature. **6.** *tv., irreg.* to cause someone or something to become completely still. **7.** *tv., irreg.* to keep the price of something at a certain level; not to allow an amount to change. **8.** *n.* a time when the temperature is 32 degrees Fahrenheit, 0 degrees centigrade, or below. **9.** ~ **over** [for a body of water] to get cold and form a layer of ice on top. **10.** ~ **up** [for something] to FREEZE as in ③ and stop functioning.

freezer ['friz ɚ] *n.* an appliance that remains at a temperature below 32 degrees Fahrenheit in order to store and preserve food and other things.

freight ['fret] **1.** *n.* cargo; products that are carried by truck, plane, train, etc. (No pl.) **2.** *n.* the cost of shipping something as ①. **3.** the *adj.* use of ① or ②.

French fry ['frɛntʃ fraɪ] *n.* a long, narrow piece of potato that has been fried in deep fat. (Usually pl. Can be shortened to FRIES.)

frenzy ['frɛn zi] *n.* a wild fury; an excited state.

178

frequency ['fri kwən si] **1.** *n.* the rate of [something] happening; how often an event occurs. (No pl.) **2.** *n.* the number of times that something occurs within a given period of time.

frequent ['fri kwənt] **1.** *adj.* happening often; occurring often; common. (Adv: *frequently*.) **2.** *tv.* to go to a certain place often.

fresh ['frɛʃ] **1.** *adj.* new; newly or recently made, done, obtained, etc., especially if not yet used or changed. (Adv: *freshly*. Comp: *fresher*; sup: *freshest*.) **2.** *adj.* not stale; not spoiled; [of foods] not canned, frozen, dried, or preserved in another way; [of fruits or vegetables] recently picked or harvested. (Adv: *freshly*. Comp: *fresher*; sup: *freshest*.)

fret ['frɛt] *iv.* to worry about something; to be upset.

friction ['frɪk ʃən] **1.** *n.* rubbing against something that resists the rubbing. (No pl.) **2.** *n.* the resistance that prevents one object from easily sliding over another object. (No pl.) **3.** *n.* a disagreement because of differences in opinions.

Friday [fraɪ de] Go to DAY.

friend ['frɛnd] **1.** *n.* someone whom someone else knows well and likes. **2.** *n.* someone or something that supports or helps someone or something.

friendly ['frɛnd li] *adj.* like a friend; nice, kind, or pleasant. (Comp: *friendlier*; sup: *friendliest*.)

friendship ['frɛnd ʃɪp] *n.* being friends with someone. (Pl only for types and instances.)

fries ['fraɪz] *n.* FRENCH FRIES. (Treated as pl.)

fright ['fraɪt] *n.* fear; terror; the condition of being scared. (No pl.)

frightened ['fraɪt nd] *adj.* scared; afraid. (Adv: *frightenedly*.)

frightening ['fraɪt n ɪŋ] *adj.* scary; filling one with fear; causing fear. (Adv: *frighteningly*.)

frill ['frɪl] **1.** *n.* a decorative edge on cloth. **2.** *n.* something that is an added bonus but is not necessary. (Usually pl.)

fringe ['frɪndʒ] **1.** *n.* a border for clothing or material, made of a row of threads or strings hanging loose. **2.** *n.* the edge of something; something that is far away from the center. (Fig. on ①. Sometimes pl with the same meaning.) **3.** *tv.* to enclose something and serve as its border.

frisk ['frɪsk] *tv.* to pat and press on the body in a search for weapons, drugs, evidence, or stolen property.

179

frog ['frɔg] *n.* a small creature, living in water and on land, that hops and has special feet for swimming.

frolic ['frɑl ɪk] **1.** *iv., irreg.* to play; to have fun; to run and jump around. (Pt/pp: *frolicked*. Pres. part. is *frolicking*.) **2.** *n.* fun; fun entertainment. (No pl form in this sense.)

from ['frʌm] **1.** *prep.* starting at a particular time or place; originating at a particular time or place. **2.** *prep.* a word indicating separation or difference. **3.** *prep.* out of someone or something. **4.** *prep.* sent by someone or something; given by someone or something. **5.** *prep.* because of something; owing to something.

front ['frʌnt] **1.** *n.* the part of something that faces forward. **2.** *n.* a border between two masses of air of different temperatures or pressures. **3.** *n.* the way one appears to other people; the way one seems to be when around other people; an outward appearance. **4.** *iv.* to face in a certain direction. **5.** *adj.* closest to ①. (Prenominal only.)

frontier [frən 'tɪr] **1.** *n.* a border; a line separating two states or countries. **2.** *n.* the line separating settled areas from wild areas; the edge of an undeveloped area.

frost ['frɔst] **1.** *n.* frozen moisture on the surface of something, especially the ground; small ice crystals on the surface of something. (Pl only for types and instances.) **2.** *iv.* to be covered with small ice crystals; to be covered with frozen moisture. **3.** *tv.* to put frosting on a cake or dessert.

frostbite ['frɔst baɪt] *n.* an injury caused by exposing skin to extremely cold weather without protection. (No pl.)

frosting ['frɔs tɪŋ] *n.* a mixture of sugar and other things that is spread on top of a cake or pastry. (Pl only for types and instances.)

froth ['frɔθ] *n.* foam; a mass of white bubbles that forms on top of liquids or around the mouth. (No pl.)

frown ['fraʊn] **1.** *n.* the opposite of a smile; the look on one's face made by pulling the eyebrows together and squinting the eyes. **2.** *iv.* to pull one's eyebrows together and squint the eyes; to scowl; to look angry.

froze ['froz] pt of FREEZE.

frozen ['froz ən] pp of FREEZE.

fruit ['frut] *n.* the part of a plant that contains seeds and can be eaten as food. (Pl only for types and instances. Number is expressed with *piece(s) of fruit*.)

fruitcake ['frut kek] *n.* a cake that has dried fruit and spices in it.

fruitful ['frut fʊl] *adj.* producing good results; beneficial; useful. (Adv: *fruitfully.*)

frustrated ['frəs tre təd] *adj.* disappointed and dissatisfied.

fry ['fraɪ] *tv.* to cook something in hot fat.

fuck ['fʌk] **1.** *tv.* to copulate [with] someone or some creature. (Taboo. Potentially offensive. Use only with discretion. A highly offensive word to many people. There are many additional meanings and constructions with the word.) **2.** *iv.* to copulate. (Comments as with ①.)

fudge ['fʌdʒ] **1.** *n.* a thick, rich chocolate candy. (No pl.) **2.** *iv.* to attempt to lie to or deceive someone. (Informal.)

fuel ['fjul] **1.** *n.* material that is burned to make heat or energy. **2.** *tv.* to supply something with ①. **3.** *tv.* to provide someone or something with energy or encouragement. (Fig. on ②.)

fugitive ['fjudʒ ɪ tɪv] **1.** *n.* someone who has run away from or is hiding from the law. **2.** *adj.* hiding or escaping from the law; fleeing.

fulfill [fʊl 'fɪl] **1.** *tv.* to carry out an order, plan, or promise. **2.** *tv.* to satisfy a demand or a need.

full ['fʊl] **1.** *adj.* completely filled; having no empty space. (Adv: *fully.* Comp: *fuller;* sup: *fullest.*) **2.** *adj.* entire; complete; whole. (Adv: *fully.*) **3.** *adj.* at the highest or greatest extent or amount possible.

full-time ['fʊl 'taɪm] **1.** *adj.* all the time; 24 hours a day. **2.** *adj.* [of a job that] takes up the working day, usually 8 hours a day, 5 days a week. **3.** *adv.* throughout the normal workweek.

fully ['fʊl i] *adv.* completely; entirely; wholly.

fun ['fʌn] **1.** *n.* enjoyment, especially from play or amusement. (No pl.) **2.** *adj.* entertaining; playful. (Colloquial.)

function ['fʌŋk ʃən] **1.** *n.* the proper use of something; the purpose of something. **2.** *n.* a social gathering; an event where people get together and do things such as talk, drink, or celebrate. **3.** *iv.* to work properly; to operate; to be in proper use.

fund ['fʌnd] **1.** *n.* an amount of money that is reserved for a specific reason. **2.** *n.* an investment that is really a combination of other investments, such as stocks and bonds. (Short for *mutual fund.*) **3.** *tv.* to provide someone or something with money; to provide money for something.

funds *n.* money; an amount or supply of money. (Treated as pl, but not countable.)

181

funeral ['fjun (ə) rəl] **1.** *n.* a ceremony performed when someone is buried. **2.** the *adj.* use of ①.

fungi ['fʌn dʒɑɪ] a pl of FUNGUS.

fungus ['fʌŋ gəs] *n., irreg.* a plant that does not have leaves and is not green, such as the mushroom. (Pl: FUNGI or *funguses*.)

funnel ['fʌn əl] *n.* a cone-shaped device with a wide mouth and a narrow spout on the bottom, used when pouring liquids from one container into another.

funny ['fʌn i] **1.** *adj.* amusing; causing laughter. (Comp: *funnier;* sup: *funniest*.) **2.** *adj.* strange; weird; unusual; odd. (Comp: *funnier;* sup: *funniest*.)

fur ['fɚ] **1.** *n.* the short, soft hair that grows on many mammals. (Pl only for types and instances.) **2.** *n.* a coat or other garment made from animal skin covered with ①. **3.** *adj.* made from animal skin covered with ①.

furious ['fjɚ i əs] *adj.* very angry; violently angry; very upset. (Adv: *furiously*.)

furnace ['fɚ nəs] *n.* an oven that can be heated at very high temperatures to melt metal, heat a building, etc.

furnish ['fɚ nɪʃ] **1.** *tv.* to provide something; to supply something. **2.** *tv.* to supply and arrange furniture in a place.

furniture ['fɚ nɪ tʃɚ] *n.* the objects in a house, apartment, or office that can be moved, such as tables, chairs, desks, etc. (No pl. Number is expressed with *piece(s) of furniture*.)

furry ['fɚ i] *adj.* covered with fur; having fur. (Adv: *furrily.* Comp: *furrier;* sup: *furriest*.)

further ['fɚ ðɚ] **1.** *adj.* more distant in space or time. (One of the comp. forms of FAR, along with FARTHER.) **2.** *adv.* more distant in space or time. (One of the comp. forms of FAR, along with FARTHER.) **3.** *adv.* to a greater degree or extent; to a more advanced level. (One of the comp. forms of FAR, along with FARTHER.) **4.** *tv.* to advance or promote someone or something.

furthermore ['fɚ ðɚ mor] *adv.* also; in addition to what has been said or stated.

furthest ['fɚ ðəst] *adj.* the most distant in space or time. (One of the sup. forms of FAR, along with FARTHEST.)

fury ['fjɚ i] **1.** *n.* violent anger; rage. (No pl.) **2.** *n.* power or force.

182

fuse ['fjuz] **1.** *tv.* to melt something together with something else; to melt two things together. **2.** *iv.* [for two or more things] to melt together. **3.** *n.* a part of an electrical circuit that melts and stops the flow of electricity when there is a dangerous amount of electricity flowing through the circuit.

fuss ['fʌs] **1.** *iv.* to whine and cry. **2.** *n.* argument; complaining. (Informal.)

fussy ['fʌs i] *adj.* hard to please; likely to complain about everything. (Adv: *fussily.* Comp: *fussier;* sup: *fussiest.*)

futile ['fjut əl] *adj.* hopeless; useless; worthless. (Adv: *futilely.*)

future ['fju tʃɚ] **1.** *adj.* coming; yet to come; later. (Prenominal only.) **2.** *n.* the time that is to come; events that will happen. (No pl.) **3.** *n.* the things that are planned for one's life. (Pl only for types and instances.) **4.** *n.* the tense of verbs that describe actions that are to happen or actions that will happen.

fuzz ['fʌz] *n.* short, soft, light hairs. (No pl.)

fuzzy ['fʌz i] *adj.* having fuzz; covered with fuzz. (Adv: *fuzzily.* Comp: *fuzzier;* sup: *fuzziest.*)

G

gadget ['gædʒ ɪt] *n.* any small, practical device, tool, or appliance.

gain ['gen] **1.** *tv.* to get something; to obtain something; to acquire something. **2.** *tv.* [for a clock or watch] to reach a later time than it should have. **3.** *tv.* to earn or save time. **4.** *iv.* to earn, get, or acquire something of value. **5.** *n.* a profit. (Often pl.) **6.** *n.* an increase in something.

galaxy ['gæl ək si] *n.* a large mass or cluster of stars and their solar systems in space.

gale ['gel] **1.** *n.* a very strong wind. **2.** *n.* an outburst, especially of laughter. (Often pl.)

gall ['gɔl] **1.** *n.* bile, a bitter liquid made by the liver. (Especially of animals. No pl form.) **2.** *n.* a sore spot on the hide of an animal, usually caused by rubbing or chafing. **3.** *n.* rudeness; impudence. (No pl form.) **4.** *tv.* to cause a sore to develop by rubbing or chafing. **5.** *tv.* to annoy or bother someone severely; to irritate someone. (Fig. on ④.)

gallant ['gæl ənt] *adj.* honorable and brave; very polite. (Refers especially to men who are very polite toward women. Adv: *gallantly.*)

gallery ['gæl ə ri] **1.** *n.* a balcony, often running along a wall or outside a window. **2.** *n.* a room or building where art is displayed.

gallon ['gæl ən] *n.* a unit of liquid measure, equal to 4 quarts, 8 pints, or almost 3.8 liters.

gallop ['gæl əp] **1.** *n.* a fast way that a horse runs. (In a GALLOP, all four of the horse's feet are off the ground at once during each stride.) **2.** *iv.* to move quickly; [for a horse] to run fast.

gambit ['gæm bɪt] an initial movement or statement made to secure a position that is to one's advantage.

game ['gem] **1.** *n.* a kind of contest, sporting event, or pastime played according to a set of rules. **2.** *n.* an instance of playing ①. **3.** *n.* wild animals that are hunted for sport or food. (No pl. Treated as a sg.)

gamut ['gæm ət] *n.* the entire range of something from one extreme to the other. (No pl form.)

gang ['gæŋ] **1.** *n.* a group of people who work, play, or do things together. **2.** *n.* a group of young criminals.

gangster ['gæŋ stɚ] *n.* a member of a gang of criminals; a thug.

gap ['gæp] **1.** *n.* an opening created by a crack; an opening created where two objects or structures do not meet. **2.** *n.* an interruption in time; a period of time between two events or the parts of an event. **3.** *n.* an easily seen difference between two things or groups of people.

garage [gə 'rɑʒ] *n.* a building, or a part of a building, used to store a car or other motor vehicle.

garbage ['gɑr bɪdʒ] *n.* trash; rubbish; useless things that are thrown away. (No pl.)

garden ['gɑrd n] **1.** *n.* a piece of land where plants, flowers, or vegetables are grown. **2.** *iv.* to raise and take care of plants grown in ①.

gardener ['gɑrd nɚ] *n.* someone who takes care of a garden; someone who plants and nourishes plants in a garden.

garlic ['gɑr lɪk] **1.** *n.* a strong-smelling plant whose bulb is made of small segments, used as a flavoring in cooking. (No pl form in this sense.) **2.** *adj.* made from or with ①.

garment ['gɑr mənt] *n.* an article of clothing; a piece of clothing.

gas ['gæs] **1.** *n.* vapor; a substance that is not in a liquid or solid state at a temperature that is comfortable for people. (Pl only for types and instances.) **2.** *n.* a naturally occurring vapor that will burn and is used for cooking and heating. (No pl.) **3.** *n.* GASOLINE, the liquid that is made from petroleum and is used to operate motors and engines. (Pl only for types and instances.)

gash ['gæʃ] **1.** *n.* a large or deep cut or wound; a slash. **2.** *tv.* to slash or cut something.

gasoline [gæs ə 'lin] *n.* a liquid that is made from oil and is used to operate motors and engines. (Pl only for types and instances.)

gasp ['gæsp] **1.** *n.* a quick, short inward breath; a quick breathing in of air. **2.** *iv.* to breathe in suddenly as in surprise, shock, fear, etc.

gate ['get] **1.** *n.* a barrier that can be opened or closed at an opening in a fence or wall. **2.** *n.* a decorative structure, including ①, serving as a formal entrance to a park, cemetery, street, etc. **3.** *n.* the place where people enter a stadium, arena, etc. **4.** *n.* the entrance to the passage to an airplane in an airport.

185

gather ['gæð ɚ] **1.** *tv.* to bring something together; to collect something; to bring people together. **2.** *tv.* to gain or increase in something, especially speed or intensity. **3.** *iv.* to come together into a big group.

gathering ['gæð ɚ ɪŋ] *n.* a group of people; a group of people who have come together for a specific purpose.

gauge ['geʤ] **1.** *n.* a device or instrument for displaying a measurement. **2.** *n.* a measurement of the scope or range of something. **3.** *n.* the diameter of the barrel of a shotgun or of a wire or the thickness of a sheet of metal. **4.** *n.* the distance between the two rails of a track or between the two wheels on an axle. **5.** *tv.* to estimate a distance.

gauze ['gɔz] *n.* a thin, loosely woven cloth. (Pl only for types and instances.)

gave ['gev] pt of GIVE.

gay ['ge] **1.** *adj.* happy; cheerful; brightly colored. (Adv: *gaily.* Comp: *gayer;* sup: *gayest.*) **2.** *adj.* [of someone, usually a male] attracted to people of the same sex. (Comp: *gayer;* sup: *gayest.*) **3.** *n.* a person who is ②, usually a male.

gaze ['gez] *n.* an intent stare.

gear ['gɪr] **1.** *n.* a wheel, with teeth along its edge, that moves similar wheels of differing diameters. **2.** *n.* equipment; tools; the things required to do a certain activity. (No pl. Treated as sg.)

geese ['gis] pl of GOOSE.

gem ['ʤɛm] **1.** *n.* a jewel; a precious stone, especially one used in jewelry. **2.** *n.* someone or something that is very beautiful or wonderful; a perfect example of someone or something. (Fig. on ①.)

gender ['ʤɛn dɚ] **1.** *n.* [in grammar] a subdivision of nouns into masculine, feminine, and, sometimes, neuter categories. **2.** *n.* SEX ③; the condition of being male or female.

gene ['ʤin] *n.* a part of a chromosome within every living cell that determines a characteristic of a plant or animal.

general ['ʤɛn ɚ rəl] **1.** *adj.* widespread; commonly known, understood, believed, or experienced. (Adv: *generally.*) **2.** *adj.* not specific; not specialized. (Adv: *generally.*) **3.** *adj.* usual; regular; appropriate to most situations. (Adv: *generally.*) **4.** *n.* a high-ranking army or air force officer.

generally ['ʤɛn (ə) rə li] **1.** *adv.* usually; commonly. **2.** *adv.* by almost everyone. **3.** *adv.* in a way that does not consider details or specifics.

generate ['dʒɛn ə ret] *tv.* to cause something to come into being.

generation [dʒɛn ə 'rе ʃən] **1.** *n.* producing or creating something. (No pl.) **2.** *n.* one stage in the history of a family. **3.** *n.* all the people of the same culture who were born around the same time, taken as a group.

generous ['dʒɛn ə rəs] **1.** *adj.* not selfish; giving freely. (Adv: *generously.*) **2.** *adj.* [of an amount] more than is needed; [of an amount] large. (Adv: *generously.*)

genius ['dʒin jəs] **1.** *n.* someone who is very smart, especially someone who is much smarter than most of the population. **2.** *n.* someone who has a very impressive talent or skill in a specific area. (Fig. on ①.) **3.** *n.* the talent or skill of ②. (No pl form in this sense.)

gentle ['dʒɛn təl] *adj.* pleasantly mild; not rough; tame; kind. (Adv: *gently* ['dʒɛnt li]. Comp: *gentler;* sup: *gentlest.*)

gentleman ['dʒɛn tl mən] **1.** *n., irreg.* a man who is refined, polite, and well mannered. (The male counterpart of LADY. Pl: GENTLEMEN.) **2.** *n., irreg.* a polite term for MAN ①.

gentlemen ['dʒɛn tl mən] pl of GENTLEMAN.

gently ['dʒɛnt li] **1.** *adv.* in a kind way; in a way that does not cause pain or worry. **2.** *adv.* smoothly; mildly; not roughly.

genuine ['dʒɛn ju ɪn] **1.** *adj.* real; actual; not fake; not artificial. (Adv: *genuinely.*) **2.** *adj.* sincere. (Adv: *genuinely.*)

geography [dʒi 'ɑ grə fi] *n.* the study of the features of the surface of earth, including the land and climate, countries, and the people and cultures of the countries. (No pl.)

geology [dʒi 'ɑl ə dʒi] *n.* the study of the origin and the structure of earth. (No pl.)

geometry [dʒi 'ɑm ɪ tri] **1.** *n.* the part of mathematics that deals with the relationships and properties of points, lines, curves, angles, surfaces, and solids. (No pl.) **2.** the *adj.* use of ①.

germ ['dʒɚm] *n.* a very small organism that causes disease.

gesture ['dʒɛs tʃɚ] **1.** *n.* a movement made with a part of the body to communicate or to emphasize a statement, emotion, or feeling. **2.** *n.* an act of kindness or courtesy; an act that demonstrates friendship. **3.** *iv.* to use hand motions and facial movements when communicating; to make ①.

get ['gɛt] **1.** *tv., irreg.* to obtain something; to receive something. (Pt: GOT; pp: GOT or GOTTEN.) **2.** *tv., irreg.* to bring something; to fetch

187

something. **3.** *tv., irreg.* to understand something; to comprehend something. **4.** *tv., irreg.* to cause something to happen to someone or something; to cause someone or something to be a certain way. **5.** *iv., irreg.* to become. **6.** *iv., irreg.* to arrive somewhere; to reach a certain point or place. (Followed by an adverb such as HOME, THERE, or SOMEWHERE or by a prepositional phrase.)

ghost ['gost] *n.* an apparent image of a dead person, moving among the living.

giant ['dʒaɪ ənt] **1.** *n.* a fictional or mythical humanlike creature who is very, very large. **2.** *n.* an unusually large person or animal. **3.** *n.* a person who is very important or known to be excellent at something. **4.** *adj.* very large; enormous. (Prenominal only.)

gift ['gɪft] **1.** *n.* a present; something that is given to someone without expecting anything in return. **2.** *n.* a special skill or talent.

giraffe [dʒə 'ræf] *n.* an African animal that has long legs and a very long neck.

girder ['gɚd ɚ] *n.* a large metal support beam used in building bridges and buildings.

girl ['gɚl] **1.** *n.* a female child. **2.** *n.* a woman. (Informal. Considered derogatory by some.) **3.** *n.* a man's girlfriend. (Informal.)

girlfriend ['gɚl frɛnd] **1.** *n.* a woman with whom someone is romantically involved. **2.** *n.* a female friend.

give ['gɪv] **1.** *tv., irreg.* to cause someone or something to have or receive something; to cause something to become owned by someone. (Pt: GAVE; pp: GIVEN.) **2.** *tv., irreg.* to supply something; to provide something. **3.** *tv., irreg.* to make some sort of a sound with the mouth. **4.** *iv., irreg.* to be flexible; to be elastic; not to break when pushed or pulled. **5.** ~ **up** to quit. **6.** ~ **in** to yield; to agree finally. **7.** ~ **out** to stop functioning; to wear out.

given ['gɪv ən] pp of GIVE.

glad ['glæd] **1.** *adj.* happy; content; pleased; joyful. (Adv: *gladly.* Comp: *gladder;* sup: *gladdest.*) **2.** *adj.* causing happiness, pleasure, or joy. (Adv: *gladly.* Comp: *gladder;* sup: *gladdest.*)

glamour ['glæm ɚ] *n.* charm and beauty. (No pl.)

glance ['glæns] *n.* a brief look toward someone or something.

glare ['glɛɚ] **1.** *n.* a harsh, angry stare. **2.** *n.* strong, bright light. (No pl.) **3.** *iv.* to stare angrily.

glass [ˈglæs] **1.** *n.* a hard, stiff, easily broken, usually clear substance, used to make windows, drinking GLASSES as in ②, eyeglasses, etc. (Pl only for types and instances.) **2.** *n.* a container that is used to drink from, usually made of ①. (The GLASS for drinking does not have a handle.) **3.** *n.* the contents of ②.

glasses *n.* EYEGLASSES. (Treated as pl. Short for EYEGLASSES. Number is expressed with *pair(s) of glasses.*)

glee [ˈgli] *n.* great happiness. (No pl.)

gleeful [ˈgli fʊl] *adj.* very happy; joyful. (Adv: *gleefully.*)

glide [ˈglaɪd] **1.** *iv.* to move smoothly. **2.** *iv.* to move through the air without engine power.

glimmer [ˈglɪm ɚ] **1.** *n.* a brief flicker of light; a faint light that glows and then fades. **2.** *n.* a tiny bit of certain abstract things. (Fig. on ①.) **3.** *iv.* to briefly flicker; to give off a faint light that glows and subsides. **4.** *iv.* [for an abstract quality] to appear only for a very short time.

glisten [ˈglɪs ən] *iv.* to shine with reflected light; to sparkle with reflected light.

global [ˈglob əl] *adj.* of or about the whole world; worldwide. (Adv: *globally.*)

globe [ˈglob] **1.** *n.* a ball; a sphere. **2.** *n.* a ball or sphere with a map of the world on it. **3.** *n.* the earth; the world.

gloom [ˈglum] *n.* the feeling of sadness and dullness. (No pl.)

gloomy [ˈglum i] *adj.* dark; dim; sad; depressing. (Adv: *gloomily.* Comp: *gloomier;* sup: *gloomiest.*)

glorify [ˈglor ə faɪ] **1.** *tv.* to honor or worship someone; to praise someone or something. **2.** *tv.* to exaggerate the importance of someone or something.

glorious [ˈglor i əs] *adj.* beautiful; splendid; wonderful. (Adv: *gloriously.*)

glory [ˈglor i] **1.** *n.* praise and honor. (No pl.) **2.** *n.* something of great beauty or wonder.

glossary [ˈglɒs ə ri] *n.* a list of words and their definitions, as used within a particular book or article.

glove [ˈglʌv] *n.* one of a pair of fitted coverings for the hand, typically made of fabric or leather and having individual "pockets" for each finger and thumb.

189

glow ['glo] **1.** *iv.* to shine; to give off a weak light. **2.** *iv.* to be very hot; to be so hot as to be red, yellow, or white with heat. **3.** *iv.* to be very excited with emotion or energy. **4.** *iv.* to show a healthy appearance; to have bright red cheeks. **5.** *n.* a weak light.

glue ['glu] **1.** *n.* a thick, sticky liquid that is used to make something stick to something else; an adhesive. (Pl only for types and instances.) **2.** *tv.* to stick something to something else using ①.

glum ['glʌm] *adj.* sad; disappointed. (Adv: *glumly.* Comp: *glummer;* sup: *glummest.*)

glut ['glʌt] **1.** *n.* too much of something. **2.** *tv.* to supply someone or something with too much of something.

glutton ['glʌt n] *n.* someone who eats or drinks too much.

gnash ['næʃ] *tv.* to bite and slash with the teeth.

gnat ['næt] *n.* a small fly that bites.

gnaw ['nɔ] **1.** *tv.* to bite or chew away at something piece by piece. **2.** ~ **at;** ~ **on** to bite or chew away at something piece by piece. **3.** ~ **at;** ~ **on** (Fig. on ②.) to cause constant pain or worry.

go ['go] **1.** *iv., irreg.* to move from one place to another; [for time] to progress or pass. **2.** *tv., irreg.* to practice or perform certain sports activities, such as running, swimming, canoeing, fencing, jogging, skiing, walking, or other activities expressed with words ending in *-ing.* (Pt: WENT; pp: GONE. The third-person sg pres. tense is GOES.) **3.** *iv., irreg.* to leave. **4.** *iv., irreg.* to reach a certain time or place; to extend to a certain time or place. **5.** *iv., irreg.* to work; to function. **6.** *iv., irreg.* to become. **7.** *iv., irreg.* to become worn-out; to weaken. **8.** *iv., irreg.* to belong in a certain place. **9.** *iv., irreg.* [for the activities in a period of time] to unfold in some way, good or bad. **10.** *iv., irreg.* to progress through a series of words or musical notes.

goal ['gol] **1.** *n.* an aim; a purpose; a result that one would like to achieve from doing something. **2.** *n.* [in sports] a place where players try to send a ball in order to score points. **3.** *n.* [in sports] an instance of sending a ball through or past ②, and the points earned by doing this. **4.** *n.* the finish line; the end point of a race.

goalie ['go li] *n.* a GOALKEEPER. (A shortening of GOALKEEPER.)

goalkeeper ['gol kip ɚ] *n.* [in sports] the player whose position is in front of the team's goal and who tries to prevent players on the other team from scoring.

goat ['got] *n.* an animal with horns, similar to a sheep.

190

gobble ['gɑb əl] **1.** ~ **down;** ~ **up** to eat all of one's food very quickly. **2.** *iv.* [for a turkey] to make a noise; to make a noise like a turkey. **3.** *n.* the noise that a turkey makes.

god ['gɑd] **1.** *n.* a male spiritual being who is worshiped. (Compare this with GODDESS.) **2.** *n.* someone or something admired as ① . **3.** *n.* [in religions such as Christianity, Islam, and Judaism] the one spiritual being that is worshiped as the creator and ruler of everything. (Capitalized. No pl.)

goddess ['gɑd əs] *n.* a female spiritual being who is worshiped.

goes ['goz] the third-person sg, pres. tense of GO.

goggles ['gɔg əlz] *n.* a pair of protective lenses that are worn during swimming, skiing, biking, and other activities. (Treated as pl. Number is expressed with *pair(s) of goggles*.)

gold ['gold] **1.** *n.* a chemical element that is a soft, yellow metal, is very valuable, and is the standard for money in many countries. (No pl.) **2.** *n.* coins or jewelry made of ① . (No pl.) **3.** *n.* a deep yellow color. (Pl only for types and instances.) **4.** *adj.* made of ① . **5.** *adj.* deep yellow in color. (Comp: *golder;* sup: *goldest.*)

golden ['gol dən] **1.** *adj.* made from gold; yellowish as if made from gold. **2.** *adj.* [of anniversaries] the fiftieth.

goldfish ['gold fɪʃ] *n., irreg.* a kind of small fish, typically orange or gold, commonly kept as a pet. (Pl: *goldfish.*)

golf ['gɔlf] **1.** *n.* a game played on a large area of land, where players use a club to hit a small ball into a hole, using as few strokes as possible. (No pl.) **2.** *iv.* to play ① .

gone ['gɔn] pp of GO.

good ['gʊd] **1.** *adj., irreg.* having positive qualities; satisfactory; suitable; not negative. (Adv: WELL. Comp: BETTER; sup: BEST.) **2.** *adj., irreg.* having proper morals; moral; not evil. **3.** *adj., irreg.* enjoyable; pleasant; satisfying. (Adv: WELL. Comp: BETTER; sup: BEST.) **4.** *adj., irreg.* complete; thorough; full. (Adv: WELL. Comp: BETTER; sup: BEST.) **5.** *adj., irreg.* skillful; talented; able to do something right. (Adv: WELL. Comp: BETTER; sup: BEST.) **6.** *adj., irreg.* properly behaved; obedient. (Comp: BETTER; sup: BEST.) **7.** *adj.* ripe; edible; not spoiled; not rotten. **8.** *n.* excellence; virtue; goodness. (No pl.)

good-bye ['gʊd 'baɪ] **1.** *interj.* farewell, as said when someone leaves. **2.** *adj.* of or about leaving; of or about a departure.

191

goodness ['gʊd nəs] *n.* being good, ethical, and right. (No pl form in this sense.)

goods *n.* items for sale; products that are made to be sold. (Treated as pl, but not countable.)

goose ['gus] *n., irreg.* a bird having a long neck and similar to a large duck. (Pl: GEESE.)

gorilla [gə 'rɪl ə] *n.* the largest kind of ape.

Gospel ['gɑs pəl] *n.* one of the first four books of the New Testament of the Bible.

gossip ['gɑs əp] **1.** *n.* talk about other people, which may or may not be true; rumors about other people. (No pl.) **2.** *n.* someone who often talks about other people and other people's private lives. **3.** *iv.* to talk about other people and their private lives; to spread rumors about other people.

got ['gɑt] pt and a pp of GET.

gotten ['gɑt n] a pp of GET.

gourmet [gʊr 'me] **1.** *n.* someone who enjoys fine foods and wine. **2.** *adj.* [of food and drink] produced according to the highest cooking standards.

govern ['gʌv ərn] **1.** *iv.* to rule [over someone or something]; to be the leader of a group of people. **2.** *tv.* to rule or lead a group of people. **3.** *tv.* to guide, control, or regulate something.

government ['gʌv ərn mənt] **1.** *n.* the system of rule over a country and its people. (No pl.) **2.** *n.* the political organization ruling in a particular area. **3.** the *adj.* use of ① or ②. (Also *governmental.*)

governor ['gʌv ər nər] **1.** *n.* the title of the executive officer of each state of the United States. **2.** *n.* someone who governs or rules certain organizations. **3.** *n.* a device that controls the speed of a car or other vehicle, either keeping it at a constant speed or not allowing it to go over a certain speed.

gown ['gaʊn] **1.** *n.* a formal dress for a woman. **2.** *n.* a NIGHTGOWN. **3.** *n.* a type of loose ceremonial covering or robe such as is worn at graduation ceremonies.

grab ['græb] **1.** *tv.* to seize and hold someone or something; to snatch someone or something; to take something rudely. **2.** *tv.* to get and bring something; to fetch something. (Informal.) **3.** *n.* an act of seizing as in ①.

grace ['gres] **1.** *n.* elegance, smoothness, or attractiveness of form or motion. (No pl.) **2.** *n.* calm and tolerant elegance. (No pl.) **3.** *n.* favor; mercy; favorable regard. (No pl.) **4.** *n.* a prayer said before eating. (No pl.) **5.** *tv.* to make something more beautiful or elegant; to add beauty or elegance to something.

graceful ['gres ful] *adj.* moving with smoothness and grace; elegant in appearance. (Adv: *gracefully.*)

gracious ['gre ʃəs] **1.** *adj.* kind; courteous; pleasant. (Adv: *graciously.*) **2.** *adj.* of or about great comfort and good taste. (Adv: *graciously.*) **3.** *adj.* merciful; showing love and mercy. (Adv: *graciously.*) **4.** *interj.* a mild expression of wonder or surprise.

grade ['gred] **1.** *n.* a level in school corresponding to a year of study. **2.** *n.* a mark, given to a student for a class, test, paper, or assignment, that shows how well or how poorly the student did. **3.** *n.* a degree of quality. **4.** *n.* the slope of a road, roof, terrace, etc. **5.** *tv.* to give ② for the work of a student.

gradual ['græ dʒu əl] *adj.* moving, happening, or changing a little bit at a time; slow. (Adv: *gradually.*)

graduate 1. ['græ dʒu ət] *n.* someone who has completed high school, college, or university. **2.** ['græ dʒu et] *tv.* to depart from a school, college, or university with a degree.

graduation [græ dʒu 'e ʃən] **1.** *n.* the ceremony where students become GRADUATES ①. **2.** *n.* one of a series of marks on something, showing the units of measurement.

grain ['gren] **1.** *n.* grass or cereal plants grown for their edible seeds. (Pl only for types and instances.) **2.** *n.* seeds of ①. (Pl only for types and instances.) **3.** *n.* an individual seed of ①. **4.** *n.* a tiny particle of something, such as sand or salt. **5.** *n.* a very small unit of weight, equal to about 64.8 milligrams. **6.** *n.* the pattern or direction of the fibers of wood. (Pl only for types and instances.)

gram ['græm] *n.* the basic unit for measuring weight in the metric system, equal to $\frac{1}{1,000}$ of a kilogram or about $\frac{1}{28}$ of an ounce.

grammar ['græm ɚ] **1.** *n.* a system of rules and principles in a language that determines how sentences are formed; the study of sentence structure and the relationships between words within sentences. (Pl only for types and instances.) **2.** *n.* a statement of the rules of a language that accounts for how sentences are formed, especially the description of what the standard form of the language is

grand

like. **3.** *n.* following the rules of ② in the use of written and spoken language. (No pl.)

grand ['grænd] **1.** *adj.* impressive; magnificent. (Adv: *grandly.* Comp: *grander;* sup: *grandest.*) **2.** *n.* a thousand dollars. (Slang. No pl.)

grandchild ['græn(d) tʃaɪld] *n., irreg.* a child of one's child. (Pl: GRAND-CHILDREN.)

grandchildren ['græn(d) tʃɪl drən] pl of GRANDCHILD.

granddad ['græn dæd] *n.* grandfather; the father of one's mother or father. (Also a term of address. Capitalized when written as a proper noun.)

granddaughter ['græn dɔt ɚ] *n.* the daughter of one's son or daughter.

grandfather ['græn(d) fɑ ðɚ] *n.* the father of one's mother or father. (Also a term of address. Capitalized when written as a proper noun.)

grandma ['græm mɑ] *n.* grandmother; the mother of one's mother or father. (Also a term of address. Capitalized when written as a proper noun.)

grandmother ['græn(d) məð ɚ] *n.* the mother of one's mother or father. (Also a term of address. Capitalized when written as a proper noun.)

grandpa ['græm pɑ] *n.* grandfather; the father of one's mother or father. (Also a term of address. Capitalized when written as a proper noun.)

grandparent ['græn(d) per ənt] *n.* a grandmother or a grandfather; the parent of one's parent. (The pl usually refers to one or more pairs consisting of a GRANDMOTHER and a GRANDFATHER.)

grandson ['græn(d) sən] *n.* the son of one's child.

grandstand ['græn(d) stænd] *n.* the area where people sit at a race-track, ball field, and the like.

grant ['grænt] **1.** *n.* money that is given by a government or a private agency for a worthy purpose. **2.** *tv.* to give something formally to someone. **3.** *tv.* to give permission for something to someone; to give someone permission for something. **4.** *tv.* to concede that something is true; to admit to someone that something is true. (The object is a clause with THAT ⑦.)

grape ['grep] **1.** *n.* a red, green, or purple fruit that grows in bunches on vines. **2.** *adj.* made of or flavored with ①.

194

graph ['græf] **1.** *n.* a drawing that shows the difference between two or more amounts or the changes in amounts through time. **2.** *tv.* to place information on ①; to make ①.

graphic arts AND **graphics** ['græf ɪk 'ɑrts] *n.* the arts that involve painting, drawing, and images displayed by various means. (Treated as sg or pl.)

graphics Go to GRAPHIC ARTS.

grass ['græs] *n.* a plant with thin blades instead of leaves. (Pl only for types and instances.)

grateful ['gret fʊl] *adj.* feeling or showing gratitude toward someone or something; feeling or showing appreciation; thankful. (Adv: *gratefully.*)

gratitude ['græt ə tud] *n.* the quality of being thankful; a feeling or expression of thanks. (No pl.)

grave ['grev] **1.** *n.* the place where someone is buried; a burial site. **2.** *n.* the actual hole that someone is buried in. **3.** *adj.* very serious; dire. (Adv: *gravely.*)

gravel ['græv əl] *n.* crushed rock; pebbles about the size of peas. (Pl only for types and instances.)

graveyard ['grev jɑrd] *n.* a cemetery; a place where dead people are buried.

gravity ['græv ə ti] **1.** *n.* the force that pulls things toward the center of planets, stars, moons, etc.; the force that pulls things toward the center of the earth. (No pl.) **2.** *n.* seriousness; importance. (No pl.)

gravy ['gre vi] **1.** *n.* the juice that drips from meat when it cooks. (Pl only for types and instances.) **2.** *n.* a sauce made from ①, often thickened with flour or something similar. (Pl only for types and instances.)

gray ['gre] **1.** *n.* the color made when white is mixed with black. (Pl only for types and instances.) **2.** *n.* the color GRAY as in ①, when found in the hair. (No pl.) **3.** the *adj.* form of ①. (Adv: *grayly.* Comp: *grayer;* sup: *grayest.*) **4.** *iv.* [for hair] to become ③; [for someone] to develop ②.

grease 1. ['gris] *n.* melted animal fat or any similarly oily substance. (No pl.) **2.** ['gris, 'griz] *tv.* to coat something with ①.

greasy ['gris i] *adj.* oily; like grease; coated with grease. (Adv: *greasily.* Comp: *greasier;* sup: *greasiest.*)

195

great ['gret] **1.** *adj.* large in size or importance. (Adv: *greatly.* Comp: *greater;* sup: *greatest.*) **2.** *adj.* good; very good. (Adv: *greatly.* Comp: *greater;* sup: *greatest.*) **3.** *interj.* Super!; Wonderful! (Sometimes used sarcastically.)

greatly ['gret li] *adv.* very much.

greed ['grid] *n.* a strong desire for money, possessions, or power. (No pl.)

greedy ['gri di] *adj.* showing greed; desiring money, possessions, or power too strongly. (Adv: *greedily.* Comp: *greedier;* sup: *greediest.*)

green ['grin] **1.** *n.* the color of grass or of the leaves of trees in the summer; the color made when blue and yellow are mixed together. (Pl only for types and instances.) **2.** *n.* a grassy area. **3.** *adj.* of the color of grass. (Comp: *greener;* sup: *greenest.*) **4.** *adj.* unripe; not yet ripe or mature. (Comp: *greener;* sup: *greenest.*) **5.** *adj.* without experience; young. (Fig. on ④. Comp: *greener;* sup: *greenest.*)

greenhouse ['grin haʊs] *n., irreg.* a building with a glass roof and glass walls where the temperature is controlled so that plants can grow inside all year round. (Pl: [...haʊ zəz].)

greens *n.* the leaves of certain plants eaten as food. (Treated as pl.)

greet ['grit] *tv.* to welcome someone; to address someone, especially upon meeting or arrival.

greeting ['gri tɪŋ] *n.* a word, phrase, or action—such as *Hello*—said or done when meeting someone or when answering the telephone.

grew ['gru] pt of GROW.

grid ['grɪd] **1.** *n.* a series of lines arranged vertically and horizontally forming squares, especially as found on maps or graphs. **2.** *n.* a series of rods, bars, or wires arranged as in ①. **3.** *n.* a network of electrical lines spread over a large area; a network of roads.

grief ['grif] *n.* sorrow; distress. (No pl.)

grill ['grɪl] **1.** *n.* a grid of metal rods set over a fire, on which food is placed to cook; a BARBECUE ①. **2.** *n.* an outdoor stove that cooks food placed on a framework of rows of metal bars. **3.** *tv.* to cook food on ① or ②. **4.** *tv.* to question someone forcefully and thoroughly. **5.** *iv.* [for food] to be cooked on ① or ②.

grille ['grɪl] **1.** *n.* a grate above the front bumper of a car in front of the radiator. (Compare this with GRILL.) **2.** *n.* a grid of metal bars placed in a door or window.

grim ['grɪm] 1. *adj.* not likely to turn out well. (Adv: *grimly.* Comp: *grimmer;* sup: *grimmest.*) 2. *adj.* [looking] stern and harsh. (Adv: *grimly.* Comp: *grimmer;* sup: *grimmest.*)

grime ['graɪm] *n.* thick, oily dirt. (No pl.)

grin ['grɪn] 1. *n.* a big smile. 2. *iv.* to smile widely so that one's teeth show.

grind ['graɪnd] 1. *tv., irreg.* to make something into a powder or tiny chunks, by crushing or pounding it. (Pt/pp: GROUND.) 2. *tv., irreg.* to rub things together with force.

grindstone ['graɪnd ston] *n.* a thick, round wheel of stone that is used to sharpen knives.

grip ['grɪp] 1. *tv.* to hold someone or something tightly with one's hands. 2. *n.* a tight hold on someone or something.

gripe ['graɪp] *n.* a complaint.

groan ['gron] 1. *n.* a loud, deep noise of pain, disappointment, or disapproval. 2. *iv.* to make a loud, deep noise of pain, disappointment, or disapproval. 3. *iv.* [for an enormous bulk] to make a deep noise or creak.

grocer ['gro sɚ] *n.* someone who owns or runs a grocery store; someone who sells food and basic supplies.

groceries ['gros riz] *n.* items bought at a grocery store. (Treated as pl, but not countable.)

grocery ['gros ri] *adj.* having to do with food bought and sold at a store.

groom ['grum] 1. *n.* a man who is getting married. 2. *tv.* to clean and comb a horse. 3. *tv.* to make someone's hair neat. 4. *tv.* to prepare someone for a specific duty.

groove ['gruv] 1. *n.* a long, narrow channel cut into a surface. 2. *n.* the continuous, circular channel on a phonograph record in which the needle rests. 3. *tv.* to cut ① into something.

grope ['grop] 1. *iv.* to search with one's hands. 2. ~ **for** to search for something with one's hands.

ground ['graʊnd] 1. pt/pp of GRIND. 2. *adj.* broken or chopped into powder or into tiny chunks by grinding. 3. *n.* the surface of the earth. (No pl.) 4. *tv.* to cause a pilot, airplane, or bird to stay on the surface of the earth. (Pt/pp: *grounded.*) 5. *tv.* to make someone stay in a certain place as punishment. (Fig. on ④. Pt/pp: *grounded.*) 6. *tv.* to make an electrical device safer by extending a wire into ③. (Pt/pp: *grounded*.)

grounds *n.* the remains of powdered coffee beans after coffee has been made from them. (Treated as pl, but not countable.)

group ['grup] **1.** *n.* a number of people or things considered as a unit; a category. **2.** *tv.* to arrange people or things into categories; to place things or people together in ①.

grove ['grov] *n.* a small forest; woods; a group of trees.

grow ['gro] **1.** *tv., irreg.* to care for plants, causing them to mature. (Pt: GREW; pp: GROWN.) **2.** *iv., irreg.* to become bigger, larger, or more powerful; to increase. **3.** *iv., irreg.* to become a certain way.

growl ['graʊl] **1.** *n.* a deep, threatening sound, especially one made in anger. **2.** *iv.* to make a deep, threatening sound; to say something in a deep, threatening way, especially when angry or irritated.

grown ['gron] **1.** pp of GROW. **2.** *adj.* fully developed; adult; mature; ripe.

growth ['groθ] **1.** *n.* development; the amount someone or something develops in a certain period of time. (No pl.) **2.** *n.* an increase; the process of becoming bigger, larger, or more powerful. (No pl.) **3.** *n.* an unnatural or unhealthy lump of tissue; a tumor.

grudge ['grʌdʒ] *n.* a resentment held toward someone.

gruff ['grʌf] **1.** *adj.* rough in behavior; surly. (Adv: *gruffly.* Comp: *gruffer;* sup: *gruffest.*) **2.** *adj.* [of a voice or sound] deep and hoarse. (Adv: *gruffly.* Comp: *gruffer;* sup: *gruffest.*)

grumble ['grʌm bəl] **1.** *iv.* to speak with a low, indistinct, and possibly complaining voice. **2.** *iv.* [for something] to make a low rumbling noise, indicating stress or heaviness. (Fig. on ①.) **3.** *n.* a low, indistinct voice.

guarantee [gɛr ən 'ti] **1.** *n.* a written document that promises that a certain product will operate properly for a certain amount of time. **2.** *n.* a written or verbal promise that one will be responsible for something, especially for certain debts or actions. **3.** *tv.* to promise that something will be done. (The object can be a clause with THAT ⑦.) **4.** *tv.* to promise to be responsible for certain debts, actions, or results. **5.** *tv.* to provide ①, promising that a product will work properly for a period of time.

guard ['gɑrd] **1.** *n.* someone or some creature that watches and protects someone or something. **2.** the *adj.* use of ①. **3.** *tv.* to protect someone or something; to keep someone or something from escaping.

guess ['gɛs] **1.** *n.* an opinion or statement that is given without really knowing what is true. **2.** *tv.* to make a successful try at figuring out the right answer to a question. (The object can be a clause with THAT ⑦.) **3.** *tv.* to think that something will probably happen; to suppose that something will happen. (The object is a clause with THAT ⑦.)

guest ['gɛst] **1.** *n.* someone who visits another person's home because of an invitation. **2.** *n.* someone who is taken to dinner or to a place of entertainment by someone else, who is paying for it. **3.** *n.* someone who is invited by an organization or government to make a visit. **4.** *n.* a customer of a hotel, motel, etc.

guide ['gaɪd] **1.** *n.* someone who shows someone else the way. **2.** *n.* someone who leads tours. **3.** *n.* a book or chart of information about a thing or a place. **4.** *tv.* to lead someone to the right place. **5.** *tv.* to lead a tour. **6.** *tv.* to direct the business of something; to control something. **7.** *tv.* to advise someone.

guilt ['gɪlt] **1.** *n.* the feeling that one has done something wrong or bad. (No pl.) **2.** *n.* the burden or responsibility of having done something wrong or bad. (No pl.)

guilty ['gɪl ti] *adj.* having broken a rule or done something wrong; judged in a court to have done a crime; not innocent. (Adv: *guiltily.* Comp: *guiltier;* sup: *guiltiest.*)

gulf ['gʌlf] **1.** *n.* an area of sea, larger than a bay, surrounded by land on two or three sides. **2.** *n.* a large or wide separation. (Fig. on ①.)

gulp ['gʌlp] **1.** *n.* the swallowing of a large amount of food, drink, or air. **2.** *n.* a large mouthful; a large breath of air; a large bite of food or drink. **3.** ~ **down** to swallow food, drink, or air quickly.

gum ['gʌm] **1.** *n.* a soft, sticky, flavored substance that people chew. (Pl only for types and instances.) **2.** *n.* the upper or lower ridge of flesh that covers the jaw bones and surrounds the bases of the teeth.

gun ['gʌn] **1.** *n.* a weapon that shoots bullets. **2.** *n.* a device or tool that has a handle and trigger like ①, used for applying or installing something.

gush ['gʌʃ] **1.** *n.* a large flow of a fluid. **2.** *iv.* to flow out rapidly and in large amounts. **3.** *tv.* to allow a fluid to flow; to make fluid flow.

gust ['gʌst] **1.** *n.* a strong rush of wind or smoke. **2.** *iv.* [for the wind] to move in short, strong bursts.

gut [ˈgʌt] **1.** *n.* the area of the intestine or stomach. (No pl.) **2.** *tv.* to take the intestines and organs out of an animal.

guts 1. *n.* the intestines. (Treated as pl, but not countable. Colloquial.) **2.** *n.* courage. (Treated as pl, but not countable. Colloquial.)

gutter [ˈgʌt ɚ] **1.** *n.* a metal channel hanging on the edge of a roof to carry away water when it rains. **2.** *n.* the wide, wooden channel on either side of a bowling lane. **3.** *n.* on a street, a lower, formed channel that leads water and other waste to the entrance of a sewer.

guy [ˈgɑɪ] **1.** *n.* a man; a boy. (Informal.) **2.** *n.* a person, male or female, especially in the pl. (Informal.)

gym [ˈdʒɪm] **1.** *n.* a gymnasium. **2.** the *adj.* use of ①.

gymnasium [dʒɪm ˈnez i əm] *n.* a large room or building for physical education, physical training, or certain sports events such as basketball and wrestling. (Can be shortened to GYM.)

H

habit ['hæb ɪt] **1.** *n.* an action that is done over and over, usually without thinking about it. **2.** *n.* an addiction; a strong need for drugs, tobacco, alcohol, etc. **3.** *n.* the uniform worn by a monk or a nun.

had ['hæd] **1.** pt/pp of HAVE. **2.** *aux.* the pt form of HAVE (5), used in forming the past PERFECT verb form. (Used before the pp of a verb. Reduced to *'d* in contractions. See also HAS.)

hadn't ['hæd nt] *cont.* had not.

hag ['hæg] *n.* an ugly old woman; a witch.

hail ['hel] **1.** *n.* round pellets of ice that fall from the sky like rain. (No pl. Number is expressed with HAILSTONE(S).) **2.** *n.* a group of things that come in small, sharp units. **3.** *n.* a continual series of demands, objections, questions, etc. **4.** *tv.* to greet or welcome someone with cheers, joy, and approval. **5.** *tv.* to honor and praise someone or something; to praise and approve something eagerly. **6.** *iv.* [for (1)] to fall from the sky.

hailstone ['hel ston] *n.* a small, round ball of ice that falls from the sky like rain.

hailstorm ['hel storm] *n.* a storm that produces or includes hail.

hair ['hɛr] **1.** *n.* the strands or fibers that grow on the body of an animal, especially the ones that grow on top of the heads of humans. (No pl. Treated as sg.) **2.** *n.* one of the strands or fibers that grow on the body of an animal as in (1).

hairbrush ['hɛr brəʃ] *n.* a brush used for smoothing hair and making it look orderly.

haircut ['hɛr kət] **1.** *n.* an act or instance of cutting hair, especially the hair on top of someone's head. **2.** *n.* the particular way that one's hair has been cut; a hairstyle.

hairdo ['hɛr du] *n.* the style of one's hair; the way one's hair has been cut or shaped. (Pl in -s.)

hairdresser ['hɛr drɛs ɚ] *n.* someone who cuts and styles hair; a hair stylist.

hairy ['hɛr i] *adj.* covered with hair; having a lot of hair. (Comp: *hairier;* sup: *hairiest.*)

201

half ['hæf] **1.** *n., irreg.* either of two equal parts that form a complete thing. (Pl: HALVES.) **2.** *n.* a portion—as described in ①—of the amount of people or things already mentioned or referred to. (Treated as sg or pl.) **3.** *adj.* being ① of an amount; being one of two equal parts. **4.** *adv.* part of the way; not completely.

halfhearted ['hæf 'hɑrt ɪd] *adj.* not too enthusiastic; without excitement. (Adv: *halfheartedly.*)

halfway ['hæf 'we] **1.** *adj.* at the middle; in the middle. **2.** *adv.* to the point that is ①.

hall ['hɔl] **1.** *n.* a passage that connects rooms and stairways inside a house or building. (See also HALLWAY.) **2.** *n.* a large room for big meetings, lectures, dances, etc. **3.** *n.* a building where college students live, sleep, study, or have classes.

hallway ['hɔl we] *n.* a HALL; a passage that connects rooms and stairways inside a house or building.

halt ['hɔlt] **1.** *iv.* to stop. **2.** *tv.* to cause someone or something to stop.

halve ['hæv] **1.** *tv.* to cut something into two halves; to split something into two equal halves. **2.** *tv.* to reduce something by half.

halves ['hævz] pl of HALF.

ham ['hæm] **1.** *n.* the upper part of a hog's rear hip and thigh, preserved by salt and a special kind of wood smoke. **2.** *n.* ① eaten as food. (Pl only for types and instances.)

hamburger ['hæm bɚ gɚ] **1.** *n.* beef that has been ground into tiny bits. (No pl.) **2.** *n.* a sandwich made of cooked ground beef and a specially shaped bun.

hammer ['hæm ɚ] **1.** *n.* a tool with a heavy metal head that is used to pound nails or to break things. **2.** *tv.* to hit something with ①.

hand ['hænd] **1.** *n.* the structure at the end of the arm, used for grasping; the most distant part of the arm, below the wrist. **2.** *n.* the cards given or dealt to someone in a card game; one session in a game of cards. **3.** *n.* side; direction. (No pl.) **4.** *n.* one of the pointers on a clock or watch. **5.** *tv.* to give something to someone by using one's ①. **6.** the *adj.* use of ① or ④. **7.** ~ **out** to pass something, usually papers, out to people.

handbag ['hænd bæg] *n.* a purse; a container that serves as a purse.

handful ['hænd fʊl] *n.* the amount of something that can be held in the hand.

202

handicap ['hæn di kæp] **1.** *n.* a disability; a disadvantage; something that hinders someone from doing something in the usual way. **2.** *n.* [in sports or games] a restriction placed on a better player in order to make the event more competitive. **3.** *tv.* to prevent someone from doing something in the usual way; to hinder someone.

handkerchief ['hæŋ kɚ tʃɪf] *n.* a square of soft fabric used to wipe one's nose or face.

handle ['hæn dəl] **1.** *n.* the part of an object that is held on to so that the object can be used, moved, picked up, pushed, pulled, opened, or closed. **2.** *tv.* to feel someone or something with one's hands; to use one's hands on someone or something. **3.** *iv.* [for something] to work in a certain way while being used; [for a vehicle or boat] to be guided, driven, or steered.

handlebar ['hæn dəl bɑr] *n.* the curved metal tube by which one steers a bicycle or motorcycle. (Usually pl.)

handsome ['hæn səm] **1.** *adj.* very attractive; [of a male] very good-looking. (Adv: *handsomely.* Comp: *handsomer;* sup: *handsomest.*) **2.** *adj.* ample; generous; more than enough. (Adv: *handsomely.* Comp: *handsomer;* sup: *handsomest.*)

handwriting ['hænd raɪt ɪŋ] **1.** *n.* writing done by hand with a pen or pencil instead of with a typewriter or computer. (No pl form.) **2.** *n.* one's own style of writing; a sample of one's own ①. (No pl form.)

hang ['hæŋ] **1.** *tv., irreg.* to suspend something from a higher place, using a rope, chain, etc. (Pt/pp: HUNG.) **2.** *tv., irreg.* to attach something to a wall. **3.** *tv.* to execute a person by suspending the person by the neck. (Pt/pp: *hanged* for this sense.) **4.** *iv., irreg.* to be suspended over something; to remain above someplace or thing. **5.** ~ **around** to loiter someplace; to be in a place or in an area, doing nothing in particular.

hangar ['hæŋ ɚ] *n.* a large building where airplanes are stored and serviced.

hanger ['hæŋ ɚ] *n.* a wooden, metal, or plastic frame for suspending clothing inside a closet.

haphazard ['hæp 'hæz ɚd] *adj.* random; without being planned. (Adv: *haphazardly.*)

happen ['hæp ən] *iv.* to occur; to take place.

happiness ['hæp i nəs] *n.* being happy; being glad or joyful. (No pl.)

happy [ˈhæp i] **1.** *adj.* [of someone or some creature] feeling or showing joy or being in a good mood; [of someone] glad, pleased, or willing. (Adv: *happily.* Comp: *happier;* sup: *happiest.*) **2.** *adj.* causing joy; joyful. (Adv: *happily.* Comp: *happier;* sup: *happiest.*)

harbor [ˈhɑr bɚ] **1.** *n.* a sheltered port where ships and boats can anchor safely. **2.** *tv.* to keep something in one's mind, especially bad feelings toward someone.

hard [ˈhɑrd] **1.** *adj.* firm; solid; not soft. (Comp: *harder;* sup: *hardest.*) **2.** *adj.* difficult; not easy to do. (Comp: *harder;* sup: *hardest.*) **3.** *adj.* severe; harsh; demanding. (Comp: *harder;* sup: *hardest.*) **4.** *adj.* forceful; violent; not gentle. (Comp: *harder;* sup: *hardest.*) **5.** *adj.* [of water] having a high mineral content. (Comp: *harder;* sup: *hardest.*) **6.** *adv.* with great force or energy. (Comp: *harder;* sup: *hardest.*)

hardly [ˈhɑrd li] *adv.* barely; almost not at all.

hardware [ˈhɑrd wer] **1.** *n.* tools, nails, screws, door handles, electrical supplies, brackets, buckets, utensils, and similar things used in building and maintenance. (No pl form.) **2.** *n.* computer equipment; the machinery of a computer, as opposed to software programs. (No pl form.)

hardy [ˈhɑrd i] **1.** *adj.* robust; able to live under difficult conditions. (Adv: *hardily.* Comp: *hardier;* sup: *hardiest.*) **2.** *adj.* [of a plant] able to survive a severe winter freeze. (Adv: *hardily.* Comp: *hardier;* sup: *hardiest.*)

hare [ˈheɚ] *n.* an animal, such as the jackrabbit, that is very similar to a rabbit, but larger.

harm [ˈhɑrm] **1.** *n.* mental or physical damage to someone or something. (No pl.) **2.** *tv.* to damage someone or something.

harmful [ˈhɑrm fʊl] *adj.* causing damage or harm to someone or something. (Adv: *harmfully.*)

harmless [ˈhɑrm ləs] *adj.* not causing damage or harm. (Adv: *harmlessly.*)

harmony [ˈhɑr mə ni] **1.** *n.* the effect of different musical notes that are played or sung together, creating a pleasant sound. (Pl only for types and instances.) **2.** *n.* agreement; peace. (No pl. Fig. on ①.)

harp [ˈhɑrp] *n.* a musical instrument having strings attached to a frame of wood.

harsh [ˈhɑrʃ] **1.** *adj.* rough; unpleasant to look at or listen to; unpleasant to touch, taste, or smell. (Adv: *harshly.* Comp: *harsher;* sup: *harsh-*

est.) **2.** *adj.* mean; cruel; severe. (Adv: *harshly.* Comp: *harsher;* sup: *harshest.*)

harvest ['hɑr vəst] **1.** *n.* the gathering of a crop of grain, fiber, fruit, vegetables, etc. **2.** *n.* the total amount of grain, fiber, fruit, or vegetables produced in an area. **3.** *tv.* to collect a crop of grain, fiber, fruit, or vegetables when it is ready.

has ['hæz] **1.** *tv.* the present-tense form of HAVE used for the third-person sg, that is, with *he, she, it,* and sg nouns. **2.** *aux.* the present-tense form of HAVE ⑤ used for the third-person sg, that is, with *he, she, it,* and sg nouns, in forming the present PERFECT verb form. (Used before the pp of a verb. Reduced to *'s* in contractions.)

hasn't ['hæz ənt] *cont.* has not.

haste ['hest] *n.* speed; hurry. (No pl form in this sense.)

hasten ['hes ən] **1.** *tv.* to cause someone or something to hurry; to cause something to happen sooner. **2.** ~ **to do** to hurry to do something.

hasty ['he sti] **1.** *adj.* quick; speedy. (Adv: *hastily.* Comp: *hastier;* sup: *hastiest.*) **2.** *adj.* carelessly fast; without proper thought. (Adv: *hastily.* Comp: *hastier;* sup: *hastiest.*)

hat ['hæt] *n.* an article of clothing shaped to cover the head.

hatch ['hætʃ] **1.** *n.* an opening in a wall, ceiling, or floor. **2.** *iv.* [for a baby bird or reptile] to break an eggshell from the inside and come out.

hatchet ['hætʃ ɪt] *n.* a short axe.

hate ['het] **1.** *n.* intense dislike. (No pl.) **2.** *tv.* to dislike someone or something intensely.

hatred ['he trɪd] *n.* intense dislike; hate. (No pl form in this sense.)

haul ['hɔl] **1.** *tv.* to carry something, using force; to drag something heavy. **2.** *tv.* to carry or bring someone or something by truck or other vehicle. **3.** *n.* an instance of traveling from one place to another, and the distance, time, or effort involved.

haunt ['hɔnt] **1.** *tv.* [for a ghost or spirit] to remain in a certain place and appear occasionally. **2.** *tv.* [for someone or something annoying or disquieting] to remain in one's thoughts. (Fig. on ①.) **3.** *tv.* to visit a place often; to be in a place for long periods. (Fig. on ①.) **4.** *n.* a place that is visited by a certain person often; a place where someone goes frequently.

205

haunted ['hɔnt ɪd] *adj.* bothered by a ghost or an evil spirit; frequented by a ghost.

have ['hæv] **1.** *tv., irreg.* to own something; to possess something; to possess a quality. (Pt/pp: HAD; in the pres. tense, the third-person sg form is HAS.) **2.** *tv., irreg.* to undergo something; [for something] to happen to oneself; to experience something. **3.** *tv., irreg.* to eat or drink something; to consume something. **4.** *tv., irreg.* to cause something to be done; to cause someone or something to do something. **5.** *aux.* a verb that is used to form the PERFECT verb forms, which show that an action is completed. (Used before the pp of a verb.)

hawk ['hɔk] **1.** *n.* a bird of prey, similar to a falcon, with strong beak and claws, a long tail, and good eyesight. **2.** *tv.* to sell something, especially in the street.

hay ['he] *n.* grass or plants cut, dried, and used as food for cattle, horses, etc. (No pl.)

haystack ['he stæk] *n.* a large amount of hay that is piled together to dry.

hazard ['hæz ɚd] **1.** *n.* the risk of something bad happening. **2.** *tv.* to risk something; to put something in danger. **3. at ~** risked; in danger; at risk.

he ['hi] **1.** *pron.* a third-person sg masculine pronoun. (Refers to male creatures. Used as a subject of a sentence or a clause. See also HIM, HIMSELF, and HIS.) **2.** *pron.* a third-person sg pronoun. (Used when the sex of a grammatical subject is unimportant, indeterminate, undetermined, or irrelevant. Objected to by some as actually referring only to males in this sense. See also THEY ②.) **3.** *n.* a male person or creature.

head ['hɛd] **1.** *n.* the part of the body of humans and animals above the neck, including the face, eyes, nose, mouth, ears, brain, and skull. **2.** *n.* the brain; the mind. **3.** *n.* an individual animal, used especially in counting cows, horses, and sheep. (No pl. Always a sg form preceded by words that tell how many.) **4.** *n.* the leader of a company, country, organization, group, etc.; a chief; someone who is in charge. **5.** *n.* the top, front, or upper part of something, such as a table, a page, a sheet of paper, a line [of people], or a [school] class. **6.** *adj.* primary; chief; foremost. (Prenominal only.) **7.** *tv.* to lead a group of people; to be in charge of a group of people or part of a company. **8.** *iv.* to move in a certain direction. **9. a ~; per ~** for each person; for each individual.

206

headache ['hɛd ek] 1. *n.* a pain in the head, especially one that lasts a long time. 2. *n.* a problem; a bother; a worry. (Fig. on ①.)

headline ['hɛd laɪn] 1. *n.* the title of a newspaper article, especially at the top of the front page. 2. *tv.* to have a major part in a play or movie, and thus have one's name written in large print, like ①, in the advertising for the play or movie.

health ['hɛlθ] 1. *n.* freedom from diseases of the mind or the body. (No pl.) 2. *n.* vigor; general condition. (No pl. Fig. on ①.) 3. the *adj.* use of ① or ②.

heap ['hip] *n.* a large pile of things; a stack of things piled together.

hear ['hɪr] 1. *iv., irreg.* to be able to sense or experience sounds by means of the ears. (Pt/pp: HEARD.) 2. *tv., irreg.* to sense or receive a certain sound or a certain utterance. 3. *tv., irreg.* to learn that something has happened. (The object can be a clause with THAT ⑦.) 4. *tv., irreg.* [for a court of law] to listen to the two sides of a court case. 5. *tv., irreg.* to pay attention to someone or something; to listen to someone or something. (The object can be a clause with THAT ⑦.)

heard ['hɚd] pt/pp of HEAR.

hearing ['hɪr ɪŋ] 1. *n.* the sense that allows one to recognize sound; the ability to hear. (No pl form.) 2. *n.* an examination of basic evidence in a court of law. 3. the *adj.* use of ①.

heart ['hɑrt] 1. *n.* a large, four-chambered muscle that pumps blood throughout the body. 2. *n.* ① considered as a symbol of the center of a person's emotions, thoughts, and love. (Fig. on ①.) 3. *n.* the shape ♥. 4. *n.* [in a deck of playing cards] one card of a group of cards that bears a red ♥.

heartbeat ['hɑrt bit] 1. *n.* one full pulse of the heart. 2. *n.* a moment; a second or two.

hearty ['hɑr ti] 1. *adj.* energetic; vigorous; strong and lively. (Adv: *heartily.* Comp: *heartier;* sup: *heartiest.*) 2. *adj.* [of a meal] large and satisfying. (Adv: *heartily.* Comp: *heartier;* sup: *heartiest.*)

heat ['hit] 1. *n.* hotness; the quality that is felt as a higher temperature. (No pl.) 2. *n.* hot weather. (No pl.) 3. *n.* a grouping of contestants in a sporting event. (The winners of groups compete in other HEATS or the final event.) 4. *tv.* to cause something to become hotter. 5. *iv.* to become hotter or warmer.

heater ['hit ɚ] *n.* a device that provides heat for heating a room, usually electric or powered by a liquid fuel.

207

heaven ['hɛv ən] *n.* [in certain religions] the place where God resides and where the souls of good people go after death. (Usually associated with the sky. No pl.)

heavy ['hɛv i] **1.** *adj.* weighing a lot; of great weight. (Adv: *heavily.* Comp: *heavier;* sup: *heaviest.*) **2.** *adj.* [of sound] strong, deep, and ponderous. (Adv: *heavily.* Comp: *heavier;* sup: *heaviest.*) **3.** *adj.* great in amount; dense; intense; thick. (Adv: *heavily.* Comp: *heavier;* sup: *heaviest.*) **4.** *adj.* serious; requiring a lot of thought to understand. (Adv: *heavily.* Comp: *heavier;* sup: *heaviest.*)

hectic ['hɛk tɪk] *adj.* very active; very excited; very busy. (Adv: *hectically* […ɪk li].)

he'd ['hid] **1.** *cont.* he would. **2.** *cont.* he had, where HAD is an auxiliary.

hedge ['hɛdʒ] **1.** *n.* a row of bushes planted closely together, separating two parcels of land. **2.** *n.* a statement that protects against a risk or danger; a statement that equivocates. **3.** *tv.* to make a statement in an evasive way to avoid committing oneself to a certain belief or decision. **4.** ~ **in** to enclose or surround something with a hedge. **5.** ~ **in** to restrict or contain someone; to limit someone. (Fig. on ④.) **6.** *iv.* to speak in an evasive way, avoiding the risks of being more specific.

heed ['hid] *tv.* to pay close attention to something, such as advice.

heel ['hil] **1.** *n.* the back part of the foot; the part of the foot that bears the weight of the body. **2.** *n.* the part of a shoe or sock that covers the back part of the foot. **3.** *n.* the part of a shoe that supports the back part of the foot.

heels *n.* shoes with a tall HEEL ③, worn by women, usually on formal occasions. (Short for *high heels.* Treated as pl, but not countable. Number is expressed with *pair(s) of heels.*)

height ['haɪt] **1.** *n.* the amount that someone or something is tall; vertical length [of a person or of a vertical object]. (No pl.) **2.** *n.* the length of something from bottom to top; the distance to a higher point from a lower level.

heighten ['haɪt n] **1.** *tv.* to cause something to become more intense or exciting. **2.** *iv.* to become more intense or exciting.

heir ['ɛr] *n.* someone, male or female, who inherits something from its owner; someone who receives something when the owner dies.

heiress ['ɛr ɪs] *n.* the feminine form of HEIR; a female who has inherited a fortune.

held ['hɛld] pt/pp of HOLD.

helicopter ['hɛl ə kɑp tɚ] *n.* an aircraft with large, rotating blades that can lift and hold the aircraft in the air.

he'll ['hil] *cont.* he will.

hell ['hɛl] **1.** *n.* [in certain religions] the place where the devil resides and where the souls of wicked people go after death. (No pl. Sometimes capitalized.) **2.** *n.* suffering, misery, and despair. (Fig. on ①. No pl.) **3.** *interj.* a word used to indicate anger or surprise. (Colloquial.)

hello [hɛ 'lo] **1.** *n.* an act of greeting someone; an act of saying ②. (Pl ends in -s.) **2.** *interj.* a word used in greeting someone or in answering the telephone.

helm ['hɛlm] *n.* the wheel or lever used to control the direction of a ship. (No pl form.)

helmet ['hɛl mət] *n.* a protective covering for the head; a covering for the head, worn for protection.

help ['hɛlp] **1.** *n.* aid; assistance. (No pl. Treated as sg.) **2.** *n.* someone or a group hired to do a job, usually a service job. (No pl. Treated as sg or pl, but not counted.) **3.** *iv.* to give assistance. **4.** *tv.* to give assistance to someone or something; to aid someone or something. **5.** *tv.* to relieve an illness or condition; to ease the discomfort caused by something; to make a sickness or discomfort less severe. **6.** *interj.* a cry used when one needs aid or assistance.

hem ['hɛm] **1.** *n.* the folded and sewn edge of a piece of cloth. **2.** *tv.* to make a nice, even edge on a piece of cloth by folding and sewing.

hemisphere ['hɛm əs fɪr] **1.** *n.* half of a sphere; half of a ball. **2.** *n.* one of two halves of the earth.

hen ['hɛn] *n.* a female bird, especially a female chicken.

her ['hɚ] **1.** *pron.* an objective form of SHE, referring to females. (Used after prepositions and as the object of verbs.) **2.** *pron.* an objective form of SHE, referring to ships and certain countries. (Also other informal uses.) **3.** *pron.* a possessive form of SHE, referring to females. (Used as a modifier before a noun. Compare this with HERS.)

herb ['ɚb] *n.* a plant whose seeds or leaves are used for flavoring food or for medicines.

herd ['hɚd] **1.** *n.* a large group of cattle or other similar large animals such as elk, buffalo, zebra, elephants, etc. **2.** *tv.* to cause a large group of people or animals to move together. **3.** *tv.* to take care of cattle,

209

sheep, or other groups of animals. **4.** *iv.* to form into a group; to move as a group.

here ['hɪr] **1.** *adv.* in, at, to, or from the location of the speaker or writer who uses this word. **2.** *adv.* now; at this point in time or in a process. **3.** *adv.* a form that begins a sentence and is followed by a verb, which then is followed by the subject of the sentence. (Often used to point out or offer something. Takes *be, go, stand, rest,* or a similar verb.) **4.** *n.* this place.

heritage ['hɛr ɪ tɪdʒ] *n.* the cultural background of a group of people. (No pl.)

hermit ['hɚ mɪt] *n.* someone who moves away from society and who lives alone.

hero ['hɪr o] **1.** *n.* someone who is honored and respected for bravery or courage. (Compare this with HEROINE. Pl ends in *-es.*) **2.** *n.* the main male character in a story, movie, or play. (See also HEROINE. Pl ends in *-es.*)

heroic [hɪ 'ro ɪk] *adj.* courageous; brave; valiant. (Adv: *heroically* […ɪk li].)

heroine ['hɛr o ɪn] **1.** *n.* a brave and courageous woman; a woman who does heroic actions. (Compare this with HERO.) **2.** *n.* the main female character in a story, movie, or play. (See also HERO.)

heroism ['hɛr o ɪz əm] **1.** *n.* a heroic act; a brave or courageous act. (No pl form in this sense.) **2.** *n.* the quality of being a hero or a heroine. (No pl form in this sense.)

hers ['hɚz] *pron.* a possessive form of SHE. (Used in place of a noun. Compare this with HER.)

herself [hɚ 'sɛlf] **1.** *pron.* the reflexive form of SHE. (Used after a verb or a preposition when the subject of the sentence is the same female to which the pronoun refers.) **2.** *pron.* an emphatic form of SHE. (Follows the nominal that is being emphasized.)

he's ['hiz] **1.** *cont.* he is. **2.** *cont.* he has. (Where HAS is an auxiliary.)

hesitate ['hɛz ə tet] **1.** *iv.* to waver; to pause for a moment before doing something, especially because one is unsure of something. **2.** *iv.* to be unwilling to do something; to be reluctant to do something.

hid ['hɪd] pt of HIDE.

hidden ['hɪd n] pp of HIDE.

hide ['haɪd] **1.** *tv., irreg.* to place something out of view; to place something so that it cannot be seen; to conceal something. (Pt: HID; pp:

HIDDEN.) **2.** *iv., irreg.* to place oneself so that one cannot be seen; to conceal oneself. **3.** *n.* the skin of an animal, especially when used to make leather.

high ['haɪ] **1.** *adj.* far above the ground; further above than average; not low. (Comp: *higher;* sup: *highest.*) **2.** *adj.* extending a certain distance upward; at or reaching a particular distance above the ground or above sea level. (Follows the measure of height. Comp: *higher;* sup: *highest.*) **3.** *adj.* great in power, rank, or importance. (Adv: *highly.* Comp: *higher;* sup: *highest.*) **4.** *adj.* [of heat, number, pitch, price, velocity, intelligence, standards, etc.] great or strong, or greater or stronger than what is normal or average. (Adv: *highly.* Comp: *higher;* sup: *highest.*) **5.** *n.* the top point; a peak. **6.** *adv.* to or at a place that is far up. (Comp: *higher;* sup: *highest.*)

highly ['haɪ li] the *adv.* form of HIGH ③; very much. (Comp: *higher;* sup: *highest.*)

highway ['haɪ we] *n.* a main road—especially one designed for high speed—used to get from one city to another.

hike ['haɪk] **1.** *n.* a long walk, especially in the woods, mountains, etc. **2.** *iv.* to travel or walk as in ①.

hiker ['haɪk ɚ] *n.* someone who hikes.

hill ['hɪl] **1.** *n.* a raised part of the earth's surface, smaller than a mountain. **2.** *n.* a heap or mound of soil, especially one made by an animal.

hilltop ['hɪl tɑp] *n.* the top of a hill.

him ['hɪm] **1.** *pron.* an objective form of HE ①. (The pronoun used to refer to males. Used after prepositions and as the object of verbs.) **2.** *pron.* an objective form of HE ②. (Used when the sex of a grammatical object of a verb or preposition is unimportant, indeterminate, undetermined, or irrelevant. Objected to by some as actually referring only to males in this sense. See also THEM ②.)

himself [hɪm 'sɛlf] **1.** *pron.* the reflexive form of HE ①. (Used after a verb or a preposition when the subject of the sentence is the same male to which the pronoun refers.) **2.** *pron.* the reflexive form of HE ②. (Used after a verb or a preposition when the sex of the subject of the sentence is unimportant, indeterminate, undetermined, or irrelevant. This sense is objected to by some as actually referring only to males.) **3.** *pron.* an emphatic form of HIM. (Follows the nominal being emphasized.)

hind [ˈhaɪnd] *adj.* positioned at the rear or back of something. (Prenominal only.)

hinder [ˈhɪn dɚ] **1.** *tv.* to attempt to prevent someone or something from doing something; to block someone or something from doing something. **2.** *tv.* to attempt to prevent something from happening, progressing, or succeeding; to make it difficult for something to happen, progress, or succeed.

hinge [ˈhɪndʒ] *n.* a jointed device that fits two things together so that one of the things, such as a door or gate, can move.

hint [ˈhɪnt] **1.** *n.* a clue; a suggestion that helps solve a puzzle or answer a question. **2.** *n.* a small trace; a little bit of something; a small amount. **3.** *tv.* to suggest ①; to provide ①. (The object is a clause with THAT ⑦.)

hip [ˈhɪp] **1.** *n.* the joint that connects the leg with the body; the area on each side of the body, below the waist, where the leg joins the trunk of the body. **2.** *adj.* in style; fashionable. (Older slang. Comp: *hipper*; sup: *hippest*.)

hippopotami [hɪp ə ˈpɑt ə maɪ] a pl of HIPPOPOTAMUS.

hippopotamus [hɪp ə ˈpɑt ə məs] *n., irreg.* a large, round-shaped African mammal that lives in and near rivers, having thick skin and very little hair. (Pl: *hippopotamuses* or HIPPOPOTAMI.)

hire [ˈhaɪɚ] *tv.* to employ someone at a job; to pay someone to do work.

his [ˈhɪz] **1.** *pron.* the possessive form of HE, referring to a male who has already been mentioned. (Comes before a noun.) **2.** *pron.* the possessive form of HE, referring to a male who has already been mentioned. (Used in place of a noun.) **3.** *pron.* the possessive form of HE, referring to a person who has already been mentioned. (Used when the sex of the person referred to is unimportant, indeterminate, undetermined, or irrelevant. Objected to by some as referring only to males in this sense. See also THEIR ②.) **4.** *pron.* the possessive form of HE, referring to a person who has already been mentioned. (Used in place of a noun. Used when the sex of the person referred to is unimportant, indeterminate, undetermined, or irrelevant. Objected to by some as actually referring only to males in this sense.)

hiss [ˈhɪs] **1.** *n.* the sound that a snake makes; a long *s* sound. **2.** *iv.* to make ①.

historian [hɪ ˈstor i ən] *n.* someone who studies history; someone who writes about history.

history ['hɪs tə ri] **1.** *n.* the study of events that have happened. (No pl.) **2.** *n.* a record of events that have happened. **3.** *n.* background; facts about the past of someone or something.

hit ['hɪt] **1.** *tv., irreg.* to strike someone or something; to contact someone or something violently or with force. (Pt/pp: *hit*.) **2.** *tv., irreg.* to reach something. **3.** *n.* someone or something that is very successful. **4.** *n.* [in baseball] a play where the batter HITS as in ① the ball with a bat and is able to get to a base safely. **5.** *adj.* [of music or performances] popular. (Prenominal only.)

hive ['haɪv] *n.* the box, container, or structure that bees live in. (See also BEEHIVE, HIVES.)

hives *n.* any one of various skin diseases characterized by a rash. (Treated as sg or pl, but not countable. See also HIVE.)

hoard ['hord] **1.** *tv.* to store a large amount of something secretly for future use. **2.** *n.* a large amount of something that has been secretly stored for future use.

hoarse ['hors] **1.** *adj.* [of a voice] rough and raspy sounding from illness or misuse. (Adv: *hoarsely.* Comp: *hoarser;* sup: *hoarsest.*) **2.** *adj.* [of a person] having a voice that is rough and raspy sounding from illness or misuse. (Adv: *hoarsely.* Comp: *hoarser;* sup: *hoarsest.*)

hobby ['hab i] *n.* an activity that is done in one's spare time; an activity that one likes to do.

hobo ['ho bo] *n.* a tramp; someone who travels from city to city looking for food or work. (Usually male. Pl ends in *-s* or *-es.*)

hockey ['hak i] *n.* a game, played on ice, where skaters try to hit a rubber disk into a goal area. (No pl.)

hoe ['ho] **1.** *n.* a garden tool consisting of a small blade attached to a long handle, used to remove weeds or to break up soil. **2.** *tv.* to use ① on something; to remove weeds or break up soil with ①.

hog ['hɔg] **1.** *n.* a full-grown pig, especially one raised for food or to produce young. **2.** *n.* someone who is very greedy or messy. (Fig. on ①.) **3.** *tv.* to take more than one's fair share of something. (Informal.)

hoist ['hɔɪst] **1.** *n.* a device for lifting heavy things. **2.** *tv.* to raise something using ropes or chains.

hold ['hold] **1.** *tv., irreg.* to keep someone or something in one's arms or hands. (Pt/pp: HELD.) **2.** *tv., irreg.* to support the weight of someone or something; to bear the weight of someone or something. **3.** *tv.,* *irreg.* to grasp something so it remains in a certain position. **4.** *tv., irreg.* to reserve something; to set something aside, waiting for further action. **5.** *tv., irreg.* to contain something; to have enough room for something. **6.** *tv., irreg.* to cause an event to take place. **7.** *tv., irreg.* to retain a certain position or condition. **8.** *tv., irreg.* to restrain someone or something; to keep someone or something under control. **9.** *iv., irreg.* to withstand a strain; not to break under pressure. **10.** *iv., irreg.* to remain connected to a telephone line while one's call has been temporarily suspended—so the caller or the person who was called can talk on another telephone line. **11.** *n.* a grasp; a grip. **12.** *n.* a good or secure grasp of something. **13.** *n.* the place in a ship or plane where cargo is stored.

holder ['hold ɚ] *n.* something that holds something; something that keeps something in a certain position.

holdup ['hold əp] **1.** *n.* a robbery, especially one committed with a gun; a stickup. **2.** *n.* a delay; the reason that something is not moving properly.

hole ['hol] *n.* an opening made in or through a solid object; an opening in the surface of something.

holiday ['hɑl ə de] **1.** *n.* a period of time when most businesses and schools are closed in honor of someone or something. **2.** *n.* a holy day; a religious celebration.

hollow ['hɑl o] **1.** *n.* an open space inside an object; a cavity. **2.** *n.* a small valley; a sunken area of land. **3.** *adj.* having an open space inside; not solid. (*Adv: hollowly.* Comp: *hollower;* sup: *hollowest.*) **4.** *adj.* sunken. (*Adv: hollowly.* Comp: *hollower;* sup: *hollowest.*) **5.** *adj.* empty; without meaning or substance. (*Adv: hollowly.* Comp: *hollower;* sup: *hollowest.*) **6.** ~ **out** to scoop something out; to form an open space inside an object.

holster ['hol stɚ] *n.* a fabric or leather case for a gun, worn on the body or attached to a saddle.

holy ['hol i] *adj.* sacred; associated with divine matters. (Comp: *holier;* sup: *holiest.*)

homage ['ɑm ɪdʒ] praise, respect, and honor.

home ['hom] **1.** *n.* the place where one lives; one's house or apartment. **2.** *n.* the place where someone was born; the place that someone comes from; the place where someone grew up. **3.** *n.* an institution or building where people who need special care live. **4.** *n.* a place where something is found, based, or located; a place where something originated or was invented. **5.** the *adj.* use of ①, ②, ③, or ④. **6.** *adv.* at ① or ②; to ① or ②.

homemaker ['hom mek ɚ] *n.* a person who manages a home, especially a married woman who manages her home and, possibly, children.

homeowner ['hom o nɚ] *n.* someone who owns a home.

homesick ['hom sɪk] *adj.* sad and depressed because one is away from one's home.

homework ['hom wɚk] **1.** *n.* schoolwork that is to be completed at home or elsewhere outside the school building. (No pl.) **2.** *n.* preparation that should be done before a meeting or discussion. (Fig. on ①. No pl.)

honest ['ɑn əst] **1.** *adj.* always telling the truth; not lying; able to be trusted. (Adv: *honestly.*) **2.** *adj.* obtained fairly and legally; not stolen. (Adv: *honestly.*) **3.** *adj.* sincere; appearing fair and ①. (Adv: *honestly.*)

honesty ['ɑn ɪs ti] *n.* the quality of being honest; truthfulness. (No pl.)

honey ['hʌn i] *n.* a sweet, sticky substance made by bees. (Pl only for types and instances.)

honeymoon ['hʌn i mun] **1.** *n.* the vacation that two newly married people take after the wedding. **2.** *n.* a calm period of good business or political relations, especially right after someone new has come to power.

honk ['hɔŋk] **1.** *n.* the sound made by a horn or a goose. **2.** *iv.* to make the sound of a horn or a goose. **3.** *tv.* to sound a horn; to cause a horn to make a noise.

honor ['ɑn ɚ] **1.** *n.* the respect or regard shown to someone or something. (No pl.) **2.** *n.* character and integrity; honesty and fairness; a way of being that earns trust. (No pl.) **3.** *n.* a pleasure; a privilege. **4.** *tv.* to hold someone in high regard; to respect someone. **5.** *tv.* to make a payment as agreed; for a bank to accept a check and pay out the money that the check was written for.

honorable ['ɑn ɚ ə bəl] *adj.* worthy of honor; deserving honor. (Adv: *honorably.*)

honors ['ɑn ɚz] praise, awards, and recognition.

hood ['hʊd] **1.** *n.* a covering for the head and neck, sometimes attached to a coat and sometimes also covering the face. **2.** *n.* the metal panel that covers the top of the front of a car.

215

hoof ['hʊf, 'huf] *n., irreg.* the hard part on the bottom of the foot of a horse, deer, and certain other animals. (Pl: HOOVES.)

hook ['hʊk] **1.** *n.* a bent or curved piece of plastic, wood, wire, or metal, used to catch, pull, or hold something. **2.** *n.* [in boxing] a short blow given while one's elbow is bent. **3.** *tv.* to catch and pull something with ①.

hoot ['hut] **1.** *n.* the noise that an owl makes. **2.** *iv.* to make ①; to make a noise like ①.

hooves ['huvz] pl of HOOF.

hop ['hɑp] **1.** *n.* a small movement upward, like a jump. **2.** *n.* an airplane flight, especially a short one. **3.** *iv.* to jump up and down; to jump forward a small distance. **4.** *iv.* [for frogs, rabbits, kangaroos, etc.] to move by jumping.

hope ['hop] **1.** *n.* the happy feeling that something one wants to happen will actually happen. (No pl.) **2.** *n.* something that is desired; something that one wants to happen; an expectation. **3.** *tv.* to feel happy about and wish for something that one wants to happen in the future. (The object is a clause with THAT ⑦.)

hopeful ['hop fʊl] **1.** *adj.* full of hope; showing hope; optimistic. (Adv: *hopefully*.) **2.** *adj.* causing hope; seeming as if what is hoped for will happen.

horizon [hə 'raɪ zən] *n.* the line in the distance where the sky seems to meet the earth.

horizontal [hor ə 'zɑn təl] *adj.* flat; parallel to flat ground; not up and down. (Adv: *horizontally*.)

horn ['hɔrn] **1.** *n.* a hard, usually pointed growth on the heads of cattle, goats, antelope, sheep, etc. **2.** *n.* the hard substance that an animal's hoof or HORN as in ① is made of. (No pl.) **3.** *n.* a device that makes noise, as in a car or other vehicle. **4.** *n.* one of the brass musical instruments, such as the trumpet, the cornet, the tuba, the French horn, and the trombone, played by blowing air through a shaped tube. (Often in compounds.)

hornet ['hɔr nɪt] *n.* a large kind of stinging wasp.

horrible ['hɔr ə bəl] **1.** *adj.* causing horror or terror. (Adv: *horribly*.) **2.** *adj.* awful; bad. (Adv: *horribly*.)

horrify ['hɔr ə faɪ] *tv.* to frighten someone very badly; to terrify someone.

horror ['hɔr ɚ] **1.** *n.* intense dread or fear; fright. (Pl only for types and instances.) **2.** *n.* someone or something that causes fear or fright; an experience of ①.

horse ['hɔrs] *n.* an animal, larger than a donkey, that is used for carrying people and pulling heavy things, especially on farms.

hose ['hoz] **1.** *n.* a flexible tube used to direct water or some other liquid. (Treated as sg. Pl: *hoses*.) **2.** *n.* men's socks, especially to go with formal clothing. (No pl. Treated as pl, but not countable. Number is expressed with *pair(s) of hose*.) **3.** *n.* women's long, sheer stockings, made of silk or nylon. (No pl. Treated as pl, but not countable. Number is expressed with *pair(s) of hose*.) **4.** *n.* PANTYHOSE. (No pl. Treated as pl, but not countable.)

hospital ['hɑs pɪt əl] *n.* a building where medical care for serious diseases and illnesses is provided.

host ['host] **1.** *n.* someone who receives and welcomes guests. (Male or female. Sometimes *hostess* is used for a female.) **2.** *n.* the person arranging a party or gathering, especially where food is served. (Male or female. Sometimes *hostess* is used for a female.) **3.** *n.* someone who introduces people on a television show; someone who has a talk show on television. **4.** *n.* a large number of people or things. **5.** *tv.* to be ③ on a television show. **6.** *tv.* to be ① or ② at a party.

hostage ['hɑs tɪdʒ] **1.** *n.* someone or something held by force, to be released only when stated demands are met. **2.** the *adj.* use of ①.

hostile ['hɑs təl] **1.** *adj.* easily angered; unfriendly; antagonistic. (Adv: *hostilely*.) **2.** *adj.* acting like an enemy; aggressive and threatening. (Adv: *hostilely*.)

hot ['hɑt] **1.** *adj.* having a high temperature; not cold or warm. (Adv: *hotly*. Comp: *hotter*; sup: *hottest*.) **2.** *adj.* [of food] very spicy, causing a burning feeling in the mouth. (Adv: *hotly*. Comp: *hotter*; sup: *hottest*.) **3.** *adj.* very intense; excited or angry. (Fig. on ①. Adv: *hotly*. Comp: *hotter*; sup: *hottest*.) **4.** *adj.* currently popular. (Informal. Comp: *hotter*; sup: *hottest*.)

hotel [ho 'tɛl] *n.* a building where people can rent a place to stay while away from home on business or vacation.

hound ['haʊnd] **1.** *n.* a dog, especially one used for hunting. **2.** *n.* a fan; someone who is very excited about a hobby or activity. (Informal.) **3.** *tv.* to chase someone; to worry someone; to harass someone.

hour ['aʊ ɚ] **1.** *n.* a unit of time measurement equal to 60 minutes or $\frac{1}{24}$ of a day. **2.** *n.* a period of time set aside for some activity. **3.** *n.* the distance that can be traveled in ①.

hourly ['aʊ ɚ li] **1.** *adj.* happening every hour; happening once an hour. **2.** *adv.* every hour; once an hour.

house 1. ['haʊs] *n., irreg.* a building where a person or a family lives; a home. (Pl: ['haʊ zəz] or ['haʊ səz].) **2.** ['haʊs] *n.* a household; all the people who live in ①. (No pl.) **3.** ['haʊs] *n., irreg.* a legislature; a legislative body. **4.** ['haʊs] *n., irreg.* the part of a theater where the audience sits. **5.** ['haʊz] *tv.* to provide shelter to someone or some creature.

housebreak ['haʊs brek] *tv., irreg.* to train a pet not to defecate or urinate in the house, or in the case of a cat, outside its special place. (Pt: HOUSEBROKE; pp: HOUSEBROKEN.)

housebroke ['haʊs brok] pt of HOUSEBREAK.

housebroken ['haʊs brok ən] pp of HOUSEBREAK.

household ['haʊs hold] **1.** *n.* the group of people who live in a house or apartment. **2.** *adj.* found in ①; associated with ①.

housekeeper ['haʊs kip ɚ] **1.** *n.* someone who is paid to manage household chores. **2.** *n.* someone who manages the cleaning in a hotel, resort, hospital, or large building. **3.** *n.* a person who is paid to clean someone's house. (Euphemistic.)

houseplant ['haʊs plænt] *n.* a plant usually grown indoors.

housework ['haʊs wɚk] *n.* cooking, cleaning, washing, and other household tasks. (No pl.)

hover ['hʌv ɚ] **1.** *iv.* to stay in one place in the air; to float in place over someone or something. **2.** *iv.* to linger somewhere; to stay near someone or something.

how [haʊ] **1.** *interrog.* in what way?; by what means? **2.** *interrog.* to what extent?; to what degree? **3.** *interrog.* in what condition? **4.** *conj.* the way in which; the manner in which.

however [haʊ 'ɛv ɚ] **1.** *adv.* but; nevertheless; in spite of something. **2.** *adv.* no matter how. (Followed by an adjective or adverb.) **3.** *conj.* in whatever way; by whatever means.

howl ['haʊl] **1.** *n.* a long wail, as with the cry of a wolf or the sound of a high wind. **2.** *iv.* to make ①.

huddle ['hʌd l] **1.** *n.* a group of people crowded together. **2.** *n.* [in football] a group of players close together, planning the next play.

3. *iv.* [for a number of people] to stand closely together in a small space, especially to keep warm. **4.** *iv.* [for a creature] to curl up somewhere; to bring one's arms and legs close to the body, as if to keep warm.

hue ['hju] *n.* color; a variety, shade, or intensity of a color.

hug ['hʌg] **1.** *n.* an act of holding someone or something in one's arms in a friendly or loving way. **2.** *tv.* to hold someone as in ①. **3.** *tv.* to stay close to a curb, railing, wall, or some other object as one moves along.

huge ['hjudʒ] **1.** *adj.* [of size] very large or enormous. (Adv: *hugely*. Comp: *huger;* sup: *hugest*.) **2.** *adj.* of a notable extent; [of extent, degree, or amount] notably large. (Adv: *hugely*. Comp: *huger;* sup: *hugest*.)

hum ['hʌm] **1.** *n.* a long, vibrating sound, like a long "mmmmmmm"; a low murmur; a quiet buzzing sound. (No pl.) **2.** *iv.* to make a long, vibrating sound, like a long "mmmmmmmmmm"; to sing with one's mouth closed, as in ②. **3.** *tv.* to sing musical notes with one's mouth closed, as in ②.

human ['hju mən] **1.** *n.* a person. **2.** the *adj.* use of ①. (Adv: *humanly*.) **3.** *adj.* showing feelings that people normally show. (Adv: *humanly*.) **4.** ~ **being** a human creature; a person.

humble ['hʌm bəl] **1.** *adj.* aware of one's faults; modest. (Adv: *humbly*. Comp: *humbler;* sup: *humblest*.) **2.** *adj.* simple; lowly; not elegant. (Adv: *humbly*. Comp: *humbler;* sup: *humblest*.) **3.** *tv.* to lower the position of someone; to cause someone to become ①.

humid ['hju mɪd] *adj.* [of weather] damp; [of air] containing much moisture. (Adv: *humidly*.)

humidity [hju 'mɪd ə ti] *n.* moisture in air; water vapor carried in the air. (No pl form in this sense.)

humility [hju 'mɪl ə ti] *n.* being humble; modesty. (No pl form in this sense.)

humor ['hju mɚ] **1.** *n.* the quality of being funny. (No pl.) **2.** *tv.* to tolerate someone who behaves oddly; to accept someone who has strange whims or desires.

humorous ['hju mə rəs] *adj.* funny; amusing; having humor. (Adv: *humorously*.)

hump ['hʌmp] *n.* a large, rounded bump or swelling.

hunch ['hʌntʃ] *n.* a guess based on how one feels.

hundred ['hʌn drəd] **1.** *n.* the number 100; the number between 99 and 101. (Additional forms as with *two hundred, three hundred, four hundred*, etc.) **2.** *n.* 100 people or things.

hung ['hʌŋ] **1.** a pt/pp of HANG. **2.** *adj.* [of a jury] unable to reach a decision; [of a jury] not having a majority.

hunger ['hʌŋ gɚ] **1.** *n.* a general lack of food. (No pl.) **2.** *n.* the feeling of a need for something. (Fig. on ①. No pl.)

hungry ['hʌŋ gri] *adj.* wanting food; lacking food; having an empty stomach. (Adv: *hungrily.* Comp: *hungrier;* sup: *hungriest.*)

hunk ['hʌŋk] *n.* a large, solid amount of something.

hunt ['hʌnt] **1.** *tv.* to search for and kill animals for food or for sport. **2.** *iv.* to search for and kill animals as in ①.

hunter ['hʌn tɚ] *n.* someone who hunts; someone who searches for and kills animals for food or sport.

hurl ['hɚl] **1.** *tv.* to throw someone or something with force. **2.** *tv.* to shout something negative, such as an insult or bad words.

hurry ['hɚ i] **1.** *iv.* to move quickly or briskly. **2.** *tv.* to cause someone or something to move quickly or briskly. **3.** *n.* a rush; an effort to be fast or faster. **4.** ~ **up;** ~ **on** to move faster.

hurt ['hɚt] **1.** *n.* pain of the body or emotions; an ache. (Pl only for types and instances.) **2.** *tv., irreg.* to injure a part of the body; to harm one's mental processes or emotional well-being. (Pt/pp: *hurt.*) **3.** *tv., irreg.* to have a bad effect on someone or something; to be bad for someone or something. **4.** *tv., irreg.* to cause pain in something; to give someone pain. **5.** *iv., irreg.* to feel pain.

husband ['hʌz bənd] *n.* a married man; the man that a woman is married to.

hush ['hʌʃ] **1.** *n.* silence; quiet; calm. (No pl.) **2.** *tv.* to cause someone or something to be calm and quiet. **3.** *iv.* to become calm and quiet.

husky ['hʌs ki] **1.** *adj.* [of a voice] low sounding as if the speaker has a sore throat. (Adv: *huskily.* Comp: *huskier;* sup: *huskiest.*) **2.** *adj.* big and strong; muscular. (Adv: *huskily.* Comp: *huskier;* sup: *huskiest.*) **3.** *n.* a kind of dog that pulls sleds in the far north.

hustle ['hʌs əl] **1.** *tv.* to move someone or something to someplace quickly. **2.** *tv.* to sell something in an aggressive manner. **3.** *iv.* to move quickly. (Informal.)

hut ['hʌt] *n.* a small shelter; a humble dwelling.

hutch [ˈhʌtʃ] **1.** *n.* a cage for rabbits or other small animals. **2.** *n.* a cupboard or cabinet with shelves.

hyena [haɪ ˈi nə] *n.* a wild, doglike animal of Africa that eats meat and has a loud cry that sounds like laughter.

hymn [ˈhɪm] *n.* a religious song of praise meant to be sung by worshipers.

hype [ˈhaɪp] **1.** *n.* an extreme amount of publicity; exaggerated praise used for publicity. (No pl.) **2.** *tv.* to provide ① for someone or something.

hyphen [ˈhaɪ fən] *n.* the mark of punctuation (-). (It is placed between the parts of some compound words, between the words in certain phrases, or between syllables where a word has been split between two lines of print.)

hypnotism [ˈhɪp nə tɪz əm] **1.** *n.* hypnotizing people as a method of exploring and influencing the mind. (No pl.) **2.** *n.* the process of hypnotizing someone. (No pl.)

hypnotize [ˈhɪp nə taɪz] *tv.* to place someone in a sleeplike condition.

hypotheses [haɪ ˈpɑθ ə siz] pl of HYPOTHESIS.

hypothesis [haɪ ˈpɑθ ə sɪs] *n., irreg.* a conjecture; a possible explanation; an idea that has not been proved but that explains the facts about something. (Pl: HYPOTHESES.)

I

I ['aɪ] *pron.* the first-person sg pronoun—in writing, it refers to the writer, and in speaking, it refers to the speaker. (Used as the subject of a sentence or a clause. Compare this with ME.)

ice ['aɪs] **1.** *n.* frozen water. (No pl. Number is expressed with *piece(s)* or *cube(s)* of *ice*.) **2.** *tv.* to cover a cake with icing or frosting. (See also ICING.)

iceberg ['aɪs bɚg] *n.* an enormous piece of ice floating in the sea.

icicle ['aɪs sɪ kəl] *n.* a pointed spike of ice that hangs from something such as a tree branch.

icing ['aɪ sɪŋ] *n.* cake frosting; a sweet coating for cakes, cookies, and other desserts. (No pl.)

icy ['aɪ si] **1.** *adj.* covered with or made of ice. (Adv: *icily.* Comp: *icier*; sup: *iciest.*) **2.** *adj.* very cold; freezing cold. (Adv: *icily.* Comp: *icier*; sup: *iciest.*)

I'd ['aɪd] **1.** *cont.* I would. **2.** *cont.* I had. (Where HAD is an auxiliary.)

idea [aɪ 'di ə] **1.** *n.* a thought produced by the mind; an opinion. **2.** *n.* a picture of something produced by the mind; a mental picture. **3.** *n.* a suggestion; a plan.

ideal [aɪ 'dil] *adj.* perfect; perfectly suitable. (Adv: *ideally.*)

ideals *n.* high moral standards; strong moral beliefs.

identical [aɪ 'dɛn tɪ kəl] *adj.* equal; exactly alike. (Adv: *identically* [...ɪk li].)

identification [aɪ dɛn tə fə 'ke ʃən] **1.** *n.* identifying someone or something; the condition of being identified. (Pl only for types and instances.) **2.** *n.* some kind of document that identifies someone; something that proves who someone is. (No pl.)

identify [aɪ 'dɛn tə faɪ] **1.** *tv.* to state who or what someone or something is; to allow the identification of someone or something. **2.** *tv.* to reveal someone's identity.

identity [aɪ 'dɛn tə ti] *n.* who or what a certain person or thing is. (No pl form.)

222

idiom ['ɪd i əm] **1.** *n.* a phrase whose meaning is different from the combined literal meanings of the separate words that make up the phrase. **2.** *n.* a mode of expression or design.

idiot ['ɪd i ət] *n.* a foolish person; a stupid person.

idle ['aɪd l] **1.** *adj.* not working; unemployed; not kept busy; [of machinery] not operating or not being used. (Adv: *idly.* Comp: *idler;* sup: *idlest.*) **2.** *adj.* habitually lazy; not liking work. (Adv: *idly.* Comp: *idler;* sup: *idlest.*) **3.** *adj.* not having a purpose or result; of little significance; useless; pointless. (Adv: *idly.*) **4.** *tv.* to run an engine at low speed in neutral.

idol ['aɪd l] **1.** *n.* something that is worshiped as sacred in an organized religion. **2.** *n.* someone who is extremely popular; someone whom people honor or praise. (Fig. on ①.)

if ['ɪf] **1.** *conj.* in the event [that something is the case]; on the condition [that something is the case]. **2.** *conj.* whether. (Often introduces an indirect question.) **3.** *conj.* although; even though.

ignite [ɪg 'naɪt] **1.** *tv.* to set fire to something; to cause something to start to burn. **2.** *iv.* to start to burn.

ignorant ['ɪg nə rənt] **1.** *adj.* without knowledge; without information; uninformed. (Adv: *ignorantly.*) **2.** *adj.* caused by a lack of knowledge; resulting from a lack of knowledge. (Adv: *ignorantly.*)

ignore [ɪg 'nor] *tv.* to pay no attention to someone or something.

I'll ['aɪl] *cont.* I will.

ill ['ɪl] **1.** *adj.* sick; not well; not healthy. **2.** *adv.* badly. (Before a participle or certain adjectives. Usually hyphenated.) **3.** *n.* harm. (No pl.)

illegal [ɪ 'li gəl] *adj.* not legal; against the law. (Adv: *illegally.*)

illness ['ɪl nəs] **1.** *n.* a sickness; a disease. **2.** *n.* a period of being sick.

ills *n.* troubles.

illuminate [ɪ 'lum ə net] **1.** *tv.* to spread light on someone or something; to spread light throughout a place. **2.** *tv.* to make something clearer or easier to understand. (Fig. on ①.)

illusion [ɪ 'lu ʒən] **1.** *n.* a vision of something that is not really there; a false image. **2.** *n.* a false belief; something that seems to be true but is not true.

illustrate ['ɪl ə stret] **1.** *tv.* to decorate a book with pictures. **2.** *tv.* to use an example to explain something.

223

illustration [ɪl ə 'stre ʃən] **1.** *n.* a picture or drawing in a book, magazine, newspaper, etc. **2.** *n.* an example that explains something; a demonstration of something.

I'm ['aɪm] *cont.* I am.

image ['ɪm ɪdʒ] **1.** *n.* that which is seen in a mirror or similar surface. **2.** *n.* a sculpture, painting, or other form of art that represents someone or something; a picture or photograph of someone or something. **3.** *n.* a picture of something in one's mind; a mental picture. **4.** *n.* the opinion that people have about a certain person or thing; someone's or something's reputation.

imagery ['ɪm ɪdʒ ri] *n.* words, music, or pictures that represent or create images, often making one think about situations or feelings. (No pl. Treated as sg.)

imaginary [ɪ 'mædʒ ə nɛr i] *adj.* existing only in the mind; not real. (Adv: *imaginarily* [ɪ mædʒ ə 'nɛr ə li].)

imagination [ɪ mædʒ ə 'ne ʃən] **1.** *n.* the part of the mind that produces thoughts and images that are not real or not experienced; the part of the mind that imagines things. (No pl.) **2.** *n.* the ability to think of new and interesting ideas; the ability to imagine something. (No pl.)

imagine [ɪ 'mædʒ ɪn] **1.** *tv.* to think of someone or something; to form an image of someone or something in one's mind. (The object can be a clause with THAT ⑦.) **2.** *tv.* to think something; to believe something; to suppose something; to guess something. (The object is a clause with THAT ⑦.)

imitate ['ɪm ə tet] **1.** *tv.* to attempt to copy the style, behavior, or success of someone whom one admires or wants to be like. **2.** *tv.* to copy the behavior, speech, and movement of someone for amusement.

imitation [ɪm ə 'te ʃən] **1.** *n.* copying someone's actions or deeds; copying something. (No pl.) **2.** *n.* a copy; a duplicate. **3.** *n.* an act of imitating someone or something. **4.** *adj.* fake; artificial; resembling something.

immaculate [ɪ 'mæk jə lɪt] *adj.* pure; absolutely clean; spotless. (Adv: *immaculately*.)

immaterial [ɪm ə 'tɪr i əl] *adj.* not relevant; having nothing to do with something. (Adv: *immaterially*.)

immediate [ɪ 'mid i ɪt] **1.** *adj.* happening now; happening at once. (Adv: *immediately*.) **2.** *adj.* closest to someone or something in space or time; next to someone or something. (Adv: *immediately*.)

immediately [ɪ 'mid i ɪt li] *adv.* at this very time; at this instance.

immemorial [ɪm mə 'mor i əl] *adj.* [since a time] so long ago that no one can remember the details, origin, date, issues, etc.

immense [ɪ 'mɛns] *adj.* very large; huge; enormous. (Adv: *immensely*.)

immersion [ɪ 'mɚ ʒən] **1.** *n.* placing something under water or in a liquid. (Pl only for types and instances.) **2.** *n.* being completely involved in something. (Fig. on ①. No pl.)

immigrate ['ɪm ə gret] *iv.* to come into a new country to live.

immodest [ɪ 'mɑd əst] **1.** *adj.* not modest; revealing; shameless. (Adv: *immodestly*.) **2.** *adj.* not modest about oneself; often bragging. (Adv: *immodestly*.)

immoral [ɪ 'mor əl] *adj.* without morals; not moral; breaking moral rules. (Adv: *immorally*.)

immortal [ɪ 'mor təl] **1.** *adj.* everlasting; lasting forever; never dying; living forever. (Adv: *immortally*.) **2.** *adj.* continuing to be remembered forever; never forgotten. (Adv: *immortally*.)

impact 1. ['ɪm pækt] *n.* the crash of objects striking one another with force. **2.** ['ɪm pækt] *n.* the influence or effect of someone or something. (Fig. on ①.) **3.** [ɪm 'pækt] *tv.* to crash into something.

impasse ['ɪm pæs] *n.* a place where movement or progress is blocked by something; a deadlock. (No pl form.)

impatient [ɪm 'pe ʃənt] *adj.* not patient; not able to wait for someone or something. (Adv: *impatiently*.)

implement 1. ['ɪm plə mənt] *n.* a tool; a utensil; a piece of equipment; an instrument. **2.** ['ɪm plə mənt] *tv.* to put something in action; to carry out something, such as a plan.

implore to do [ɪm 'plor tu] to beg someone to do something.

imply [ɪm 'plɑɪ] *tv.* to suggest something; to indicate something without actually saying it. (The object is a clause with THAT ⑦.)

impolite [ɪm pə 'lɑɪt] *adj.* rude; not polite; not courteous. (Adv: *impolitely*.)

import 1. [ɪm 'port] *tv.* to bring in (to one country) a product from a foreign country. **2.** ['ɪm port] *n.* a product that is brought into one country from another country.

importance [ɪm 'port ns] **1.** *n.* the condition of being important. (No pl.) **2.** *n.* the relative position or rank of someone or something. (No pl.)

225

important [ɪm 'pɔrt nt] *adj.* having a great effect, value, or influence. (Adv: *importantly.*)

impossible [ɪm 'pɑs ə bəl] **1.** *adj.* not possible; not able to happen. (Adv: *impossibly.*) **2.** *adj.* unpleasant; unendurable. (Adv: *impossibly.*)

impress [ɪm 'prɛs] **1.** *tv.* to make a good impression on someone; to have a strong effect on someone; to cause someone to feel admiration. **2.** ~ **upon** to stress the importance of something to someone. **3.** ~ **into** to press something, such as a design, into something.

impressive [ɪm 'prɛs ɪv] *adj.* [of someone or something notably] large, strong, excellent, or important; [of someone or something] arousing admiration. (Adv: *impressively.*)

improve [ɪm 'pruv] **1.** *tv.* to cause someone or something to become better. **2.** *iv.* to become better.

improvement [ɪm 'pruv mənt] **1.** *n.* getting better; improving. (No pl form in this sense.) **2.** *n.* something that makes someone or something better.

impulse ['ɪm pəls] **1.** *n.* a short burst of electrical energy. **2.** *n.* the sudden desire to do something; a whim. (Fig. on ①.)

impure [ɪm 'pjʊr] **1.** *adj.* not pure; dirty; mixed with other things. (Adv: *impurely.*) **2.** *adj.* not morally pure. (Adv: *impurely.*)

in [ɪn] **1.** *prep.* inside something; within something; surrounded by something else. **2.** *prep.* into something; entering into a space; going through a boundary and to a position that is surrounded by something else. **3.** *prep.* at some point during a certain time period. **4.** *prep.* after a certain period of time. **5.** *prep.* with something or using something, especially a language or a way of writing or expressing something. **6.** *adv.* inward; indoors; going into something; in a way that someone or something will be in a position that is surrounded by something else. **7.** *adv.* at home; at one's office; available.

inaccurate [ɪn 'æk jə rɪt] *adj.* not accurate; incorrect. (Adv: *inaccurately.*)

inactive [ɪn 'æk tɪv] **1.** *adj.* not active; not moving. (Adv: *inactively.*) **2.** *adj.* [of someone] not or no longer working actively or being actively involved. (Adv: *inactively.*) **3.** *adj.* having no effect; [of a chemical] not reacting. (Adv: *inactively.*)

inadequate [ɪn 'æd ə kwɪt] *adj.* not adequate; not enough; not good enough. (Adv: *inadequately.*)

inch ['ɪntʃ] **1.** *n.* a unit of measurement of distance, equal to ¹⁄₁₂ of a foot or approximately 2.54 centimeters. **2.** *iv.* to move very slowly; to move a distance equal to ① at a time.

incident ['ɪn sɪ dənt] **1.** *n.* an event; something that happens. **2.** *n.* a disturbance; an accident.

incline 1. ['ɪn klaɪn] *n.* a slant; a slope; a surface that is on an angle to flat ground. **2.** [ɪn 'klaɪn] *iv.* to slant; to slope. **3.** ~**d to do** to tend to do something; to "lean toward" doing something.

include [ɪn 'klud] **1.** *tv.* [for something] to contain something or to have something among its parts. **2.** *tv.* [for someone] to cause someone or something to be a part of something; to add something to something else.

income ['ɪn kəm] *n.* the amount of money received as wages, interest, or similar payments; money received in exchange for goods or services.

incorrect [ɪn kə 'rɛkt] *adj.* not correct; wrong; false. (Adv: *incorrectly.*)

increase 1. ['ɪn kris] *n.* growth; becoming larger. (Pl only for types and instances.) **2.** [ɪn 'kris] *iv.* to become larger, faster, or more powerful; to become larger in number or amount. **3.** [ɪn 'kris] *tv.* to cause something to become larger, faster, or more powerful; to cause something to become larger in number or amount.

incubator ['ɪŋ kjə bet ɚ] **1.** *n.* a container that keeps eggs warm until they hatch. **2.** *n.* a special container or device in which babies that are born too early are kept for warmth and care.

indeed [ɪn 'did] **1.** *adv.* very much so; quite. **2.** *adv.* in fact; actually. **3.** *interj.* Amazing!

indent [ɪn 'dɛnt] *tv.* [in writing or typing] to begin a line a few spaces farther from the edge or margin than the other lines, as at the beginning of a paragraph.

indentation [ɪn dɛn 'te ʃən] **1.** *n.* a notch; a dent; a cut. **2.** *n.* indenting lines of type or writing. (Pl only for types and instances.)

independence [ɪn dɪ 'pɛn dəns] *n.* freedom from someone or some government; liberty. (No pl.)

independent [ɪn dɪ 'pɛn dənt] **1.** *adj.* not dependent on someone or something; not controlled by others; not ruled by other people or countries. (Adv: *independently.*) **2.** *adj.* not needing the support of others; self-supporting. (Adv: *independently.*) **3.** *adj.* separate; dis-

227

tinct from other things. (Adv: *independently*.) **4.** *n.* a politician or a voter who does not belong to a political party.

index ['ɪn dɛks] **1.** *n., irreg.* an alphabetical list of topics showing where each topic can be found in the main part of a book, report, magazine, journal, etc. (Pl: *indexes* or INDICES.) **2.** *n., irreg.* a scale where prices or amounts of certain things are compared with the prices or amounts of those same things at an earlier date. **3.** *tv.* to locate important topics and list them and their locations, as in ①.

indicate ['ɪn də ket] **1.** *tv.* to point something out verbally; to state a fact. (The object is a clause with THAT ⑦.) **2.** *tv.* to make something known; to draw someone's attention to something. (The object can be a clause with THAT ⑦.) **3.** *tv.* [for a meter, chart, signal] to show specific information. (The object can be a clause with THAT ⑦.)

indices ['ɪn dɪ siz] a pl of INDEX.

indigestion [ɪn də 'dʒɛs tʃən] *n.* an upset stomach; the digestion of food that causes pain. (No pl.)

indignant [ɪn 'dɪg nənt] *adj.* feeling anger or resentment at something. (Adv: *indignantly*.)

individual [ɪn də 'vɪ dʒu əl] **1.** *n.* a person; one person. **2.** *adj.* separate; single. (Adv: *individually*.)

indoor [ɪn dor] *adj.* inside a building; kept within walls and under a roof. (Prenominal only.)

indoors [ɪn 'dorz] *adv.* in or into a building.

industry ['ɪn də stri] **1.** *n.* the production of goods; the manufacture of products. (No pl.) **2.** *n.* the business activity concerning a specific kind of product or service. **3.** *n.* hard work or labor.

inedible [ɪn 'ɛd ə bəl] *adj.* not able to be eaten; not good for eating. (Adv: *inedibly*.)

inf. an abbreviation of *infinitive form*.

infant ['ɪn fənt] **1.** *n.* a baby; a young child. **2.** the *adj.* use of ①.

infect [ɪn 'fɛkt] *tv.* to contaminate someone or something with an organism that causes disease.

infection [ɪn 'fɛk ʃən] **1.** *n.* the entrance and growth of disease-producing organisms in the body. (Pl only for types and instances.) **2.** *n.* a disease caused by ①.

inferior [ɪn 'fɪr i ɚ] **1.** *adj.* lower in amount, rank, power, quality, or strength than someone or something else. (Adv: *inferiorly*.) **2.** *n.* someone who has a lower-ranking job than someone else.

inferno [ɪn ˈfɚ no] **1.** *n.* a large, fierce fire. (Pl ends in *-s.*) **2.** *n.* a place that is very hot. (Fig. on ①. Pl ends in *-s.*)

infinity [ɪn ˈfɪn ə ti] **1.** *n.* infiniteness; boundlessness; limitlessness. (No pl form in this sense.) **2.** *n.* an endless amount of time or space. (No pl form in this sense.)

inflammable [ɪn ˈflæm ə bəl] *adj.* able to catch fire; FLAMMABLE; not fireproof. (The opposite is NONFLAMMABLE. Adv: *inflammably.* This *in* shows emphasis, not negativeness.)

inflation [ɪn ˈfle ʃən] **1.** *n.* the process of putting air or gas into something; blowing something up. (No pl.) **2.** *n.* an economic condition in which too much money is available for purchasing too few goods. (No pl.)

inflict (up)on [ɪn ˈflɪkt (əp) ˈɑn] to impose something on someone.

influence [ˈɪn flu əns] **1.** *n.* the power or ability to cause certain results or to affect what happens. (Pl only for types and instances.) **2.** *n.* a cause of some behavior. **3.** *tv.* to affect someone or something.

influenza [ɪn flu ˈɛn zə] *n.* the flu; an easily spread sickness caused by a virus. (No pl.)

informal [ɪn ˈform əl] **1.** *adj.* not formal, official, or final. (Adv: *informally.*) **2.** *adj.* [of words, language, or speech] used every day but a little more relaxed than more formal speech. (Adv: *informally.*) **3.** *adj.* [of dress] not formal; casual. (Adv: *informally.*)

information [ɪn fɚ ˈme ʃən] *n.* news; knowledge about something; facts. (No pl. Number is expressed by *piece(s)* or *bit(s) of information.*)

ingredient [ɪn ˈgrid i ənt] *n.* something that is part of a mixture.

inhale [ɪn ˈhel] **1.** *iv.* to breathe in. **2.** *tv.* to breathe something in.

inherit [ɪn ˈher ɪt] **1.** *tv.* to receive the assets of a person when the person dies. **2.** *tv.* to receive a characteristic or feature from one's parents or ancestors.

initial [ɪ ˈnɪʃ əl] **1.** *n.* the first letter of a word or name when standing alone, representing the whole word or name. (Used also for a series of first letters taken from a series of words.) **2.** *adj.* first; occurring or appearing at the beginning of something. (Adv: *initially.*) **3.** *tv.* to sign something with the ① of each word in one's name rather than with one's full name.

inject [ɪn ˈdʒɛkt] **1.** *tv.* to put a liquid into a living body through a hollow needle. **2.** *tv.* to introduce a fluid into something under pressure.

229

injection [ɪn ˈdʒɛk ʃən] *n.* injecting something. (Pl only for types and instances.)

injure [ˈɪn dʒɚ] *tv.* to harm someone or something; to damage someone or something.

injury [ˈɪn dʒə ri] *n.* physical or mental damage or harm; a specific instance of damage or harm.

ink [ˈɪŋk] **1.** *n.* a colored liquid used for writing or printing. (Pl only for types and instances.) **2.** *n.* a liquid that is injected into the water by an octopus—and by some other sea animals—to confuse pursuers. (No pl.)

inn [ˈɪn] *n.* a small hotel; a place that offers rooms to rent for travelers.

inner [ˈɪn ɚ] *adj.* on the inside; nearer to the center; further inside.

inning [ˈɪn ɪŋ] *n.* [in baseball] a period of playing time that ends after the two teams have received three outs each during their turns batting.

innocent [ˈɪn ə sənt] **1.** *adj.* free from guilt or sin; not guilty. (Adv: *innocently.*) **2.** *adj.* harmless; not meant to cause harm. (Adv: *innocently.*) **3.** *adj.* too trusting; not recognizing things that are evil; inexperienced. (Adv: *innocently.*)

inoculate [ɪ ˈnɑk jə let] *tv.* to inject someone or something with a weakened or dead disease-causing agent in order to stimulate antibodies against the disease.

input [ˈɪn pʊt] **1.** *n.* addition; the act of putting something into something. (No pl.) **2.** *n.* advice; opinions; ideas or suggestions. (Informal. No pl.) **3.** *n.* information; data; information that is put into a computer. (No pl.) **4.** *n.* an electronic signal that is fed into a circuit. **5.** *tv.,* *irreg.* to put data into a computer. (Pt/pp: *inputted* or *input.*)

inquire [ɪn ˈkwaɪɚ] *iv.* to ask someone about something. (Also spelled *enquire.*)

inquiry [ɪn ˈkwaɪɚ i] **1.** *n.* a question. (Also spelled *enquiry.*) **2.** *n.* an investigation; a search for truth; a search for an answer.

inquisitive [ɪn ˈkwɪz ɪ tɪv] *adj.* asking a lot of questions; curious; eager to learn. (Adv: *inquisitively.*)

insane [ɪn ˈsen] **1.** *adj.* crazy; not sane. (Adv: *insanely.*) **2.** *adj.* owing to insanity; done because of insanity. (Adv: *insanely.*) **3.** *adj.* very stupid; very foolish; very idiotic. (Informal. Adv: *insanely.*)

insanity [ɪn ˈsæn ə ti] *n.* the state or condition of being insane. (No pl.)

230

insect ['ɪn sɛkt] **1.** *n.* a small creature with wings and six legs. **2.** *n.* a bug; any creature similar to ①.

inside 1. ['ɪn 'saɪd] *n.* the interior of a building or an object; the part of an object that is within something. **2.** [ɪn 'saɪd, 'ɪn saɪd] *adj.* interior; in, of, or about ①. **3.** [ɪn 'saɪd] *adv.* in or into a room or building; in or into an object. **4.** [ɪn 'saɪd, 'ɪn saɪd] *prep.* within a room or building; within an object; within the interior; in an interior position.

insight ['ɪn saɪt] **1.** *n.* wisdom; the ability to observe and identify things that are important. (No pl.) **2.** *n.* a statement showing that one has observed and identified something important.

insipid [ɪn 'sɪp ɪd] *adj.* boring; dull; bland; uninteresting. (Adv: *insipidly.*)

inspect [ɪn 'spɛkt] *tv.* to examine someone or something carefully.

inspection [ɪn 'spɛk ʃən] *n.* study; inspecting and reviewing. (Pl only for types and instances.)

inspire [ɪn 'spaɪr] **1.** *tv.* to influence someone to do something. **2.** *tv.* to fill someone with a certain spiritual emotion or feeling; to arouse a certain emotion in someone.

install [ɪn 'stɔl] **1.** *tv.* to set up a piece of equipment for use; to make something ready for use. **2.** *tv.* to put someone in a certain job or position.

installment [ɪn 'stɔl mənt] **1.** *n.* an episode; one part of a series of stories or reports. **2.** *n.* one of a series of payments on a debt.

instance ['ɪn stəns] *n.* an example; a case; an occurrence.

instant ['ɪn stənt] **1.** *n.* one moment in time; a very short amount of time. **2.** *adj.* immediate; without delay. (Adv: *instantly.*) **3.** *adj.* [of food or drink] easily and quickly prepared.

instantly ['ɪn stənt li] *adv.* right now; at this very moment.

instead [ɪn 'stɛd] *adv.* in place of something; as another choice.

instinct ['ɪn stɪŋkt] *n.* an ability someone or some creature is born with to act or respond in a particular way.

institution [ɪn stɪ 'tu ʃən] **1.** *n.* an organization that serves a special purpose. **2.** *n.* an established tradition; a habit; a custom.

instruct [ɪn 'strʌkt] *tv.* to teach someone something; to educate someone about something.

231

instruction [ɪn 'strʌk ʃən] **1.** *n.* education; teaching. (No pl.) **2.** *n.* an order or set of orders; a direction or set of directions. (Usually pl.)

instructor [ɪn 'strʌk tɚ] *n.* a teacher; someone who instructs people about something.

instrument ['ɪn strə mənt] **1.** *n.* a thing that is used to help someone do something; a tool; a device. **2.** *n.* something that shows a measurement. **3.** *n.* an object that produces musical notes when played.

insulate ['ɪn sə let] **1.** *tv.* to cover something with a material that prevents the passage of electricity, heat, or sound. **2.** ~ **from** to separate someone or something from other things or people by distance or a barrier. (Fig. on ①.)

insulation [ɪn sə 'le ʃən] *n.* material that prevents the passage of electricity, heat, or sound. (No pl form in this sense.)

insult [ɪn 'sʌlt] **1.** *n.* an offensive remark; a rude statement that offends someone. **2.** *tv.* to offend someone; to say something rude or offensive to someone.

insurance [ɪn 'ʃɚ əns] **1.** *n.* a contract that pays a sum of money in the case of a loss or injury. (No pl. Number is expressed with *insurance policy* or *insurance policies*.) **2.** *n.* something that protects against a loss or an injury. (No pl.) **3.** *n.* the business of writing and selling ①. (No pl.) **4.** the *adj.* use of ①, ②, or ③.

insure [ɪn 'ʃɚ] **1.** *tv.* to purchase insurance for someone or something. (Compare this with ENSURE.) **2.** *tv.* [for an insurance company] to sell insurance on someone or something.

intelligence [ɪn 'tɛl ɪ dʒəns] **1.** *n.* the level of someone's ability to learn and understand. (No pl.) **2.** *n.* information about an enemy and the enemy's plans. (No pl.) **3.** *n.* a department within a military service that gathers ②. (No pl.)

intelligent [ɪn 'tɛl ə dʒənt] *adj.* smart; able to learn and understand things well. (Adv: *intelligently*.)

intensity [ɪn 'tɛn sə ti] *n.* the degree or amount of power or strength. (Pl only for types and instances.)

intention [ɪn 'tɛn ʃən] *n.* a purpose; a plan.

intercourse ['ɪn tɚ kɔrs] *n.* copulation, usually human copulation. (Short for *sexual intercourse*.)

interest ['ɪn trəst] **1.** *n.* the attention or concern shown toward someone or something. (No pl.) **2.** *n.* something that causes ①; something that attracts one's curiosity or attention as in ⑤. **3.** *n.* the money—

232

usually a percentage of the amount borrowed—that a lender charges to someone who borrows money. (No pl.) **4.** *n.* the money—usually a percentage of the amount held—that a bank or other financial institution pays for holding someone's money for a period of time. (No pl.) **5.** *tv.* to capture the attention or curiosity of someone or something.

interested ['ɪn trəs tɪd] **1.** *adj.* involved; [of someone] dependent on the outcome or decision. **2.** ~ **(in)** curious about something; willing to hear or learn more information; willing to participate; willing to purchase.

interesting ['ɪn trəs tɪŋ] *adj.* causing interest or curiosity; worthy of interest; keeping someone's interest. (Adv: *interestingly*.)

interestingly ['ɪn trəs tɪŋ li] **1.** *adv.* in a way that causes or keeps someone's interest. **2.** *adv.* strangely; curiously.

interfere [ɪn tɚ 'fɪr] *iv.* to get involved [with something that is private or restricted].

interference [ɪn tɚ 'fɪr əns] **1.** *n.* interfering; serving as a problem; getting involved and making oneself a bother. (No pl.) **2.** *n.* an electronic disturbance that prevents the clear reception of a radio or television signal. (No pl.)

interim ['ɪn tɚ əm] *n.* the time in between events; the meantime; the meanwhile; an interval.

interior [ɪn 'tɪr i ɚ] **1.** *n.* a part or surface that is within something; a part or surface that is inside of something. **2.** *n.* the area within something; the space that is inside something. **3.** the *adj.* use of ① or ②.

interj. an abbreviation of INTERJECTION.

interjection [ɪn tɚ 'dʒɛk ʃən] *n.* a word, expression, or phrase that is used to express something with force or emotion. (Abbreviated *interj.* here.)

intermediate [ɪn tɚ 'mid i ɪt] *adj.* between two stages, levels, sizes, weights, etc. (Adv: *intermediately*.)

intermission [ɪn tɚ 'mɪ ʃən] *n.* a pause between the parts of a play, movie, opera, or other performance.

internal [ɪn 'tɚ nəl] **1.** *adj.* inside; inner. (Adv: *internally*.) **2.** *adj.* coming from within. (Adv: *internally*.) **3.** *adj.* domestic; not foreign. (Adv: *internally*.)

233

international [ɪn tɚ ˈnæʃ ə nəl] **1.** *adj.* of or about two or more countries; between two countries; among three or more countries. (Adv: *internationally.*) **2.** *adj.* global; in all nations. (Adv: *internationally.*)

Internet [ˈɪn tɚ net] *n.* a digital system of high-speed global communication and data transfer. (No pl. Not a proper noun, but usually capitalized. Can be shortened to NET.)

interpret [ɪn ˈtɚ prət] **1.** *tv.* to explain the meaning of something. **2.** *tv.* to translate what someone is saying in one language into another language.

interrog. an abbreviation of INTERROGATIVE.

interrogative [ɪn tə ˈrɑg ə tɪv] *n.* a word or expression used to ask a question. (WHO, WHAT, WHEN, WHERE, WHY, and HOW are the most common INTERROGATIVES. Abbreviated *interrog.* here.)

interrupt [ɪn tə ˈrʌpt] **1.** *iv.* to break into a conversation; to start talking while someone else is talking. **2.** *tv.* to stop the flow or movement of something; to stop something temporarily.

interruption [ɪn tə ˈrʌp ʃən] **1.** *n.* interrupting; stopping and interfering in a conversation or an activity. **2.** *n.* a break in the flow of something.

intersection [ɪn tɚ ˈsek ʃən] **1.** *n.* a junction of two or more roads, streets, highways, etc.; a place where roads or streets come together or cross. **2.** *n.* the point at which two or more things join.

interval [ˈɪn tɚ vəl] **1.** *n.* a period of time between two events. **2.** *n.* the distance between two points in a series of points. **3.** *n.* the distance between two musical tones.

interview [ˈɪn tɚ vju] **1.** *n.* a meeting between an employer and a job seeker, where the employer asks questions of the job seeker. **2.** *n.* a meeting where a reporter asks questions of someone. **3.** *tv.* to ask questions of someone, possibly about employment; to make direct inquiries of someone. **4.** *tv.* to ask questions of someone for a television or radio program, a newspaper or magazine article, etc.

intestine [ɪn ˈtes tɪn] *n.* the tube or channel between the stomach and the rectum. (Often pl with the same meaning.)

intimate **1.** [ˈɪn tə mɪt] *adj.* close; very personal; private. (Adv: *intimately.*) **2.** [ˈɪn tə mɪt] *adj.* [of a place] quiet, private, friendly, and inviting. (Adv: *intimately.*) **3.** [ˈɪn tə met] *tv.* to hint something; to suggest something. (Takes a clause.)

into [ˈɪn tu] **1.** *prep.* to the inner part of something; to the interior of something. **2.** *prep.* up against someone or something. **3.** *prep.* interested in something. (Informal.)

introduce [ɪn trə ˈdus] *tv.* to establish something; to bring something into use; to make something known or familiar to someone.

introduction [ɪn trə ˈdʌk ʃən] **1.** *n.* an instance of presenting one person to another person. **2.** *n.* making the availability of something known to people. **3.** *n.* the part of a book, chapter, or lecture that comes at the beginning and explains its purpose. **4.** *n.* the basic and important information about a subject.

intrusion [ɪn ˈtru ʒən] **1.** *n.* entering into a situation where one is not wanted; a visit that is not welcome. **2.** *n.* breaking into a house or other building.

invalid 1. [ˈɪn və lɪd] *n.* someone who is weak because of sickness. **2.** [ˈɪn və lɪd] *adj.* the *adj.* use of ①. **3.** [ɪn ˈvæl ɪd] *adj.* not valid; useless; worthless. (Adv: *invalidly.*)

invasion [ɪn ˈve ʒən] **1.** *n.* a military attack. **2.** *n.* the attack and spread of something bad or dangerous. (Fig. on ①.)

invent [ɪn ˈvɛnt] **1.** *tv.* to create something that has never been made before. **2.** *tv.* to make up a story, an excuse, or a lie. (Fig. on ①.)

invention [ɪn ˈvɛn ʃən] **1.** *n.* the creation of a new device; the production of a new machine or a new process. (No pl.) **2.** *n.* a new device; something that has been created for the first time.

inventor [ɪn ˈvɛn tɚ] *n.* someone who INVENTS ① something; someone who has invented something.

inventory [ˈɪn vən tor i] **1.** *n.* goods and supplies on hand or stored in a warehouse; stock waiting to be sold. (No pl form.) **2.** *n.* a list showing the number of each item that has been packed, received, shipped, etc.

investigate [ɪn ˈvɛs tə get] *tv.* to conduct an investigation; to try to find the facts of something.

investment [ɪn ˈvɛst mənt] *n.* money that is assigned to a project, stocks, a bank account, etc., with the hope and expectation of profit.

investor [ɪn ˈvɛs tɚ] *n.* someone who puts money into an investment.

invisible [ɪn ˈvɪz ə bəl] *adj.* not visible; unable to be seen; not seen and imaginary. (Adv: *invisibly.*)

invitation [ɪn vɪ ˈte ʃən] *n.* a written, printed, or spoken statement asking someone to attend an event or to do something.

235

invite [ɪn 'vɑɪt] **1.** *tv.* to request someone to attend an event; to ask someone to come for a visit; to ask someone to join in doing something. **2.** *tv.* to tempt something to happen; to provoke something to happen, especially disaster or trouble. (Fig. on ①.)

invoice ['ɪn vɔɪs] **1.** *n.* a bill; a document showing how much money is owed for goods or services. **2.** *tv.* to present someone or a business firm with ①.

involve [ɪn 'vɑlv] *tv.* to include someone or something; to make someone or something a part of something.

irk ['ɚk] *tv.* to annoy, upset, or irritate someone.

iron ['ɑɪɚn] **1.** *n.* an element that is a common metal, used to make steel. (No pl.) **2.** *n.* a small device with a flat metal bottom, heated and used to press the wrinkles out of cloth. **3.** *adj.* made from ①. **4.** *tv.* to smooth the wrinkles out of clothes with ②.

irony ['ɑɪ rə ni] **1.** *n.* using words in a funny or sarcastic way to create a meaning opposite from their combined literal meaning. (No pl.) **2.** *n.* an event that has the opposite result of what was planned or expected.

irradiate [ɪ 'red i et] *tv.* to treat something with radiation; to treat food with radiation to keep it from spoiling.

irreg. an abbreviation of IRREGULAR ④.

irregular [ɪr 'rɛg jə lɚ] **1.** *adj.* not regular; oddly shaped; uneven. (Adv: *irregularly.*) **2.** *adj.* happening at differing intervals of time; not happening regularly. (Adv: *irregularly.*) **3.** *adj.* different from what is normal, and therefore unacceptable. (Euphemistic.) **4.** *adj.* [of the form of a noun, verb, adjective, or adverb] not regular in the way it changes form, such as with the pl, pt, comp, or sup. (Abbreviated *irreg.* here. Adv: *irregularly.*)

irrigate ['ɪr ə get] *tv.* to supply land or crops with water; to bring water to land or crops.

irritate ['ɪr ɪ tet] **1.** *tv.* to cause a part of the body to become red or swollen. **2.** *tv.* to bother or annoy someone or something.

irritation [ɪr ɪ 'te ʃən] **1.** *n.* a bother; something that irritates. **2.** *n.* the condition of being sore or itchy; soreness or tenderness of skin or other body tissues. (Pl only for types and instances.)

is [ɪz] *iv.* a form of BE, used in the pres. tense of the third-person sg, that is, with *he, she, it,* and sg nouns. (Reduced to *'s* in contractions.)

island ['ɑɪ lənd] **1.** *n.* a piece of land surrounded by water and smaller than a continent. **2.** *n.* something that is completely surrounded by something else. (Fig. on ①.)

isle ['ɑɪl] *n.* an island.

isn't ['ɪz ənt] *cont.* is not.

isolate ['ɑɪ sə let] *tv.* to keep someone or something separate from other people or things; to separate someone or something from other people or things.

isolation [ɑɪ sə 'le ʃən] *n.* the state of being isolated; keeping someone or something away from other people or things. (No pl.)

issue ['ɪ ʃu] **1.** *n.* one of a set of publications that are available regularly. **2.** *n.* the number of stamps or magazines printed at one time. **3.** *n.* a topic; the topic being discussed; a concern. **4.** *tv.* to assign something to someone; to supply something to someone. **5.** *tv.* to speak or utter a command; to deliver or publish a written command or order. **6.** *tv.* to publish a magazine, bulletin, newsletter, or newspaper.

it [ɪt] **1.** *pron.* a form referring to something that is not human; a form referring to a plant, an animal, or something that is not living. (However, IT is sometimes used to refer to a baby or a small child. See also ITS and ITSELF. The pl is THEY.) **2.** *pron.* a form used as the subject of a sentence where there is no real actor or doer. (Usually with the verb BE, but with others also.) **3.** *n.* the player who must find or chase everyone else in various children's games.

italic [ɪ 'tæl ɪk] **1.** *adj.* [of letters] slanted; printed with slanted letters. **2.** ~s *n.* slanted printing. (Treated as sg or pl.)

itch ['ɪtʃ] **1.** *n.* a feeling on the skin that makes one want to scratch. **2.** *iv.* [for the skin] to have ①.

itchy ['ɪtʃ i] *adj.* with the feeling of itching; constantly itching. (Comp: *itchier*; sup: *itchiest*.)

it'd ['ɪt ɪd] **1.** *cont.* it would. **2.** *cont.* it had, where HAD is an auxiliary.

item ['ɑɪ təm] *n.* one thing that is part of a list or a series; a unit; a piece of information; a piece of news.

it'll ['ɪt əl] *cont.* it will.

it's ['ɪts] **1.** *cont.* it is. (Compare this with ITS.) **2.** *cont.* it has. (This HAS is an auxiliary. Compare this with ITS.)

its ['ɪts] *pron.* the possessive form of IT; belonging to it. (Compare this with IT's.)

237

itself [ɪt 'sɛlf] **1.** *pron.* the reflexive form of ɪᴛ. **2.** *pron.* an emphatic form of ɪᴛ. (Follows the nominal that is being emphasized.)

iv. an abbreviation of *intransitive verb.*

I've ['ɑɪv] *cont.* I have. (This ʜᴀᴠᴇ is an auxiliary.)

ivory ['ɑɪ vri] **1.** *n.* the hard, white substance of which an elephant's tusk is made. (No pl.) **2.** *n.* the color of ①. **3.** the *adj.* use of ① or ②.

ivy ['ɑɪv i] *n.* a plant that holds onto walls, trees, etc., and climbs as it grows. (Pl only for types and instances.)

J

jack ['dʒæk] **1.** *n.* a device used to lift heavy things off the ground, especially to push up a car wheel in order to change a tire. **2.** *n.* [in a deck of playing cards] a card that has a picture of a young man on it and is signified by the letter *J*.

jacket ['dʒæk ɪt] **1.** *n.* a light coat; the light coat that is part of a suit. **2.** *n.* a covering for a book or a sound recording.

jail ['dʒel] **1.** *n.* a building where criminals are locked up or where people are locked up while waiting for a trial. **2.** *tv.* to put someone in ①; to order someone to spend time in ①.

jam ['dʒæm] **1.** *n.* a sweet food made by boiling fruit and sugar until it is thick. (Pl only for types and instances.) **2.** *tv.* to cause something to become stuck; to force something to fit someplace. **3.** *iv.* to become stuck; to be unable to work properly because something is stuck; to be unable to move because something is stuck.

janitor ['dʒæn ɪ tɚ] *n.* someone who cleans and takes care of a building.

January ['dʒæn ju ɛr ɪ] Go to MONTH.

jar ['dʒɑr] **1.** *n.* a container with a wide, circular top, usually made of glass or clay, and usually without handles. **2.** *n.* the contents of ①. **3.** *tv.* to hit (lightly) or shake someone or something.

jaw ['dʒɔ] **1.** *n.* the upper or lower bones that form the mouth and support the teeth. **2.** *n.* one of the two parts of a device that holds something tight, such as a vise or pliers.

jawbone ['dʒɔ bon] *n.* the upper or especially, the lower bones that form the mouth and support the teeth.

jazz ['dʒæz] **1.** *n.* a style of music characterized by its rhythms, harmony, and the creative ways its players work together while it is being played. (No pl.) **2.** the *adj.* use of ①.

jealous ['dʒɛl əs] *adj.* not liking anyone who, one believes, might try to take away one's things or the people one loves. (Adv: *jealously*.)

jealousy ['dʒɛl ə si] *n.* the condition of being jealous; not liking someone who has something one wants. (No pl.)

jeans ['dʒinz] *n.* a pair of cloth pants, often dark blue, made of sturdy material. (Treated as pl. Number is expressed by *pair(s) of jeans*.)

jelly ['dʒɛl i] **1.** *n.* a soft food that is made by boiling fruit juice and sugar together and is often spread on bread. (Pl only for types and instances.) **2.** *adj.* made with ①.

jeopardy ['dʒɛp ɚ di] *n.* a state of risk or hazard.

jerk ['dʒɚk] **1.** *n.* a sudden push or pull of the muscles; a movement made when something starts or stops quickly. **2.** *tv.* to push or pull someone or something suddenly. **3.** *iv.* to move with ①; make a movement like ①.

jest ['dʒɛst] **1.** *n.* a joke; a statement or action said or done in fun. **2.** *iv.* to make jokes.

jet ['dʒɛt] **1.** *n.* a stream of air, water, steam, or another fluid that is shot out from a small opening at high pressure. **2.** *n.* an airplane that moves at high speed using engines similar to a rocket. (Short for *jet plane.*) **3.** *iv.* [for water, steam, or another fluid] to form a stream by being forced out of a small opening under pressure. **4.** *iv.* to travel by ②. **5.** *tv.* to cause water, steam, or another fluid to form a stream by forcing it out of a small opening under pressure.

jet-black ['dʒɛt 'blæk] *adj.* deep, shiny black in color.

jewel ['dʒu əl] *n.* a gem; a valuable stone; a piece of jewelry.

jeweler ['dʒu (ə) lɚ] *n.* someone who deals in watches, valuable gems, and precious metals.

jewelry ['dʒu (ə)l ri] *n.* objects usually made of valuable metals or stones, such as rings, earrings, necklaces, bracelets, and pins. (No pl. Treated as sg. Number is expressed with *piece(s) of jewelry*.)

jiggle ['dʒɪg əl] **1.** *tv.* to move someone or something up and down or from side to side. **2.** *iv.* to move up and down or from side to side.

jingle ['dʒɪŋ gəl] **1.** *n.* the ringing noise of metal objects gently hitting together; the noise of a small bell being struck. **2.** *n.* a tune or song used in advertising. **3.** *tv.* to make ringing noises by hitting metal objects together. **4.** *iv.* [for metal objects] to make noises when struck together; [for a small bell] to make a noise when shaken.

job ['dʒɑb] **1.** *n.* a career; an occupation; regular employment. **2.** *n.* a task; a duty; a responsibility; a piece of work. **3.** *n.* the performance or result of one's work.

240

jog ['dʒɔg] **1.** *n.* a slow, gentle run usually done for exercise; a [human] trot. **2.** *n.* a bend to the right or the left; something that causes a line not to be straight. **3.** *iv.* to exercise by running slowly.

jogger ['dʒɔg ɚ] *n.* someone who exercises by jogging.

join ['dʒɔɪn] **1.** *iv.* to come together; to connect; to unite. **2.** *tv.* to connect someone or something to someone or something else; to unite people or things into a single unit. **3.** *tv.* to enroll in a club, class, the military, or some other organization; to become a member of an organization.

joint ['dʒɔɪnt] **1.** *n.* a place where two things, especially bones, join. **2.** *adj.* done or owned together; joined; united. (Adv: *jointly.*)

joke ['dʒok] **1.** *n.* something said or done to make people laugh, especially a short story told to make people laugh. **2.** *tv.* to say something in a teasing or playful manner; to say something that is meant to be funny. (The object is a clause with THAT ⑦.) **3.** *iv.* to tell ①; to kid or tease [someone]; to say or do things that are meant to be funny.

jolly ['dʒɑl i] *adj.* very happy; very cheerful. (Comp: *jollier;* sup: *jolliest.*)

jostle ['dʒɑs əl] **1.** *tv.* to bump into someone, especially in a crowd. **2.** *iv.* to move somewhere quickly, especially through a crowded area, while bumping into people or pushing people out of the way.

journal ['dʒɚ nl] **1.** *n.* a diary; a book where one writes down one's feelings, thoughts, or activities. **2.** *n.* a magazine, periodical, or scholarly publication.

journey ['dʒɚn i] **1.** *n.* a trip; a voyage. **2.** *iv.* to travel.

joy ['dʒɔɪ] **1.** *n.* extreme pleasure or happiness. (No pl.) **2.** *n.* someone or something that causes extreme pleasure or happiness.

joyful ['dʒɔɪ fəl] **1.** *adj.* [of someone] full of joy; extremely happy; very glad. (Adv: *joyfully.*) **2.** *adj.* [for something] causing joy; causing extreme happiness.

joyous ['dʒɔɪ əs] *adj.* full of joy; extremely happy; very glad. (Adv: *joyously.*)

judge ['dʒʌdʒ] **1.** *n.* an official who hears and settles cases in a court of law and who presides over trials. **2.** *n.* someone who helps decide the winner of a contest or competition. **3.** *tv.* to hear and settle a case in a court of law; to preside over a trial in a court of law. **4.** *tv.* to help decide the winner of a contest or competition. **5.** *tv.* to state an opinion about someone or something; to evaluate someone or something.

6. *tv.* to estimate something; to make a guess that something will happen. (The object is a clause with THAT ⑦.)

judgment ['dʒʌdʒ mənt] **1.** *n.* the ability to make the proper decisions; the ability to judge. (No pl.) **2.** *n.* the result of judging; the decision made by a judge or a jury. **3.** *n.* an opinion. (No pl.)

juggle ['dʒʌg əl] **1.** *tv.* to keep three or more objects moving through the air by catching and throwing them in a circle. **2.** *tv.* to deal with several things at the same time. **3.** *iv.* to toss objects in the air as in ①.

juice ['dʒus] *n.* the liquid part of fruit, vegetables, or meat. (Pl only for types and instances.)

July [dʒə 'laɪ] Go to MONTH.

jumble ['dʒʌm bəl] **1.** *tv.* to mix things up; to cause things to be out of order. **2.** *n.* a group of things that are mixed up; a group of things that are out of order.

jumbo ['dʒʌm bo] *adj.* extra large; larger than regular.

jump ['dʒʌmp] **1.** *iv.* to leap up; to spring up; to push off the ground with one's legs. **2.** *iv.* to move suddenly, as if surprised or scared. **3.** *iv.* to go up sharply; to increase sharply; to rise sharply. (Fig. on ①.) **4.** *tv.* to start a car by connecting its battery to another car's battery. **5.** *n.* a leap off the ground; a leap off the ground and over, through, or across something. **6.** *n.* a sudden rise; an increase. (Fig. on ⑤.)

junction ['dʒʌŋk ʃən] *n.* a place where two or more things come together, especially the place where roads or train tracks come together or cross.

June ['dʒun] Go to MONTH.

jungle ['dʒʌŋ gəl] *n.* a tropical forest of thick, lush plant growth, usually near the equator.

junior ['dʒun jɚ] **1.** *n.* someone who is younger or who has a lower rank or position than someone else. **2.** *n.* a student in the third year of high school (11th grade) or the third year of college. **3.** *adj.* of or about someone who is younger or who has a lower rank or position. **4.** *adj.* of or about the third year of high school or college. (Prenominal only.)

junk ['dʒʌŋk] **1.** *n.* things that are worthless; things that should be thrown away. (No pl.) **2.** *tv.* to throw something away.

jury ['dʒɚ i] **1.** *n.* a group of people who listen to evidence at a trial in a court of law and make a decision about the truth of the facts of the case. **2.** the *adj.* use of ①.

just ['dʒʌst] **1.** *adj.* fair; not biased; honest; right; in accordance with the law. (Adv: *justly.*) **2.** *adj.* as someone deserves; appropriate. (Adv: *justly.*) **3.** *adv.* only. **4.** *adv.* barely; by a small amount. **5.** *adv.* exactly [the right amount and no more].

justice ['dʒʌs tɪs] **1.** *n.* the quality or condition of being just; fairness, especially in a court of law. (No pl.) **2.** *n.* the administration of law; the practice of law within the court system. (No pl.) **3.** *n.* a judge. (Also a title and term of address.)

justify ['dʒʌs tɪ faɪ] *tv.* to explain why one did something; to give a good reason for something.

jut out ['dʒʌt aʊt] to stick out from something.

juvenile ['dʒu və naɪl] **1.** *n.* a child [from a legal point of view]. **2.** *n.* a young animal. **3.** *adj.* youthful; for young people.

K

kangaroo [kæŋ gə 'ru] *n.* a large animal of Australia that hops on its hind legs. (Pl ends in -s.)

keel ['kil] *n.* the main beam along the bottom of a boat or ship on which the frame is built.

keen ['kin] **1.** *adj.* [of a cutting edge] sharp. (Adv: *keenly.* Comp: *keener;* sup: *keenest.*) **2.** *adj.* [of a sense of taste, vision, hearing, touch, or smell] very sensitive or sharp. (Fig. on ①. Adv: *keenly.* Comp: *keener;* sup: *keenest.*)

keep ['kip] **1.** *tv., irreg.* to cause someone or something to remain somewhere. (Pt/pp: KEPT.) **2.** *tv., irreg.* to have something for a period of time; to continue to have something. **3.** *iv.* to continue to do something.

keeper ['kip ɚ] *n.* someone who keeps someone or something; a protector; a guard; someone who cares for animals in a zoo. (See also ZOOKEEPER.)

keepsake ['kip sek] *n.* something that is kept to remind the owner of someone or something; a memento.

keg ['kɛg] **1.** *n.* a small wooden barrel, especially one that holds 100 pounds of nails. **2.** *n.* a small metal barrel, especially one that holds beer.

kennel ['kɛn əl] *n.* a place where dogs are kept.

kept ['kɛpt] pt/pp of KEEP.

ketchup AND **catsup** ['kɛtʃ əp, 'kæt səp] *n.* a thick liquid, made from tomatoes, that is put on food for flavoring. (Pl only for types and instances.)

kettle ['kɛt əl] *n.* a large cooking pot; a pot for heating liquids.

key ['ki] **1.** *n.* a device that unlocks or locks a lock; something that unlocks something that is locked. **2.** *n.* something that gives access to an answer or a solution; something that provides the answers or solutions for something. (Fig. on ①.) **3.** *n.* a part of a machine or instrument that is pressed down to make something happen, as on a computer keyboard, a typewriter, or a piano. **4.** *n.* a musical scale that begins on a particular note; a set of related musical notes. **5.** *adj.* important; essential; basic.

244

keyboard ['ki bord] **1.** *n.* a row of keys that make a certain musical sound when pressed. **2.** *n.* an electronic device that creates music. **3.** *n.* the rows of keys standing for letters, symbols, and numbers as found on typewriters, computers, etc.

keynote ['ki not] *adj.* [of a speech or a speaker] primary or main. (Prenominal only.)

keypad ['ki pæd] **1.** *n.* [on a computer] a special, separate set of number keys arranged as on a calculator. **2.** *n.* any small control panel having an arrangement of push buttons, as found on a telephone or a calculator.

kick ['kɪk] **1.** *tv.* to strike someone or something with the foot, usually the toe of a shoe or boot. **2.** *iv.* to move one's legs back and forth as if KICKING something as in ①. **3.** *n.* an act of striking someone or something with the foot, as in ①.

kid ['kɪd] **1.** *n.* a child; a youngster. (Informal.) **2.** *n.* a baby goat. **3.** *n.* the skin of ②. (No pl.) **4.** *tv.* to tease someone; to joke with someone; to trick someone. **5.** *adj.* [of a brother or sister] younger. (Informal. Prenominal only.)

kidnap ['kɪd næp] *tv.* to take someone away by force, especially in order to make a demand for something; to abduct someone. (Pt/pp: *kidnapped*.)

kidney ['kɪd ni] **1.** *n.* one of the two organs that separate waste and water from the bloodstream, creating urine. **2.** the *adj.* use of ①.

kill ['kɪl] **1.** *tv.* to cause the death of someone or something directly. **2.** *tv.* to end something; to cause something to end. (Fig. on ①.) **3.** *iv.* to cause death. **4.** *n.* an animal that is hunted and KILLED as in ①. (No pl.)

killer ['kɪl ɚ] *n.* someone or something that kills; someone or something that causes death.

kilogram ['kɪl ə græm] *n.* a metric unit of weight, equal to 1,000 grams or about 2.2 pounds.

kilometer [kɪ 'lɑm ə tɚ] *n.* a metric unit of distance, equal to 1,000 meters or about ⅝ of a mile.

kilowatt ['kɪl ə wɑt] *n.* a metric unit of electrical power, equal to 1,000 watts per hour.

kin ['kɪn] *n.* family; relatives. (No pl form. Treated as pl.)

kind ['kɑɪnd] **1.** *n.* a sort; a type; a variety. **2.** *adj.* thoughtful; helpful. (Adv: *kindly*. Comp: *kinder;* sup: *kindest*.)

kindergarten [ˈkɪn dɚ gɑrd n] *n.* the grade before first grade, usually for children between the ages of 4 and 6.

kindle [ˈkɪnd əl] **1.** *tv.* to set fire to something; to set something on fire. (Fig. on ①.) **2.** *tv.* to cause something to happen; to bring something into action. (Fig. on ①.) **3.** *iv.* to catch fire.

kindness [ˈkɑɪnnəs] *n.* the quality of being kind; politeness and caring.

king [ˈkɪŋ] **1.** *n.* the male ruler of a nation where the head of the country inherits his office from a previous ruler. **2.** *n.* a playing card with a picture of ① on it. **3.** *n.* a playing piece in chess that can move one space in any direction.

kingdom [ˈkɪŋ dəm] **1.** *n.* a country ruled by a king or queen. **2.** *n.* one of three kinds of life forms—such as the animal or plant KINGDOM.

kiss [ˈkɪs] **1.** *n.* a touching of one's lips to someone or something, especially someone else's lips. **2.** *tv.* to touch one's lips to someone or something, especially someone else's lips. **3.** *iv.* [for two people] to KISS each other on the lips, as in ②.

kit [ˈkɪt] **1.** *n.* a container or carrying device that holds tools, equipment, or supplies for a specific purpose. **2.** *n.* the parts and instructions needed to build a particular thing, such as a model airplane.

kitchen [ˈkɪtʃ ən] **1.** *n.* a room where food is stored and cooked. **2.** the *adj.* use of ①.

kite [ˈkɑɪt] *n.* a small wooden frame covered with cloth, paper, or plastic and attached to a long string—flown in the wind for amusement.

kitten [ˈkɪt n] *n.* a baby cat; a young cat.

knead [ˈnid] **1.** *tv.* to mix something together by squeezing it with one's hands. **2.** *tv.* to massage a muscle. (Fig. on ①.)

knee [ˈni] **1.** *n.* the front part of the joint in the middle of the leg. **2.** *n.* the part of a pants leg that covers ①.

kneecap [ˈni kæp] *n.* the flat bone at the front of the knee.

kneel [ˈnil] *iv., irreg.* to put the weight of one's body on one or both knees. (Pt/pp: *kneeled* or KNELT.)

knelt [ˈnɛlt] a pt/pp of KNEEL.

knew [ˈnu] pt of KNOW.

knife [ˈnɑɪf] **1.** *n., irreg.* a long, flat utensil or tool that has a handle and a sharp edge used for cutting. (Pl: KNIVES.) **2.** *tv.* to stab someone or something.

knit ['nɪt] *tv.* to make a fabric or clothing by using long needles to loop yarn or thread together.

knives ['naɪvz] pl of KNIFE.

knob ['nɑb] *n.* a round handle or control button.

knock ['nɑk] **1.** *iv.* to hit one's knuckles against something. **2.** *n.* the noise made by rapping or tapping as with ①. **3.** *n.* a sharp hit; a rap; a thump. **4.** *tv.* to hit or bump something and make it move or fall; to hit something against someone or something.

knot ['nɑt] **1.** *n.* a tight lump made where pieces of rope, cord, hair, string, etc., are tied together. **2.** *n.* a hard circle of wood in a board, where a small branch was joined. **3.** *n.* a unit of speed equal to 1.15 miles per hour, used to measure the movement of ships and wind at sea. **4.** *tv.* to tie something with ①; to fasten something with ①. **5.** *iv.* to become tied or twisted into ①.

know ['no] **1.** *tv., irreg.* to have met and become familiar with someone. (Pt: KNEW; pp: KNOWN.) **2.** *tv., irreg.* to understand something; to have had experience with something. **3.** *tv., irreg.* to recognize someone or something. **4.** *tv., irreg.* to have knowledge about someone or something; to have information about someone or something. (The object can be a clause with THAT ⑦.)

know-how knowledge and skill. (Informal.)

knowledge ['nɑl ɪdʒ] *n.* the information that is known about someone or something. (No pl.)

known ['non] pp of KNOW.

knuckle ['nʌk əl] *n.* the joint between the bones of a finger or the joint between a finger and the hand.

L

lab ['læb] *n.* LABORATORY.

label ['leb əl] **1.** *n.* a small notice bearing important information. **2.** *tv.* to attach ① to something.

labor ['leb ɚ] **1.** *n.* a kind of work, especially hard, physical work. (No pl.) **2.** *n.* workers, especially in contrast to people in management. (No pl. Treated as sg.) **3.** *n.* the work a woman's body does to bring about birth; the contractions of the womb in the process of giving birth. (No pl.) **4.** the *adj.* use of ①, ②, or ③. **5.** *iv.* to work hard.

laboratory ['læb rə tor i] **1.** *n.* a room or building that contains scientific equipment for experiments, tests, manufacture, or instruction. (Often shortened to LAB.) **2.** the *adj.* use of ①.

lace ['les] **1.** *n.* a delicate web of cotton or other thread woven into a design or pattern. (No pl.) **2.** *n.* a string used for tying something closed, especially for tying one's shoes closed; a SHOELACE. **3.** *adj.* made of ①.

lack ['læk] **1.** *n.* a shortage of something; the condition of not having any of something. **2.** *tv.* to need something; not to have enough of something; to be without something.

lacy ['les i] **1.** *adj.* made of lace. (Adv: *lacily.* Comp: *lacier;* sup: *laciest.*) **2.** *adj.* delicate and complex like lace; having a delicate pattern. (Fig. on ①. Adv: *lacily.* Comp: *lacier;* sup: *laciest.*)

ladder ['læd ɚ] *n.* a set of steps attached to two side pieces, used for climbing up to reach something or climbing down from something.

ladle ['led l] **1.** *n.* a large, deep spoon with a long handle, used for serving a liquid from a bowl. **2.** *tv.* to serve a liquid using ①.

lady ['led i] **1.** *n.* a refined woman. (Compare this with GENTLEMAN.) **2.** *n.* a woman. (Also a term of address.)

lag ['læg] *n.* a delay; the period of time between the end of one event and the start of another.

laid ['led] pt/pp of LAY.

lain ['len] a pp of LIE ③.

lair ['lɛr] *n.* an animal's shelter; the place where an animal sleeps.

lake ['lek] *n.* a large body of water surrounded by land.

248

lamb ['læm] **1.** *n.* a young sheep. **2.** *n.* the meat of ① used as food. (No pl.)

lame ['lem] *adj.* not able to walk properly; limping; crippled. (Adv: *lamely.* Comp: *lamer;* sup: *lamest.*)

lamp ['læmp] **1.** *n.* a device that makes light; an electric light bulb. **2.** *n.* a stand—often ornamental—that holds an electric light bulb.

lamppost ['læmp post] *n.* a post that supports a street light.

lampshade ['læmp ʃed] *n.* a cover that fits over the electric light bulb in a lamp to soften the glare of the light.

land ['lænd] **1.** *n.* the dry, solid part of the earth's surface; the part of the earth's surface that is not covered with water. (No pl.) **2.** *n.* ground; dirt; soil. (No pl.) **3.** *n.* a portion of ①; an area of ground. (No pl.) **4.** *n.* a country. **5.** *iv.* [for someone or something that is moving or falling through the air] to stop and come to rest somewhere, especially on the ground. **6.** *iv.* [for an airplane] to return to the ground safely. **7.** *tv.* [for a pilot] to return an airplane to the ground safely.

landing ['læn dɪŋ] *n.* [an airplane's] coming to earth; [a pilot's] act of bringing a plane to earth.

landlady ['lænd led i] *n.* a woman who owns and rents out space where people can live, such as houses and apartments; a woman who manages residential rental property. (See also LANDLORD.)

landlord ['lænd lord] *n.* a person or a company that manages and collects rent for houses, apartments, and offices.

landscape ['lænd skep] **1.** *n.* the land and the things visible on it, such as trees, bodies of water, rocks, hills, etc. (Pl only for types and instances.) **2.** *n.* a painting or drawing of the land or other outdoor scenes. **3.** *tv.* to arrange flowers, trees, bushes, hills, rocks, and other objects to make a yard or park look beautiful.

lane ['len] **1.** *n.* a road, path, or route. **2.** *n.* a section of a road wide enough for one line of traffic; a section of a running track wide enough for one person to run; a division of a swimming pool wide enough for one person to swim.

language ['læŋ gwɪdʒ] **1.** *n.* the system of spoken and written symbols used by people to express thoughts, meaning, and emotions. (Pl only for types and instances.) **2.** *n.* any system of symbols used in a computer program. **3.** *n.* a specific style of expression. (No pl.)

lantern ['læn tɚn] *n.* a protective case with clear sides, containing a source of light.

lap ['læp] **1.** *n.* the flat surface formed by the tops of the upper legs when someone is sitting. **2.** *n.* one trip around a track; two lengths of a swimming pool. **3.** *iv.* [for water] to move in small waves, making a gently splashing noise.

lapel [lə 'pɛl] *n.* on a coat or jacket, one of the flaps that is folded back toward the shoulders, just below the collar.

lapse ['læps] **1.** *n.* a brief failure; a small mistake. **2.** *n.* the period of time it takes for something to happen; the passing of time. **3.** *n.* the return to one's bad habits or actions after a period of not doing them. **4.** *iv.* [for something to expire] because it was not used or renewed by a certain time. **5.** *iv.* to fail at an attempt to reform (oneself) and return to one's old bad habits or actions.

large ['lɑrdʒ] **1.** *adj.* greater in size than average; more than average; big. (Comp: *larger;* sup: *largest.*) **2.** *n.* an object, especially one for sale, that is ① in size.

largely ['lɑrdʒ li] *adv.* primarily; mainly.

lash ['læʃ] **1.** *n.* a blow from a whip. **2.** *n.* an EYELASH. **3.** *tv.* to hit someone or something with a whip. **4.** *tv.* to tie someone or something [to something]; to bind someone or something.

last ['læst] **1.** *adj.* final; at the end; after all other people or things. (Adv: *lastly.*) **2.** *adj.* the most recent; nearest in the past; latest. **3.** *adj.* least likely; least appropriate. **4.** *iv.* to continue for a length of time; to remain; to endure.

latch ['lætʃ] **1.** *n.* a device for holding a door or window closed; a lock for a door or window that can be locked and unlocked with a key. **2.** *tv.* to close a door or window so that the LATCH as in ① seizes and holds the door or window closed firmly. **3.** *iv.* [for ①] to seize and hold [something]; [for something] to close firmly with ①.

late ['let] **1.** *adj.* not on time; past the time that something is supposed to happen; past the time that someone or something is to be in a place. (Comp: *later;* sup: *latest.*) **2.** *adj.* far into a certain period of time; toward the end of a certain period of time. **3.** *adj.* no longer living; dead, especially having died recently; now dead. (Prenominal only.) **4.** *adv.* after the time that something is supposed to happen.

lately ['let li] *adv.* recently.

later ['let ɚ] *adv.* at a time after the present time; at a future time.

250

lather ['læð ɚ] **1.** *n.* white foam that is made by mixing soap with water. (No pl.) **2.** *tv.* to cover something with ①.

laugh ['læf] **1.** *iv.* to express pleasure or amusement by making short, happy sounds with the voice. **2.** *n.* the noise that someone makes when amused, as in ①.

laughter ['læf tɚ] *n.* the sound(s) made when people laugh. (No pl. Treated as sg.)

launch ['lɔntʃ] **1.** *tv.* to set a new boat or ship into the water for the first time. **2.** *tv.* to send a rocket or its cargo into the air. **3.** *tv.* to begin a project; to start carrying out a plan. (Fig. on ①.) **4.** *n.* an instance of sending something as in ① or ②.

launder ['lɔn dɚ] *tv.* to wash clothes or fabric; to wash and iron clothes or fabric.

laundry ['lɔn dri] **1.** *n.* clothes that need to be washed; clothes that have just been washed and dried. (No pl.) **2.** *n.* a business where clothes can be taken to be washed. **3.** *n.* a location in a house or apartment building where clothes are washed.

lavatory ['læv ə tor i] **1.** *n.* a sink used for washing one's hands; a wash basin with running water available. **2.** *n.* a bathroom; a room with a toilet. (Euphemistic.)

lavish ['læv ɪʃ] *adj.* in or involving large amounts; grand and excessive. (Adv: *lavishly.*)

law ['lɔ] **1.** *n.* a rule; a statement of obligation within a legal system. **2.** *n.* a principle that describes something that happens as a regularity in mathematics or the natural world. **3.** *n.* the study of the system of LAWS as in ①. (No pl.)

lawful ['lɔ fʊl] *adj.* legal; permitted by law; sanctioned by law. (Adv: *lawfully.*)

lawn ['lɔn] *n.* an area of ground with cut grass; a yard.

lawsuit ['lɔ sut] *n.* a claim or complaint brought into a court of law. (Can be shortened to SUIT.)

lawyer ['lɔ jɚ] *n.* someone who is trained in law and is a member of the bar.

lax ['læks] *adj.* loose; not strict; not demanding. (Adv: *laxly.* Comp: *laxer;* sup: *laxest.*)

lay ['le] **1.** a pt of LIE. **2.** *adj.* not trained in a profession, such as law or medicine; not ordained as a religious leader. **3.** *tv., irreg.* to place something on a surface or in a flat position. (Compare this with ④

251

and LIE ③. Pt/pp: LAID.) **4.** *tv., irreg.* [for a hen] to produce and deposit an egg.

layer ['leɚ] *n.* a level; one level of thickness that is placed on a surface.

lazy ['lez i] **1.** *adj.* doing almost no work; avoiding work. (Adv: *lazily.* Comp: *lazier;* sup: *laziest.*) **2.** *adj.* moving slowly. (Fig. on ①. Adv: *lazily.* Comp: *lazier;* sup: *laziest.*)

lead 1. ['lɛd] *n.* a heavy, soft, grayish metallic element. (No pl.) **2.** ['lid] *n.* a clue; a hint; information that can be used to help solve a crime. **3.** ['lid] *n.* the distance or amount by which someone or something is ahead of someone or something else, especially in a race or contest. **4.** ['lid] *n.* the main role in a movie or play. **5.** ['lid] *tv., irreg.* to guide someone or something; to show someone or something the way. (Pt/pp: LED.) **6.** ['lid] *tv., irreg.* to be the leader of someone or something; to be in charge of someone or something. **7.** ['lid] *tv., irreg.* to be ahead of another team or other players in a competition. **8.** ['lid] *iv., irreg.* to guide; to show the way.

leader ['lidɚ] *n.* a ruler; someone who leads or is in charge of a group of people.

leaf ['lif] **1.** *n., irreg.* the flat, usually green, part of a tree or plant that is attached to a branch or stem. (Pl: LEAVES.) **2.** *n., irreg.* an extra section that can be placed in the top of a table to make it larger.

leafy ['lif i] *adj.* having a lot of leaves; covered with leaves. (Comp: *leafier;* sup: *leafiest.*)

league ['lig] **1.** *n.* a group of people, organizations, or countries that work together because they have a common interest or goal. **2.** *n.* a group of sports teams that play against each other.

leak ['lik] **1.** *n.* an opening in a channel, pipe, tire, container, etc., that allows something to escape. **2.** *n.* an instance of something escaping from an opening as in ①. **3.** *n.* an instance of secret information being revealed secretly. (Fig. on ②.) **4.** *iv.* [for a container] to have an opening as in ① that allows water, air, or something else to escape. **5.** *tv.* [for a container with an opening as in ①] to allow water, air, or something else to escape or enter. **6.** *tv.* to secretly reveal secret information. (Fig. on ⑤.)

leakage ['lik ɪdʒ] **1.** *n.* the process of leaking. (No pl.) **2.** *n.* something that is leaked. (No pl.)

leaky ['lik i] *adj.* tending to leak; likely to leak. (Comp: *leakier;* sup: *leakiest.*)

lean ['lin] **1.** *iv.* to be slanting; to be sloped. **2.** *adj.* [of someone or something] very thin or skinny. (Adv: *leanly.* Comp: *leaner;* sup: *leanest.*) **3.** *adj.* [of meat] having almost no fat. (Adv: *leanly.* Comp: *leaner;* sup: *leanest.*)

leap ['lip] **1.** *iv., irreg.* to jump from one place to another. (Pt/pp: *leaped* or LEAPT.) **2.** *tv., irreg.* to jump over something. **3.** *n.* a jump; an instance of leaping.

leapt ['lɛpt] a pt/pp of LEAP.

learn ['lɚn] *tv.* to receive knowledge; to gain a particular piece of knowledge. (The object can be a clause with THAT ⑦.)

lease ['lis] *n.* a rental contract.

least ['list] **1.** *adj.* a sup. form of LITTLE; the smallest [amount]. **2.** *adv.* in the smallest amount; to the smallest degree; the opposite of MOST. **3.** *pron.* the smallest amount.

leather ['lɛð ɚ] **1.** *n.* a material made from the skin of an animal, used to make shoes, coats, belts, gloves, etc. (Pl only for types and instances.) **2.** *adj.* made of ①.

leave ['liv] **1.** *iv., irreg.* to go away; to exit from a place. (Pt/pp: LEFT.) **2.** *tv., irreg.* to depart from a place. **3.** *tv., irreg.* to depart [from a place], letting someone or something remain in the place. **4.** *tv., irreg.* to depart from and abandon someone, such as a husband or wife. **5.** *tv., irreg.* to cause someone or something to be in a certain condition. **6.** *tv., irreg.* to will something to someone or something; to give something to someone or something after one dies. **7.** *n.* an extended period of time away from one's duties.

leaves ['livz] pl of LEAF.

lecture ['lɛk tʃɚ] **1.** *n.* a long talk about a certain subject; a speech. **2.** *n.* a speech that warns or scolds. **3.** *iv.* to give ①; to talk about a certain subject. **4.** *tv.* to talk to people about a certain subject, especially to talk to an audience or a class. **5.** *tv.* to scold someone about something; to give ① to someone.

lecturer ['lɛk tʃɚ ɚ] **1.** *n.* someone who gives a lecture. **2.** *n.* someone who gives lectures; especially someone below the rank of professor or instructor who teaches at a university or college.

led ['lɛd] pt/pp of LEAD.

ledge ['lɛdʒ] *n.* a narrow surface that sticks out along a wall or under a window; a shelf.

leer ['lɪr] *n.* a look of sexual desire or interest.

left [ˈlɛft] **1.** pt/pp of LEAVE. **2.** *n.* the direction to the west when you are facing north. (No pl.) **3.** *adj.* toward ②; located at ②. **4.** *adv.* toward ②.

left-hand [ˈlɛft hænd] *adj.* left; on, to, or at one's left side. (Prenominal only.)

left-handed [ˈlɛft hæn dɪd] **1.** *adj.* favoring the use of the left hand. (Adv: *left-handed* or *left-handedly.*) **2.** *adj.* designed for people who are ①. **3.** *adv.* [of writing] done with the left hand.

leftover [ˈlɛft ov ɚ] *adj.* remaining; unused and therefore extra. (Prenominal only.)

leftovers [ˈlɛft ov ɚz] *n.* portions of food left over from a meal; portions of food remaining after a meal. (Treated as pl. Rarely countable.)

leg [ˈlɛg] **1.** *n.* one of the two body parts that support a human; one of the four body parts that support most other mammals, or similar parts that support certain other animals, such as insects. **2.** *n.* the part of a piece of clothing that wraps around ①. **3.** *n.* [in furniture or other structures] a vertical piece that supports weight. **4.** *n.* a part of a trip; a part of a distance to be covered.

legal [ˈlig əl] **1.** *adj.* lawful; according to the law. (Adv: *legally.*) **2.** *adj.* of or about law. (Adv: *legally.*)

legend [ˈlɛdʒ ənd] **1.** *n.* an old and often repeated story; a fable; a myth. **2.** *n.* an explanation of symbols used on a map, plan, chart, etc.

legislate [ˈlɛdʒ ɪ slet] **1.** *tv.* to make laws. **2.** *tv.* to pass a law about something. (The object can be a clause with THAT ⑦.)

legislation [lɛdʒ ɪ ˈsle ʃən] **1.** *n.* writing and making laws. (No pl.) **2.** *n.* laws that have been made; a set of laws. (No pl. Number is expressed with *piece(s) of legislation.*)

legislative [ˈlɛdʒ ɪ sle tɪv] *adj.* of or about making laws or the people who make laws. (Adv: *legislatively.*)

legislator [ˈlɛdʒ ɪ sle tɚ] *n.* someone who makes laws; a member of a legislature.

legislature [ˈlɛdʒ ɪ sle tʃɚ] *n.* the group of people who are elected or appointed to make laws.

legitimate [lɪ ˈdʒɪt ə mət] **1.** *adj.* lawful; according to the law. (Adv: *legitimately.*) **2.** *adj.* correct; valid; reasonable. (Adv: *legitimately.*)

3. *adj.* [of a person] born to legally married parents; [of the birth of a person] legal. (Adv: *legitimately.*)

leisure [ˈli ʒɚ] 1. *n.* free time; time that is not spent at work or sleeping; time when one can do what one wants. (No pl.) 2. the *adj.* use of ①.

lemon [ˈlɛm ən] 1. *n.* a sour, yellow citrus fruit. 2. *n.* a product, such as a car, that does not work properly and cannot be repaired. (Informal.) 3. *adj.* made or flavored with ①.

lemonade [lɛm ən ˈed] *n.* a drink made from the juice of lemons, sugar, and water. (No pl.)

lend [ˈlɛnd] 1. *tv., irreg.* to grant someone permission to use or borrow something for a period of time. (Pt/pp: LENT.) 2. *tv., irreg.* to contribute an effect to something; to add a quality to something. (Fig. on ①.)

length [ˈlɛŋkθ] 1. *n.* the measurement of something from end to end; the amount of time that has passed. (The opposite of WIDTH. Pl only for types and instances.) 2. *n.* a piece of something of a certain or known ①.

lengthen [ˈlɛŋk θən] 1. *tv.* to make something longer. 2. *iv.* to become longer.

lens [ˈlɛnz] 1. *n.* a piece of curved glass, or some other clear material, that bends rays of light. 2. *n.* the clear, curved part of the eye—located behind the pupil—that focuses light rays on the retina.

lent [ˈlɛnt] pt/pp of LEND.

leopard [ˈlɛp ɚd] *n.* a large animal in the cat family, typically having yellowish fur with black spots.

less [ˈlɛs] 1. *adj.* the comp. form of LITTLE; a smaller amount. (Used with things that are measured in quantities. Compare this with *fewer*, at FEW, which is used with things that can be counted.) 2. *adv.* to a smaller extent or degree; not as much. 3. *suffix* a form meaning *without* that can be added to nouns and to adjectives that have come from verbs. (The resulting adjectives can be made into nouns with the *-ness* suffix and into adverbs with the suffix *-ly*.)

lessen [ˈlɛs ən] 1. *iv.* to become less; to decrease in size, amount, or power. 2. *tv.* to cause something to become less.

lesson [ˈlɛs ən] 1. *n.* a session of instruction with a teacher; the material to be covered in one session of instruction; something, such as a school assignment, that is to be learned, studied, or prepared. 2. *n.*

something that one learns from an experience; an experience that one learns something from.

let [ˈlɛt] **1.** *tv., irreg.* to allow someone or something to do something; to allow something to happen. (Pt/pp: *let*.) **2.** *tv., irreg.* to rent an apartment or room (to someone).

let's [ˈlɛts] *cont.* let us; we will [do something]. (A gentle command or request. A response is usually expected.)

letter [ˈlɛt ɚ] **1.** *n.* a written or printed symbol in an alphabet. **2.** *n.* a written message sent to a person or a group.

lettuce [ˈlɛt ɪs] *n.* a leafy, green vegetable, often used in salads. (No pl. Number is expressed with *leaf* or *leaves of lettuce* and *head(s) of lettuce*.)

level [ˈlɛv əl] **1.** *n.* a flat surface; a horizontal plane. **2.** *n.* one of the floors of a building or other structure. **3.** *n.* a layer; a step or a stage. **4.** *n.* the amount of a measurement; a position on a scale of measurement. **5.** *n.* a tool or device that shows when a surface is exactly horizontal or vertical. **6.** *adj.* [of a surface] exactly horizontal, so every point is the same height. **7.** *adj.* [of a measurement] steady; not changing. (Fig. on ⑥.) **8.** *tv.* to knock down trees, buildings, or other objects until the land is flat; to clear land by knocking down trees or buildings.

lever [ˈlɛv ɚ] **1.** *n.* a bar of metal or wood, positioned so that it increases one's power in lifting or moving heavy objects. **2.** *n.* a bar or handle that serves as a control device.

liability [laɪ ə ˈbɪl ə ti] **1.** *n.* a kind of danger to people that could cause a lawsuit against whoever is responsible for creating the danger. (No pl form.) **2.** *n.* a cost or [monetary] charge; a potential cost; a negative consideration. (No pl form.)

liar [ˈlaɪ ɚ] *n.* someone who tells lies; someone who does not tell the truth.

liberal [ˈlɪb (ə) rəl] **1.** *adj.* tolerant; broad-minded; progressive. (Adv: *liberally.*) **2.** *adj.* generous; abundant; plenty; ample. (Adv: *liberally.*) **3.** *adj.* of or about political views that favor social and economic progress, very often through government control and management. (Adv: *liberally.*) **4.** *n.* someone who has LIBERAL ③ viewpoints.

liberate [ˈlɪb ə ret] *tv.* to set someone or something free; to release someone or something from control.

256

liberty [ˈlɪb ɚ ti] **1.** *n.* the freedom from control; the freedom to think or act for oneself. (No pl.) **2.** *n.* the permission to do something; a right or a privilege that one has been given.

librarian [laɪ ˈbrɛr i ən] *n.* someone who manages or helps operate a library.

library [ˈlaɪ brɛr i] **1.** *n.* a building or room that has a supply of books or similar materials available for use by a number of people. **2.** *n.* a collection of books, records, videotapes, etc.

license [ˈlaɪ səns] **1.** *n.* a document that proves that someone has official permission to do or own something. **2.** *n.* a freedom to do something. (No pl.) **3.** *tv.* to give or sell someone a ① for something; to authorize someone or something; to permit someone or something.

lick [ˈlɪk] **1.** *tv.* to move the tongue along someone or something; to taste something by moving one's tongue along it; to make something wet by moving one's tongue along it. **2.** *n.* the movement of the tongue along the surface of something as in ①. **3.** *n.* a small amount of something that one gets by moving the tongue as in ①.

lid [ˈlɪd] **1.** *n.* a cover for a container, surface, hole, etc. **2.** *n.* the fold of skin over the eye; an EYELID.

lie [ˈlaɪ] **1.** *n.* a statement that is not true and that the speaker knows is not true; a false statement. **2.** *iv.* to say something that is not true; to tell ①. (Pt/pp: LIED. Pres. part.: LYING.) **3.** *iv., irreg.* to be in a flat position; to place oneself in a flat position. (Pt: LAY; pp LAIN. See also LAY. Pres. part.: LYING.) **4.** *iv., irreg.* to be located; to be in a certain place. **5.** *iv., irreg.* to remain in a place or condition; to stay in a certain condition or position.

lied [ˈlaɪd] pt/pp of LIE ②.

life [ˈlaɪf] **1.** *n.* the power that causes plants and animals to exist, in general. (No pl.) **2.** *n., irreg.* an individual instance of ① that can be lived, lost, saved, spent, wasted, etc.; the period of time between the time of one's birth and one's death or between the time of one's birth and the present. (Pl: LIVES.) **3.** *n., irreg.* the activities, experiences, and habits of a person. **4.** *n.* excitement; vigor. (No pl.) **5.** *n.* a kind of living; a quality of living. (No pl.)

lifeboat [ˈlaɪf bot] *n.* a boat used to carry people away from a sinking ship; a boat used to save people in danger of drowning.

lifeguard [ˈlaɪf ɡard] *n.* someone who works at a beach or swimming pool to encourage water safety and rescue people from danger in the water.

257

lifesaver ['laɪf sev ɚ] **1.** *n.* someone or something that saves someone's life. **2.** *n.* something that serves well in an emergency. (Fig. on ①.)

lifetime ['laɪf taɪm] **1.** *n.* the time that a person or animal is living. **2.** *n.* the period of time that something works or can be used. (Fig. on ①.)

lift ['lɪft] **1.** *tv.* to pick someone or something up from the ground; to raise someone or something to a higher level. **2.** *iv.* [for clouds, fog, smoke, smog] to rise or go away. **3.** *n.* a free ride in a car or truck. (Informal.) **4.** *n.* something that makes someone feel happier, stronger, or more awake.

light ['laɪt] **1.** *n.* a form of radiation or energy that makes things visible. (No pl.) **2.** *n.* something that produces ①, such as a lamp or a flame. **3.** *n.* something, such as a match, that produces fire. (No pl.) **4.** *n.* the period of time when the sun is in the sky; daytime. (No pl.) **5.** *n.* a traffic signal that uses ② that are red, yellow, and green to control people and vehicles. (Short for *traffic light*.) **6.** *n.* a view; the way that something is seen or thought of. (No pl.) **7.** *adj.* pale in color; not dark or deep; mixed with white. (Adv: *lightly*.) **8.** *adj.* not heavy; not weighing much; easy to carry. (Adv: *lightly*.) **9.** *adj.* not having much force; gentle. (Fig. on ⑧. Adv: *lightly*.) **10.** *iv., irreg.* [for a creature] to land on a surface after flight. (Pt/pp: *lighted* or *lɪt*.) **11.** *tv., irreg.* to set something on fire; to cause something to begin to burn.

lighter ['laɪt ɚ] *n.* a device that makes a flame to light cigarettes or cigars.

lighthouse ['laɪt haʊs] *n., irreg.* a tall structure near the sea, with a bright light near the top that warns ships away from danger. (Pl: [...haʊ zəz].)

lighting ['laɪt ɪŋ] **1.** *n.* light that makes things and people visible; illumination; the type or quality of light in a room or other place. (No pl.) **2.** *n.* the equipment that directs light, especially for effect in a television or movie studio or on a stage. (No pl.)

lightning ['laɪt nɪŋ] *n.* a flash or streak of light in the sky, especially during a thunderstorm. (No pl. Number is expressed with *bolt(s)* or *flash(es) of lightning*.)

likable ['laɪk ə bəl] *adj.* easy to like; pleasant. (Adv: *likably*.)

like ['laɪk] **1.** *tv.* to enjoy someone or something; to find someone or something pleasant. **2.** *n.* a desire; something that one enjoys having or doing. **3.** *adj.* similar; same. (Prenominal only.) **4.** *prep.* similar to someone or something; in the same way as someone or something. **5.** *prep.* for instance, the following people or things; such as the following people or things. **6.** *conj.* in the same way as someone or something does; similar to the way someone or something is. (Viewed as incorrect by some people.) **7.** *conj.* as though; as if. (Viewed as incorrect by some people.)

likelihood ['laɪk li hʊd] *n.* the chance of being likely; the state of something being probable. (No pl.)

likely ['laɪk li] **1.** *adj.* probable. **2.** *adj.* suitable; apt.

limb ['lɪm] **1.** *n.* a large tree branch. **2.** *n.* an arm, leg, or wing.

lime ['laɪm] **1.** *n.* a small, green citrus fruit. **2.** *n.* a white substance, made by burning a kind of rock, which is used to make plaster, cement, and mortar. (No pl.) **3.** *adj.* made or flavored with ①.

limit ['lɪm ɪt] **1.** *n.* a boundary; the edge; the farthest point of something; the greatest amount allowed or possible. **2.** *tv.* to prevent someone or something from passing a certain point or amount; to restrict something to a certain amount of space or time; to restrict choices.

limp ['lɪmp] **1.** *n.* an uneven walk; a way of walking where one's foot drags or moves as if it is injured. **2.** *iv.* to walk to somewhere showing ①. **3.** *adj.* not stiff; having no resistance. (Adv: *limply.* Comp: *limper;* sup: *limpest.*)

line ['laɪn] **1.** *n.* a thin mark, straight or curved, made on the surface of something. **2.** *n.* a border; a mark that shows the limit, border, or end of something. **3.** *n.* a wide band; a stripe. **4.** *n.* a string, rope, or cord. (On boats and ships, ropes are called *lines.*) **5.** *n.* a wire, pipe, or cable that carries a public utility company's product, such as electricity, water, gas, telephone, etc. **6.** *n.* a telephone connection. **7.** *n.* a row or series of people standing and waiting for a turn to do something. **8.** *n.* a row of words in printing or writing. **9.** *n.* something that is said by an actor onstage or in a film. **10.** *tv.* to put a lining in something; to cover the inside of something with something else.

linen ['lɪn ən] **1.** *n.* a fabric made from flax. (No pl form.) **2.** *n.* tablecloths and sheets made of ① or some other fabric; underwear. (Sometimes pl with the same meaning.) **3.** the *adj.* use of ① or ②.

linger ['lɪŋ gɚ] *iv.* to remain someplace; to loiter; to be slow in moving or leaving.

lining ['laɪn ɪŋ] *n.* a fabric or other material put on the inside surface of something for protection, warmth, etc.

259

link ['lɪŋk] **1.** *n.* one of the loops or circles that make up a chain. **2.** *n.* someone or something that connects someone or something to someone or something else. (Fig. on ①.) **3.** *tv.* to connect someone or something to someone or something else.

lint ['lɪnt] *n.* a tiny piece of thread; a small cluster of threads, dirt, hair, etc. (No pl.)

lion ['laɪ ən] *n.* a large, tan-colored wild animal in the cat family, native to Africa.

lioness ['laɪ ən əs] *n.* a female LION.

lip ['lɪp] **1.** *n.* one of the two ridges of flesh on the outside of the mouth. **2.** *n.* a rim; an edge, especially a part of an edge of a container.

lipstick ['lɪp stɪk] *n.* makeup that is put on the lips to give them a different color. (No pl form in this sense.)

liquid ['lɪk wɪd] **1.** *n.* a flowing substance, such as water, that is not a gas or a solid. **2.** *adj.* in the form of ①. **3.** *adj.* [of an asset that can be] easily converted to cash.

liquor ['lɪk ɚ] **1.** *n.* broth or juices from cooking. (No pl.) **2.** *n.* alcohol for drinking. (Pl only for types and instances.)

list ['lɪst] **1.** *n.* a printed or written series of words, names, or items. **2.** *n.* a slant or tilt to one side, as with a ship. **3.** *tv.* to write things on ①. **4.** *iv.* to lean to one side.

listen ['lɪs ən] *iv.* to pay attention to a source of sound.

lit ['lɪt] a pt/pp of LIGHT.

liter ['lit ɚ] *n.* a metric unit of liquid measurement equal to 1.06 quarts.

literacy ['lɪt ə rə si] *n.* the ability to read and write. (No pl.)

literal ['lɪt ə rəl] **1.** *adj.* [of the meaning of a word or phrase] basic instead of secondary or figurative. (Adv: *literally.*) **2.** *adj.* exact, especially pertaining to translations; translating or interpreting one word at a time. (Adv: *literally.*)

literature ['lɪt ə rə tʃɚ] **1.** *n.* writing considered as art, such as fiction, plays, and poetry. (No pl.) **2.** *n.* all the written material of a specific subject or region. (No pl.) **3.** *n.* information; a brochure or small book that has information about something. (No pl.)

litter ['lɪt ɚ] **1.** *n.* bits of trash; rubbish; things that are thrown away. (No pl form in this sense.) **2.** *n.* all the babies that an animal has from one pregnancy. **3.** *n.* a sandlike substance that is placed in a box for domestic cats to excrete wastes into. (No pl form in this sense.) **4.** *tv.* to throw bits of trash on the floor or ground. **5.** *iv.* to throw bits of trash on the ground as a habit.

little ['lɪt əl] **1.** *adj.* small in size. (Comp: *littler*; sup: *littlest*.) **2.** *adj.*, *irreg.* not much. (Without *a*. Comp: LESS; sup: LEAST. Used with items that cannot be counted. Compare this with FEW ①.) **3.** *adj.*, *irreg.* some; a small amount. (With *a*. Comp: LESS; sup: LEAST. Used with items that cannot be counted. Compare this with FEW ②.) **4.** *adv.*, *irreg.* not much; not a lot. (Comp: LESS; sup: LEAST.)

livable ['lɪv bəl] *adj.* suitable to be lived in or with. (Adv: *livably*.)

live 1. ['laɪv] *adj.* not dead; having life. **2.** ['laɪv] *adj.* carrying electricity; electrically charged. (Fig. on ①.) **3.** ['laɪv] *adj.* on the air; not taped; broadcast at the same time something is happening. **4.** ['laɪv] *adv.* while something is really happening; broadcast at the moment that something is happening. **5.** ['lɪv] *iv.* to be; to exist; to be alive; to survive. **6.** ['lɪv] *iv.* to reside at a certain address; to reside in or at a certain place. **7.** ['lɪv] *iv.* to exist in a certain way.

lively ['laɪv li] *adj.* showing energy or excitement; cheerful; active. (Comp: *livelier*; sup: *liveliest*.)

liver ['lɪv ər] **1.** *n.* an organ, in the body of an animal, that produces fluids used in digestion and performs other important functions. **2.** *n.* a whole ①, eaten as food. **3.** *n.* ①, eaten as food. (No pl.)

lives 1. ['laɪvz] pl of LIFE. **2.** ['lɪvz] the third-person sg of LIVE.

livestock ['laɪv stɑk] *n.* animals that are kept on a farm or ranch, usually for the production of food. (No pl. Treated as sg or pl, but not countable.)

living room ['lɪv ɪŋ rum] *n.* the main room of a house or apartment, large enough to hold a number of people.

lizard ['lɪz ərd] *n.* a reptile with legs, scaly skin, and a tail.

load ['lod] **1.** *n.* something that is carried; a burden; a weight. **2.** *n.* the amount of something that can be carried; one large portion of something for carrying. **3.** *n.* the amount of electricity used by an electrical device. **4.** *tv.* to put bullets into a gun; to put film or videotape into a camera; to install computer software into a computer. **5.** *tv.* to fill something with something.

loaf ['lof] **1.** *n., irreg.* a mass of bread dough baked in one piece. (Pl: LOAVES.) **2.** *n., irreg.* a mass of food cooked in a shape like ①. (Often part of a compound.) **3.** *iv.* to waste time.

loan ['lon] **1.** *n.* something, especially money, that is lent to someone. **2.** *tv.* to lend something to someone; to let someone borrow something. (Some people object to the use of LOAN in this sense rather than LEND, reserving LOAN for the lending of money.)

loathe ['loð] *tv.* to hate someone or something very much.

loaves ['lovz] pl of LOAF.

lobby ['lɑb i] **1.** *n.* the entrance room of a building. **2.** *tv.* to try to influence someone who makes laws or regulations to vote a certain way.

lobster ['lɑb stɚ] **1.** *n.* an edible sea animal with six legs and (possibly) two large claws. **2.** *n.* the meat of ① used as food. (No pl.) **3.** *adj.* made or flavored with ②.

local ['lok əl] **1.** *adj.* of or about the nearby area. (Adv: *locally.*) **2.** *n.* a bus or train that stops at every station. **3.** *n.* a person who lives in the area that something is in. (Often pl.)

locate ['lo ket] **1.** *tv.* to find someone or something; to learn where someone or something is. **2.** *tv.* to place someone or something in a particular place.

location [lo 'ke ʃən] *n.* the place where someone or something is; the place where someone or something is found.

lock ['lɑk] **1.** *n.* a device on a door opening that prevents the door from being opened without a key. **2.** *n.* a device similar to a ① that controls access to something. **3.** *n.* a part of a canal or river between two heavy, watertight gates where the level of the water can be raised or lowered, allowing boats to move from one level of water to another. **4.** *n.* a small bundle of [head] hair; a strand or curl of hair.

locker ['lɑk ɚ] *n.* a cabinet like a tiny closet that can be locked, where clothes and valuables are kept.

locomotive [lok ə 'mot ɪv] **1.** *n.* a train engine. **2.** the *adj.* use of ①.

locust ['lok əst] *n.* a kind of insect that travels in large swarms and destroys crops.

lodge ['lɑdʒ] **1.** *n.* a small, privately owned cabin for campers, hunters, skiers, and others who like to stay in the country. **2.** *n.* the place where a men's organization meets. **3.** *n.* the structure that beavers build to live in. **4.** *iv.* to become stuck somewhere; to become wedged in something.

loft ['lɔft] **1.** *n.* an upper level in a barn or stable, where hay is kept. **2.** *n.* a large apartment with high ceilings and few walls, usually renovated from an old warehouse.

lofty ['lɔf ti] **1.** *adj.* high; very tall. (Adv: *loftily.* Comp: *loftier;* sup: *loftiest.*) **2.** *adj.* noble; dignified. (Fig. on ①. Adv: *loftily.* Comp: *loftier;* sup: *loftiest.*)

log ['lɔg] **1.** *n.* a length of the trunk or main branch of a tree with all of the branches removed. **2.** *n.* a detailed record of a trip, written by the captain of a ship, plane, train, etc. **3.** *tv.* to note something in ②.

logic ['lɑdʒ ɪk] **1.** *n.* the science of reasoning; the part of philosophy that deals with reason. (No pl.) **2.** *n.* a method of argument or reasoning. (No pl.) **3.** *n.* sense; rational thought; the ability to reason. (No pl.)

logical ['lɑdʒ ɪ kəl] *adj.* making sense; according to the rules of logic. (Adv: *logically* [...ɪk li].)

lollipop ['lɑl i pɑp] *n.* a piece of hard candy on the end of a stick.

lone ['lon] *adj.* only; alone; without others. (Prenominal only. See also ALONE. No comp. or sup.)

lonely ['lon li] **1.** *adj.* sad because one is alone; lonesome. (Comp: *lonelier;* sup: *loneliest.*) **2.** *adj.* isolated; away from other people. (Comp: *lonelier;* sup: *loneliest.*)

lonesome ['lon səm] *adj.* lonely; sad because one is alone. (Adv: *lonesomely.*)

long ['lɔŋ] **1.** *adj.* great in length or in amount of time. (Comp: *longer;* sup: *longest.*) **2.** *adj.* having a certain length; lasting a certain amount of time. (Follows the measure of length or time. Comp: *longer.*) **3.** *adv.* for a great extent of time before or after the time indicated. **4.** *adj.* seeming to take more time than normal; seeming to be farther than normal. (Comp: *longer;* sup: *longest.*)

look ['lʊk] **1.** *n.* an act of seeing [someone or something]; an act of trying to see someone or something. **2.** *n.* a manner or style of appearing. **3.** *n.* an expression on the face. **4.** *iv.* to seem; to appear [to be]. **5.** *iv.* to face a certain direction; to be positioned in a certain direction.

loom ['lum] **1.** *n.* a machine used for weaving cloth, blankets, or rugs. **2.** *iv.* to appear somewhere in a threatening or unfriendly way.

loop ['lup] *n.* anything that looks like a circular figure formed by a line that curves and possibly crosses itself.

263

loose ['lus] **1.** *adj.* not tight; having room to move. (Adv: *loosely.* Comp: *looser;* sup: *loosest.*) **2.** *adj.* free; escaped and not confined. **3.** *adj.* not exact. (Fig. on ①. Adv: *loosely.* Comp: *looser;* sup: *loosest.*) **4.** *adj.* [of morals] lax or not restrained. (Adv: *loosely.* Comp: *looser;* sup: *loosest.*) **5.** *adv.* freely.

loosen ['lus ən] **1.** *tv.* to cause something to be less tight or restraining; to untie someone or something. **2.** *iv.* to become less tight or restraining; to unfasten.

loot ['lut] **1.** *n.* stolen money or objects. (No pl.) **2.** *tv.* to rob things or places, especially during a war or a riot. **3.** *iv.* to steal [something], especially during a war or riot.

lose ['luz] **1.** *tv., irreg.* to permit someone or something to "escape" from one's care, ownership, or possession. (Pt/pp: LOST.) **2.** *tv., irreg.* to have less of something after doing something or after something happens. **3.** *tv., irreg.* not to win something; not to gain or receive something. **4.** *iv., irreg.* not to win; to be defeated.

loss ['lɔs] **1.** *n.* an instance of losing something. **2.** *n.* the value of something that was lost; how much something lost costs; money that is lost or never earned. **3.** *n.* the death of someone; the death of a loved one. **4.** *n.* a defeat; the failure to win.

lost ['lɔst] **1.** pt/pp of LOSE. **2.** *adj.* unable to be found. **3.** *adj.* no longer owned; no longer in one's possession. **4.** *adj.* not knowing where one is; not knowing how to get to where one wants to be.

lot ['lɑt] **1.** *n.* a part of the available goods; a group of goods. **2.** *n.* fate; destiny; the kind of life that one has been granted. **3.** *n.* an area of land; a share of land; a piece of property. **4. a ~; ~s** *n.* many of the people or things already mentioned; much of something already mentioned. (Treated as sg or pl, but not countable.) **5. a ~; ~s** *adv.* much; often.

lotion ['lo ʃən] *n.* a creamy liquid that is rubbed on the body to soothe, add moisture, or clean the skin. (Pl only for types and instances.)

loud ['lɑʊd] **1.** *adj.* [of sound] having much volume or intensity; not quiet. (Adv: *loudly.* Comp: *louder;* sup: *loudest.*) **2.** *adj.* too bright; showy. (Fig. on ①. Adv: *loudly.* Comp: *louder;* sup: *loudest.*) **3.** *adv.* sounding as in ①. (Comp: *louder;* sup: *loudest.*)

lovable ['lʌv ə bəl] *adj.* able to be loved; deserving of being loved. (Adv: *lovably.*)

love ['lʌv] **1.** *n.* a strong emotion of attraction, care, romance, or desire toward someone. (No pl.) **2.** *n.* a strong interest in something. (No pl.) **3.** *n.* [in tennis] a score of zero. **4.** *tv.* to care deeply for someone romantically. **5.** *tv.* to care deeply for someone; to care very much about someone. **6.** *tv.* to care about or like something very much.

lovely ['lʌv li] *adj.* beautiful; pretty; attractive. (Comp: *lovelier;* sup: *loveliest.*)

lover ['lʌv ɚ] **1.** *n.* one of two people who love each other in a romantic way. **2.** *n.* someone whom one loves in a romantic way; a mate to whom one may or may not be married. **3.** *n.* someone who enjoys something; someone who enjoys doing something.

low ['lo] **1.** *adj.* only a little way above the ground or sea level; not high. (Comp: *lower;* sup: *lowest.*) **2.** *adj.* near the bottom of something. (Comp: *lower;* sup: *lowest.*) **3.** *adj.* less than average in amount, power, volume, height, intensity, cost, etc. (Comp: *lower;* sup: *lowest.*) **4.** *adj.* [feeling] weak or unhappy. (Comp: *lower;* sup: *lowest.*) **5.** *adj.* mean; unkind; cruel. (Comp: *lower;* sup: *lowest.*) **6.** *adj.* [of a supply or of strength] inadequate or not enough. (Comp: *lower;* sup: *lowest.*) **7.** *adv.* to or at a position below or near the bottom of something.

lower ['lo ɚ] **1.** *iv.* [for something] to go from a high level to a low level. **2.** *tv.* to cause something to go from a high level to a low level; to move something down.

lowercase ['lo ɚ 'kes] *adj.* [of a letter or letters] in the smaller size as with *i* in *Bill;* not capitalized. (Compare this with UPPERCASE.)

lowly ['lo li] *adj.* humble; low in rank; simple; meek. (Comp: *lowlier;* sup: *lowliest.*)

loyal ['lɔɪ əl] *adj.* true to one's friends, country, or promises. (Adv: *loyally.*)

loyalty ['lɔɪ əl ti] *n.* the quality of being loyal. (Pl only for types and instances.)

lubricate ['lu brə ket] *tv.* to put oil or another lubricant on something so that it can move against something else smoothly.

lubrication [lu brə 'ke ʃən] **1.** *n.* applying something that will make things slippery; applying oil or grease. (No pl.) **2.** *n.* something like oil or grease that makes things slippery. (Pl only for types and instances.)

luck ['lʌk] **1.** *n.* random chance; fortune; chance. (No pl.) **2.** *n.* good or bad fortune; success or failure. (No pl.)

265

lucky ['lʌk i] **1.** *adj.* [of someone] having good luck; fortunate. (Comp: *luckier*; sup: *luckiest*.) **2.** *adj.* causing good luck; bringing good fortune. (Comp: *luckier*; sup: *luckiest*.) **3.** *adj.* showing, having, or being good luck. (Adv: *luckily*. Comp: *luckier*; sup: *luckiest*.)

lug ['lʌg] **1.** *n.* a small piece that sticks out of something. **2.** *tv.* to carry or move someone or something heavy.

luggage ['lʌg ɪdʒ] *n.* baggage; suitcases. (No pl. Number is expressed with *piece(s) of luggage*.)

lukewarm ['luk 'worm] **1.** *adj.* slightly warm. **2.** *adj.* without excitement; without enthusiasm. (Fig. on ①. Adv: *lukewarmly*.)

lull ['lʌl] *n.* a quiet moment between long periods of noise or activity; a temporary calm.

lullaby ['lʌl ə baɪ] *n.* a quiet song that is sung to help someone fall asleep.

lumber ['lʌm bɚ] **1.** *n.* timber, logs, and boards used for building. (No pl.) **2.** *iv.* to move in a heavy or clumsy way.

lump ['lʌmp] *n.* a hard mass of some substance having no specific shape.

lunar ['lun ɚ] *adj.* of or about the moon.

lunatic ['lun ə tɪk] **1.** *n.* someone who is insane; someone who is CRAZY ①. (No longer commonly used for a mental patient.) **2.** *n.* someone who acts wild and CRAZY ②. (Fig. on ①.)

lunch ['lʌntʃ] **1.** *n.* a meal eaten around noon; a meal eaten in the middle of the day. **2.** *iv.* to eat a meal around noon; to eat ①.

luncheon ['lʌn tʃən] *n.* a formal meal in the middle of the day. (Fancier than a LUNCH, and usually involving a number of people.)

lunchroom ['lʌntʃ rum] *n.* a room where people in a school, office, or factory eat lunch.

lung ['lʌŋ] *n.* one of a pair of organs in the body that are used when breathing.

lunge ['lʌndʒ] **1.** *iv.* to move forward suddenly with force. **2.** *n.* a sudden forward movement with force.

lurch ['lɚtʃ] **1.** *n.* a sudden movement like a jerk or a jump. **2.** *iv.* to move in a way that is out of control; to move without control.

lure ['lʊr] **1.** *tv.* to try to attract or catch a person or an animal by offering something the person or animal wants; to tempt someone or something. **2.** *n.* someone or something that attracts; something that is used to attract a person or animal.

lurk ['lɚk] **1.** *iv.* to hang out someplace without being noticed; to be someplace without being noticed. **2.** *iv.* to connect to an Internet discussion and just read messages without ever sending any.

lush ['lʌʃ] **1.** *adj.* [of a place] very comfortable; [of a place] richly comfortable. (Adv: *lushly.* Comp: *lusher;* sup: *lushest.*) **2.** *adj.* covered with plants and thick vegetation. (Adv: *lushly.* Comp: *lusher;* sup: *lushest.*)

luxury ['lʌg ʒə ri] **1.** *n.* expensive comfort; elegance; the very best of things. (Pl only for types and instances.) **2.** *n.* something that is not necessary but is desired.

lying ['laɪ ɪŋ] pres. part. of LIE.

lynch ['lɪntʃ] *tv.* to capture and hang someone who is thought to have committed a crime. (Outside the legal system.)

lynx ['lɪŋks] *n.* a type of wild cat with a short tail, long legs, and ears that have fluffy fur at the tips.

lyric ['lɪr ɪk] **1.** *adj.* of or about poetry that expresses the feelings of the poet. (Adv: *lyrically* [...ɪk li].) **2.** *n.* a short poem.

lyrics *n.* the words of a song. (Treated as pl.)

M

ma'am ['mæm] *cont.* a polite form of address for a woman. (A contraction of *madam*.)

macaroni [mæk ə 'ron i] *n.* pasta in the shape of curved tubes. (No pl.)

machine [mə 'ʃin] *n.* a device created to do some kind of work.

machinery [mə 'ʃin (ə) ri] *n.* machines and parts of machines, in general. (No pl.)

mad ['mæd] **1.** *adj.* crazy; insane; mentally ill. (Adv: *madly.* Comp: *madder;* sup: *maddest.*) **2.** *adj.* angry; upset. (Comp: *madder;* sup: *maddest.* Not prenominal.)

made ['med] pt/pp of MAKE.

magazine [mæg ə 'zin] *n.* a booklet that is published at regular intervals of time.

maggot ['mæg ət] *n.* the larva of a fly; a fly before it develops into an adult fly.

magic ['mædʒ ɪk] **1.** *n.* sorcery or the use of special, unnatural, or evil powers. (No pl.) **2.** *n.* the art of performing tricks that use illusion to fool an audience. (No pl.) **3.** *n.* a special quality or power that lures or interests people. (Fig. on ①. No pl.) **4.** the *adj.* use of ①, ②, or ③. (Adv: *magically* […ɪk li].)

magical ['mædʒ ɪ kəl] **1.** *adj.* having or using MAGIC ①. (Adv: *magically* […ɪk li].) **2.** *adj.* exciting and interesting; romantic. (Adv: *magically* […ɪk li].)

magician [mə 'dʒɪ ʃən] **1.** *n.* someone who practices magic or sorcery. **2.** *n.* a performer who entertains by creating illusions.

magnet ['mæg nət] **1.** *n.* an iron or steel object that draws other iron or steel objects toward it. **2.** *n.* someone or something that people or things are attracted toward. (Informal. Fig. on ①.)

magnetic [mæg 'nɛt ɪk] **1.** *adj.* able to draw or attract iron or steel in the way that a magnet does. (Adv: *magnetically* […ɪk li].) **2.** *adj.* able to be affected or harmed by magnetism. (Adv: *magnetically* […ɪk li].) **3.** *adj.* [of someone's personality] attracting or drawing people [to oneself].

268

magnetism ['mæg nə tiz əm] **1.** *n.* the physical laws of how magnets attract metal. (No pl.) **2.** *n.* a charm or attraction that draws people toward someone. (Fig. on ①. No pl.)

magnificent [mæg 'nɪf ɪ sənt] **1.** *adj.* impressive; grand; splendid; stately. (Adv: *magnificently.*) **2.** *adj.* excellent; superb; brilliant. (Adv: *magnificently.*)

magnify ['mæg nə faɪ] **1.** *tv.* to cause someone or something to seem or look larger, especially by looking through a lens. **2.** *tv.* to exaggerate something; to make something seem better or worse than it is. (Fig. on ①.)

maid ['med] *n.* a woman who is paid to cook, clean, and do other work around the house.

mail ['mel] **1.** *n.* letters and packages that are delivered by the post office. (No pl. Number is expressed with *piece(s) of mail.*) **2.** *tv.* to send (someone) a letter or package by ①.

mailbox ['mel bɑks] **1.** *n.* a place where mail is put so it can be picked up and taken to the post office and then delivered. **2.** *n.* a container into which a mail carrier delivers mail. **3.** *n.* the electronic version of ②, where e-mail is received.

main ['men] **1.** *adj.* most important; primary; chief. (Prenominal only. Adv: *mainly.*) **2.** *n.* an important pipe that carries water, sewage, gas, etc.

maintain [men 'ten] **1.** *tv.* to continue something as before; to keep doing something. **2.** *tv.* to take care of something; to make sure that something works properly. **3.** *tv.* to support someone or something, especially with money. **4.** *tv.* to assert an opinion; to defend one's opinion and continue to assert it when someone argues against it. (The object can be a clause with THAT ⑦.)

maintenance ['men tə nəns] *n.* keeping equipment and supplies in good condition. (No pl.)

majesty ['mædʒ ə sti] *n.* dignity; greatness and importance, especially of royalty. (No pl.)

major ['me dʒɚ] **1.** *adj.* large in size or amount; great; important; serious. **2.** *adj.* primary; more important. (Prenominal only.) **3.** *n.* an officer in the army, air force, or marines who is above a captain and below a lieutenant colonel. (Sometimes a term of address. Capitalized when written as a proper noun.) **4.** *n.* a student's primary area of study. **5.** *n.* someone whose ④ is in a certain subject.

majority [mə 'dʒɔr ə ti] **1.** *n.* those people who are part of the largest group or division of people, considered as a single group. (No pl. Treated as sg.) **2.** *n.* [in a group] a number of people or things equal to more than half of the whole group, considered as individuals. (No pl.) **3.** *n.* the largest number of votes; a number of votes equal to a specific proportion of all the votes. (No pl.)

make ['mek] **1.** *tv., irreg.* to bring something into being; to put something together from other parts; to form something; to build something; to produce something. (Pt/pp: MADE.) **2.** *tv., irreg.* to cause someone or something to be in a certain condition. **3.** *tv., irreg.* to cause someone or something [to] do something; to force someone or something [to] do something. **4.** *tv., irreg.* to assign someone to a job; to appoint someone to a position. **5.** *tv., irreg.* to earn money; to acquire something. **6.** *tv., irreg.* to arrive at a place; to arrive at a place in time for something; to reach something; to manage to get to something. **7.** *tv., irreg.* to become something; to assume a certain status or job. **8.** *n.* a brand; a certain style or kind.

makeup ['mek əp] **1.** *n.* substances applied to the face to improve its appearance. (No pl. Treated as sg.) **2.** *n.* the contents of something; the parts or substances that form something. (No pl. Treated as sg.) **3.** the *adj.* use of ①.

malaria [mə 'lɛr i ə] *n.* a parasitic disease carried by infected mosquitoes in tropical areas, causing chills and fever. (No pl form in this sense.)

male ['mel] **1.** *adj.* of or about men or boys; of or about animals of the sex that is, at maturity, capable of causing a female to become pregnant. **2.** *adj.* [of an electrical or electronic connector] having short metal rods to be inserted into or between electrical contacts. **3.** *n.* a human or animal that is ①.

malice ['mæl ɪs] *n.* the desire to harm someone or something; the desire to do something evil. (No pl.)

mall ['mɔl] **1.** *n.* a large building with many stores inside; a shopping center. **2.** *n.* a wide, formal walkway, usually lined with trees.

mallet ['mæl ət] *n.* a tool shaped like a hammer with a large head.

mammal ['mæm əl] *n.* one of a large class of warm-blooded animals whose females are able to produce milk to feed their young.

man ['mæn] **1.** *n., irreg.* an adult male person. (Pl: MEN.) **2.** *n.* the human race; all people. (No pl. Treated as sg.) **3.** *n., irreg.* a strong and brave human male. **4.** *tv.* to provide a business or organization with one's services or labor.

manage ['mæn ɪdʒ] *tv.* to be in charge of someone or something; to guide someone or something.

manager ['mæn ɪ dʒɚ] *n.* someone who manages or controls someone or something.

mangle ['mæn gəl] *tv.* to crush something; to mutilate something; to cut or tear something.

maniac ['men i æk] **1.** *n.* someone who has a dangerous, sometimes violent, mental illness. **2.** *n.* someone who is wild, foolish, and too eager. (Fig. on ①.)

manicure ['mæn ə kjɚ] **1.** *n.* a beauty treatment of the hands and fingernails. **2.** *tv.* to give someone ①. **3.** *tv.* to trim something, especially trees, shrubs, grass, or hedges. (Fig. on ②.)

mankind ['mæn 'kaɪnd] *n.* the human race; all people. (No pl. Treated as sg.)

manner ['mæn ɚ] *n.* a method; a style; a way of doing something; a way of being.

mannerism ['mæn ə rɪz əm] *n.* a gesture or movement of a certain person; a habit or trait of a certain person.

manners *n.* the elements of proper and polite behavior.

mansion ['mæn ʃən] *n.* a very large house; a large, elegant house.

mantel ['mæn təl] *n.* the frame around a fireplace, and especially the shelf above the fireplace.

mantle ['mæn təl] *n.* something that completely covers or weighs down someone or something, such as a heavy coat.

manual ['mæn j(u)əl] **1.** *n.* a book that explains how to do or use something; an instruction book; a book of information about something. **2.** *adj.* of or about the hand or hands. (Adv: *manually.*)

manufacture [mæn jə 'fæk tʃɚ] **1.** *n.* the science and business of making products in factories or industry. (No pl.) **2.** *tv.* to make something in large amounts in a factory or by using machines.

manufacturer [mæn jə 'fæk tʃɚ ɚ] *n.* a person, business, or company that manufactures products.

manure [mə 'nu ɚ] *n.* animal feces, especially when used as fertilizer. (No pl form in this sense.)

271

manuscript ['mæn jə skrıpt] **1.** *n.* a book or text that is written by hand. **2.** *n.* the original copy of a book or article that is sent to a publisher.

many ['mɛn i] **1.** *adj., irreg.* numerous; of a large number. (See also MORE and MOST for the comp. and sup. MANY is used with things that can be counted. Compare this with MUCH.) **2.** *pron.* a large number of people; a large number of people or things already referred to.

map ['mæp] **1.** *n.* a drawing that shows certain features of the earth's surface; a sketch or drawing that shows locations or the relations between things or places. **2.** *tv.* to draw ①.

marble ['mɑr bəl] **1.** *n.* a kind of stone that can be cut, shaped, and polished. (Pl only for types and instances.) **2.** *n.* a small, solid ball of colored glass, used in MARBLES. **3.** *adj.* made of ①.

marbles *n.* a game that involves directing one MARBLE ② into a group of them.

march ['mɑrtʃ] **1.** *iv.* to walk in rigid steps, in the manner of a soldier. **2.** *iv.* to walk someplace with a certain goal in mind; to walk someplace for a certain reason. **3.** *tv.* to force someone to move or walk. **4.** *n.* an act of walking in a line, like soldiers. **5.** *n.* a demonstration or protest where people are walking with signs or chanting. **6.** *n.* music that has a strong beat and is used in parades or while soldiers MARCH as in ①. **7.** Go to MONTH. (Capitalized.)

margarine ['mɑr dʒə rın] *n.* a food made from animal or vegetable fats, used in place of butter; a spread for bread. (Pl only for types and instances.)

margin ['mɑr dʒın] **1.** *n.* the space between the edge of a text and the edge of the page. **2.** *n.* an extra amount; the amount that is more than what is needed.

marine [mə 'rin] **1.** *adj.* of or about salt water and the creatures that live in salt water. **2.** *adj.* of, about, from, or concerning the sea. **3.** *adj.* of or about ships and shipping on the sea. **4.** *n.* someone who is a member of the U.S. Marine Corps, a branch of the United States military services that serves on land and sea and in the air.

mark ['mɑrk] **1.** *n.* a spot; a stain; a dent; something that spoils a clear or clean surface. **2.** *n.* a line or figure made by a pencil, crayon, pen, or other writing device. **3.** *n.* something that is a sign of something; something that stands for something else. **4.** *iv.* to draw or make ①. **5.** *tv.* to put a spot on something; to stain something; to spoil an otherwise clear or clean surface with ①. **6.** *tv.* to indicate something; to show something; to symbolize or represent something; to stand for something.

market ['mɑr kɪt] **1.** *n.* a place or building where people gather to buy and sell things. **2.** *n.* the business, building, or system through which company shares are traded. (Short for *stock market*.) **3.** *n.* an area or a country where a product is needed or used; a certain group of people for which a product is needed or by which a product is used. **4.** *n.* the demand for a certain product. **5.** *tv.* to advertise a product; to promote a product; to make a plan for selling a product.

marketplace ['mɑr kɪt ples] **1.** *n.* a place, usually outside, where things are bought and sold. **2.** *n.* trade; buying and selling. (No pl.)

markup ['mɑrk əp] *n.* a price increase; the amount a price is raised.

marriage ['mer ɪdʒ] **1.** *n.* the religious or legal union of a husband and a wife. **2.** *n.* the ceremony that joins a man and a woman in ①; a wedding.

marry ['mer i] **1.** *iv.* to unite with someone in a marriage. **2.** *tv.* to unite two people in a marriage; to perform a wedding ceremony. **3.** *tv.* to take someone as a husband or a wife.

marsh ['mɑrʃ] *n.* a low area of land sometimes covered with water.

marshmallow ['mɑrʃ mel o] *n.* a soft, spongy candy made from sugar. (Originally made from the roots of a flower called the *marsh mallow*.)

marshy ['mɑr ʃi] *adj.* low and moist, like a MARSH.

marvel ['mɑr vəl] *n.* someone or something that is amazing or surprising.

marvelous ['mɑr və ləs] *adj.* wonderful; super; great; fantastic; excellent. (Adv: *marvelously*.)

masculine ['mæs kjə lɪn] **1.** *adj.* having features usually associated with a male; manly. (Adv: *masculinely*.) **2.** *adj.* a grammar term describing a certain class of nouns, some of which refer to males. (See also GENDER.)

mash ['mæʃ] *tv.* to crush something until it is a soft paste; to beat something into a pulp or paste.

mask ['mæsk] **1.** *n.* a covering that disguises the face. **2.** *n.* a covering that protects the face, eyes, nose, or mouth. **3.** *tv.* to conceal something; to hide something; to put ② on someone or something.

mason ['me sən] *n.* someone who makes walls of stones or bricks for a living.

mass ['mæs] **1.** *n.* an amount of something with no specific shape; a lump; a heap. **2.** *n.* the scientific term for the amount of matter that makes up an object. (No pl.) **3.** *adj.* suitable for many people or things; involving many people or things. (Prenominal only.) **4.** *n.* a Christian church service with communion. (Capitalized.)

massacre ['mæs ə kɚ] **1.** *n.* the brutal killing of many people in one battle or instance. **2.** *tv.* to brutally kill many people in one battle or instance.

massive ['mæs ɪv] *adj.* very large; enormous; powerful. (Adv: *massively*.)

mast ['mæst] *n.* [on a ship] an upright beam or pole to which sails are attached.

master ['mæst ɚ] **1.** *n.* a person who has authority over people, animals, or things; a man who has authority over people, animals, or things. **2.** *n.* someone who is very skilled at something. **3.** *n.* an original page or document that copies are made from. **4.** the *adj.* use of ①, ②, or ③. (Prenominal only.) **5.** *adj.* primary; main; chief; controlling everything else. (Prenominal only.) **6.** *adj.* of professional standing or quality. (Prenominal only.) **7.** *tv.* to become skilled in something; to learn how to do something well; to gain control of an ability.

mat ['mæt] **1.** *n.* a piece of material for covering part of a floor, especially in front of a door. **2.** *n.* a piece of thick, padded material used to cushion falls in certain sports. **3.** *n.* a tangled mass of hair, weeds, strings, or other things.

match ['mætʃ] **1.** *n.* a sporting event; a competition. **2.** *n.* someone or something that is the equal of or just like someone or something else; two people or things that are equal or alike. **3.** *n.* a thin stick with a chemical substance on one end, which, when struck against a hard surface, creates fire. **4.** *tv.* [for something] to be exactly like something else; to fit something exactly; to go with something well. **5.** *iv.* to be exactly alike; to go together well; to fit together well.

mate ['met] **1.** *n.* the sexual partner of a living creature. **2.** *n.* a spouse; a husband or a wife. **3.** *n.* one of a pair. **4.** *n.* a friend or colleague; a person who shares someplace or some activity with someone. **5.** *iv.* to have sex; to breed. (Used primarily of animals.) **6.** *tv.* to bring a male and female animal together so that breeding will result.

material [mə 'tɪr i əl] **1.** *n.* a substance that an object is made of; a substance that can be used to make things. **2.** *n.* cloth; fabric. (No pl.) **3.** *n.* information, knowledge, experience, or imagination used to

274

develop a story, movie, book, program, etc. (No pl.) **4.** *adj.* of or about the physical world. (Adv: *materially.*) **5.** *adj.* of importance or relevance. (Adv: *materially.*)

maternal [mə 'tɚ nəl] **1.** *adj.* of or about mothers or motherhood. (Adv: *maternally.*) **2.** *adj.* related through the mother's side of the family. (Adv: *maternally.*)

math ['mæθ] **1.** *n.* MATHEMATICS. (No pl. Treated as sg.) **2.** the *adj.* use of ①.

mathematic [mæθ ə 'mæt ɪk] *adj.* having the exactness or precision of mathematics. (See also MATHEMATICS.)

mathematics [mæθ ə 'mæt ɪks] *n.* the science that studies the properties and relationships of numbers and shapes. (Treated as sg.)

matter ['mæt ɚ] **1.** *n.* anything that takes up space. (No pl.) **2.** *n.* a certain kind of substance. (No pl.) **3.** *n.* a concern; an issue; an affair. **4.** *iv.* to be important; to have meaning.

mattress ['mæ trɪs] *n.* a large, rectangular pad that is used to sleep on.

mature [mə 'tʃur] **1.** *adj.* [of someone] adult or fully grown; [of fruit or vegetables] ripe or ready to eat. (Adv: *maturely.*) **2.** *adj.* characteristic of an adult; sensible; responsible. (Adv: *maturely.*) **3.** *tv.* to cause someone or something to become ① or ②. **4.** *iv.* to become ①. **5.** *iv.* [for a bond] to reach full value; [for a payment] to be due.

maturity [mə 'tʃur ə ti] **1.** *n.* the state of being mature or developed; the degree to which someone or something is mature. (No pl.) **2.** *n.* human wisdom; adult thinking. (No pl.) **3.** *n.* the date when an amount of money becomes due and must be paid.

maximum ['mæk sə məm] **1.** *n.* the highest amount or degree possible; the upper limit or boundary. **2.** *adj.* greatest; highest; most.

may ['me] **1.** *aux.* be allowed to do something; have permission to do something. (Often CAN is used in place of MAY, even though, in standard English, CAN refers to ability, and MAY refers to permission. See also MIGHT.) **2.** *aux.* be possible. (See also MIGHT.) **3.** *aux.* a form used to extend a wish or express a hope; let it be that.... **4.** Go to MONTH. (Capitalized.)

maybe ['me bi] *adv.* perhaps; possibly yes, possibly no.

mayonnaise [me ə 'nez] *n.* a creamy sauce for salads and sandwiches; a sauce made from eggs, oil, and vinegar. (No pl.)

mayor ['me ɚ] *n.* the elected leader of a city, town, or village.

maze ['mez] **1.** *n.* a network of connected passages, arranged so that it is hard to get from one place to another because most of the paths are blocked. **2.** *n.* something that is as confusing as ①. (Fig. on ①.)

me ['mi] **1.** *pron.* the objective form of I, the first-person sg pronoun. (Used after prepositions and transitive verbs and as an indirect object. **2.** *pron.* a first-person sg form. (Used after a shortened form of BE to refer to the speaker or writer. Usually, either "It's me" or the more formal "It is I." Rarely, if ever, "It's I" or "It is me.")

meadow ['mɛd o] *n.* an area of grass-covered land; an area of land where cows, sheep, or goats can eat.

meal ['mil] **1.** *n.* a regular occasion where food is eaten, especially breakfast, lunch, or dinner. **2.** *n.* the food that is eaten at ①. **3.** *n.* crushed grain; flour. (Pl only for types and instances.)

mean ['min] **1.** *adj.* cruel; not kind; selfish. (Adv: *meanly.* Comp: *meaner;* sup: *meanest.*) **2.** *adj.* average. (Prenominal only.) **3.** *n.* an average; the average of a group of numbers. **4.** *tv., irreg.* [for language] to represent, indicate, or express something; [for someone] to indicate, express, or intend something by words or actions. (Pt/pp: MEANT.) **5.** *tv., irreg.* [for something] to indicate or signal something. **6.** *iv., irreg.* to intend to do something.

meaning ['min ɪŋ] *n.* the sense of a word, statement, or symbol; what a word, statement, or symbol means.

means ['minz] *n.* one's [financial] ability to accomplish something.

meant ['mɛnt] pt/pp of MEAN.

meantime ['min taɪm] the period of time between two things; the period of time between now and when something is supposed to happen.

meanwhile ['min ʍaɪl] *adv.* at the same time; during the same time.

measles ['mi zəlz] *n.* an easily spread disease common in children, characterized by fever and red spots on the skin. (Treated as sg or pl, but not countable. Often preceded by *the.*)

measure ['mɛ ʒɚ] **1.** *n.* a unit in a system that determines the amount of something. **2.** *n.* one of the series of groups of musical notes that makes up a piece of music. **3.** *n.* the extent, amount, or quantity of something. **4.** *n.* a course of action; a plan. **5.** *n.* a law; a proposed law; a resolution. **6.** *tv.* to determine the size, extent, amount, degree, etc., of something. **7.** *iv.* to be a certain size, extent, amount, degree, etc.

276

measurement ['mɛ ʒɚ mənt] **1.** *n.* a system of measuring. (No pl.) **2.** *n.* the process of measuring. (No pl.) **3.** *n.* the size, length, weight, or amount of something, as determined by measuring.

meat ['mit] **1.** *n.* the flesh of animals used as food. (Pl only for types and instances.) **2.** *n.* the main idea or content of something. (Fig. on ①. No pl.)

meatloaf ['mit lof] **1.** *n.* a dish of chopped meat shaped like a loaf of bread and baked. (Pl only for types and instances.) **2.** *n.* a unit or loaf of ①.

medal ['mɛd l] *n.* a small piece of metal—usually flat and having a design or words on it—that is given to someone as an honor.

medallion [mə 'dæl jən] **1.** *n.* a large medal. **2.** *n.* a large design or decorative element; a decorative element resembling a large coin or medal.

meddle ['mɛd l] **1.** ~ **(in)** to interfere in someone's business; to involve oneself in someone's business when one is not wanted. **2.** ~ **with** to play with and interfere with something.

media ['mid i ə] **1.** *n.* the Latin pl of MEDIUM ①. (Although it is a Latin pl, MEDIA can be treated as sg or pl in English. Not countable.) **2.** *n.* the Latin pl of MEDIUM ②. (Often treated as sg. Not countable.) **3.** *n.* the Latin pl of MEDIUM ③. (Often treated as sg. Not countable.)

mediator ['mid i et ɚ] *n.* someone who helps negotiate the settlement of a disagreement.

medical ['mɛd ə kəl] *adj.* of or about medicine or the study and practice of medicine. (Adv: *medically* [...ɪk li].)

medicate ['mɛd ə ket] *tv.* to put medicine on or in someone or something; to treat someone or something with medicine or drugs.

medication [mɛd ə 'ke ʃən] **1.** *n.* the use or application of medicine. (No pl.) **2.** *n.* a kind of medicine; a dose of medicine.

medicine ['mɛd ə sən] **1.** *n.* the science and study of preventing, identifying, and curing diseases in the body. (No pl.) **2.** *n.* something that is used to treat a disease, especially something that is taken by the mouth or injected into the body. (Pl only for types and instances.)

medieval [mid i 'i vəl] *adj.* of or about the Middle Ages in Europe, from about A.D. 500 to 1450. (Adv: *medievally*.)

mediocre [mi di 'o kɚ] *adj.* only average; halfway between good and bad; just acceptable.

medium ['mid i əm] **1.** *n., irreg.* a channel or pathway for sending information—such as newspapers, radio, television, print advertising, etc. (The Latin pl is MEDIA, and the English pl is *mediums.*) **2.** *n., irreg.* a substance in which organisms such as bacteria can be grown and kept alive. (Rarely used in the sg. Pl: MEDIA.) **3.** *n., irreg.* the [different kinds of] materials used by an artist. (The Latin pl is MEDIA, and the English pl is *mediums.*) **4.** *n.* the middle size of an object for sale that comes in different sizes. (Pl: *mediums.*)

meek ['mik] *adj.* letting others do as they want; not protesting. (Adv: *meekly.* Comp: *meeker;* sup: *meekest.*)

meet ['mit] **1.** *tv., irreg.* to come together with someone either by chance or on purpose; to encounter someone. (Pt/pp: MET.) **2.** *tv., irreg.* [for something] to touch someone or something; to come into contact with someone or something. **3.** *tv., irreg.* to be introduced to someone. **4.** *iv., irreg.* to come together; to join; to connect; to make contact; to touch.

meeting ['mit ɪŋ] **1.** *n.* a group of people who have come together for a specific reason. **2.** *n.* an instance of people coming together, perhaps by accident.

megabyte ['mɛg ə baɪt] *n.* a unit consisting of about one million BYTES. (The abbreviation is *MB,* and the word can be shortened to *meg.*)

mellow ['mɛl o] **1.** *adj.* [of colors, sounds, textures, or tastes that are] soft, deep, relaxing, or muted. (Adv: *mellowly.* Comp: *mellower;* sup: *mellowest.*) **2.** *adj.* relaxed and quiet. (Informal. Fig. on ①. Adv: *mellowly.* Comp: *mellower;* sup: *mellowest.*) **3.** *tv.* to cause someone or a group to become ②. **4.** *iv.* to become ②.

melody ['mɛl ə di] *n.* the series of notes that make up the tune of a song; a song; a tune.

melon ['mɛl ən] **1.** *n.* one of a family of large round or oval fruits with thick rinds and juicy, edible insides. **2.** *n.* the edible part of ①; ① used as food. (No pl. Number is expressed with *piece(s)* or *slice(s)* of *melon.*)

melt ['mɛlt] **1.** *iv.* [for a solid] to become liquid; to turn into a liquid. **2.** *tv.* to cause something solid to become liquid; to cause something solid to turn into a liquid. **3.** *tv.* to cause something to disappear or fade. (Fig. on ②.) **4.** *n.* an instance of turning into a liquid as in ①.

member ['mɛm bɚ] *n.* someone who belongs to a group or an organization.

278

membership ['mɛm bɚ ʃɪp] 1. *n.* the connection between one person and an organization to which the person belongs. (Pl only for types and instances.) 2. *n.* all of the members of a group or organization. (No pl.)

memento AND **momento** [mə 'mɛn to] *n.* a souvenir; something that reminds one of someone else or of a place that one has been to.

memo ['mɛm o] *n.* a note or announcement, especially in an office. (A shortened form of the word *memorandum*. Pl ends in *-s.*)

memorable ['mɛm ə rə bəl] *adj.* worth remembering; easy to remember. (Adv: *memorably.*)

memorial [mə 'mɔr i əl] 1. *adj.* [of something] used to remind someone of a person, thing, place, or event. (Prenominal only.) 2. *n.* something that is a reminder of an event in the past or of a person no longer living.

memory ['mɛm ə ri] 1. *n.* the brain or mind, thought of as a place where ideas, words, images, and past events reside. (No pl.) 2. *n.* the functioning or quality of ①; the ability of ① to function. 3. *n.* an instance of remembering a past event, experience, person, or sensation; someone or something that is remembered. 4. *n.* the part of a computer where information is kept until it is needed. (No pl.)

men ['mɛn] pl of MAN.

menace ['mɛn ɪs] 1. *n.* a threat; someone or something that threatens harm, violence, or danger. 2. *tv.* to threaten someone or something with harm, violence, or danger.

mend ['mɛnd] 1. *tv.* to fix something; to repair something. 2. *iv.* to become healthy; to become well.

menstrual ['mɛn str(u)əl] *adj.* associated with menstruation. (Adv: *menstrually.*)

menstruate ['mɛn stru et] *iv.* to experience menstruation; to have a menstrual period.

menstruation [mɛn stru 'e ʃən] *n.* the monthly process in sexually mature women who are not pregnant in which the lining of the uterus is shed. (No pl.)

mental ['mɛn təl] 1. *adj.* of or about the mind; done by the mind. (Adv: *mentally.*) 2. *adj.* of or about illness of the mind.

mention ['mɛn ʃən] 1. *tv.* to say or write something; to tell about something briefly. (The object can be a clause with THAT ⑦.) 2. *tv.* to

279

refer to someone or something. **3.** *n.* an instance of saying or writing something as in ②; a brief statement; a reference.

menu ['mɛn ju] **1.** *n.* a list of food and drink available at a restaurant. **2.** *n.* a list of options or functions available in a computer program. (Fig. on ①.)

meow [mi 'aʊ] **1.** *n.* the sound a cat makes. **2.** *iv.* [for a cat] to make its characteristic sound.

merchandise ['mɚ tʃən daɪs] *n.* products for sale or trade; things that are for sale. (No pl. Treated as sg.)

merchant ['mɚ tʃənt] *n.* someone who buys and sells products in order to make money; a retailer.

mercury ['mɚ kjə ri] **1.** *n.* a silver-gray element that is liquid at room temperature. (No pl.) **2.** *n.* the closest planet to the sun in our solar system. (Capitalized.)

mercy ['mɚ si] *n.* kindness; pity; compassion. (No pl except when referring to *God's mercies*.)

mere ['mɪr] *adj.* only; nothing more than. (Prenominal only. Adv: MERELY. Comp: none; sup: *merest.*)

merely ['mɪr li] *adv.* this only; only this and nothing else; just.

merge ['mɚdʒ] **1.** *iv.* to join with something else. **2.** *iv.* to enter the flow of traffic. **3.** *tv.* to cause two or more things to come together and become one.

merger ['mɚ dʒ ɚ] *n.* an act or process of joining two organizations into one.

merit ['mɛr ɪt] **1.** *n.* worth; value. (No pl.) **2.** *n.* a good point; a virtue. (Usually pl.) **3.** *tv.* to deserve something; to be worthy of something.

merry ['mɛr i] *adj.* happy; cheerful; joyful. (Adv: *merrily.* Comp: *merrier;* sup: *merriest.*)

mesh ['mɛʃ] *n.* material that is woven in such a way that there are holes between the threads or wires. (Pl only for types and instances.)

mess ['mɛs] **1.** *n.* something or someplace that is dirty or untidy. **2.** *n.* a group of things that are not in order; a situation that is not organized; confusion. **3.** *n.* [in the military services] a meal, eaten by a group.

message ['mɛs ɪdʒ] **1.** *n.* a communication between two or more people; a piece of written or spoken information for someone. **2.** *n.* the moral of a story; a lesson that is to be learned from a story.

messenger ['mɛs ən dʒɚ] *n.* someone who delivers messages, documents, parcels, or flowers.

messy ['mɛs i] *adj.* dirty or not organized; not clean and tidy. (Adv: *messily*. Comp: *messier*; sup: *messiest*.)

met ['mɛt] pt/pp of MEET.

metal ['mɛt əl] **1.** *n.* a solid mineral substance that can be cast or beaten into different shapes. (Pl only for types and instances.) **2.** *adj.* made from ①.

metallic [mə 'tæl ɪk] *adj.* associated with metal; made of metal.

meteor ['mit i ɚ] *n.* a large rock from space that enters the earth's atmosphere.

meter ['mit ɚ] **1.** *n.* the basic unit of the measurement of length in the metric system, equal to 39.37 inches. **2.** *n.* a device that measures and displays the amount of something that is used. **3.** *n.* the rhythms caused by accents in poetry and music. (Pl only for types and instances.) **4.** *tv.* to measure the flow of something with ②.

method ['mɛθ əd] *n.* a way of doing something; a system; a procedure.

metric ['mɛ trɪk] *adj.* of or about the system of measurement based on the meter. (Adv: *metrically* [...ɪk li].)

mice ['maɪs] a pl of MOUSE.

microphone ['maɪ krə fon] *n.* a device that changes sound waves into electrical waves so that the sound can be broadcast, recorded, or made louder. (Can be shortened to MIKE.)

microscope ['maɪ krə skop] *n.* a device that makes very small objects appear much larger.

microwave ['maɪ kro wev] **1.** *n.* a very short radio wave, used in sending radio messages, radar, and cooking. **2.** *n.* an oven that uses ① to cook or heat food quickly. **3.** the *adj.* use of ①. **4.** *tv.* to cook or heat something in ②.

midair ['mɪd 'ɛr] *adj.* in the air; not touching the ground.

midday 1. ['mɪd 'de] *n.* noon; the middle of the day. (No pl.) **2.** ['mɪd de] *adj.* happening in the middle of the day; happening at noon. (Prenominal only.)

middle ['mɪd l] **1.** *n.* a place or time halfway between two ends or sides; the center. **2.** *n.* the area of the waist; halfway along the body of a human or other creature. **3.** *adj.* central; at the same distance from either end; halfway between the beginning and the end. (Prenominal only.)

midnight ['mɪd naɪt] **1.** *n.* 12:00 at night; twelve o'clock at night. **2.** *adj.* happening at ①; beginning at ①. (Prenominal only.)

Midwest ['mɪd 'wɛst] **1.** *n.* the middle part of the United States. (No pl.) **2.** the *adj.* use of ①.

might ['maɪt] **1.** *n.* power; strength. (No pl.) **2.** *aux.* a form that expresses possibility. (See also MAY and COULD.) **3.** *aux.* a form expressing permission. (See also MAY and COULD.)

mighty ['maɪt i] *adj.* powerful; strong; very great. (Adv: *mightily.* Comp: *mightier;* sup: *mightiest.*)

migration [maɪ 'greɪ ʃən] *n.* the movement of numbers of people or creatures from place to place.

mike ['maɪk] *n.* a device for converting sounds to electronic audio signals. (Short for MICROPHONE.)

mild ['maɪld] **1.** *adj.* gentle or calm; not extreme, powerful, or severe. (Adv: *mildly.* Comp: *milder;* sup: *mildest.*) **2.** *adj.* [of food] plain and not spicy. (Adv: *mildly.* Comp: *milder;* sup: *mildest.*) **3.** *adj.* light; not severe or harsh. (Adv: *mildly.* Comp: *milder;* sup: *mildest.*)

mile ['maɪl] *n.* a unit of measurement of length, equal to 5,280 feet or about 1.6 kilometers.

mileage ['maɪl ɪdʒ] **1.** *n.* a distance expressed in miles. (Pl only for types and instances.) **2.** *n.* the total number of miles that can be traveled using one gallon of gasoline. (No pl.)

military ['mɪl ə tɛr i] *adj.* having to do with the armed forces. (Adv: *militarily* [mɪl ə 'tɛr ə li].)

militia [mə 'lɪʃ ə] *n.* a group of citizens who are not part of the professional army but who are trained as soldiers.

milk ['mɪlk] **1.** *n.* the white liquid made by female mammals to feed their young. (Usually refers to cows' milk used as food. No pl.) **2.** *n.* a white liquid from certain plants. (No pl.) **3.** *tv.* to take ① from an animal.

mill ['mɪl] **1.** *n.* a building containing the machinery needed to turn grain into meal. **2.** *n.* a machine or device that crushes grains, seeds, or coffee beans.

milligram ['mɪl ə græm] *n.* a unit of measurement of weight; one one-thousandth ($\frac{1}{1,000}$) of a gram.

millimeter ['mɪl ə mit ɚ] *n.* a unit of measurement of length; one one-thousandth ($\frac{1}{1,000}$) of a meter.

282

million ['mɪl jən] **1.** *n.* the number 1,000,000. (Additional numbers are formed as with *two million, three million, four million,* etc.) **2.** *adj.* 1,000,000; consisting of 1,000,000 things; having 1,000,000 things.

millionaire [mɪl jə 'nɛr] *n.* someone who has $1,000,000 in assets after debt is subtracted.

mincemeat ['mɪns mit] **1.** *n.* a mixture of fruit, spices, and sometimes chopped meat, as a filling for pies. (No pl form.) **2.** the *adj.* use of ①.

mind ['maɪnd] **1.** *n.* the part of humans that thinks and has feelings. **2.** *n.* the center of intelligence and memory; the imagination; the creative part of humans. **3.** *tv.* to care for someone or something; to tend to someone or something. **4.** *tv.* to be opposed to something; to care if someone does something. **5.** *iv.* to be opposed [to something]; to object.

mine ['maɪn] **1.** *n.* an opening into the earth from which precious metals, minerals, or gems are recovered. **2.** *n.* a source of something in large amounts; someone, something, or someplace that supplies large amounts of something. (Fig. on ①.) **3.** *n.* a bomb that is placed under the surface of the soil or water and explodes when it is touched. **4.** *tv.* to remove precious metals, minerals, or gems from the earth. **5.** *tv.* to place bombs under the surface of the soil or water at a particular location. **6.** *pron.* the first-person sg possessive pronoun. (Used in place of a noun.)

miner ['maɪn ɚ] *n.* someone who digs underground for precious metals, minerals, or gemstones; someone who works in a mine.

mineral ['mɪn (ə) rəl] **1.** *n.* one of many kinds of crystallike substances dug from the earth; a substance that is gotten by mining. **2.** *n.* an element that plants and animals need in order to function properly. **3.** the *adj.* use of ①.

mingle ['mɪŋ gəl] **1.** *iv.* to blend or mix. **2.** *tv.* to blend or mix things together. **3.** ~ **(with)** to talk to different people; to associate with different people.

miniature ['mɪn i ə tʃɚ] **1.** *adj.* small; on a small scale; smaller than other things of the same kind. **2.** *n.* something that is small; something that is smaller than other things of the same kind.

minimal ['mɪn ə məl] *adj.* smallest possible [amount]. (Adv: *minimally.*)

minimum ['mɪn ə məm] **1.** *n.* the least amount or degree possible; the smallest amount or degree possible. **2.** *adj.* minimal; smallest; lowest; least.

283

minister ['mɪn ɪ stɚ] **1.** *n.* a pastor; a preacher; the leader of a Christian church. **2.** *n.* [in many countries] someone who is the head of a government department.

mink ['mɪŋk] **1.** *n., irreg.* a small, long, furry animal similar to the weasel or ferret. (Pl: *mink* or *minks*.) **2.** *n.* the fur of ①. (No pl.) **3.** *n.* a coat made from ②. **4.** *adj.* made from ②.

minnow ['mɪn o] *n.* a kind of very small, thin fish that lives in fresh water.

minor ['maɪn ɚ] **1.** *adj.* small in size or amount; not serious; not very important. **2.** the *adj.* use of ①. **3.** *n.* a student's secondary area of study. **4.** *n.* someone who is younger than the legal age of responsibility.

minority [maɪ 'nor ə ti] **1.** *n.* a smaller part of a group of people or things; a subgroup of things or people that are less than half of the whole amount. (No pl form in this sense.) **2.** *n.* someone who is a member of a different race, religion, or ethnic group from the majority of a population. **3.** *n.* the state of being younger than the legal age of responsibility. (No pl form in this sense.) **4.** *adj.* the *adj.* use of ②.

mint ['mɪnt] **1.** *n.* a small plant with leaves that have a fresh, strong flavor, and the leaves themselves. (No pl.) **2.** *n.* a candy that is flavored with ①. **3.** *n.* a building where the government makes coins and paper money. **4.** *adj.* tasting like ①; flavored with ①. **5.** *adj.* perfect; in excellent condition. **6.** *tv.* to make something, especially coins, from metal.

minus ['maɪn əs] **1.** *prep.* reduced by some amount; decreased by some amount; made less by some amount; with something omitted or subtracted. (Symbolized by "−".) **2.** *adj.* below zero; less than zero; [of a number] negative. (Precedes the amount. Symbolized by "−".) **3.** *adj.* [of a school letter grade] less than the full grade. (Follows the letter. Symbolized by "−".) **4.** *n.* a negative factor; a lack.

minute 1. ['mɪn ɪt] *n.* a unit of the measurement of time, equal to 60 seconds or ¹⁄₆₀ hour. **2.** [maɪ 'nut] *adj.* very small. (Adv: *minutely*.)

minutes ['mɪn ɪts] *n.* a written account of what happened at a meeting. (Treated as pl, but not countable.)

miracle ['mɪr ə kəl] **1.** *n.* a remarkable event that cannot be explained by the laws of nature. **2.** *n.* an unexpected, lucky event. (Fig. on ①.)

miraculous [mɪ 'ræk jə ləs] **1.** *adj.* not able to be explained by the laws of science or nature. (Adv: *miraculously*.) **2.** *adj.* unexpectedly excellent. (Fig. on ①. Adv: *miraculously*.)

mirage [mɪ 'rɑʒ] n. an image of something that does not really exist, especially an image of water in the desert; something that fools one's vision.

mirror ['mɪr ɚ] 1. n. a piece of polished glass, treated in a way that makes it reflect images perfectly. 2. n. someone or something that shows what someone or something thinks, looks like, acts like, or is. (Fig. on ①.) 3. tv. to show something as though it were seen in ①; to represent something.

mirth ['mɚθ] n. fun and laughter. (No pl.)

mischief ['mɪs tʃɪf] 1. n. playful trouble; slightly bad tricks or deeds. (No pl.) 2. n. someone—usually a child—who is a source of trouble or problems.

misconduct [mɪs 'kɑn dəkt] n. bad behavior; behavior that is not good or moral. (No pl.)

miser ['mɑɪz ɚ] n. someone who is very selfish and has a lot of money.

miserable ['mɪz ə rə bəl] 1. adj. unhappy; very sad; depressed. (Adv: miserably.) 2. adj. unpleasant; depressing. (Adv: miserably.) 3. adj. poor; squalid; wretched. (Adv: miserably.)

misery ['mɪz ə ri] 1. n. a state of unhappiness, depression, and suffering. (No pl form in this sense.) 2. n. something that causes unhappiness, depression, and suffering. (No pl form in this sense.)

misfit ['mɪs fɪt] n. someone who does not seem to belong with other people or fit a situation.

misfortune [mɪs 'for tʃən] n. bad luck; bad fortune. (Pl only for types and instances.)

mishap ['mɪs hæp] n. an unlucky event or accident; bad luck; an unfortunate accident.

misjudge [mɪs 'dʒʌdʒ] tv. to make the wrong judgment about someone or something.

mislaid [mɪs 'led] pt/pp of MISLAY.

mislay [mɪs 'le] tv., irreg. to put something in a location that is later forgotten. (Pt/pp: MISLAID.)

mismanage [mɪs 'mæn ɪdʒ] tv. to manage someone or something badly; to deal with someone or something badly.

misplace [mɪs 'ples] tv. to put something someplace and then forget where it is.

285

miss ['mɪs] **1.** *tv.* to fail to hit, catch, meet, or reach someone or something. **2.** *tv.* to fail to locate or observe people or things that are where they are meant to be. **3.** *tv.* to notice the absence of someone or something. **4.** *tv.* to feel sad about the loss, departure, or absence of someone or something. **5.** *tv.* to avoid or escape something; to avoid doing something. **6.** *tv.* to lack something; to fail to acquire or experience something that is available. **7.** *n.* a failure to hit, reach, catch, or do something. **8.** *n.* a polite form of address for girls and young women. **9.** *n.* a title for a girl or unmarried woman. (Capitalized when written as a proper noun.)

missile ['mɪs əl] **1.** *n.* something that is thrown, shot, or fired at a target. **2.** *n.* a rocket carrying bombs or weapons that can be shot at a target very far away.

mission ['mɪ ʃən] **1.** *n.* a journey to a place to do an important task. **2.** *n.* a specific task or duty; a specific aim or objective.

misspell [mɪs 'spɛl] *tv.* to spell something wrongly.

mist ['mɪst] **1.** *n.* a light spray of water or other liquid; a small cloud formed by spraying water or other liquid. **2.** *tv.* to spray someone or something with water or other liquid; to cover something with ① or water vapor.

mistake [mɪ 'stek] **1.** *n.* an error; something that is wrong; something that is not correct. **2.** *tv., irreg.* to have the wrong idea about something. (Pt: MISTOOK; pp: MISTAKEN.)

mistaken [mɪ 'stek ən] pp of MISTAKE.

mister ['mɪs tɚ] *n.* a title for an adult male; a form of address for men. (The abbreviation, MR., is used in writing.)

mistook [mɪs 'tʊk] pt of MISTAKE.

mistreat [mɪs 'trit] *tv.* to treat someone or something badly; to abuse someone or something.

mistrust [mɪs 'trʌst] **1.** *tv.* not to trust someone or something; to doubt someone or something. **2.** *n.* lack of trust; doubts about someone or something; distrust. (No pl.)

misty ['mɪs ti] *adj.* [of a surface] covered with mist; [of air] filled with mist. (Adv: *mistily.* Comp: *mistier;* sup: *mistiest.*)

misunderstand [mɪs ən dɚ 'stænd] *tv., irreg.* to understand someone or something incorrectly. (Pt/pp: MISUNDERSTOOD.)

misunderstanding [mɪs ən dɚ 'stænd ɪŋ] **1.** *n.* the failure to understand something. (No pl form in this sense.) **2.** *n.* an argument; a disagreement.

misunderstood [mɪs ən dɚ 'stʊd] pt/pp of MISUNDERSTAND.

misuse 1. [mɪs 'jus] *n.* incorrect use; improper use; using something wrongly. (No pl.) **2.** [mɪs 'juz] *tv.* to use something the wrong way; to use something for a purpose for which it was not meant to be used.

mitten ['mɪt n] *n.* a piece of clothing for one's hand, without separate parts for each finger but with a separate area for the thumb.

mix ['mɪks] **1.** *n.* a mixture; a combination of different people or things. **2.** *n.* a combination of different foods that is ready to be cooked or used in cooking. **3.** *tv.* to combine or blend different things so that they form one thing. **4.** *tv.* to do two things at the same time. **5.** *iv.* to be friendly and comfortable with other people; to be with other people. **6.** ~ **up with** to confuse one person or thing with another.

mixed ['mɪkst] **1.** *adj.* combined; blended. **2.** *adj.* [of the thoughts or feelings that someone has about someone or something] combining very different things, such as liking and disliking. **3.** *adj.* having both males and females; for both sexes.

mixture ['mɪks tʃɚ] *n.* a combination or blend of different people or things.

moan ['mon] **1.** *n.* a deep, long cry of sadness, suffering, pain, or grief. **2.** *iv.* to make a deep, long cry of sadness, suffering, pain, or grief.

mob ['mɑb] **1.** *n.* a large group of people crowded around someone or something. **2.** *tv.* [for a large group of people] to crowd around someone or something.

mobile 1. ['mob əl] *adj.* able to move easily; able to be moved easily; movable. **2.** ['mo bil] *n.* a hanging arrangement of balanced objects that move with air currents. (Refers to decorations, works of art, or devices to entertain infants.)

mock ['mɑk] **1.** *tv.* to make fun of someone; to laugh at or ridicule someone, especially by copying how that person speaks or acts. **2.** *tv.* to copy or imitate someone or something. **3.** *adj.* not real.

mockery ['mɑk ə ri] *n.* something that is a poor substitute for the real thing or person.

mockingbird ['mɑk ɪŋ bɚd] *n.* a bird native to the Americas, so called because it imitates the calls or songs of other birds.

mode

mode ['mod] **1.** *n.* a way of doing something; a method; a manner. **2.** *n.* a feature of a verb that shows whether it is a statement, command, or wish; MOOD ②.

model ['mɑd l] **1.** *n.* a copy of an object, usually made smaller than the original. **2.** *n.* someone or something that is the perfect example of something; someone or something that is to be copied or imitated; a standard. **3.** *n.* someone who is paid to wear and show off clothing that is available for sale. **4.** *n.* someone who poses for artists and photographers. **5.** *n.* one style of a certain product in a series of styles. **6.** *adj.* perfect; worthy of imitation; regarded as the perfect example. (Prenominal only.) **7.** *adj.* built to a smaller scale than normal. (Prenominal only.) **8.** *iv.* to work as ③ or ④. **9.** *tv.* [for ③] to wear and show off clothing.

modem ['mod əm] *n.* a device that connects a computer with a telephone line or a television cable system so that information can be sent or received over that line.

moderate 1. ['mɑd ə rɪt] *adj.* not extreme; in the center; average or medium. (Adv: *moderately.*) **2.** ['mɑd ə rɪt] *n.* someone whose political or social views are not extreme. **3.** ['mɑd ə ret] *tv.* to reduce something; to cause something to be less strong. **4.** ['mɑd ə ret] *tv.* to lead a discussion; to lead a meeting.

moderation [mɑd ə 're ʃən] *n.* being moderate; [doing things] within reasonable limits. (No pl.)

modern ['mɑd ən] *adj.* up-to-date; new; of or about the present or very recent time. (Adv: *modernly.*)

modest ['mɑd ɪst] **1.** *adj.* shy; humble; not bragging about oneself. (Adv: *modestly.*) **2.** *adj.* not excessive; moderate; not large. (Adv: *modestly.*) **3.** *adj.* decent; not revealing too much of one's body. (Adv: *modestly.*)

moist ['mɔɪst] *adj.* damp; a little bit wet. (Adv: *moistly.* Comp: *moister;* sup: *moistest.*)

moisten ['mɔɪ sən] *tv.* to make something moist; to make something damp.

moisture ['mɔɪs tʃɚ] *n.* wetness; water in the air; vapor. (No pl.)

molar ['mol ɚ] *n.* one of the teeth in the back of the mouth, used for grinding food.

molasses [mə 'læs ɪz] *n.* a sweet, dark, sticky liquid made in the process of making sugar. (This is sg. No pl.)

288

mold ['mold] **1.** *n.* a fuzzy or slimy growth that forms on animal or plant matter. (Pl only for types and instances.) **2.** *n.* a hollow object that has a certain shape. (Certain liquids—such as clay, resin, cement, rubber, etc.—are poured into it, and when the liquid hardens, it will have the same shape as the mold.) **3.** *n.* something that was shaped by or made in ②. **4.** *tv.* to shape something; to form something into a certain shape; to shape something using ②. **5.** *iv.* to be covered with ①.

mole ['mol] *n.* a small, furry mammal that lives underground, eats worms and bugs, and cannot see well.

molecule ['mɑl ə kjul] *n.* the smallest part into which a chemical compound can be divided without changing its chemical composition.

molt ['molt] **1.** *tv.* [for an animal] to shed feathers, skin, or fur. **2.** *iv.* [for animals] to shed [something], as with ①.

molten ['molt n] *adj.* melted; made into liquid. (Adv: *moltenly*.)

mom ['mɑm] *n.* mother. (Informal. Also a term of address. Capitalized when written as a proper noun.)

moment ['mo mənt] **1.** *n.* an instant in time; a brief period of time. **2.** *n.* a certain point in time.

momento [mə 'mɛn to] Go to MEMENTO.

momentum [mo 'mɛn təm] *n.* the force and speed of movement or progress. (No pl.)

monarch ['mɑn ɑrk] *n.* a king or a queen.

Monday ['mʌn de] Go to DAY.

monetary ['mɑn ə tɛr i] *adj.* of or about money. (Adv: *monetarily* [mɑn ə 'tɛr ə li].)

money ['mʌn i] **1.** *n.* currency; coins and bills issued by a government. (No pl.) **2.** *n.* wealth; riches. (No pl.)

monitor ['mɑn ə tɚ] **1.** *n.* a device that looks somewhat like a television set and is used to display computer information. **2.** *n.* a measuring device that keeps a record of something. **3.** *tv.* to watch, listen to, or keep a record of something.

monk ['mʌŋk] *n.* a man who devotes his life to religion as part of an all-male religious organization.

monkey ['mʌŋ ki] *n.* a small, hairy primate with a long tail.

monopoly [mə 'nɑp ə li] **1.** *n.* the condition existing when someone or something has complete control over something. **2.** *n.* a business

289

that is the only provider of a service or product. **3.** *n.* the right to be the only provider of a service or product, as authorized by a government.

monster ['mɑn stɚ] *n.* a large creature that scares people.

monstrosity [mɑn 'strɑs ə ti] *n.* someone or something that is huge and very ugly.

month ['mʌnθ] **1.** *n.* one of the 12 divisions of a year. (The months of the year, in order, are JANUARY, FEBRUARY, MARCH, APRIL, MAY, JUNE, JULY, AUGUST, SEPTEMBER, OCTOBER, NOVEMBER, DECEMBER.) **2.** *n.* a period of about 30 or 31 days; a period of four weeks.

monthly ['mʌnθ li] **1.** *adj.* happening every month; happening once a month. **2.** *adv.* every month; once a month.

monument ['mɑn jə mənt] **1.** *n.* a structure that is built in memory of a person or event. **2.** *n.* something that preserves the memory of a person, culture, or event. (Fig. on ①.)

mood ['mud] **1.** *n.* a state of mind; the way one is feeling. **2.** *n.* a feature of a verb that shows whether it is a statement, a command, or a wish; MODE ②.

moon ['mun] **1.** *n.* a large natural satellite that orbits around a planet. **2.** *n.* the natural satellite that orbits around the earth.

moonlight ['mun lɑɪt] **1.** *n.* the light from a moon. (No pl.) **2.** *adj.* done at night, while the moon is shining; happening while the moon is shining. (Prenominal only.) **3.** *iv.* to have a second job in the evening or at night in addition to the job one has during the day. (Pt/pp: *moonlighted*.)

moose ['mus] *n., irreg.* a northern animal—similar to a large deer—the males of which have wide, flat horns on their heads. (Pl: *moose*. See also ELK ②.)

mop ['mɑp] *n.* a group of thick, heavy strings or a sponge, attached to a pole, used wet or dry for cleaning floors.

moral ['mɔr əl] **1.** *adj.* of or about good and bad, according to society's standards of right and wrong. (Adv: *morally*.) **2.** *adj.* showing or representing good behavior and values. (Adv: *morally*.) **3.** *n.* the lesson that can be learned from a story.

morale [mə 'ræl] *n.* confidence; the amount of confidence felt by a person or group of people. (No pl.)

morality [mə 'ræl ə ti] *n*. the goodness or rightness of someone's behavior; good behavior measured by society's standards of right and wrong. (No pl.)

morals *n*. a person's MORAL ① principles of behavior, especially concerning sex. (Treated as pl, but not countable.)

more ['mor] **1.** *adj*. the comp. form of MUCH or MANY; a greater amount or number. (Prenominal only.) **2.** *pron*. the comp. form of MUCH or MANY; a greater amount or number. **3.** *n*. an additional amount or number. (No pl.) **4.** *adv*. a word used to form the comp. form of some adjectives and adverbs; to a greater extent. **5.** *adv*. of a greater amount.

morning ['mor nɪŋ] **1.** *n*. the period of the day from midnight to noon. **2.** *n*. dawn; sunrise. **3.** *adj*. happening during ①. (Prenominal only.)

mornings *adv*. every MORNING ①.

morsel ['mor səl] *n*. a small piece of something, especially food.

mortal ['mor təl] **1.** *n*. a human being; someone or something that must die; someone or something that will not live forever. **2.** *adj*. unable to live forever; having to die at some time. (Adv: *mortally*.)

mortar ['mor tɚ] **1.** *n*. a kind of cement that binds bricks or stones to each other, especially when a wall is being built. (Pl only for types and instances.) **2.** *n*. a short, wide cannon that shoots shells in a high arc. **3.** *n*. a hard bowl used to hold substances being ground into powder.

mortgage ['mor gɪdʒ] **1.** *n*. an agreement by which a borrower grants a lender the ownership of an asset in exchange for a loan of money, thus protecting the loan with the asset. (When the loan is repaid, the ownership of the property is returned to the borrower. If the borrower is unable to pay the loan, the asset then belongs to the lender.) **2.** *tv*. to use an asset to secure a loan.

mosaic [mo 'ze ɪk] *n*. a design made from many pieces of colored substances, especially glass or stone.

mosque ['mɑsk] *n*. an Islamic building of worship; a building where Muslims worship.

mosquito [mə 'skit o] *n*. a small insect, the female of which sucks blood from warm-blooded creatures. (Pl ends in *-s* or *-es*.)

moss ['mɔs] *n*. a small, soft green plant without flowers that grows in masses on rocks and other surfaces. (Pl only for types and instances.)

most ['most] **1.** *adj.* the sup. form of MUCH or MANY; the greatest amount or number. (Prenominal only.) **2.** *adj.* over half; almost all. (Prenominal only. Adv: *mostly*.) **3.** *n.* over half or almost all of a certain group of things or people; over half or almost all of something. (No pl. Treated as sg or pl, but not countable.) **4.** *adv.* a word used to form the sup. form of some adjectives and adverbs; to the greatest extent. (Usually with *the*.) **5.** *adv.* very. (Used for emphasis.)

mostly ['most li] **1.** *adv.* more than half; for the most part. **2.** *adv.* most of the time; usually.

motel [mo 'tɛl] *n.* a hotel for people traveling by car; a hotel alongside a highway.

moth ['mɔθ] *n., irreg.* a small insect with large, broad wings and antennae, similar to a butterfly, but usually not as colorful. (Pl: ['mɔðz].)

mothball ['mɔθ bɔl] *n.* a small ball made of a substance that keeps moths away from clothes.

mother ['mʌð ɚ] **1.** *n.* a female who has given birth to a child or offspring. **2.** *n.* a term of address used with one's own ①. (Capitalized when written as a proper noun.) **3.** *adj.* [of one's language or country] native. (Prenominal only.) **4.** *tv.* to take care of someone in the manner of ①.

motherhood ['mʌð ɚ hʊd] *n.* the state of being a mother. (No pl.)

motion ['mo ʃən] **1.** *n.* movement; moving. (Pl only for types and instances.) **2.** *n.* a formal proposal that something be done, made during a meeting. **3.** *tv.* to direct someone by moving a part of one's body, usually the hands. **4.** *iv.* to point or indicate by moving a part of one's body, usually the hands.

motive ['mot ɪv] *n.* a reason for doing something; something—such as an idea, a need, or a way of thinking—that causes a person to do something.

motor ['mot ɚ] *n.* an engine; a machine that changes some kind of fuel into power that can lift, turn, or move things.

motorboat ['mot ɚ bot] *n.* a boat that is powered by a motor or engine.

motorcycle ['mot ɚ saɪ kəl] *n.* a vehicle that has two wheels and a frame larger and heavier than a bicycle, and that is powered by a motor.

motorist ['mot ə rɪst] *n.* someone who drives a car.

motto ['mɑt o] *n.* a short statement that expresses a belief or a rule of behavior. (Pl ends in *-s* or *-es.*)

mound ['maʊnd] *n.* a small hill or pile.

mount ['maʊnt] **1.** *n.* a support; an object that something is attached to or hung from. **2.** *n.* a (particular) mountain. (Abbreviated *Mt.*) **3.** *tv.* to get on an animal or vehicle that one must ride with one leg on either side of the animal or vehicle. **4.** *tv.* to climb something; to go up something. **5.** *tv.* to hang something to a fixed support; to attach something to a fixed support.

mountain ['maʊnt n] **1.** *n.* a very tall mass of land that pushes up from the surface of the earth; a very tall hill. **2.** *n.* a very tall pile of something; a very large amount of something. (Fig. on ①.)

mourn ['morn] **1.** *tv.* to feel sorrow or sadness about the death or loss of someone or something. (E.g., to *mourn the death of someone.*) **2.** *tv.* to feel sorrow or sadness about someone who has died. (E.g., to *mourn someone.*) **3.** *iv.* to feel sorrow or sadness, especially about someone's death. (E.g., to *mourn because of a death.*)

mourner ['mor nɚ] *n.* someone who mourns; someone who attends a funeral.

mouse ['maʊs] **1.** *n., irreg.* a small, furry rodent with tiny eyes and a long tail, like a rat but smaller. (Pl: MICE.) **2.** *n., irreg.* a device that can be moved around by one hand to control the movements of a pointer on a computer screen. (Pl: MICE or *mouses.*)

mousetrap ['maʊs træp] *n.* a simple device that is used to trap mice that are indoor pests.

mousse ['mus] *n.* a rich, creamy dessert made from cream, eggs, and fruit or chocolate. (Pl only for types and instances.)

mouth 1. ['maʊθ] *n., irreg.* the opening on the faces of animals where food and air enter the body. (Pl: ['maʊðz].) **2.** ['maʊθ] *n., irreg.* an opening of something; the entrance to something. (Fig. on ①.) **3.** ['maʊθ] *n., irreg.* the place where a river joins a lake, sea, or ocean. **4.** ['maʊð] *tv.* to move ① as if one were speaking but without producing actual speech.

mouthpiece ['maʊθ pis] **1.** *n.* the part of a musical instrument that is blown into; the part of a musical instrument that is put on or between one's lips. **2.** *n.* the part of a machine or device that is placed on or next to someone or something's mouth.

mouthwash ['maʊθ wɑʃ] *n.* a liquid that is used to rinse one's mouth in order to make the breath smell better or to kill germs in the mouth.

293

move ['muv] **1.** *iv.* to go to a different time or space; to change position in time or space. **2.** *iv.* to be in motion. **3.** *iv.* to change where one lives or works. **4.** *tv.* to transport someone or something to a different time or space; to cause someone or something to change position. **5.** *tv.* to cause someone or something to remain in motion. **6.** *tv.* to affect someone's emotions or feelings. **7.** *tv.* to formally make a suggestion at a meeting; to formally propose something. (The object is a clause with THAT ⑦.) **8.** *n.* an instance of changing position as in ①; a movement. **9.** *n.* the act of going to a new house to live. **10.** *n.* one step in a plan; an action that has a specific result. **11.** *n.* a player's turn in a game.

movement ['muv mənt] **1.** *n.* moving; changing position in time or space. (Pl only for types and instances.) **2.** *n.* a division of a symphony or other classical work of music. **3.** *n.* a common social or political goal and the people who work together to promote it.

movie ['muv i] **1.** *n.* a film; a motion picture; a story on film. **2.** the *adj.* use of ①.

mow ['mo] *tv., irreg.* to cut grass. (Pp: mowed or MOWN.)

mower ['mo ɚ] *n.* a machine used to cut grass evenly. (Short for *lawn mower*.)

mown ['mon] a pp of MOW.

Mr. ['mɪst ɚ] *n.* a title for an adult male. (The abbreviation of MISTER.)

Mrs. ['mɪs əz] *n.* a title for a married woman.

Ms. ['mɪz] *n.* a title for an adult female.

much ['mʌtʃ] **1.** *adv., irreg.* to a great extent; to a great degree; a lot. (Comp: MORE; sup: MOST.) **2.** *adj., irreg.* a lot; to quite an extent or degree. (Comp: MORE; sup: MOST.) **3.** *n.* a large extent; a large degree; a large amount. (No pl.)

mucus ['mju kəs] *n.* the slimy substance secreted by the body to protect and moisten certain tissues. (No pl.)

mud ['mʌd] *n.* a mixture of dirt and water; very wet soil. (No pl.)

muddle ['mʌd l] **1.** *n.* a confused mess; a condition of confusion. **2.** *tv.* to confuse something; to get things out of order. **3.** *iv.* to progress or move along in a confused or disorganized fashion.

muddy ['mʌd i] **1.** *adj.* covered with mud. (Adv: *muddily.* Comp: *muddier;* sup: *muddiest.*) **2.** *adj.* not clear; cloudy. (Said especially of colors or liquids. Fig. on ①. Adv: *muddily.* Comp: *muddier;* sup: *muddiest.*)

294

muffler ['mʌf lɚ] **1.** *n.* part of the exhaust system of a car that softens the noises of the engine. **2.** *n.* a scarf that can be wrapped around the neck for warmth.

mug ['mʌg] **1.** *n.* a drinking cup with a handle. **2.** *n.* the contents of ①. **3.** *tv.* to attack and rob someone.

mugger ['mʌg ɚ] *n.* someone who attacks and robs people on the street.

muggy ['mʌg i] *adj.* hot and humid. (Adv: *muggily.* Comp: *muggier;* sup: *muggiest.*)

mulch ['mʌltʃ] **1.** *n.* plant matter or other material spread on plants to protect them and to retain the moisture in the soil. (Pl only for types and instances.) **2.** *tv.* to spread ① around plants in a garden.

mule ['mjul] *n.* the offspring of one horse and one donkey.

multiple ['mʌl tə pəl] **1.** *adj.* involving many parts; consisting of many parts. (Adv: *multiply* ['mʌl tə pli].) **2.** *n.* a number that can be divided by another number without a remainder; a number that can be divided evenly by another number.

multiply ['mʌl tə plaɪ] **1.** *tv.* to increase something. **2.** *iv.* to reproduce; to have offspring; to breed. **3.** *iv.* to increase. **4.** ~ **by** to add an amount to itself the number of times shown by another number; to perform multiplication.

mumble ['mʌm bəl] **1.** *iv.* to speak in an unclear manner; to speak softly with poor pronunciation. **2.** *tv.* to say something that cannot be heard clearly. **3.** *n.* speech that cannot be heard clearly.

munch ['mʌntʃ] **1.** *tv.* to eat a crisp food that makes a noise; to eat something noisily. **2.** ~ **on** to eat something; to chew on something.

municipal [mju 'nɪs ə pəl] *adj.* of, for, or serving a city, town, or village. (Adv: *municipally.*)

mural ['mjʊr əl] *n.* a picture or scene that is painted on the surface of a wall.

murder ['mɚ dɚ] **1.** *n.* the killing of a human, done on purpose and against the law. **2.** *tv.* to kill someone on purpose and against the law.

murderer ['mɚ dɚ ɚ] *n.* someone who kills someone else; someone who is found guilty of murder.

murmur ['mɚ mɚ] **1.** *n.* a low, quiet sound. **2.** *n.* an irregular sound made by the heart, caused by defects in the heart. **3.** *iv.* to make low, quiet sounds; to speak very quietly. **4.** *tv.* to say something very quietly. (The object can be a clause with THAT ⑦.)

295

muscle ['mʌs əl] **1.** *n.* a group of long tissues in the body that can be shortened to make parts of the body move. **2.** *n.* strength; power. (No pl. Fig. on ①.)

muscular ['mʌs kjə lɚ] **1.** *adj.* in or of the muscles. **2.** *adj.* having muscles that are strong and well developed. (Adv: *muscularly.*)

museum [mju 'zi əm] *n.* a building where art or things of or about science, history, or some other subject are placed on display for the public to see and learn about.

mushroom ['mʌʃ rum] **1.** *n.* a kind of fungus that is often used as food. **2.** *iv.* to grow very quickly or suddenly.

mushy ['mʌʃ i] *adj.* soft and pulpy. (Adv: *mushily.* Comp: *mushier;* sup: *mushiest.*)

music ['mju zɪk] **1.** *n.* the sounds of the voice or of instruments making pleasant tones in a series or a series of groups. (No pl in standard English. Number is expressed with *piece(s) of music.*) **2.** *n.* a piece of paper that shows the notes of a particular song or melody. (No pl.)

musical ['mju zɪ kəl] **1.** *adj.* causing music to be made; producing notes or tones. (Adv: *musically* [...ɪk li].) **2.** *adj.* of or about music. (Adv: *musically* [...ɪk li].) **3.** *n.* a play or movie in which the actors sing songs, usually as a way of moving the story forward.

musician [mju 'zɪ ʃən] *n.* someone who plays a musical instrument; someone who writes music; someone who is in a band or an orchestra.

muss up ['mʌs əp] to make something messy, especially one's hair; to move someone's hair out of place.

mussel ['mʌs əl] *n.* a kind of shellfish, usually having very dark shells, that can be eaten as food.

must ['mʌst] **1.** *aux.* a form showing a requirement to do something; [to] have to [do something]. (Uses *had to* for a pt.) **2.** *aux.* a form indicating probability or likelihood. (Uses the form *has to have* plus the pp or *must have* plus the pp for a pt.) **3.** *n.* something that is necessary or essential.

mustache ['mʌs tæʃ] *n.* hair that grows on the upper lip.

mustard ['mʌs tɚd] **1.** *n.* a plant with a bright yellow flower. (No pl.) **2.** *n.* a seasoning or sauce made from the powdered seeds of ①, water or vinegar, and spices. (Pl only for types and instances.)

mustn't ['mʌs ənt] *cont.* must not. (Indicates what one is not allowed to do or what one may not do.)

296

musty ['mʌs ti] *adj.* smelling old and stale; smelling like mold. (Adv: *mustily.* Comp: *mustier;* sup: *mustiest.*)

mutiny ['mjut n ni] **1.** *n.* rebellion against someone in power, especially by sailors or soldiers. (No pl form in this sense.) **2.** *iv.* to be part of ①.

mutter ['mʌt ɚ] **1.** *iv.* to speak in a low, grumbling way that is hard to understand. **2.** *tv.* to say something as in ①.

mutual ['mju tʃu əl] **1.** *adj.* shared by two or more people; equally felt or done by each person toward the other. (Adv: *mutually.*) **2.** *adj.* common to two or more people; known to two or more people. (Adv: *mutually.*)

muzzle ['mʌz əl] **1.** *n.* [in certain animals] the part of the face that sticks out. **2.** *n.* a cover put over the mouth of an animal so that it will not bite someone or something. **3.** *n.* the front end of a gun; the barrel of a gun. **4.** *tv.* to put ② on an animal.

my ['maɪ] **1.** *pron.* the first-person sg possessive pronoun. (Describes people or things belonging to the speaker or writer. Used as a modifier before a noun. Compare this with MINE ⑥.) **2.** *interj.* a word used to show surprise.

myself [maɪ 'sɛlf] **1.** *pron.* the first-person sg reflexive pronoun. **2.** *pron.* ① used to emphasize the speaker or the writer as subject of the sentence.

mystery ['mɪs tə ri] **1.** *n.* the quality of not being explained, known, or understood; the quality of being hidden or secret. (Pl only for types and instances.) **2.** *n.* a book that involves a crime or murder that is solved in the story. **3.** the *adj.* use of ①.

myth ['mɪθ] **1.** *n.* a fable; a story that explains a mystery of nature or tells how something came into existence. **2.** *n.* someone or something that is imaginary or invented; something that is not based in fact. (Fig. on ①.)

mythical ['mɪθ ə kəl] *adj.* imaginary; [of a character, story, or situation] invented. (Adv: *mythically* [...ɪk li].)

mythology [mɪθ 'ɑl ə dʒi] **1.** *n.* the study of myths. (Pl only for types and instances.) **2.** *n.* a collection of myths about someone, something, or some culture.

297

N

n. an abbreviation of NOMINAL.

nag ['næg] **1.** *tv.* to continue to bother someone; to demand, by complaining all the time, that someone do something. **2.** *iv.* to continue to be a bother and a pest by making demands.

nail ['nel] **1.** *n.* a thin rod of metal, pointed on one end. **2.** *n.* one of the hard, flat tips at the ends of fingers and toes. **3.** *tv.* to attach or secure something with ①.

naked ['nek əd] *adj.* nude; wearing no clothes.

name ['nem] **1.** *n.* the word that indicates someone, something, or someplace. **2.** *n.* [someone's] fame or reputation. **3.** *n.* someone who is famous or important. **4.** *tv.* to give or apply a NAME as in ① to someone, something, or someplace. **5.** *tv.* to state or recite the ① of someone or something. **6.** *tv.* to appoint someone; to choose someone or something.

nanny ['næn i] *n.* a woman whose job is to take care of someone else's children.

nap ['næp] **1.** *iv.* to sleep for a short period of time, especially during the day. **2.** *n.* a short amount of sleep, especially during the day. **3.** *n.* the upright threads of a carpet or of a piece of material, such as velvet. (No pl.)

nape ['nep] *n.* the back [of the neck].

napkin ['næp kɪn] *n.* a square of fabric or paper used for protecting one's clothes and keeping tidy at meals.

narrate ['nɛr et] **1.** *tv.* to tell a story. **2.** *iv.* to tell about events that are being shown in a film, a slide show, on television, or in some other performance setting.

narrative ['nɛr ə tɪv] **1.** *n.* telling a story or giving an account of something that happened; narration. (No pl form in this sense.) **2.** *n.* an instance of ①.

narrow ['nɛr o] **1.** *adj.* not wide; short from side to side in comparison with the length of something from one end to the other. (Adv: *narrowly.* Comp: *narrower;* sup: *narrowest.*) **2.** *adj.* limited; not broad. (Fig. on ①. Adv: *narrowly.* Comp: *narrower;* sup: *narrowest.*) **3.** *tv.*

to cause something to become ①. **4.** *iv.* to become ①. **5.** *iv.* to become ②.

nasal ['nez əl] **1.** *adj.* of or about the nose. (Adv: *nasally.*) **2.** *adj.* of the quality of sound heard when making the speech sounds [m], [n], or [ŋ]. (Adv: *nasally.*) **3.** *n.* a speech sound, such as [m] or [n], made by opening the passage to the nose at the back of the throat.

nasty ['næs ti] **1.** *adj.* mean; angry; unpleasant. (Adv: *nastily.* Comp: *nastier;* sup: *nastiest.*) **2.** *adj.* dirty-minded; offensive to one's morals. (Adv: *nastily.* Comp: *nastier;* sup: *nastiest.*) **3.** *adj.* very serious; bad; dangerous. (Adv: *nastily.* Comp: *nastier;* sup: *nastiest.*) **4.** *adj.* not pleasant to see, hear, smell, taste, or touch. (Adv: *nastily.* Comp: *nastier;* sup: *nastiest.*)

nation ['ne ʃən] **1.** *n.* a country; a country that governs itself. **2.** *n.* the people of a country; a group of people who are ruled by the same government.

national ['næ ʃ ə nəl] **1.** *adj.* of or about a nation; belonging to a nation; throughout a nation. (Adv: *nationally.*) **2.** *n.* a citizen of a specific nation or a particular group of nations.

nationality [næ ʃ ə 'næl ə ti] *n.* the status that arises from having citizenship in a particular country or being born in a particular country.

native ['ne tɪv] **1.** *n.* something that comes from a certain country or region. **2.** *n.* someone born in a particular place. **3.** *adj.* born or raised in a certain country or region; belonging to a certain country or region. (Adv: *natively.*)

natural ['nætʃ ə rəl] **1.** *adj.* made by nature; existing in nature; not artificial; not made by people; not affected by people. (Adv: *naturally.*) **2.** *adj.* existing since birth; not learned. (Adv: *naturally.*) **3.** *n.* someone who is thought of as perfect for a certain job; someone who does something very well, especially through inborn ability. **4.** *n.* a musical note that is not a sharp or a flat; one of the white keys on the piano.

nature ['ne tʃɚ] **1.** *n.* everything in the world except the material products of human work and thought: people, animals, plants, rocks, land, water, the weather, etc. (No pl.) **2.** *n.* land that has not been affected by humans. (No pl.) **3.** *n.* [someone's or something's] character; the essential qualities of someone or something; what someone or something really is.

naughty ['nɔ ti] **1.** *adj.* bad; behaving badly; not obeying rules. (Usually used to describe the behavior of children. Adv: *naughtily.* Comp: *naughtier;* sup: *naughtiest.*) **2.** *adj.* vulgar; indecent. (Adv: *naughtily.* Comp: *naughtier;* sup: *naughtiest.*)

nausea ['nɔ zi ə] *n.* a feeling of sickness; the feeling that one has to vomit. (No pl.)

nauseous ['nɔ ʃəs, 'nɔ zi əs] **1.** *adj.* causing nausea; sickening; causing someone to feel sick. (Adv: *nauseously.*) **2.** *adj.* experiencing nausea; sickened. (Adv: *nauseously.*)

nautical ['nɔt ɪ kəl] *adj.* of or about ships, shipping, or sailors. (Adv: *nautically* [...ɪk li].)

naval ['ne vəl] *adj.* of or about a navy.

navel ['ne vəl] *n.* the depression in the center of the belly where a baby is attached to its mother until shortly after birth.

navigate ['næv ə get] **1.** *tv.* to steer a ship, airplane, or other vehicle in some direction. **2.** *tv.* to travel or follow a route on the water, over land, or in the air. **3.** *iv.* to determine the proper direction or route.

navigation [næv ə 'ge ʃən] *n.* the rules, skills, and science of navigating. (No pl.)

navy ['nev i] *n.* the branch of the military that deals with protecting the sea or fighting at sea.

near ['nɪr] **1.** *prep.* at a place that is not far away from someone or something; at a time that is not far away from something. **2.** *adj.* close in distance, time, relationship, or effect. (Comp: *nearer;* sup: *nearest.*) **3.** *adv.* at or to a place that is not far away; at or to a time that is not too distant. (Comp: *nearer;* sup: *nearest.*) **4.** *tv.* to come closer to someone or something; to approach someone or something. **5.** *iv.* to come closer in time or space; to approach.

nearby ['nɪr 'baɪ] **1.** *adv.* near; close; not far away. **2.** *adj.* near; close; not far away.

nearly ['nɪr li] *adv.* almost; not quite.

nearsighted ['nɪr saɪt ɪd] *adj.* unable to see things in the distance clearly; myopic. (Adv: *nearsightedly.*)

neat ['nit] *adj.* clean; tidy; orderly. (Adv: *neatly.* Comp: *neater;* sup: *neatest.*)

necessary ['nɛs ə sɛr i] *adj.* required; needed. (Adv: *necessarily* [nɛs ə 'sɛr ə li].)

300

necessity [nə 'sɛs ə ti] **1.** *n.* the quality of being necessary or needed. (No pl.) **2.** *n.* something that is required; something that is needed or necessary.

neck ['nɛk] **1.** *n.* the narrow part of the body that connects the head to the rest of the body; the outside of the throat. **2.** *n.* the narrowest part of something; something narrow that connects two things. (Fig. on ①.)

necklace ['nɛk ləs] *n.* a decorative band, chain, or similar object that is worn around the neck.

necktie ['nɛk taɪ] *n.* a specially made strip of decorative cloth, typically worn under the collar of a man's shirt. (Also a TIE. Originally served the purpose of keeping the collar closed.)

need ['nid] **1.** *n.* something that is required or necessary; something that must be done or had; a requirement. **2.** *tv.* to require something; to have to have something; to want something for a certain reason.

needle ['nid l] **1.** *n.* a thin, pointed spike of metal having a narrow slit that thread fits through, used for sewing. **2.** *n.* a thin, hollow, pointed spike of metal used for injecting and removing body fluids. **3.** *n.* a thin, pointed spike used to show a position on a scale or meter. **4.** *n.* the part of a record player that "rides" on a (vinyl) record as it is played. **5.** *n.* a long, thin, sharply pointed leaf of a pine tree. **6.** *n.* a long, thin, sharp thorn as found on a cactus. **7.** *tv.* to annoy someone.

needlework ['nid l wɚk] *n.* crafts that are done with a needle, such as sewing. (No pl.)

needy ['nid i] *adj.* [of someone] very poor; [of someone] needing the basic things in life. (Adv: *needily.* Comp: *needier*; sup: *neediest*.)

negative ['nɛg ə tɪv] **1.** *adj.* meaning "not" or "no"; expressing "not" or "no"; showing refusal or denial. (Adv: *negatively.*) **2.** *adj.* not positive; the opposite of positive; lacking something that makes a thing positive; not good. (Adv: *negatively.*) **3.** *adj.* less than zero; minus; below the number zero. **4.** *adj.* cynical; not having hope; having a sad or gloomy outlook. (Adv: *negatively.*) **5.** *adj.* showing that a certain disease or condition is not present. (Adv: *negatively.*) **6.** *adj.* [of some part of an electrical circuit] lower in electrical charge than other points in the same circuit, allowing electrical energy to flow from other parts of the circuit. (Adv: *negatively.*) **7.** *n.* a word or statement that means "not" or "no." **8.** *n.* a piece of film (for photography). **9.** *n.* a quality or factor that is ②.

301

neglect [nɪ ˈglɛkt] **1.** *tv.* not to take care of someone or something; not to pay attention to someone or something; to ignore someone or something. **2.** *n.* the lack of taking care of someone or something; a lack of paying attention to someone or something. (No pl.)

negotiate [nə ˈgo ʃi et] **1.** *iv.* to discuss the matters that need to be settled before reaching an agreement. **2.** *tv.* to make an agreement through discussions as in ①. **3.** *tv.* to move around or through a difficult route successfully.

neighbor [ˈne bɚ] **1.** *n.* someone who lives very close by. **2.** *n.* someone who is sitting or standing next to oneself.

neighborhood [ˈne bɚ hʊd] **1.** *n.* a specific area within a larger city or town where people live. **2.** *n.* the people who live in a certain area of the city.

neighboring [ˈne bɚ ɪŋ] *adj.* adjacent; bordering.

neither [ˈni ðɚ] **1.** *adj.* not EITHER; not one person or thing nor the other; not either of two people or things. **2.** *pron.* not EITHER; not either one (of two people or things). (Treated as sg.) **3.** *conj.* not. (Used before a sequence of two words or phrases connected by NOR.)

nephew [ˈnɛf ju] *n.* the son of one's brother or sister; the son of one's spouse's brother or sister.

nerve [ˈnɚv] **1.** *n.* a fiber in the body that carries messages to and from the brain. **2.** *n.* courage; bravery. (No pl.)

nervous [ˈnɚv əs] **1.** *adj.* apprehensive; worried; jumpy; edgy. (Adv: *nervously.*) **2.** *adj.* of or about the nerves.

-ness [nəs] *suffix* a form that can be added freely to adjectives to create a noun with a parallel meaning.

nest [ˈnɛst] **1.** *n.* a structure made of twigs that is built by a bird as a shelter for its eggs and that is typically rounded and bowl-shaped. **2.** *n.* a place where certain animals live with their young. **3.** *iv.* to build or live in ① or ②.

net [ˈnɛt] **1.** *n.* a piece of mesh fabric—made of string, wire, or cord and sometimes attached to something—that is typically used to catch, trap, or block something. **2.** *n.* a system for fast electronic communication connecting people, businesses, and institutions. (Short for INTERNET. Usually capitalized.) **3.** *adj.* remaining after all factors have been considered, deducted, or added, as with weight, income, cost, effect, results, outcome, etc.

network ['nɛt wɚk] **1.** *n.* a pattern of crossing lines, paths, or similar structures; a system of lines, paths, or similar structures that are connected together. **2.** *n.* a group of computers connected to each other and the systems that connect them. **3.** *n.* a group of radio or television stations that broadcast the same programs. **4.** *n.* a collection of friends or business contacts. **5.** *iv.* to make social and business contacts; to talk with people in one's area of business or interest.

neurotic [nʊ 'rɑt ɪk] **1.** *adj.* of or about a mild psychological problem or illness, such as having obsessions or irrational fears; affected by such a problem or illness. (Adv: *neurotically* [...ɪk li].) **2.** *n.* someone who has irrational fears or obsessions or some other mild psychological problem or illness.

neuter ['nut ɚ] **1.** *adj.* neither masculine nor feminine; not having a SEX ③. **2.** *adj.* [of a class of words] not masculine or feminine.

neutral ['nu trəl] **1.** *adj.* not joining with either side in a war, conflict, or argument. (Adv: *neutrally*.) **2.** *adj.* at neither extreme; in the middle of a scale. (Adv: *neutrally*.)

neutron ['nu trɑn] *n.* in the nucleus of an atom, a particle that has no electrical charge.

never ['nɛv ɚ] *adv.* not ever; at no time.

new ['nu] **1.** *adj.* recently done, made, bought, acquired, discovered, or built; not existing or known of before. (Adv: *newly*. Comp: *newer;* sup: *newest*. See also NEWS.) **2.** *adj.* the more recent of two or more things. (Comp: *newer;* sup: *newest*.) **3.** *adj.* not familiar; strange; unknown. (Adv: *newly*. Comp: *newer;* sup: *newest*.) **4.** *adj.* different; changed. (Adv: *newly*. Comp: *newer;* sup: *newest*.) **5.** *adj.* beginning again; starting over. (Adv: *newly*. Comp: *newer;* sup: *newest*.)

newborn ['nu born] **1.** *n.* an infant; a baby that has just been born. **2.** *adj.* having just been born.

newcomer ['nu kəm ɚ] *n.* someone who has recently arrived at a certain place.

newly ['nu li] *adv.* recently; as of late; just.

newlywed ['nu li wɛd] *n.* someone who has recently married.

news ['nuz] **1.** *n.* information, particularly current information about a person or a recent event. (Treated as sg. No other sg form in this sense.) **2.** *n.* a television or radio program where information about recent events is broadcast. (Treated as sg. No other sg form in this sense.)

303

newspaper ['nuz pe pɚ] *n.* a daily or weekly publication consisting of news, articles, and advertisements printed on large sheets of paper.

newt ['nut] *n.* a small amphibian with four legs and a tail.

next ['nɛkst] **1.** *adj.* following; nearest in sequence after; soonest after. **2.** *adj.* located in the nearest position to something; [of someone or something] beside someone or something [else]. **3.** *adv.* at the soonest time after now; in the nearest place or position after this one.

nibble ['nɪb əl] **1.** *n.* a small bite of something; a little taste of something. **2.** *iv.* to eat only a tiny bit. **3.** *tv.* to eat a tiny bite of something; to eat something in tiny bites; to bite something gently with tiny bites.

nice ['naɪs] **1.** *adj.* pleasant; agreeable; enjoyable. (Adv: *nicely.* Comp: *nicer;* sup: *nicest.*) **2.** *adj.* kind; friendly. (Adv: *nicely.* Comp: *nicer;* sup: *nicest.*) **3.** *adj.* good; clever; well done. (Informal. Adv: *nicely.* Comp: *nicer;* sup: *nicest.*)

nick ['nɪk] **1.** *n.* a small dent or chip on the surface of something. **2.** *tv.* to put or cause a small dent or chip on the surface of something.

nickel ['nɪk əl] **1.** *n.* a metallic element that does not rust easily. (No pl.) **2.** *n.* a U.S. coin worth five cents.

nickname ['nɪk nem] **1.** *n.* a secondary, familiar, or intimate name for someone or something. **2.** *tv.* to give someone, something, or someplace a NICKNAME as in ①.

niece ['nis] *n.* the daughter of one's brother or sister; the daughter of one's spouse's brother or sister.

night ['naɪt] **1.** *n.* the time between sunset and sunrise; the darkness between sunset and sunrise; nighttime. (No pl.) **2.** *n.* the period of time between sunset and midnight. **3.** *n.* a specific ① or ② when something happens or is planned. **4.** *n.* a unit of measure based on the number of NIGHTS ① but also including the period of time between NIGHTS ①. (E.g., stay at a hotel *for seven nights.*) **5.** *adj.* happening during ① or ②.

nightclub ['naɪt kləb] *n.* a bar or club open at night where there is entertainment, dancing, performances, etc.

nightgown ['naɪt gaʊn] *n.* an item of clothing like a dress, usually for women, that is worn in bed.

nightlife ['naɪt laɪf] *n.* entertainment and social activities that take place during the night. (No pl.)

nightmare ['naɪt mɛr] **1.** *n.* a frightening dream. **2.** *n.* a real event that is frightening or awful. (Fig. on ①.)

304

nights *adv.* every night; during every night; only at night.

nighttime ['naɪt taɪm] **1.** *n.* the time during the night; the time from after sunset until sunrise. (No pl.) **2.** the *adj.* use of ①.

nimble ['nɪm bəl] *adj.* able to move quickly and easily; agile. (Adv: *nimbly.* Comp: *nimbler;* sup: *nimblest.*)

nine ['naɪn] 9. Go to FOUR.

nineteen ['naɪn 'tin] 19. Go to FOUR.

nineteenth ['naɪn 'tinθ] 19th. Go to FOURTH.

ninetieth ['naɪn ti əθ] 90th. Go to FOURTH.

ninety ['naɪn ti] 90. Go to FORTY.

ninth ['naɪnθ] 9th. Go to FOURTH.

nip ['nɪp] **1.** *tv.* to pinch or bite someone or something. **2.** *tv.* to remove something by pinching or biting.

nitwit ['nɪt wɪt] *n.* an idiot; someone who is foolish or stupid.

nix ['nɪks] *tv.* to put a stop to something; to end something; to reject something.

no ['no] **1.** *adj.* not any; not a; not one; not any amount of. **2.** *adv.* a word that is used as an answer to show that one does not agree. **3.** *adv.* a word that is used to stress a negative statement. **4.** *n.* a negative answer. (Pl ends in -*s* or -*es*.)

nobility [no 'bɪl ə ti] *n.* dignity; the quality of being noble. (No pl.)

noble ['nob əl] **1.** *adj.* refined; moral; showing dignity. (Adv: *nobly.* Comp: *nobler;* sup: *noblest.*) **2.** the *adj.* use of ①. (Adv: *nobly.* Comp: *nobler;* sup: *noblest.*) **3.** *adj.* [of a chemical element] not able to mix with other elements; [of a chemical element] not able to react with other elements.

nobody ['no bad i] **1.** *pron.* no person; no one; not anybody. (No pl.) **2.** *n.* someone who is not important; someone who has no power.

nod ['nad] **1.** *n.* a quick downward or up-and-down movement of the head, usually to show agreement. **2.** *tv.* to express something by moving one's head as in ④. **3.** *tv.* to move one's head in agreement as in ④. **4.** *iv.* to move one's head down, or up and down, quickly, especially to show agreement or approval, or as a greeting. **5.** *iv.* to let one's head jerk down as one begins to fall asleep. **6.** *iv.* [for one's head] to jerk down as one begins to fall asleep while sitting or standing.

noise ['nɔɪz] *n.* annoying or unwanted sound. (Pl only for types and instances.)

noisy ['nɔɪz i] *adj.* [of a sound or of someone or something making sounds] loud; [of someone or something] making much noise. (Adv: *noisily.* Comp: *noisier*; sup: *noisiest.*)

nominal ['nɑm ə nəl] **1.** *n.* a noun or expression that can serve as the subject of a sentence, the direct or indirect object of a verb, or the object of a preposition. (Abbreviated *n.* here.) **2.** *adj.* functioning as ①. (Adv: *nominally.*) **3.** *adj.* in name only; in theory, but not in reality. (Adv: *nominally.*) **4.** *adj.* [of a fee or charge] very small, especially as compared with what something is worth. (Adv: *nominally.*)

nominate ['nɑm ə net] **1.** *tv.* to formally propose someone for a job or an office. **2.** *tv.* to propose that someone or something receive an award.

none ['nʌn] **1.** *pron.* not one; not any; no person; no thing. **2.** *pron.* not one part; no part.

nonflammable [nɑn 'flæm ə bəl] *adj.* difficult to burn; impossible to burn; not flammable. (Adv: *nonflammably.*)

nonprofit [nɑn 'prɑf ɪt] *adj.* not making a profit; not organized or established for the purpose of making money.

nonsense ['nɑn sɛns] *n.* something that does not make sense; something that is foolish. (No pl.)

nonstop ['nɑn 'stɑp] **1.** *adj.* without stopping or pausing; continuous. **2.** *adv.* without stopping; continuously.

noodle ['nud l] *n.* a strip or piece of pasta.

noon ['nun] *n.* the time in the middle of the day between morning and afternoon; 12:00 in the daytime; midday. (No pl.)

noonday ['nun de] *adj.* happening at noon; happening in the middle of the day. (Prenominal only.)

noontime ['nun taɪm] **1.** *n.* noon; the middle of the day. (No pl.) **2.** *adj.* happening at noon; happening in the middle of the day. (Prenominal only.)

noose ['nus] *n.* a loop tied at the end of a rope, used to trap or hang someone or something.

nor ['nɔr] *conj.* a word used to connect a series of persons or things that are not options or possibilities.

normal ['nɔr məl] **1.** *adj.* regular; typical; usual; expected. (Adv: *normally.*) **2.** *adj.* sane; not sick in the mind. (Adv: *normally.*)

north ['nɔrθ] **1.** *n.* the direction to the left of someone or something facing the rising sun. (No pl.) **2.** *n.* the northern part of a region,

306

country, or planet. (No pl form. Capitalized when referring to a specific region of the United States.) **3.** *adj.* at ①; in ②; on the side toward ①; facing toward ①. **4.** *adj.* from ①. (Used especially to describe wind.) **5.** *adv.* toward ①; into the northern part of something.

northeast [norθ 'ist] **1.** *n.* a direction halfway between north and east. (No pl.) **2.** *n.* an area in the northeastern part of a city, region, or country. (No pl. Capitalized when referring to a specific region of the United States.) **3.** *adj.* in ②; toward ①; facing ①. **4.** *adj.* [of wind] blowing from ①. **5.** *adv.* toward ①.

northeastern [norθ 'ist ən] *adj.* in the northeast; toward the northeast; facing northeast.

northern ['nor ðən] **1.** *adj.* in the north; toward the north; facing the north. **2.** *adj.* [of wind] blowing from the north.

northwest [norθ 'wɛst] **1.** *n.* a direction halfway between north and west. (No pl.) **2.** *n.* an area in the northwestern part of a country. (No pl. Capitalized when referring to a region of the United States.) **3.** *adj.* in ②; toward ①; facing ①. **4.** *adj.* [of wind] blowing from ①. **5.** *adv.* toward ①.

northwestern [norθ 'wɛs tən] *adj.* in the northwest; toward the northwest; facing northwest.

nose ['noz] **1.** *n.* the structure between the mouth and the eyes in humans, being the organ used for smelling and breathing, and a similar structure in other animals. **2.** *n.* the sense of smell; ① used for smelling something. **3.** *n.* the front end of an airplane, a rocket, a ship, or some other similar thing. (Fig. on ①.)

nosedive ['noz daɪv] **1.** *n.* a sudden drop or decline, especially the sudden fall of an airplane with the nose pointing downward. **2.** *iv.* to plunge with the nose pointing downward. **3.** *iv.* [for a measurement] to decline or drop suddenly. (Fig. on ②.)

nostril ['nɑs trəl] *n.* one of the two outside holes of the nose.

nosy ['noz i] *adj.* trying to find out (private) things about people or things; snooping; prying. (Adv: *nosily.* Comp: *nosier;* sup: *nosiest.*)

not ['nɑt] **1.** *adv.* a negative particle used with verbs, adverbs, participles, prepositions, nominals, and adjectives. (Contracted to *n't.*) **2.** *adv.* a negative particle that stands for a part of a sentence that is being refused, denied, or negated.

307

notable [ˈnot ə bəl] **1.** *adj.* deserving to be noted; noteworthy; remarkable. (Adv: *notably.*) **2.** *n.* someone who is worth noting; someone who is remarkable.

notation [no ˈte ʃən] *n.* a set of signs or symbols that is used to represent something.

notch [ˈnɑtʃ] **1.** *n.* a V-shaped cut in a surface, made for a specific reason. **2.** *n.* a degree of quality or quantity. (Fig. on ①.) **3.** *tv.* to make a V-shaped cut for a specific reason.

note [ˈnot] **1.** *n.* a short written message. **2.** *n.* a comment (on the bottom of a page or at the end of a book) that explains, clarifies, or provides the source of something in the text. (See also FOOTNOTE.) **3.** *n.* a piece of paper money; a bill. **4.** *n.* the written symbol for a specific musical tone. **5.** *n.* a specific musical tone; one sound made by singing or playing a musical instrument. **6.** *n.* a sign of something; a hint of something. **7.** *tv.* to write something as a short message. (The object can be a clause with THAT ⑦.) **8.** *tv.* to remark about something; to state something; to observe something. (The object is a clause with THAT ⑦.) **9.** *tv.* to pay attention to something; to remember something. (The object can be a clause with THAT ⑦.)

notebook [ˈnot bʊk] *n.* a book in which notes are written.

notepaper [ˈnot pe pɚ] *n.* paper that notes, such as thank-you notes, are written on. (Pl only for types and instances.)

notes *n.* information that is written down by someone while listening to a lecture or reading a book.

nothing [ˈnʌθ ɪŋ] **1.** *pron.* not one thing; not a thing; not anything. (No pl. Treated as sg.) **2.** *n.* something that is without meaning; something that is not significant or important; not anything that is significant or important. (No pl. Treated as sg.) **3.** *n.* zero; no amount. (No pl.)

notice [ˈnot ɪs] **1.** *tv.* to see, hear, taste, or smell someone or something; to be aware of someone or something. (The object can be a clause with THAT ⑦.) **2.** *n.* an announcement; a sign that warns or informs; a warning. **3.** *n.* attention; a state of awareness [about something]. (No pl.)

noticeable [ˈnot ɪs ə bəl] *adj.* able to be seen; easily seen; easily noticed. (Adv: *noticeably.*)

notify [ˈnot ə fɑɪ] *tv.* to inform someone about something; to tell someone officially about something.

notion [ˈno ʃən] **1.** *n.* an opinion; a belief. **2.** *n.* a whim; an intention.

noun [ˈnɑʊn] *n.* a word that refers to a person, place, thing, or idea. (See also NOMINAL.)

nourish [ˈnɚ ɪʃ] **1.** *tv.* to feed someone or something; to give someone or something the things necessary for life and health. **2.** *tv.* to encourage something; to support something as it develops. (Fig. on ①. Used especially with feelings and emotions.)

novel [ˈnɑv əl] **1.** *n.* a relatively long, written story. **2.** *adj.* new; original; not known before.

novelty [ˈnɑv əl ti] **1.** *n.* the quality of being novel; the quality of being new or original. (Pl only for types and instances.) **2.** *n.* a small item, often inexpensive and usually interesting or amusing. **3.** the *adj.* use of ① or ②. (Prenominal only.)

November [no ˈvɛm bɚ] Go to MONTH.

novice [ˈnɑv ɪs] **1.** *n.* someone who is new at a job or responsibility. **2.** *n.* someone who has just joined a religious order and will become a monk or a nun. **3.** *adj.* [of someone] new to a task or activity. (Prenominal only.)

now [ˈnɑʊ] **1.** *adv.* at this moment; at this point in time; immediately. **2.** *adv.* in these days; in modern times; in present times. **3.** *adv.* a word used for emphasis, to get someone's attention, with commands, and to move on to the next topic. **4.** *n.* the present; this time. (No pl.)

nowhere [ˈno ʍɛr] *adv.* at no place; to or toward no place; not to or at any place.

nuclear [ˈnu kli ɚ] *adj.* of or about the nucleus of an atom or the energy created by splitting or fusing the nuclei of atoms.

nuclei [ˈnu kli ɑɪ] pl of NUCLEUS.

nucleus [ˈnu kli əs] **1.** *n., irreg.* the center of something; the core of something. (Pl: NUCLEI.) **2.** *n., irreg.* the core of an atom, consisting of protons and neutrons. **3.** *n., irreg.* the control center of a living cell.

nude [ˈnud] **1.** *adj.* naked; not wearing any clothes. **2.** *n.* someone who is not wearing any clothes; a statue or a painting of someone who is not wearing any clothes.

nuisance [ˈnu səns] *n.* a bother; someone or something that is annoying.

numb [ˈnʌm] **1.** *adj.* unable to feel anything; unable to sense anything. (Adv: *numbly* [ˈnʌm li]. Comp: *number* [ˈnʌm ɚ]; sup: *numbest* [ˈnʌm əst].) **2.** *tv.* to cause someone or something to be unable to feel anything.

number ['nʌm bɚ] **1.** *n.* a symbol or a word that expresses an amount; a symbol or a word that shows how many; a digit or series of digits that has an assigned significance. **2.** *n.* a specific ① that identifies someone or something in a series. (Also appears as the symbol "#".) **3.** *n.* a song; a piece of music. **4.** *n.* a grammatical category showing whether one or more than one person or thing is being referred to. (Pl only for types and instances.) **5.** *tv.* to assign something a ①. (Refers especially to things in a series.) **6.** *tv.* to reach a total of a certain amount; to be a certain amount.

numeral ['num ə rəl] *n.* the symbol or figure that represents a number.

numerous ['num ə rəs] *adj.* many; several; a lot. (Adv: *numerously.*)

nun ['nʌn] *n.* a woman who is a member of a religious order.

nurse ['nɚs] **1.** *n.* someone, usually a woman, trained to provide medical care, often under the supervision of a physician. **2.** *n.* a woman who raises other people's children; a woman who helps a family raise its children. **3.** *tv.* to feed a baby milk from one's breast. **4.** *tv.* [for anyone] to treat a disease or a sick person. **5.** *iv.* [for a female mammal] to feed a baby mammal as in ③. **6.** *iv.* [for a baby mammal] to suck or take milk from a female mammal.

nursery ['nɚs (ə) ri] **1.** *n.* a room for babies in a hospital or residence. **2.** *n.* a place where children are watched while their parents are busy at something else. **3.** *n.* a place where plants are grown and sold.

nut ['nʌt] **1.** *n.* a hard, woody shell containing an edible part. **2.** *n.* the edible part of ①, used as food. **3.** *n.* someone who is crazy, insane, or foolish. (Slang.)

nutrition [nu 'trɪ ʃən] *n.* the science of providing people with information about healthy food. (No pl.)

nutshell ['nʌt ʃɛl] *n.* the hard, woody shell around the edible part of a nut.

nutty ['nʌt i] **1.** *adj.* tasting like a nut; made from nuts. (Adv: *nuttily.* Comp: *nuttier;* sup: *nuttiest.*) **2.** *adj.* crazy; insane. (Slang. Adv: *nuttily.* Comp: *nuttier;* sup: *nuttiest.*)

nylon ['nɑɪ lɑn] **1.** *n.* a very strong but light, often flexible fiber made from chemicals, that is used especially to make clothes and fabric. (No pl.) **2.** *adj.* made from ①.

O

oak ['ok] **1.** *n.* a kind of strong tree that produces an edible nut. **2.** *n.* wood from ①. (Pl only for types and instances.) **3.** *adj.* made from ②.

oar ['or] *n.* a long pole with one wide, flat end—similar to a paddle—used to steer and row boats.

oases [o 'e siz] pl of OASIS.

oasis [o 'e sɪs] **1.** *n., irreg.* in a desert, a place that has water and trees. (Pl: OASES.) **2.** *n., irreg.* a place that is free of problems or difficulties. (Fig. on ①.)

oat ['ot] **1.** *n.* a cereal grain used as food for humans and cattle. **2.** *n.* a single grain of ①. **3.** *adj.* made of ①.

oath ['oθ] *n., irreg.* a promise that one will speak only the truth; a promise that one will do something. (Pl: ['oðz].)

oatmeal ['ot mil] **1.** *n.* crushed oats. (No pl.) **2.** *n.* cooked ①, usually eaten with milk and sugar. (No pl.) **3.** *adj.* made with crushed oats.

oats *n.* a cereal grain used as food for humans and cattle. (Treated as pl, but not countable.)

obedience [o 'bid i əns] *n.* the condition of being obedient. (No pl.)

obedient [o 'bid i ənt] *adj.* obeying; following orders. (Adv: *obediently.*)

obey [o 'be] **1.** *tv.* to yield to someone and do as one has been instructed; to follow instructions, commands, or rules. **2.** *iv.* to do as one is told.

object 1. ['ɑb dʒɛkt] *n.* a thing; something that can be seen or touched. **2.** ['ɑb dʒɛkt] *n.* a goal; an aim; someone or something that a thought or an action is directed toward. **3.** ['ɑb dʒɛkt] *n.* a noun or nominal that is affected by the action or condition of a verb; a noun or nominal within a prepositional phrase. **4.** ~ **to** [əb 'dʒɛkt tu] to oppose something; to argue against something; to make an objection about something.

objection [əb 'dʒɛk ʃən] *n.* a stated reason for not wanting to do something.

311

oblige [ə 'blaɪdʒ] **1.** *iv.* to do something nice for someone; to do someone a favor. **2.** ~ **to do** to require someone to do something.

oblong ['ɑb lɔŋ] *adj.* [especially of a circle or a rectangle] long and a little narrow. (Adv: *oblongly.*)

obnoxious [əb 'nɑk ʃəs] *adj.* very annoying; very irritating. (Adv: *obnoxiously.*)

oboe ['o bo] *n.* a musical instrument that has a long, thin wooden body and a mouthpiece holding a double reed.

obscure [əb 'skjʊr] **1.** *adj.* [of reasoning or explanation] hard to understand or not clearly stated. (Adv: *obscurely.*) **2.** *adj.* not well known; not famous. (Adv: *obscurely.*) **3.** *adj.* hard to see; hidden, especially by darkness. (Adv: *obscurely.*) **4.** *tv.* to make something hard to see; to keep something from view; to dim or darken something. **5.** *tv.* to make something difficult to understand; to cloud one's meaning. (Fig. on ④.)

observe [əb 'zɔv] **1.** *tv.* to watch something; to see something; to notice something. **2.** *tv.* to obey a law or custom; to pay attention to a law or custom. (The object can be a clause with THAT ⑦.) **3.** *tv.* to celebrate a holiday. **4.** *tv.* to make a comment or a remark; to state something. (The object is a clause with THAT ⑦.)

obsessed [əb 'sɛst] *adj.* thinking about someone or something too much, as if one were forced to do so.

obstacle ['ɑb stə kəl] *n.* something that is in the way of someone, something, or some action; a hindrance; a block.

obstinate ['ɑb stə nɪt] *adj.* stubborn; not willing to change one's mind; not willing to listen to other people's ideas. (Adv: *obstinately.*)

obstruct [əb 'strʌkt] *tv.* to get in the way of someone or something; to block someone or something.

obstruction [əb 'strʌk ʃən] *n.* something that is in the way; something that is blocking the way.

obtain [əb 'ten] *tv.* to get something; to gain possession of something; to come to own something.

obvious ['ɑb vi əs] *adj.* easily recognized; easily seen or understood; plain; clear. (Adv: *obviously.*)

occasion [ə 'ke ʒən] **1.** *n.* a time when something happens; a time when something occurs; an instance. **2.** *n.* a special event.

occasional [ə 'ke ʒə nəl] *adj.* happening from time to time; happening once in a while; not happening all the time or regularly. (Adv: *occasionally*.)

occult [ə 'kʌlt] *adj.* hidden from regular knowledge; filled with mystery.

occupancy ['ɑk jə pən si] **1.** *n.* occupying a house, building, or other piece of property. (No pl.) **2.** *n.* the number of people that a room or building is allowed to hold. (No pl.)

occupant ['ɑk jə pənt] *n.* someone who lives in a certain place; a business that occupies a certain building or space.

occupation [ɑk jə 'pe ʃən] **1.** *n.* a job; a career; what one does for a living. **2.** *n.* taking or keeping possession of a region or a country.

occupy ['ɑk jə paɪ] **1.** *tv.* to use or consume time by doing something. **2.** *tv.* to keep someone busy doing something. **3.** *tv.* to be in a certain place; to take up the space in a certain place; to live in a certain place; to have one's business in a certain place. **4.** *tv.* to move into and take control of another country.

occur [ə 'kɚ] **1.** *iv.* to happen; to take place. **2.** *iv.* to be; to exist; to be found.

occurrence [ə 'kɚ əns] *n.* an event; something that happens; an incident.

ocean ['o ʃən] *n.* a large body of salt water that covers ¾ of the earth's surface, or one of that body's four divisions: the Arctic Ocean, the Atlantic Ocean, the Indian Ocean, and the Pacific Ocean.

o'clock [ə 'klɑk] *adv.* a word used to indicate the time of day. (It follows a number from 1 to 12 and means that it is that time exactly, or zero minutes past the hour. Literally, *of the clock*.)

octagon ['ɑk tə gɑn] *n.* a flat figure or shape with eight sides.

octave ['ɑk tɪv] *n.* a musical interval of two notes where the higher note is twelve half tones above the lower note; [on a piano] the first and eighth key in a row of eight white keys.

October [ɑk 'to bɚ] Go to MONTH.

octopi ['ɑk tə paɪ] a pl of OCTOPUS.

octopus ['ɑk tə pəs] *n., irreg.* a boneless sea creature with eight legs. (Greek for "eight-footed." The English pl is *octopuses* or OCTOPI.)

odd ['ɑd] **1.** *adj.* strange; different; unusual; out of place. (Adv: *oddly*. Comp: *odder*; sup: *oddest*.) **2.** *adj.* not even; [of a number] not able to be divided by two without an amount (one) being left over. **3.** *adj.*

313

not regular; [of occasions or events] random; occasional. (Prenominal only. Comp: *odder;* sup: *oddest.*)

oddity ['ʊd ə ti] **1.** *n.* the state of being unusual or strange. (No pl.) **2.** *n.* something that is odd; something that is unusual or strange.

odor ['o dɚ] *n.* a smell; a scent; an aroma.

of [əv] **1.** *prep.* belonging to someone; owned by someone; closely associated with someone. (Takes a nominal in the possessive form. Pronouns that can follow OF in this sense are *mine, yours, his, hers, ours,* and *theirs.*) **2.** *prep.* connected to someone or something; relating to someone or something; associated with someone or something; representing someone or something; being a portion or part from something. **3.** *prep.* made from something. **4.** *prep.* containing something; including someone or something; having people or things as the members or parts. **5.** *prep.* a preposition expressing a measurement or an amount. **6.** *prep.* a preposition linking a type of location to the name of a location. **7.** *prep.* referring to someone or something; about someone or something; concerning someone or something. **8.** *prep.* having a certain quality or aspect. **9.** *prep.* before a certain hour.

off ['ɔf] **1.** *prep.* away from someone or something; not on someone or something. (① through ④ are often *off of,* a construction objected to by some.) **2.** *prep.* less than something; deducted from something. **3.** *prep.* leading away from a place or path; turning from a place or path; connecting to a place or path. **4.** *prep.* in or over the water near land. **5.** *adj.* stopped; not being used; causing something not to function or operate, especially by stopping the flow of electricity. (Not prenominal.) **6.** *adj.* wrong; not accurate. (Not prenominal.) **7.** *adj.* canceled. (Not prenominal.) **8.** *adj.* [of a time period] free of work. (Not prenominal.)

offend [ə 'fɛnd] *tv.* to shock someone, especially through one's actions, attitude, or behavior.

offense 1. [ə 'fɛns] *n.* the breaking of a law; a crime; an illegal act. **2.** [ə 'fɛns] *n.* something that is shocking or disgusting. **3.** ['ɔ fɛns] *n.* a way of attacking; an attack.

offensive 1. [ə 'fɛn sɪv] *adj.* shocking; annoying; offending someone. (Adv: *offensively.*) **2.** ['ɔ fɛn sɪv] *adj.* of or about attacking. (Adv: *offensively.*) **3.** [ə 'fɛn sɪv] *n.* an attack.

offer ['ɔf ɚ] **1.** *tv.* to present something that can be taken or refused. **2.** *tv.* to propose a price for something that is being sold. **3.** *n.* something that is OFFERED as in ①. **4.** *n.* a price or amount that is OFFERED as in ②.

offering [ˈɔf ə ɪŋ] *n.* something that is offered, especially to a church, to a charity, or as part of a religious ceremony.

office [ˈɔf ɪs] **1.** *n.* a room—usually assigned to one person—where business is done. **2.** *n.* the combined workplaces of a number of people. **3.** *n.* a position of power and responsibility, especially in a government or an organization.

officer [ˈɔ fə sə] *n.* someone in a position of authority, especially in the military, the government, or some other organization.

official [ə ˈfɪ ʃəl] **1.** *n.* an officer; someone in a position of authority. **2.** *adj.* of or about the power, authority, and responsibility of an office or an officer. (Adv: *officially.*)

offshore [ˈɔf ˈʃor] *adj.* located or occurring in, on, or over the water away from the shore.

offspring [ˈɔf sprɪŋ] *n.* [a person's] child or children; [an animal's] young. (No pl. Treated as sg or pl.)

offstage [ˈɔf ˈstedʒ] **1.** *adj.* next to the visible part of the stage of a theater, but not visible to the audience. **2.** *adv.* at, to, or toward the area next to the visible part of the stage.

often [ˈɔf ən] *adv.* frequently; happening many times.

oh [ˈo] *interj.* a form expressing surprise or other feelings.

oil [ˈɔɪl] **1.** *n.* a slick, greasy liquid that does not dissolve in water. (Pl only for types and instances.) **2.** *tv.* to put lubrication on something using ①; to make something slippery by putting ① on it; to put ① on something.

oilcan [ˈɔɪl kæn] *n.* a can that is used to apply oil as lubrication.

oily [ˈɔɪl i] *adj.* made of oil; containing oil; soaked with oil. (Comp: *oilier;* sup: *oiliest.*)

oink [ˈɔɪŋk] **1.** *n.* the sound made by a pig. **2.** *iv.* to make the sound of a pig.

ointment [ˈɔɪnt mənt] *n.* a substance that is put on the skin to heal it, soothe it, or soften it.

OK Go to OKAY.

okay AND **OK** [o ˈke] **1.** *adv.* all right; adequately. **2.** *adv.* to a degree of intensity below "very good" but above "poor." **3.** *adj.* just good, but not excellent. **4.** *interj.* a word used to confirm that one understands something. **5.** *n.* approval. **6.** *tv.* to approve something.

315

old [ˈoʊld] **1.** *adj.* having been alive for a long time; not recently born; not young. (Comp: *older;* sup: *oldest.*) **2.** *adj.* having existed for a long time; not recently made; not new. (Comp: *older;* sup: *oldest.*) **3.** *adj.* of a certain age. Comp: *older.*) **4.** *adj.* previous; former. (Comp: *older;* sup: *oldest.*)

old-fashioned [ˈoʊld ˈfæʃ ənd] *adj.* belonging to the style, actions, behavior, or rules of the past. (Adv: *old-fashionedly.*)

olive [ˈɑ lɪv] **1.** *n.* a tree grown in warm climates for its fruit. **2.** *n.* the fruit of ①, used for food.

omelet [ˈɑm lɪt] *n.* a dish made of beaten eggs, cooked flat and folded over, sometimes stuffed with other foods.

omission [oʊ ˈmɪʃ ən] **1.** *n.* not listing or not including someone or something; omitting someone or something. **2.** *n.* something that has been left out; something that has been omitted.

omit [oʊ ˈmɪt] *tv.* to leave someone or something out; to forget to list or include something.

on [ˈɑn] **1.** *prep.* above and supported by someone or something; covering or partially covering someone or something; touching the surface of someone or something. **2.** *prep.* traveling by [plane, train, boat, bus, motorcycle, bicycle, etc.]. (But one travels *in* an automobile.) **3.** *prep.* near something; at the edge of [a body of water]. **4.** *prep.* about someone or something. **5.** *prep.* [happening] at a specific time, identified by the date or the day. **6.** *prep.* as a member or part of some group. **7.** *adj.* operating; turned on as in ⑨. **8.** *adj.* still happening; not canceled; continuing as scheduled. **9.** *adv.* so that something operates; so that something has the power to operate.

once [ˈwʌns] **1.** *adv.* one time. **2.** *adv.* at a time in the past; formerly.

oncoming [ˈɑn kəm ɪŋ] *adj.* coming toward [oneself]; approaching.

one [ˈwʌn] **1.** 1. Go to FOUR. **2.** *n.* a BILL ③ or NOTE ③ worth a single dollar. **3.** *adj.* happening on or at a particular time. (Prenominal only.) **4.** *adj.* united; together; joined. (Not prenominal.) **5.** *pron.* a person or thing that is referred to. **6.** *pron.* you; anybody; a person.

oneself [wən ˈsɛlf] *pron.* the reflexive form of the pronoun ONE ⑥. (Used when *one* is the subject of the sentence.)

onion [ˈʌn jən] **1.** *n.* a plant with a large, round edible bulb and thin green stalks. **2.** *n.* the edible bulb of ①, sometimes sliced or chopped. **3.** *adj.* made with or flavored with ②.

only ['on li] **1.** *adj.* sole; single. **2.** *adv.* [this and] nothing more. **3.** *conj.* except that.

onset ['on sɛt] *n.* the beginning of something; the start of something.

onstage [ɔn 'stedʒ] **1.** *adj.* located or happening on a part of a stage that an audience can see. **2.** *adv.* on, to, or toward a part of the stage that an audience can see.

onto ['ɔn tu] *prep.* to a position that is on something.

onward ['ɔn wɚd] *adv.* further in space or time; forward in space or time.

ooze ['uz] **1.** *n.* mud; slime; a thick liquid. (No pl.) **2.** *iv.* to flow slowly, like mud or a very thick liquid; to seep out of a hole slowly.

opaque [o 'pek] **1.** *adj.* not able to be seen through; not allowing light to pass through; not clear. (Adv: *opaquely.*) **2.** *adj.* hard to understand. (Fig. on ①. Adv: *opaquely.*)

open ['o pən] **1.** *adj.* not shut; not closed; not sealed. **2.** *adj.* allowing customers to enter; ready for business. **3.** *adj.* not decided. **4.** *adj.* available; free and not restricted. (Adv: *openly.*) **5.** *adj.* sincere; honest about one's feelings. (Adv: *openly.*) **6.** *tv.* to cause something to become ①; to allow a place to be entered into or exited from. **7.** *tv.* to establish the beginning of something; to cause something to start. **8.** *iv.* to be accessible; to become ready for business or use.

opener ['o pə nɚ] *n.* someone or something that opens something.

opening ['o pə nɪŋ] **1.** *n.* a way into a container, compartment, or room; a way through a wall or barrier. **2.** *n.* something that is available; a job that is available. **3.** *n.* an opportunity to do something or say something. (Fig. on ①.) **4.** *adj.* at the beginning; the first; the earliest.

opera ['ɑ prə] **1.** *n.* the branch of theater or music in which lengthy performances include solo and choral singing, orchestra music, and sometimes dance. (No pl.) **2.** *n.* a presentation or performance of a musical production as in ①.

operate ['ɑp ə ret] **1.** *iv.* [for a machine or device] to work or function. **2.** *iv.* to perform surgery; to perform an operation. **3.** *tv.* to cause something to work or function; to direct or manage something.

operation [ɑ pə 're ʃən] **1.** *n.* surgery; a medical procedure where something is done to the body, usually involving cutting. **2.** *n.* the way something works; the way something is used.

317

operator [ˈɑp ə ret ɚ] **1.** *n.* someone who operates a machine. **2.** *n.* someone who handles telephone calls; the person one talks to when one dials "0" on a telephone.

opinion [ə ˈpɪn jən] **1.** *n.* thoughts, ideas, or attitudes concerning someone or something. (Pl only for types and instances.) **2.** *n.* advice from a professional or an expert.

opossum [ə ˈpɑs əm] *n.* a small, gray, furry animal with a hairless, flexible tail.

opponent [ə ˈpon ənt] *n.* someone who is on the opposite side in a contest, fight, or argument.

opportunity [ɑp ɚ ˈtu nə ti] *n.* a good chance for doing something; a favorable time for doing something.

oppose [ə ˈpoz] *tv.* to be against someone or something; to fight against someone or something; to argue against someone or something. (Often passive.)

opposite [ˈɑp ə sɪt] **1.** *adj.* completely different in at least one major respect. (Adv: *oppositely*.) **2.** *adj.* of or about a location that is the farthest point away within a defined area. (Adv: *oppositely*.) **3.** *prep.* across from someone or something; facing someone or something. **4.** *n.* someone or something that is OPPOSITE as in ① as compared to someone or something else.

opposition [ɑp ə ˈzɪ ʃən] **1.** *n.* a state of being against someone or something; resistance. (No pl.) **2.** *n.* the people who are against something. (No pl.)

oppress [ə ˈprɛs] *tv.* to rule someone or a group of people harshly or cruelly; to keep someone from succeeding.

optic [ˈɑp tɪk] *adj.* of or about the eye or vision. (Adv: *optically* [...ɪk li].)

optical [ˈɑp tɪ kəl] *adj.* of or about the eye or vision. (Adv: *optically* [...ɪk li].)

optimist [ˈɑp tɪ məst] *n.* someone who believes that everything will be fine; someone who looks on the positive side of everything.

option [ˈɑp ʃən] *n.* a choice; something [else] that is available for choosing.

or [ˈor] **1.** *conj.* a word used in a list of items to show a choice or difference. **2.** *conj.* otherwise; if not. **3.** *conj.* that is to say.

oral [ˈor əl] **1.** *adj.* of or about the mouth. (Adv: *orally*.) **2.** *adj.* spoken. (Adv: *orally*.)

orange ['or ɪndʒ] **1.** *n.* a color of the rainbow between red and yellow, and the color of ②. (Pl only for types and instances.) **2.** *n.* a round, juicy citrus fruit—of the color ①—that grows on a tree. **3.** *adj.* of the color ①. **4.** *adj.* made with ②; flavored with ②.

orbit ['or bɪt] **1.** *n.* a pathway around a planet or a star, such as that taken by a planet, a moon, or a rocket. **2.** *tv.* to move in a circle around a star or planet. **3.** *iv.* to move in a circle around a star or planet.

orchard ['or tʃə·d] *n.* a farm of fruit or nut trees.

orchestra ['or kə strə] *n.* a group of several musicians and the instruments they play, usually including strings.

orchid ['or kɪd] *n.* a flower with unusually shaped and brightly colored petals.

ordain [or 'den] **1.** *tv.* to confer the status of being a priest or a minister on someone. **2.** *tv.* to order something; to make something a law. (The object can be a clause with THAT ⑦.)

ordeal [or 'dil] *n.* a very difficult experience.

order ['or də·] **1.** *n.* the sequence in which a series of things is arranged. **2.** *n.* a state of everything being in its proper place. (No pl.) **3.** *n.* a state of being able to be used; condition. (No pl.) **4.** *n.* a state wherein people are following rules and behaving properly. (No pl.) **5.** *n.* a command. **6.** *n.* a request for certain goods or services. **7.** *n.* one serving of a kind of food. **8.** *tv.* to request goods or services. **9.** *tv.* to request a serving of food or a full meal. **10.** *tv.* to arrange someone or something into a certain sequence.

orderly ['or də· li] **1.** *adj.* neat; in order. **2.** *n.* a hospital worker who assists doctors and nurses in caring for patients.

ordinal number Go to ORDINAL NUMERAL.

ordinal number AND **ordinal numeral** ['or dɪ nəl 'nʌm bə·, 'or dɪ nəl 'nu mə rəl] *n.* the number used to show rank or position in a series, such as *first, second, third*, etc. (See also CARDINAL NUMBER.)

ordinary ['ord n ner i] *adj.* usual; common; typical; regular. (Adv: *ordinarily* [ord n 'ner ə li].)

organ ['or gən] **1.** *n.* a part of an animal that performs a specific function. **2.** *n.* a musical instrument with keyboards that control the air flow into many pipes of different lengths, each sounding a different note. (Also **pipe organ**.)

organism ['or gə nɪz əm] *n.* a plant or an animal; a living thing.

organization [or gə nə 'ze ʃən] *n.* a group of people, such as those in a club or society; a company; a department of government.

organize ['or gə naɪz] **1.** *tv.* to arrange different parts in a way so that they work properly; to arrange different parts into a system. **2.** *tv.* to form an organization or meeting.

oriental [or i 'ɛn təl] *adj.* of or about the peoples and cultures of eastern Asia and the islands to the south and east. (Adv: *orientally*. Objected to by some. *Asian* is often substituted for this term.)

origin ['or ə dʒən] *n.* the starting point; something that other things develop from.

original [ə 'rɪdʒ ə nəl] **1.** *adj.* not copied or based on something else. **2.** *adj.* first; earliest. (Adv: *originally*.) **3.** *n.* something that copies are made from; the first example of something that other examples are based on.

originate [ə 'rɪdʒ ə net] **1.** *tv.* to cause something to exist; to found something; to establish something, such as an organization. **2.** *iv.* to start; to begin.

ornament ['or nə mənt] **1.** *n.* decorations, in general. (No pl form in this sense.) **2.** *n.* a decoration; something that makes someone or something look prettier. **3.** *tv.* to add ① to something; to put ② on something; to adorn something.

ornamental [or nə 'mɛn təl] *adj.* used as an ornament; decorative. (Adv: *ornamentally*.)

orphan ['or fən] **1.** *n.* a young child whose parents are dead or missing. **2.** *tv.* to cause someone to become ①. (Typically passive.)

ostrich ['ɑs trɪtʃ] *n.* a large bird that runs very quickly but cannot fly.

other ['ʌð ɚ] **1.** *pron.* the second of two people or things; the remaining person or things. **2.** the *adj.* use of ①. **3.** *adj.* more of the same or similar kind of thing or people.

otherwise ['ʌð ɚ waɪz] **1.** *conj.* or else; or it is that. **2.** *adv.* in another way; in a different way; differently. **3.** *adv.* in every regard except [this one]; in every way except [this one].

otter ['ɑt ɚ] **1.** *n.* a long, thin, furry animal that lives in and near water, and eats fish. **2.** *n.* the skin and fur of ①. (No pl.) **3.** *adj.* made from ②.

ought to ['ɔt tu] **1.** have to do something; obliged to do something. **2.** likely to happen; should happen.

ounce ['aʊns] **1.** *n.* a unit of measurement of weight equal to $1/16$ of a pound or about 28 grams. **2.** *n.* a unit of measurement of liquid equal to $1/16$ of a pint or $1/8$ of a cup.

our ['aɚ] *pron.* the first-person pl possessive pronoun including the speaker or writer. (Used as a modifier before a noun.)

ours *pron.* the first-person pl possessive pronoun. (Used in place of a noun.)

ourselves ['aɚ 'sɛlvz] **1.** *pron.* the first-person pl reflexive pronoun. **2.** *pron.* a form used to emphasize WE.

oust ['aʊst] *tv.* to get rid of someone or something; to remove someone or something by force.

out ['aʊt] **1.** *adv.* away from a place; not in a place; not in the usual condition; not at the usual position; to a point beyond a limit. **2.** *adv.* in the open air; into the open air; outside; not inside. **3.** *adj.* not at the usual position; not at home; not at work. (Not prenominal.) **4.** *adj.* no longer in style; old-fashioned. (Not prenominal.) **5.** *adj.* not a possible choice. (Not prenominal. Informal.) **6.** *adj.* no longer burning; no longer giving off light. (Not prenominal.) **7.** *adj.* not working; not functioning properly. (Not prenominal.) **8.** *adj.* [in baseball, of someone] no longer permitted to play in a particular turn. (Not prenominal.) **9.** *adj.* used up; no longer having more of a substance. (Not prenominal.) **10.** *adj.* unconscious; not aware; not awake. (Not prenominal.)

outcast ['aʊt kæst] *n.* someone who has been rejected, abandoned, or deserted.

outcome ['aʊt kəm] *n.* the final result; the effect of something.

outcry ['aʊt kraɪ] **1.** *n.* a strong protest; an uproar. **2.** *n.* a loud cry.

outdoor [aʊt 'dor] *adj.* not inside; not in a building; used or done OUT-DOORS.

outdoors ['aʊt 'dorz] *adv.* in or into the open air; not inside a building.

outer ['aʊ tɚ] **1.** *adj.* farther away from the center. **2.** *adj.* exterior; on the outside.

outfit ['aʊt fɪt] **1.** *n.* different items of clothing that are worn together. **2.** *n.* equipment needed for a certain job or activity. **3.** *n.* a group of people; a company or organization. (Informal.) **4.** *tv.* to provide someone with ②.

outgrew [aʊt 'gru] pt of OUTGROW.

321

outgrow [aʊt 'gro] **1.** *tv., irreg.* to no longer fit into one's clothes because one has grown. (Pt: OUTGREW; pp: OUTGROWN.) **2.** *tv., irreg.* to become too mature to do certain things meant for younger children. (Fig. on ①.) **3.** *tv., irreg.* to grow to be taller or to grow faster than someone else.

outgrown [aʊt 'gron] pp of OUTGROW.

outlaw ['aʊt lɔ] **1.** *tv.* to make something illegal; to declare that something is against the law. **2.** *n.* a criminal.

outlay ['aʊt le] *n.* money spent for a certain reason; time or energy spent for a certain reason.

outlet ['aʊt let] **1.** *n.* the socket in a wall where something can be plugged in for electrical power. **2.** *n.* a way out for something. **3.** *n.* a way to let one's feelings out; a way to use one's creativity. (Fig. on ②.)

outline ['aʊt laɪn] **1.** *n.* the shape of someone or something; the border of someone or something. **2.** *n.* a list of the main topics of a speech or text; a plan. **3.** *tv.* to draw the shape of someone or something; to draw the border of someone or something. **4.** *tv.* to list the main topics of a speech or text. **5.** *tv.* to describe a plan.

outlive [aʊt 'lɪv] *tv.* to live longer than someone else; to work, function, or last longer than something else.

outlook ['aʊt lʊk] **1.** *n.* an imagined view of the future course that something may take. (No pl.) **2.** *n.* a way of looking at things that happen.

output ['aʊt pʊt] **1.** *n.* the amount of something that is made; production. (No pl.) **2.** *n.* something that is produced. (No pl.) **3.** *n.* the energy that is produced by a machine. (No pl.) **4.** *n.* information that is produced by a computer. (No pl.)

outrage ['aʊt redʒ] **1.** *n.* a very cruel or horrible deed. **2.** *n.* anger caused by a very cruel or horrible action. (No pl.) **3.** *tv.* to anger someone greatly by doing a very cruel or horrible deed.

outright ['aʊt raɪt] **1.** *adj.* complete; direct; openly and without delay. **2.** *adj.* [of money given] without limitations. **3.** *adv.* without limitations.

outside ['aʊt 'saɪd] **1.** *n.* the part of something that faces away from the center of something; the surface of something that is out. (Also pl with the same meaning, but not countable.) **2.** *adj.* on ①; external; not inside a building. **3.** *adj.* farther from the center than something else. **4.** *adj.* not associated with the inner group. (Prenominal only.) **5.** *adv.* to or toward ①; on or at ①; in or into the outdoors. **6.** *prep.* past the limit of something; beyond something; on or toward the exterior of something.

outward [ˈɑʊt wɚd] **1.** *adv.* away; away from someplace; toward the outside. **2.** *adj.* of or about one's appearance instead of one's feelings or thoughts. (Adv: *outwardly.*)

outweigh [ɑʊt ˈwe] **1.** *tv.* to weigh more than someone or something else. **2.** *tv.* to be more important than someone or something else. (Fig. on ①.)

outwit [ɑʊt ˈwɪt] *tv.* to be more clever than someone and therefore win at something.

oval [ˈo vəl] **1.** *adj.* shaped like an egg; almost shaped like a circle, but flatter. (Adv: *ovally.*) **2.** *n.* a shape like that of an egg; the shape of a flattened circle.

oven [ˈʌv ən] **1.** *n.* an appliance or enclosed space within an appliance that can be heated to cook food. **2.** *n.* an appliance that is heated to dry and harden pottery or other objects.

over [ˈo vɚ] **1.** *prep.* above someone or something; higher than someone or something. **2.** *prep.* on someone or something; covering someone or something. **3.** *prep.* across something; from one side of something to the other; above and to the other side of something. **4.** *prep.* off and down from something. **5.** *prep.* during something; throughout some period of time. **6.** *prep.* more than a certain measurement; greater than something. (Some people prefer *more than* to OVER in this sense.) **7.** *prep.* with something noisy in the background. **8.** *prep.* from [the radio, the Internet, or a telephone]. **9.** *prep.* covering the surface of someone or something. **10.** *adv.* at some other place; on the other side of something. **11.** *adv.* down; so that a surface faces down. **12.** *adv.* again. **13.** *prefix* too; too much. (Usually in a compound.) **14.** *adj.* done; finished; at the end. (Not prenominal.)

overate [o vɚ ˈet] pt of OVEREAT.

overboard [ˈov ɚ bord] *adv.* [falling, dropping, or being thrown] from a boat or ship into the water.

overcame [o vɚ ˈkem] pt of OVERCOME.

overcharge [o vɚ ˈtʃɑrdʒ] *tv.* to charge someone more money for something than it really costs.

overcoat [ˈo vɚ kot] *n.* a heavy coat that is worn over other clothes.

323

overcome [o vɚ ˈkʌm] **1.** *tv., irreg.* to defeat someone or something; to fight and win against someone or something. (Pt: OVERCAME; pp: *overcome*.) **2.** *tv., irreg.* to cause someone to become helpless, especially because of emotion.

overdose [ˈo vɚ dos] **1.** *n.* a large dose of a drug that causes someone to faint or die. **2.** *iv.* to become unconscious or die because one has taken too many drugs or too much medicine.

overeat [o vɚ ˈit] *iv., irreg.* to eat too much. (Pt: OVERATE; pp: OVEREATEN.)

overeaten [o vɚ ˈit n] pp of OVEREAT.

overhead 1. [ˈo vɚ hɛd] *n.* the costs of running a business; business expenses. (No pl. Treated as sg.) **2.** [ˈo vɚ hɛd] the *adj.* use of ①. **3.** [ˈo vɚ hɛd] *adj.* above one's head. (Prenominal only.) **4.** [ˈo vɚ ˈhɛd] *adv.* above one's head; in the air; passing through the air.

overheat [o vɚ ˈhit] **1.** *iv.* to become too hot; to break or stop working because of being worked too hard. **2.** *tv.* to cause something to become too hot.

overkill [ˈo vɚ kɪl] *n.* the condition of having or doing more than is necessary. (No pl.)

overlap 1. [o vɚ ˈlæp] *iv.* [for parts of two or more things] to happen at the same time. **2.** [o vɚ ˈlæp] *iv.* [for parts of two or more things] to cover the same space. **3.** [o vɚ ˈlæp] *tv.* [for something] to partially cover something [else]. **4.** [o vɚ ˈlæp] *tv.* [for something] to begin before something else finishes; to place the beginning of something over the end of something else. **5.** [ˈo vɚ læp] *n.* the extra part of something that extends over something else. (No pl.) **6.** [ˈo vɚ læp] *n.* the amount by which something extends over something else. (No pl.)

overlook 1. [ˈo vɚ lʊk] *n.* a high place that provides a good view of a lower place. **2.** [o vɚ ˈlʊk] *tv.* to forget or neglect something. **3.** [o vɚ ˈlʊk] *tv.* to ignore something.

overnight 1. [ˈo vɚ naɪt] *adj.* done during the night; lasting through the night. **2.** [o vɚ ˈnaɪt] *adv.* through the night; during the night. **3.** [o vɚ ˈnaɪt] *adv.* in just one night.

oversaw [o vɚ ˈsɔ] pt of OVERSEE.

overseas [o vɚ ˈsiz] **1.** *adv.* across the sea; on the other side of the ocean. **2.** *adj.* done, used, or about a place on the other side of the ocean.

oversee [o vɚ 'si] *tv., irreg.* to supervise someone or something; to watch over someone or something so that something is done properly. (Pt: OVERSAW; pp: OVERSEEN.)

overseen [o vɚ 'sin] pp of OVERSEE.

oversight ['o vɚ saɪt] *n.* something that is not noticed or thought of.

oversleep [o vɚ 'slip] *iv., irreg.* to sleep longer than one wanted to; to sleep too long. (Pt/pp: OVERSLEPT.)

overslept [o vɚ 'slɛpt] pt/pp of OVERSLEEP.

overtake [ov ɚ 'tek] *tv., irreg.* to catch up to and pass someone or something else. (Pt: OVERTOOK; pp: OVERTAKEN.)

overtaken [ov ɚ 'tek ən] pp of OVERTAKE.

overthrew [o vɚ 'θru] pt of OVERTHROW.

overthrow [o vɚ 'θro] *tv., irreg.* to remove someone or something from power; to seize power from a government. (Pt: OVERTHREW; pp: OVERTHROWN.)

overthrown [o vɚ 'θron] pp of OVERTHROW.

overtime ['o vɚ taɪm] **1.** *n.* time at work past the time when one normally finishes. (No pl.) **2.** *n.* money earned by working past the time when one normally finishes. (No pl.) **3.** *n.* [in a sporting event] an extra amount of playing time allowed in order to break a tie score. (No pl.) **4.** *adv.* past the hours when one normally finishes. **5.** *adj.* of or about working extra as in ①.

overtook [ov ɚ 'tʊk] pt of OVERTAKE.

overture ['o vɚ tʃɚ] **1.** *n.* the piece of music at the beginning of an opera, symphony, ballet, etc., that introduces key melodies and themes. **2.** *n.* the communication of an intention to make an offer of something.

owe ['o] **1.** *tv.* to be in debt for a sum of money; to have to pay someone for something. **2.** *tv.* to be obliged to give someone something.

owl ['aʊl] *n.* a bird that has large eyes that face the front and a short, curved beak, and is active at night.

own ['on] **1.** *tv.* to possess something; to have something as a belonging. **2.** *adj.* belonging to oneself or itself. **3.** *adj.* a form indicating something already mentioned as belonging to oneself or itself.

owner ['o nɚ] *n.* someone who owns something.

ownership ['o nɚ ʃɪp] *n.* the state of being an owner; the right one has to own something. (No pl.)

325

ox [ˈɑks] *n., irreg.* an adult male of a kind of cattle. (An ox has been made unable to breed. Pl: OXEN.)

oxen [ˈɑk sən] pl of ox.

oxygen [ˈɑks ɪ dʒən] *n.* a gas that makes up about 20 percent of the air we breathe. (No pl.)

oyster [ˈɔɪs tɚ] **1.** *n.* a small sea creature that lives between two hinged shells and sometimes produces pearls. **2.** *n.* ① used as food.

ozone [ˈo zon] *n.* a kind of oxygen produced when an electrical spark, such as lightning, passes through the air. (No pl.)

P

pace ['pes] **1.** *n.* the speed at which someone or something moves. (No pl.) **2.** *n.* a distance of one step when running or walking. **3.** *iv.* to walk back and forth slowly and regularly.

pack ['pæk] **1.** *n.* a group of things that have been placed together—in a case, for example—so they can be carried. **2.** *n.* a group of animals that live, hunt, and travel together. **3.** *tv.* to fill a container completely. **4.** *tv.* to gather, assemble, and arrange things and place them in a space or container.

package ['pæk ɪdʒ] **1.** *n.* a group of things that are wrapped together or boxed; a container in which goods are sold or shipped. **2.** *n.* a parcel, especially one that is wrapped in paper or something similar. **3.** *tv.* to place something in a container, especially to make it available for sale.

pact ['pækt] *n.* an agreement; a treaty.

pad ['pæd] **1.** *n.* a small cushion or mass of soft material used to protect something, make something comfortable, absorb fluid, or give something a certain shape. **2.** *n.* a tablet of paper; a stack of pieces of paper that are glued together along one edge. **3.** *iv.* to walk softly and very quietly. **4.** *tv.* to make a movie, book, program, etc., longer by adding extra words, longer pauses, extra performance material, etc.

paddle ['pæd l] **1.** *n.* a kind of oar used to steer and move a canoe or other small boat. **2.** *n.* a round or long flat object used to spank someone. **3.** *tv.* to move a canoe with ①. **4.** *tv.* to spank someone with ② or with the hand. **5.** *iv.* to propel [something] with ①.

pagan ['pe gən] **1.** *n.* someone whose religion is not Christianity, Islam, or Judaism; someone who has no religion. **2.** *adj.* of, by, for, or about ①.

page ['pedʒ] **1.** *n.* one sheet of paper in a book. **2.** *n.* one side of one sheet of paper in a book. **3.** *n.* a sheet of paper suitable for writing or printing or having writing or printing. **4.** *n.* a signal that someone has a waiting message or telephone call, especially a beep from a pager. **5.** *tv.* to alert someone that a message or telephone call is waiting.

pager ['pe dʒɚ] *n.* an electronic device that makes a signal to alert someone to a waiting message or telephone call.

paid ['ped] **1.** pt/pp of PAY. **2.** *adj.* hired; employed; receiving money.

pail ['pel] **1.** *n.* a bucket; a container without a lid and with a curved handle that connects to opposite sides of the rim. **2.** *n.* the contents of ①.

pain ['pen] *n.* hurt or ache caused by injury, sickness, or mental distress. (Pl only for types and instances.)

painful ['pen fʊl] *adj.* causing pain; hurting. (Adv: *painfully.*)

painkiller ['pen kɪl ɚ] *n.* a type of a medicine or drug that ends or relieves pain.

paint ['pent] **1.** *n.* a colored liquid that is spread on a surface to give the surface color and protection and that gets hard when it dries. (Pl only for types and instances.) **2.** *tv.* to cover something with ①, using a brush or something similar. **3.** *tv.* to make a picture of someone or something using ①. **4.** *iv.* to cover walls or other objects with ①. **5.** *iv.* to make pictures with ①.

paintbrush ['pent 'brʌʃ] *n.* a brush used to apply paint to a surface.

painting ['pen tɪŋ] **1.** *n.* the art and study of making pictures with paint. (No pl.) **2.** *n.* a picture that is made with paint.

pair ['per] **1.** *n.* a set of two similar or matching things; two people or two things. **2.** *n.* [in card games] two cards with the same number or value. **3.** *tv.* to sort or order people or things into sets of two.

pajama *adj.* of, by, for, or about PAJAMAS.

pajamas [pə 'dʒɑ məz] *n.* clothes worn in bed or worn at night before one goes to bed. (Treated as pl. Number is expressed by *pair(s) of pajamas.*)

pal ['pæl] *n.* a friend; a chum. (Informal.)

palace ['pæl ɪs] *n.* a very large, luxurious house, especially one where a king, queen, or important political leader lives or once lived.

pale ['pel] **1.** *adj.* having a lighter color than usual; faded. (Adv: *palely.* Comp: *paler;* sup: *palest.*) **2.** *iv.* to become lighter in color; to whiten or weaken in color; to fade. **3.** *iv.* [for someone] to become ① and appear faint. **4.** *iv.* [for something] to appear to be weak or inadequate.

palm ['pɑm] **1.** *n.* the front of the hand between the wrist and the bottom of the fingers. **2.** *n.* a tree with a long trunk and long, pointed leaves at the top, attached to a hard stem. (Short for *palm tree.*) **3.** *tv.* to hide something in one's ①.

pan ['pæn] **1.** *n.* a wide, shallow vessel used for cooking. **2.** *tv.* to give a bad review about a movie, book, or play; to criticize something harshly. **3.** *iv.* [for a camera] to move while filming, traveling over a scene as one's eyes might move.

pancake ['pæn kek] *n.* a thin, round cake (made of flour, eggs, and milk) that is cooked on both sides.

pane ['pen] *n.* a section of glass in a window or door.

panel ['pæn əl] **1.** *n.* a thin, flat square or rectangular section of hard material. **2.** *n.* a group of people who are selected to talk about something or judge someone or something. **3.** *tv.* to cover the walls of a room with ①.

panic ['pæn ɪk] **1.** *n.* a fear that is out of control; a sense of terror. (No pl.) **2.** *iv., irreg.* to feel ①; to experience fear that is frantic and out of control. (Pt/pp: PANICKED. Pres. part.: *panicking*.) **3.** *tv., irreg.* to cause someone or some creature to experience ①.

panicked ['pæn ɪkt] pt/pp of PANIC.

pant ['pænt] **1.** *iv.* to make quick, shallow breaths, as an overheated dog does. **2.** *n.* a gasp; a quick, shallow breath.

panties *n.* a pair of women's underpants. (Treated as pl. Number is expressed with *pair(s) of panties.* Also countable.)

pantry ['pæn tri] *n.* a small room near a kitchen, where pots, pans, dishes, silverware, tablecloths, food, and other kitchen items are kept.

pants *n.* trousers; clothing worn below the waist, having a separate tube, hole, or compartment for each leg. (Treated as pl. Number is expressed with *pair(s) of pants.* Also countable.)

pantyhose ['pæn ti hoz] *n.* a garment that is made of sheer stockings extending from a pair of panties. (No pl. Treated as pl, but not countable. Number is expressed with *pair(s) of pantyhose.*)

paper ['pe pɚ] **1.** *n.* processed fiber and other substances, pressed into sheets, used for writing, printing, drawing on, and other things. (No pl. Number is usually expressed with *piece(s)* or *sheet(s) of paper.*) **2.** *n.* WALLPAPER; decorated ① that is glued to walls. (No pl.) **3.** *n.* a newspaper. **4.** *n.* an article; an essay. **5.** *adj.* made from ①. **6.** *tv.* to cover something with wallpaper.

papers 1. *n.* documents; sheets of PAPER ① in groups or stacks, bearing information. (Treated as pl, but not countable.) **2.** *n.* documents that prove who one is; one's passport or visa, carried while visiting a foreign country. (Treated as pl, but not countable.)

paperweight ['pe pɚ wet] *n.* a heavy object placed on a stack of papers to keep them from blowing away.

par ['pɑr] *n.* [in golf] the normal number of strokes that it takes to get the golf ball from the tee into the hole. (No pl form. A number may follow PAR.)

parable ['pɛr ə bəl] *n.* a story in the form of an analogy that presents a moral lesson.

parachute ['pɛr ə ʃut] **1.** *n.* a large bowl-shaped piece of fabric attached to and supporting someone who jumps from an airplane or some other very high place. **2.** *iv.* to drift downward, wearing ①.

parade [pə 'red] **1.** *n.* a public event where people march or ride down a street with people watching from both sides. **2.** *iv.* to march somewhere in ①. **3.** *tv.* to make someone march in front of people.

paradise ['pɛr ə dɑɪs] **1.** *n.* heaven. (No pl.) **2.** *n.* somewhere on earth that seems as lovely and wonderful as ①. (No pl.)

paragraph ['pɛr ə græf] *n.* a sentence or group of sentences usually related some way in meaning.

parallel ['pɛr ə lɛl] **1.** *adj.* [lines or plane surfaces] at the same distance apart or at an equal distance apart everywhere. **2.** *adj.* similar; like [a situation]; analogous. **3.** *tv.* to go or be on a route or in a direction that is beside something else as in ①. (E.g., a road that *parallels the railroad tracks.*)

paralyzed ['pɛr ə lɑɪzd] *adj.* unable to move, as if frozen.

paraphrase ['pɛr ə frez] **1.** *n.* something that someone has said or has written in a different way. **2.** *tv.* to restate something as in ①.

parasite ['pɛr ə sɑɪt] **1.** *n.* a plant or animal completely dependent on another species of plant or animal for food or support. (PARASITES on humans and animals cause diseases or health disorders.) **2.** *n.* someone who depends on other people for food and shelter; a useless person who is supported by other people. (Fig. on ①.)

parcel ['pɑr səl] **1.** *n.* a package, especially one that is mailed or delivered; something that is wrapped up. **2.** *n.* an amount of land that is sold as a unit.

pardon ['pɑr dn] **1.** *n.* forgiving someone. (Pl only for types and instances.) **2.** *n.* an act that keeps someone from being punished under the law. **3.** *tv.* to forgive someone; to excuse someone. **4.** *tv.* to release someone from jail; to order that someone not be executed; to keep someone from being punished.

parent ['pɛr ənt] **1.** *n.* the father or the mother of a living creature. **2.** *n.* a business that owns another business; the main office of one or more businesses or other organizations. **3.** *adj.* serving as a ②.

parentheses [pə 'rɛn θə siz] pl of PARENTHESIS.

parenthesis [pə 'rɛn θə sɪs] *n., irreg.* either of the pair of symbols "**(**" and "**)**" used to enclose information of secondary importance in writing or printing. (Pl: PARENTHESES.)

park ['pɑrk] **1.** *n.* a piece of land set aside by a city, state, county, or nation for use by the public, usually having trees, grass, and other natural features. **2.** *tv.* to stop a car or other vehicle and leave it in a certain place for a period of time. **3.** *iv.* to leave a car or other vehicle in a certain place for a period of time.

parliament ['pɑr lə mənt] *n.* a government body that makes the laws for a country.

parlor ['pɑr lɚ] **1.** *n.* a living room; a place in a home where guests can sit and talk. (Old-fashioned.) **2.** *n.* a store that sells a certain product or service, such as hair care, ice cream, or funerals.

parrot ['pɛr ət] **1.** *n.* a kind of tropical bird, often brightly colored, that can copy human speech. **2.** *tv.* to repeat someone else's words or ideas without thinking. (Fig. on ①. The object can be a clause with THAT ⑦.)

parsley ['pɑrs li] *n.* an herb used in cooking to add flavor to food or as a decoration. (No pl. Number is expressed with *sprig(s) of parsley.*)

part ['pɑrt] **1.** *n.* one piece of the whole; one section of the entire amount. **2.** *n.* one of a set of equal divisions. **3.** *n.* an actor's role in a play or movie. **4.** *n.* the line between two sections of hair on the head, established when combing it. **5.** *tv.* to make a pathway or an opening through a group of people or things. **6.** *tv.* to separate one's hair along a line, especially when combing it into two sides. **7.** *iv.* to divide or separate, making an opening.

partial ['pɑr ʃəl] **1.** *adj.* not complete; only part of the entire thing. (Adv: *partially.*) **2.** *adj.* favoring someone or something; biased. (Not prenominal. Adv: *partially.*) **3.** ~ **to** favoring or preferring something.

participation [pɑr tɪs ə 'pe ʃən] *n.* joining in and doing something with other people. (No pl.)

participle ['pɑr tə sɪp əl] *n.* either the *pres. part.* (the *-ing* form) or the *pp.*

331

particle ['part ɪ kəl] **1.** *n.* a small piece of something. **2.** *n.* a kind of short, basic word or a part of a word—such as a conjunction, article, or preposition—that affects the meaning of another word. **3.** *n.* a basic unit of matter, such as a proton, neutron, or electron.

particular [pər 'tɪk jə lɚ] **1.** *adj.* specific; distinct [from others]. (Adv: *particularly.*) **2.** *adj.* unusual; noticeable; worth noticing. (Adv: *particularly.*) **3.** *adj.* hard to please. (Adv: *particularly.*)

particularly [pər 'tɪk jə lɚ li] *adv.* especially; in a way that is worth mentioning.

partition [pɑr 'tɪ ʃən] **1.** *n.* a divider; something that separates two spaces; a wall. **2.** *tv.* to split something into two or more parts.

partner ['pɑrt nɚ] **1.** *n.* someone with whom one shares a business; one of the owners of a business. **2.** *n.* someone who shares an activity with someone else.

part-time ['pɑrt 'tɑɪm] **1.** *adj.* for only part of the time and not full-time. **2.** *adv.* [working] only part of the workweek; not as full-time.

party ['pɑr ti] **1.** *n.* a social gathering of people; a gathering of people who are having fun. **2.** *n.* a group of people who are together for a specific reason. **3.** *n.* a group of people united with a common goal or with common ideas, especially in politics. **4.** *n.* a person. **5.** the *adj.* use of ① or ③. **6.** *iv.* to celebrate; to have fun with other people. (Informal.)

pass ['pæs] **1.** *tv.* to reach someone or something and go beyond. **2.** *tv.* to succeed in a [school] course or examination; to have a medical examination where no problems are discovered. **3.** *tv.* to use up a period of time [doing something]; to occupy a period of time [doing something]. **4.** *tv.* to approve of or agree to something, such as a motion, law, or regulation, by means of a vote. **5.** *tv.* to hand something over to someone; to give something to someone. **6.** *tv.* to throw a ball to someone in a game. **7.** *iv.* to reach and go beyond. **8.** *iv.* to meet the requirements for successfully completing a [school] course. **9.** *iv.* [for a motion or law] to be approved by means of a vote. **10.** *iv.* [for time] to progress or proceed. **11.** *n.* a ticket or document showing that one is allowed to go somewhere. **12.** *n.* the transfer of a ball or something similar in various sports. **13.** *n.* a narrow road or pathway, especially through mountains.

passable ['pæs ə bəl] **1.** *adj.* able to be crossed or passed through; able to be traveled over. **2.** *adj.* [a motion or proposition] likely to get enough votes to pass. **3.** *adj.* only adequate; fair; okay. (Adv: *passably.*)

passage ['pæs ɪdʒ] **1.** *n.* a path or hallway. **2.** *n.* the progress or movement of time. (No pl.) **3.** *n.* the approval of a law or motion, usually by a vote. (No pl.) **4.** *n.* a short section of a piece of music, a speech, or a written work.

passbook ['pæs bʊk] *n.* a book for keeping track of one's savings account in a bank.

passenger ['pæs ən dʒɚ] *n.* someone who is riding in a vehicle but is not driving it.

passion ['pæʃ ən] **1.** *n.* strong romantic and sexual feeling. (Pl only for types and instances.) **2.** *n.* a very strong interest in something.

passive ['pæs ɪv] **1.** *adj.* not resisting; not active; letting others take charge or control a situation. (The opposite of ACTIVE ②. Adv: *passively.*) **2.** *adj.* of or about a grammatical state where the verb acts on the subject of the sentence. (The opposite of ACTIVE ③. Adv: *passively.*) **3.** *n.* a verb phrase that is ②.

passport ['pæs pɔrt] *n.* a document shaped like a small book, showing what country one is a citizen of. (It is needed to enter certain countries.)

password ['pæs wɚd] *n.* a secret word, phrase, or set of symbols that allows someone access to something.

past ['pæst] **1.** *n.* a time that has gone by; things that have happened; history. (No pl.) **2.** *adj.* most recent; occurring in the time just before this time. **3.** *adj.* occurring or completed at some previous time. **4.** the *adj.* use of ①. **5.** *adv.* by; toward or alongside someone or something and then beyond. **6.** *prep.* farther [in space, time, ability, or quality] than someone or something; beyond [in space, time, ability, or quality] someone or something.

pasta ['pɑs tə] *n.* a food prepared by mixing flour, water, and sometimes egg to make a dough or paste, and then shaping it into different forms; noodles. (Pl only for types and instances.)

paste ['pest] **1.** *n.* a soft mixture that is easily spread. (Pl only for types and instances.) **2.** *n.* a soft mixture that causes objects to stick together. (Pl only for types and instances.) **3.** *tv.* to cause something to stick to something else with ②.

pastime ['pæs taɪm] *n.* an activity that one enjoys; an enjoyable activity that is done to pass the time.

pastor ['pæs tɚ] *n.* a minister in a Christian church.

pastry ['pe stri] **1.** *n.* rich dough that is made with flour and butter or fat and is baked. (Pl only for types and instances.) **2.** *n.* baked foods, typically sweet, usually made with ①. (Pl only for types and instances. Number is expressed with *piece(s) of pastry*.) **3.** *n.* a piece or item of ②; a sweet roll, small cake, or other sweetened, baked food, often with fruit or with a sweet coating or filling.

pasture ['pæs tʃɚ] *n.* a field of grass, especially one where animals eat.

pat ['pæt] **1.** *n.* a gentle tap, especially with the palm of one's hand. **2.** *tv.* to touch or tap someone or something gently a few times, especially with the palm of the hand. **3.** *adj.* perfectly, as if rehearsed or from memory. (Adv: *patly*.)

patch ['pætʃ] **1.** *n.* a piece of cloth or other material used to repair a hole or a tear or to cover something. **2.** *n.* a small area of land. **3.** *n.* a small area on a surface that is different from the area around it.

patent ['pæt nt] **1.** *n.* the exclusive right, registered with the government, to benefit from the ownership of a process or invention. **2.** *tv.* to seek and gain ① on something.

path ['pæθ] **1.** *n., irreg.* a track or trail along the earth. (Pl: ['pæðz] or ['pæθs].) **2.** *n., irreg.* the route someone or something takes to achieve a result. (Fig. on ①.)

pathway ['pæθ we] *n.* a PATH ① or ②.

patience ['pe ʃəns] *n.* the quality of being patient and not becoming anxious or annoyed. (No pl.)

patient ['pe ʃənt] **1.** *adj.* able to wait for something to happen without complaining or becoming anxious or annoyed. (Adv: *patiently*.) **2.** *n.* someone who is getting medical help from a doctor, nurse, or hospital.

patio ['pæt i o] *n.* a paved surface connected to one's house where one can relax, gather with others, barbecue food, etc. (From Spanish. Pl ends in -*s*.)

patrol [pə 'trol] **1.** *tv.* to watch over an area by walking or driving around. **2.** *iv.* to watch over [an area] by walking or driving around. **3.** *n.* people who watch over an area as in ①.

patronize ['pe trə naɪz] **1.** *tv.* to be a regular customer of a store, restaurant, hotel, or other business. **2.** *tv.* to act as if one is superior to someone else.

patter ['pæt ɚ] **1.** *n.* a series of quick tapping sounds. (No pl.) **2.** *iv.* [for falling rain] to make quick tapping sounds as it strikes something.

pattern ['pæt ɚn] **1.** *n.* a design; an arrangement of shapes and colors, especially one that is repeated. **2.** *n.* a repeated element in a series of events. **3.** *n.* a printed or drawn outline of the parts of a garment or something that is to be built.

patty ['pæt i] *n.* a thin, flat disk of ground or mashed food, especially one formed of ground meat.

pause ['pɔz] **1.** *n.* a brief delay; a moment in which someone or something stops talking, moving, or working. **2.** *iv.* to stop for a moment; to stop moving or talking for a moment.

pave ['pev] *tv.* to build or cover a road, street, driveway, highway, etc., with cement, concrete, or some other hard surface.

pavement ['pev mənt] *n.* a flat surface of concrete, cement, or some other hard material covering an area, especially covering a street or sidewalk. (No pl.)

paw ['pɔ] **1.** *n.* the foot of a clawed animal. **2.** *tv.* to handle someone or something with hands or ①.

pay ['pe] **1.** *tv., irreg.* to give money (to someone) in exchange for a product or a service or to settle a debt. (E.g., to *pay twelve dollars.* Pt/pp: PAID.) **2.** *tv., irreg.* to give someone an amount of money in exchange for a product or service or to settle a debt. (E.g., to *pay someone.*) **3.** *tv., irreg.* to settle a bill or a debt. **4.** *tv., irreg.* [for something] to yield a certain amount of money or a certain benefit. **5.** *n.* wages; salary; the amount of money that one earns from a job. (No pl. Treated as sg.) **6.** *adj.* requiring money in order to be used.

payday ['pe de] *n.* the day on which a company pays its workers.

payment ['pe mənt] **1.** *n.* transferring money [to someone]. (Pl only for types and instances.) **2.** *n.* an amount of money paid or to be paid; something that is paid [to someone or something].

payroll ['pe rol] *n.* the list of a company's employees and their salaries.

pea ['pi] **1.** *n.* a small, round, green vegetable that grows in a pod on a vinelike plant. **2.** *n.* the plant that ① grows on. (No sg in this sense. Number is expressed with *pea plant(s).*)

peace ['pis] **1.** *n.* a condition where there is no war or fighting; a time when there is order and harmony. (No pl.) **2.** *n.* silence; freedom from anxiety. (No pl.)

335

peaceful ['pis fʊl] **1.** *adj.* without war or fighting; not at war; orderly. (Adv: *peacefully.*) **2.** *adj.* happy and calm; free from anxiety. (Adv: *peacefully.*)

peach ['pitʃ] **1.** *n.* a soft, sweet, juicy, round fruit with a fuzzy skin, yellow-orange pulp, and a large pit in the middle. **2.** *adj.* made with ①; tasting like ①.

peacock ['pi kɑk] **1.** *n.* a large male peafowl having a large, beautifully colored tail that fans out. **2.** *n.* any peafowl.

peafowl ['pi fɑʊl] *n., irreg.* a large bird from Southeast Asia, the males of which have large, showy tails. (Pl: *peafowl* or *peafowls.*)

peahen ['pi hɛn] *n.* a female peafowl.

peak ['pik] **1.** *n.* the top of something, especially a mountain; the highest point of something. **2.** *n.* the maximum amount of effort or accomplishment. **3.** *iv.* to form or rise to ①. **4.** *iv.* to reach ②.

peal ['pil] **1.** *n.* the [loud], ringing sound that bells make. **2.** *n.* a long, loud sound, such as with laughter. **3.** *iv.* to ring loudly; to sound loudly.

peanut ['pi nʌt] **1.** *n.* a plant with seedpods that grow underground. **2.** *n.* the nut meat of ①; the nut meat and shell of ①.

pear ['per] *n.* a yellow, brown, or green fruit that is rounded at the bottom and narrower toward the top.

pearl ['pɚl] *n.* a hard, white, round substance formed inside an oyster, usually used in jewelry.

pebble ['pɛb əl] *n.* a small stone.

pecan [pɪ 'kɑn] **1.** *n.* a tall tree native to the southern United States and Mexico. **2.** *n.* the edible part of ①; the nutmeat and shell of ①. **3.** *n.* the wood of ①. (Pl only for types and instances.) **4.** *adj.* made with ②. **5.** *adj.* made from ③.

peculiar [pɪ 'kjul jɚ] *adj.* odd; strange; unusual. (Adv: *peculiarly.*)

pedal ['pɛd l] **1.** *n.* a device that controls something and is operated with the feet. **2.** *tv.* to ride a bicycle. **3.** *iv.* to ride [a bicycle] somewhere.

pedestal ['pɛd ə stəl] *n.* a base that supports a statue, vase, column, etc.

pedestrian [pə 'dɛs tri ən] **1.** *n.* someone who walks as a means of travel; someone who is walking. **2.** *adj.* designed for ①; serving ①. **3.** *adj.* boring; unimaginative. (Adv: *pedestrianly.*)

336

peek ['pik] **1.** *n.* a quick, sly look; a quick look at something that one is not supposed to look at. **2.** *iv.* to look quickly at something that one is not supposed to look at.

peel ['pil] **1.** *n.* the outer skin of certain fruits and vegetables. (No pl. See also PEELING.) **2.** *tv.* to remove ①. **3.** *tv.* to remove an outer layer from something. (Fig. on ②.) **4.** *iv.* [for an outer layer] to come off.

peeling ['pi lɪŋ] *n.* a part of something, especially fruits and vegetables, that has been peeled off. (Often pl.)

peep ['pip] **1.** *n.* a high noise, such as that made by a baby chicken or other birds. **2.** *iv.* to have a quick look at something, especially in secret; a peek. **3.** *iv.* to make a noise, as with ①.

peeve ['piv] *n.* something that irritates or annoys someone.

peg ['pɛg] **1.** *n.* a thick wooden or plastic pin used to hold objects together. **2.** *tv.* to attach something to something with ①.

pelican ['pɛl ɪ kən] *n.* a bird that lives on or near the water and that has a bill with a large scoop on the lower part.

pellet ['pɛl ɪt] *n.* a hard, small ball of something, such as ice, wax, dirt, or metal.

pelt ['pɛlt] **1.** *n.* the complete fur-covered skin of an animal. **2.** ~ **with** to target someone or something with something. **3.** *tv.* to hit against someone or something repeatedly with force.

pen ['pɛn] **1.** *n.* a thin writing instrument that uses ink. **2.** *n.* a confined area where certain animals are kept. **3.** *tv.* to write something, usually with ①.

penalty ['pɛn əl ti] *n.* a punishment for breaking a rule or law.

pencil ['pɛn səl] **1.** *n.* a thin writing instrument with a pointed core made of a soft black material. **2.** *tv.* to write something with ①.

(pencil) sharpener ['pɛn səl 'ʃɑr pən ɚ] *n.* a machine that sharpens things, usually pencils.

penny ['pɛn i] *n.* a cent; ¹⁄₁₀₀ of a dollar in the United States and various other nations.

pension ['pɛn ʃən] *n.* money that is paid to a former employee, from retirement until death, or some other period of time, to replace a salary.

penthouse ['pɛnt hɑʊs] *n., irreg.* a special apartment on the top floor of a building. (Pl: [...hɑʊ zəz].)

337

people ['pip əl] **1.** *n.* persons. (No pl. Treated as a pl. Used as a pl of PERSON.) **2.** *n.* a specific group of ①; a race or ethnic group of ①. (Sg or pl with the same meaning.)

pep ['pɛp] *n.* energy; vigor. (No pl.)

pepper ['pɛp ɚ] **1.** *n.* a vegetable, often green or red, that is mostly hollow and often very hot and spicy. **2.** *n.* the dried berries of various plants, usually ground, used to season food. (Usually black in the United States and white in Europe. Pl only for types and instances.) **3.** *tv.* to sprinkle ② on food as a seasoning. **4.** *tv.* [for many tiny things] to strike something lightly.

peppy ['pɛp i] *adj.* full of energy; active; excited. (Adv: *peppily.* Comp: *peppier;* sup: *peppiest.*)

per ['pɚ] *prep.* for each; for every.

per head Go to a HEAD.

perceive [pɚ 'siv] *tv.* to be aware of someone or something with one's mind; to be aware of someone or something through one's senses.

percent [pɚ 'sɛnt] *n.* a one-hundredth part. (No pl. Usually expressed with a number ranging from 0 through 100. Also expressed as "%".)

percentage [pɚ 'sɛn tɪdʒ] *n.* a part that is less than the whole amount.

perch ['pɚtʃ] **1.** *n.* a branch or rod that a bird grasps with its feet when it is at rest. **2.** *n.* a place to sit that is high off the floor or ground; a high ledge. (Fig. on ①.) **3.** *n., irreg.* any one of several species of edible fish. (Pl: *perch,* except when referring to a number of species.) **4.** *iv.* to sit on top of something; to stand on top of something, as does a bird.

percussion [pɚ 'kʌʃ ən] **1.** *n.* the impact of the hitting of one object against another. (No pl form in this sense.) **2.** *n.* musical instruments that are struck, such as drums, bells, and xylophones, as a group in a band or orchestra. (No pl form in this sense.)

perfect 1. ['pɚ fɪkt] *adj.* being the best; completely correct; without flaws. (Adv: *perfectly.*) **2.** ['pɚ fɪkt] *adj.* exactly suitable; exactly what is needed. (Adv: *perfectly.*) **3.** ['pɚ fɪkt] *adj.* complete; total. (Adv: *perfectly.*) **4.** ['pɚ fɪkt] *n.* a grammatical construction showing a completed action or condition; a form of the verb that shows that something was completed, is completed, or will be completed. (In English, it consists of the pp of the verb that follows a form of HAVE ⑤. No pl.) **5.** [pɚ 'fɛkt] *tv.* to make something without flaws as in ①.

perfection [pɚ ˈfɛk ʃən] **1.** *n.* the condition of being perfect. (No pl.) **2.** *n.* becoming perfect; making something perfect. (No pl.)

perform [pɚ ˈform] **1.** *tv.* to do something; to do an action. **2.** *tv.* to present a play, sing a song, play a piece of music, do a dance, etc., for an audience. **3.** *iv.* to act, sing, dance, or play music, especially in front of people. **4.** *iv.* to function; to do what is expected or has been assigned.

performance [pɚ ˈfor məns] **1.** *n.* a presentation of a play, a piece of music, a song, a dance, etc. **2.** *n.* the quality of performing or functioning; how well someone or something performs. (Pl only for types and instances.)

performer [pɚ ˈfor mɚ] *n.* someone who performs, such as an actor, a singer, a musician, a dancer.

perfume 1. [ˈpɚ fjum, pɚ ˈfjum] *n.* a mixture of pleasant-smelling natural or artificial oils and alcohol that is put on people's skin. (Pl only for types and instances.) **2.** [pɚ ˈfjum] *tv.* to place a pleasant-smelling substance on someone; to add a pleasant-smelling substance to the air in a room.

perhaps [pɚ ˈhæps] *adv.* maybe; possibly; maybe yes, maybe no.

peril [ˈpɛr əl] **1.** *n.* great danger. (No pl form in this sense.) **2.** *n.* something that causes danger; a great danger.

period [ˈpɪr i əd] **1.** *n.* a punctuation mark (.) used at the end of a sentence or at the end of an abbreviation. **2.** *n.* a certain length of time, including certain times in history. **3.** *n.* a section or part of certain games, such as basketball. **4.** *n.* a division of the school day. **5.** *n.* the time during the month when a woman menstruates. (Short for *menstrual period*.) **6.** *adj.* [of art, architecture, crafts, or literature] having to do with a certain time in history.

perish [ˈpɛr ɪʃ] **1.** *iv.* to die. **2.** *iv.* [for something] to go away or fade away.

perjury [ˈpɚ dʒə ri] *n.* lying in court after one has taken an oath promising not to lie. (No pl.)

permanent [ˈpɚ mə nənt] **1.** *adj.* intended or designed to last forever or for a long time; not temporary. (Adv: *permanently*.) **2.** *n.* a type of hair treatment where the hair is caused to stay in a particular arrangement for a long time. (From *permanent wave*.)

permission [pɚ ˈmɪ ʃən] *n.* consent; agreement that something may be done. (No pl.)

permit 1. ['pɚ mɪt] *n.* an official document that allows someone to do something. **2.** [pɚ 'mɪt] *tv.* to allow someone to do something; to let someone do something.

persecute ['pɚ sə kjut] *tv.* to oppress or harass someone or some group of people, especially because of race, religion, or some other belief or status.

persevere [pɚ sə 'vɪr] *iv.* to continue working to reach a goal, even though it is difficult; to struggle with a problem or difficulty.

persist [pɚ 'sɪst] **1.** *iv.* to continue to do something; not to give up, even if the task is difficult or if one faces opposition. **2.** *iv.* to continue to exist.

person ['pɚ sən] **1.** *n.* a human being; a man, a woman, a boy, or a girl. (PEOPLE is sometimes used as the pl.) **2.** *n.* a grammar term, used to show the relationship of the speaker or writer to the receiver of the message.

personal ['pɚ sən əl] **1.** *adj.* of or about the private affairs of a particular person; belonging to or used by a particular person. (Adv: *personally.*) **2.** *adj.* done by a certain person, instead of by someone else. (Adv: *personally.*)

personality [pɚ sə 'næl ə ti] **1.** *n.* aspects of one's thinking and behavior that make one different from everyone else. **2.** *n.* someone who is well known; a famous person.

personnel [pɚ sə 'nɛl] *n.* the people who work for a company or organization. (No pl.)

perspire [pɚ 'spaɪɚ] *iv.* to sweat.

persuade [pɚ 'swed] *tv.* to use argument or discussion to cause someone to do or think something.

persuasion [pɚ 'swe ʒən] *n.* efforts to persuade someone of something. (No pl.)

pesky ['pɛs ki] *adj.* being a PEST ① or ②; irritating; annoying; troublesome. (Adv: *peskily.* Comp: *peskier;* sup: *peskiest.*)

pest ['pɛst] **1.** *n.* any animal or insect that destroys crops, spreads disease, or enters people's homes. **2.** *n.* someone or something that causes trouble; someone or something that is a nuisance.

pester ['pɛs tɚ] *tv.* to bother someone; to annoy someone.

pet ['pɛt] **1.** *n.* an animal that is kept in one's home or yard as a companion. **2.** *adj.* [of an animal] kept as ①. (Prenominal only.) **3.** *adj.*

special; particular; favorite. (Prenominal only.) **4.** *tv.* to stroke or pat someone or some creature.

petal ['pɛt əl] *n.* one of the colored sections of the blossom of a flower.

petite [pə 'tit] **1.** *adj.* [of a woman] small; [of a woman] short. (From French. Adv: *petitely.*) **2.** *adj.* [of a clothing size or range of sizes] fitting women who are ①.

petition [pə 'tɪ ʃən] **1.** *n.* a document signed by many people who are demanding something from someone. **2.** *tv.* to request something formally of a government or of an authority, often through the use of ①. (The object can be a clause with THAT ⑦.)

petroleum [pə 'tro li əm] *n.* oil that is pumped from under the ground, used to make gasoline and other substances. (No pl.)

phantom ['fæn təm] **1.** *n.* a ghost; an image or memory that is "seen" by the mind in a dream or in a vision, but is not real. **2.** *adj.* like a ghost; unreal; apparent, but not real.

phase ['fez] **1.** *n.* a stage in the development of someone or something; a stage in a sequence of events. **2.** *n.* any of the stages of the appearance of the moon as seen from earth.

philosophy [fɪ 'las ə fi] **1.** *n.* the science and study of the meaning of truth, knowledge, reality, and existence. (No pl.) **2.** *n.* the way one looks at life; the principles one uses to live one's life. (Pl only for types and instances.)

phobia ['fob i ə] *n.* an unreasonable fear; a strong dread. (Also in combinations, such as *claustrophobia, hydrophobia.*)

phone ['fon] **1.** *n.* a TELEPHONE. **2.** *tv.* to call someone by ①; to TELEPHONE someone.

photo ['fo to] *n.* a photograph; a snapshot; a picture made by a camera.

photograph ['fo tə græf] **1.** *n.* a picture made by a camera; a photo; a snapshot. (Can be shortened to PHOTO.) **2.** *tv.* to take a picture, with a camera, of someone or something.

photographer [fə 'tɑ grə fɚ] *n.* someone who takes pictures with a camera, especially for a living.

photography [fə 'tɑ grə fi] *n.* the science, study, art, or act of taking a picture with a camera. (No pl.)

phr. an abbreviation of PHRASE ① and ②.

phrase ['frez] **1.** *n.* a group of words that functions as a unit of grammar within a sentence. **2.** *n.* an expression usually including several

341

words. **3.** *n.* a series of notes that is a part of a piece of music. **4.** *tv.* to put communication into words. **5.** *tv.* to perform music, grouping into a series the notes that belong to ③.

physical [ˈfɪz ɪ kəl] **1.** *adj.* of or about the body; of the body. (Adv: *physically* […ɪk li].) **2.** *adj.* of or about the laws of nature; of or about the study of physics. **3.** *adj.* of or about real objects; of or about matter. (Adv: *physically* […ɪk li].) **4.** *n.* a thorough examination by a doctor. (Short for *physical examination*.)

physician [fɪ ˈzɪ ʃən] *n.* a medical doctor.

physics [ˈfɪz ɪks] *n.* the science and study of the properties of and relationships between matter and energy. (Treated as sg.)

pianist [ˈpi ə nɪst] *n.* someone who plays the piano, especially a professional piano player.

piano [pi ˈæ no] *n.* a large musical instrument in which small, soft hammers connected to a keyboard strike tuned metal strings. (Pl ends in *-s*.)

pick [ˈpɪk] **1.** *n.* a tool that is a heavy, pointed metal bar attached to a handle, used for breaking apart ice, rocks, and other objects. **2.** *n.* a choice; a selection. (Pl only for types and instances.) **3.** *tv.* to choose a particular person or thing. **4.** *tv.* to remove something from someplace, especially using one's fingers or a pointed tool. **5.** *tv.* to gather or harvest flowers, fruit, cotton, peas, beans, etc.

pickle [ˈpɪk əl] **1.** *n.* a cucumber—whole, sliced, chopped, or in sections—that has been preserved in salt water or vinegar. **2.** *tv.* to preserve food, especially vegetables, in salt water or vinegar.

picnic [ˈpɪk nɪk] **1.** *n.* a meal prepared to be eaten informally outdoors. **2.** *iv., irreg.* to have ①. (Pt/pp: PICNICKED. Pres. part.: PICNICKING.) **3.** *adj.* used for ①.

picnicked [ˈpɪk nɪkt] pt/pp of PICNIC.

picnicking [ˈpɪk nɪk ɪŋ] pres. part. of PICNIC.

picture [ˈpɪk tʃɚ] **1.** *n.* a drawing, a painting, or a photograph; an image of someone or something. **2.** *n.* a movie; a motion picture. **3.** *n.* the image on a television screen. **4.** *tv.* to think of someone or something; to make a mental image of someone or something; to imagine something. **5.** *tv.* to show someone or something in ①.

pie [ˈpaɪ] **1.** *n.* a kind of food that has a crust of pastry or something similar and is filled with meat, fruit, or some sweet substance. (The

342

crust can be on the bottom or on both the bottom and top. Pl only for types and instances.) **2.** *n.* a single, complete, round unit of ①.

piece ['pis] **1.** *n.* a part of something; a part broken off of or removed from something; an object that is put together with other objects to make something. **2.** *n.* an example of something, especially of an art or craft, such as music. **3.** *n.* [in games such as chess or checkers that are played on a special board] an object that is placed on the board and, typically, moved to different places on the board according to the rules of the particular game.

piecrust ['paɪ krəst] *n.* a piece of pastry found on the bottom and often the top of a pie.

pier ['pɪr] *n.* a dock; a structure like a bridge that extends into the water from the shore, supported by posts or columns.

pierce ['pɪrs] *tv.* to make a hole through someone or something; to cause something to go through something else.

pig ['pɪg] **1.** *n.* a farm animal with short legs and a curled tail, raised for food, especially bacon, ham, and pork. (Thought of as greedy and messy.) **2.** *n.* someone who eats a lot of food. (Fig. on ①.) **3.** *n.* someone who is dirty or messy. (Fig. on ①.)

pigeon ['pɪdʒ ən] *n.* a bird, commonly found in cities, with short legs and a heavy body, whose head bobs as it walks.

pigment ['pɪg mənt] *n.* a substance that causes paint, skin, dye, or plant tissue to have a certain color. (Pl only for types and instances.)

pile ['paɪl] **1.** *n.* a mound, stack, or heap of something, such as clothing, leaves, dirt. **2.** *n.* a beam of wood or steel that is driven into the ground to support a building, bridge, or other structure. **3.** *tv.* to place or form things or matter into a shape like ①.

pilgrim ['pɪl grɪm] **1.** *n.* someone who travels, especially to a holy place, as a religious act. **2.** *n.* one of the settlers of Plymouth Colony in 1620. (Capitalized.)

pill ['pɪl] *n.* a small, formed mass containing vitamins, medicine, or some other drug that is swallowed.

pillar ['pɪl ɚ] *n.* a column; a strong upright structure used to support something or as decoration.

pillow ['pɪl o] *n.* a cloth bag filled with feathers or a similar soft material, typically used to support one's head while sleeping, or for decoration.

pillowcase ['pɪl o kes] *n.* a fabric cover for a pillow.

pilot ['paɪ lət] **1.** *n.* someone who flies a plane; someone who guides a boat along a channel. **2.** *tv.* to fly an airplane; to guide a boat through a channel. **3.** *adj.* experimental; serving as a test.

pimple ['pɪm pəl] *n.* a small, round infection on the skin.

pin ['pɪn] **1.** *n.* a thin, stiff, pointed wire occurring in a variety of forms, such as with a flat top, a plastic end, a safety cover on the end, etc. (The simple ① is also called a *straight pin*.) **2.** *n.* a piece of jewelry that is attached to clothing with a variety of ①. **3.** *tv.* to attach something to something else with some variety of ①. **4.** *tv.* to press someone or something against something.

pinch ['pɪntʃ] **1.** *n.* an act of squeezing a fold of skin, usually causing pain. **2.** *n.* a small amount of something, such as a spice, that can be held between one's first finger and one's thumb. **3.** *tv.* to squeeze or hold something, such as a fold of flesh, between two surfaces.

pine ['paɪn] **1.** *n.* a kind of tree that has long, thin, sharp needles for leaves. **2.** *n.* wood from ①. (Pl only for types and instances.) **3.** *adj.* made from ②; composed of ②.

pineapple ['paɪn æp əl] **1.** *n.* a large, juicy tropical fruit that is yellow on the inside and has a very rough skin. **2.** *n.* the edible part of ①. (No pl.) **3.** *adj.* made from ②; containing or flavored with ②.

pink ['pɪŋk] **1.** *n.* the color of red mixed with white; a light, pale red. (Pl only for types and instances.) **2.** the *adj.* use of ①. (Comp: *pinker*; sup: *pinkest*.)

pint ['paɪnt] **1.** *n.* a unit of liquid measure, equal to half a quart or ⅛ of a gallon or 16 fluid ounces. **2.** *n.* a unit of dry measure, equal to half a quart or ¼₆₄ of a bushel. **3.** the *adj.* use of ① or ②.

pioneer [paɪ ə 'nɪr] **1.** *n.* someone who is one of the first of a particular group of people to settle a new area. (From the point of view of the particular group.) **2.** *n.* someone who is one of the first to investigate an area of science that has never been examined; someone who is one of the first people to do something, preparing the way for other people to do the same. **3.** *tv.* to prepare the way for other people to do something; to help develop something for other people.

pious ['paɪ əs] *adj.* very religious; expressing respect for God. (Adv: *piously*.)

pipe ['paɪp] **1.** *n.* a hollow tube that is used to carry a fluid from one place to another. **2.** *n.* a tube connected to a small bowl, used to smoke tobacco.

pirate ['paɪ rət] **1.** *n.* someone who robs ships at sea. **2.** *tv.* to steal or capture something, especially while at sea. **3.** *tv.* to take something; to use something when one does not have the right to use it. (Fig. on ②.) **4.** *tv.* to duplicate and sell copies of books, records, videos, and software without the permission of the original publisher. (Fig. on ②.)

piss ['pɪs] **1.** *iv.* to urinate. (Potentially offensive. The topic and the word are not heard in polite company. Use with caution.) **2.** *n.* urine. (Offensive as with ①.)

pistol ['pɪs təl] *n.* a small gun that can be held and shot with one hand.

piston ['pɪs tən] *n.* a solid cylinder that is moved up and down inside a tube by some force, such as that found in an engine.

pit ['pɪt] **1.** *n.* a large hole in the ground. **2.** *n.* a large, hard seed at the center of some kinds of fruit. **3.** *tv.* to remove ② from fruit.

pitch ['pɪtʃ] **1.** *tv.* to toss something toward someone or something. **2.** *tv.* [in baseball] to toss or throw a ball toward the batter. **3.** *tv.* to toss or throw someone or something. **4.** *iv.* [in baseball] to throw a baseball toward a batter. **5.** *iv.* [for a ship] to plunge up and down; [for the front of a ship] to rise and fall in rough water. **6.** *n.* [in baseball] the movement of the ball from the pitcher toward the batter or the throw that moves the ball toward the batter. **7.** *n.* slope; the amount that something is slanted. (Pl only for types and instances.) **8.** *n.* the measure of the highness or lowness of a sound. (Pl only for types and instances.) **9.** *n.* the standard number of vibrations each second that makes a certain tone; the standard musical sound for a given note. **10.** *n.* tar.

pitch-dark *adj.* very dark; as dark as pitch (tar).

pitcher ['pɪtʃ ɚ] **1.** *n.* the baseball player who pitches the baseball toward the other team's players, who then may strike it with the bat. **2.** *n.* a tall container with a handle, used for serving liquids. **3.** *n.* the contents of ②.

pitiful ['pɪt ə fʊl] **1.** *adj.* causing pity; worthy of pity; piteous. (Adv: *pitifully.*) **2.** *adj.* worthless; worthy of contempt. (Adv: *pitifully.*)

pity ['pɪt i] **1.** *n.* a feeling of sorrow caused by seeing or learning about the suffering of other people; sympathy. (No pl.) **2.** *tv.* to be sorry for someone or something; to feel ① for someone or something.

pizza ['pit sə] *n.* a food made of a baked disk of dough covered with spicy tomato sauce, cheese, and perhaps other foods. (Pl only for types and instances.)

345

pl the abbreviation of PLURAL.

place ['ples] 1. *n.* a position in space; a location; a certain area. 2. *n.* a house or apartment; a location where one lives. 3. *n.* a position in relation to other positions in a numbered series. 4. *tv.* to put something in a certain position; to put something on a certain surface. 5. *tv.* to remember when and where one has met someone or something in the past.

plague ['pleg] *n.* a disease that kills people and is quickly spread. (No pl. Treated as sg.)

plaid ['plæd] 1. *n.* a design of stripes that cross each other at right angles. 2. the *adj.* use of ①.

plain ['plen] 1. *n.* a flat area of land; a prairie. (Often pl with the same meaning, but not countable.) 2. *adj.* obvious; easy to see or understand. (Adv: *plainly.* Comp: *plainer;* sup: *plainest.*) 3. *adj.* simple; not complex; not decorated. (Adv: *plainly.* Comp: *plainer;* sup: *plainest.*) 4. *adj.* not attractive; average looking. (Adv: *plainly.* Comp: *plainer;* sup: *plainest.*) 5. *adv.* simply; clearly; obviously. (Colloquial.)

plaintiff ['plen tɪf] *n.* someone who sues someone else; someone who brings a lawsuit against someone else; someone who charges a defendant with doing wrong.

plan ['plæn] 1. *n.* the ideas for a future action or event; a detailed schedule for doing something. 2. *n.* a program or structure that provides a benefit to workers. 3. *tv.* to make ① for an event. 4. *iv.* to arrange [something] in advance.

plane ['plen] 1. *n.* a flat surface. 2. *n.* an airplane. 3. *n.* a tool equipped with a blade that is scraped over wood to make it flat or smooth. 4. *tv.* to make something flat or smooth by using ③.

planet ['plæn ɪt] *n.* a huge sphere of matter that circles a single star in a permanent orbit.

plank ['plæŋk] 1. *n.* a board; a long, thin, narrow, flat piece of wood. 2. *n.* an issue or policy that a political party officially supports. (A figurative ① in the party PLATFORM ③.)

plans *n.* a set of drawings of a house or building before it is built, used to help someone build the building. (Treated as pl.)

plant ['plænt] 1. *n.* a stationary living thing that makes its own food using sunlight and material from the soil or other substance that supports it. 2. *n.* a factory. 3. *tv.* to put a seed or a small ① in the ground so that it will grow; to place [the seeds or young ① of] a crop into the soil. **4.** *tv.* to place someone or something firmly in position. (Fig. on ③.)

plaster ['plæs tɚ] **1.** *n.* a mixture of lime, water, and sand, which hardens when it dries. (Pl only for types and instances.) **2.** *tv.* to apply ① to something.

plastic ['plæs tɪk] **1.** *n.* an artificial material, made from a variety of chemicals, that can be formed into different shapes. (Pl only for types and instances.) **2.** *adj.* made of ①. **3.** *adj.* [of something] easily molded or shaped. (Adv: *plastically* [...ɪk li].)

plate ['plet] **1.** *n.* an almost flat, round dish for holding food. **2.** *n.* a sheet of metal or glass. **3.** *n.* a metal plate that goes on the back of a vehicle, showing the license number of the vehicle. (Short for *license plate.*) **4.** *tv.* to give one sort of metal a thin outer layer of a more valuable metal.

plateau [plæ 'to] **1.** *n.* a flat area of land that is raised up higher than the surrounding land. **2.** *iv.* [for a number or a measurement] to reach a higher level and then remain unchanged.

platform ['plæt form] **1.** *n.* a flat structure that is higher than the area around it, especially one that people can occupy standing or sitting. **2.** *n.* the flat surface next to a railroad track where people get on and off trains. **3.** *n.* a formal statement of the ideas and policies of a political party. (See also PLANK ②.)

platter ['plæt ɚ] **1.** *n.* a large plate used for serving food. **2.** *n.* the contents of ①.

play ['ple] **1.** *n.* fun; recreation; something that is done for fun or amusement. (No pl.) **2.** *n.* one movement or action in a game or sport. **3.** *n.* a piece of writing that is written as a series of lines that people say, for performance in a theater. **4.** *n.* a performance of ③. **5.** *iv.* [for a sound-making device] to operate or reproduce sounds that have been recorded. **6.** *iv.* to perform on the stage or in public; to perform. **7.** *iv.* [for a performance] to be performed; [for a movie] to be shown. **8.** *iv.* to take one's turn in a game; to lay down a card in a card game. **9.** *iv.* to perform [on a musical instrument as in ⑬]. **10.** *iv.* to have fun; to amuse oneself; to be active in a sport or game. **11.** *tv.* to perform a role in the theater or in a movie. **12.** *tv.* to take part in a certain game, sport, or activity; to participate in a certain game, sport, or activity. **13.** *tv.* to make music with a musical instrument; to perform a particular piece of music on an instrument. (E.g., to *play a song.*) **14.** *tv.* to perform on a musical instrument. (E.g., to *play a violin.*) **15.** *tv.* [for an electronic device] to process tapes,

347

records, or CDs in a way that produces the sounds or pictures that have been recorded. **16.** *tv.* [for someone] to cause an electronic device to produce sounds and pictures as in ⑮.

player ['ple ɚ] **1.** *n.* someone who plays a game or sport. **2.** *n.* someone who plays a particular musical instrument. **3.** *n.* something that plays a recording. (Compare this with RECORDER ③.)

playful ['ple fʊl] **1.** *adj.* liking to play; full of fun. (Adv: *playfully.*) **2.** *adj.* funny; humorous; not serious. (Adv: *playfully.*)

playground ['ple grɑʊnd] **1.** *n.* an outdoor place for children to play. **2.** the *adj.* use of ①.

playmate ['ple met] *n.* a child with whom another child plays.

plaything ['ple θɪŋ] *n.* a toy; something that is played with.

plea ['pli] **1.** *n.* a request; an appeal. **2.** *n.* a statement in court in which one declares that one is guilty or innocent.

plead ['plid] **1.** *tv., irreg.* to declare in court that one is guilty or not guilty before the trial actually begins. (Pt/pp: *pleaded* or PLED.) **2.** *tv., irreg.* to claim something as an excuse. (The object can be a clause with THAT ⑦. Pt/pp: *pleaded* or PLED.)

pleasant ['plɛz ənt] **1.** *adj.* [of something] bringing or causing enjoyment and pleasure. (Adv: *pleasantly.*) **2.** *adj.* [of someone] friendly and nice. (Adv: *pleasantly.*)

please ['pliz] **1.** *adv.* a word used to make requests or commands more polite. **2.** *tv.* to cause someone to be happy or satisfied.

pleasure ['plɛʒ ɚ] *n.* a feeling of happiness because of something that one likes; enjoyment; a pleasing feeling or emotion. (Pl only for types and instances.)

pleat ['plit] *n.* a flat fold in a fabric, especially one fold in a series of folds, as found in skirts, draperies, and curtains.

pled ['plɛd] a pt/pp of PLEAD.

pledge ['plɛdʒ] **1.** *n.* a promise; a vow; a statement that one will do something. **2.** *tv.* to promise something. (The object can be a clause with THAT ⑦.)

plentiful ['plɛn tɪ fʊl] *adj.* having enough or more than enough; ample. (Adv: *plentifully.*)

plenty ['plɛn ti] **1.** *n.* a full supply; more than enough. (No pl.) **2.** *adj.* enough; almost too much. (Not prenominal.)

pliers ['plaɪ ɚz] *n.* a tool with rough jaws, used to grasp objects. (Usually treated as pl. Number is expressed with *pair(s) of pliers.* Also countable.)

plot ['plɑt] **1.** *n.* the story of a movie, book, opera, television show, play, etc. **2.** *n.* a secret plan to do something wrong or illegal. **3.** *n.* a small garden or part of a garden; a small area of land. **4.** *iv.* to plan in secret. **5.** *iv.* to make plans to do something, especially secretly. **6.** *tv.* to plan in secret to do something. **7.** *tv.* to determine the position of something on a map, chart, or graph.

plotter ['plɑt ɚ] *n.* a machine that marks points, lines, or curves on a graph.

plow ['plaʊ] **1.** *n.* a farm tool made of a heavy metal blade used to break up and turn over soil. **2.** *n.* a large, curved blade in front of a vehicle that is used to move snow off a road or path. **3.** *n.* a vehicle equipped with ②. **4.** *iv.* to use ①. **5.** *tv.* to cut into land, making rows for planting crops, with ①. **6.** *tv.* to clear a road or path of snow with ②.

pluck ['plʌk] **1.** *tv.* to remove the feathers from a bird; to remove hairs from the body of a person or an animal. **2.** *tv.* to clean a bird of its feathers. **3.** *tv.* to pull something from someplace.

plug ['plʌg] **1.** *n.* a small device for closing a hole, drain, or other opening. **2.** *n.* the connector that is pushed into an electric receptacle. (Short for *electric plug.*) **3.** *n.* a statement made while speaking on television or radio that encourages people to buy something or do something. **4.** *tv.* to mention a product and to encourage people to buy it.

plum ['plʌm] **1.** *n.* a fruit with a smooth skin and a soft, sweet, juicy pulp with a large pit. **2.** *n.* a deep purple color. **3.** *adj.* deep purple in color.

plumber ['plʌm ɚ] *n.* someone who is trained to install and repair sewer pipes, water pipes, and fixtures such as sinks, toilets, bathtubs, and drains.

plumbing ['plʌm ɪŋ] **1.** *n.* the work that a plumber does. (No pl.) **2.** *n.* water pipes, sewer pipes, gas pipes, and related fixtures. (No pl.)

plume ['plum] **1.** *n.* a feather, especially a bright, colorful one. **2.** *n.* something that looks like a feather, especially a cloud of smoke or a jet of water.

plump ['plʌmp] *adj.* a little fat or swollen.

349

plunder ['plʌn dɚ] **1.** *tv.* to rob someone or some place. **2.** *n.* loot; things that are stolen. (No pl form in this sense.) **3.** *n.* stealing; robbery. (No pl form in this sense.)

plunge ['plʌndʒ] **1.** *n.* a dive; a jump into water. **2.** *iv.* to dive into a liquid.

plural ['plɚ əl] **1.** *n.* a form of a word that refers to more than one thing or person. **2.** the *adj.* use of ①.

plus ['plʌs] **1.** *prep.* in addition to someone or something; added to someone or something. (Symbolized by "+".) **2.** *conj.* and also. **3.** *adj.* above zero; [marking a number] greater than zero. (Symbolized as "+".) **4.** *n.* an advantage; an extra.

ply ['plaɪ] **1.** *n.* a layer of something. (Hyphenated after a number.) **2.** *tv.* to work doing one's job, especially at one's trade.

plywood ['plaɪ wʊd] *n.* a wooden panel made of several thin sheets of wood that are glued together. (No pl.)

pneumonia [nə 'mon jə] *n.* an infection of the lungs involving fluid in the lungs. (No pl form in this sense.)

pocket ['pɑk ɪt] **1.** *n.* a small cloth bag that is sewn into clothing and is used to hold things, such as a wallet or keys. **2.** *n.* a small amount of something that is separated from other amounts of it; an isolated amount of something. **3.** *adj.* small enough to fit in ①; meant to be put in ①. **4.** *tv.* to put something in one's ①. **5.** *tv.* to steal something by putting it in one's ①.

pod ['pɑd] *n.* a long, soft, narrow shell that holds the seeds of certain plants, such as peas and beans.

poem ['po əm] *n.* a piece of writing in a form that sometimes rhymes and often has a rhythm, usually expressing feelings, emotions, or imagination.

poet ['po ɪt] *n.* someone who writes poetry.

poetic [po 'ɛt ɪk] **1.** *adj.* [of thoughts] expressed as a poem. (Adv: *poetically* [...ɪk li].) **2.** the *adj.* form of POETRY.

poetry ['po ə tri] **1.** *n.* a poem; poems; a collection of poems. (No pl. Treated as sg.) **2.** *n.* the art of writing poems. (No pl.)

point ['pɔɪnt] **1.** *n.* the sharp end of something. **2.** *n.* the main idea of something; the purpose of something. **3.** *n.* one idea, argument, or statement in a series of ideas, arguments, or statements. **4.** *n.* a certain position in space or moment in time; a certain degree or position of something. **5.** *n.* [in geometry] the place where two lines cross

350

each other. **6.** *n.* a dot; a DECIMAL POINT. **7.** *n.* a feature, trait, or ability of someone or something. **8.** *n.* a unit of scoring in a game. **9.** *n.* a helpful hint; a piece of advice. **10.** *tv.* to aim someone at someone or something; to direct someone to someone or something. **11.** *iv.* to indicate the location of someone or something by directing one's finger toward the location. **12.** *iv.* to be facing in a certain direction.

pointed ['pɔɪn tɪd] **1.** *adj.* having a point; sharp; sharpened to a point. **2.** *adj.* straightforward; directed in an obvious way. (Adv: *pointedly.*)

poison ['pɔɪ zən] **1.** *n.* a substance that can injure or kill a living creature, especially if eaten, drunk, breathed in, or absorbed through the skin. (Pl only for types and instances.) **2.** *tv.* to kill or harm someone or something with ①. **3.** *tv.* to put ① in something, especially food, in order to kill or harm someone or something. **4.** *tv.* to have a harmful effect on someone or something; to corrupt someone or something. (Fig. on ②.)

poisonous ['pɔɪ zən əs] *adj.* toxic; containing poison. (Adv: *poisonously.*)

poke ['pok] **1.** *n.* a push with one's finger, fist, or elbow, or with a blunt object. **2.** *tv.* to push someone or something with one's finger, fist, or elbow, or with a blunt object.

poker ['pok ɚ] **1.** *n.* a long, narrow metal rod that is used to move logs or coal in a fire. **2.** *n.* a card game where players win by having cards with the highest value. (No pl.)

polar ['po lɚ] *adj.* of or about the areas near the north or south pole.

pole ['pol] **1.** *n.* a long, thin, solid tube of wood, steel, plastic, or other material. **2.** *n.* one of the two places where the imaginary axis on which a planet spins meets the surface of the planet—at the north and south ends of the planet. **3.** *n.* either side of a magnet; either end of a magnet; one of the two strongest points of a magnet that either pulls or pushes metal objects.

police [pə 'lis] **1.** *tv.* to patrol an area; to control, regulate, or protect an area. **2.** *tv.* to regulate or control people, their behavior, or their actions.

policeman [pə 'lis mən] *n., irreg.* a police officer; a male member of a police force. (Pl: POLICEMEN or *police officers.*)

policemen [pə 'lis mən] pl of POLICEMAN.

policewoman [pə 'lis wʊm ən] *n., irreg.* a female police officer; a female member of a police force. (Pl: POLICEWOMEN or *police officers.*)

policewomen [pə 'lis wɪm ən] pl of POLICEWOMAN.

policy ['pɑl ə si] n. a plan of action used by management or government; a regulation.

polish ['pɑl ɪʃ] **1.** n. a substance that is used to make something shiny. (Pl only for types and instances.) **2.** tv. to make a surface shiny or glossy, especially by rubbing it. **3.** tv. to improve something; to make something better or perfect; to refine something. (Fig. on ②.)

Polish ['po lɪʃ] adj. of or about Poland; describing a person born in Poland.

polite [pə 'laɪt] adj. courteous; having good behavior; having good manners; doing things in a helpful and kind way. (Adv: politely.)

political [pə 'lɪ tɪ kəl] adj. of or about politics, politicians, or government. (Adv: politically [...ɪk li].)

politician [pɑl ə 'tɪ ʃən] n. a person whose business is politics, especially someone holding or seeking a government office.

politics ['pɑl ə tɪks] **1.** n. the business or operation of government; the study of the management of government. (Treated as sg or pl, but not countable.) **2.** n. someone's beliefs about political issues. (Treated as sg or pl, but not countable.)

poll ['pol] **1.** n. a survey that determines the popular opinion about an issue. **2.** tv. to ask someone questions as part of a survey.

pollen ['pɑl ən] n. a yellow powder made by flowers that is part of the process of making seeds. (Pl only for types and instances.)

polls n. the places where people vote. (Treated as pl.)

pollute [pə 'lut] **1.** tv. to cause something to become dirty or impure. **2.** iv. to make something dirty or impure.

pompous ['pɑmp əs] adj. arrogant; too formal; too grand. (Adv: pompously.)

pond ['pɑnd] n. a small body of water; a body of water smaller than a lake.

ponder ['pɑn dɚ] **1.** iv. to think carefully; to consider. **2.** tv. to think about something carefully; to consider something.

ponderous ['pɑn dɚ əs] adj. slow and awkward, especially because of being large or heavy. (Adv: ponderously.)

pony ['pon i] n. a small horse.

ponytail ['pon i tel] n. a bunch of hair pulled toward the back of the head and tied.

poodle ['pud l] *n.* a kind of dog that has curly fur.

pool ['pul] **1.** *n.* a puddle of water or other liquid. **2.** *n.* a game played with a number of hard balls on a felt-covered table having six pockets and raised sides. **3.** *tv.* to put money or things together for common use.

poor ['por] **1.** *adj.* not rich; having very little money; not owning many things. (Comp: *poorer;* sup: *poorest.*) **2.** *adj.* below a certain level of quality; inferior in operation or function. (Adv: *poorly.* Comp: *poorer;* sup: *poorest.*) **3.** *adj.* worthy of pity or sympathy.

pop ['pɑp] **1.** *n.* a quick, loud noise, like an explosion. **2.** *n.* father. (Informal. Also a term of address. Capitalized when written as a proper noun.) **3.** *n.* popular music. (No pl.) **4.** *n.* a fizzy drink; a soft drink. (Informal. No pl.) **5.** *adj.* popular; well liked; favored. **6.** *iv.* to make a sound as in ①; [for something with air in it] to burst suddenly. **7.** *tv.* to cause something to make ①; to cause something with air in it to burst suddenly.

popcorn ['pɑp kɔrn] **1.** *n.* seeds of various kinds of corn that explode into a soft, white, fluffy mass when heated. (Pl only for types and instances.) **2.** *n.* exploded and puffed-up kernels of ① eaten as food. (No pl. Treated as sg.)

poplar ['pɑp lɚ] **1.** *n.* a kind of tall, thin tree that grows quickly. **2.** *n.* wood from ①. (Pl only for types and instances.) **3.** *adj.* made from ②.

poppy ['pɑp i] *n.* a flowering herb with large red blossoms.

popular ['pɑp jə lɚ] *adj.* liked by many people; favored by many people; well liked. (Adv: *popularly.*)

populate ['pɑp jə let] *tv.* [for living creatures] to occupy an area. (Usually passive.)

population [pɑp jə 'le ʃən] **1.** *n.* the living creatures of one kind that live in a certain area. **2.** *n.* the number of people or creatures living in a certain place. (No pl.)

porch ['portʃ] *n.* a covered structure built in front of a house, usually at a doorway.

porcupine ['por kjə pɑɪn] *n.* a large rodent covered with sharp needles or spines that it uses to defend itself.

pore ['por] *n.* a tiny opening in the skin of plants and animals.

pork ['pork] *n.* the meat of a pig, eaten as food. (No pl.)

353

porpoise ['pɔr pəs] *n.* a mammal that lives in the sea, swimming in groups.

port ['pɔrt] **1.** *n.* a city on an ocean, sea, or lake that has a harbor where ships can be loaded and unloaded. **2.** *n.* a harbor. **3.** *adj.* on, at, or toward the left side of a ship or aircraft when one is facing the front of the ship or aircraft.

portable ['pɔrt ə bəl] *adj.* able to be moved from place to place; able to be carried; not permanently placed in one position. (Adv: *portably.*)

porter ['pɔr tɚ] *n.* someone who carries luggage for other people, especially at a hotel, airport, or train station.

portion ['pɔr ʃən] **1.** *n.* a part of something; a section. **2.** *n.* the amount of food given to someone at one time.

portrait ['pɔr trɪt] *n.* a painting, especially of a person or a person's face.

pose ['poz] **1.** *n.* a certain way that someone sits or stands, especially when one is getting one's picture taken or painted. **2.** *iv.* to sit or stand in a certain way when someone is taking or painting one's picture. **3.** *tv.* to place someone or something, as in ①.

posh ['pɑʃ] *adj.* very lavish; elegant; full of style. (Adv: *poshly.* Comp: *posher;* sup: *poshest.*)

position [pə 'zɪ ʃən] **1.** *n.* the place where someone or something is or where someone or something belongs. **2.** *n.* the way that someone or something is placed or situated. **3.** *n.* a point of view; an opinion; the way someone thinks about a certain subject or issue. **4.** *n.* a job. **5.** *tv.* to put someone or something in a certain place.

positive ['pɑz ɪ tɪv] **1.** *adj.* meaning "yes." **2.** *adj.* certain. (Adv: *positively.*) **3.** *adj.* in favor of something; accepting something. (Adv: *positively.*) **4.** *adj.* greater than zero; plus; above zero. (Adv: *positively.*) **5.** *adj.* optimistic; having a happy or confident outlook. (Adv: *positively.*) **6.** *adj.* practical; helpful. (Adv: *positively.*) **7.** *adj.* [of some part of an electrical circuit] higher in electrical charge than other points in the same circuit, allowing electrical energy to flow to other parts of the circuit. (Adv: *positively.*) **8.** *n.* the simple form of an adjective or adverb. **9.** *n.* an image, especially a photograph, where dark and light are the same in the picture as they are in reality. **10.** *n.* an advantage; a good quality; a benefit. **11.** *n.* a quantity greater than zero.

possess [pə 'zɛs] **1.** *tv.* to have something; to own something. **2.** *tv.* to influence someone or something completely; [for someone or something, especially an evil spirit or the devil] to control someone or something completely.

possession [pə 'zɛ ʃən] **1.** *n.* ownership. (No pl.) **2.** *n.* a belonging; something that belongs to someone; something that is owned by someone.

possessive [pə 'zɛs ɪv] **1.** *adj.* selfish; unwilling to share. (Adv: *possessively*.) **2.** *adj.* [of a word] showing possession or belonging [to someone or something]. (Adv: *possessively*.) **3.** *n.* the form of a word that shows possession.

possible ['pɑs ə bəl] *adj.* able to be done; able to exist; able to happen; able to be true, but not necessarily true. (Adv: *possibly*.)

possibly ['pɑs ə bli] *adv.* perhaps; maybe.

post ['post] **1.** *n.* an upright, thick length of wood, steel, or other material. **2.** *n.* a job; a position in a company or a government. **3.** *tv.* to place a written notice where people can see it. **4.** *tv.* to mail something; to send something by mail.

postage ['pos tɪdʒ] **1.** *n.* the cost of sending something through the mail, usually paid for with stamps. (No pl.) **2.** *n.* the stamp or stamps that are placed on something that is mailed. (No pl. Number is expressed with *postage stamp(s)*.)

postal ['pos təl] *adj.* of or about mail or the post office.

postcard ['post kɑrd] *n.* a card that is thicker than paper, sometimes has a picture on one side of it, and is used to mail someone a short letter, especially when one is traveling.

poster ['pos tɚ] *n.* a large sheet of thick paper carrying a message or a picture.

postmaster ['post mæ stɚ] *n.* someone who is in charge of a post office; the head of a post office.

posture ['pɑs tʃɚ] **1.** *n.* the way that one sits, stands, or moves; the position of the body. (Pl only for types and instances.) **2.** *iv.* to sit or stand in a certain way; to strike a pose.

pot ['pɑt] **1.** *n.* a large, deep, round container, usually used to cook or hold food or liquid. **2.** *n.* a round container that holds soil and a flower or plant. **3.** *n.* the contents of ① or ②. **4.** *tv.* to put a plant in soil in ②.

355

potato [pə 'te to] **1.** *n.* a vegetable root shaped like a large egg. (Pl ends in -*es*.) **2.** *n.* the plant that produces ①. (Pl ends in -*es*.) **3.** *adj.* made of or with ①.

potent ['pot nt] **1.** *adj.* powerful; having a strong effect. (Adv: *potently*.) **2.** *adj.* [of a male] able to copulate. (Adv: *potently*.)

pottery ['pɑt ə ri] **1.** *n.* dishes, bowls, vases, and other objects that are made from baked clay. (No pl.) **2.** *n.* the craft or art of making objects out of clay and baking them so that the clay hardens. (No pl.)

pouch ['paʊtʃ] *n.* a small bag that is used to hold a small amount of something.

poultry ['pol tri] *n.* chickens, ducks, geese, and other birds that are used as meat or for providing eggs for humans to eat. (No pl.)

pound ['paʊnd] **1.** *n.* a unit of measure of weight, equal to 16 ounces or about 0.454 kilogram. **2.** *n.* the basic unit of money in the United Kingdom. (Symbolized as £.) **3.** *n.* a place where stray animals are kept. **4.** *tv.* to hit someone or something very hard again and again; to beat something into a certain shape by hitting it very hard again and again. **5.** *iv.* [for the heart or blood pressure] to beat very hard.

pour ['por] **1.** *iv.* to flow from a place; to come out of a place quickly and continuously. **2.** *tv.* to cause something to POUR as in ① out of a place quickly and continuously.

poverty ['pɑv ɚ ti] *n.* the lack of the necessities for life. (No pl.)

powder ['paʊ dɚ] **1.** *n.* a substance that consists of tiny particles. (Pl only for types and instances.) **2.** *tv.* to cover or dust something with ① or a substance that has been crushed or ground into ①.

power ['paʊ ɚ] **1.** *n.* the ability to do something; strength. (Pl only for types and instances. Typically sg or pl with the same meaning.) **2.** *n.* the authority to do something; control. (Pl only for types and instances. Sg or pl with the same meaning.) **3.** *n.* the number of times that a number is multiplied by itself. **4.** *tv.* to supply energy to a machine or other device that uses energy.

powerful ['paʊ ɚ fʊl] *adj.* having a lot of power, energy, or force; full of strength or influence. (Adv: *powerfully*.)

practical ['præk tɪ kəl] **1.** *adj.* useful; able to be used; of or about actions and results, as opposed to ideas or theories. (Adv: *practically* [...ɪk li].) **2.** *adj.* sensible; having common sense. (Adv: *practically* [...ɪk li].)

practice ['præk tɪs] **1.** *n.* doing an action many times so that one will do it better and better. (No pl.) **2.** *n.* a custom; a tradition; the way something is usually done; a habit. **3.** *n.* the business of a doctor or a lawyer. **4.** *iv.* to rehearse. **5.** *tv.* to work at a skill over and over in order to become better at it. **6.** *tv.* to do something; to make a habit of something. **7.** *tv.* to work in medicine or law.

prairie ['prer i] *n.* a very large area of land that is covered with different kinds of grasses and other plants.

praise ['prez] **1.** *n.* saying that someone or something is good; the use of words to express satisfaction or a favorable judgment. (Sg or pl with the same meaning, but not countable.) **2.** *tv.* to express satisfaction with someone or something; to talk about the good things someone or something does or how good someone or something is. **3.** *tv.* to worship someone or God with words or songs.

prank ['præŋk] *n.* a trick or joke that is played on someone.

prankster ['præŋk stɚ] *n.* someone who plays a trick or joke on someone.

pray ['pre] **1.** *iv.* to give thanks to God; to say a prayer to God; to ask God or some religious being or figure for something. **2.** *tv.* to PRAY as in ①, asking that something will happen the way one wants. (The object is a clause with THAT ⑦.)

prayer ['prer] **1.** *n.* communication with God or some other religious being or figure. **2.** *n.* the words one uses when worshiping or praying to God.

preach ['pritʃ] **1.** *iv.* to give a sermon; to talk about something religious. **2.** *tv.* to deliver a sermon; to deliver a particular message through a sermon. (The object can be a clause with THAT ⑦.)

preacher ['pritʃ ɚ] *n.* someone who preaches; the leader of a church; a minister. (Less formal than MINISTER.)

precious ['prɛʃ əs] **1.** *adj.* very valuable; worth a lot of money. (Adv: *preciously*.) **2.** *adj.* very much loved; very dear to someone; cherished. (Fig. on ①. Adv: *preciously*.) **3.** *adj.* charming and cute. (Adv: *preciously*.)

precise [prɪ 'saɪs] *adj.* exact; carefully and accurately detailed. (Adv: *precisely*.)

precision [prɪ 'sɪ ʒən] *n.* accuracy; the quality of being precise; doing something precisely. (No pl.)

357

predict [prɪ 'dɪkt] *tv.* to say that something is going to happen before it happens; to prophesy that something will happen. (The object can be a clause with THAT ⑦.)

prediction [prɪ 'dɪk ʃən] *n.* a statement made about something that is going to happen in the future; a prophecy.

preface ['prɛf ɪs] **1.** *n.* an introduction to a speech or to something that is written. **2.** *tv.* to begin a speech or written piece with an introduction.

prefer [prɪ 'fɚ] *tv.* to like someone or something better than one likes someone or something else. (The object can be a clause with THAT ⑦.)

preferable ['prɛf ə rə bəl] *adj.* more preferred; more desirable. (Adv: *preferably.*)

preference ['prɛf ə rəns] **1.** *n.* special attention that is given to certain people or things; favor. (No pl.) **2.** *n.* someone or something that is preferred over someone or something else.

prefix ['pri fɪks] *n.* a letter or a group of letters at the beginning of a word that usually changes the meaning of the word.

pregnant ['prɛg nənt] *adj.* [of a woman or female creature] carrying developing offspring within.

prehistoric [pri hɪ 'stor ɪk] *adj.* happening before history was first recorded. (Adv: *prehistorically* […ɪk li].)

prejudice ['prɛdʒ ə dɪs] **1.** *n.* opinion formed about someone or something before learning all the facts. (Pl only for types and instances.) **2.** *tv.* to cause someone to have ①.

preliminary [prɪ 'lɪm ə nɛr i] **1.** *adj.* happening before something else; being an introduction to something that is more important or more difficult. (Adv: *preliminarily* [prɪ lɪm ə 'nɛr ə li].) **2.** *n.* an action or a preparation that is done before something that is more difficult or more important.

prelude ['pre lud] *n.* an introduction, especially a short piece of music that comes before a longer work of music.

premier [prɪ 'mɪr] **1.** *adj.* best; most respected. (Prenominal only.) **2.** *n.* the prime minister of a country.

premiere [prɪ 'mɪr] **1.** *n.* the first performance or presentation of a play, film, symphony, etc. **2.** *iv.* [for a play, film, symphony, etc.] to be performed for the first time.

premise ['prɛm ɪs] *n.* a statement that an argument or another statement is based on; a statement that is assumed to be true and on which

358

another statement is based. **2.** *n.* a basic theme that is developed or built on. **3.** ~**s** *n.* a location; a piece of property, including the buildings that are built on it. (Treated as pl.)

premium ['prim i əm] **1.** *n.* a regular payment to an insurance company for some kind of protection. **2.** *n.* an additional cost in addition to the regular cost. **3.** *n.* a small prize or reward that is given to someone to buy something or use a service. **4.** *adj.* of high quality; costing more; of greater value.

prenominal [pri 'nɑm ə nəl] *adj.* [of an adjective] occurring before the noun it modifies. (Adv: *prenominally.*)

prep. an abbreviation of PREPOSITION.

prepaid [pri 'ped] pt/pp of PREPAY.

prepare [pri 'pɛr] **1.** *tv.* to make something ready for someone or something; to make something ready for use. **2.** *iv.* to make oneself ready to do something.

prepay [pri 'pe] *tv., irreg.* to pay some amount before it is due; to pay for something in advance; to pay for something before one receives it. (Pt/pp: PREPAID.)

preposition [prɛp ə 'zɪ ʃən] *n.* a word that is used to show the relationship of one word or phrase to another word or phrase. (Abbreviated *prep.* here.)

preschool ['pri skul] *n.* a school for small children before they are old enough to go to kindergarten.

prescribe [pri 'skraɪb] **1.** *tv.* [for a physician] to recommend or order that a certain medication be sold to and taken by a patient. **2.** *tv.* [for a doctor] to advise a patient to do something to become or stay healthy. (The object can be a clause with THAT ⑦.) **3.** *tv.* to state something as a law; to establish something as a law. (The object can be a clause with THAT ⑦.)

prescription [pri 'skrɪp ʃən] **1.** *n.* ordering or prescribing something, especially medicine or medical treatment. **2.** *n.* an order to do something or take medicine, especially a written order for medicine given to a patient by a doctor. **3.** *n.* the actual medicine that is ordered by ②.

presence ['prɛz əns] **1.** *n.* the state of being present; being in the same place as someone or something else. (No pl.) **2.** *n.* the power or influence one has in a group of people or in an institution. **3.** *n.* something that can be felt or sensed but not seen, such as a spirit.

present 1. ['prɛz ənt] *adj.* being in the same room or place as someone or something else; not absent. **2.** ['prɛz ənt] *adj.* now; at this time; happening now. (Adv: *presently.*) **3.** ['prɛz ənt] *n.* now; this time; this moment in time. (No pl.) **4.** ['prɛz ənt] *n.* a gift; something that is given to someone else. **5.** ['prɛz ənt] *n.* the state of a verb that indicates that something is happening now. (Short for *present tense.*) **6.** [prɪ 'zɛnt] *tv.* to give something to someone, especially as part of a ceremony. **7.** [prɪ 'zɛnt] *tv.* to make something available for the public to see; to bring something to someone's attention. **8.** [prɪ 'zɛnt] *tv.* to introduce someone to someone else.

presentation [prɛz ən 'te ʃən] **1.** *n.* the way that something is shown to other people; the manner or style in which something is shown to other people. (No pl.) **2.** *n.* a session of showing or explaining something to other people. **3.** *n.* the ceremony of giving something to someone else.

present-day ['prɛz ənt 'de] *adj.* current; happening now; of or about the present time.

presently ['prɛz ənt li] **1.** *adv.* now; at this time. **2.** *adv.* soon. (Formal.)

preservation [prɛ zɚ 've ʃən] *n.* the process of preserving something; keeping something safe or in good condition. (No pl.)

preserve [prɪ 'zɚv] **1.** *tv.* to keep someone or something alive, healthy, safe, or in good condition. **2.** *tv.* to do something or add something to something to keep it from spoiling or decaying. **3.** *n.* an area of land where plants and animals are protected.

preserves *n.* fruit cooked in sugar and sealed in a jar. (Treated as pl, but not countable.)

preside [prɪ 'zaɪd] **1.** *iv.* to be in charge of a meeting or a business; to be in control. **2.** ~ **over** to oversee something, such as a meeting.

president ['prɛz ə dənt] **1.** *n.* the leader of the government of a republic, including the leader of the government of the United States of America. **2.** *n.* the leader or head officer of an organization, club, company, university, etc. **3.** *n.* the office and position of power occupied by ① or ②.

presidential [prɛz ə 'dɛn ʃəl] *adj.* of or about a president; associated with a president. (Adv: *presidentially.*)

press ['prɛs] **1.** *n.* a machine that prints letters and pictures on paper for newspapers, magazines, books, etc. (Short for *printing press.*) **2.** *n.* the coverage of an action or event by newspapers and other media.

(No pl.) **3.** *tv.* to push something against something else; to push something with force; to weigh down heavily on something. **4.** *tv.* to move a hot iron over wrinkled clothing or fabric in order to make it smooth. **5.** *iv.* to push against something else; to push with force; to weigh down heavily; to push forward.

pressure ['prɛʃ ɚ] **1.** *n.* the effect of a force or a weight that is pushed against someone or something. (No pl.) **2.** *n.* strong influence; strong persuasion. (Fig. on ①.)

pretend [prɪ 'tɛnd] **1.** *iv.* to act [as if something were so]. **2.** *iv.* to act as if one were doing something; to try to look as if one were doing something. **3.** *tv.* to act as if something were so; to play by acting as if something were so. (The object is a clause with THAT ⑦.)

pretty ['prɪt i] **1.** *adj.* attractive; pleasing; beautiful. (Adv: *prettily.* Comp: *prettier;* sup: *prettiest.*) **2.** *adv.* rather; quite; very.

pretzel ['prɛt səl] *n.* a salted, baked stick of bread, often twisted in the shape of a loose knot.

prevail [prɪ 'vel] **1.** *iv.* to exist in many places; to be widespread. **2.** ~ **(over)** to triumph [over someone or something]; to win [beating someone or something].

prevent from [prɪ 'vɛnt frəm] *tv.* not to allow something to happen; not to allow someone to do something; to keep something from happening; to keep someone from doing something; to stop something before it begins.

preventable [prɪ 'vɛnt ə bəl] *adj.* able to be prevented. (Adv: *preventably.*)

prevention [prɪ 'vɛn ʃən] *n.* preventing something. (No pl.)

preview ['pri vju] **1.** *n.* an opportunity to see something before it is available to the public. **2.** *iv.* [for something] to be shown as ①. **3.** *tv.* to watch or listen to something as ①.

previous ['pri vi əs] *adj.* earlier; happening before something else; coming before. (Adv: *previously.*)

prey ['pre] **1.** *n.* an animal that is hunted, killed, or eaten by another animal. (No pl. Compare this with PRAY.) **2.** *n.* someone who is a victim of someone else. (No pl. Fig. on ①.)

price ['praɪs] **1.** *n.* the amount of money that something costs; the amount of money that something will be sold for. **2.** *tv.* to determine how much something will cost; to set the amount of money that something will cost.

pride ['praɪd] **1.** *n.* the pleasure that one feels when one does something well; the feeling one has when one does something good. (No pl.) **2.** *n.* someone or something for which one has ①. (No pl.) **3.** *n.* a good opinion of oneself; too high an opinion of oneself. (No pl.)

priest ['prist] *n.* someone who is trained to perform religious duties. (In the United States, especially in the Roman Catholic, Orthodox Catholic, and Episcopal Churches.)

prim ['prɪm] *adj.* very proper; very formal; very exact; very precise; easily shocked by rude or rough behavior. (Adv: *primly.* Comp: *primmer;* sup: *primmest.*)

primary ['praɪ mɛr i] **1.** *adj.* the most important; chief; main; principal. (Adv: *primarily* [praɪ 'mɛr ə li].) **2.** *n.* an election that is held to determine who will represent a political party in the election for a political office.

prime ['praɪm] **1.** *adj.* [of a state or condition] best or excellent; of the highest quality. **2.** *adj.* most important; chief; first in time, order, or importance. **3.** *tv.* to add water or liquid to a pump to replace the air that is inside so that the pump is able to draw fluid. **4.** *tv.* to make someone or something ready for something. **5.** *tv.* to cover a surface with primer before painting it.

primer ['praɪm ɚ] *n.* a liquid that is spread over wood before one covers the wood with paint. (Pl only for types and instances.)

primitive ['prɪm ə tɪv] **1.** *adj.* early in the development of something; early in the history of humans. (Adv: *primitively.*) **2.** *adj.* very simple; not complicated. (Adv: *primitively.*)

primp ['prɪmp] *iv.* to dress and get ready for a social event very carefully.

prince ['prɪns] **1.** *n.* the son or grandson of a king or a queen. **2.** *n.* the husband of a woman who inherits the throne and becomes queen.

princely ['prɪns li] **1.** *adj.* like a prince; having great charm and manners. **2.** *adj.* elegant; refined; noble. (Fig. on ①.)

princess ['prɪns ɛs] **1.** *n.* the daughter or granddaughter of a king or queen. **2.** *n.* the wife of a prince.

principal ['prɪns ə pəl] **1.** *n.* the head of an elementary, middle, or high school. (Compare this with PRINCIPLE.) **2.** *n.* an amount of borrowed money on which the borrower must pay interest. **3.** *n.* the most important or major person in a group. **4.** *adj.* main; chief; primary; most important. (Adv: *principally* ['prɪns ə pli].)

362

principle ['prɪns ə pəl] **1.** *n.* obedience to ② and ③; honor. (No pl. Compare this with PRINCIPAL.) **2.** *n.* a general or fundamental law or rule. **3.** *n.* a rule of behavior or conduct.

print ['prɪnt] **1.** *tv.* to make letters of the alphabet by hand so that each letter is separate. **2.** *tv.* to put words or pictures on a blank piece of paper, one page at a time, using some kind of machine. **3.** *tv.* to publish a book, magazine, or newspaper using a printing press or a computer printer. **4.** *tv.* to publish something that is written in a book, newspaper, magazine, etc. **5.** *tv.* to make a photograph from film. **6.** *tv.* to cause a computer to PRINT something as in ②. **7.** *iv.* to make letters of the alphabet so that each letter is separate. **8.** *iv.* to make books, magazines, newspapers, etc., with a printing press. **9.** *iv.* [for a computer printer] to operate as in ②. **10.** *n.* fabric that has a pattern on it. **11.** *n.* a photograph that is made from film; a photograph. **12.** *n.* a FINGERPRINT.

printer ['prɪn tɚ] **1.** *n.* a business or person that prints books, magazines, and other materials. **2.** *n.* a machine that causes computer information to be put onto paper.

printing ['prɪn tɪŋ] **1.** *n.* letters or words that are printed by hand; letters that are put on paper so that the letters are separate and distinct. (No pl.) **2.** *n.* letters that are put on a page by a press or a machine. (No pl.) **3.** *n.* all the copies of a book printed by machine at one time.

printout ['prɪnt aʊt] *n.* a copy of information from a computer, printed on paper.

prison ['prɪz ən] **1.** *n.* a building that criminals are kept in; a large jail. **2.** *n.* a place where someone is not allowed to leave; a place where someone has no freedom. (Fig. on ①.)

prisoner ['prɪz nɚ] **1.** *n.* someone who is kept in a prison. **2.** *n.* someone or a creature that is not free to go. (Fig. on ①.)

pristine ['prɪs tin] *adj.* as fresh and clean as when it was new; spotless. (Adv: *pristinely.*)

privacy ['praɪv ə si] *n.* a state of being away from other people or away from the attention of the public. (No pl.)

private ['praɪv ɪt] **1.** *adj.* not shared among everyone; meant only for a small number of people; not public. (Adv: *privately.*) **2.** *adj.* individual; concerning only one person. (Adv: *privately.*) **3.** *adj.* secluded; isolated; quiet; away from other people. (Adv: *privately.*) **4.** *adj.* not owned, controlled, or managed by the government. (Adv: *privately.*)

privilege ['prɪv (ə) lɪdʒ] *n.* special rights; special and honored status. (Pl only for types and instances.)

prize ['praɪz] **1.** *n.* an award that is given to a winner; an award that is given to someone who does well in a competition. **2.** *tv.* to consider something to be worth very much; to place a great value on something.

pro ['pro] *n.* a PROFESSIONAL; having great skill or training. (Pl ends in -*s*.)

probable ['prɑb ə bəl] *adj.* having a great chance of happening; likely to happen; likely to be true. (Adv: *probably*.)

probably ['prɑb ə bli] *adv.* very likely; likely to happen or likely to be true.

probation [pro 'be ʃən] **1.** *n.* a situation where an offender remains out of jail and just under observation as long as no further crimes are committed. (No pl form.) **2.** *n.* a trial period. (Fig. on ①. No pl form.)

probe ['prob] **1.** *n.* a complete examination or detailed search for facts. **2.** *n.* a thin rod with a rounded end that is used to examine the inside of a hole, wound, or cavity. **3.** *n.* a rocket or satellite that is sent into space to relay information about space or other planets to scientists on earth. **4.** *tv.* to examine a hole, wound, or cavity, using ② or a similar object. **5.** *iv.* to examine; to search.

problem ['prɑb ləm] **1.** *n.* a question that must be answered; a difficulty. **2.** *n.* a question put forward for solving, as in a school exercise or test. **3.** *adj.* difficult to deal with; difficult to work with; causing difficulty.

procedure [prə 'si dʒɚ] *n.* the way that something is done; the way that a process is done; a method.

proceed [prə 'sid] *iv.* to begin to do something.

proceeds ['pro sidz] *n.* money that is collected or received from someone or something. (Treated as pl, but not countable.)

process ['prɑ ses] **1.** *n.* a series of actions; a set of procedures used to do, make, achieve, prepare, or develop something. **2.** *tv.* to do a series of actions to something; to prepare, achieve, or develop something.

procession [prə 'se ʃən] *n.* a moving line of people or things; a steady movement of people or things in a line.

proclaim [prə 'klem] *tv.* to declare something officially; to make something public knowledge. (The object can be a clause with THAT ⑦.)

procure [pro 'kjʊr] *tv.* to get something by work or effort.

produce 1. ['pro dus] *n.* food or food products that are farmed or grown; fruits and vegetables. (No pl.) **2.** [prə 'dus] *tv.* to grow something; to create something. **3.** [prə 'dus] *tv.* to cause something to be; to create a result. **4.** [prə 'dus] *tv.* to make something from parts or materials. **5.** [prə 'dus] *tv.* to coordinate and organize the details involved in making or presenting a movie, play, or other performance. **6.** [prə 'dus] *iv.* to do what is expected or required, especially in terms of business goals.

producer [prə 'dus ɚ] **1.** *n.* someone or something that produces something. **2.** *n.* someone who coordinates and organizes the details involved in making or presenting a movie, television show, play, or other performance.

product ['prɑ dəkt] **1.** *n.* something that is produced; something that is made, created, or grown. **2.** *n.* someone or something that is the result of certain conditions; a result. **3.** *n.* the number that is determined by multiplying two or more numbers together.

production [prə 'dʌk ʃən] **1.** *n.* producing something; making something. (No pl.) **2.** *n.* the amount of or rate of ①. (No pl.) **3.** *n.* a movie, television show, play, or other performance.

profess [prə 'fɛs] *tv.* to declare something; to claim something. (The object can be a clause with THAT ⑦.)

profession [prə 'fɛ ʃən] **1.** *n.* a job or career, especially one that requires education or training. **2.** *n.* all or most of the people who work in a certain ①.

professional [prə 'fɛʃ ə nəl] **1.** the *adj.* form of PROFESSION ①. (Adv: *professionally.*) **2.** *adj.* showing the skill and standards of ③. (Adv: *professionally.*) **3.** *n.* someone who works in a profession. (Shortened to PRO informally.)

professor [prə 'fɛs ɚ] *n.* someone who holds a faculty position in a university or college. (Also a term of address.)

profile ['pro faɪl] **1.** *n.* a side view of someone or something, especially of someone's face. **2.** *n.* a short description of someone or something.

profit ['prɑf ɪt] **1.** *n.* the amount of money made by a person or business after all expenses are paid. **2.** *tv.* to benefit someone or something.

program ['pro græm] **1.** *n.* a broadcast show, such as on radio or television. **2.** *n.* a booklet provided to members of an audience, giving

365

information about the performance. **3.** *n.* a schedule of the parts of a performance. **4.** *n.* a set of coded instructions given to a computer.

programmer ['proʊ græm ɚ] *n.* someone who writes a computer program.

progress 1. ['prɑ grɛs] *n.* the movement made toward a result or goal. (No pl.) **2.** ['prɑ grɛs] *n.* the improvement that someone or something makes when moving toward a goal. (No pl.) **3.** [prə 'grɛs] *iv.* to move forward; to advance. **4.** [prə 'grɛs] *iv.* to develop; to become better.

prohibit [proʊ 'hɪb ɪt] *tv.* to forbid something.

prohibition [proʊ ə 'bɪ ʃən] **1.** *n.* forbidding or not allowing something. (Pl only for types and instances.) **2.** *n.* the period of time in U.S. history when it was illegal to make, sell, or transport alcohol. (Capitalized. No pl.)

project 1. ['prɑ dʒɛkt] *n.* an assignment or task that must be planned, researched, and executed. **2.** [prə 'dʒɛkt] *tv.* to cast a light onto something. **3.** [prə 'dʒɛkt] *tv.* to make one's voice or words louder and carry farther. **4.** [prə 'dʒɛkt] *tv.* to forecast something; to estimate something. **5.** [prə 'dʒɛkt] *iv.* to be louder when speaking. **6.** [prə 'dʒɛkt] *iv.* to stick out; to extend from a surface.

projection [prə 'dʒɛk ʃən] **1.** *n.* something that sticks out or projects. **2.** *n.* a prediction; an estimate of a future state.

projector [prə 'dʒɛk tɚ] *n.* a machine that casts an image on a screen, wall, etc. (The image may have been recorded on film or digitally on tape.)

prolong [proʊ 'lɔŋ] *tv.* to cause something to last longer than it normally would; to lengthen the time it takes to do something.

prominent ['prɑm ə nənt] **1.** *adj.* famous; well known; respected. (Adv: *prominently*.) **2.** *adj.* noticeable; easy to see. (Adv: *prominently*.)

promise ['prɑm ɪs] **1.** *n.* a sign that someone will be successful or do good work. (No pl.) **2.** *n.* a pledge to do something. **3.** *tv.* to pledge to do something; to vow that one will do something. (The object is a clause with THAT ⑦.) **4.** *tv.* to cause someone to expect something.

promote [prə 'moʊt] **1.** *tv.* to work for the acceptance of someone or something through advertising and other public contacts. **2.** *tv.* to raise someone to a new and higher level in employment or schooling.

promotion [prə 'moʊ ʃən] **1.** *n.* the movement of someone to a higher level of employment or schooling. (Pl only for types and instances.)

366

2. *n.* advertising and other activity intended to sell something. (No pl.)

prompt ['prɑmpt] **1.** *adj.* doing something, such as arriving, at the right time; on time. (Adv: *promptly.*) **2.** *tv.* to encourage or cause someone to do something. **3.** *tv.* to give someone a quiet reminder of what is to be said next. (Especially in stage performances.) **4.** *n.* a symbol on a computer screen that shows that the computer is ready to receive information.

pron. an abbreviation of PRONOUN.

pronoun ['pro nɑʊn] *n.* a word that takes the place of a noun or nominal and refers to someone or something already mentioned. (Abbreviated *pron.* here.)

pronounce [prə 'nɑʊns] **1.** *tv.* to speak the sound of a letter or a word; to make the sound of a letter or a word. **2.** *tv.* to declare something about someone or something officially.

pronunciation [prə nən si 'e ʃən] *n.* the way a letter, group of letters, or a word sounds when spoken; the way someone says things. (Pl only for types and instances.)

proof ['pruf] **1.** *n.* something that shows that something is definitely true. (No pl.) **2.** *n.* a printed copy of something that is checked for mistakes before the final copy is printed; a first or sample version of a photograph. **3.** *tv.* to proofread something.

proofread ['pruf rid] **1.** *tv., irreg.* to read something very carefully to look for and correct mistakes. (Pt/pp: *proofread* ['pruf rɛd].) **2.** *iv., irreg.* to read very carefully to look for mistakes.

prop ['prɑp] *n.* an object that is used in a play or in a movie by an actor.

propaganda [prɑp ə 'gæn də] *n.* information that tries to influence or change how people think. (No pl.)

propel [pro 'pɛl] *tv.* to cause someone or something to move ahead; to cause someone or something to move forward; to move something ahead.

propeller [pro 'pɛl ɚ] *n.* a set of blades that rotate very fast in air or water, used to push or move a boat or an airplane.

proper ['prɑp ɚ] **1.** *adj.* right; suitable; correct; appropriate. (Adv: *properly.*) **2.** *adj.* [in grammar, of a noun] referring to a person or place. (Such nouns are capitalized.) **3.** *adj.* referring to a particular place itself, and not an area outside of that place. (Not prenominal. Adv: *properly.*)

367

properly ['prɑp ɚ li] **1.** *adv.* in the right way; suitably; appropriately; according to what is expected. **2.** *adv.* strictly.

property ['prɑp ɚ ti] **1.** *n.* something that is owned. (No pl.) **2.** *n.* an amount of land and any structures that have been built on it. (No pl.)

prophecy ['prɑf ə si] *n.* the ability to foresee the future. (Pl only for types and instances.)

prophesy ['prɑf ə saɪ] *tv.* to predict what will happen in the future; to say that something is going to happen. (The object can be a clause with THAT ⑦.)

prophet ['prɑf ɪt] **1.** *n.* someone who has the talent of being able to see into the future. **2.** *n.* [in some religions] a person chosen to speak for God.

proportion [prə 'por ʃən] **1.** *n.* the relationship between the sizes of different parts of someone or something. **2.** *tv.* to adjust the amount, degree, or size of something in comparison to something else.

proposal [prə 'poz əl] **1.** *n.* a suggestion; a plan. **2.** *n.* an offer of marriage made to someone.

propose [prə 'poz] *tv.* to suggest something; to say something so that it is considered. (The object can be a clause with THAT ⑦.)

proposition [prɑp ə 'zɪ ʃən] **1.** *n.* a proposal; something that is being considered; a suggestion. **2.** *n.* a statement; a statement that is to be proved either true or false.

propulsion [prə 'pʌl ʃən] *n.* a force that causes something to move forward. (No pl form.)

prose ['proz] *n.* the usual form of written language; writing that is not in verse. (No pl.)

prosecute ['prɑs ə kjut] *tv.* to seek to enforce a law against someone or some group in a court of law.

prospect ['prɑs pɛkt] **1.** *n.* something that is probable; something that is likely; a possibility; a likelihood. **2.** *n.* the likelihood that something will be successful; the possibility that something will be successful. **3.** *n.* someone who will probably use a product or a service; someone who could become a customer. **4.** ~ **for** to search for minerals, oil, gold, silver, or precious stones in the earth.

prosper ['prɑs pɚ] *iv.* to become successful; to earn enough money so that one can live well; to thrive.

prosperity [prɑs 'pɛr ə ti] *n.* the condition of being prosperous; success; monetary success. (No pl.)

prosperous ['prɑs pə rəs] *adj.* thriving; earning or having enough money so that one can live well. (Adv: *prosperously.*)

protect [prə 'tɛkt] *tv.* to keep someone or something safe; to guard someone or something.

protection [prə 'tɛk ʃən] *n.* keeping someone or something safe; the quality offered by someone or something that protects. (Pl only for types and instances.)

protective [prə 'tɛk tɪv] *adj.* protecting; giving protection; defending; keeping someone or something safe. (Adv: *protectively.*)

protein ['pro tin] *n.* one of many chemical substances important to the cells of all living plants and animals. (Usually thought of in terms of food.)

protest 1. ['pro tɛst] *n.* a group of people displaying opposition or anger. **2.** ['pro tɛst] *n.* a complaint. **3.** [prə 'tɛst] *tv.* to complain about something; to show disapproval of something. (The object can be a clause with THAT ⑦.) **4.** [prə 'tɛst] *iv.* to complain about something.

proton ['pro tɑn] *n.* a particle in the NUCLEUS ② of an atom that carries a positive electrical charge.

prototype ['pro tə tɑɪp] *n.* the original example of something from which later examples are developed.

proud ['prɑʊd] **1.** *adj.* showing or feeling pride; having a good opinion about oneself and what one has accomplished. (Adv: *proudly.* Comp: *prouder;* sup: *proudest.*) **2.** *adj.* causing someone to feel pride. (Adv: *proudly.* Comp: *prouder;* sup: *proudest.*) **3.** *adj.* having too high an opinion about oneself; arrogant. (Adv: *proudly.* Comp: *prouder;* sup: *proudest.*)

prove ['pruv] *tv., irreg.* to provide proof of something; to be the proof of something. (Pp: *proved* or PROVEN. The object can be a clause with THAT ⑦.)

proven ['pruv ən] a pp of PROVE.

proverb ['prɑ vɚb] *n.* a short saying that makes a wise comment.

provide [prə 'vɑɪd] **1.** *tv.* to furnish or supply someone or something with something. **2.** *tv.* to state or tell something.

province ['prɑ vɪns] **1.** *n.* one of the main divisions of a country, such as Canada, similar to a state. **2.** *n.* an area of study, knowledge, or activity.

369

provincial [prə 'vɪn ʃəl] **1.** *adj.* of or about a province or provinces of a country. (Adv: *provincially.*) **2.** *adj.* of limited, local experience; rural in attitude and outlook. (Usually derogatory. Adv: *provincially.*)

provision [prə 'vɪ ʒən] **1.** *n.* a condition; a detail or statement. **2.** *n.* an arrangement that is made ahead of time. (Often pl.)

provisions *n.* food and supplies needed for everyday living. (Treated as pl, but not countable.)

provoke [prə 'vok] **1.** *tv.* to make someone angry; to irritate someone. **2.** *tv.* to cause an action to start or to happen. (Usually leading to negative results.)

prowl ['praʊl] *iv.* to sneak around quietly, like an animal hunting for food or a thief looking for something to steal.

prowler ['praʊl ɚ] *n.* a thief; a burglar who sneaks about in the night.

prude ['prud] *n.* someone who is easily offended or shocked; someone who is overly modest or proper.

prudence ['prud ns] *n.* wisdom; care in thought and action; thoughtful judgment. (No pl.)

prudent ['prud nt] *adj.* wise; thinking carefully before one does something. (Adv: *prudently.*)

prudish ['prud ɪʃ] *adj.* too easily shocked or offended; too modest. (Adv: *prudishly.*)

prune ['prun] **1.** *n.* a dried plum, eaten as food. **2.** *iv.* to remove extra branches or leaves from a plant; to trim a tree, flower, bush, or shrub so that it has a nice, even shape. **3.** *tv.* to make a plant look nice by removing extra branches or leaves.

pry ['praɪ] *iv.* to be too curious; to ask personal questions about things that should not concern one.

psychiatrist [sɪ 'kaɪ ə trɪst] *n.* a doctor who treats people who have sicknesses of the mind.

psychiatry [sɪ 'kaɪ ə tri] *n.* the science of treating people who have sicknesses of the mind. (No pl.)

psychological [saɪ kə 'ladʒ ɪ kəl] **1.** the *adj.* form of PSYCHOLOGY ①. (Adv: *psychologically* [...ɪk li].) **2.** the *adj.* form of PSYCHOLOGY ②. (Adv: *psychologically* [...ɪk li].)

psychologist [saɪ 'kal ə dʒɪst] *n.* someone who is trained in psychology; a specialist in behavior.

370

psychology [saɪ 'kɑl ə dʒi] **1.** *n.* the study and science of the mind and the behavior of individuals. (No pl.) **2.** *n.* the way people behave, think, and feel; the way a person behaves, thinks, and feels. (No pl.)

public ['pʌb lɪk] *adj.* available to everyone; available to people in general; not restricted; not private. (Adv: *publicly.*)

publication [pəb lə 'ke ʃən] **1.** *n.* making information in written form, such as in a book, magazine, or newspaper, available to the public. (No pl.) **2.** *n.* any written document that is published.

publicity [pəb 'lɪs ə ti] *n.* information that is brought to everyone's attention. (No pl.)

publicly ['pʌb lɪk li] *adv.* [done] in public; [done] where people can see.

publish ['pʌb lɪʃ] **1.** *tv.* to assemble, print, and sell books, magazines, newspapers, or other printed materials. **2.** *tv.* to make something well known.

publisher ['pʌb lɪ ʃɚ] *n.* someone or a company that assembles, prints, and makes written materials available for sale.

pudding ['pʊd ɪŋ] *n.* a soft, sweet, creamy food, usually eaten as a dessert. (Pl only for types and instances.)

puddle ['pʌd l] *n.* a collection of water or other liquid on the ground or the surface of something.

puff ['pʌf] **1.** *n.* a short blast of air, smoke, steam, gas, etc., that is blown out from something. **2.** *tv.* to blow air, steam, smoke, etc., out a little bit at a time. **3.** *iv.* to pull smoke from a cigarette or a cigar with small breaths. **4.** *iv.* to breathe when one is out of breath; to breathe with short, quick breaths.

pull ['pʊl] **1.** *tv.* to move someone or something in some direction. **2.** *tv.* to drag someone or something behind oneself; to move someone or something behind oneself while one is moving. **3.** *n.* a tug.

pulp ['pʌlp] **1.** *n.* the soft part inside a fruit, vegetable, or plant. (No pl.) **2.** *n.* any soft, partially solid, wet substance. (No pl.) **3.** *tv.* to make ② from something.

pulpit ['pʊl pɪt] *n.* a raised platform that a preacher, priest, minister, etc., stands on when preaching.

pulse ['pʌls] **1.** *n.* the rhythm of the flow of blood through one's body, caused by the beating of the heart. (No pl.) **2.** *n.* a rhythm with a regular beat; a movement of something with regular stops and starts. **3.** *iv.* to beat regularly, like the beating of the heart; to beat in rhythm.

371

pump ['pʌmp] **1.** *n.* a device that forces air, liquid, or gas through a tube or pipe. **2.** *tv.* to force air, liquid, or gas through a tube or pipe.

pumpkin ['pʌmp kɪn] **1.** *n.* a large, round, heavy orange fruit that grows on a vine. **2.** *adj.* made with ①.

punch ['pʌntʃ] **1.** *n.* a sweet drink made by mixing many different things, usually including some kind of fruit juice. (No pl.) **2.** *n.* a tool or machine that pierces holes through objects or that stamps designs on objects. **3.** *n.* a quick, powerful hit. **4.** *n.* impact; effective power; strength. (Fig. on ③.) **5.** *tv.* to hit someone or something powerfully with one's fist.

punctuate ['pʌŋk tʃu et] **1.** *tv.* to use punctuation marks in something that one writes. **2.** *tv.* to emphasize something; to stress something.

punctuation [pʌŋk tʃu 'e ʃən] *n.* the use of special marks to make writing easier to understand. (No pl.)

puncture ['pʌŋk tʃɚ] **1.** *n.* a hole in the surface of something made by a sharp or pointed object. **2.** *tv.* to make a hole in the surface of something by using a sharp or pointed object.

punish ['pʌn ɪʃ] **1.** *tv.* to give someone a penalty for doing something wrong. **2.** *tv.* to use or handle something roughly. (Fig. on ①.)

punishment ['pʌn ɪʃ mənt] **1.** *n.* punishing; the practice of giving penalties for doing something wrong. (No pl.) **2.** *n.* rough treatment. (Fig. on ①. No pl.)

punk ['pʌŋk] **1.** *n.* a young criminal; a young person who gets into trouble a lot. **2.** *n.* a loud, harsh style of music first made popular in the late 1970s by young people. (No pl.) **3.** the *adj.* use of ① or ②.

puny ['pju ni] *adj.* smaller and weaker than average. (Adv: *punily.* Comp: *punier;* sup: *puniest.*)

pup ['pʌp] *n.* a young dog; a PUPPY; the young of certain animals, including the seal.

pupil ['pju pəl] **1.** *n.* a student; someone who studies in school; someone who is taught by a teacher. **2.** *n.* the round, black opening in the middle of the colored part of the eye that allows light into the eye.

puppy ['pʌp i] *n.* a young dog.

purchase ['pɚ tʃəs] **1.** *n.* an instance of buying something. **2.** *n.* something that is bought. **3.** *tv.* to buy something.

purchaser ['pɚ tʃə sɚ] *n.* a buyer; someone who buys something.

pure ['pjʊr] **1.** *adj.* completely made from only one thing; not mixed with anything. (Adv: *purely.* Comp: *purer;* sup: *purest.*) **2.** *adj.* [of a

372

color] clear and not cloudy. (Adv: *purely.* Comp: *purer;* sup: *purest.*) **3.** *adj.* mere; absolute; nothing but. (Adv: *purely.* Comp: *purer;* sup: *purest.*) **4.** *adj.* without sin; without evil. (Adv: *purely.* Comp: *purer;* sup: *purest.*) **5.** *adj.* not having had sex. (Adv: *purely.* Comp: *purer;* sup: *purest.*)

purge ['pɚdʒ] **1.** *n.* an instance of forcing unwanted people to leave a government, university, society, or other group. **2.** *tv.* to make something clean by getting rid of what is dirty; to clean something out. **3.** *tv.* to destroy records or files.

purity ['pjʊr ə ti] *n.* the quality of being pure; the degree to which something is pure. (No pl.)

purple ['pɚ pəl] **1.** *n.* the color made by mixing blue and red; the color of ripe grapes that are not green or red. (Pl only for types and instances.) **2.** *adj.* of the color ①.

purpose ['pɚ pəs] *n.* an intention; the reason that someone does something; a kind of goal.

purse ['pɚs] **1.** *n.* a bag used, especially by women, to hold money and other personal items. **2.** *n.* an amount of money that is offered as a prize.

pursue [pɚ 'su] **1.** *tv.* to chase someone or something; to follow and attempt to catch someone or something. **2.** *tv.* to continue to work toward something; to seek something. **3.** *tv.* to follow a plan of action.

pursuit [pɚ 'sut] **1.** *n.* pursuing someone or something; chasing after someone or something. (No pl.) **2.** *n.* a hobby or job that fills one's time.

push ['pʊʃ] **1.** *iv.* to force movement in a certain direction. **2.** *tv.* to apply pressure to something, as if to move it. **3.** *tv.* to move something or someone by applying pressure. **4.** *n.* a shove; a powerful movement that causes something to move. (No pl.)

put ['pʊt] **1.** *tv., irreg.* to place something in a certain position; to cause something to be in a certain place or position; to move something to a certain place or position. (Pt/pp: *put.*) **2.** *tv., irreg.* to express something; to say something in a certain way. **3.** ~ **off** to postpone or delay something until something happens or until some future time. **4.** ~ **away** to store something; to put something where it can be found again. **5.** ~ **on** to dress in a particular garment. **6.** ~ **up with** to endure; to tolerate. **7.** ~ **out** to send someone or something out. **8.** ~ **over** to do something convincingly.

373

putty ['pʌt i] *n.* a soft, oily substance used to seal pipe connections, to seal the edges of glass in window frames, and to fill uneven surfaces. (No pl form.)

puzzle ['pʌz əl] **1.** *n.* something that confuses people; a problem that is confusing or difficult to solve. **2.** *n.* something similar to ① that people try to understand or solve for entertainment. **3.** *tv.* to confuse someone.

pyramid ['pɪr ə mɪd] **1.** *n.* a four-sided structure with sides that are shaped like triangles and meet at one point on top. **2.** *n.* one of a group of large Egyptian tombs—shaped like ①—in which Egyptian kings and queens were once buried.

python ['paɪ θən] *n.* a large snake found in tropical areas of Asia, southeast India, Africa, and Australia that uses its powerful muscles to constrict and kill its prey.

Q

quack ['kwæk] **1.** *iv.* to make the characteristic noise of a duck. **2.** *n.* the noise that a duck makes. **3.** *n.* someone who claims to be a doctor but who is not trained to be a doctor.

quadruped ['kwɑ drə pɛd] an animal having four feet.

quaint ['kwent] *adj.* strange in an interesting or funny way; charming in an old-fashioned way. (Adv: *quaintly*. Comp: *quainter*; sup: *quaintest*.)

quake ['kwek] **1.** *n.* a shaking of the earth; an EARTHQUAKE. (Short for EARTHQUAKE.) **2.** *iv.* to shake; to tremble.

qualify ['kwɑl ə faɪ] **1.** *tv.* to limit something; to restrict something; to narrow the meaning of something. **2.** *iv.* to meet the requirements for something.

quality ['kwɑl ɪ ti] **1.** *n.* a characteristic property of someone or something. **2.** *n.* a degree or level of excellence. (No pl.) **3.** *adj.* of ② that is good.

quantity ['kwɑn tə ti] *n.* an amount; a certain number of something that can be counted or measured.

quarantine ['kwɑr ən tin] **1.** *tv.* to isolate a living thing that has a disease or has been around another creature with a disease. **2.** *n.* a period of isolation of living things that have an illness or have been exposed to an illness. (Pl only for types and instances.)

quarrel ['kwɑr əl] **1.** *n.* an angry argument; an angry disagreement. **2.** *iv.* to argue with someone angrily; for two or more people to argue angrily.

quarry ['kwɑr i] **1.** *n.* a place where marble, granite, and other kinds of stone are removed from the earth. **2.** *n.* the object of a hunt or search. **3.** *tv.* to remove stone from ①.

quart ['kwɔrt] *n.* a unit of measure of liquids, equal to one-fourth gallon, 32 ounces, or about 0.95 liter.

quarter ['kwɔr tɚ] **1.** *n.* one-fourth of something; one of four equal parts; one of four parts. **2.** *n.* a coin equal to 25 cents or one-fourth of a dollar. **3.** *n.* fifteen minutes; one-fourth of an hour. (Limited to *quarter to, quarter till, quarter of, quarter after,* and *quarter past.* No pl.) **4.** *n.* three months; one-fourth of a year. **5.** *n.* one of the four periods in professional football, basketball, and other games. **6.** *n.* a neighborhood; a section of a town; a district. **7.** *n.* a period equal to one-quarter of the school or academic year. **8.** *tv.* to divide something into four parts; to cut something into four parts; to split something into four parts. **9.** *tv.* to give someone, especially soldiers, a place to stay or live.

quarters *n.* the place where someone lives. (Treated as pl.)

queasy ['kwiz i] *adj.* feeling sick, nauseated, or uneasy. (Adv: *queasily.* Comp: *queasier;* sup: *queasiest.*)

queen ['kwin] **1.** *n.* the female ruler of a country or the wife of a king. **2.** *n.* the sole egg-laying female in a colony or hive of certain species of insects, such as bees, termites, or ants. **3.** *n.* a playing card that has a picture of ① on it. **4.** *n.* a chess piece that can move any number of spaces in a straight line in any direction.

queer ['kwɪr] *adj.* odd; strange; unusual; weird. (Adv: *queerly.* Comp: *queerer;* sup: *queerest.*)

quell ['kwɛl] *tv.* to calm or put an end to chaos, confusion, or some other problem.

quench ['kwɛntʃ] **1.** *tv.* to put out a fire by using water. **2.** *tv.* to ease or eliminate one's thirst by drinking something.

quest ['kwɛst] *n.* a search for someone or something.

question ['kwɛs tʃən] **1.** *n.* an inquiry; a speech utterance used to make an inquiry. **2.** *n.* a doubt; a concern; something that one is not sure about. (No pl.) **3.** *n.* a matter to be considered; a problem for solving. **4.** *tv.* to ask ① of someone. **5.** *tv.* to doubt something; to express one's doubts or concerns about something.

questionable ['kwɛs tʃə nə bəl] **1.** *adj.* in doubt; inviting questions or scrutiny. (Adv: *questionably.*) **2.** *adj.* possibly not honest or true. (Adv: *questionably.*)

questionnaire [kwɛs tʃə 'nɛr] *n.* a printed set of questions.

quick ['kwɪk] **1.** *adj.* fast; rapid; swift. (Adv: *quickly.* Comp: *quicker;* sup: *quickest.*) **2.** *adj.* lasting only for a short period of time; beginning and ending in a short period of time. (Adv: *quickly.* Comp: *quicker;* sup: *quickest.*) **3.** *adj.* able to understand or learn things in a short amount of time. (Adv: *quickly.* Comp: *quicker;* sup: *quickest.*) **4.** *n.* the flesh under one's fingernails or toenails. (No pl.) **5.** *adv.* very rapidly; with great speed. (Colloquial. Comp: *quicker;* sup: *quickest.*)

quicken ['kwɪk ən] **1.** *iv.* to become faster; to move more quickly; to do something more quickly; to increase the speed of something. **2.** *tv.* to cause something to become faster; to cause something to occur more quickly.

quickness ['kwɪk nəs] *n.* the quality of being quick. (No pl.)

quicksand ['kwɪk sænd] *n.* wet sand, often under water, into which living creatures can sink. (No pl.)

quiet ['kwɑɪ ɪt] **1.** *adj.* not loud; making only a small amount of sound. (Adv: *quietly.* Comp: *quieter;* sup: *quietest.*) **2.** *adj.* [of a person] shy and not talkative. (Adv: *quietly.* Comp: *quieter;* sup: *quietest.*) **3.** *adj.* not active; not moving; calm; still. (Adv: *quietly.* Comp: *quieter;* sup: *quietest.*) **4.** *adj.* peaceful; restful. (Adv: *quietly.* Comp: *quieter;* sup: *quietest.*) **5.** *tv.* to cause someone or something to become ①. **6.** *n.* silence. (No pl.)

quilt ['kwɪlt] **1.** *n.* a bed covering made from a soft pad between two layers of decorative cloth, stitched together. **2.** *iv.* to work at making ①.

quip ['kwɪp] *n.* a clever, witty, or sarcastic remark.

quirk ['kwɚk] *n.* a strange habit; a strange characteristic.

quit ['kwɪt] **1.** *tv., irreg.* to stop doing something. (Pt/pp: *quit.*) **2.** *tv., irreg.* to leave a job; to resign from a job. **3.** *iv., irreg.* [for someone or something] to cease [doing something].

quite ['kwɑɪt] *adv.* very; rather; completely.

quiz ['kwɪz] **1.** *n.* a small test; an informal test. (Pl: *quizzes.*) **2.** *tv.* to test someone on or about something; to ask someone questions about someone or something.

quota ['kwot ə] *n.* a required amount of something; a required number of things or people.

quotation [kwo 'te ʃən] *n.* a statement that was said or written, used again by someone else; a statement that is quoted from someone or from someone's writing.

quote ['kwot] **1.** *tv.* to use a quotation; to repeat part of something that someone else has said or written, at the same time telling who said or wrote it. **2.** *tv.* to cite someone or a written source as the origin of a quotation. **3.** *n.* a quotation; a statement that was said or written by someone else. **4.** *n.* an estimate of the price of something.

377

R

rabbi ['ræb ɑɪ] *n.* the leader of a Jewish synagogue; a Jewish religious leader. (Also a term of address. Capitalized when written as a proper noun.)

rabbit ['ræb ət] *n.* a small animal with soft fur, long ears, and a fluffy tail.

race ['res] **1.** *n.* a contest that has to do with speed; a contest that has to do with how fast people, animals, or machines can move. **2.** *n.* a political election, and the time during the campaign leading up to the election. **3.** *n.* the physical differences among humans that have to do with dividing people into different groups, especially groups based on the color of skin. (Pl only for types and instances.) **4.** *iv.* to run rapidly, as if in a race; to move or operate very fast. **5.** *tv.* to cause someone or something to take part in ①. **6.** *tv.* to cause an engine to run very rapidly. **7.** *tv.* to compete against someone to reach a specific goal.

racetrack ['res træk] *n.* the place, usually a large oval, where a race takes place, and the stadium or arena that contains it.

racial ['reʃ əl] *adj.* of or about RACE ③. (Adv: *racially.*)

racism ['res ɪz əm] *n.* prejudice, hatred, or violence shown against someone of a particular race. (No pl.)

racist ['res ɪst] **1.** *n.* someone who believes one race is better than another. **2.** *adj.* exhibiting racism; showing prejudice against someone's race.

rack ['ræk] *n.* a frame with shelves, rods, hooks, or pegs that is used to hang things from or put things on.

racket ['ræk ət] **1.** AND **racquet** *n.* a device used to hit a ball or something similar back and forth, usually over a net. **2.** *n.* a dishonest or illegal activity, such as fraud, done to make money.

racquet ['ræk ət] Go to RACKET.

radar ['re dɑr] *n.* a device that uses radio waves to detect an object, usually a car or an aircraft, and to determine that object's location, distance, and speed. (An acronym for *radio detecting and ranging.* No pl.)

378

radiant ['re di ənt] **1.** *adj.* bright; shining; giving off light. (Adv: *radiantly.*) **2.** *adj.* looking very happy; glowing. (Fig. on ①. Adv: *radiantly.*)

radiate ['re di et] *tv.* to cause something to spread out in all directions from a center point; to give off rays of something such as heat or light.

radiation [re di 'e ʃən] **1.** *n.* the release of heat, light, or other energy. (No pl.) **2.** *n.* radioactive particles and energy used in medical treatment. (No pl.)

radiator ['re di et ɚ] **1.** *n.* a device that sends out radiation, usually in the form of heat. **2.** *n.* the part of an automobile that transfers engine heat to the surrounding air.

radical ['ræd ɪ kəl] **1.** *adj.* complete and thorough; extreme. (Adv: *radically* […ɪk li].) **2.** *adj.* [of someone] favoring extreme change. (Adv: *radically* […ɪk li].) **3.** *n.* someone who favors complete change; someone who favors extreme change.

radii ['re di ɑɪ] a pl of RADIUS.

radio ['re di o] **1.** *n.* the sending and receiving of sound through the air by using electromagnetic waves. (No pl.) **2.** *n.* a device that is used to receive electromagnetic waves and turn them into sound. (Pl ends in *-s*.) **3.** the *adj.* use of ① or ②. **4.** *tv.* to send a message by ①. **5.** *tv.* to send [a message] to someone using ②. **6.** *iv.* to use ② to send a message.

radioactive [re di o 'æk tɪv] *adj.* of or about an element, or its compounds, that releases energy as the result of naturally occurring changes in the nuclear structure of the atoms of the element. (Adv: *radioactively.*)

radius ['re di əs] **1.** *n., irreg.* the distance from the center of a circle to any point on the circle. (Pl: RADII or *radiuses*.) **2.** *n., irreg.* a line that goes from the center of a circle to any point on the circle.

raffle ['ræf əl] *n.* a way of raising money where people buy tickets to win items or prizes that have been donated. (The winning ticket is chosen at random.)

raft ['ræft] **1.** *n.* boards or logs that are tied together so they will float on water; a rubber boat that is filled with air and floats on water. **2.** *iv.* to travel across water on ①.

rafter ['ræf tɚ] *n.* one of a series of parallel boards or beams that support a roof.

379

rag ['ræg] *n.* a piece of cloth, especially one that has no value or is used for cleaning.

rage ['reʤ] **1.** *n.* extreme, violent anger. **2.** *iv.* to show extreme, violent anger toward something.

ragged ['ræg əd] *adj.* torn; [of cloth] torn or damaged. (Adv: *raggedly.*)

raid ['red] **1.** *n.* a surprise attack, especially by police or soldiers. **2.** *tv.* to enter someone's property or space and attack quickly, suddenly, and by surprise.

rail ['rel] **1.** *n.* a thick strip of wood or metal, usually used to support or guide someone or something. **2.** *n.* one of a pair of metal strips on which a train travels.

railing ['rel ɪŋ] *n.* a thick strip, rail, or tube of wood or metal that people can hold on to for support, usually found on a staircase.

railroad ['rel rod] **1.** *n.* two parallel metal rails on which a train travels. **2.** *n.* a network or system of train tracks, train stations, and trains. **3.** *n.* a business that operates trains. **4.** *tv.* to move something quickly and forcefully; to force someone to do something quickly. **5.** the *adj.* use of ①, ②, or ③.

railway ['rel we] **1.** *n.* a railroad; a railroad of a short length. **2.** the *adj.* use of ①.

rain ['ren] **1.** *n.* water that falls down from the sky in drops. (No pl.) **2.** *n.* an instance or period of ①. (The pl usually indicates a season of RAIN that occurs annually.) **3.** *iv.* [for drops of water] to fall from the sky. (The subject must be IT.) **4.** *tv.* to cause something to fall from the sky like ①.

rainbow ['ren bo] **1.** *n.* an arch of different colors of light that appears in the sky, caused by rays of sunlight passing through rain or mist. **2.** *adj.* consisting of the colors of ①; from the group of colors of ①.

raincoat ['ren kot] *n.* a waterproof coat that people wear when it rains to keep their clothes dry.

raindrop ['ren drɑp] *n.* one drop of rain.

rainfall ['ren fɔl] **1.** *n.* the drops of rain that fall when it rains; a period of falling rain. (No pl.) **2.** *n.* the amount of rain that falls in a certain place over a certain length of time. (No pl.)

rainstorm ['ren storm] *n.* a storm that has a large amount of rain.

rainy ['re ni] *adj.* having a lot of rain. (Adv: *rainily.* Comp: *rainier;* sup: *rainiest.*)

raise ['rez] **1.** *tv.* to lift someone or something up; to move someone or something to a higher level; to move someone or something upward; to cause someone or something to rise. (Compare this with RISE.) **2.** *tv.* to increase the amount of something; to increase the degree of something; to increase the force of something. **3.** *tv.* to cause plants to grow; to breed animals. **4.** *tv.* to bring up a child; to rear a child. **5.** *tv.* to collect or gather a certain amount of money. **6.** *tv.* to bring up a subject or issue; to mention something; to address a subject or an issue; to begin talking about something. **7.** *n.* an increase in one's salary; an increase in the amount of money one earns at a job.

raisin ['re zɪn] *n.* a dried grape, eaten as food.

rake ['rek] **1.** *n.* a tool that has a long handle that is attached to a row of curved metal or plastic "fingers," used to collect fallen leaves, loose grass, etc. **2.** *tv.* to collect something, especially leaves, hay, grass, or other objects on the ground, using ① or something similar. **3.** *tv.* to smooth or clean something by using ①. **4.** *iv.* to use ①; to scrape with ①.

rally ['ræl i] **1.** *tv.* to bring people together for a certain reason or cause. **2.** *n.* a large meeting, especially a large political meeting, held for a special reason.

ram ['ræm] **1.** *n.* a male sheep. **2.** *n.* a heavy pole or beam, the end of which is thrust against something. **3.** *tv.* to hit someone or something; to crash into someone or something.

ramble ['ræm bəl] **1.** *iv.* to talk or write about many different things with no connection between the different ideas; to talk or write in a way that is not organized. **2.** *iv.* to wander around in no particular direction; to go on a relaxing walk. **3.** *iv.* [for a pathway or road] to wander about, taking an indirect route.

ramp ['ræmp] **1.** *n.* a slanted path that is built or made to connect two surfaces with different heights. **2.** *n.* a road that is an entrance or exit to an expressway or tollway.

rampage ['ræm pedʒ] *n.* a period of wild, angry, or violent behavior.

rampant ['ræm pənt] *adj.* growing, moving, or spreading out of control. (Adv: *rampantly.*)

ran ['ræn] pt of RUN.

ranch ['ræntʃ] *n.* a very large farm where cattle or other animals are raised.

rancher ['ræntʃɚ] *n.* someone who works on a ranch; someone who owns a ranch.

random ['ræn dəm] *adj.* selected by chance. (Adv: *randomly.*)

rang ['ræŋ] pt of RING.

range ['rendʒ] **1.** *n.* the area between two extremes; the choices, possibilities, or selections available. **2.** *n.* the distance that something can operate or be used in, especially the distance that someone can see or hear, that a weapon can fire, or that something can travel without needing more fuel. (No pl.) **3.** *n.* a field where cattle or other animals can walk about and look for food. (No pl.) **4.** *n.* a stove with one or more ovens attached. **5.** *iv.* to vary between two limits or extremes; to be located between an upper limit and a lower limit.

rank ['ræŋk] **1.** *n.* one level in a series of levels; one level on a scale of authority, value, or importance. **2.** *iv.* to occupy a certain position on a scale of authority, value, or importance; to be on a list in a certain position. **3.** *tv.* to place someone or something on a list in its proper order or place. **4.** *adj.* smelling or tasting very bad or unpleasant. (Adv: *rankly.*) **5.** *adj.* [of vegetation] growing thickly or coarsely.

ransom ['ræn səm] **1.** *n.* money demanded by kidnappers in exchange for releasing a hostage or someone who has been kidnapped. (No pl form in this sense.) **2.** *tv.* to pay money in order to release a hostage or someone who has been kidnapped. **3.** *tv.* [for a kidnapper] to offer to release someone who has been kidnapped upon payment of ①.

rant ['rænt] to talk in a loud, violent way, about someone or something.

rap ['ræp] **1.** *n.* a style of music where the words of the song are spoken in a strong rhythm instead of being sung. (No pl.) **2.** *n.* the sound made by a quick, strong knock or hit.

rape ['rep] **1.** *n.* the act and crime of forcing someone to have sex. **2.** *tv.* to force someone to have sex.

rapid ['ræp ɪd] *adj.* quick; swift; moving fast; done quickly; happening quickly. (Adv: *rapidly.*)

rapidity [rə 'pɪd ə ti] *n.* quickness; speed. (No pl.)

rapids *n.* the part of a river where the water moves very fast and is very active. (Treated as pl.)

rapture ['ræp tʃɚ] *n.* a feeling or expression of complete joy or delight. (No pl.)

rare ['rɛr] **1.** *adj.* not common; not often found, seen, or done. (Adv: *rarely.* Comp: *rarer;* sup: *rarest.*) **2.** *adj.* [of meat] cooked only a little. (Comp: *rarer;* sup: *rarest.*)

rascal ['ræs kəl] **1.** *n.* someone who is bad or not honest; a villain. **2.** *n.* a playful or mischievous child. (Fig. on ①.)

rash ['ræʃ] **1.** *n.* a disease or condition of the skin, making it red, itchy, and bumpy. **2.** *adj.* not thinking about something carefully or long enough; done without careful thought. (Adv: *rashly.* Comp: *rasher;* sup: *rashest.*)

raspberry ['ræz bɛr i] **1.** *n.* a small, sweet, usually red or purple fruit that grows on a bush, and the bush itself. **2.** *adj.* made or flavored with ①.

rat ['ræt] **1.** *n.* a small rodent with a long tail. **2.** *n.* someone who is mean, worthless, not honest, or not loyal. (Fig. on ①.)

rate ['ret] **1.** *n.* the relation of an amount to another amount, such as speed in relation to time. **2.** *n.* a price [for each unit of something]. **3.** *tv.* to assign a value or rank to someone or something. **4.** *tv.* to deserve something; to be worthy of something.

rather ['ræð ɚ] **1.** *adv.* instead; on the contrary. **2.** *adv.* to an extent; to a degree; too; very; quite.

ratify ['ræt ə faɪ] *tv.* to approve something officially; to make something be valid officially.

ratio ['re ʃi o] *n.* the relationship between one amount as compared to another amount; a proportion. (Pl in *-s.*)

ration ['ræ ʃən] **1.** *n.* an amount of something; an amount of something as prescribed by policy, rule, or law. **2.** *tv.* to make a substance available to people only in certain small amounts.

rational ['ræʃ ə nəl] **1.** *adj.* using the mind or the brain; sensible; reasonable; logical. (Adv: *rationally.*) **2.** *adj.* able to use sense or reason; aware. (Adv: *rationally.*)

rationale [ræʃ ə 'næl] *n.* a reason; the reason for doing something; reasoning or explanation. (No pl.)

rattle ['ræt əl] **1.** *n.* a noisemaking device, usually a toy for babies, consisting of a small container with bits of hard matter inside. **2.** *n.* the noise made when a number of small things tap against something, as with ①. **3.** *iv.* to make a quick set of short noises. **4.** *tv.* to cause something to make a quick set of short noises.

rattlesnake ['ræt əl snek] *n.* a venomous snake with hard rings of skin on its tail that make a rattling sound when it shakes its tail.

raw ['rɔ] **1.** *adj.* not cooked. (Comp: *rawer;* sup: *rawest.*) **2.** *adj.* [of something that has been] rubbed until sore; having a layer of skin rubbed off. (Adv: *rawly.* Comp: *rawer;* sup: *rawest.*)

ray ['re] *n.* a beam of something that comes from a source, especially a beam of light, heat, or radiation.

raze ['rez] *tv.* to tear down a building completely.

razor ['re zɚ] **1.** *n.* a tool that holds a sharp blade that is used to shave whiskers or hair. **2.** the *adj.* use of ①.

reach ['ritʃ] **1.** *tv.* to arrive at someplace; to get to someplace. **2.** *tv.* to get hold of someone by some means of communication; to contact someone. **3.** *tv.* to stretch out to a certain place in space or time; to extend to a certain place in space or time. **4.** *tv.* to affect or influence someone; to make someone else understand something. **5.** *tv.* to total a certain amount. **6.** *iv.* to extend all the way. **7.** *n.* the distance that someone or something is able to stretch or extend; the range or capacity of someone or something.

react [ri 'ækt] **1.** *iv.* to show a response [to something]; to make a response [to someone or something]. **2.** *iv.* [for a chemical] to do something when it touches another substance; [for two chemicals] to do something when they are brought together.

reaction [ri 'æk ʃən] **1.** *n.* a response to someone or something; an action that is done in response to someone or something; a feeling that is felt in response to someone or something. **2.** *n.* the result of a chemical touching another substance; the result when two chemicals are brought together.

read 1. ['rid] *tv., irreg.* to understand what is meant by written words; to get meaning from written words. (Pt/pp: *read* ['rɛd].) **2.** ['rid] *tv., irreg.* to say written words out loud. **3.** ['rid] *iv., irreg.* to be able to understand writing and printing. **4.** ['rid] *iv., irreg.* to say written words aloud. **5.** ~ **through** to look through some reading material.

readily ['rɛd ə li] **1.** *adv.* without difficulty or problems; easily. **2.** *adv.* without delay or doubt; eagerly.

readiness ['rɛd i nəs] *n.* the state of being ready; the state of being prepared. (No pl.)

reading ['rid ɪŋ] **1.** *n.* something written that is meant to be read. **2.** *n.* a measurement shown on a meter or other similar device. **3.** the *adj.* use of ① or ②.

readjust [ri ə 'dʒʌst] *tv.* to adjust something again; to put something back where it belongs.

readjustment [ri ə 'dʒʌst mənt] **1.** *n.* the process of getting used to something again. (No pl.) **2.** *n.* an act of readjusting something; a movement or change that is made when putting something back where it belongs.

ready ['rɛd i] **1.** *adj.* [of something] able to be used right now. (Comp: *readier;* sup: *readiest.*) **2.** *tv.* to prepare something for use.

real ['ril] **1.** *adj.* existing; actual; true. (Adv: *really.*) **2.** *adj.* genuine; not fake. (Adv: *really.*) **3.** *adv.* really; very; extremely. (Colloquial.)

realism ['ri ə lɪz əm] *n.* the point of view concerned with reality in life and art. (No pl.)

realistic [ri ə 'lɪs tɪk] **1.** *adj.* appearing or seeming to be real or authentic. (Adv: *realistically* […ɪk li].) **2.** *adj.* accepting life as it really is; practical. (Adv: *realistically* […ɪk li].)

reality [ri 'æl ə ti] *n.* everything that is real; something that is real; that which exists. (Pl only for types and instances.)

realization [ri əl ə 'ze ʃən] *n.* an understanding that something exists or has happened.

realize ['ri ə laɪz] **1.** *tv.* to understand something; to be aware of something. (The object can be a clause with THAT ⑦.) **2.** *tv.* to make something real; to cause something to exist.

really ['ri (ə) li] **1.** *adv.* actually; truly; in reality. **2.** *adv.* very; completely.

realm ['rɛlm] **1.** *n.* an area that someone rules over; an area where a certain person is the most powerful. **2.** *n.* domain; category. (Fig. on ①.)

reap ['rip] **1.** *tv.* to cut and gather crops from a field. **2.** *tv.* to get something in return for doing something. (Fig. on ①.)

reappear [ri ə 'pɪr] **1.** *iv.* to appear again. **2.** *iv.* to occur again.

rear ['rɪr] **1.** *n.* the part of the body one sits on. (Euphemistic.) **2.** *adj.* in back; hind. **3.** *tv.* to raise offspring. **4.** *iv.* to rise up, especially for a horse to stand on its back legs.

rearrange [ri ə 'rendʒ] *tv.* to arrange something again or in a different way, especially to place people or things in a different order or in different positions with respect to each other.

rearrangement [ri ə 'rendʒ mənt] *n.* creating a new or different arrangement; changing the way that people or things are ordered or positioned with respect to each other. (No pl.)

reason ['ri zən] **1.** *n.* the power or ability to think, understand, and form opinions and conclusions from facts. (No pl.) **2.** *n.* a cause; a motive; an explanation; a rationale. **3.** *iv.* to think; to be able to think; to use the power or ability to think, understand, and form opinions and conclusions. **4.** *tv.* to have an opinion or conclusion based on ①. (The object is a clause with THAT ⑦.) **5.** ~ **with** to persuade someone by using ①; to argue with someone by using ①.

reasonable ['ri zə nə bəl] **1.** *adj.* sensible; making sense; according to reason. (Adv: *reasonably.*) **2.** *adj.* not expensive; having an acceptable cost. (Adv: *reasonably.*)

reasoning ['ri zə nɪŋ] *n.* the process or ability of thinking and forming conclusions from facts and evidence. (No pl.)

reassure [ri ə 'ʃʊr] *tv.* to restore someone's courage or confidence.

rebel **1.** ['rɛb əl] *n.* someone who fights or resists power, authority, or government. **2.** [rɪ 'bɛl] *iv.* to fight or resist power, authority, or government.

rebellion [rɪ 'bɛl jən] *n.* rebelling; challenging authority. (Pl only for types and instances.)

rebirth [rɪ 'bɚθ] *n.* seeming to be born again. (No pl.)

rebound **1.** ['ri baʊnd] *n.* the return movement of something that bounced off something. **2.** [rɪ 'baʊnd] *iv.* to bounce back after hitting something. **3.** [rɪ 'baʊnd] *iv.* to recover. (Fig. on ②.)

rebuild [rɪ 'bɪld] *tv., irreg.* to build something again. (Pt/pp: REBUILT.)

rebuilt [rɪ 'bɪlt] pt/pp of REBUILD.

rebuke [rɪ 'bjuk] **1.** *n.* scolding; disapproval; chiding. (No pl form in this sense.) **2.** *n.* a scolding. **3.** *tv.* to scold someone or some creature.

receipt [rɪ 'sit] **1.** *n.* a state of having been received. (No pl.) **2.** *n.* a document that proves that something has been received or paid for.

receipts *n.* money that a business receives from customers; money that is collected by a business or at a performance. (Treated as pl, but not countable.)

receive [rɪ 'siv] **1.** *tv.* to get something; to take something that is given. **2.** *tv.* to accept someone as a member of a group or organization; to welcome someone as a visitor.

receiver [rɪ ˈsiv ɚ] **1.** *n.* someone or something that receives something. **2.** *n.* the part of a telephone that one holds while one is talking. **3.** *n.* a radio or television set; something that receives broadcast signals.

recent [ˈri sənt] *adj.* happening only a short time ago; having existed for only a short time; not long ago. (Adv: *recently.*)

receptacle [rɪ ˈsɛp tə kəl] **1.** *n.* a container designed to receive something. **2.** *n.* a place to plug in an electric cord. (Short for *electric receptacle.*)

reception [rɪ ˈsɛp ʃən] **1.** *n.* receiving or welcoming someone. **2.** *n.* the quality of broadcast signals that are received by a television set, a radio, or other receiver. (No pl.) **3.** *n.* a party, gathering, or celebration where people are welcomed.

receptionist [rɪ ˈsɛp ʃə nəst] *n.* someone who sits at the desk near the front door of an office, answers phone calls, and greets, helps, or directs clients or patients.

recess 1. [ˈri sɛs] *n.* a period of time during the school day when the children are allowed to play, usually outside. **2.** [ˈri sɛs] *n.* a period of time during the workday when someone stops working for a few minutes and takes a break; a BREAK ②. **3.** [ˈri sɛs] *n.* a space cut or built into a wall; a space that is set back from a wall. **4.** [rɪ ˈsɛs] *iv.* to take a break; to stop working for a short time.

recipe [ˈrɛs ə pi] **1.** *n.* a set of directions for making something to eat. **2.** *n.* a set of directions for preparing or causing anything. (Fig. on ①.)

recipient [rɪ ˈsɪp i ənt] *n.* someone who or something that receives something.

recital [rɪ ˈsɑɪt əl] **1.** *n.* the telling of a story; a verbal account of something. **2.** *n.* a concert or performance, often by a single performer playing an instrument, singing, or reading poetry.

recite [rɪ ˈsɑɪt] *tv.* to verbally deliver an answer in school; to repeat something, such as a poem, from memory.

reckless [ˈrɛk ləs] *adj.* careless; not concerned about safety or danger. (Adv: *recklessly.*)

recklessness [ˈrɛk ləs nəs] *n.* being reckless; taking risks on purpose. (No pl.)

reckon [ˈrɛk ən] **1.** *tv.* to calculate something; to figure the amount of something; to determine the cost or the amount of something. **2.** *tv.*

to think something; to suppose something. (Colloquial. Takes a clause.)

reclaim [rɪ ˈklem] **1.** *tv.* to save or reuse something that would otherwise be thrown away. **2.** *tv.* to demand or claim the return of something that has been given away or taken away.

recognition [rɛk ɪg ˈnɪʃ ən] **1.** *n.* realization. (No pl.) **2.** *n.* acknowledgment of the existence of someone or something. (No pl.) **3.** *n.* acknowledgment of service or excellence. (No pl.)

recognizable [ˈrɛk ɪg naɪz ə bəl] *adj.* in adequate amount or degree to be noticed or identified. (Adv: *recognizably*.)

recognize [ˈrɛk ɪg naɪz] **1.** *tv.* to identify someone or something. **2.** *tv.* to make an acknowledgment that something exists. (The object can be a clause with THAT ⑦.) **3.** *tv.* to give someone the right to speak, especially at a meeting.

recollect [rɛk ə ˈlɛkt] *tv.* to remember someone or something; to bring something back into one's mind; to recall something.

recommend [rɛk ə ˈmɛnd] **1.** *tv.* to suggest [making] a particular choice from a range of choices. **2.** *tv.* to suggest a particular course of action. (The object can be a clause with THAT ⑦.)

recommendation [rɛk ə mɛn ˈde ʃən] *n.* a suggestion of which selection someone should choose from a range of choices; someone or something that is recommended.

reconcile [ˈrɛk ən saɪl] **1.** *tv.* to make peace between people or groups of people by solving problems and ending disagreements. **2.** *tv.* to bring accounts into balance. **3.** ~ **with** to make up with someone; to bring a disagreement with someone to an end.

reconsider [ri kən ˈsɪd ɚ] **1.** *tv.* to consider something again; to think about something again. **2.** *iv.* to consider again; to think about again.

record 1. [ˈrɛk ɚd] *n.* a written account of facts or information about someone or something. **2.** [ˈrɛk ɚd] *n.* a flat plastic disk that has sound stored on it and is played on a machine that makes the recorded sounds able to be heard. **3.** [ˈrɛk ɚd] *n.* the most extreme example of something; the highest, lowest, fastest, slowest, longest, shortest, or any other extreme example of something. **4.** [rɪ ˈkord] *tv.* to write down information about someone or something so that other people will be able to read the information. **5.** [rɪ ˈkord] *tv.* to store sound on audiotape or to store images on film or videotape; to put a sound or an image into a permanent form.

388

recorded [rɪ ˈkɔr dɪd] **1.** *adj.* written down; having information about someone or something written down; known. **2.** *adj.* stored on cassette, film, or videotape; stored in a permanent form.

recorder [rɪ ˈkɔr dɚ] **1.** *n.* someone who writes down and stores information. **2.** *n.* a musical instrument, consisting of a hollow tube of wood that has holes down one side. **3.** *n.* a machine that records sounds or images and usually is able to play the sounds and images back.

recording [rɪ ˈkɔr dɪŋ] *n.* a record; music, speech, or other sound that has been recorded.

recount 1. [ˈri ˈkaʊnt] *n.* another counting; a second count; another count, especially in an election when the votes are counted for a second time because the first count is thought to be faulty. **2.** [ri ˈkaʊnt] *tv.* to tell a story; to tell the story of something that happened. **3.** [ˈri ˈkaʊnt] *tv.* to count something again.

recover [ri ˈkʌv ɚ] **1.** *iv.* to get better after a sickness or injury; to return to good health. **2.** *tv.* to get something back that went away or was lost, stolen, or taken away. **3.** *tv.* to reclaim something; to pull out something useful from something that is not useful.

recovery [ri ˈkʌv ə ri] **1.** *n.* the process of getting something back that went away or was lost, stolen, or taken; receiving someone or something that went away or was lost, stolen, or taken. (No pl.) **2.** *n.* the return to someone's or something's regular condition, especially the return of good health after sickness or injury or the return of a good economy after a bad period of time. (No pl.)

recreation [rɛk ri ˈe ʃən] *n.* amusement; play; activities that are done for pleasure, enjoyment, or fun. (No pl.)

recreational [rɛk ri ˈe ʃə nəl] *adj.* of or about RECREATION. (Adv: *recreationally.*)

recruit [rɪ ˈkrut] **1.** *tv.* to cause or persuade someone to become a new member of a group, or organization such as the military. **2.** *n.* someone who has just joined a group or organization, especially the military.

rectangle [ˈrɛk tæŋ gəl] *n.* a four-sided figure with four right angles, having opposite sides that are parallel and the same length.

rectangular [rɛk ˈtæŋ gjə lɚ] *adj.* shaped like a RECTANGLE. (Adv: *rectangularly.*)

rectify [ˈrɛk tə faɪ] *tv.* to make something right; to correct something.

389

rectum ['rɛk təm] *n.* the end of the lower intestine, through which waste passes.

recuperate [ri 'kup ə ret] to recover from something; to be cured or to heal after something.

recur [ri 'kɚ] *iv.* to repeat; to happen again; to continue to happen.

recycle [ri 'saɪk əl] **1.** *tv.* to change glass, plastic, paper, or other material into a form that can be used again; to recover a resource; to find a further use for something that might otherwise be wasted. **2.** *tv.* to collect or set aside used glass, plastic, paper, or other material so that it can be made into something useful. **3.** *iv.* to collect and set aside [trash] as in ②.

recycled [ri 'saɪk əld] *adj.* made from a substance that has already been used.

red ['rɛd] **1.** *n.* the color of blood and the traffic signal that means stop. (Pl only for types and instances.) **2.** the *adj.* use of ①. (Adv: *redly.* Comp: *redder;* sup: *reddest.*) **3.** *adj.* [of hair] copper colored or rusty orange. (Comp: *redder;* sup: *reddest.*)

redbird ['rɛd bɚd] *n.* any of various birds having red feathers.

redden ['rɛd n] **1.** *iv.* to become red; to turn red. **2.** *tv.* to cause someone or something to become red; to cause someone or something to turn red.

reddish ['rɛd ɪʃ] *adj.* having some of the qualities of the color red. (Adv: *reddishly.*)

redeem [rɪ 'dim] **1.** *tv.* to convert something to cash, especially to convert a coupon, token, ticket, or other thing that is not money but represents money. **2.** *tv.* to do something that restores other people's good opinion of oneself. (Takes a reflexive object.)

redeeming [rɪ 'dim ɪŋ] *adj.* making up for other faults or problems.

redevelop [ri dɪ 'vɛl əp] **1.** *tv.* to develop something again. **2.** *tv.* to build in an area again; to construct buildings in an area again.

redhead ['rɛd hɛd] *n.* someone who has red hair.

redid ['ri 'dɪd] pt of REDO.

redirect [ri dɪ 'rɛkt] *tv.* to direct or send someone or something to a different place; to send someone or something in a different direction.

redness ['rɛd nəs] *n.* being red; the condition of having the color red. (No pl.)

redo [ri 'du] *tv., irreg.* to do something again; to do something over. (Pt: REDID; pp: REDONE.)

redone [ri 'dʌn] pp of REDO.

redouble [ri 'dʌb əl] **1.** *tv.* to double the amount of something; to increase the amount of something. **2.** *iv.* to double; to increase.

reduce [rɪ 'dus] **1.** *tv.* to make something smaller or less important; to decrease something. **2.** *iv.* to lose [weight].

reduction [rɪ 'dʌk ʃən] **1.** *n.* making something smaller; reducing something. **2.** *n.* the amount by which something is made smaller.

redundant [rɪ 'dʌn dənt] *adj.* extra; not needed; doing the same thing as someone or something else. (Adv: *redundantly.*)

redwood ['rɛd wʊd] **1.** *n.* a tall evergreen tree, found in the western United States, that lives to be very old. **2.** *n.* the wood of ①. (Pl only for types and instances.) **3.** the *adj.* use of ① or ②.

reed ['rid] **1.** *n.* a tall grasslike plant with hollow stems that grows in marshes and other wet places. **2.** *n.* a thin piece of wood in the mouthpiece of woodwind instruments like clarinets, saxophones, and oboes or a similar metal piece in harmonicas, accordions, and pipe organs. **3.** the *adj.* use of ① or ②.

reef ['rif] *n.* a ridge of rocks, sand, or coral that extends from the bottom of a sea or ocean to or almost to the surface of the water.

reek ['rik] *iv.* to smell very bad.

reel ['ril] **1.** *n.* a round frame around which string, thread, yarn, fishing line, film, audiotape, videotape, or other long materials are wound. **2.** *iv.* to twist or turn, as when struck by a powerful blow.

reelect ['ri ə 'lɛkt] *tv.* to elect someone again.

reelection [ri ə 'lɛk ʃən] *n.* the election of someone to the same position for another term.

reestablish [ri ə 'stæb lɪʃ] *tv.* to establish something again.

refer to [rɪ 'fɚ tu] **1.** to go to someone, such as an adviser, or something, such as a book, for help or information. **2.** to have to do with something; to apply to something; to be related to something; to concern something. **3.** to direct someone to use something for help or information; to direct someone to go to someone or something for help or information.

referee [rɛf ə 'ri] **1.** *n.* someone who judges the playing of sports events; an umpire. **2.** *tv.* to judge the playing of a sports event. **3.** *iv.* to serve as ①.

reference ['rɛf (ə) rəns] **1.** *n.* words that refer to something else; something that has to do with something else; something that relates to something else. **2.** *n.* something, such as a book, that is used for help or information; someone or something that provides information about something. **3.** *n.* a statement that someone writes about someone else for that other person's use when applying for something; a statement about someone or someone's character.

refill 1. [rɪ 'fɪl] *iv.* to fill again; to become full again. **2.** [rɪ 'fɪl] *tv.* to fill something again; to provide what is requested or needed. **3.** ['ri fɪl] *n.* an amount of something that is used to REFILL a container as in ②. **4.** ['ri fɪl] *n.* an additional set of doses of medicine, as prescribed by a doctor.

refine [rɪ 'faɪn] **1.** *tv.* to make something purer. **2.** *tv.* to make something more detailed, rational, or effective.

refined [rɪ 'faɪnd] **1.** *adj.* made purer; pure; having impure substances removed. **2.** *adj.* elegant; very proper and civilized. (Adv: *refinedly.*)

refinish [ri 'fɪn ɪʃ] *tv.* to remove an old paint or varnish finish and apply a new one.

reflect [rɪ 'flɛkt] **1.** *tv.* to show an image in the manner of a mirror. **2.** *tv.* to throw back heat, light, sound, or energy; to bounce back heat, light, sound, or energy. **3.** *tv.* [for something] to show or reveal a personal characteristic of someone. **4.** ~ **on** to think deeply or carefully; to ponder; to examine one's thoughts.

reflection [rɪ 'flɛk ʃən] **1.** *n.* a reflected glare; reflected light. **2.** *n.* something, especially an image, that is reflected.

reform [ri 'form] **1.** *tv.* to change someone or something for the better; to make someone or something better; to improve someone or something. **2.** *iv.* to improve; to become better; to change for the better. **3.** *n.* a planned improvement; a change that gets rid of past flaws or errors.

reformer [ri 'for mɚ] *n.* someone who reforms and improves people or things.

refrain [ri 'fren] *iv.* to hold back from doing something; to choose not to do something as planned.

refresh [rɪ 'frɛʃ] **1.** *tv.* to make someone feel better or fresher. **2.** *tv.* to bring something into memory; to restore something to someone's memory.

refreshed [rɪ 'frɛʃt] *adj.* made to feel fresh again; made to feel better because of food, drink, sleep, etc.

392

refreshing [rɪ 'frɛʃ ɪŋ] *adj.* new and exciting; giving the feeling of being fresh. (Adv: *refreshingly.*)

refreshment [rɪ 'frɛʃ mənt] **1.** *n.* the process of making someone or something fresh; renewing someone or something. (No pl form in this sense.) **2.** *n.* ~s food or drink that satisfies one's thirst or hunger.

refreshments [rɪ 'frɛʃ mənts] *n.* food or drink that satisfies one's thirst or hunger.

refrigerate [rɪ 'frɪdʒ ə ret] *tv.* to put something in a refrigerator; to keep something cold.

refrigerator [rɪ 'frɪdʒ ə ret ɚ] *n.* an appliance into which food is placed to keep it cold.

refund **1.** ['ri fənd] *n.* the money that is given back when someone returns a product to a store. **2.** [rɪ 'fʌnd] *tv.* to give someone money back when a product is returned.

refuse **1.** [rɪ 'fjuz] *tv.* not to accept something; to reject something. **2.** [rɪ 'fjuz] *tv.* to deny someone something; not to allow someone to have something. **3.** ['rɛf jus] *n.* garbage; trash; things that are thrown away. (No pl.)

regard [rɪ 'gɑrd] **1.** *tv.* to think of someone or something in a certain way. **2.** *n.* respect; esteem. (No pl.)

regardless [ri 'gɑrd ləs] *adv.* without considering something; at any rate; whatever is done; whatever option is chosen.

region ['ri dʒən] **1.** *n.* an area of land that has a common social, cultural, economic, political, or natural feature throughout it; sometimes a political division of a country. **2.** *n.* a part; an area that has a common feature throughout it.

regional ['ridʒ ə nəl] *adj.* of or about a REGION. (Adv: *regionally.*)

register ['rɛdʒ ɪ stɚ] **1.** *n.* a machine (in a store) that cashiers use to keep track of money taken in or paid out. (Short for *cash register.*) **2.** *n.* the book that a list or record of something is kept in. **3.** *tv.* to show something such as a feeling or an attitude; to express something. **4.** *iv.* to put one's name and perhaps other information on an official list.

registered ['rɛdʒ ɪ stɚd] *adj.* listed as in REGISTER ④; approved by the government; enrolled.

registration [rɛdʒ ɪ 'stre ʃən] **1.** *n.* the process of registering; the condition of being registered. (No pl.) **2.** *n.* the time when people choose and reserve classes at a school, college, or university. (No pl.)

393

regret [rɪ 'grɛt] **1.** *n.* sorrow; the feeling of being sad or sorry about something that one has done. (No pl.) **2.** *n.* something that one is sorry about; something that causes sorrow. **3.** *tv.* to feel sad or sorry about having or not having done something; to feel ① about having or not having done something. (The object can be a clause with THAT ⑦.)

regretful [rɪ 'grɛt fʊl] *adj.* full of regret; feeling sad or sorry about something. (Adv: *regretfully.*)

regular ['rɛg jə lɚ] **1.** *adj.* usual; normal. (Adv: *regularly.*) **2.** *adj.* not changing; even in size, shape, or speed; uniform. (Adv: *regularly.*) **3.** *adj.* [in grammar] following the usual pattern, especially concerning verb forms. (Adv: *regularly.*)

regularity [rɛg jə 'lɛr ə ti] *n.* the quality of being regular. (Pl only for types and instances.)

regulate ['rɛg jə let] **1.** *tv.* to control someone or something by a rule or system; to limit someone or something by a rule or system. **2.** *tv.* to fix or adjust something so that it will work at a certain level or standard.

regulation [rɛg jə 'le ʃən] **1.** *n.* the control or order caused by rules, laws, principles, or systems. (No pl form in this sense.) **2.** *n.* a rule; a law; an official principle that regulates someone or something. **3.** *adj.* according to a rule, law, system, or standard; suitable according to a rule, law, system, or standard; standard.

rehearsal [rɪ 'hɚs əl] **1.** *n.* a practice performance of a play, opera, concert, etc., devoted to perfecting the performance for an audience. **2.** the *adj.* use of ①.

rehearse [rɪ 'hɚs] **1.** *tv.* to practice a part in a play, concert, dance, or performance before performing it for the public; [for performers] to practice performing. **2.** *tv.* to cause a group of performers to practice; to cause performers to practice something that is to be performed. **3.** *iv.* to practice [a role, play, piece of music, etc.].

reign ['ren] **1.** *iv.* to rule, especially as king, queen, emperor, or empress. **2.** *iv.* to be the current winner of a contest or holder of a title. **3.** *n.* the period of the rule of a king, queen, emperor, empress, as in ①.

rein ['ren] *n.* one of a pair of long straps attached to either side of the bridle of a horse, mule, donkey, etc. (Used to control the direction of movement of the animal.)

394

reinforce [ri ɪn 'fɔrs] *tv.* to make something stronger, more able to resist wear, or longer lasting by adding something to it.

reins ['renz] *n.* the straps that are used to control a horse.

reject 1. [rɪ 'dʒɛkt] *tv.* to refuse to take or accept someone or something. **2.** ['ri dʒɛkt] *n.* someone or something that has been refused as in ①.

rejection [ri 'dʒɛk ʃən] *n.* refusal to accept someone or something. (No pl.)

rejoice [ri 'dʒɔɪs] *iv.* to be very happy [about something]; to celebrate [something] joyfully.

rejoicing [ri 'dʒɔɪs ɪŋ] *n.* great joy or happiness expressed by one or more people. (No pl.)

relate [rɪ 'let] **1.** *tv.* to tell a story; to tell what was heard. (The object can be a clause with THAT ⑦.) **2.** ~ **to** to feel a bond of some type with someone because of shared experiences.

related [rɪ 'let ɪd] **1.** *adj.* connected. (Adv: *relatedly.*) **2.** *adj.* part of the same family; in the same family. **3.** ~ **to** connected to someone as a relative; linked or connected to something.

relation [rɪ 'le ʃən] **1.** *n.* someone who is a member of one's family; a relative. **2.** *n.* a connection between two or more things; relationship.

relationship [rɪ 'le ʃən ʃɪp] **1.** *n.* a personal, romantic, business, or social connection between two people. **2.** *n.* a connection between two or more things.

relative ['rɛl ə tɪv] **1.** *n.* someone who is a member of one's family. **2.** *adj.* compared to something else; having meaning only as compared with something else. (Adv: *relatively.*)

relax [rɪ 'læks] **1.** *iv.* to become less tight, less stiff, less firm, less tense, or more loose. **2.** *iv.* to become less worried, less busy with work, or less active; to rest, be calm, or slow down. **3.** *tv.* to cause something to become less tight, less stiff, less firm, or less tense. **4.** *tv.* to cause something to become less strict, less harsh, or less severe. **5.** *tv.* to cause someone to become less worried, less busy with work, or less active; to cause someone to rest, be calm, or slow down.

relaxation [rɪ læk 'se ʃən] **1.** *n.* rest, especially after work or busy activity. (No pl.) **2.** *n.* the lessening of tightness, stiffness, tenseness, or firmness; the release of tension from something tight, stiff, tense, or firm. (No pl.) **3.** *n.* making something less severe; the easing of strict rules. (No pl.)

395

relaxing [rɪ ˈlæk sɪŋ] *adj.* calming; soothing; restful; making one feel less tense, tight, stiff, or firm. (Adv: *relaxingly.*)

relay [rɪ ˈle] *tv.* to receive something and give it to someone else; to receive something and transfer it to something else or move it further along in a process.

release [rɪ ˈlis] **1.** *tv.* to let someone or something free; to let someone or something go; to let someone or something loose. **2.** *tv.* to make a book, a movie, information, or a publication available to the public. **3.** *n.* an act of letting someone or something go; an act of setting someone or something free.

relent [rɪ ˈlɛnt] **1.** *iv.* to show pity; to be less mean or cruel; to be more merciful. **2.** *iv.* to become less severe; to become more mild; to lose strength.

relevant [ˈrɛl ə vənt] *adj.* connected to something; of or about the subject being discussed. (Adv: *relevantly.*)

reliable [rɪ ˈlɑɪ ə bəl] *adj.* able to be relied on; able to be trusted; loyal; dependable. (Adv: *reliably.*)

reliance [ri ˈlɑɪ əns] *n.* trust in and dependence on someone or something.

relief [rɪ ˈlif] **1.** *n.* the feeling that is felt when pain, a burden, a strain, or a problem is eased. (No pl.) **2.** *n.* something that eases pain, a burden, a strain, or a problem. (No pl.) **3.** *n.* money, clothing, food, or other aid that is made available to help poor people or to help people who are victims of a disaster. (No pl.)

relieve [rɪ ˈliv] **1.** *tv.* to ease or get rid of pain, anxiety, or strain. **2.** *tv.* to begin working at a job as a replacement so that the person who was working can have some time to relax.

religion [rɪ ˈlɪdʒ ən] *n.* belief in or worship of one or more gods or spirits. (Pl only for types and instances.)

religious [rɪ ˈlɪdʒ əs] **1.** the *adj.* form of RELIGION. (Adv: *religiously.*) **2.** *adj.* believing in or worshiping one or more gods or spirits. (Adv: *religiously.*)

relish [ˈrɛl ɪʃ] **1.** *tv.* to enjoy something very much. **2.** *n.* a mixture of chopped pickled cucumbers or other pickled vegetables. (No pl form.)

relocate [ri ˈlo ket] *tv.* to move someone or something to a different place.

reluctant [rɪ ˈlʌk tənt] *adj.* unwilling to do something; not wanting to do something.

rely (up)on [rɪ ˈlaɪ (əp) ɔn] to depend on someone or something; to trust that someone will do something; to trust that something will happen.

remain [rɪ ˈmen] **1.** *iv.* to stay in someplace; to continue to be in a certain place; to be left over after other parts or things are taken. **2.** *iv.* to continue to be something or act in a particular manner.

remainder [rɪ ˈmen dɚ] **1.** *n.* the part of something that is left over after part of it is taken. **2.** *n.* the number that is left over after a number is divided into another one.

remaining [rɪ ˈmen ɪŋ] *adj.* yet to happen; yet to occur; not yet done or taken care of; not yet taken away; not yet happening; not yet occurring.

remains **1.** *n.* things that are left behind. (Treated as pl, but not countable.) **2.** *n.* a corpse; a dead body. (Treated as pl.)

remark [rɪ ˈmɑrk] **1.** *n.* a comment; a statement; something that is said or written about something. **2.** *tv.* to say something; to comment about something; to state an opinion. (The object can be a clause with THAT ⑦.)

remarkable [rɪ ˈmɑrk ə bəl] *adj.* worth mentioning; worth talking about; noticeable; unusual. (Adv: *remarkably.*)

remedy [ˈrɛm ə di] **1.** *n.* a treatment; a cure; something that makes someone become healthy again. **2.** *n.* making bad conditions good or better; the correction of a problem. (Fig. on ①.) **3.** *tv.* to make bad conditions good or better; to correct a problem; to fix something that is wrong or bad.

remember [rɪ ˈmɛm bɚ] **1.** *tv.* to bring back the thought of someone or something into one's mind, memory, or imagination; to think about someone or something again. (The object can be a clause with THAT ⑦.) **2.** *tv.* not to forget someone or something; to keep someone or something in one's mind. (The object can be a clause with THAT ⑦.) **3.** *iv.* to bring [someone or something] back into one's mind, memory, or imagination.

remind [rɪ ˈmaɪnd] *tv.* to tell someone about something again; to cause someone to remember someone or something.

reminder [rɪ ˈmaɪn dɚ] *n.* something that reminds someone about something.

397

reminiscent [rɛm ə 'nɪs ənt] *adj.* reminding someone about someone or something; seeming like or suggesting someone or something.

remodel [ri 'mɑd l] *tv.* to decorate something in a new way; to construct something in a new way; to change a structure or room so that it looks more modern.

remote [rɪ 'mot] **1.** *adj.* far away in space or time; far off; not near; distant; isolated; secluded; not near other things or places. (Adv: *remotely.* Comp: *remoter;* sup: *remotest.*) **2.** *adj.* [of a possibility] very small. (Fig. on ①. Adv: *remotely.* Comp: *remoter;* sup: *remotest.*) **3.** *n.* an electronic device used to control audio and video equipment. (Short for *remote control.*)

remove [rɪ 'muv] **1.** *tv.* to take something away from a place; to get rid of something. **2.** *tv.* to take off something, especially a piece of clothing.

render ['rɛn dɚ] **1.** *tv.* to cause someone or something to be in a certain condition; to cause someone or something to become a certain way. **2.** *tv.* to give an official verdict or opinion. **3.** *tv.* to sing something; to play a song. **4.** *tv.* to melt down fat, purifying it by separating out the impurities. **5.** ~ **to** to give something to someone.

renew [ri 'nu] **1.** *tv.* to cause someone or something to become like new again; to restore someone or something. **2.** *tv.* to cause something that was no longer valid or effective to become useful again; to cause something to be valid for a longer period of time.

renounce [rɪ 'naʊns] *tv.* to give up something; to state formally that one is giving up something, especially a claim or a right.

renovate ['rɛn ə vet] *tv.* to fix up something so that it is in good condition; to restore something to a good condition; to repair a structure.

rent ['rɛnt] **1.** *n.* the money paid for the use of something, especially for the use of a place to live. (No pl.) **2.** *iv.* to live in an apartment that one does not own, but for which one pays ① to the owner.

rental ['rɛn təl] **1.** *adj.* [of an apartment, office space, equipment, or other thing] rented or available to be rented. **2.** *n.* the amount of money that is paid as rent for something. (No pl.)

rented ['rɛn təd] *adj.* occupied or used for a fee, rather than owned.

reorganization [ri or gə nə 'ze ʃən] *n.* reorganizing something; organizing something in a different way, especially so that it works or operates better; the condition of having been reorganized.

reorganize [ri 'ɔr gə nɑɪz] **1.** *tv.* to organize something in a different way, especially so that it works or operates better. **2.** *tv.* to reform a business, especially after it has gone bankrupt.

repaid [ri 'ped] pt/pp of REPAY.

repair [rɪ 'pɛr] **1.** *tv.* to fix something; to mend something; to cause something to work again. **2.** *n.* work that will fix or restore something. (Sg or pl with the same meaning.)

repairable [rɪ 'pɛr ə bəl] *adj.* able to be repaired; able to be fixed. (Adv: *repairably.*)

repay [rɪ 'pe] *tv., irreg.* to pay someone back for something; to pay someone for an amount that is owed. (Pt/pp: REPAID.)

repayment [rɪ 'pe mənt] *n.* paying back something to someone. (No pl.)

repeal [rɪ 'pil] *tv.* to void a law; to cause a law to no longer be valid.

repeat [rɪ 'pit] **1.** *tv.* to do or say something again. **2.** *tv.* to say something that someone else has just said, to find out if has been correctly understood. **3.** *tv.* to say something that one has learned.

repeated [rɪ 'pit ɪd] *adj.* previously done or said and being done or said again; done or said more than one time. (Adv: *repeatedly.*)

repent [rɪ 'pɛnt] *iv.* to be sorry for one's wrongs and prepare to be better in the future.

repetition [rɛp ɪ 'tɪ ʃən] *n.* repeating something. (Pl only for types and instances.)

replace [rɪ 'ples] **1.** *tv.* to take the place of someone or something else. **2.** *tv.* to exchange something for another thing that is more useful or newer. **3.** *tv.* to return something to the place where it belongs; to put something back where it belongs.

replacement [rɪ 'ples mənt] **1.** *n.* replacing someone or something. (No pl.) **2.** *n.* someone or something that takes the place of someone or something else. **3.** *adj.* used to replace someone or something else.

replay 1. ['ri ple] *n.* something that is played again; an event that is done over; a film clip that is played over, often in slow motion so one can see fast action better. **2.** ['ri ple] *tv.* to play something again, especially a game or a piece of film.

reply [rɪ 'plɑɪ] **1.** *iv.* to answer. **2.** *tv.* to say or write something as an answer. (The object is a clause with THAT ⑦.) **3.** *n.* an answer; something that is said or written when answering a question.

report [rɪ 'pɔrt] **1.** *n.* an account that gives information about something. **2.** *n.* the noise made when a shot is fired. **3.** *tv.* to describe news; to provide news. (The object can be a clause with THAT ⑦.) **4.** ~ **for** to present oneself for something. **5.** ~ **to** to go to someplace; to present oneself to someone at someplace.

reporter [rɪ 'pɔr tɚ] *n.* someone who provides a newspaper, magazine, radio station, or television station with news; someone who reports news or information.

repose [rɪ 'poz] **1.** *n.* sleep; quiet; rest; calm. (No pl form in this sense.) **2.** *iv.* to rest; to sleep; to lie dead in a grave.

repossess [ri pə 'zɛs] *tv.* [for a company] to take back something purchased on credit when the purchaser fails to make payments on time.

represent [rɛp rɪ 'zɛnt] **1.** *tv.* to portray someone or something; to express something. **2.** *tv.* to act on behalf of someone else; to speak for someone else.

reproach [rɪ 'protʃ] **1.** *n.* blame; criticism. (No pl form.) **2.** *tv.* to blame or criticize someone.

reproduce [ri prə 'dus] **1.** *tv.* to make a copy of something. **2.** *tv.* to create something again; to do something in the way it has already been done. **3.** *iv.* to have offspring.

reproduction [ri prə 'dʌk ʃən] **1.** *n.* the process of making a copy of something. (No pl.) **2.** *n.* creating offspring; reproducing. (No pl.) **3.** *n.* a copy of something, especially of a work of art or a book.

reproductive [ri prə 'dʌk tɪv] *adj.* of or about REPRODUCTION ②. (Adv: *reproductively.*)

reptile ['rɛp taɪl] *n.* a class of animals whose temperature is the same as the surrounding air, including dinosaurs, lizards, snakes, turtles, tortoises, alligators, and crocodiles.

republic [rɪ 'pʌb lɪk] **1.** *n.* a nation where the people are governed by officials whom they elect. **2.** *n.* a system of government in which the people elect officials to represent them.

reputation [rɛp jə 'te ʃən] *n.* the basis for the good or bad opinion that people have about someone or something.

request [rɪ 'kwɛst] **1.** *tv.* to ask for something politely. (The object can be a clause with THAT ⑦.) **2.** *n.* a polite demand; an instance of asking for something.

require [rɪ ˈkwaɪɚ] **1.** *tv.* to demand a particular qualification or skill. **2.** *tv.* to demand that someone do something. (The object can be a clause with THAT ⑦.)

required [rɪ ˈkwaɪɚd] *adj.* demanded and needed; ordered; necessary.

requirement [rɪ ˈkwaɪɚ mənt] *n.* something that must be done; something that is required; something that is necessary.

rerun [ˈri rən] *n.* a television program that is not new; a television program that has been on television before.

rescue [ˈrɛs kju] **1.** *tv.* to save someone or something that is in danger. **2.** *n.* an instance of saving someone or something from danger.

research 1. [ˈri sɚtʃ, rɪ ˈsɚtʃ] *n.* study and examination; the collecting of information. (No pl.) **2.** [rɪ ˈsɚtʃ] *tv.* to collect information about something in great detail.

resemble [rɪ ˈzɛm bəl] *tv.* to look like someone or something; to be like someone or something.

resent [rɪ ˈzɛnt] *tv.* to feel bitter toward someone about something; to feel insulted by someone about something. (The object can be a clause with THAT ⑦.)

resentful [rɪ ˈzɛnt fʊl] *adj.* full of anger or bitter feelings about someone or something; feeling that one has been insulted; showing anger or bitter feelings. (Adv: *resentfully.*)

reservation [rɛz ɚ ˈve ʃən] **1.** *n.* a doubt about something; a concern; something that stops someone from accepting something. **2.** *n.* a previous claim on the use of something at a specific time, such as a room in a hotel, a table at a restaurant, or a seat in a theater, on an airplane, or at a concert.

reserve [rɪ ˈzɚv] **1.** *tv.* to schedule the use of something at a certain time; to record a claim for the future use of something at a certain time. **2.** *tv.* to save something for future use. **3.** *n.* something that is saved for future use.

reserved [rɪ ˈzɚvd] **1.** *adj.* saved for a certain person or certain reason; scheduled to be used by someone at a certain time. **2.** *adj.* quiet; keeping to oneself; not talking about oneself. (Adv: *reservedly* [rɪ ˈzɚv əd li].)

reserves *n.* troops or soldiers that are prepared to be called to war. (Treated as pl, but not countable.)

401

reservoir ['rɛ zɚ vwɑr] **1.** *n.* an artificial lake where water is stored for the use of people. **2.** *n.* a place where something, such as knowledge, is stored. (Fig. on ①.)

reside [rɪ 'zaɪd] *iv.* to live in a certain place.

residence ['rɛz ə dəns] **1.** *n.* the period of time that someone lives in a certain place. (No pl. Number is expressed with *period(s) of residence*.) **2.** *n.* a house or an apartment; the place where someone lives.

resident ['rɛz ə dənt] **1.** *n.* a person who lives in a certain house or apartment. **2.** *n.* a person who lives in a certain city, state, or country. **3.** *n.* a doctor who works full time at a hospital in order to get advanced medical training. **4.** *adj.* living in or working at a certain place.

residential [rɛz ə 'dɛn ʃəl] *adj.* of or about residences; of or about homes or apartments rather than offices, farms, or factories. (Adv: *residentially*.)

resign [rɪ 'zaɪn] **1.** *tv.* to quit a position or office. **2.** ~ **oneself to** to cause oneself to accept something without complaining; to cause oneself to yield to something.

resignation [rɛz ɪg 'ne ʃən] **1.** *n.* voluntarily leaving a job, office, committee, or task. (Pl only for types and instances.) **2.** *n.* a formal statement or document made by someone who is leaving a job.

resist [rɪ 'zɪst] **1.** *tv.* to oppose something; to refuse to accept something. **2.** *tv.* to keep from doing something; to prevent something from happening; to stop something from happening. (Takes a verb with *-ing*.) **3.** *tv.* to be undamaged by something; to be able to withstand something.

resistance [rɪ 'zɪs təns] *n.* resisting someone or something; the ability to resist someone or something. (No pl.)

resolve [rɪ 'zɑlv] **1.** ~ **to do** to decide to do something. **2.** *tv.* [for a group of people] to vote to produce a statement making a request or statement. (Takes a clause.) **3.** *tv.* to settle an issue; to solve a problem; to come to an agreeable solution; to explain something. **4.** *n.* determination; the ability to do things in a determined way. (No pl form in this sense.)

resource ['ri sɔrs] *n.* someone or something that one can go to for help, information, support, or supplies.

resourceful [ri 'sɔrs fʊl] *adj.* able to think of different ways to solve a problem. (Adv: *resourcefully*.)

respect [rɪ 'spɛkt] **1.** *n.* the honor, admiration, or esteem that one feels for someone or something. (No pl.) **2.** *n.* the polite behavior one shows to someone whom one honors or admires. (No pl.) **3.** *tv.* to honor, admire, or esteem someone or something.

respectable [rɪ 'spɛk tə bəl] *adj.* worthy of respect; deserving respect; deserving honor and acceptance; admirable. (Adv: *respectably.*)

respectful [rɪ 'spɛkt fʊl] *adj.* showing respect; honoring. (Adv: *respectfully.*)

respond [rɪ 'spɑnd] *tv.* to answer a question; to give an answer; to say something as a response. (The object is a clause with THAT ⑦.)

response [rɪ 'spɑns] **1.** *n.* an answer; a reply; something that is said or done to answer a question. **2.** *n.* a reaction; something that is done when something happens.

responsibility [rɪ spɑn sə 'bɪl ə ti] **1.** *n.* the authority for something; the duty to take care of someone or something. (Pl only for types and instances.) **2.** *n.* accountability for something wrong or bad; blame for causing something bad or, sometimes, credit for causing something good. (No pl.) **3.** *n.* the quality of being responsible. (No pl.) **4.** *n.* someone or something that one must care for.

responsible [rɪ 'spɑn sə bəl] *adj.* reliable; able to do something without being told what to do. (Adv: *responsibly.*)

rest ['rɛst] **1.** *n.* sleep. (No pl.) **2.** *n.* relaxation; a period of calm or quiet after work or activity. (No pl.) **3.** *iv.* to relax after work or activity. **4.** *iv.* to remain somewhere. **5.** *tv.* to cause someone or an animal to relax. **6. the ~** *n.* the remainder [of something]; the things that are left over. (Sg form. Treated like a sg or pl, but not countable.)

restaurant ['rɛs tə rɑnt] *n.* a place where one buys and eats a meal, which is usually served at a table.

restful ['rɛst fʊl] *adj.* causing one to feel rested; peaceful; calm; quiet. (Adv: *restfully.*)

restore [rɪ 'stor] *tv.* to return something to its original or regular condition; to put something back.

restrain [rɪ 'stren] *tv.* to prevent someone or something from moving or doing something.

restrict [rɪ 'strɪkt] *tv.* to limit what someone or something can do; to make something—such as one's rights, one's movement, one's speech—less than it was.

403

restriction [rɪ 'strɪk ʃən] *n.* a condition that limits action or movement; a rule against doing something; a regulation.

restroom ['rɛst rum] *n.* a room with a toilet, especially in a public building. (A euphemism.)

result [rɪ 'zʌlt] **1.** *n.* the outcome of an event; something that is caused by something else. **2.** *n.* the answer to a math problem; a solution.

resulting [rɪ 'zʌl tɪŋ] *adj.* happening because of something else; being a result.

résumé ['rɛz u me] *n.* a document that lists one's education, work history, and other important information.

resume [rɪ 'zum] **1.** *tv.* to do something again after having stopped for a time. **2.** *iv.* to begin again after having stopped for a time.

retail ['ri tel] *adj.* [of a store] selling products to consumers directly.

retailer ['ri tel ɚ] *n.* a shopkeeper; someone or a business that sells products directly to consumers.

retain [rɪ 'ten] **1.** *tv.* to keep something; to continue to have something. **2.** *tv.* to hire a lawyer.

retake 1. ['ri tek] *n.* an act of filming a part of a movie or television show again. **2.** ['ri 'tek] *tv., irreg.* to take a picture again or to film a part of a movie or television show again. (Pt: RETOOK; pp: RETAKEN.)

retaken ['ri 'tek ən] pp of RETAKE.

retire [rɪ 'tɑɪɚ] **1.** *iv.* to stop working permanently and live on the money one has saved. **2.** *iv.* to go to bed. **3.** *tv.* to cause something to no longer be used; to remove something from use. **4.** *tv.* to pay a debt; to finish paying a debt.

retired [rɪ 'tɑɪɚd] *adj.* having quit working permanently.

retirement [rɪ 'tɑɪɚ mənt] *n.* the period of time in one's life after one has stopped work permanently. (No pl.)

retook ['ri 'tʊk] pt of RETAKE.

retreat [rɪ 'trit] **1.** *iv.* to go back, especially because one cannot fight or go forward. **2.** *n.* an act of going back, especially during a battle, because one cannot fight or move forward. **3.** *n.* a quiet, isolated place; a place that one can go to for quiet, rest, or safety.

return [rɪ 'tɚn] **1.** *iv.* to go back or come back to a previous time, location, position, or condition. **2.** *tv.* to give something back to the person it came from; to put something back in the place it came from. **3.** *tv.* to cause someone or something to go back or come back to a

404

previous time, location, position, or condition. **4.** *n.* an act of coming back or going back as in ①. **5.** *n.* a set of tax forms. (Short for *tax return*.)

return(s) *n.* the amount of money that is made from a business.

reunion [ri 'jun jən] *n.* a party or gathering of people who are coming together again, especially of people who have not seen each other in a long time.

reunite [ri ju 'naɪt] **1.** *tv.* to bring people or things together again; to unite people or things again. **2.** *iv.* to bring together again; to come together again; to unite again.

reveal [rɪ 'vil] **1.** *tv.* to allow or cause something to be seen. **2.** *tv.* to make information known; to tell a piece of information. (The object can be a clause with THAT ⑦.)

revealing [rɪ 'vil ɪŋ] **1.** *adj.* allowing or causing something to be seen; showing something, especially skin. (Adv: *revealingly*.) **2.** *adj.* giving much information; allowing concealed information to be seen or known. (Adv: *revealingly*.)

revenge [rɪ 'vɛndʒ] *n.* harm done to a person as punishment for a bad deed the person has done to oneself. (No pl.)

revenue ['rɛv ə nu] **1.** *n.* income; money that is made from a business or an investment. (Usually sg.) **2.** *n.* money that is collected by the government from taxes. (Either sg or pl with the same meaning, but not countable.)

reverberate [rɪ 'vɚb ə ret] *iv.* [for sound] to roll through or pass through a space.

reverence ['rɛv rəns] *n.* respect; admiration; awe. (No pl form in this sense.)

reverse [rɪ 'vɚs] **1.** *tv.* to cause something to go or operate backwards. **2.** *tv.* to cause something to move the opposite way; to turn something the other way; to turn something upside down; to turn something inside out. **3.** *iv.* to go or move backwards; to move in the opposite direction. **4.** *n.* the opposite. **5.** *n.* the back of something; the back side.

review [rɪ 'vju] **1.** *tv.* to examine something again. **2.** *tv.* to study information again, especially before a test. **3.** *tv.* to write or prepare a written evaluation of a play, movie, book, dance, or other work of art. **4.** *iv.* to study again. **5.** *n.* a formal examination or inspection. **6.** *n.* an essay that evaluates a book, play, movie, dance, or other work.

revise [rɪ 'vaɪz] *tv.* to make something current or up-to-date; to change something to include different information.

revised [rɪ 'vaɪzd] *adj.* updated; made current; changed to include new information.

revision [rɪ 'vɪʒ ən] **1.** *n.* a change—usually an improvement—made to a document or a manuscript. **2.** *n.* a document that has been revised.

revival [rɪ 'vaɪ vəl] **1.** *n.* reviving someone or something; the process of returning life or energy to someone. **2.** *n.* a new production of a play or musical that has been done before; something that has been revived. (Fig. on ①.)

revive [rɪ 'vaɪv] **1.** *tv.* to cause someone to return to a conscious state, with normal breathing and heart activity. **2.** *tv.* to bring something back into use; to bring something back into style. **3.** *iv.* to return to a conscious state, as in ①.

revolt [rɪ 'volt] **1.** *iv.* to fight against authority or the government. **2.** *tv.* to cause someone to feel sick with disgust; to offend someone strongly. **3.** *n.* a rebellion; a riot; an instance of fighting as in ① against authority.

revolting [rɪ 'vol tɪŋ] *adj.* sickening; very offensive. (Adv: *revoltingly.*)

revolution [rɛv ə 'lu ʃən] **1.** *n.* an act of seizing a government by force and replacing it with new rulers. **2.** *n.* a complete change. (Fig. on ①.) **3.** *n.* the circular or rotating movement made by an object going around a fixed object or position.

revolve [rɪ 'valv] *iv.* [for someone or something] to turn [around an axis].

revolver [rɪ 'val vɚ] *n.* a gun having spaces for bullets in a cylinder that revolves.

reward [rɪ 'word] **1.** *n.* something, especially money, given to someone who has done something good. **2.** *tv.* to give someone ①.

rewarding [rɪ 'wor dɪŋ] *adj.* satisfying; valuable. (Adv: *rewardingly.*)

rewind [ri 'waɪnd] **1.** *tv., irreg.* to cause something, especially an audiotape, videotape, or film, to wind backward. (Pt/pp: REWOUND.) **2.** *iv., irreg.* [for something that winds around an object, such as an audiotape, videotape, or film] to run backward. **3.** *n.* a button or device that causes a reverse movement as in ②.

rewound [ri 'waʊnd] pt/pp of REWIND.

rewrite 1. [ri 'raɪt] *tv., irreg.* to revise something that has been written. (Pt: REWROTE; pp: REWRITTEN.) **2.** ['ri raɪt] *n.* a copy of writing that has been revised.

rewritten ['ri 'rɪt n] **1.** pp of REWRITE. **2.** *adj.* written in a different way; revised.

rewrote ['ri 'rot] pt of REWRITE.

rhinoceros [raɪ 'nɑs ə rəs] *n., irreg.* a large animal of Africa and South Asia that has one or two large horns on its nose. (Pl: *rhinoceros* or *rhinoceroses.*)

rhyme ['raɪm] **1.** *n.* a state existing where two or more words end in similar or identical sounds. (No pl.) **2.** *iv.* [for a word or phrase] to end with the same sound or sounds as another word or phrase; [for a poem] to include words or phrases ending with the same sound or sounds, especially at the ends of pairs of lines.

rhythm ['rɪð əm] *n.* beats that occur in a pattern, such as in music. (Pl only for types and instances.)

rib ['rɪb] **1.** *n.* one of the several pairs of bones that are attached to the backbone and curve around to the front of the chest. **2.** *n.* meat that contains ①, eaten as food.

ribbon ['rɪb ən] **1.** *n.* a narrow band of fabric or material, often used as a decoration. **2.** *n.* a special kind of ①, coated with ink, used in a typewriter or computer printer; a special, thin strip of plastic film used in an electric typewriter.

rice ['raɪs] **1.** *n.* a grasslike plant that produces edible seeds. (Pl only for types and instances.) **2.** *n.* the edible grain of ①. (No pl. Number is expressed with *grain(s) of rice.*)

rich ['rɪtʃ] **1.** *adj.* having a lot of money; wealthy; not poor. (Adv: *richly.* Comp: *richer;* sup: *richest.*) **2.** *adj.* [for food] having a lot of cream, butter, or other fats. (Adv: *richly.* Comp: *richer;* sup: *richest.*) **3.** *adj.* [of soil] good for growing plants; fertile. (Adv: *richly.* Comp: *richer;* sup: *richest.*) **4.** *adj.* [of a color] vivid or deep. (Adv: *richly.* Comp: *richer;* sup: *richest.*) **5.** *adj.* plentiful; causing or yielding plenty, benefit, or value.

riches *n.* wealth; an ample amount of anything good, especially money and property. (Treated as pl, but not countable.)

ricochet ['rɪk ə ʃe] *iv.* [for some rapidly moving object, such as a bullet] to bounce off something at an angle.

407

rid ['rɪd] **1.** *tv., irreg.* to free something or a place of something. (Pt/pp: *rid.*) **2.** *tv., irreg.* to make oneself free of someone or something. (Takes a reflexive object.)

ridden ['rɪd n] **1.** pp of RIDE. **2.** *adj.* burdened with something; full of something. (Only in combinations.)

riddle ['rɪd l] **1.** *n.* a puzzling question whose answer usually requires one to think in an unusual or clever way. **2.** *n.* someone or something that is difficult to understand; someone or something that is puzzling. (Fig. on ①.)

ride ['raɪd] **1.** *tv., irreg.* to sit on or in something that moves; to be a passenger on or in a vehicle that moves or travels. (Pt: RODE; pp: RIDDEN. With HORSE, DONKEY, ELEPHANT, and other animals. With TRAIN, BICYCLE, ELEVATOR, MOTORCYCLE, TROLLEY but *ride in* a CAR, TAXI, TRUCK, or Jeep.) **2.** *tv., irreg.* to travel along on something. **3.** *n.* a journey using a vehicle or an animal. **4.** *n.* a kind of entertainment in which people travel in some kind of vehicle to experience interesting sights and sounds, thrills, or learning.

ridge ['rɪdʒ] **1.** *n.* a long, narrow hill or mountain. **2.** *n.* a long, narrow, raised part of something. **3.** *n.* the line where two surfaces slanted upward meet, as with the top edge of a roof.

ridicule ['rɪd ə kjul] **1.** *tv.* to make fun of someone or something; to mock someone or something. **2.** *n.* laughter or mockery directed at someone or something, especially in a cruel way. (No pl.)

ridiculous [rɪ 'dɪk jə ləs] *adj.* deserving to be laughed at or mocked; deserving ridicule. (Adv: *ridiculously.*)

rifle ['raɪ fʊl] **1.** *n.* a gun with a long barrel. **2.** *tv.* to search an area thoroughly, stealing valuable things.

right ['raɪt] **1.** *adj.* the opposite of LEFT; to the east when someone or something faces north. (Only prenominal.) **2.** *adj.* correct; true; not wrong; not false. (Adv: *rightly.*) **3.** *adj.* morally good; according to the law or social standards. (Adv: *rightly.*) **4.** *adj.* proper; suitable; being good for a situation. **5.** *adv.* toward the side described in ①. **6.** *adv.* correctly; not wrongly. **7.** *adv.* properly; suitably; in a way that is good for a situation. **8.** *adv.* directly; straight. **9.** *n.* that which is correct, proper, or good. (No pl.) **10.** *tv.* to cause something to be upright; to fix something that is leaning or has fallen, so that it is standing up again.

408

right-handed ['rɑɪt hæn dɪd] **1.** *adj.* able to use the right hand better than the left; using the right hand to write with. (Adv: *right-handed(ly).*) **2.** *adj.* made to be used by the right hand.

right(s) *n.* something that is due a person according to civil or moral law. (*Right* is sg; *rights* is pl.)

rigid ['rɪdʒ ɪd] **1.** *adj.* stiff; not bending; hard to bend; not flexible. (Adv: *rigidly.*) **2.** *adj.* stubborn and determined. (Fig. on ①. Adv: *rigidly.*)

rigorous ['rɪg ə rəs] **1.** *adj.* harsh; strict; severe; demanding. (Adv: *rigorously.*) **2.** *adj.* thorough; exact; according to strict scientific standards; scientifically accurate. (Adv: *rigorously.*)

rim ['rɪm] **1.** *n.* the edge of something, especially of something that is circular. **2.** *n.* the part of a wheel that a tire is put around.

ring ['rɪŋ] **1.** *n.* something made from a circle of material; a circular band. **2.** *n.* a piece of jewelry made from a circle of metal that is usually worn around a person's finger. **3.** *n.* a circle. **4.** *n.* a group of people or things that are in a circle. **5.** *n.* an enclosed place where boxing and wrestling matches, circuses, or other forms of entertainment take place. **6.** *n.* the sound made by a bell or a chime. (No pl.) **7.** *n.* a group of criminals, especially ones who work together as an illegal business. **8.** *tv., irreg.* to cause a bell to RING as in ⑨. (Pt: RANG; pp: RUNG.) **9.** *iv., irreg.* to make a noise like a bell; [for a bell] to produce a noise.

rinse ['rɪns] *n.* an act of washing with clean water, either for cleaning or to remove soap.

riot ['rɑɪ ət] **1.** *n.* a violent, uncontrolled disturbance by a crowd of angry people; a large, violent protest. **2.** *iv.* to participate in ①; to be part of ①.

rip ['rɪp] **1.** *n.* a tear; a gash; a ragged cut. **2.** *tv.* to tear something apart; to tear something off; to cause something to come apart by pulling on it. **3.** *iv.* to become torn; to be torn apart.

ripe ['rɑɪp] *adj.* ready to be eaten or used; having developed enough so that it can be eaten or used; ready. (Adv: *ripely.* Comp: *riper;* sup: *ripest.*)

ripen ['rɑɪ pən] *iv.* to become ripe.

ripple ['rɪp əl] **1.** *n.* a small, gentle wave in water or fabric, caused by a light wind or by something falling onto the surface of water. **2.** *iv.* to develop into a series of ①. **3.** *iv.* to make a sound of gently running water; to flow like gently flowing water. **4.** *tv.* to cause something to have small waves.

rise ['raɪz] **1.** *iv., irreg.* to go upward; to move upward; to go to a higher level. (Pt: ROSE; pp: RISEN. Compare this with RAISE.) **2.** *iv., irreg.* to wake up and get out of bed. **3.** *iv., irreg.* [for the sun, moon, stars, and other objects in space] to appear to come up past the horizon. **4.** *iv., irreg.* [of dough] to become higher and lighter.

risen ['rɪz ən] pp of RISE.

rising ['raɪ zɪŋ] **1.** *adj.* going higher; moving higher; going to a higher level; increasing in amount, strength, or intensity. **2.** *adj.* coming up above the horizon; moving above the horizon.

risk ['rɪsk] **1.** *n.* a danger; a chance of harm or loss; a possibility of harm or loss. **2.** *tv.* to expose someone or something to loss, harm, or death.

risky ['rɪsk i] *adj.* dangerous; having a possibility of harm or loss; not safe. (Adv: *riskily.* Comp: *riskier;* sup: *riskiest.*)

rival ['raɪv əl] **1.** *n.* a person or team that one works or plays against; someone against whom one competes or plays. **2.** the *adj.* use of ①. **3.** *tv.* to be as good as someone or something else; to equal someone or something else.

river ['rɪv ɚ] *n.* a large natural passage of fresh water that flows into a larger passage or body of water.

road ['rod] **1.** *n.* a path or way that people can drive cars and other vehicles on to get from one place to another. **2.** *n.* a way to reach something or to achieve some result; a way of being or acting that leads to something. (Fig. on ①.)

roam ['rom] **1.** *tv.* to travel someplace with no definite destination in mind; to wander someplace. **2.** *iv.* to travel around with no specific goal; to wander.

roar ['ror] **1.** *n.* a very loud, deep noise. **2.** *iv.* to make ①. **3.** *iv.* to laugh very hard and very long because someone or something is very funny.

roast ['rost] **1.** *tv.* to cook something by using dry heat; to bake; to cook in an oven; to prepare something by using heat. (Most meats and vegetables are roasted. Bread and ham are baked. Potatoes are either roasted or baked.) **2.** *iv.* to become cooked by using dry heat; to become cooked over fire. **3.** *n.* meat that is suitable for cooking in dry heat; meat that has been cooked with dry heat.

rob ['rɑb] *tv.* to steal something from someone; to take something from someone by force.

robber ['rɑb ɚ] *n.* someone who robs people or places; a thief.

410

robbery ['rɑb (ə) ri] *n.* stealing something that belongs to someone else; theft.

robe ['rob] **1.** *n.* a long, one-piece garment, especially worn to show one's rank or position. **2.** *n.* BATHROBE.

robin ['rɑb ən] *n.* a songbird with orange feathers on its breast.

robot ['ro bɑt] *n.* a machine that does the work of a human and often moves like or looks like a human.

rock ['rɑk] **1.** *n.* the mineral substances of which a planet is made. (No pl.) **2.** *n.* a stone; a hard piece of earth; a piece of mineral. **3.** *adj.* made of ①; consisting of ① or ②. **4.** *iv.* to move back and forth; to move from side to side; to sway. **5.** *tv.* to move something back and forth or from side to side.

rocker Go to ROCKING CHAIR.

rocket ['rɑk ət] **1.** *n.* a device used to travel through space or to carry weapons through the air. **2.** *iv.* to travel by ①.

rocking chair AND **rocker** ['rɑk ɪŋ 'tʃɛr, 'rɑk ɚ] *n.* a chair whose legs are set into two curved pieces of wood so that it can rock back and forth.

rod ['rɑd] *n.* a long, narrow cylinder of wood, metal, plastic, or other material.

rode ['rod] pt of RIDE.

rodent ['rod nt] *n.* a member of a group of mammals with large, strong, sharp front teeth.

rodeo ['ro di o] *n.* an event that includes contests involving roping cattle and riding horses or bulls. (Pl ends in -*s.*)

role ['rol] **1.** *n.* a part in a play or movie; the part that an actor plays in a play or movie. **2.** *n.* the duty someone has in a group or organization.

roll ['rol] **1.** *n.* a small loaf of bread made for one person; a small, round piece of bread for one person. **2.** *n.* a unit of something that has been formed into a tube. **3.** *iv.* to move forward by turning over and over; for a ball to move forward along a surface. **4.** *iv.* to move on wheels. **5.** *tv.* to move something forward by turning it over and over; to move a ball forward along a surface. **6.** *tv.* to move something on wheels; to cause something to move on wheels. **7.** *tv.* to cause something to form the shape of a tube or cylinder.

romance [ro 'mæns] **1.** *n.* an interest in love and adventure. (No pl.) **2.** *n.* a love story. **3.** *n.* a love experience with someone. **4.** *n.* a group of languages that includes French, Italian, Spanish, Portuguese, and Romanian. (Capitalized.) **5.** *tv.* to treat someone in a romantic way; to show someone love. **6.** the *adj.* use of ①, ②, ③, or ④. (Capitalized with ④.)

romantic [ro 'mæn tɪk] **1.** *adj.* full of love and adventure; of or about a love experience; of or about love. (Adv: *romantically* […ɪk li].) **2.** *adj.* causing romance; used to create a feeling of romance. (Adv: *romantically* […ɪk li].)

roof ['ruf, 'rʊf] **1.** *n.* the outside covering of the top of a building, vehicle, or other enclosed space. **2.** *n.* the top part of the inside of something, such as the mouth or a cave. **3.** *tv.* to put ① over something; to build ①.

room ['rum] **1.** *n.* a part of a building that is separated from other parts of the building by a wall with a door in it. **2.** *n.* space that is or could be taken up by someone or something.

roommate ['rum met] *n.* someone with whom one shares an apartment or room.

roomy ['rum i] *adj.* having plenty of room; having a lot of space; having a comfortable amount of space; not crowded. (Adv: *roomily*. Comp: *roomier*; sup: *roomiest*.)

roost ['rust] **1.** *n.* a place, such as a nest or branch, where birds rest or sleep. **2.** *iv.* to occupy ① for rest or sleep.

rooster ['rust ɚ] *n.* an adult male chicken.

root 1. ['rut, 'rʊt] *n.* the part of a plant that is under the ground, taking water from the soil and supporting the plant. **2.** ['rut, 'rʊt] *n.* the part of a strand of hair that is under the surface of the skin. (Fig. on ①.) **3.** ['rut, 'rʊt] *n.* the origin of something; the source of something; something that causes something else. **4.** ['rut, 'rʊt] *n.* the form of a word that other words are made from. **5.** ['rut, 'rʊt] *tv.* to cause a plant to grow. **6.** ['rut] *iv.* to cheer for someone; to provide encouragement for someone or a team, especially for someone or a team in a contest or sports event.

rope ['rop] **1.** *n.* a strong, thick cord made by twisting smaller cords together. (Pl only for types and instances.) **2.** *tv.* to catch someone or something by swinging a loop of ①.

rose ['roz] **1.** pt of RISE. **2.** *n.* a bright, sweet-smelling flower that grows on a plant having thorns. **3.** *n.* the bush that ② grows on.

412

rosy ['roz i] **1.** *adj.* pink; rose-colored. (Adv: *rosily.* Comp: *rosier;* sup: *rosiest.*) **2.** *adj.* full of hope; optimistic. (Adv: *rosily.* Comp: *rosier;* sup: *rosiest.*)

rot ['rɑt] **1.** *n.* decay; something that is rotten. (No pl.) **2.** *iv.* to decay; [for plant or animal material] to lose its form because of bacteria. **3.** *tv.* to cause something to decay.

rotate ['ro tet] **1.** *iv.* to move in a circle around a fixed point; to move around the center of something in a circle. **2.** *iv.* to go in sequence; to occur in order or in sequence. **3.** *tv.* to move something in a circle around a fixed point; to cause something to revolve; to move something around an axis.

rotten ['rɑt n] **1.** *adj.* decayed; spoiled. (Adv: *rottenly.*) **2.** *adj.* very bad; evil; nasty. (Adv: *rottenly.*)

rough ['rʌf] **1.** *adj.* not smooth; not even; having a surface that is uneven or bumpy. (Adv: *roughly.* Comp: *rougher;* sup: *roughest.*) **2.** *adj.* using force; harsh; violent. (Adv: *roughly.* Comp: *rougher;* sup: *roughest.*) **3.** *adj.* coarse; not delicate; not refined. (Adv: *roughly.* Comp: *rougher;* sup: *roughest.*) **4.** *adj.* hard; difficult; severe; not easy. (Comp: *rougher;* sup: *roughest.*) **5.** *adj.* not in final form; not finished; not exact; not detailed; approximate. (Adv: *roughly.* Comp: *rougher;* sup: *roughest.*)

round ['raʊnd] **1.** *adj.* shaped like a circle; circular; curved. (Adv: *roundly.* Comp: *rounder;* sup: *roundest.*) **2.** *adj.* shaped like a ball; spherical; curved. (Adv: *roundly.* Comp: *rounder;* sup: *roundest.*) **3.** *n.* the bullet or shell for a single shot from a gun. **4.** *n.* a song that people begin singing at different times so that the words and music of the different parts overlap. **5.** *prep.* AROUND. (Informal. ROUND can be used informally for any of the preposition senses listed under AROUND.) **6.** *adv.* AROUND. (Informal.)

route ['rut, 'raʊt] **1.** *n.* a road; a path; the way one travels; the way something is sent. **2.** *tv.* to send something by a particular ①.

routine [ru 'tin] **1.** *n.* a regular habit; something that is done regularly. (Pl only for types and instances.) **2.** *n.* a piece of entertainment; a skit; a sequence of actions in a performance. **3.** *adj.* normal; as a habit; as usually done. (Adv: *routinely.*)

row 1. ['ro] *n.* a series of people or things in a line; a line of people or things. **2.** ['ro] *n.* a line of seats in a theater, church, auditorium, classroom, or other place where people sit in a line. **3.** ['raʊ] *n.* a quarrel; an argument. **4.** ['ro] *iv.* to move through water in a boat by using oars. **5.** ['ro] *tv.* to move a boat by using oars.

413

rowboat ['ro bot] *n.* a small boat that is moved by using oars.

royal ['rɔɪ əl] **1.** *adj.* belonging to kings, queens, princes, princesses, etc.; of or about kings, queens, princes, princesses, etc. (Adv: *royally.*) **2.** *adj.* elegant; fit for royalty. (Fig. on ①. Adv: *royally.*)

royalty ['rɔɪ əl ti] **1.** *n.* the rank and power of kings, queens, princes, princesses, etc. (No pl.) **2.** *n.* people who have attained ①. (No pl.) **3.** *n.* money earned from the publication of a copyright holder's work.

rub ['rʌb] *tv.* to push or slide something against something else.

rubber ['rʌb ɚ] **1.** *n.* a waterproof material that goes back to its original shape when stretched or pressed. (No pl.) **2.** *adj.* made from ①.

rubbish ['rʌb ɪʃ] *n.* trash; garbage; things that are thrown away. (No pl.)

ruby ['rub i] **1.** *n.* a red gemstone. **2.** the *adj.* use of ①.

rudder ['rʌd ɚ] *n.* a blade (at the back of a ship or airplane) that can be moved back and forth to control direction.

rude ['rud] **1.** *adj.* not polite; not well mannered; not courteous. (Adv: *rudely.* Comp: *ruder;* sup: *rudest.*) **2.** *adj.* simple; not complex; primitive; coarse; rough; made without complex tools. (Adv: *rudely.* Comp: *ruder;* sup: *rudest.*)

rudeness ['rud nəs] *n.* not being polite; bad manners; bad behavior. (No pl.)

rug ['rʌg] *n.* a carpet; a thick piece of woven fabric that is used to cover a floor.

rugged ['rʌg əd] **1.** *adj.* [of a trail] rough and jagged. (Adv: *ruggedly.*) **2.** *adj.* [of something] strong and lasting a long time; [of something] not easily broken. (Adv: *ruggedly.*) **3.** *adj.* [of someone] sturdy and strong. (Adv: *ruggedly.*)

ruin ['ru ɪn] **1.** *tv.* to destroy someone or something completely; to make something worthless. **2.** *n.* the remaining part of an old building. (Often pl.) **3.** *n.* a great amount of destruction. (No pl.)

ruined ['ru ɪnd] *adj.* destroyed; completely damaged; made worthless.

rule ['rul] **1.** *n.* a statement that says what one is or is not allowed to do; a regulation. **2.** *n.* government; the control of someone in authority. (No pl.) **3.** *tv.* to decide something officially. (The object is a clause with THAT ⑦.) **4.** *tv.* to govern a country or its people.

ruler ['rul ɚ] **1.** *n.* someone who rules; someone, such as a king or queen, who runs a government. **2.** *n.* a straight strip of wood, plastic, metal, or other material that has marks on it that show measurement.

rumble ['rʌm bəl] **1.** *n.* a low vibrating sound, like the sound of thunder. **2.** *iv.* to make a low vibrating sound, like the sound of thunder.

rumor ['rum ɚ] *n.* news about someone or something that may or may not be true; information that is passed from person to person about someone and that may or may not be true.

rump ['rʌmp] **1.** *n.* the rear part of a person or an animal; the buttocks. **2.** *n.* meat from the rear part of an animal, used as food. (No pl. Number is expressed with *rump roast(s)*.)

run ['rʌn] **1.** *iv., irreg.* to move quickly in such a way that both feet are off the ground during each stride. (Pt: RAN; pp: run.) **2.** *iv., irreg.* to work; to be working; to function; to be in operation. **3.** *iv., irreg.* to extend to a certain length or distance; to reach a certain distance or time. **4.** *iv., irreg.* to flow; [for liquids] to move. **5.** *iv., irreg.* [for a liquid color] to spread, flow, or bleed. **6.** *iv., irreg.* to move quickly as a form of exercise or as a sport. **7.** *iv., irreg.* [for one's nose] to drip fluid. **8.** *tv., irreg.* to extend something to a certain length or distance; to cause something to reach a certain distance or time. **9.** *tv., irreg.* to control, own, or manage a business. **10.** *tv., irreg.* to publish something in a newspaper or magazine. **11.** *n.* an instance of RUNNING as in ①. **12.** *n.* a trip; a journey. **13.** ~ **for** to be a candidate for an office in an election. **14.** ~ **out** to leave something or a place, running. **15.** ~ **out** to use all of something and have none left.

run-down ['rʌn 'daʊn] **1.** *adj.* in poor health. **2.** *adj.* [of something] in bad condition owing to neglect.

rung ['rʌŋ] **1.** pp of RING. **2.** *n.* one of the poles or boards forming a step of a ladder.

running ['rʌn ɪŋ] **1.** *n.* the activity of someone who runs for sport, health, or pleasure. (No pl.) **2.** the *adj.* use of ①. **3.** *adj.* [of talk] continuous. (Fig. on ②.)

runny ['rʌn i] *adj.* [of eggs] not completely cooked and still somewhat liquid. (Comp: *runnier;* sup: *runniest.*)

run-of-the-mill [rən əv ðə 'mɪl] *adj.* average; ordinary; typical; normal; regular.

runway ['rʌn we] *n.* a landing strip for an airplane; a track that an airplane takes off from and lands on.

rural ['rɚ əl] *adj.* in the country; not like the city; not urban or suburban. (Adv: *rurally.*)

rush ['rʌʃ] **1.** *n.* hurry; haste; movement in a fast and urgent manner. (No pl.) **2.** *n.* a very sudden movement or flow.

rust ['rʌst] **1.** *n.* a dark red or dark orange layer that forms on iron or steel when it is exposed to air or water. (No pl.) **2.** *iv.* to acquire a coating of ①. **3.** *tv.* to cause something to be covered with ①.

rustle ['rʌs əl] **1.** *n.* a soft noise, like the sound that leaves make when they are blown by the wind or the sound made when objects are rubbed together. (No pl.) **2.** *iv.* [for objects] to make a soft noise when rubbed together or blown by the wind. **3.** *tv.* to cause objects to make a noise as in ②. **4.** *tv.* to steal cattle.

rusty ['rʌs ti] **1.** *adj.* covered with rust; rusted. (Adv: *rustily.* Comp: *rustier;* sup: *rustiest.*) **2.** *adj.* [of a skill or knowledge] poor or lacking because it has been unused for so long a time. (Adv: *rustily.* Comp: *rustier;* sup: *rustiest.*)

rut ['rʌt] *n.* a deep track that a wheel makes in soft ground; a groove.

ruthless ['ruθ ləs] *adj.* without pity; without mercy; cruel; evil. (Adv: *ruthlessly.*)

rye ['rɑɪ] **1.** *n.* a tall grass that is farmed for its light brown grain. (No pl.) **2.** *n.* grain from ①. (No pl. Number is expressed with *grain(s) of rye.*) **3.** *adj.* made from ②.

S

sack ['sæk] **1.** *n.* a bag or pouch made of paper, cloth, etc. **2.** *n.* the contents of ①.

sacred ['se krɪd] *adj.* holy; blessed. (Adv: *sacredly.*)

sacrifice ['sæ krə faɪs] **1.** *n.* giving up something; not having something that is wanted or needed. (Pl only for types and instances.) **2.** *n.* something that is offered to a god or spirit. **3.** *tv.* to take the life of a creature as in ②. **4.** *tv.* to give up something of value [for someone else's benefit].

sad ['sæd] **1.** *adj.* not happy; feeling sorrow. (Adv: *sadly.* Comp: *sadder*; sup: *saddest.*) **2.** *adj.* unfortunate; [of something] not bringing pleasure. (Adv: *sadly.* Comp: *sadder*; sup: *saddest.*)

sadden ['sæd n] **1.** *iv.* to become sad. **2.** *tv.* to cause someone to become sad.

saddle ['sæd l] **1.** *n.* a leather seat that fits on the back of a horse or other animal that carries people. **2.** *n.* a bicycle or motorcycle seat. **3.** *tv.* to place ① on a horse or a similar animal.

sadness ['sæd nəs] *n.* sorrow; having feelings of gloom or depression; a lack of happiness. (No pl.)

safe ['sef] **1.** *n.* a solid, sturdy, steel or iron box—with a strong lock—that money, jewelry, papers, or other valuable objects are kept in for protection. **2.** *adj.* not dangerous; not risky; not causing or creating danger. (Adv: *safely.* Comp: *safer*; sup: *safest.*) **3.** *adj.* protected; secure. (Adv: *safely.* Comp: *safer*; sup: *safest.*)

safeguard ['sef gɑrd] **1.** *n.* something that protects someone or something from danger. **2.** *tv.* to protect someone or something from danger; to keep someone or something safe.

safekeeping ['sef 'kip ɪŋ] *n.* keeping someone or something safe; a place or state where something is safe. (No pl.)

safety ['sef ti] **1.** *n.* the state of being safe; freedom from harm or danger. (No pl.) **2.** *the adj.* use of ①.

sag ['sæg] *iv.* to bend, hang, or curve downward.

said ['sɛd] pt/pp of SAY.

417

sail ['sel] **1.** *n.* a sheet of cloth that is stretched on a mast of a ship to catch the energy of the wind. **2.** *iv.* to travel by boat or ship on the water. **3.** *iv.* [for a ship or boat] to travel on the water. **4.** *iv.* to glide through the air the way a boat moves through water. **5.** *tv.* to steer a boat or ship on the water. **6.** *tv.* to cause something to glide through the air.

sailboat ['sel bot] *n.* a boat that has at least one sail and that moves by the power of the wind.

sailor ['se lɚ] **1.** *n.* someone who works on a boat or a ship. **2.** *n.* someone who is in the navy.

sake ['sek] *n.* [someone's] benefit, demands, or welfare.

salad ['sæl əd] *n.* a dish of mixed vegetables, especially lettuce, or other food mixed with vegetables, usually with a sauce called *salad dressing.*

salary ['sæl (ə) ri] *n.* the amount of money that someone is paid for working. (Compare to WAGE.)

sale ['sel] **1.** *n.* the exchange of a product or service for money; an act of selling. **2.** *n.* a special event where products or services are sold for less money than normal.

sales *n.* the amount of products or services sold during a certain period of time. (Treated as pl, but not countable.)

salesclerk ['selz klɚk] *n.* someone who works in a store, helping customers and selling products.

salesman ['selz mən] *n., irreg.* someone whose job is selling things; a man whose job is selling things. (Pl: SALESMEN.)

salesmen ['selz mən] pl of SALESMAN.

salespeople ['selz pi pəl] a pl of SALESPERSON.

salesperson ['selz pɚ sən] *n., irreg.* someone whose job is selling things. (Pl: SALESPEOPLE or *salespersons.*)

saleswoman ['selz wʊ mən] *n., irreg.* a woman whose job is selling things. (Pl: SALESWOMEN.)

saleswomen ['selz wɪ mən] pl of SALESWOMAN.

salmon ['sæm ən] **1.** *n., irreg.* a large food fish with soft, pale pink flesh. (Pl: *salmon.*) **2.** *n.* the meat of ①. (No pl.)

salt ['sɔlt] **1.** *n.* a white substance used to season or preserve food and to melt snow and ice. (No pl.) **2.** *n.* a chemical substance made by combining an acid with a metal. (Pl only for types and instances.)

3. *tv.* to season something by putting ① on it. **4.** *tv.* to cover something with ①.

salted [ˈsɔl tɪd] *adj.* [of food] having salt added.

salty [ˈsɔl ti] *adj.* tasting like salt; having salt. (Adv: *saltily.* Comp: *saltier;* sup: *saltiest.*)

salute [sə ˈlut] **1.** *tv.* to show respect for someone by bringing the right hand to one's head. **2.** *n.* an act of moving the hand to the head as in ①.

same [ˈsem] **1.** *adj.* not different; being the identical person or thing. **2.** *adj.* being exactly like someone or something else; not different from someone or something else; alike.

sameness [ˈsem nəs] *n.* the quality of being the same; the degree of being very similar to someone or something. (No pl.)

sample [ˈsæm pəl] **1.** *n.* a small portion of something that shows what the rest of it is like. **2.** *tv.* to take, try, or taste a small portion of something.

sanctuary [ˈsæŋk tʃu ɛr i] **1.** *n.* a sacred or holy building; a holy place of worship. **2.** *n.* a place of safety or preservation, especially for birds and other wild animals.

sand [ˈsænd] **1.** *n.* very tiny particles of rock or seashells, such as are found on beaches and in deserts. (Pl only for types and instances.) **2.** *tv.* to rub something with sandpaper to make it smooth; to smooth something with sandpaper. **3.** *tv.* to put or sprinkle ① on a surface, such as an icy street.

sandpaper [ˈsænd pe pɚ] *n.* a paper lightly coated with sand particles, used to polish or smooth a surface. (Pl only for types and instances.)

sandwich [ˈsænd wɪtʃ] **1.** *n.* two pieces of bread with some kind of food in between. **2.** *tv.* to put someone or something tightly between or among other persons or objects.

sane [ˈsen] **1.** *adj.* having a healthy mind; not crazy. (Adv: *sanely.* Comp: *saner;* sup: *sanest.*) **2.** *adj.* rational; sensible; having or showing common sense. (Adv: *sanely.* Comp: *saner;* sup: *sanest.*)

sang [ˈsæŋ] pt of SING.

sanitary [ˈsæn ə tɛr i] **1.** *adj.* very clean; not dangerous to one's health. (Adv: *sanitarily.*) **2.** *adj.* used for the disposal of waste that is harmful to health.

419

sanitation [sæn ə 'te ʃən] *n.* the study and practice of preserving the health of the public, especially concerning the removal of waste. (No pl.)

sanity ['sæn ə ti] *n.* sound mental health. (No pl.)

sank ['sæŋk] a pt of SINK.

sap ['sæp] **1.** *n.* a fluid in a tree that carries important nutrients to its parts. (No pl.) **2.** *tv.* to take away someone's or something's strength or energy.

sarcasm ['sɑr kæz əm] *n.* the use of words that have the opposite meaning from what is said. (No pl.)

sarcastic [sɑr 'kæs tɪk] *adj.* using sarcasm; using irony; mocking. (Adv: *sarcastically* [...ɪk li].)

sardine [sɑr 'din] *n.* a small, edible fish, usually sold in flat cans.

sat ['sæt] pt/pp of SIT.

Satan ['set n] *n.* the devil.

satellite ['sæt ə laɪt] **1.** *n.* a natural body of rock and minerals that orbits around a planet; a moon. **2.** *n.* a spacecraft that orbits a planet. **3.** *adj.* dependent on something else that has more power.

satin ['sæt n] **1.** *n.* a soft, silky, smooth cloth that is shiny on one side. (Pl only for types and instances.) **2.** *adj.* made from ①.

satisfaction [sæt ɪs 'fæk ʃən] *n.* a feeling that one is content; fulfillment. (Pl only for types and instances.)

satisfactory [sæt ɪs 'fæk tə ri] *adj.* adequate; meeting certain needs or requirements. (Adv: *satisfactorily*.)

satisfy ['sæt ɪs faɪ] **1.** *tv.* to make someone content; to please someone; to make someone happy with something. **2.** *tv.* to meet or fulfill certain needs or requirements.

Saturday ['sæt ə de] Go to DAY.

sauce ['sɔs] *n.* a liquid that is put on food to add flavor. (Pl only for types and instances.)

saucepan ['sɔs pæn] *n.* a round metal pan with a handle, used for cooking and boiling food.

saucer ['sɔ sə] *n.* a small dish that cups are set on.

sausage ['sɔ sɪdʒ] **1.** *n.* a food made of chopped meat mixed with spices (in the United States). (No pl.) **2.** *n.* a food made of ① stuffed into a thin tube of animal intestine or artificial material and made into segments. **3.** *adj.* made with ①.

savage ['sæv ɪdʒ] **1.** *adj.* wild; not tamed; not civilized; primitive. (Adv: *savagely.*) **2.** *adj.* fierce; ready to fight; violent; vicious. (Adv: *savagely.*) **3.** *n.* someone who is wild, not tamed, and not civilized.

save ['sev] **1.** *tv.* to make someone or something safe from harm or danger; to rescue someone or something. **2.** *tv.* to keep a supply of something, especially money, for future use; to place something aside, especially money, for future use. **3.** *tv.* not to spend something; not to use something; to reserve something. **4.** *tv.* to cause something to be unnecessary (for someone); to prevent the need (for someone) to do something.

savings ['sev ɪŋz] *n.* money that is saved for future use; money that is set aside, especially in a bank account, for future use. (Treated as pl, but not countable.)

saw ['sɔ] **1.** pt of SEE. **2.** *n.* a cutting tool with a thin blade that is notched with tiny, sharp teeth. **3.** *iv., irreg.* to cut with ②. (Pt: *sawed;* pp: *sawed* or SAWN.) **4.** *tv., irreg.* to cut something with ②.

sawdust ['sɔ dəst] *n.* tiny flakes of wood that are made when wood is sawed. (No pl form in this sense.)

sawn ['sɔn] a pp of SAW.

say ['se] **1.** *tv., irreg.* to pronounce words; to speak words. (Pt/pp: SAID.) **2.** *tv., irreg.* to state something; to declare something; to express something in words. (The object can be a clause with THAT ⑦.) **3.** *n.* a role of authority or influence [in making a decision]. (No pl.)

scale ['skel] **1.** *n.* a series of numbers at different levels, used for measuring something. **2.** *n.* the relation between a measurement on a map or design compared to the actual measurement it corresponds to. **3.** *n.* a series of musical notes, from low notes to high notes or from high notes to low notes. **4.** *n.* the size or extent of something, especially as compared to something else or an average. (No pl.) **5.** *n.* a device that measures how much something weighs. (Sg or pl with the same meaning.) **6.** *n.* one of the small, thin pieces of hardened skin on the bodies of most fish and snakes. **7.** *n.* a flake of something, especially dead skin. **8.** *tv.* to climb something. **9.** *tv.* to remove ⑥ from a fish.

scalp ['skælp] *n.* the skin and any hair growing on it on the top and back of the head.

scan ['skæn] **1.** *tv.* to examine something closely and carefully, as though one were searching for something. **2.** *tv.* to look through something quickly and carelessly; to glance at something; to read through something quickly. **3.** *tv.* to put a picture or a text into a computer file by placing the picture or book on a scanner.

scandal ['skæn dəl] *n.* an event that causes disgrace; an instance of actions that are not legal, moral, or ethical and that become known by other people.

scanner ['skæn ɚ] *n.* a machine that converts a page of a book or a picture to an image that can be stored, viewed, or changed on a computer.

scant ['skænt] *adj.* not enough of something. (Adv: *scantly*. Comp: *scanter;* sup: *scantest*.)

scanty ['skæn ti] *adj.* not sufficient; falling short of an amount that is needed. (Adv: *scantily*. Comp: *scantier;* sup: *scantiest*.)

scapegoat ['skep got] **1.** *n.* someone who is blamed for the mistakes of others; someone who takes the blame for the mistakes of others. **2.** *tv.* to blame someone for the mistakes of others.

scar ['skɑr] **1.** *n.* a mark that is left on the surface of something, such as skin, that has been torn, cut, burned, or otherwise damaged. **2.** *tv.* to cause someone or something to have ①.

scarce ['skɛrs] *adj.* rare; hard to find. (Adv: *scarcely*. Comp: *scarcer;* sup: *scarcest*.)

scarcely ['skɛrs li] *adv.* hardly; barely; just almost. (Not used with other negative adverbs.)

scarcity ['skɛr sɪ ti] *n.* a lack; a very small supply.

scare ['skɛr] **1.** *tv.* to cause someone to feel fear or fright; to cause someone to be afraid. **2.** *n.* a bad fright; an instance of being afraid; a feeling of fear.

scared ['skɛrd] *adj.* feeling fright; filled with fear.

scarf ['skɑrf] *n., irreg.* a long strip of cloth that is wrapped around the neck or face for decoration or to keep warm when it is cold. (Pl: SCARVES.)

scarlet ['skɑr lɪt] **1.** *n.* a bright red color. (No pl form in this sense.) **2.** *adj.* bright red in color.

scarves ['skɑrvz] pl of SCARF.

scary ['skɛr i] *adj.* causing fear; filling one with fear; causing one to be afraid. (Adv: *scarily*. Comp: *scarier;* sup: *scariest*.)

scatter ['skæt ɚ] **1.** *tv.* to cause each person or thing in a group to move in a different direction. **2.** *tv.* to spread things—such as seeds,

422

papers, ashes, etc.—over a wide area by throwing them. **3.** *iv.* [for each person or thing in a group] to move in a different direction.

scene ['sin] **1.** *n.* all that can be seen from one place. **2.** *n.* the place where something happens; a setting. **3.** *n.* a division of an act of a play; an incident in a movie or play. **4.** *n.* a display of emotion or action, especially an angry or violent action.

scenery ['sin (ə) ri] **1.** *n.* the natural surroundings—trees, mountains, valleys—of an area. (No pl.) **2.** *n.* the things that are built or bought and put on a stage to represent the place where the action of a play takes place. (No pl.)

scent ['sɛnt] **1.** *n.* a smell; an aroma; an odor; the way someone or something smells. **2.** *tv.* to sense the smell of someone or something.

schedule ['skɛ dʒəl] **1.** *n.* a list showing the times that events are supposed to happen. **2.** *tv.* to put someone or something on ①.

scheme ['skim] **1.** *n.* a plan; a method for doing something; a way of doing something, possibly dishonestly. **2.** *iv.* to plot; to make plans, especially dishonest ones.

scholar ['skɑl ɚ] **1.** *n.* someone who studies a subject thoroughly. **2.** *n.* a student; a pupil. **3.** *n.* someone who has a scholarship.

scholarly ['skɑl ɚ li] **1.** *adj.* concerning scholarship and schoolwork. **2.** *adj.* having a lot of knowledge about a certain subject.

scholarship ['skɑl ɚ ʃɪp] **1.** *n.* knowledge that a person receives by studying; evidence of one's knowledge. (No pl.) **2.** *n.* a sum of money given by an organization to a student for school fees or other expenses related to studying.

school ['skul] **1.** *n.* a building for education and instruction. **2.** *n.* all the people who work at or attend ①; all the people who teach or study at ①. **3.** *n.* a group of fish that swim together. **4.** *n.* the education system; participation in the education system. (No pl.)

schoolchild ['skul tʃɑɪld] *n., irreg.* a child of school age, especially a child in grades kindergarten through eighth grade; a child who attends school. (Pl: SCHOOLCHILDREN.)

schoolchildren ['skul tʃɪl drɪn] pl of SCHOOLCHILD.

schoolroom ['skul rum] *n.* a room in a school building, especially one where students are taught.

schoolteacher ['skul titʃ ɚ] *n.* someone who teaches in a school.

schoolwork ['skul wɚk] *n.* work that a student must do for a class; the assigned projects that a student must do. (No pl. See also HOME-WORK.)

science ['saɪ əns] **1.** *n.* a system of knowledge obtained by testing and proving facts that describe the way something acts, functions, or exists. (No pl.) **2.** *n.* a kind of study that results in a system of knowl-edge obtained by testing and proving facts that describe the way something acts, functions, or exists.

scientific [saɪ ən 'tɪf ɪk] **1.** *adj.* using the laws or facts of a science. (Adv: *scientifically* [...ɪk li].) **2.** *adj.* of or about science. (Adv: *scien-tifically* [...ɪk li].)

scientist ['saɪ ən tɪst] *n.* someone who is skilled in a science; some-one who works in a science.

scissors ['sɪz ɚz] *n.* a set of two sharp blades that have handles on one end and are connected in the middle. (Treated as sg or pl. Number is expressed with *pair(s) of scissors*.)

scold ['skold] **1.** *tv.* to speak angrily to someone who has done some-thing wrong. **2.** *n.* someone who speaks as in ①.

scolding ['skol dɪŋ] *n.* speaking angrily to someone as punishment.

scoop ['skup] **1.** *n.* a shovellike utensil or tool. **2.** *n.* the contents of ①.

scope ['skop] *n.* the range of something; the limit of something; the extent of something. (No pl.)

scorch ['skortʃ] **1.** *tv.* to burn something so that burn marks are made but the object is not destroyed. **2.** *iv.* to be burned as in ①.

score ['skor] **1.** *n.* the number of points that a person or team has received in a game or contest; the number of points that a person has received on a test. **2.** *n.* a written piece of music for instruments or voices. **3.** *n.* a group of twenty things. **4.** *tv.* to earn one or more points in a game or contest. **5.** *tv.* to cut lines or grooves into a sur-face; to cut a surface with a series of lines. **6.** *tv.* to earn a certain number of points on a test. **7.** *iv.* to achieve [a level of performance in academic grades]. **8.** *iv.* to earn [a point in a game or contest].

scoundrel ['skaʊn drəl] *n.* a rascal; a villain; someone who is wicked or dishonest.

scowl ['skaʊl] **1.** *n.* a frown; an angry look. **2.** *iv.* to look angry; to frown.

424

scrap ['skræp] **1.** *n.* a small piece of something, especially a small piece of something that is left over from a larger piece, especially of food or cloth. **2.** *n.* material, such as metal, that can be reused. (No pl.) **3.** *tv.* to throw something away that is no longer wanted, needed, or able to be used.

scrape ['skrep] **1.** *tv.* to damage something by rubbing a sharp or rough object against it. **2.** *tv.* to remove something by rubbing with a sharp or rough object. **3.** *iv.* to rub with force against something else. **4.** *n.* damage or injury to an object or the skin caused by rubbing something sharp or rough against it. **5.** *n.* the sound that is made when a rough object rubs hard against something else.

scratch ['skrætʃ] **1.** *tv.* to damage an object's surface by causing a sharp object to make a cut or tear in it; to make a cut or tear in the surface of something with a sharp object. **2.** *tv.* to remove something from the surface of something using a sharp object to cut or tear into it. **3.** *tv.* to rub a location of the body that itches with one's fingers, fingernails, or a sharp object. **4.** *iv.* to rub [a part of the body that itches]. **5.** *n.* a cut, tear, or damage as caused by ①.

scrawl ['skrɔl] **1.** *n.* bad handwriting; writing that is hard to read because it is messy. **2.** *tv.* to write something in a messy way; to write something using bad handwriting. **3.** *iv.* to write in a messy way; to write using bad handwriting.

scream ['skrim] **1.** *iv.* [for someone] to make a very loud noise, especially when hurt, afraid, excited, surprised, or filled with emotion. **2.** *iv.* to speak very loudly; to talk in a very loud voice. **3.** *tv.* to say something in a very loud voice. (The object can be a clause with THAT ⑦.) **4.** *n.* a very loud noise, especially made by someone who is hurt, afraid, excited, surprised, or filled with emotion.

screech ['skritʃ] **1.** *n.* a shrill, high-pitched scream; a shrill, high-pitched noise made by a machine or when something rubs against something else. **2.** *iv.* to make a shrill, high-pitched noise as in ①. **3.** *tv.* to say something in a shrill, high-pitched voice.

screen ['skrin] **1.** *n.* a mesh made of thin wires crossing each other. **2.** *n.* a piece of cloth stretched over a frame, used to block, protect, or separate someone or something from someone or something else. **3.** *n.* a large white surface that movies are projected onto. **4.** *n.* the glass part of a television set or computer monitor on which images are seen. **5.** *tv.* to determine if someone will be allowed to speak or meet with someone else. **6.** *tv.* to show a movie; to make a movie available to the public.

screw ['skru] **1.** *n.* a piece of metal, similar to a nail, having a sharp RIDGE ② wrapped around its shaft. (A screw has a flat or rounded head that has a single groove or two crossed grooves.) **2.** *tv.* to fasten something to something else with ①. **3.** *tv.* to twist ① into wood or metal with a screwdriver. **4.** *tv.* to turn the lid, cap, or top of a container to close it tightly.

screwdriver ['skru draɪ vɚ] *n.* a common tool used to tighten and loosen screws.

scribble ['skrɪb əl] **1.** *tv.* to draw or write something quickly or in a messy way, especially so that it is hard to recognize or read. (The object can be a clause with THAT ⑦.) **2.** *iv.* to draw or write quickly or in a messy way so that the result is hard to recognize or read. **3.** *n.* marks or words that are hard to recognize or read because they were drawn or written quickly or in a messy way.

script ['skrɪpt] **1.** *n.* a document containing the words of a play, movie, or speech. **2.** *n.* a way of writing in which the letters of a word are joined together.

scripture ['skrɪp tʃɚ] *n.* holy writings; one or more holy writings. (Pl only for types and instances. Sg or pl with the same meaning.)

scrub ['skrʌb] **1.** *tv.* to clean or wash the surface of someone or something by rubbing. **2.** *tv.* to remove something from something by rubbing. **3.** *iv.* to clean or wash [oneself] by rubbing, usually with a stiff brush, cloth, or sponge. **4.** *n.* an area of small trees and low bushes; a collection of small trees and bushes. (No pl.)

scrutinize ['skrut n aɪz] *tv.* to examine someone or something closely; to look at something very closely; to inspect someone or something.

scrutiny ['skrut n i] *n.* a close examination; an inspection; looking at something closely. (No pl.)

scuba ['sku bə] **1.** *iv.* to dive and explore underwater. (Pt/pp: *scubaed*.) **2.** the *adj.* use of ①.

scuff ['skʌf] **1.** *tv.* to make scratches in the surface of something clean and smooth; to make marks on the surface of something clean and smooth. **2.** *iv.* to walk somewhere without picking up one's feet; to slide one's feet along as one walks.

sculptor ['skʌlp tɚ] *n.* an artist who makes art out of clay, stone, metal, or other solid materials.

sculpture ['skʌlp tʃɚ] **1.** *n.* the art of making art from clay, stone, metal, or another solid material. (No pl.) **2.** *n.* a piece of art that is

426

made out of clay, stone, metal, or another solid material. (Often sg with a pl meaning.)

sea ['si] **1.** *n.* a large body of salt water that is smaller than an ocean. **2.** *n.* one of the large bodies of salt water that cover almost three-fourths of the earth's surface; an ocean.

seafood ['si fud] *n.* animals from the sea, including fish, shellfish, and octopus, that are eaten as food. (No pl.)

seal ['sil] **1.** *n.* a large animal that has thick, coarse fur, lives in and near the sea, and has flat legs. **2.** *n.* an official mark or design of a government, business, organization, or person that is printed or stamped on objects for identification. (A signature usually serves as a seal for an individual.) **3.** *n.* a piece of wax, metal, or other material that has the mark or design of a government, business, organization, or person printed or stamped on it. **4.** *n.* something that causes an opening in an object to remain closed; something that prevents an opening from being opened secretly. **5.** *tv.* to close something tightly; to fasten something tightly, often with glue or pressure. **6.** *tv.* to fill cracks in an object with a substance so that air, water, or other things cannot pass through the cracks.

seam ['sim] **1.** *n.* the line of thread where two pieces of cloth have been sewn together. **2.** *n.* the line where two edges of anything meet.

search ['sɚtʃ] **1.** *iv.* to look carefully, trying to find someone or something. **2.** *tv.* to examine someone or something closely to try to find something. **3.** *n.* an attempt to find someone or something.

seashell ['si ʃɛl] *n.* a shell of an animal that lives in the sea; a hard, protective covering made by an animal that lives in the sea, such as an oyster.

seashore ['si ʃor] *n.* the land that borders the sea; the shore that runs along a sea.

seasick ['si sɪk] *adj.* being sick while on a boat or a ship because of the movement of the sea.

seaside ['si saɪd] **1.** *n.* the land that borders a sea; the seashore. (No pl.) **2.** *adj.* located on the seashore; at the side of the sea.

season ['siz ən] **1.** *n.* one of the four times of the year: winter, spring, summer, and fall. **2.** *n.* a period of time marked by a certain kind of weather, an activity, or condition. **3.** *tv.* to add spices to food to make it taste better or different.

seasonal ['siz ə nəl] the *adj.* form of SEASON ②. (Adv: *seasonally*.)

427

seasoning ['siz (ə) nıŋ] *n.* a spice; an herb; something that is added to food to make it taste better or different.

seat ['sit] **1.** *n.* something that is used for sitting on; a place where someone can sit. **2.** *n.* the part of a pair of pants that one sits on. **3.** *n.* the part of the body that one sits on; the behind; the buttocks. **4.** *n.* a place where someone is a member, such as in Congress or on a stock exchange. **5.** *tv.* to provide someone with ①; to lead someone to ①; to help someone sit down. **6.** *tv.* to have a certain number of places to sit; to have room for a certain number of seated people.

seated ['sit ɪd] *adj.* sitting down in or on something.

seating ['sit ɪŋ] **1.** *n.* a particular arrangement of seats. (No pl.) **2.** *n.* the number of seats that are available in a place. (No pl.)

seawater ['si wɔt ɚ] *n.* salt water as found in the sea.

seaweed ['si wid] *n.* a plant that grows in or at the edge of the sea. (Pl only for types and instances.)

seclude [sɪ 'klud] *tv.* to keep someone away from other people; to keep something away from other things or places.

secluded [sɪ 'klud ɪd] *adj.* private; remote; set apart from other places; kept away from other places or people. (Adv: *secludedly.*)

seclusion [sɪ 'klu ʒən] *n.* the condition of being private and hidden; a place away from other people. (No pl.)

second ['sɛk ənd] **1.** *n.* a basic unit of the measurement of time; ¹⁄₆₀ of a minute; ¹⁄₃,₆₀₀ of an hour. **2.** *n.* a moment; a very short period of time. **3.** *n.* a unit of measurement of an angle equal to ¹⁄₆₀ of a minute or ¹⁄₃,₆₀₀ of a degree. **4.** *n.* someone or something that comes after the first [one] as in ⑤. **5.** *adj.* coming, happening, or being immediately after the first. (Adv: *secondly.*) **6.** *adv.* in a position that is immediately after the first position.

secondary ['sɛk ən der i] **1.** *adj.* second in importance; not primary. (Adv: *secondarily.*) **2.** *adj.* [of the education of students] from the 6th to 12th or from the 9th to 12th grades, depending on the school district.

secondhand ['sɛk ənd 'hænd] **1.** *adj.* [of goods] already used by someone else; not new. **2.** *adj.* [of stores] selling used products. **3.** *adj.* not experienced directly but heard from another person. **4.** *adv.* learned from someone else.

second-rate *adj.* not of the best quality; inferior.

seconds *n.* an additional serving of food. (Treated as pl.)

secrecy ['si krı si] *n.* the quality of being secret; keeping something a secret. (No pl.)

secret ['si krıt] **1.** *n.* information known by a small number of people, especially people who have promised not to tell anyone else. **2.** *n.* a mystery; something that cannot be explained. **3.** *adj.* known only by a small number of people who have promised not to tell anyone else. (Adv: *secretly.*) **4.** *adj.* working at a job without others knowing what one does; doing something without others knowing what one is doing. (Adv: *secretly.*)

secretary ['sɛk rı tɛr i] **1.** *n.* someone who is employed to type letters, answer telephones, organize schedules and meetings, and do other office work. **2.** *n.* someone who keeps a written record of the things that are discussed at the official meetings of an organization. **3.** *n.* someone who is in charge of a department of the United States government. **4.** *n.* a writing desk with drawers and shelves.

secrete [sı 'krit] **1.** *tv.* [for a part of a plant or an animal] to produce and release a fluid. **2.** *tv.* to hide something; to put something in a place where others cannot see it or find it.

secretion [sı 'kri ʃən] *n.* a fluid that is produced and released by a part of a plant or an animal, such as sap or mucus. (Sg or pl with the same meaning, but not countable.)

secretive ['si krə tıv] *adj.* tending to do things secretly; tending not to do things publicly or openly. (Adv: *secretively.*)

secretly ['si krət li] *adv.* without being known or seen by others.

section ['sɛk ʃən] **1.** *n.* a separate part of a larger group, place, or thing; a division. **2.** *n.* a unit of measurement of land equal to one square mile or 640 acres. **3.** *tv.* to divide something into separate parts as in ①.

secure [sı 'kjʊr] **1.** *adj.* safe from danger, harm, loss, injury, or theft. (Adv: *securely.*) **2.** *tv.* to safely fasten or close something. **3.** *tv.* to obtain something.

security [sı 'kjʊr ə ti] **1.** *n.* the state of being or feeling safe from danger, harm, loss, injury, or theft. (No pl.) **2.** *n.* an office or department concerned with the protection of people and property. (No pl.) **3.** *n.* property that is promised to a bank or lender when money is borrowed. (If the money is not paid back, then the bank or lender will be given the property. No pl.) **4.** *n.* a monetary asset or debt agreement, such as a stock or a bond. **5.** the *adj.* use of ①, ②, ③, or ④.

sedan [sɪ 'dæn] *n.* a car with four doors, a front seat and a backseat, a fixed roof, and room for at least four people.

sedate [sɪ 'det] **1.** *adj.* quiet; calm; relaxed; not excited; not moved by excitement. (Adv: *sedately*.) **2.** *tv.* to give someone or an animal a drug that causes relaxation.

sedative ['sɛd ə tɪv] **1.** *n.* a drug or medicine that causes one to sleep or relax. **2.** the *adj.* use of ①.

sedentary ['sɛd n̩ tɛr i] **1.** *adj.* [of a creature] not very active and keeping still most of the time. (Adv: *sedentarily* [sɛd n̩ 'tɛr ə li].) **2.** *adj.* [of activity] not requiring a lot of movement. (Adv: *sedentarily* [sɛd n̩ 'tɛr ə li].)

see ['si] **1.** *iv., irreg.* to sense or experience with the eyes. (Pt: SAW; pp: SEEN.) **2.** *tv., irreg.* to observe someone or something by the use of the eyes; to sense or experience someone or something with the eyes. **3.** *tv., irreg.* to understand something; to comprehend something. (The object can be a clause with THAT ⑦.) **4.** *tv., irreg.* to learn something by reading or through direct observation. (The object can be a clause with THAT ⑦.) **5.** *tv., irreg.* to visit someone; to stop by the place where someone lives. **6.** *tv., irreg.* to meet with someone for an appointment. **7.** *tv., irreg.* to date someone; to have a romantic relationship with someone.

seed ['sid] **1.** *n.* a part of a plant that a new plant will grow from if it is fertilized. **2.** *tv.* to plant crops on an area of land by scattering ①.

seedling ['sid lɪŋ] *n.* a young plant or tree that is newly grown from a seed.

seedy ['si di] **1.** *adj.* having a lot of seeds. (Comp: *seedier*; sup: *seediest*.) **2.** *adj.* run-down; shabby. (Adv: *seedily.* Comp: *seedier*; sup: *seediest*.)

seek ['sik] *tv., irreg.* to try to find someone or something; to look for someone or something. (Pt/pp: SOUGHT.)

seem ['sim] *iv.* to appear to be a certain way; to give the impression of being a certain way.

seen ['sin] pp of SEE.

seep ['sip] *iv.* [for a liquid] to pass through something slowly; to leak.

segment ['sɛg mənt] **1.** *n.* a part of something; a part of something that can be easily separated. **2.** *tv.* to separate something into parts; to divide something into parts.

segregate [ˈsɛ grɪ get] **1.** *tv.* to separate someone or a group of people from other people; to isolate someone or a group of people. **2.** *tv.* to separate people of one race from people of another race.

segregated [ˈsɛ grɪ get ɪd] *adj.* [of human races] separated by law or other forces. (Adv: *segregatedly.*)

segregation [sɛ grɪ ˈge ʃən] **1.** *n.* the state existing in a segregated society; the state of races being separated by law or other causes. (No pl.) **2.** *n.* the separation of someone or something from other people or things. (No pl.)

seize [ˈsiz] **1.** *tv.* to grab, take, and hold on to someone or something. **2.** *tv.* to take control of something by force or by authority; to capture something by force or by authority.

seizure [ˈsi ʒɚ] **1.** *n.* an act of seizing someone or something. **2.** *n.* a sudden attack of a sickness; a convulsion caused by a sudden attack of a sickness.

seldom [ˈsɛl dəm] *adv.* almost never; rarely.

select [sə ˈlɛkt] **1.** *tv.* to pick someone or something from a group of choices. **2.** *adj.* specifically chosen; exclusive; specially chosen. (Adv: *selectly.*)

selection [sə ˈlɛk ʃən] **1.** *n.* a choice; someone or something that is chosen; someone or something that is selected. **2.** *n.* a variety of things to choose from, especially in a store.

selective [sə ˈlɛk tɪv] *adj.* choosing carefully; making careful choices. (Adv: *selectively.*)

self [ˈsɛlf] *n.* a reference to a person as an individual or being. (Usually in compounds. See also MYSELF, YOURSELF, HERSELF, HIMSELF, ITSELF, ONESELF, OURSELVES, YOURSELVES, THEMSELVES. No pl.)

self-addressed [ˈsɛlf ə ˈdrɛst] *adj.* addressed to oneself.

self-centered [ˈsɛlf ˈsɛn tɚd] *adj.* selfish; often thinking only of oneself instead of anyone else. (Adv: *self-centeredly.*)

self-confidence [sɛlf ˈkɑn fɪ dəns] *n.* the belief that one is able to do something; confidence in one's own ability. (No pl.)

self-conscious [sɛlf ˈkɑn ʃəs] *adj.* aware that one is being seen by other people, especially when one is shy or embarrassed around other people. (Adv: *self-consciously.*)

self-contained [sɛlf kən ˈtend] *adj.* containing within itself everything that is necessary.

431

self-control [sɛlf kən 'trol] *n.* the control of one's own actions or feelings. (No pl.)

self-discipline ['sɛlf 'dɪs ə plɪn] *n.* the discipline needed to control one's feelings and actions. (No pl.)

self-employed [self ɛm 'plɔɪd] *adj.* working for one's own business; not working for other people.

self-esteem [sɛlf ə 'stim] *n.* the good opinion one has of oneself; the respect one shows for oneself. (No pl.)

self-help ['sɛlf 'hɛlp] **1.** *n.* helping oneself without the help of others. (No pl.) **2.** *adj.* [of books or techniques] showing people how to help themselves without the help of others.

selfish ['sɛl fɪʃ] *adj.* too concerned with oneself; too concerned with what one wants instead of what other people want; showing more care for oneself than for other people. (Adv: *selfishly.*)

selfishness ['sɛl fɪʃ nəs] *n.* the state of being too greedy and concerned with oneself. (No pl.)

self-reliant [sɛlf rɪ 'lɑɪ ənt] *adj.* able to get along or do something without the help of others. (Adv: *self-reliantly.*)

self-respect [sɛlf rɪ 'spɛkt] *n.* the respect and pride one has for oneself. (No pl.)

self-service ['sɛlf 'sɚ vɪs] **1.** *n.* the system by which one must serve oneself in a store or business. (No pl.) **2.** the *adj.* use of ①.

sell ['sɛl] **1.** *tv., irreg.* to transfer a product in exchange for money; to transfer a product to someone in exchange for money. (Pt/pp: SOLD.) **2.** *tv., irreg.* to make something available for purchase. **3.** *tv., irreg.* to cause something to be more likely to be used or bought.

seller ['sɛl ɚ] *n.* someone who sells something for money.

semester [sɪ 'mɛs tɚ] *n.* half of a school year; a term; a 16-week to 18-week period of classes.

semicircle ['sɛm ɪ sɚk əl] *n.* half of a circle; a shape like half of a circle.

semicolon ['sɛm ɪ ko lən] *n.* a punctuation mark (;) that shows separation between two clauses, indicating more of a pause than a comma but less of a pause than a period. (It is also used to separate items in a list if any of the items uses a comma, so that the reader is not confused.)

seminar ['sɛm ə nɑr] **1.** *n.* one of the meetings of a type of (college) course that meets regularly with a professor to discuss theories, studies, or research. **2.** *n.* a meeting where a speaker, or panel of speakers, talks and information or ideas about a particular topic is exchanged.

senate ['sɛn ɪt] **1.** *n.* the smaller of the two groups of people who are elected to make the federal laws in the U.S. **2.** *n.* the professors who are the governing body at some schools and universities.

senator ['sɛn ə tə˞] *n.* someone who is a member of a senate.

send ['sɛnd] *tv., irreg.* to cause someone or something to be transported or to go from one place to another. (Pt/pp: SENT.)

senile ['si naɪl] *adj.* tending to forget things or be confused because of advancing age. (Adv: *senilely.*)

senility [sə 'nɪl ə ti] *n.* a state of confusion and loss of memory associated with old age. (No pl.)

senior ['sin jə˞] **1.** *adj.* [of people] older; [of employees] having served an employer longer than most other employees. **2.** *adj.* higher in rank or position. **3.** *adj.* of or for students in the fourth year of high school or college. **4.** *adj.* for very old or elderly people; serving elderly people. **5.** *n.* an older person; a *senior citizen.* **6.** *n.* a student in the fourth year of high school (12th grade) or the fourth year of college.

seniority [sin 'jor ə ti] *n.* the quality of having been employed at one's place of work for a relatively longer period of time than someone else. (No pl.)

sensation [sɛn 'se ʃən] **1.** *n.* the use of the senses; the ability to see, hear, touch, taste, or smell. **2.** *n.* an awareness of someone or something because of sight, sound, touch, taste, or smell. **3.** *n.* a vague feeling of awareness; a general feeling in the mind. **4.** *n.* someone or something that causes people to become very excited or interested.

sensational [sɛn 'se ʃə nəl] **1.** *adj.* very exciting or interesting; attracting a lot of attention. (Adv: *sensationally.*) **2.** *adj.* exaggerated and designed to excite and appeal to a mass audience. (Adv: *sensationally.*)

sense ['sɛns] **1.** *n.* each of the abilities allowing creatures to see, hear, touch, taste, or smell. **2.** *n.* a special feeling or sensation, especially one that cannot be described. (No pl.) **3.** *n.* the ability to understand or appreciate something. (No pl.) **4.** *n.* good judgment; the ability to make good decisions. (No pl.) **5.** *n.* the meaning or definition of something; a meaning. **6.** *n.* a belief shared by a group of people. **7.** *tv.* to be aware of something with the help of ①. (The object can be a clause with THAT ⑦.) **8.** *tv.* to determine something; to have a feeling about a situation. (The object can be a clause with THAT ⑦.)

senseless ['sɛns ləs] **1.** *adj.* without reason; having no purpose; stupid; foolish. (Adv: *senselessly.*) **2.** *adj.* unconscious. (Adv: *senselessly.*)

sensible ['sɛn sə bəl] **1.** *adj.* representing or showing common sense; wise. (Adv: *sensibly.*) **2.** *adj.* practical instead of stylish. (Adv: *sensibly.*)

sensitive ['sɛn sə tɪv] **1.** *adj.* able to feel the effect of something, especially light, sound, smell, taste, or texture; easily affected or harmed by something. (Adv: *sensitively.*) **2.** *adj.* easily offended; [of someone] easily affected by something. (Fig. on ①. Adv: *sensitively.*) **3.** *adj.* easily able to sense a small change in something.

sensitivity [sɛn sə 'tɪv ɪ ti] **1.** *n.* the ability to sense or perceive something. (No pl.) **2.** *n.* the tendency to perceive or imagine even the smallest offense. (Sometimes pl with the same meaning.)

sensory ['sɛn sə ri] *adj.* of the senses; of the ability to see, hear, taste, touch, or smell.

sensual ['sɛn ʃu əl] *adj.* providing pleasure to the body; concerning the pleasures of eating, drinking, sex, etc. (Adv: *sensually.*)

sensuous [sɛn 'ʃu əs] *adj.* affecting the senses; experienced through the senses. (Adv: *sensuously.*)

sent ['sɛnt] pt/pp of SEND.

sentence ['sɛnt ns] **1.** *n.* a group of words that forms an independent thought, usually including at least a subject and a verb. **2.** *n.* the punishment given to a criminal by a judge in a court of law. **3.** *tv.* [for a judge] to assign a punishment to a criminal.

sentiment ['sɛn tə mənt] *n.* a tender feeling or emotion. (No pl.)

sentimental [sɛn tə 'mɛn təl] *adj.* having tender feelings or emotions, often sad or romantic ones. (Adv: *sentimentally.*)

sentiments *n.* a written or spoken expression of SENTIMENT. (Treated as pl.)

sentry ['sɛn tri] *n.* someone, usually a soldier, who guards a place; a soldier who stands guard.

separable ['sɛp ɚ ə bəl] *adj.* able to be separated; able to be divided. (Adv: *separably.*)

separate 1. ['sɛp rət] *adj.* not together; not joined; apart; single; individual. (Adv: *separately.*) **2.** ['sɛp ə ret] *tv.* to be between two or more people or things; to keep two or more people or things apart. **3.** ['sɛp

434

ə ret] *tv.* to cause two or more people or things to be apart. **4.** ['sɛp ə ret] *iv.* to break apart; to divide; to split. **5.** ['sɛp ə ret] *iv.* [for a husband and wife] to stop living together, often as a trial before beginning to divorce each other.

separated ['sɛp ə ret ɪd] *adj.* [of a married couple] no longer living together but not divorced.

separation [sɛp ə 're ʃən] **1.** *n.* the state of being separated. (Pl only for types and instances.) **2.** *n.* a period of time when two people who are married no longer live together but have not yet divorced.

September [sɛp 'tɛm bɚ] Go to MONTH.

sequence ['si kwəns] **1.** *n.* the order in which a group of people or things are placed; the order in which a series of events happen. **2.** *tv.* to put people or things into ①.

sequester [sɪ 'kwɛs tɚ] *tv.* to keep someone apart from other people, especially to isolate members of a jury from the public during a trial.

serenade [sɛr ə 'ned] **1.** *n.* a song sung to someone; a love song. **2.** *tv.* to sing a romantic song to someone; to play a romantic piece of music for someone.

serene [sə 'rin] *adj.* quiet; calm; peaceful. (Adv: *serenely.*)

serenity [sə 'rɛn ɪ ti] *n.* the quality of being serene. (No pl.)

serial ['sɪr i əl] **1.** *n.* a story that is presented in separate parts. **2.** the *adj.* use of ①. (Adv: *serially.*)

series ['sɪr iz] **1.** *n.* a group of similar things that happen or appear one after the other in a certain order; a group of similar things that are arranged in a row. (Treated as sg.) **2.** *n.* a set of television programs that is broadcast one at a time, usually once per week.

serious ['sɪr i əs] **1.** *adj.* stern; not humorous or playful. (Adv: *seriously.*) **2.** *adj.* important; not minor. (Adv: *seriously.*)

seriousness ['sɪr i əs nəs] *n.* importance; gravity; a state of being SERIOUS ① or ②. (No pl.)

sermon ['sɚ mən] **1.** *n.* a speech about religion or morals, especially one given by a member of the clergy. **2.** *n.* a long speech by someone who is giving advice or who is scolding someone else. (Fig. on ①.)

serpent ['sɚ pənt] *n.* a snake.

servant ['sɚ vənt] *n.* someone who serves a person, the public, or God, especially someone who is paid to work for someone else in that person's house.

435

serve ['sɚv] **1.** *tv.* to provide someone with a service. **2.** *tv.* to bring (previously ordered) food to someone, as in a restaurant. **3.** *tv.* to provide a useful service or function. **4.** *iv.* to perform military service. **5.** *iv.* to begin a play in a sport like tennis by hitting the ball toward the other player.

server ['sɚ vɚ] **1.** *n.* a utensil used to serve certain foods. **2.** *n.* a WAITRESS; a WAITER.

service ['sɚ vɪs] **1.** *n.* the work that someone does for the benefit of someone; work done by servants, clerks, food servers, taxi drivers, etc. (No pl. See ③.) **2.** *n.* the repair of a machine or device; maintenance. (No pl.) **3.** *n.* the benefit provided by a company or organization that fulfills the needs of people but does not usually manufacture products. (This includes *electric service, natural gas service, telephone service, water service, sewer service, message service, diaper service, lawn-care service,* etc.) **4.** *n.* a religious meeting or ceremony. **5.** *tv.* to repair or adjust something mechanical or electronic.

services *n.* work that is done to help someone, especially the work done by a professional person. (Treated as pl, but not countable.)

serving ['sɚ vɪŋ] *n.* the amount of food or drink that is usually served to one person.

session ['sɛ ʃən] *n.* a period of time during which a meeting is held or an activity is pursued.

set ['sɛt] **1.** *tv., irreg.* to put someone or something on a surface; to place someone or something somewhere. (Pt/pp: SET.) **2.** *tv., irreg.* to move someone or something into a certain position. **3.** *tv., irreg.* to join the ends of a broken bone and place them in the proper position. **4.** *tv., irreg.* to determine or establish a value, a standard, a time, an amount, etc. **5.** *tv., irreg.* to adjust a machine so that it works correctly; to adjust something so that it will show the correct measurement, time, amount, etc. **6.** *iv., irreg.* [for a liquid] to take a certain shape; to become shaped; [for concrete or plaster] to get hard. **7.** *iv., irreg.* [for the sun] to drop below the horizon at night; to sink out of sight. **8.** *n.* a collection of related things; a group of things that are found or belong together. **9.** *n.* the location of the performing area for a play, TV show, or movie. **10.** *adj.* ready. (Not prenominal.) **11.** *adj.* established; determined in advance; arranged. **12.** ~ **off;** ~ **out** to begin on a journey or expedition. **13.** ~ **up** to place something, someone, or oneself upright. **14.** ~ **up** to construct or assemble something.

setback ['sɛt bæk] *n.* something that causes something to change for the worse.

settle ['sɛt əl] **1.** *tv.* to decide something, especially an argument; to resolve something. **2.** *tv.* to pay a bill or account. **3.** *tv.* to place oneself in a comfortable position. (Takes a reflexive object.) **4.** *tv.* to occupy land or a town and live there, often as a pioneer. **5.** *tv.* to cause something to be calm, still, or less active. **6.** *iv.* to sink, especially into the ground or to the bottom of something.

settlement ['sɛt əl mənt] **1.** *n.* the establishing of towns or communities in new areas. (No pl.) **2.** *n.* a town established by people who have moved to an area where there was no town before. **3.** *n.* an agreement that ends an argument, disagreement, or fight.

settler ['sɛt lɚ, 'sɛt l ɚ] *n.* a pioneer; someone who is one of the first people to live in a location.

setup ['sɛt əp] *n.* an arrangement; the way something is arranged or organized.

seven ['sɛv ən] 7. Go to FOUR.

seventeen ['sɛv ən 'tin] 17. Go to FOUR.

seventeenth [sɛv ən 'tinθ] 17th. Go to FOURTH.

seventh ['sɛv ənθ] 7th. Go to FOURTH.

seventieth ['sɛv ən ti əθ] 70th. Go to FOURTH.

seventy ['sɛv ən ti] 70. Go to FORTY.

sever ['sɛv ɚ] **1.** *tv.* to cut through something; to cut something apart. **2.** ~ **ties with** to end a relationship or agreement suddenly.

several ['sɛv (ə) rəl] **1.** *adj.* some; a few, but not many. **2.** *n.* some people or things; a few people or things. (No pl.)

severe [sə 'vɪr] **1.** *adj.* harsh; strict; not gentle. (Adv: *severely.* Comp: *severer;* sup: *severest.*) **2.** *adj.* strong; violent; causing harm; not mild. (Adv: *severely.* Comp: *severer;* sup: *severest.*)

severed ['sɛv ɚd] *adj.* cut off; cut from; separated.

severity [sɪ 'vɛr ɪ ti] *n.* the quality of being severe. (No pl.)

sew ['so] **1.** *tv., irreg.* to attach two pieces of material together or to attach something to a piece of material by making stitches using a needle and thread. (Pt: *sewed;* pp: *sewed* or SEWN.) **2.** *iv., irreg.* to attach with stitches using a needle and thread.

sewage ['su ɪdʒ] *n.* water and human waste that is carried away by sewers from homes and businesses. (No pl.)

437

sewer 1. ['su ɚ] *n.* a pipe that carries waste away from homes and businesses. **2.** ['so ɚ] *n.* someone who sews.

sewing ['so ɪŋ] **1.** *n.* the work that is done with a needle and thread; the stitches made in material with a needle and thread. (No pl.) **2.** *n.* a piece of clothing or material that is being sewed. (No pl.) **3.** the *adj.* use of ① or ②.

sewn ['son] a pp of SEW.

sex ['sɛks] **1.** *n.* human sexual responses and activity. (No pl.) **2.** *n.* copulation; sexual arousal leading to copulation; the urge to copulate; the subject of copulation. (No pl.) **3.** *n.* the state of being male or female. **4.** the *adj.* use of ①.

sexism ['sɛks ɪz əm] *n.* discrimination against someone, usually a woman, because of that individual's sex. (No pl.)

sexist ['sɛk sɪst] **1.** *n.* someone, usually a male, who practices SEXISM. **2.** the *adj.* use of ①. (Adv: *sexistly*.)

sexual ['sɛk ʃu əl] **1.** *adj.* of or about copulation or reproduction and the associated feelings and urges. (Adv: *sexually*.) **2.** *adj.* requiring two creatures or organisms for reproduction.

sexuality [sɛk ʃu 'æl ə ti] *n.* human sexual matters and feelings; the involvement or interest a person has in sex. (No pl.)

sexually ['sɛk ʃu (ə) li] *adv.* in a sexual manner; in a way that concerns sex.

sexy ['sɛk si] *adj.* of or about sex appeal; causing an interest in sex; sexually exciting. (Comp: *sexier*; sup: *sexiest*.)

sg the abbreviation of SINGULAR.

shabby ['ʃæb i] *adj.* having a messy appearance; looking run-down or worn-out. (Adv: *shabbily*. Comp: *shabbier*; sup: *shabbiest*.)

shack ['ʃæk] *n.* a small house, hut, or shed that has been built quickly or poorly.

shade ['ʃed] **1.** *n.* a place that is not directly exposed to sunlight because an object between that place and the sun blocks the sunlight. (No pl.) **2.** *n.* a variety of a color; the lightness or darkness of a color. **3.** *n.* a slight amount of a quality. **4.** *n.* a device that can be rolled down over a window so that light will not get in or so that people cannot see in. (Short for *window shade*.) **5.** *tv.* to prevent light from reaching an area; to make something darker or harder to see by blocking light. **6.** *tv.* to make something darker by painting or drawing on it with a darker color.

shading [ˈʃed ɪŋ] *n.* the use of darker colors in paintings and drawings to make shadows and darker areas. (No pl.)

shadow [ˈʃæd o] **1.** *n.* the patch of shade created by someone or something blocking light. **2.** *n.* a slight suggestion; a trace. (Fig. on ①.)

shady [ˈʃe di] **1.** *adj.* in the shade; blocked from direct exposure to light; shaded. (Comp: *shadier;* sup: *shadiest.*) **2.** *adj.* not honest; always making schemes and deceiving people. (Comp: *shadier;* sup: *shadiest.*)

shaft [ˈʃæft] **1.** *n.* a rod or pole, such as part of an arrow. **2.** *n.* a pole that is used as a handle, such as with an axe or a golf club. **3.** *n.* a ray [of light]. **4.** *n.* a long, narrow passage, often vertical.

shaggy [ˈʃæg i] *adj.* covered with long, thick, messy hair; [of hair] long, thick, and messy. (Adv: *shaggily.* Comp: *shaggier;* sup: *shaggiest.*)

shake [ˈʃek] **1.** *iv., irreg.* [for something large] to move up and down, back and forth, or side to side many times very quickly. (Pt: SHOOK; pp: SHAKEN.) **2.** *iv., irreg.* [for someone] to move as in ① or seem less secure. **3.** *tv., irreg.* to cause someone or something to move up and down, back and forth, or side to side many times very quickly.

shaken [ˈʃek ən] **1.** pp of SHAKE. **2.** *adj.* greatly upset; disturbed; bothered.

shaker [ˈʃek ɚ] *n.* a small container that has a few tiny holes on one end, from which salt, pepper, or sometimes another spice is spread on food by shaking.

shake-up [ˈʃek əp] *n.* a large change in the arrangement of an organization, including the movement, firing, or addition of people who have important jobs.

shaky [ˈʃe ki] **1.** *adj.* shaking a small amount; not steady. (Comp: *shakier;* sup: *shakiest.*) **2.** *adj.* risky; not certain; not able to be relied on. (Comp: *shakier;* sup: *shakiest.*)

shall [ˈʃæl] **1.** *aux.* a form used with *I* and *we* to indicate something in the future. (Formal. See also WILL and SHOULD.) **2.** *aux.* a form used with *you, he, she, it, they,* and names of people or things to indicate something one must do, a command, or a promise. (Formal. See also WILL and SHOULD.) **3.** *aux.* a verb form used with *I* and *we* in questions that ask the hearer or reader to decide something concerning the speaker or writer. (Formal. See also WILL and SHOULD.)

shallow [ˈʃæl o] **1.** *adj.* not deep; having only a small distance from the top of something to the bottom, especially used to describe water.

(Adv: *shallowly.* Comp: *shallower;* sup: *shallowest.*) **2.** *adj.* [of thoughts] trivial; not having deep, important thoughts. (Fig. on ①. Adv: *shallowly.* Comp: *shallower;* sup: *shallowest.*)

sham ['ʃæm] **1.** *n.* a ruse; a trick; a hoax; a fraud. **2.** *n.* a fake; a counterfeit; a phony; something that is not the real object that it is said to be; someone who pretends to be someone else. **3.** the *adj.* use of ②.

shame ['ʃem] **1.** *n.* a feeling that someone has done something wrong or bad; a bad feeling of guilt. (No pl.) **2.** *n.* an unfortunate situation. (No pl.) **3.** *n.* disgrace; loss of honor. (No pl.) **4.** *tv.* to cause someone to feel ①.

shameful ['ʃem fʊl] *adj.* causing or deserving shame or disgrace. (Adv: *shamefully.*)

shameless ['ʃem ləs] *adj.* without shame, especially when one should feel shame; not modest. (Adv: *shamelessly.*)

shampoo [ʃæm 'pu] **1.** *n.* a liquid soap used for washing hair. (Pl only for types and instances. Pl ends in -*s.*) **2.** *n.* a washing of one's own or someone else's hair with ①. (Pl ends in -*s.*) **3.** *tv.* to wash someone's hair with ①. **4.** *iv.* to wash [hair] with ①.

shape ['ʃep] **1.** *n.* a form; a figure; a mass; an object. **2.** *n.* condition; a state of being—good or bad. (No pl.) **3.** *tv.* to cause something to have a certain form; to form something.

shapeless ['ʃep ləs] *adj.* without a shape; having no definite form. (Adv: *shapelessly.*)

shapely ['ʃep li] *adj.* having an attractive body; attractive in shape. (Especially used to describe women. Comp: *shapelier;* sup: *shapeliest.*)

share ['ʃɛr] **1.** *n.* one person's part of something that belongs to more than one person; a portion. **2.** *n.* a unit of STOCK ③; a unit into which the capital of a company or business is divided, and that is owned by a person or corporation. **3.** *tv.* to use something together with another person or other people; to own something together with another person or other people. **4.** *tv.* to divide something between two or among three or more people so that each person has a portion of it. **5.** *iv.* to use together with another person or other people; to own together with another person or other people.

shared ['ʃɛrd] *adj.* belonging to two or more people; divided among two or more people.

shark ['ʃɑrk] *n.* a large, dangerous fish with a pointed fin on its back and long, sharp teeth.

sharp [ˈʃɑrp] **1.** *adj.* having an edge that cuts things easily or having a point that pierces things easily; not dull. (Adv: *sharply.* Comp: *sharper;* sup: *sharpest.*) **2.** *adj.* having a sudden change in direction; turning at a narrow angle. (Adv: *sharply.* Comp: *sharper;* sup: *sharpest.*) **3.** *adj.* intelligent; smart; able to learn things quickly; aware. (Adv: *sharply.* Comp: *sharper;* sup: *sharpest.*) **4.** *adj.* feeling like a sting, bite, or cut; causing a stinging, biting, or cutting feeling. (Adv: *sharply.* Comp: *sharper;* sup: *sharpest.*) **5.** *adj.* distinct; clear; easily seen or heard. (Adv: *sharply.* Comp: *sharper;* sup: *sharpest.*) **6.** *adj.* [of speech or language] bitterly negative. (Adv: *sharply.* Comp: *sharper;* sup: *sharpest.*) **7.** *adj.* slightly higher in tone. (Comp: *sharper;* sup: *sharpest.*) **8.** *adj.* excellent looking. (Adv: *sharply.* Comp: *sharper;* sup: *sharpest.*) **9.** *n.* a tone that is half a step higher than the next lowest natural tone. **10.** *adv.* exactly at a stated time.

sharpen [ˈʃɑr pən] *tv.* to cause something to become sharp.

shatter [ˈʃæt ɚ] **1.** *iv.* to break into many tiny pieces. **2.** *tv.* to break something into many tiny pieces.

shave [ˈʃev] **1.** *tv., irreg.* to remove someone's or something's hair with a sharp blade; to scrape off hair by moving a razor over the skin. (Pt: *shaved;* pp: *shaved* or SHAVEN.) **2.** *tv., irreg.* to cut a thin slice from something. **3.** *iv., irreg.* to move a razor over one's skin to remove hair. **4.** *n.* an instance of removing hair from the face or body by using a razor.

shaven [ˈʃev ən] a pp of SHAVE.

she [ˈʃi] **1.** *pron.* the third-person feminine sg pronoun. (Refers to female persons or creatures. Used as the subject of a sentence or a clause. See also HER, HERSELF, and HERS.) **2.** *pron.* the third-person feminine sg pronoun. (Informal. Used to refer to certain objects, such as ships and cars.) **3.** *n.* a female.

sheaf [ˈʃif] *n., irreg.* a stack or bundle of things that are tied together. (Pl: SHEAVES.)

shear [ˈʃɪr] **1.** *tv., irreg.* to cut or remove something with SHEARS or scissors, especially wool from a sheep. (Pp: *sheared* or SHORN.) **2.** *tv., irreg.* to trim a sheep totally, removing its wool.

shears *n.* large scissors; a heavy pair of scissors used for cutting thick materials. (Treated as pl. Number is usually expressed with *pair(s) of shears.*)

sheath [ˈʃiθ] *n., irreg.* a covering for the blade of a knife or sword. (Pl: [ˈʃiðz].)

sheaves ['ʃivz] pl of SHEAF.

she'd ['ʃid] **1.** *cont.* she had, where HAD is an auxiliary. **2.** *cont.* she would.

shed ['ʃed] **1.** *n.* a small building, usually used for storage. **2.** *iv., irreg.* to release or lose hair, or skin in the case of a reptile. (Pt/pp: *shed.*) **3.** *tv., irreg.* [for an animal] to lose skin or hair. **4.** *tv., irreg.* to release a fluid, especially tears or blood. **5.** *tv., irreg.* to rid oneself of a burden or something embarrassing. (Fig. on ③.) **6.** *tv., irreg.* to remove clothing.

sheep ['ʃip] *n., irreg.* an animal that grows wool on its body and is raised on farms for its wool and meat. (Pl: *sheep.*)

sheepish ['ʃip ɪʃ] *adj.* weak; timid; easily scared; shy; easily embarrassed. (Adv: *sheepishly.*)

sheer ['ʃɪr] **1.** *adj.* complete; utter. (Comp: *sheerer;* sup: *sheerest.*) **2.** *adj.* transparent; very thin; easy to see through. (Adv: *sheerly.* Comp: *sheerer;* sup: *sheerest.*) **3.** *adj.* straight up and down; vertical but not slanting or sloping. (Adv: *sheerly.* Comp: *sheerer;* sup: *sheerest.*)

sheet ['ʃit] **1.** *n.* a large, thin piece of fabric that is used in pairs on beds. (People sleep between SHEETS.) **2.** *n.* a thin, flat piece of something, such as paper, metal, glass, ice, etc., usually rectangular.

shelf ['ʃelf] *n., irreg.* a horizontal, flat piece of wood, metal, etc., that is put against or attached to a wall or is found in bookcases or other furniture. (Pl: SHELVES.)

she'll ['ʃil] *cont.* she will.

shell ['ʃel] **1.** *n.* the hard covering on the outside of seeds, nuts, eggs, and shellfish. **2.** *n.* an exploding object that is shot out of a large gun. **3.** *tv.* to free something from ① [by removing ①]. **4.** *tv.* to attack people or a place with SHELLS as in ②.

shellfish ['ʃel fɪʃ] **1.** *n., irreg.* an animal that lives in the water and has a shell, including clams, crabs, lobsters, and oysters. (Pl: *shellfish.*) **2.** *n.* the meat of ①. (No pl.)

shelter ['ʃel tɚ] **1.** *n.* protection from the weather, danger, or harm. (No pl.) **2.** *n.* a place or structure where one can find ①. **3.** *tv.* to protect someone or something from the weather, danger, or harm.

sheltered ['ʃel tɚd] *adj.* [of an area] protected, especially from the weather.

442

shelve ['ʃɛlv] **1.** *tv.* to place something on a shelf. **2.** *tv.* to delay something until a later time. (Fig. on ①.)

shelves ['ʃɛlvz] pl of SHELF.

shelving ['ʃɛl vɪŋ] *n.* shelves; a set of shelves. (No pl.)

shepherd ['ʃɛp ɚd] **1.** *n.* someone who raises and protects sheep. **2.** *tv.* to guide someone in the way that a shepherd leads sheep. (Fig. on ①.)

sherbet ['ʃɚ bət] *n.* a sweet, frozen dessert usually made of or flavored with fruit juice. (Pl only for types and instances.)

sheriff ['ʃɛr ɪf] *n.* the most important officer elected to enforce the law in a U.S. county.

she's ['ʃiz] **1.** *cont.* she is. **2.** *cont.* she has, where HAS is an auxiliary.

shield ['ʃild] **1.** *n.* a cover for something (such as a part of a machine) that protects someone from being hurt. **2.** *n.* a large piece of metal or wood carried in front of the body to protect it during fighting. **3.** *tv.* to protect someone or something from someone or something; to keep someone or something safe from someone or something.

shift ['ʃɪft] **1.** *n.* a change in policy, position, opinion, or behavior. **2.** *n.* a period during which a worker completes a day at work, such as day shift, night shift, afternoon shift. (In a workplace that operates more than 8 hours per day.) **3.** *tv.* to change the position of someone or something. **4.** *iv.* to experience changes in behavior or opinion.

shimmer ['ʃɪm ɚ] **1.** *iv.* to shine with small waves of light; to shine with reflected light that moves slightly. **2.** *n.* a gleam or glow that seems to move back and forth slightly.

shin ['ʃɪn] *n.* the front of the leg between the knee and the ankle.

shine ['ʃaɪn] **1.** *iv., irreg.* to be bright with light; to reflect light. (Pt/pp: *shined* or SHONE.) **2.** *iv.* to do very well; to excel; to be excellent. (Fig. on ①.) **3.** *tv., irreg.* to direct a beam or source of light in a certain direction. (Pt/pp: *shined* or SHONE.) **4.** *tv.* to polish something; to cause something to become shiny. **5.** *n.* the brightness of a surface that has been polished.

shingle ['ʃɪŋ gəl] *n.* a thin panel of wood or another material used to cover a roof in overlapping rows.

shingles *n.* a severe, painful disease of the nerves, causing blisters to form on the skin. (Treated as sg or pl, but not countable.)

shiny ['ʃaɪ ni] *adj.* bright; polished; reflecting a lot of light. (Adv: *shinily.* Comp: *shinier;* sup: *shiniest.*)

443

ship ['ʃɪp] **1.** *n.* a large boat that travels on water and carries people and cargo. **2.** *tv.* to send something from one place to another by train, truck, plane, or ①.

shipment ['ʃɪp mənt] *n.* a load of goods or products ready to be shipped, being shipped, or just received.

shipping ['ʃɪp ɪŋ] **1.** *n.* the activity or business of delivering products by ship, train, plane, or truck. (No pl.) **2.** *n.* the cost of transporting something. (No pl.) **3.** the *adj.* use of ① or ②.

shipwreck ['ʃɪp rɛk] **1.** *n.* the destruction of a ship caused by running into something. **2.** *n.* the remains of a ship that has undergone ①. **3.** *tv.* to cause someone to be harmed or stranded owing to ①.

shirt ['ʃɚt] *n.* a piece of clothing worn above the waist, worn either next to the skin or over an undershirt, and sometimes worn beneath a sweater, jacket, vest, or coat.

shit ['ʃɪt] **1.** *n.* dung; feces. (All senses are taboo in polite company. Use only with caution.) **2.** *n.* something poor in quality; junk. **3.** *n.* nonsense; bullshit. **4.** *exclam.* a general expression of disgust. (Potentially offensive. Use only with caution.)

shiver ['ʃɪv ɚ] **1.** *iv.* [for a living creature] to shake a little bit, especially because of cold, sickness, or fear. **2.** *n.* a slight shaking movement, especially because of cold, sickness, or fear.

shock ['ʃak] **1.** *n.* a sudden surprise, especially one that is violent or disturbing. **2.** *n.* a weakened condition of the body caused by a violent or disturbing event. (No pl.) **3.** *n.* a strong, violent force, especially that caused by an earthquake or bomb. **4.** *n.* the passing of electricity through someone's body. **5.** *tv.* to surprise someone, especially in a disturbing or violent way. **6.** *tv.* to offend someone; to disgust someone. **7.** *tv.* to give someone or some creature electricity as in ④.

shocking ['ʃak ɪŋ] *adj.* causing surprise, especially in a disturbing or violent way; offensive; causing disgust. (Adv: *shockingly*.)

shoddy ['ʃad i] *adj.* done carelessly; poorly made or done. (Adv: *shoddily*. Comp: *shoddier*; sup: *shoddiest*.)

shoe ['ʃu] *n.* an outer covering for one's foot, usually having a firm base, but less sturdy than a boot.

shoelace ['ʃu les] *n.* a fabric band or string that is put through the holes on top of a shoe or boot and tied.

shoestring [ˈʃuˌstrɪŋ] *n.* a cord or string used in tightening the shoe to the foot.

shone [ˈʃon] a pt/pp of SHINE.

shook [ˈʃʊk] pt of SHAKE.

shoot [ˈʃut] **1.** *tv., irreg.* to fire a gun or similar weapon. (Pt/pp: SHOT.) **2.** *tv., irreg.* [for a weapon] to send something, such as a bullet or arrow, with great force. **3.** *tv., irreg.* to send something forward as though from a weapon; to thrust something forward. (Fig. on ②.) **4.** *tv., irreg.* to strike someone or some creature with something, such as a bullet or an arrow, that has been sent from a weapon. **5.** *iv., irreg.* to discharge [a weapon]. **6.** *iv., irreg.* to move somewhere very quickly. **7.** *iv., irreg.* to fire guns as a hobby, as for target practice. **8.** *n.* a new bud or stem that sprouts from the ground or from an older part of a plant; a bit of new plant growth.

shooting [ˈʃut ɪŋ] **1.** *n.* the sport or skill of hitting targets by firing a gun at them. (No pl.) **2.** *n.* an act of murder, attempted murder, or other harm using a gun.

shop [ˈʃɑp] **1.** *n.* a small store, especially one where a single class of products is sold. **2.** *n.* a place where things are built or repaired. **3.** *iv.* to go to a store to buy things. **4.** *tv.* to visit a particular store, mall, or area in order to buy things.

shopkeeper [ˈʃɑp kip ɚ] *n.* someone who owns or manages a shop.

shoplift [ˈʃɑp lɪft] **1.** *tv.* to steal merchandise from a shop or store. **2.** *iv.* to steal [something] as in ①.

shoplifter [ˈʃɑp lɪft ɚ] *n.* someone who steals merchandise from a shop or store.

shopping [ˈʃɑp ɪŋ] *n.* buying things; searching for the right thing to purchase. (No pl.)

shopworn [ˈʃɑp worn] *adj.* ruined or damaged from being on display in a store.

shore [ˈʃor] *n.* the land along the edge of a body of water.

shoreline [ˈʃor laɪn] *n.* the land along the edge of a body of water, especially of an ocean, lake, or sea; the line where the land meets the water.

shorn [ˈʃorn] a pp of SHEAR.

short [ˈʃort] **1.** *adj.* not tall; less than average height from top to bottom. (Comp: *shorter*; sup: *shortest*.) **2.** *adj.* not long; less than average length from side to side. (Comp: *shorter*; sup: *shortest*.) **3.** *adj.* not

445

long in time; less than average duration; happening only for a small amount of time; brief. (Comp: *shorter;* sup: *shortest.*) **4.** *adj.* not having enough of something; lacking enough of something. (Comp: *shorter;* sup: *shortest.*) **5.** *adv.* not close enough; not far enough; not enough. **6.** *n.* a flaw in an electrical circuit that allows electricity to go where it should not go. (Short for *short circuit.*)

shortage ['ʃɔr tɪdʒ] **1.** *n.* a lack; a state of not having enough of something. **2.** *n.* the amount by which something is SHORT ④; the amount of something that is needed in order to have enough.

shortchange ['ʃɔrt 'tʃendʒ] *tv.* to give less than is due someone; to give someone less CHANGE ③ than is due.

shortcoming ['ʃɔrt kəm ɪŋ] *n.* a fault; a flaw; a defect.

shortcut ['ʃɔrt kət] *n.* a path that is shorter, more direct, or quicker to travel than a different or more established route.

shorten ['ʃɔrt n] **1.** *iv.* to become shorter. **2.** *tv.* to cause something to become shorter.

shortening ['ʃɔrt nɪŋ] **1.** *n.* causing something to become shorter. (No pl.) **2.** *n.* butter or some other kind of oily substance, used in frying and baking foods. (Pl only for types and instances.)

short-lived ['ʃɔrt 'lɪvd] *adj.* not lasting very long.

shorts **1.** *n.* a pair of pants whose legs end about at the knees. (Treated as pl. Number is expressed with *pair(s) of shorts.* Also countable.) **2.** *n.* underpants for men and boys. (Treated as pl. Number is expressed with *pair(s) of shorts.* Also countable.)

shortsighted ['ʃɔrt 'saɪt ɪd] **1.** *adj.* not able to see things clearly in the distance; able to see things that are near but not able to see things that are far away. (Adv: *shortsightedly.*) **2.** *adj.* acting without considering what will happen in the future. (Fig. on ①. Adv: *shortsightedly.*)

short-staffed ['ʃɔrt 'stæft] *adj.* not having enough people to do a job properly; not having enough employees to run a business properly; needing more people in order to do a job properly.

short-tempered ['ʃɔrt 'tɛm pɚd] *adj.* easily made angry.

short-term ['ʃɔrt 'tɚm] *adj.* only for a short period of time; not permanent; temporary.

shot ['ʃɑt] **1.** pt/pp of SHOOT. **2.** *n.* the firing of a weapon; the shooting of a gun or other weapon. **3.** *n.* someone who shoots in a particular way, such as good or bad. **4.** *n.* an injection of medicine, a vaccine, or a drug. **5.** *n.* in a game, a ball or similar object that is

446

aimed and sent toward a goal in order to score a point. **6.** *n.* a photograph or a length of film or video.

should ['ʃʊd] **1.** *aux.* ought to be somehow. (Indicating that something is expected.) **2.** *aux.* ought to do something. (Indicating that something must be done.)

shoulder ['ʃol dɚ] **1.** *n.* one of two parts of the body where an arm connects with the top of the chest below the neck. **2.** *n.* the dirt or pavement along the side of a road. **3.** *tv.* to have responsibility for something; to take responsibility for something.

shouldn't ['ʃʊd nt] *cont.* should not.

should've ['ʃʊd əv] *cont.* should have, where HAVE is an auxiliary.

shout ['ʃaʊt] **1.** *iv.* to speak, laugh, or make spoken noises loudly. **2.** *tv.* to speak something loudly; to say something by shouting. (The object can be a clause with THAT ⑦.) **3.** *n.* a loud utterance; a loud cry.

shove ['ʃʌv] **1.** *iv.* to push with force. **2.** *tv.* to push someone or something with force in some direction. **3.** *n.* a push made with force.

shovel ['ʃʌv əl] **1.** *n.* a tool—having a wide, flat blade attached to a handle—used to lift, move, or remove earth or loose objects. **2.** *iv.* to work by using ①; to move, lift, or remove [something] by using ①. **3.** *tv.* to move, lift, or remove something by using ①. **4.** *tv.* to clear something with ①.

show ['ʃo] **1.** *tv., irreg.* to cause someone to see something; to put something in someone's sight. (Pt: *showed;* pp: SHOWN or *showed.*) **2.** *tv., irreg.* to reveal something; to let something be known. (The object can be a clause with THAT ⑦.) **3.** *tv., irreg.* to lead someone; to guide someone to a place. **4.** *tv., irreg.* to prove something; to make something clear. (The object can be a clause with THAT ⑦.) **5.** *tv., irreg.* to display or deliver a kind of treatment, such as sympathy, to someone. **6.** *tv., irreg.* to reveal a condition or illness. **7.** *tv., irreg.* [for a movie theater] to present a movie. **8.** *iv., irreg.* [for a condition] to appear or be visible; to be noticeable. **9.** *iv., irreg.* [for a play or a film] to be presented or displayed. **10.** *n.* a movie, television program, or theater performance. **11.** *n.* a grand spectacle; a noticeable display. **12.** *n.* something that is put on display for the public. **13.** *n.* a display of something, such as raised hands, regard, praise, etc. **14.** ~ **off** to attempt to get attention from someone by one's actions and speech.

shower ['ʃaʊ ɚ] **1.** *n.* a device [part of the plumbing] that sprays water onto someone who is bathing. **2.** *n.* a bath using ①. **3.** *n.* the place or compartment where one bathes. **4.** *n.* a brief fall of rain, snow, or other liquids in drops. **5.** *n.* a party for a woman who is about to get married or have a baby. **6.** *iv.* to rain; to fall like rain. **7.** *iv.* to wash under ①.

showing ['ʃo ɪŋ] **1.** *n.* a display of something. **2.** *n.* a display of one's success or lack of success.

shown ['ʃon] a pp of SHOW.

showroom ['ʃo rum] *n.* a room where products that are available for purchase are displayed.

showy ['ʃo i] *adj.* very noticeable; designed to get attention. (Adv: *showily.* Comp: *showier;* sup: *showiest.*)

shrank ['ʃræŋk] pt of SHRINK.

shred ['ʃrɛd] **1.** *n.* a very small piece of something; a scrap of something; a fragment. **2.** *tv.* to rip or cut something into scraps or small pieces; to make something into bits by rubbing against a rough or sharp surface.

shredded ['ʃrɛd əd] *adj.* ripped or cut into shreds; made into shreds by rubbing against a rough or sharp object.

shrewd ['ʃrud] *adj.* clever and intelligent; showing good judgment and common sense. (Adv: *shrewdly.* Comp: *shrewder;* sup: *shrewdest.*)

shrewdness ['ʃrud nəs] *n.* the quality of being shrewd. (No pl.)

shriek ['ʃrik] *n.* a loud, shrill, high-pitched scream or sound.

shrill ['ʃrɪl] *adj.* high-pitched and irritating; annoying or loud to the point of causing pain. (Adv: *shrilly.* Comp: *shriller;* sup: *shrillest.*)

shrimp ['ʃrɪmp] **1.** *n., irreg.* a shellfish, about the size and shape of a finger, with a thin body, commonly eaten as food. (Pl: *shrimp* or *shrimps.*) **2.** the *adj.* use of ①.

shrine ['ʃraɪn] *n.* an altar, chapel, or other place of worship, especially one where there is a connection to a god, saint, or other revered being.

shrink ['ʃrɪŋk] **1.** *iv., irreg.* to become smaller in size. (Pt: SHRANK or SHRUNK; pp: SHRUNK or SHRUNKEN. SHRUNK is usually used with auxiliary verbs, and SHRUNKEN is usually used as an adjective.) **2.** *tv., irreg.* to cause someone or something to become smaller in size.

shrivel ['ʃrɪv əl] **1.** *iv.* to become wrinkled while drying up; to wither. **2.** *tv.* to cause someone or something to wither.

shrub ['ʃrʌb] *n.* a plant similar to a very small tree that has many stems coming from the ground; a bush.

448

shrubbery ['ʃrʌb (ə) ri] *n.* a group of shrubs; shrubs in general. (No pl.)

shrug ['ʃrʌg] **1.** *n.* the lifting of one's shoulders to indicate doubt or a lack of caring or interest. **2.** *tv.* to lift one's shoulders as in ①. **3.** *iv.* to gesture with ①.

shrunk ['ʃrʌŋk] a pt/pp of SHRINK.

shrunken ['ʃrʌŋ kən] a pp of SHRINK.

shudder ['ʃʌd ɚ] **1.** *iv.* to shake with fear, cold, or disgust. **2.** *n.* a brief, uncontrolled shaking of the body because of fear or disgust.

shuffle ['ʃʌf əl] **1.** *iv.* to walk without picking up one's feet; to walk in a way that one's feet never leave the ground. **2.** *iv.* to mix up [playing cards so that they are] in a different order. **3.** *tv.* to move one's feet without picking them up from the ground. **4.** *tv.* to mix up playing cards so that they are not in any specific order.

shun ['ʃʌn] *tv.* to avoid someone or something; to stay away from someone or something.

shut ['ʃʌt] **1.** *tv., irreg.* to close something, such as a door, window, or drawer. (Pt/pp: *shut.*) **2.** *tv., irreg.* to close something, such as a door, an eye, or the mouth. **3.** *iv., irreg.* to become closed. **4.** *adj.* closed; moved into a closed position. (Not prenominal.)

shutdown ['ʃʌt daʊn] *n.* an instance of closing a factory or other place of industry, business, or government for a period of time.

shut-in ['ʃʌt ɪn] *n.* someone who is not able or not allowed to go outside because of sickness.

shutter ['ʃʌt ɚ] **1.** *n.* one of a pair of doors or panels that can be closed over the outside of a window. **2.** *n.* a device in a camera that opens and shuts quickly behind the lens in order to allow the proper amount of light when someone takes a picture.

shuttle ['ʃʌt əl] *n.* a bus or an airplane making regular trips back and forth between two places.

shy ['ʃaɪ] **1.** *adj.* nervous around other people; not likely to talk around other people; timid; reserved. (Adv: *shyly.* Comp: *shier, shyer;* sup: *shiest, shyest.*) **2.** *adj.* not quite reaching a stated amount; almost having enough of something, but not quite. (Not prenominal. Comp: *shier, shyer;* sup: *shiest, shyest.*)

shyness ['ʃaɪ nəs] *n.* the quality of being shy; the quality of being timid or nervous around other people. (No pl.)

sibling ['sɪb lɪŋ] *n.* a brother or sister.

sick ['sɪk] **1.** *adj.* not healthy; ill; having a disease. (Comp: *sicker;* sup: *sickest.*) **2.** *adj.* having an upset stomach and feeling like one has to vomit. (Comp: *sicker;* sup: *sickest.*)

sicken ['sɪk ən] **1.** *tv.* to cause someone or some creature to become sick. **2.** *tv.* to disgust someone. **3.** *iv.* to become sick; to become ill. **4.** *iv.* to become disgusted [with something].

sickening ['sɪk (ə) nɪŋ] *adj.* causing disgust; disgusting; nauseating. (Adv: *sickeningly.*)

sickness ['sɪk nəs] *n.* the condition of being sick; illness; disease.

side ['saɪd] **1.** *n.* one of the flat surfaces of an object shaped like a box, not including the top or the bottom. **2.** *n.* any of the flat surfaces of a three-dimensional object. **3.** *n.* either surface of something that is thin and flat. **4.** *n.* a particular surface of something. **5.** *n.* the shore along either edge of a river. **6.** *n.* a position or area that is to the right, left, or a certain direction from a central or reference point. **7.** *n.* the entire left or right part of a body. **8.** *n.* a group of people that opposes another group, including sports teams, countries at war, or groups involved with political or social causes. **9.** *adj.* [of a location] at, toward, or beside something.

sideline ['saɪd laɪn] **1.** *n.* an activity done in addition to one's primary interest or work. **2.** *tv.* to prevent a player from playing in a sporting event.

sidelines *n.* the line along the side of something, especially the line at the boundary of the playing area of a sport. (Treated as pl.)

sidestep ['saɪd stɛp] **1.** *tv.* to avoid injury or a crash by stepping to the side. **2.** *tv.* to avoid or evade something. (Fig. on ①.)

sideswipe ['saɪd swaɪp] *tv.* to hit something along its side; to hit something with one's side.

sidetrack ['saɪd træk] **1.** *tv.* to move a train from a main track to a minor one that runs parallel to the main track. **2.** *tv.* to cause someone to change from the main topic of conversation. (Fig. on ①.) **3.** *tv.* to cause the subject of a conversation or speech to shift away from the original subject.

sidewalk ['saɪd wɔk] *n.* a paved path, usually along the side of a street, for people to walk on.

sideways ['saɪd wez] **1.** *adj.* to or from a side. **2.** *adv.* to, on, or from a side or both sides; positioned with the side or edge toward the front.

siege ['sidʒ] *n.* the surrounding of a city, fort, or other place by people who are trying to capture it; an attack.

sift ['sɪft] *tv.* to separate small pieces from larger pieces by shaking the smaller ones through a tool containing a screen.

sigh ['saɪ] **1.** *iv.* to breathe out slowly and noisily, especially to indicate that one is bored, relieved, sad, or tired. **2.** *n.* the sound of breathing out as in ①.

sight ['saɪt] **1.** *n.* the ability to see; the power to see; vision. (No pl.) **2.** *n.* something that is seen; something in one's range of vision; a view. **3.** *n.* something that is worth seeing. (Often pl.) **4.** *n.* something that looks funny or strange. (No pl.) **5.** *tv.* to see someone or something for the first time, especially when one is looking for that person or thing.

sighted ['saɪt ɪd] *adj.* [of someone] able to see; [of someone] not blind.

sightless ['saɪt ləs] *adj.* unable to see; without sight; blind. (Adv: *sightlessly.*)

sightseeing ['saɪt si ɪŋ] *n.* visiting famous or interesting places, especially when one is on vacation. (No pl.)

sign ['saɪn] **1.** *n.* a mark that represents something; a mark that indicates something. **2.** *n.* something that indicates something else. **3.** *n.* a flat object that has information printed on it, placed where everyone can see it. **4.** *n.* a gesture used to communicate. **5.** *tv.* to write one's name [somewhere]. **6.** *tv.* to mark or write on something with one's name. **7.** *tv.* to communicate something by using SIGN ④ language.

signal ['sɪg nəl] **1.** *n.* something that conveys a message by affecting one of the senses; a sound, light, movement, etc., that conveys a message. **2.** *n.* the waves sent by a radio or television transmitter. **3.** *tv.* to indicate something. (The object can be a clause with THAT ⑦.)

signature ['sɪg nə tʃɚ] *n.* a person's name, handwritten by the person.

signed ['saɪnd] *adj.* marked with someone's signature.

significance [sɪg 'nɪf ə kəns] *n.* importance; meaning. (No pl.)

significant [sɪg 'nɪf ə kənt] *adj.* important; having meaning. (Adv: *significantly.*)

signify ['sɪg nə faɪ] *tv.* to mean something; to indicate something; to be a sign of something. (The object can be a clause with THAT ⑦.)

451

silence ['saɪ ləns] **1.** *n.* absolute quiet; the absence of all sound. (No pl.) **2.** *n.* the absence of comments about something. (No pl.) **3.** *tv.* to cause someone to be quiet; to cause someone to stop talking or to stop making noise.

silent ['saɪ lənt] **1.** *adj.* quiet; not speaking or making noise; done without making noise. (Adv: *silently.*) **2.** *adj.* [of a (spelling) letter] not pronounced; not representing a sound. (Adv: *silently.*)

silk ['sɪlk] **1.** *n.* a smooth, fine thread that is created by a silkworm when making its cocoon. (No pl.) **2.** *n.* cloth woven from ①. (Pl only for types and instances.) **3.** *adj.* made of ②.

silkworm ['sɪlk wəm] *n.* a creature that makes a cocoon of silk.

silky ['sɪl ki] *adj.* like silk; soft and smooth; [of cloth] soft and shimmering. (Adv: *silkily.* Comp: *silkier;* sup: *silkiest.*)

sill ['sɪl] *n.* the bottom ledge of a window or door frame.

silly ['sɪl i] *adj.* foolish; not sensible. (Comp: *sillier;* sup: *silliest.*)

silver ['sɪl və] **1.** *n.* a bright, white, valuable metallic element, which in its pure form is soft and easily shaped. (No pl.) **2.** *n.* coins, rather than paper money. (From a time when major U.S. coins were made of ①. No pl.) **3.** *adj.* made of ①.

silverware ['sɪl və wɛr] **1.** *n.* eating or serving utensils that are made from or plated with silver. (No pl.) **2.** *n.* knives, forks, and spoons made of steel, nickel, or metals other than silver. (No pl.)

silvery ['sɪl və ri] *adj.* looking like silver.

similar ['sɪm ə lə] *adj.* resembling something else, but not exactly the same. (Adv: *similarly.*)

similarity [sɪm ə 'lɛr ɪ ti] *n.* a way or an aspect in which someone or something is like or resembles someone or something else.

simmer ['sɪm ə] **1.** *tv.* to boil something gently; to cook something at or just below its boiling point. **2.** *iv.* to boil gently; to cook at or just below the boiling point. **3.** *iv.* to be angry without letting other people know that one is angry. (Fig. on ②.) **4.** *iv.* [for a situation] to be currently somewhat calm but progressing toward violence.

simple ['sɪm pəl] **1.** *adj.* easy; not complicated; not complex. (Adv: *simply.* Comp: *simpler;* sup: *simplest.*) **2.** *adj.* plain; not complicated; not fancy. (Adv: *simply.* Comp: *simpler;* sup: *simplest.*)

simplicity [sɪm 'plɪs ɪ ti] *n.* the quality of being simple or not complicated. (No pl.)

452

simplify ['sɪm plə faɪ] *tv.* to make something simpler; to make something easier to do or understand; to make something clearer.

simplistic [sɪm 'plɪs tɪk] *adj.* too simple; having been simplified too much. (Adv: *simplistically* [...ɪk li].)

simply ['sɪm pli] **1.** *adv.* easily; without difficulty. **2.** *adv.* merely; only. **3.** *adv.* absolutely; completely; very.

simulate ['sɪm jə let] *tv.* to show the nature or effects of something, allowing the observer to learn about it without experiencing it.

simulation [sɪm jə 'le ʃən] **1.** *n.* a demonstration of the nature or effects of an event without anyone really experiencing it. **2.** *n.* something that has been simulated.

simultaneous [saɪ məl 'te ni əs] *adj.* happening or existing at the same time. (Adv: *simultaneously.*)

sin ['sɪn] **1.** *n.* evil; something that is wicked or wrong; an act that is in opposition to a religious or moral principle. (Pl only for types and instances.) **2.** *iv.* to break a religious or moral principle.

since ['sɪns] **1.** *conj.* from a certain time in the past until now. **2.** *conj.* because. **3.** *prep.* from a certain time in the past until now. **4.** *adv.* from a certain time in the past until now.

sincere [sɪn 'sɪr] *adj.* honest; real; genuine; true. (Adv: *sincerely.* Comp: *sincerer;* sup: *sincerest.*)

sincerely [sɪn 'sɪr li] **1.** *adv.* honestly; really; genuinely; truly. **2.** *adv.* a word used as a polite way to finish a letter, before one's signature.

sincerity [sɪn 'sɛr ɪ ti] *n.* the quality of being sincere; honesty. (No pl.)

sinful ['sɪn fʊl] **1.** *adj.* full of sin; having committed a sin. (Adv: *sinfully.*) **2.** *adj.* wicked; bad; evil; leading people into sin. (Adv: *sinfully.*)

sing ['sɪŋ] **1.** *iv., irreg.* to make music with one's voice, uttering a melody with words. (Pt: SANG; pp: SUNG.) **2.** *tv., irreg.* to make music as in ①.

singe ['sɪndʒ] *tv.* to burn something slightly; to burn the edge or end of something.

single ['sɪŋ gəl] **1.** *adj.* one and only one. (Adv: *singly.*) **2.** *adj.* individual; meant for one thing or person. (Adv: *singly.*) **3.** *adj.* not married. (Adv: *singly.*) **4.** *adj.* having only one part; not double; not multiple. (Adv: *singly.*) **5.** *n.* something that is meant for one person. **6.** *n.* a $1 bill. **7.** *n.* someone who is not married.

single-minded ['sɪŋ gəl 'maɪn dɪd] *adj.* having only one purpose. (Adv: *single-mindedly.*)

453

singular ['sɪŋ gjə lɚ] **1.** *adj.* referring to only one person or thing. **2.** *adj.* unusual; exceptional; remarkable. **3.** *n.* the form of a noun that refers to only one person or thing.

sink ['sɪŋk] **1.** *iv., irreg.* to go beneath a surface; to fall beneath a surface. (Pt: SANK or SUNK; pp: SUNK.) **2.** *iv., irreg.* to become smaller in number; to decrease. **3.** *iv., irreg.* [for someone] to collapse or fall to the ground because of weakness, fear, respect, etc. **4.** *tv., irreg.* to cause something to go lower and lower beneath the surface of water or some other liquid. **5.** *n.* a permanent hollow bowl or basin, especially in a kitchen or bathroom, for washing dishes, one's hands or face, etc.

sinking ['sɪŋ kɪŋ] *adj.* going further downward into a liquid.

sinner ['sɪn ɚ] *n.* someone who sins.

sinus ['saɪ nəs] **1.** *n.* one of a number of spaces inside the bones of the face that are connected to the outside air by way of the nose. **2.** the *adj.* use of ①.

sip ['sɪp] **1.** *tv.* to drink something a little bit at a time. **2.** *n.* a small drink of something; a little taste of something liquid.

siphon AND **syphon** ['saɪ fən] *n.* a tube that has one end in a container of liquid and, through pressure and gravity, pulls the liquid downward into another container placed at a lower level.

sir ['sɚ] *n.* a word used to address a male politely.

siren ['saɪ rən] *n.* a device that makes a loud noise of warning, found on police cars, fire trucks, and ambulances.

sissy ['sɪs i] *n.* a weak and shy boy; a boy who behaves like a girl. (Derogatory.)

sister ['sɪs tɚ] **1.** *n.* a female sibling; a daughter of one's mother or father. **2.** *n.* a nun. (Also a term of address. Capitalized when written as a proper noun.)

sit ['sɪt] **1.** *iv., irreg.* to be in a position where the upper part of the body is straight, and the buttocks are supported by a chair, a seat, the floor, or some other surface. (Pt/pp: SAT.) **2.** *iv., irreg.* [for something] to be in a certain position; to be in a place. **3.** *iv., irreg.* [for an animal] to be positioned with the back end resting on a surface. **4.** *tv., irreg.* to make someone SIT as in ① in a location.

site ['saɪt] *n.* a location where something is, or was happening, has happened, or will happen.

situate ['sɪt ʃu et] *tv.* to place something; to have or make a place for something.

situation [sɪt ʃu 'e ʃən] *n.* a condition; the circumstances of an event; a state of affairs.

six ['sɪks] 6. Go to FOUR.

six-pack ['sɪks pæk] *n.* a package of six things, especially six cans of beer or soft drinks.

sixteen ['sɪks 'tin] 16. Go to FOUR.

sixteenth ['sɪks 'tinθ] 16th. Go to FOURTH.

sixth ['sɪksθ] 6th. Go to FOURTH.

sixtieth ['sɪks ti əθ] 60th. Go to FOURTH.

sixty ['sɪks ti] 60. Go to FORTY.

sizable ['sɑɪz ə bəl] *adj.* large; rather large; much. (Adv: *sizably.*)

size ['sɑɪz] **1.** *n.* the degree to which someone or something is large or small. (No pl.) **2.** *n.* one measurement in a series of measurements, used to describe ① of a product one wants, such as an article of clothing, a portion of food or drink, certain hardware, etc.

sizzle ['sɪz əl] **1.** *n.* the hissing noise made when frying fat or frying food in fat. (No pl.) **2.** *iv.* [for fat or cooking oil] to make a hissing noise when it is fried; to sound like fat when it fries.

sizzling ['sɪz lɪŋ] **1.** *adj.* frying; making the noise that fat does when it is heated. **2.** *adj.* very hot.

skate ['sket] **1.** *n.* an ice skate; a roller skate. **2.** *iv.* to move (over a surface) while wearing ice skates or roller skates.

skater ['sket ɚ] *n.* someone who ice-skates or roller-skates.

skeleton ['skɛl ə tən] **1.** *n.* the bones of a person or an animal, usually connected in their proper arrangement. **2.** *n.* an outline; the basic structure that supports something. (Fig. on ①.)

skeptic ['skɛp tɪk] *n.* someone who doubts faith, claims, theories, or facts; someone who questions the truth of something, especially religion.

skeptical ['skɛp tɪ kəl] *adj.* doubting; questioning; finding something hard to believe. (Adv: *skeptically* […ɪk li].)

skepticism ['skɛp tə sɪz əm] *n.* doubt; the condition of being skeptical; skeptical attitude or behavior. (No pl.)

sketch ['skɛtʃ] **1.** *n.* a simple drawing; a rough drawing that is quickly made. **2.** *n.* a brief description; an outline. **3.** *n.* a short skit; a very short play that is usually funny. **4.** *tv.* to draw someone or something roughly and quickly; to make a quick drawing. **5.** *iv.* to draw roughly and quickly.

sketchy ['skɛtʃ i] *adj.* not complete; without details. (Adv: *sketchily.* Comp: *sketchier;* sup: *sketchiest.*)

ski ['ski] **1.** *n.* one of two long, narrow, thin strips of wood or plastic used to travel on the surface of snow or water. **2.** *iv.* to move on the surface of snow or water on a pair of ①.

skid ['skɪd] **1.** *iv.* [for a wheel of a vehicle] to continue to move over a surface after the brakes have been applied. **2.** *iv.* to slip forward or sideways while moving. **3.** *n.* a forward or sideways slipping movement as with ① or ②.

skier ['ski ɚ] *n.* someone who skis on water or snow.

skiing ['ski ɪŋ] *n.* the sport or activity of moving over snow or water on skis. (No pl.)

skill ['skɪl] *n.* the ability to do something well, especially because of talent, experience, or practice.

skilled ['skɪld] *adj.* having skill; experienced.

skillet ['skɪl ət] *n.* a shallow pan used for frying foods.

skillful ['skɪl fʊl] *adj.* having skill; experienced; able to do something very well. (Adv: *skillfully.*)

skim ['skɪm] **1.** *tv.* to remove something from the surface of a liquid. **2.** *tv.* to glide over the surface of something; to go over the surface of something quickly. **3.** *tv.* to scan reading material; to read something quickly.

skin ['skɪn] **1.** *n.* the outer covering of humans and most animals; the outer covering of many fruits and vegetables. (Pl only for types and instances.) **2.** *tv.* to remove the skin from something.

skinny ['skɪn i] *adj.* very thin; without much fat. (Comp: *skinnier;* sup: *skinniest.*)

skip ['skɪp] **1.** *iv.* to move so that one takes a step with one foot, hops on that foot, takes a step with the second foot, and then hops on the second foot, repeatedly. **2.** *tv.* to pass someone or something over; to omit something. **3.** *tv.* to avoid attending a school class or other event and go someplace else.

skirmish ['skɚ mɪʃ] *n.* a small battle or argument.

skirt ['skɚt] **1.** *n.* an item of women's clothing that wraps around the waist and hangs down, without separate sections for each leg. **2.** *tv.*

to move along the edge of something; not to move through the center of something. **3.** *tv.* to evade an issue, topic, or question; to fail to address an issue, topic, or question.

skit ['skɪt] *n.* a short performance that is usually funny or that addresses a certain topic.

skull ['skʌl] *n.* the bones of the head; the bones that protect the brain.

skunk ['skʌŋk] *n.* a small animal that has black fur with a white stripe down its back and a bushy tail, and that releases a very bad smell when attacked or frightened.

sky ['skaɪ] *n.* the space above the earth; the air above the earth. (Sometimes pl.)

skydive ['skaɪ daɪv] **1.** *iv.* to jump from an airplane, fall through the air, and then open a parachute. (Pt/pp: *skydived.*) **2.** *n.* an instance of jumping from an airplane as in ①.

skylight ['skaɪ laɪt] *n.* a window in the roof or ceiling of a building.

skyscraper ['skaɪ skre pɚ] *n.* a very tall building.

slab ['slæb] *n.* a thick slice of something; a thick, flat piece of something.

slack ['slæk] **1.** *adj.* loose; not tight; not taut. (Adv: *slackly.* Comp: *slacker;* sup: *slackest.*) **2.** *adj.* not strict; relaxed. (Fig. on ①. Adv: *slackly.* Comp: *slacker;* sup: *slackest.*) **3.** *adj.* not active; not busy. (Adv: *slackly.* Comp: *slacker;* sup: *slackest.*) **4.** *n.* looseness; a part of something that is not pulled tight.

slacken ['slæk ən] *iv.* to reduce, especially in speed or tightness; to become slower or looser.

slacks *n.* pants; trousers. (Treated as pl. Number is expressed with *pair(s) of slacks.* Also countable. Rarely sg.)

slain ['slen] pp of SLAY.

slam ['slæm] **1.** *tv.* to shut something noisily and with force. **2.** *tv.* to insult or criticize someone or something very strongly. (Informal.) **3.** *iv.* [for something] to shut very noisily and with force. **4.** *n.* a loud and violent closing or crash.

slander ['slæn dɚ] **1.** *n.* a spoken or written lie that is meant to hurt someone's reputation; something false that is said in order to hurt someone's reputation. (No pl.) **2.** *tv.* to damage someone's reputation by lying about that person.

slanderous ['slæn dɚ əs] *adj.* understood or intended to be slander. (Adv: *slanderously.*)

457

slang ['slæŋ] **1.** *n.* words or expressions that are not expected in formal, educational, or business settings. (Not usually pl.) **2.** the *adj.* use of ①.

slant ['slænt] **1.** *n.* a slope; an angle. (No pl.) **2.** *iv.* to slope; to angle; to move at an angle; to rise or fall while moving in a certain direction. **3.** *tv.* to cause something to be angled; to cause something to move at an angle. **4.** *tv.* to express something in a way that favors one point of view over another.

slap ['slæp] **1.** *tv.* to hit someone or something with one's open hand; to hit someone or something with something flat. **2.** *tv.* to put something on a surface carelessly and with force. **3.** *n.* a hit with one's open hand or with something flat. **4.** *n.* the noise made when someone or something is hit with someone's open hand or with something flat.

slash ['slæʃ] **1.** *tv.* to cut something violently with a sharp object, using large, sweeping movements. **2.** *tv.* to reduce numbers or amounts greatly. **3.** *n.* a cut made by a violent movement as in ①; a gash. **4.** *n.* the "/" symbol; the "\" symbol.

slate ['slet] **1.** *n.* a rock that splits easily into flat, thin layers. (No pl.) **2.** *n.* a group of candidates offered by a political party in an election. **3.** *adj.* made of ①.

slaughter ['slɔ tɚ] **1.** *tv.* to kill and cut up an animal for food. **2.** *tv.* to kill living creatures ruthlessly.

slave ['slev] *n.* someone who is owned by someone else; someone who is the property of someone else.

slavery ['slev (ə) ri] *n.* the ownership of slaves. (No pl.)

slay ['sle] *tv., irreg.* to kill someone or some animal; to murder someone. (Pt: SLEW; pp: SLAIN.)

slaying ['sle ɪŋ] *n.* a murder; the killing of someone or some animal.

sleazy ['sli zi] *adj.* cheap and crude; having a bad reputation. (Adv: *sleazily.* Comp: *sleazier;* sup: *sleaziest.*)

sled ['slɛd] **1.** *n.* a flat platform attached to long, thin blades that move easily over snow. **2.** *iv.* to ride somewhere on ①; to play with ①; to travel by ①.

sleek ['slik] **1.** *adj.* smooth and shiny. (Especially used to describe hair or fur—of people or animals—that is healthy or well cared for. Adv: *sleekly.* Comp: *sleeker;* sup: *sleekest.*) **2.** *adj.* having neat, smooth lines; stylish. (Adv: *sleekly.* Comp: *sleeker;* sup: *sleekest.*)

458

sleep ['slip] **1.** *n.* the period of rest when the mind is not conscious; the period of rest when the body is not awake. (No pl.) **2.** *iv., irreg.* not to be awake; to rest the body and mind in an unconscious condition. (Pt/pp: SLEPT.) **3.** *tv., irreg.* to provide space for a certain number of people to SLEEP as in ②; to have enough space for a certain number of people to SLEEP as in ②.

sleepless ['slip ləs] *adj.* without sleep; unable to sleep. (Adv: *sleeplessly.*)

sleepwalk ['slip wɔk] *iv.* to walk while sleeping.

sleepwalker ['slip wɔk ɚ] *n.* someone who walks around while sleeping.

sleepy ['slip i] *adj.* tired; drowsy; needing to sleep. (Adv: *sleepily.* Comp: *sleepier;* sup: *sleepiest.*)

sleet ['slit] **1.** *n.* partly frozen rain; partly frozen rain mixed with snow or hail. (No pl.) **2.** *iv.* [for ①] to fall from the sky.

sleeve ['sliv] *n.* the part of an item of clothing that covers the arm.

sleeveless ['sliv ləs] *adj.* without sleeves. (Adv: *sleevelessly.*)

sleigh ['sle] *n.* a large sled; a platform or carriage—usually pulled by horses or dogs—attached to long, metal blades for traveling over snow.

slender ['slɛn dɚ] *adj.* slim; thin, in a pleasant or graceful way. (Adv: *slenderly.* Comp: *slenderer;* sup: *slenderest.*)

slept ['slɛpt] pt/pp of SLEEP.

slew ['slu] **1.** pt of SLAY. **2.** *n.* a large amount of something. (Informal.)

slice ['slɑɪs] **1.** *n.* a thin, flat piece that is cut from something. **2.** *n.* a part; a portion; a share. **3.** *tv.* to cut a thin, flat piece from something; to cut something into thin, flat pieces.

slick ['slɪk] **1.** *adj.* wet and slippery; oily and slippery; icy and slippery. (Adv: *slickly.* Comp: *slicker;* sup: *slickest.*) **2.** *adj.* clever; sly; shrewd. (Informal. Adv: *slickly.* Comp: *slicker;* sup: *slickest.*) **3.** *adj.* attractive or nicely designed, but without much content or meaning; shallow. (Adv: *slickly.* Comp: *slicker;* sup: *slickest.*)

slid ['slɪd] pt/pp of SLIDE.

slide ['slɑɪd] **1.** *iv., irreg.* to move or glide along a smooth surface; to move down a surface; to move without resistance. (Pt/pp: SLID.) **2.** *iv., irreg.* to move backward or forward on a groove or track. **3.** *tv., irreg.* to cause someone or something to glide along a smooth surface or on a track; to cause someone or something to move or glide along a

459

smooth surface. **4.** *tv., irreg.* to move something quietly, especially without anyone else noticing. **5.** *n.* a downward movement; a decline. **6.** *n.* a small, square frame with a picture on a piece of film in the center, the image of which can be projected onto a screen. **7.** *n.* a small, thin, rectangular piece of glass that small objects are placed on so that they can be examined under a microscope.

slight ['slaɪt] **1.** *adj.* not very large; not very important. (Adv: *slightly.* Comp: *slighter;* sup: *slightest.*) **2.** *adj.* frail; delicate; not strong. (Adv: *slightly.* Comp: *slighter;* sup: *slightest.*) **3.** *tv.* to neglect mentioning someone or something; to insult a person by ignoring the person's presence or accomplishments. **4.** *n.* the insult of treating someone as unimportant; the lack of attention paid to someone or something.

slightly ['slaɪt li] *adv.* a little; to a small degree.

slim ['slɪm] **1.** *adj.* thin; slender. (Adv: *slimly.* Comp: *slimmer;* sup: *slimmest.*) **2.** *adj.* small in amount or quality; slight. (Adv: *slimly.* Comp: *slimmer;* sup: *slimmest.*)

slime ['slaɪm] *n.* a soft, sticky, unpleasant fluid; filth. (No pl.)

slimy ['slaɪ mi] *adj.* covered with slime; like slime; filthy. (Adv: *slimily.* Comp: *slimier;* sup: *slimiest.*)

sling ['slɪŋ] **1.** *tv., irreg.* to throw something with force; to hurl something; to fling something. (Pt/pp: SLUNG.) **2.** *tv., irreg.* to hang or suspend something from something or between two things. (Informal.) **3.** *n.* a strip of cloth that is used to support an injured arm by being looped around the neck.

slip ['slɪp] **1.** *iv.* to fall accidentally while moving or being moved; to slide from a place or position. **2.** *iv.* to move or happen quietly, quickly, smoothly, easily, secretly, or without being noticed. **3.** *iv.* to grow worse; to lower; to diminish; to decline. **4.** *n.* an accidental fall as in ①. **5.** *n.* a mistake; an error; something that was done wrong.

slipper ['slɪp ɚ] *n.* a foot covering that one wears indoors and that can be taken on and off easily; a shoe made of light materials.

slippery ['slɪp (ə) ri] **1.** *adj.* allowing people or things to slip. **2.** *adj.* hard to catch or hold; likely to slip out of one's hands.

slit ['slɪt] **1.** *n.* a straight, narrow cut or opening. **2.** *tv., irreg.* to cut or tear something in a straight line so that there is a narrow opening. (Pt/pp: *slit.*)

sliver ['slɪv ɚ] *n.* a small, thin, sharp piece or stick of something.

460

slob ['slɑb] *n.* someone who is very messy; someone who is rude and coarse.

slogan ['slo gən] *n.* a motto; a unique word or phrase used in advertising or politics.

slope ['slop] **1.** *n.* the slanted side of a mountain or hill. **2.** *n.* the amount that a line or surface SLOPES as in ③. (No pl.) **3.** *iv.* to lean, be set, or be formed at an angle. **4.** *tv.* to cause something to be at an angle; to cause something not to be level or straight up and down.

sloping ['slop ɪŋ] *adj.* at an angle; not flat or straight up and down. (Adv: *slopingly.*)

sloppy ['slɑp i] **1.** *adj.* muddy; rainy; very wet as the result of bad weather. (Adv: *sloppily.* Comp: *sloppier;* sup: *sloppiest.*) **2.** *adj.* messy; not tidy; careless. (Adv: *sloppily.* Comp: *sloppier;* sup: *sloppiest.*)

slot ['slɑt] **1.** *n.* a narrow opening in an object or machine. **2.** *n.* a place on a list or schedule. **3.** *tv.* to place someone or something on a list or schedule.

slouch ['slaʊtʃ] *iv.* to sit, stand, or move without holding one's body erect.

slovenly ['slʌv ən li] *adj.* [of someone] dirty or messy in appearance.

slow ['slo] **1.** *adj.* not fast; not quick; taking a long time; taking more time than average; moving with less speed than average. (Adv: *slowly.* See also ④. Comp: *slower;* sup: *slowest.*) **2.** *adj.* behind schedule; happening later than the time something is supposed to happen. (Comp: *slower;* sup: *slowest.*) **3.** *adj.* boring; dull; without much action or interest. (Adv: *slowly.* Comp: *slower;* sup: *slowest.*) **4.** *adv.* at the pace described in ①. (Comp: *slower;* sup: *slowest.*) **5.** *iv.* to become ①; to become less fast; to move less fast. **6.** *tv.* to cause something to become ①; to cause something to move less fast.

slug ['slʌg] **1.** *n.* a small, slimy creature, similar to a snail but without a shell. **2.** *n.* a hit or blow, especially with a closed fist. **3.** *tv.* to hit someone or something using one's closed fist.

sluggish ['slʌg ɪʃ] *adj.* moving slowly or without energy; not very active. (Adv: *sluggishly.*)

slum ['slʌm] *n.* a neighborhood where most of the people live in poverty.

slumber ['slʌm bɚ] **1.** *iv.* to sleep. **2.** *n.* sleep; deep rest.

slump ['slʌmp] **1.** *n.* a financial collapse; a sudden fall or decline. **2.** *iv.* to sink; to slouch. **3.** *iv.* [for a value] to sink lower. (Fig. on ②.)

slung ['slʌŋ] pt/pp of SLING.

slur ['slɚ] **1.** *tv.* to say something in a way that is not clear; to pronounce something in a way that is not clear. **2.** *n.* an insult.

slush ['slʌʃ] *n.* a mixture of snow and water; snow that has started to melt. (No pl.)

sly ['slaɪ] *adj.* sneaky; clever; able to do things secretly. (Adv: *slyly.* Comp: *slyer;* sup: *slyest.*)

smack ['smæk] **1.** *tv.* to hit someone or something, especially noisily; to strike someone or something noisily, as with an open hand or a flat object. **2.** *n.* the sound made when something is smacked as in ①.

small ['smɔl] **1.** *adj.* not large; less than average size or weight. (Comp: *smaller;* sup: *smallest.*) **2.** *adj.* little; slight; not a lot; having less than an average amount of something. (Comp: *smaller;* sup: *smallest.*) **3.** *adj.* [of letters] lowercase; [of letters] not capital.

small-time *adj.* small; on a small scale.

smart ['smɑrt] **1.** *adj.* intelligent; not stupid; able to learn things quickly. (Comp: *smarter;* sup: *smartest.*) **2.** *adj.* showing a current style; in style; in fashion; trendy. (Adv: *smartly.* Comp: *smarter;* sup: *smartest.*) **3.** *iv.* to sting; to feel sharp pain; to cause sharp pain.

smash ['smæʃ] **1.** *tv.* to break something into tiny pieces noisily or violently. **2.** *iv.* to break into tiny pieces noisily or violently.

smear ['smɪr] **1.** *tv.* to spread something on a surface, especially in a careless or messy fashion. **2.** *tv.* to ruin someone's reputation; to make someone look bad; to say bad things about someone. **3.** *n.* a stain; a mark made by wiping something on a surface.

smell ['smɛl] **1.** *n.* odor; something in the air, sensed with one's nose. (Pl only for types and instances.) **2.** *tv.* to sense something with the nose; to sense an odor or scent; to sense something that has an odor or scent. **3.** *iv.* to have a certain quality of scent or odor. **4.** *iv.* to stink; to have a bad smell.

smelly ['smɛl i] *adj.* having a bad or strong odor. (Comp: *smellier;* sup: *smelliest.*)

smile ['smaɪl] **1.** *n.* a facial expression where the ends of the mouth are turned up, indicating happiness, amusement, or a good mood. **2.** *iv.* to have ① on one's face; to look happy or pleased.

smiling ['smaɪl ɪŋ] *adj.* having a smile; happy; cheerful. (Adv: *smilingly.*)

smock ['smɑk] *n.* a light covering that one wears over one's clothes to protect them from becoming dirty while working, especially as worn by a doctor, nurse, painter, etc.

smog ['smɔg] *n.* smoke and fog that are trapped in the air; a mixture of fumes and smoke that are trapped like fog over a place. (A combination of *smoke* and *fog*. No pl.)

smoke ['smok] **1.** *n.* a cloud of gas that can be seen in the air when something burns. (No pl.) **2.** *n.* an act or session of burning tobacco and inhaling the ①. (Informal.) **3.** *iv.* to give off ①; to release ① into the air. **4.** *iv.* to inhale and then exhale ① from burning tobacco. **5.** *tv.* to inhale ① of burning cigarettes, tobacco, etc., into the lungs. **6.** *tv.* to preserve food by exposing it to ① from burning wood.

smoking ['smok ɪŋ] **1.** *adj.* giving off smoke. **2.** *adj.* a word used to indicate that people are permitted to SMOKE ④.

smoky ['smok i] **1.** *adj.* [of air] full of smoke; tasting or smelling like smoke. (Comp: *smokier;* sup: *smokiest.*) **2.** *adj.* giving off more smoke than normal or expected. (Adv: *smokily.* Comp: *smokier;* sup: *smokiest.*)

smolder ['smol dɚ] **1.** *iv.* [for wood or other fibers] to burn or give off smoke without having a flame. **2.** *iv.* [feelings that seem] to grow yet remain trapped and unexpressed. (Fig. on ①.)

smoldering ['smol dɚ ɪŋ] *adj.* burning or giving off smoke without having a flame. (Adv: *smolderingly.*)

smooth ['smuð] **1.** *adj.* having an even surface; having a surface without bumps; not rough. (Adv: *smoothly.* Comp: *smoother;* sup: *smoothest.*) **2.** *adj.* gentle; not rough; calm; not harsh. (Adv: *smoothly.* Comp: *smoother;* sup: *smoothest.*) **3.** *adj.* without lumps; having an even texture. (Adv: *smoothly.* Comp: *smoother;* sup: *smoothest.*) **4.** *tv.* to cause something to become ①.

smother ['smʌð ɚ] **1.** *iv.* to die because one cannot get enough oxygen, especially because something is covering one's mouth; to suffocate. **2.** *tv.* to kill a living creature by preventing it from breathing. **3.** *tv.* to cover something with a thick layer of something.

smudge ['smʌdʒ] **1.** *n.* a dirty mark or stain; a smear. **2.** *tv.* to dirty something with a mark.

smug ['smʌg] *adj.* confident and pleased with oneself and one's abilities; too satisfied with oneself. (Adv: *smugly.* Comp: *smugger;* sup: *smuggest.*)

smuggle [ˈsmʌg əl] *tv.* to bring something into or take something out of a country illegally.

smuggler [ˈsmʌg lɚ] *n.* a criminal who brings something into or takes things from a country illegally.

smuggling [ˈsmʌg lɪŋ] *n.* the illegal business of bringing something into or taking things out of a country. (No pl.)

snack [ˈsnæk] **1.** *n.* food that is eaten between meals; a small amount of food. **2.** *iv.* to eat a small amount of food between meals.

snag [ˈsnæg] **1.** *n.* a thread that is pulled away from where it belongs in a fabric. **2.** *n.* something that gets in the way; something that causes a problem in a plan or procedure. **3.** *tv.* to catch a piece of clothing or material by a thread.

snail [ˈsnel] *n.* a small, soft creature that has no limbs, has two small feelers, and lives in a hard, round shell.

snake [ˈsnek] **1.** *n.* a long, thin reptile that has no limbs. **2.** *iv.* to move in twists and turns; to curve like ①. **3.** *tv.* to move something in twists and turns; to bend something into curves like the curves of ①.

snap [ˈsnæp] **1.** *iv.* [for something] to make a sharp, popping sound, usually by breaking. **2.** *iv.* [for something that is pulled tight or is under pressure] to break suddenly. **3.** *tv.* to break something that is pulled tight or is under pressure. **4.** *tv.* to take a picture with a camera. **5.** *tv.* to close ⑧. **6.** *n.* the noise made when something SNAPS as in ① or ②; a quick, sudden, popping sound. **7.** *n.* a sudden breaking of something; the breaking of something that is pulled tight or is under pressure. **8.** *n.* a metallic or plastic fastener that closes firmly when pressed.

snapshot [ˈsnæp ʃɑt] *n.* a photograph; a picture taken with a camera.

snare [ˈsnɛr] **1.** *tv.* to trap someone or something; to catch someone or something in a trap. **2.** *n.* a trap for catching animals.

snarl [ˈsnɑrl] **1.** *iv.* to growl. **2.** *iv.* to become tangled. **3.** *n.* an angry growl.

snarling [ˈsnɑr lɪŋ] *adj.* growling angrily.

snatch [ˈsnætʃ] *tv.* to grab someone or something suddenly; to steal something or kidnap someone.

sneak [ˈsnik] **1.** *iv., irreg.* to move quietly and secretly; to move without being noticed. (Pt/pp: *sneaked* or SNUCK.) **2.** *tv., irreg.* to obtain or take something, such as a taste, a look, a peek, a touch, etc., quietly and secretly.

sneaker ['snik ɚ] *n.* one of a pair of gym shoes or tennis shoes; one of a pair of comfortable, casual canvas shoes with rubber soles.

sneaky ['snik i] *adj.* doing something dishonest or wrong, quietly and secretly. (Adv: *sneakily.* Comp: *sneakier;* sup: *sneakiest.*)

sneer ['snɪr] **1.** *iv.* to show contempt by the look on one's face. **2.** *n.* a look of contempt.

sneeze ['sniz] **1.** *n.* a sudden and uncontrollable burst of air and mucus that is pushed out of the nose and mouth. **2.** *iv.* to make ①.

snicker ['snɪk ɚ] **1.** *iv.* to laugh; to laugh at someone or something. **2.** *n.* a laugh; a small laugh.

sniff ['snɪf] **1.** *iv.* to breathe in through the nose in small, quick puffs that can be heard. **2.** *iv.* to become aware of a smell by SNIFFING as in ①. **3.** *n.* a small, quick breath made through the nose, made especially when smelling something.

snip ['snɪp] **1.** *tv.* to clip something; to cut something with scissors in short strokes; to cut something up into tiny pieces. **2.** *n.* a short cutting movement; a short stroke made with scissors.

snob ['snɑb] *n.* someone who displays arrogance; someone who acts superior to others.

snobbish ['snɑb ɪʃ] *adj.* arrogant; thinking that one is better than others. (Adv: *snobbishly.*)

snoop ['snup] *iv.* to sneak; to pry; to search through something without the owner's permission.

snooze ['snuz] **1.** *iv.* to sleep; to nap. **2.** *n.* sleep; a nap. (Informal.)

snore ['snor] *iv.* to breathe loudly while sleeping, especially to pass air through the nose so that it vibrates and makes a loud noise.

snort ['snort] **1.** *iv.* to make a short, loud noise by blowing air through the nose. **2.** *tv.* to inhale something, usually a drug, forcefully into the nose. (Informal.) **3.** *n.* the noise made by blowing through the nose.

snow ['sno] **1.** *n.* water vapor that has frozen into small white flakes that fall from the sky. (No pl.) **2.** *n.* an instance of ① falling from the sky; a coating of ① on the ground. **3.** *iv.* [for ①] to fall from the sky.

snowball ['sno bɔl] **1.** *n.* a ball of snowflakes that have been pressed together. **2.** *iv.* to grow at a rapidly increasing rate. (Fig. on ①.)

snowbank ['sno bæŋk] *n.* a big, long mound of snow.

465

snowbound ['sno baʊnd] *adj.* not able to leave home or travel because there is too much snow.

snowdrift ['sno drɪft] *n.* a ridge of snow shaped by wind blowing it along the ground.

snowflake ['sno flek] *n.* one individual piece of snow; a drop of water that freezes and falls from the sky as snow.

snowman ['sno mæn] *n., irreg.* a mass of snow that has been shaped like a person. (Pl: SNOWMEN.)

snowmen ['sno mɛn] pl of SNOWMAN.

snowplow ['sno plaʊ] *n.* a tractor or other vehicle with a large scoop or blade in front to clear snow from roads, driveways, and other surfaces.

snowshoe ['sno ʃu] *n.* a light frame with leather straps stretched across it, which attaches to the bottom of shoes or boots so that one can walk on top of snow and not sink into it.

snowstorm ['sno storm] *n.* a storm with lots of snow; a blizzard.

snuck ['snʌk] a pt/pp of SNEAK.

snug ['snʌg] **1.** *adj.* warm; cozy; comfortable. (Adv: *snugly.* Comp: *snugger;* sup: *snuggest.*) **2.** *adj.* too tight; fitting too closely. (Adv: *snugly.* Comp: *snugger;* sup: *snuggest.*)

snuggle ['snʌg əl] *iv.* to cuddle; to press against someone for warmth or to show affection.

so ['so] **1.** *adv.* to a certain degree; to such a high degree; very. **2.** *adv.* in such a way; in that way; in this way. **3.** *adv.* also; too; as well. (Comes before the verbs BE, DO, or HAVE. In negative constructions, use NEITHER or *not either.*) **4.** *conj.* in order that; with the result that. **5.** *conj.* therefore; hence; consequently. **6.** *interj.* a mild exclamation of surprise or indignation. **7.** *adj.* true. (Not prenominal.)

so long as Go to AS LONG AS.

soak ['sok] **1.** *iv.* to remain in [a container of] liquid for a period of time. **2.** *tv.* to cause something to become or remain completely wet. **3.** *n.* a period of time spent in [a container of] liquid.

soap ['sop] **1.** *n.* a substance that helps clean objects being washed. (Pl only for types and instances.) **2.** *tv.* to clean someone or something with ①; to cover someone or something with ① while washing.

soapy ['so pi] *adj.* covered with soap. (Adv: *soapily.* Comp: *soapier;* sup: *soapiest.*)

466

soar ['sor] **1.** *iv.* to fly; to fly upward; to glide. **2.** *iv.* to increase suddenly and in a large amount; to go up suddenly and in a large amount. (Fig. on ①.)

sob ['sab] **1.** *iv.* to cry while breathing short, quick breaths. **2.** *n.* a short, quick sound made while one is crying.

sober ['sob ɚ] **1.** *adj.* not drunk; not having been drinking alcohol. (Adv: *soberly.* Comp: *soberer;* sup: *soberest.*) **2.** *adj.* very serious; with dignity. (Adv: *soberly.* Comp: *soberer;* sup: *soberest.*)

soccer ['sɑk ɚ] *n.* a sport played by two teams of eleven people who move a round ball about a field. (In Europe, soccer is called *football.* No pl.)

social ['so ʃəl] **1.** *adj.* of or about friendship or interaction with other people. (Adv: *socially.*) **2.** *adj.* living together or forming groups in an organized way. (Adv: *socially.*)

society [sə 'sɑɪ ə ti] **1.** *n.* all people; all humans. (No pl.) **2.** *n.* all people in a certain culture during a certain period of time. **3.** *n.* an organization whose members have similar interests or goals; a club. **4.** *n.* the upper-class people of a community; the community of people assumed to have good manners; people who are thought to be in an exclusive or desirable social class. (No pl.)

sociology [so si 'ɑl ə dʒi] *n.* the study of the functioning and organization of human society. (No pl.)

sock ['sɑk] *n.* a fabric covering for the foot, usually worn inside a shoe.

socket ['sɑk ət] *n.* **1.** one of a number of types of opening that something round fits into. **2.** an opening into which an electrical plug is put.

sod ['sɑd] *n.* turf; a piece of ground held together by the roots of grass. (No pl.)

soda ['so də] **1.** *n.* a soft drink; a drink with lots of little bubbles, usually sweetly flavored. (Short for *soda pop.*) **2.** *n.* water containing lots of little bubbles, having little or no flavor. (Short for *soda water.*)

sofa ['so fə] *n.* a couch; a seat that is wide enough for more than one or two people.

soft ['sɔft] **1.** *adj.* not hard; yielding to pressure; less hard than average. (Adv: *softly.* Comp: *softer;* sup: *softest.*) **2.** *adj.* delicate; smooth; calm; not rough; not coarse; not harsh; gently affecting the senses. (Adv: *softly.* Comp: *softer;* sup: *softest.*) **3.** *adj.* not strong or strict; weak or lax. (Adv: *softly.* Comp: *softer;* sup: *softest.*) **4.** *adj.* [of water]

467

lacking certain minerals and able to make lather from soap easily. (Comp: *softer*; sup: *softest*.) **5.** *adj.* [of a letter] pronounced like the *c* in *cent* rather than the *c* of *cold*. **6.** *adj.* quiet; not loud. (Adv: *softly*. See also (7). Comp: *softer*; sup: *softest*.) **7.** *adv.* quietly; not as loudly. (Comp: *softer*; sup: *softest*.)

softball ['sɔft bɔl] **1.** *n.* a game that is similar to baseball but uses a bigger, softer ball. (No pl.) **2.** *n.* a ball that is like a baseball but is bigger and somewhat softer. **3.** the *adj.* use of (1).

software ['sɔft wɛr] *n.* one or more computer programs meant to be used or stored on a computer. (No pl.)

soggy ['sɑg i] *adj.* moist; wet; soaked. (Adv: *soggily*. Comp: *soggier*; sup: *soggiest*.)

soil ['sɔɪl] **1.** *n.* the ground; the top layer of dirt that plants grow in. (Pl only for types and instances.) **2.** *tv.* to make something dirty.

soiled ['sɔɪld] *adj.* dirtied; made dirty.

solar ['so lɚ] *adj.* of or about the sun, the light of the sun, or the heat of the sun.

sold ['sold] pt/pp of SELL.

soldier ['sol dʒɚ] *n.* someone who serves or fights in an army, especially one who is not an officer.

sole ['sol] **1.** *adj.* only; [the] only [one]. (Adv: *solely*.) **2.** *n.* the bottom surface of the foot; the bottom part of a shoe, boot, or other piece of footwear. **3.** *n., irreg.* a flat, edible fish. (Pl: *sole*.) **4.** *n.* the edible flesh of (3). (No pl.) **5.** *tv.* to put a new SOLE as in (2) on a shoe or boot.

solemn ['sɑl əm] **1.** *adj.* [of someone] very serious. (Adv: *solemnly*.) **2.** *adj.* very formal; associated with a religious or formal ceremony. (Adv: *solemnly*.)

solid ['sɑl ɪd] **1.** *n.* something that is hard and does not allow its shape to be changed easily; something that is not a liquid and not a gas. **2.** *adj.* not liquid or gas; having a shape that does not change on its own to fit a container. (Adv: *solidly*.) **3.** *adj.* not hollow; having an inside that is full of something. (Adv: *solidly*.) **4.** *adj.* [of a period of time] continuous and not interrupted. (Adv: *solidly*. Before or after a noun.) **5.** *adj.* sturdy; well made; dependable; able to be relied on; strong; not likely to break, collapse, or fail. (Adv: *solidly*.)

solids *n.* food that is SOLID (2) and not liquid. (Treated as pl.)

solitary ['sɑl ɪ tɛr i] *adj.* alone; by oneself. (Adv: *solitarily* [sɑl ə 'tɛr ə li].)

solo ['so lo] **1.** *n.* a musical piece performed by one person; a piece of music written primarily for one singer or one instrument. (Pl ends in -s.) **2.** *adj.* done alone; done without help. **3.** *adv.* without help; alone. **4.** *iv.* to perform by oneself; to do something by oneself.

solution [sə 'lu ʃən] **1.** *n.* an answer to a problem or question; a way to fix a problem. **2.** *n.* a liquid that has a solid or gas dissolved in it; a mixture of a liquid and a solid or gas that has been dissolved in the liquid.

solve ['sɔlv] *tv.* to find the answer to a question or a problem.

some ['sʌm] **1.** *adj.* [of a person or creature] unnamed or unknown. **2.** *adj.* a few; more than one, but not many. (Use ANY in negative statements or questions.) **3.** *adj.* [of something] excellent, exciting, or extreme. (Informal. Always stressed.) **4.** *n.* a number of people or things; a few people or things, but less than many. (No pl.)

somebody ['sʌm bɑd i] **1.** *pron.* some person; someone; a certain unnamed person. (Compare this with ANYBODY.) **2.** *n.* a famous or important person rather than just nobody. (Compare this with ANYBODY.)

someday ['sʌm de] *adv.* at some time in the future.

somehow ['sʌm haʊ] *adv.* in some way; in some manner; in a way that is not yet known.

someone ['sʌm wən] *pron.* somebody; some person; a person; a certain unnamed person. (Compare this with ANYONE.)

someplace ['sʌm ples] *adv.* SOMEWHERE; at, in, or to someplace. (Informal. SOMEWHERE is preferred by some people. Compare this with ANYPLACE.)

something ['sʌm θɪŋ] **1.** *pron.* some thing; a certain thing that is not known or named. (Compare this with ANYTHING.) **2.** *n.* a thing that is more than nothing. (Compare this with ANYTHING. No pl.) **3.** *adv.* somewhat; in some way. (E.g., *look something alike.*)

sometime ['sʌm taɪm] *adv.* at some point in time that is not known or stated.

sometimes *adv.* now and then; occasionally; from time to time.

somewhat ['sʌm mət] *adj.* rather; slightly; to some degree; kind of.

somewhere ['sʌm mɛr] *adv.* at, in, or to someplace. (Compare this with ANYWHERE.)

son ['sʌn] *n.* someone's male child; the male child of a parent. (Also used as a term of address by an older person to any boy or young man.)

song ['sɔŋ] **1.** *n.* a story or words that are set to music; words that are sung. **2.** *n.* singing; the art, practice, or action of singing. (No pl.) **3.** *n.* the musical noise that birds make.

songbird ['sɔŋ bɚd] *n.* any common bird with a characteristic song.

soon ['sun] *adv.* in a short period of time; before long; shortly. (Comp: *sooner;* sup: *soonest.*)

soot ['sʊt] *n.* a black powder that is made by burning something, such as coal or wood. (No pl form in this sense.)

soothe ['suð] **1.** *tv.* to calm someone or something; to comfort someone or something; to ease pain or discomfort. **2.** *iv.* to be a comfort; to be a relief.

soothing ['suð ɪŋ] *adj.* comforting; calming; relieving. (Adv: *soothingly.*)

soprano [sə 'præn o] **1.** *n.* someone, usually a woman, who sings the highest musical notes. (Pl ends in *-s.*) **2.** the *adj.* use of ①.

sorcerer ['sɔrs ə rɚ] *n.* a male magician who contacts evil spirits.

sorcery ['sɔr sə ri] *n.* magic practiced with the help of evil spirits. (No pl.)

sore ['sɔr] **1.** *adj.* in a state of hurting; painful; aching. (Adv: *sorely.* Comp: *sorer;* sup: *sorest.*) **2.** *n.* a painful infection or injury on the skin.

sorrow ['sɑr o] **1.** *n.* sadness; grief. **2.** *n.* a cause of sadness, grief, or misfortune.

sorry ['sɑr i] **1.** *adj.* expressing an apology. (Not prenominal. Comp: *sorrier;* sup: *sorriest.*) **2.** *adj.* sad; feeling pity; wishing that something had happened differently. (Not prenominal. Comp: *sorrier;* sup: *sorriest.*) **3.** *adj.* regretful; wishing that one had acted differently. (Not prenominal. Comp: *sorrier;* sup: *sorriest.*) **4.** *adj.* not adequate or acceptable. (Only prenominal. Comp: *sorrier;* sup: *sorriest.*)

sort ['sɔrt] **1.** *n.* a kind; a category; a group of similar persons, things, or qualities. **2.** *tv.* to put things in a particular order; to arrange things by category; to separate things by category.

sought ['sɔt] pt/pp of SEEK.

soul ['sol] **1.** *n.* the part of a human that is said to be separate from the body (and that some religions believe never dies); the part of the body that controls emotion and thought; the spirit. **2.** *n.* a person; a human being. **3.** *n.* the force or spirit that gives something depth or meaning. (Fig. on ①.)

sound [ˈsaʊnd] **1.** *n.* a property of vibrating air that can stimulate the ears and be heard. (No pl.) **2.** *n.* a noise; vibrations that stimulate the ears. **3.** *n.* a narrow channel of water that connects two larger bodies of water. **4.** *tv.* to cause something to make a noise; to cause something to be heard. **5.** *iv.* to make a characteristic noise. **6.** *iv.* to be heard in a certain way. **7.** *adj.* [of sleep] deep. (Adv: *soundly.*) **8.** *adj.* healthy; not damaged or injured; in good condition. **9.** *adj.* strong; sturdy; safe. (Adv: *soundly.* Comp: *sounder;* sup: *soundest.*) **10.** *adj.* sane; logical; reasonable; well reasoned; using good sense or judgment. (Adv: *soundly.* Comp: *sounder;* sup: *soundest.*)

soup [ˈsup] *n.* a liquid food that is made by boiling meat, fish, vegetables, or other foods. (Pl only for types and instances.)

sour [ˈsaʊɚ] **1.** *adj.* tasting like an acid; having a taste like lemons; not sweet, salty, or bitter. (Adv: *sourly.* Comp: *sourer;* sup: *sourest.*) **2.** *adj.* [of milk] spoiled. (Adv: *sourly.* Comp: *sourer;* sup: *sourest.*) **3.** *adj.* unpleasant; disagreeable. (Adv: *sourly.* Comp: *sourer;* sup: *sourest.*) **4.** *iv.* [for milk] to become ②.

source [ˈsors] *n.* the origin of something; the place where something comes from.

south [ˈsaʊθ] **1.** *n.* the direction to the right of someone or something facing east. (No pl.) **2.** *n.* the part of a region, country, or planet located toward ①. (No pl. Capitalized when referring to a region of the United States.) **3.** *adj.* to ①; toward ①; facing ①, located in ②. **4.** *adj.* coming from ①, especially used to describe wind. **5.** *adv.* toward ①.

southeast [saʊθ ˈist] **1.** *n.* the direction halfway between south and east. (No pl.) **2.** *n.* an area in the southeastern part of a region or country. (Capitalized when referring to a region of the United States.) **3.** *adj.* located in the ②; toward ①; facing ①. **4.** *adj.* from ①, especially describing wind. **5.** *adv.* toward ①.

southeastern [saʊθ ˈis tɚn] *adj.* in the southeast; toward the southeast; facing the southeast.

southern [ˈsʌð ɚn] **1.** *adj.* in the south; toward the south; facing south. **2.** *adj.* from the SOUTH ①, especially describing wind. **3.** *adj.* concerning the society and culture of the American South. (Often capitalized.)

471

southerner ['sʌð ɚ nɚ] *n.* someone who lives in the southern part of a country, especially someone from the southern United States. (Sometimes capitalized.)

southwest [saʊθ 'wɛst] **1.** *n.* the direction halfway between south and west. (No pl.) **2.** *n.* the southwestern part of a region or a country. (No pl. Capitalized when referring to a region of the United States.) **3.** *adj.* located in ①; toward ①; facing ①. **4.** *adj.* from ①, especially describing wind. **5.** *adv.* toward ①.

southwestern [saʊθ 'wɛs tɚn] *adj.* in the southwest; toward the southwest; facing the southwest.

souvenir [su və 'nɪr] *n.* something that reminds one of someplace, someone, or one's travels; a keepsake.

sovereign ['sɑv rɪn] **1.** *n.* a king or queen; a monarch; a ruler in a monarchy. **2.** *adj.* having the highest power. (Adv: *sovereignly.*) **3.** *adj.* independent; not controlled by another country; self-governing. (Adv: *sovereignly.*)

sow 1. ['so] *tv., irreg.* to drop or toss seed on the ground; to plant crops by scattering seed on the ground. (Pp: SOWN or *sowed.*) **2.** ['so] *iv., irreg.* to plant [crops] by scattering seed on the ground. **3.** ['saʊ] *n.* a female pig.

sown ['son] a pp of sow.

space ['spes] **1.** *n.* every location in existence in the universe. (No pl.) **2.** *n.* every place past the air surrounding the earth. (No pl.) **3.** *n.* a place or area that has length, width, and depth; a place where there is room for someone or something to be. (No pl.) **4.** *n.* a blank line or empty box on a piece of paper where something is to be written. **5.** *n.* an empty place between two words in a written or printed line. **6.** *tv.* to place things with distance between them.

spacecraft AND **spaceship** ['spes kræft, 'spes ʃɪp] *n., irreg.* a rocket or vehicle that travels in space. (Pl: *spacecraft* and *spaceships.*)

spaceship Go to SPACECRAFT.

spade ['sped] **1.** *n.* a tool, similar to a small shovel, used for digging. **2.** *n.* the black symbol " ♠ " found on playing cards; one of the four suits found on playing cards. **3.** *tv.* to dig something with ①.

spaghetti [spə 'gɛt i] *n.* long, thin, (often dried) sticks made of a flour and water mixture, which are boiled and then eaten as food; long sticks of pasta. (No pl.)

span ['spæn] **1.** *n.* the length of a bridge or arch between two supports. **2.** *n.* a period of time; a length of time. **3.** *tv.* to stretch over a space or a period of time; to extend across a space or a period of time.

spare ['spɛr] **1.** *adj.* surplus; extra; free; not needed. **2.** *adj.* extra; saved in case of emergency; reserved for emergency use; kept for emergency use. **3.** *n.* something that is extra and not immediately needed. **4.** *n.* an extra tire that is kept in a vehicle in case a tire loses its air. **5.** *tv.* not to permit someone to undergo punishment or execution. **6.** *tv.* to be able to give time, money, or energy.

sparrow ['spɛr o] *n.* a common, small, brown bird.

sparse ['spɑrs] *adj.* scattered; not having many people or things in a certain area; not dense; having a very small amount of people or things in an area. (Adv: *sparsely.* Comp: *sparser;* sup: *sparsest.*)

spat ['spæt] **1.** a pt/pp of SPIT. **2.** *n.* an argument; a quarrel; a disagreement.

speak ['spik] **1.** *tv., irreg.* to say something; to utter something; to express one's thoughts in words. (Pt: SPOKE; pp: SPOKEN.) **2.** *tv., irreg.* to use a language; to know how to talk in a language. **3.** *iv., irreg.* to talk; to say words.

speaker ['spik ɚ] **1.** *n.* someone who speaks; someone who makes speeches; someone who speaks a particular language. **2.** *n.* the Speaker of the U.S. House of Representatives; the presiding officer in the U.S. House of Representatives; the representative of the majority party in the House who has the most seniority. (Capitalized.) **3.** *n.* a device that reproduces sound, as found in a stereo, television, computer, etc.

special ['spɛ ʃəl] **1.** *adj.* not ordinary; not regular; set apart from other things, especially for a particular purpose or reason. (Adv: *specially.*) **2.** *n.* something that is set apart from other things, especially for a particular purpose or reason; a unique offering. **3.** *n.* the offering of something for sale at a price that is ①.

specific [spə 'sɪf ɪk] *adj.* particular; certain; definite; precise; exact. (Adv: *specifically* […ɪk li].)

specifics *n.* the details and facts of a matter. (Treated as sg.)

specimen ['spɛs ə mən] **1.** *n.* an example from a group or species of something. **2.** *n.* a small amount of something, especially a fluid from the body.

speck ['spɛk] *n.* a small particle; a very small piece of something; a small spot.

473

speckled ['spɛk əld] *adj.* marked with small dots or flecks of color.

spectacle ['spɛk tə kəl] *n.* something to be viewed; something to be seen; a display; a scene.

spectacles *n.* EYEGLASSES. (Old-fashioned. Treated as pl. Number is expressed with *pair(s) of spectacles*.)

spectator ['spɛk te təʳ] *n.* someone who watches something but does not take part in it.

speculation [spɛk jə 'le ʃən] **1.** *n.* guessing; trying to determine something, especially without knowing all of the facts. (Pl only for types and instances.) **2.** *n.* an investment in a risky business venture.

sped ['spɛd] pt/pp of SPEED.

speech ['spitʃ] **1.** *n.* the production of words by talking. (No pl.) **2.** *n.* a lecture; a formal talk to a group of listeners.

speed ['spid] **1.** *iv., irreg.* to move fast; to go fast, especially to go faster than the legal limit. (Pt/pp: SPED.) **2.** *tv., irreg.* to cause something to go or move fast; to cause something to go or move faster. **3.** *n.* the rate at which someone or something moves or does something during a period of time. (Pl only for types and instances.) **4.** *n.* rapid movement; the quickness with which someone or something moves. (No pl.)

speedboat ['spid bot] *n.* a small boat that has a powerful engine that can be driven at high speeds, especially for pleasure on lakes and rivers.

spell ['spɛl] **1.** *tv., irreg.* to say or write the letters of a word in the right order. (Pt/pp: *spelled* or, less frequently, SPELT.) **2.** *tv., irreg.* [for letters] to signify a word. **3.** *iv., irreg.* to know how to say or write the letters of many words; to be able to SPELL words as in ①.

spelt ['spɛlt] a pt/pp of SPELL.

spend ['spɛnd] **1.** *tv., irreg.* to pay an amount of money for something that one buys. (Pt/pp: SPENT.) **2.** *tv., irreg.* to pass time; to use time or energy; to consume energy.

spendthrift ['spɛnd θrɪft] *n.* someone who wastes money; someone who spends too much money.

spent ['spɛnt] **1.** pt/pp of SPEND. **2.** *adj.* exhausted.

sphere ['sfir] **1.** *n.* a perfectly round object; a globe; a ball. **2.** *n.* the area or domain where someone or something has an influence or an effect; the place or environment in which someone or something exists or acts.

spherical ['sfɛr ɪ kəl] *adj.* shaped like a sphere. (Adv: *spherically* [...ɪk li].)

spice ['spaɪs] **1.** *n.* an herb or other vegetable fiber or seed that tastes or smells unique and is used to give extra flavor to food. **2.** *n.* something that adds excitement or flavor. (Fig. on ①. No pl.) **3.** *tv.* to season or flavor food with ①.

spicy ['spaɪs i] **1.** *adj.* flavored with spices; seasoned with spices; having a sharp flavor. (Adv: *spicily*. Comp: *spicier*; sup: *spiciest*.) **2.** *adj.* somewhat vulgar; slightly sexually oriented. (Adv: *spicily*. Comp: *spicier*; sup: *spiciest*.)

spider ['spaɪ dɚ] *n.* a small creature with eight legs whose body produces a silk thread that it uses to make a web, which is then used to trap insects, which it eats.

spike ['spaɪk] **1.** *n.* a large, thick, metal nail that comes to a sharp point. **2.** *n.* a pointed metal or plastic object on the bottom of a shoe that gives the wearer extra traction. (Also called a *cleat*.) **3.** *n.* a sharp peak on a graph; an increase that can be represented as a peak on a graph.

spill ['spɪl] **1.** *tv., irreg.* to cause something, especially a liquid, to pour from a container by accident; to cause something, especially a liquid, to fall. (Pt/pp: *spilled* or, less frequently, SPILT.) **2.** *iv., irreg.* [for something, especially a liquid] to fall or be poured from a container by accident. **3.** *n.* something, especially a liquid, that has fallen or been poured from a container by accident. **4.** *n.* a fall from something.

spilt ['spɪlt] a pt/pp of SPILL.

spin ['spɪn] **1.** *iv., irreg.* to turn around in circles quickly. (Pt/pp: SPUN. *Spinned* is often heard.) **2.** *iv., irreg.* to rotate on an axis. **3.** *iv., irreg.* [for one's surroundings] to seem to revolve. **4.** *iv., irreg.* to pull and twist, making thread or yarn from wool, cotton, or other fibers. **5.** *tv., irreg.* to cause someone or something to turn around in circles quickly. **6.** *tv., irreg.* to pull and twist fibers into thread or yarn. **7.** *tv., irreg.* [for a spider] to make a web. **8.** *tv., irreg.* to create a tale, story, or lie. **9.** *n.* a short trip in or on a vehicle.

spinach ['spɪn ɪtʃ] **1.** *n.* a leafy, green vegetable. (No pl.) **2.** *adj.* made of or with ①.

spine ['spaɪn] **1.** *n.* the column of bones and the nerves within it that are at the center of the back of humans and certain other animals. **2.** *n.* any long, narrow, stiff thing that provides support, such as the side of a cover of a book where the pages are attached. (Fig. on ①.)

3. *n.* a stiff, pointed growth as found on certain plants and animals, providing protection.

spire ['spaɪɚ] *n.* the top part of a steeple; the top part of a structure on top of a building that comes to a point.

spirit ['spɪr ɪt] **1.** *n.* the part of a human that is separate from the body (and that some religions believe never dies); the part of the body that controls emotion and intellect; the soul. **2.** *n.* a being that does not have a body; a ghost. **3.** *n.* the driving force of something; something that provides energy or force to something; zeal. (Fig. on ①. No pl.)

spirits *n.* strong drink containing alcohol.

spit ['spɪt] **1.** *iv., irreg.* to expel the natural fluid from one's mouth; to push fluid out of one's mouth. (Pt/pp: spit or SPAT.) **2.** *tv., irreg.* to expel something from one's mouth; to push something out of one's mouth. **3.** *n.* fluid or mucus that comes from someone's mouth. (No pl.) **4.** *n.* a thin rod with a sharp end that food is pushed onto so that it can be roasted over a fire.

spite ['spaɪt] *n.* a desire to annoy someone else or get revenge; malice. (No pl.)

spiteful ['spaɪt fəl] *adj.* full of spite; wanting to annoy someone else or get revenge. (Adv: spitefully.)

splash ['splæʃ] **1.** *iv.* [for liquid] to scatter in many drops; [for liquid] to fall and spread in waves. **2.** *tv.* to cause a liquid to scatter in many drops or waves. **3.** *n.* an instance of a liquid scattering as in ①, and the sound that goes with it.

splatter ['splæt ɚ] **1.** *iv.* to splash, especially in a careless, clumsy, or messy way. **2.** *tv.* to splash a liquid, especially in a careless, clumsy, or messy way.

spleen ['splin] *n.* an organ in the body, near the stomach, that filters the blood and destroys old, used blood cells.

splendid ['splɛn dɪd] *adj.* excellent; very good; brilliant; wonderful; super. (Adv: splendidly.)

splice ['splaɪs] **1.** *tv.* to fasten the ends of two pieces of something together by weaving, taping, or otherwise connecting them. **2.** *n.* a joint or connection that has been made by weaving, taping, or otherwise connecting the ends of two pieces of something.

splint ['splɪnt] *n.* a flat object that is secured to a person's finger, toe, or limb in order to give support or to keep a broken bone in place.

splinter ['splɪn tɚ] 1. *n.* a sliver; a thin, sharp broken-off piece of wood, glass, or some other material. 2. *adj.* [of a group of people] separated from a larger group of people. (Prenominal only.) 3. *iv.* to separate from a larger object or group; to break into smaller pieces or groups. 4. *tv.* to break something into ①.

split ['splɪt] 1. *tv., irreg.* to separate something into sections, layers, or groups; to divide something into sections, layers, or groups. (Pt/pp: *split.*) 2. *tv., irreg.* to cut something along its length. 3. *tv., irreg.* to share something among members of a group; to divide something among members of a group. 4. *iv., irreg.* [for people or things] to separate into sections, layers, or groups. 5. *iv., irreg.* [for something] to break or tear open along its length. 6. *n.* the crack, cut, or break made by breaking or cutting something, as in ②. 7. *n.* a separation within a group. 8. *adj.* separated; divided; cut from end to end.

spoil ['spɔɪl] 1. *iv.* to become rotten; to rot; to decay. 2. *tv.* to ruin something; to destroy something; to make something so that it can no longer be used. 3. *tv.* to treat someone too well; to raise a child without discipline.

spoke ['spok] pt of SPEAK.

spoken ['spok ən] pp of SPEAK.

sponge ['spʌndʒ] 1. *n.* any of a group of small animals that live in the water, attach themselves to underwater objects, and form a soft, flexible skeleton. 2. *n.* the soft skeleton of ① used for cleaning or the absorption of liquids, or an artificial substance having the same qualities.

sponsor ['spɑn sɚ] 1. *n.* someone or an organization that supports and guides another person or organization. 2. *n.* someone who assumes responsibility for creating or developing something. 3. *n.* a business that advertises during a radio or television program. 4. *tv.* to support someone or an organization, usually with money, often for the sake of publicity.

spool ['spul] *n.* something that thread, film, wire, etc., can be wound around.

spoon ['spun] 1. *n.* a utensil that is made of a small, shallow oval bowl at the end of a handle, used for serving food, stirring drinks, and eating liquids and soft foods. 2. *tv.* to move something to a place with ①.

477

sport ['sport] **1.** *n.* competition and physical activity as found in games and some outdoor activities. (No pl.) **2.** *n.* a particular game involving physical activity and competition.

sportsman ['sports mən] *n., irreg.* a man who participates in sports events or various outdoor activities. (Pl: SPORTSMEN.)

sportsmen ['sports mən] pl of SPORTSMAN.

sporty ['spor ti] *adj.* stylish; in fashion. (Adv: *sportily.* Comp: *sportier;* sup: *sportiest.*)

spot ['spɑt] **1.** *n.* a part (typically round) of a surface that is a different color from the rest of the surface. **2.** *n.* a mark, as might be left by blood, paint, food, etc.; a dirty mark. **3.** *n.* a specific location; a place; a position. **4.** *tv.* to recognize someone or something; to happen to see someone or something.

spotless ['spɑt ləs] *adj.* totally clean; without spots. (Adv: *spotlessly.*)

spotlight ['spɑt lɑɪt] **1.** *n.* a spot or disk of strong, bright light. **2.** *n.* a lamp that produces a circle of strong, bright light. **3.** *n.* something that is the focus of public attention. **4.** *tv.* to place someone or something in the focus of attention.

spouse ['spɑʊs] *n.* a husband; a wife.

spout ['spɑʊt] **1.** *n.* the opening of something from which a liquid comes out. **2.** *tv.* to push out something, especially a liquid; to force a liquid out, especially through a narrow pipe or tube. **3.** *iv.* to flow into, out of, from, through, down, or onto someone or something.

sprain ['spren] **1.** *tv.* to twist a joint in the body in a way that causes injury or pain. **2.** *n.* a joint that has been twisted in a way that causes injury or pain.

sprang ['spræŋ] a pt of SPRING.

spray ['spre] **1.** *tv.* to direct a stream of small drops of liquid onto a surface. **2.** *tv.* to coat a surface with a stream of small drops of liquid. **3.** *n.* liquid that is pushed through the air in small drops, especially under pressure.

spread ['spred] **1.** *iv., irreg.* to move outward; to become longer, wider, or broader; to extend to a larger or to the largest area possible; to expand. (Pt/pp: *spread.*) **2.** *iv., irreg.* to be passed on to many people. **3.** *tv., irreg.* to pass along something to many people. **4.** *tv., irreg.* to stretch something out; to cause something to become longer, wider, or broader. **5.** *tv., irreg.* to apply something onto something else by moving it around, making an even layer.

478

spree ['spri] **1.** *n.* a session of wild drinking, spending, or partying. **2.** *n.* a period of activity and action.

spring ['sprɪŋ] **1.** *n.* the season of the year between winter and summer. **2.** *n.* a natural source of water from the ground; a place where water comes out of the earth. **3.** *n.* a metal coil; a metal object that is wound in the shape of a coil. **4.** *iv., irreg.* to jump; to leap. (Pt: SPRANG or SPRUNG; pp: SPRUNG.) **5.** *iv., irreg.* [for ③] to fail and lose its elastic property. **6.** the *adj.* use of ①.

sprinkle ['sprɪŋ kəl] **1.** *iv.* to fall in small drops or pieces; to scatter in small drops or pieces. **2.** *iv.* to rain a little. (With *it* as a subject.) **3.** *tv.* to cause something to fall in small drops or pieces; to scatter something in small drops or pieces. **4.** *tv.* to be scattered here and there; to be in a few locations here and there. (Usually passive.) **5.** *n.* a dust or powder that can be SPRINKLED as in ③. (No pl form in this sense.) **6.** *n.* a small amount of rain.

sprint ['sprɪnt] **1.** *iv.* to run very fast over a short distance; to run a short distance very fast. **2.** *n.* a very fast run over a short distance. **3.** *n.* a short race.

sprout ['spraʊt] **1.** *iv.* [for a plant] to bud; [for a plant] to start growing leaves, flowers, or buds; [for a plant] to grow from a seed. **2.** *tv.* to grow something, such as a leaf or branch. **3.** *n.* new growth; a new bud, leaf, flower, or stem.

spruce ['sprus] **1.** *n.* a type of pine tree having short needles. **2.** *n.* the wood of ①. (No pl.)

sprung ['sprʌŋ] pp of SPRING; a pt of SPRING.

spun ['spʌn] pt/pp of SPIN.

spur ['spɚ] **1.** *n.* a sharp object worn on the heel of a boot, used to make a horse that one is riding go faster. **2.** *n.* a highway or railroad track that branches from the main one. **3.** *tv.* to poke a horse with ①.

spy ['spaɪ] **1.** *n.* someone whose job is to secretly watch other people, organizations, or governments in order to learn information. **2.** *tv.* to see something; to discover something by sight; to secretly watch other people, organizations, or governments in order to learn information.

squabble ['skwɑb əl] **1.** *n.* a small argument; a quarrel; a disagreement. **2.** *iv.* to argue about something; to disagree over something.

squad ['skwɑd] *n.* a group of people who work together or who have been trained together for a job; a group of 11 soldiers and a leader who work together.

square ['skwɛr] **1.** *n.* a shape made with four sides that are the same length and four right angles. **2.** *n.* a four-sided area in a city surrounded by streets or buildings. **3.** *n.* an L-shaped or T-shaped tool, used for drawing and measuring right angles. **4.** *n.* a number that is the product of a number multiplied by itself. **5.** *adj.* shaped like ①. (Adv: *squarely.*) **6.** *adj.* forming a right angle; forming a 90-degree angle. (Adv: *squarely.*) **7.** *adj.* [of an area] roughly equal in size and shape to ① that has sides of the requested or demanded length. (Follows the measurement of length.) **8.** *adj.* [of an area shaped like ①] having four sides of a certain length. (A *square inch* is the area measured by a **SQUARE** ① that is one inch long and one inch wide. Adv: *squarely.*) **9.** *adj.* having no debts; having settled all debts. **10.** *tv.* to multiply a number by itself. **11.** *tv.* to make something ⑥.

squat ['skwɑt] **1.** *iv.* to crouch; to rest, sitting with one's feet on the ground and one's legs bent under one's body. **2.** *adj.* shorter or thicker than normal or expected. (Adv: *squatly.* Comp: *squatter;* sup: *squattest.*)

squawk ['skwɔk] **1.** *n.* a loud, harsh noise, especially one made by a bird. **2.** *iv.* to make a loud, harsh noise.

squeak ['skwik] **1.** *n.* a short, soft, high-pitched noise. **2.** *iv.* to make a short, soft, high-pitched noise.

squeal ['skwil] **1.** *n.* a loud, shrill noise or cry. **2.** *iv.* to make ①.

squeeze ['skwiz] **1.** *tv.* to press something with force. **2.** *tv.* to force the liquid from something by pressing it.

squint ['skwɪnt] **1.** *tv.* to close one's eyes almost all the way when looking at someone or something. **2.** *iv.* to have one's eyes almost closed because the light is so bright.

squirm ['skwɚm] *iv.* to move around uncomfortably; to writhe.

squirrel ['skwɚ əl] *n.* a rodent that lives in trees and has a large, bushy tail.

squirt ['skwɚt] **1.** *tv.* to force liquid through the air in a stream; to cause liquid to stream through the air. **2.** *tv.* to hit someone or something with a stream of liquid. **3.** *n.* a short stream of liquid that is sent through the air.

stab ['stæb] **1.** *tv.* to thrust a pointed object into someone or something. **2.** *n.* a thrust of a pointed object. **3.** *n.* a sharp, painful feeling.

stabilize ['steb ə laɪz] **1.** *tv.* to make something steady; to fix something in place; to keep something from moving or changing. **2.** *iv.* to become steady; to be fixed in place.

stable ['steb əl] **1.** *adj.* unlikely to fall, move, or shake; steady; firm. (Adv: *stably.*) **2.** *adj.* not likely to change; constant; permanent. (Adv: *stably.*) **3.** *n.* a building where horses are kept.

stack ['stæk] **1.** *n.* an orderly pile of something; a neat pile of something. **2.** *tv.* to place things in a neat, orderly pile; to arrange things into a neat, orderly pile.

stadium ['sted i əm] *n.* a playing field surrounded by rows of seats for spectators.

staff ['stæf] **1.** *n.* the workers who operate and manage an organization. (Pl but treat as sg.) **2.** *n.* a large, heavy stick used for support; a large cane. **3.** *tv.* to provide something with enough workers so that a job can be done properly. **4.** *tv.* [for workers] to provide services for a task.

stage ['stedʒ] **1.** *n.* a period of development; one part of a process. **2.** *n.* the floor, usually raised, in a theater where performers perform. **3.** *tv.* to produce a play at a theater; to put on a play. **4.** *tv.* to plan and do something that attracts public attention.

stain ['sten] **1.** *tv.* to change or add to the color of something; to make something dirty by changing its color. **2.** *tv.* to coat a wooden surface with a liquid that gives it a color. **3.** *tv.* to color tissue or an organism so it can be observed or identified. **4.** *iv.* [for a substance] to have the ability to change the color of something permanently. **5.** *n.* a mark, spot, or flaw. **6.** *n.* a liquid that is used to give color to wood. (Pl only for types and instances.)

stair ['stɛr] *n.* a step or series of steps that go from one level to another. (Usually pl.)

staircase ['stɛr kes] *n.* a set of stairs that allows one to go from one level of a building to another; a stairway.

stairway ['stɛr we] *n.* a set of stairs that allow one to go from one level of a building to another; a staircase.

stake ['stek] *n.* a pointed piece of wood or plastic that is driven into the ground.

stakes *n.* the amount of money bet in a game; the amount of risk involved in some activity. (Treated as pl, but not countable.)

stale ['stel] *adj.* no longer fresh. (Adv: *stalely.* Comp: *staler;* sup: *stalest.*)

481

stalk ['stɔk] **1.** *n.* the main stem of a plant, which is connected to the roots, and from which leaves grow. **2.** *tv.* to pursue or approach an animal or a person without being seen or heard.

stall ['stɔl] **1.** *n.* a small, enclosed space. **2.** *n.* a space within a barn or stable for one animal, especially a horse. **3.** *n.* a booth in a market, or in a building with an open wall in front, where products are sold. **4.** *iv.* [for a vehicle] to stop because of engine trouble. **5.** *iv.* to wait a while so that one has more time; to evade something by taking extra time.

stamp ['stæmp] **1.** *n.* a square of paper (issued by the government) that must be attached to certain documents to make them official or to indicate that a fee or tax has been paid, especially as used for postage. **2.** *n.* a tool that prints a design (a picture or words) onto a surface. **3.** *n.* the design that is printed onto a surface by ②. **4.** *tv.* to mark an object with ②, usually to make it official or to make an acknowledgment that a fee has been paid or that requirements have been met. **5.** *tv.* to put ① on an envelope. **6.** *tv.* to hit something or make something flat by bringing down one's foot on it with force. **7.** *iv.* to walk heavily somewhere; to walk with heavy steps.

stampede [stæm 'pid] **1.** *n.* a sudden rush of frightened horses or cattle. **2.** *n.* a sudden rush of excited, angry, or impatient people. (Fig. on ①.) **3.** *iv.* to rush as part of a large crowd of people or creatures. **4.** *tv.* to cause ① or ②.

stand ['stænd] **1.** *iv., irreg.* to be in a normal or typical vertical position. (Pt/pp: STOOD.) **2.** *iv., irreg.* to be a particular height when in a vertical position on one's feet. **3.** *iv., irreg.* to be in a particular location. **4.** *iv., irreg.* [for a law] to remain in force. **5.** *tv., irreg.* to move someone or something to a vertical position. **6.** *tv., irreg.* to withstand something; to endure something; to put up with something. **7.** *n.* the position one takes on an issue. **8.** *n.* a base, frame, or piece of furniture that supports something. **9.** *n.* the place where a witness sits in a court of law. (Short for *witness stand*.)

standard ['stæn dəd] **1.** *n.* something against which something else is tested or measured; something that is the basis of a comparison. **2.** *n.* a degree of quality or excellence. **3.** *adj.* ordinary; conforming to a certain degree or amount; normal. (Adv: *standardly*.) **4.** *adj.* correct and acceptable according to the formal rules of a language. (Adv: *standardly*.)

standby ['stænd baɪ] **1.** *n.* an extra thing or person, nearby and ready. (Pl: *standbys*.) **2.** *n.* a person traveling by waiting for space on a plane to become available. (Pl: *standbys*.) **3.** *adv.* traveling when one is not able to reserve a seat and must travel as ②.

standstill ['stænd 'stɪl] *n.* a complete stop; a condition in which nothing is moving. (No pl form.)

stank ['stæŋk] a pt of STINK.

staple ['step əl] **1.** *n.* a small, thin, U-shaped piece of wire that fastens papers together, or that fastens things to a surface. **2.** *n.* any one of the most basic foods. **3.** *tv.* to fasten papers together or to attach something else with ①.

stapler ['step lɚ] *n.* a machine that drives staples through paper or into objects.

star ['stɑr] **1.** *n.* a large object in space, such as the sun, that creates its own heat and light. **2.** *n.* a celebrity; a famous entertainer. **3.** *n.* a figure that has five or more points that radiate from a center point. **4.** *n.* ③ used as a mark of a degree of quality. **5.** *tv.* [for a movie, play, or television show] to feature a particular performer. **6.** *iv.* [for a performer] to appear as a major performer in a movie, play, or television show. **7.** *adj.* most outstanding; most excellent; best.

starch ['stɑrtʃ] **1.** *n.* a white food substance that is part of potatoes, rice, and other grains. (Pl only for types and instances.) **2.** *n.* a substance used to stiffen cloth. (Pl only for types and instances.) **3.** *n.* a food that contains ①. **4.** *tv.* to stiffen fabric or clothing by coating it with or soaking it in ②.

stare ['stɛr] *n.* a long, direct look at someone or something with one's eyes wide open.

start ['stɑrt] **1.** *n.* the beginning point of something; the time or place where something begins. **2.** *n.* a shock that may bump, jerk, or jolt the body. **3.** *tv.* to begin a process; to begin doing something; to cause something to operate, work, or move. **4.** *tv.* to originate something. **5.** *iv.* to begin a movement; to begin a journey; to begin a process; to begin at the lower limit of something. **6.** *iv.* to move or jerk suddenly, as though one were surprised or scared; to be startled.

startle ['stɑrt əl] *tv.* to cause someone to move or jump suddenly because of fear or surprise.

starvation [stɑr 've ʃən] *n.* suffering and possibly death caused by not having food. (No pl.)

starve ['stɑrv] **1.** *iv.* to die because of a lack of food; to die because one does not or cannot eat. **2.** *tv.* to cause someone or some creature to die of hunger.

483

starving ['stɑr vɪŋ] **1.** *adj.* very hungry. **2.** *adj.* dying from a lack of food.

stash ['stæʃ] *tv.* to hide something somewhere secretly for future use.

state ['stet] **1.** *n.* the condition that someone or something is in. **2.** *n.* the government of a country. (No pl.) **3.** *n.* a division of government within a country or a republic. **4.** the *adj.* use of ②. **5.** the *adj.* use of ③. **6.** *tv.* to express something; to say something. (The object can be a clause with THAT ⑦.)

stately ['stet li] *adj.* dignified; majestic; ceremonial; full of pomp. (Comp: *statelier*; sup: *stateliest*.)

statement ['stet mənt] **1.** *n.* something that is said; something that is stated. **2.** *n.* a list showing the status of an account during a period of time.

stateroom ['stet rum] *n.* a private cabin on a ship or train.

static ['stæt ɪk] **1.** *n.* the buzzing noise made when a radio or television station is not tuned in properly or when there is electronic interference. (No pl.) **2.** *adj.* [of electricity] not flowing in an electrical current; tiny electric sparks as found indoors in cold, dry weather. **3.** *adj.* not changing; stable; steady. (Adv: *statically* [...ɪk li].)

station ['ste ʃən] **1.** *n.* the building or platform where a train or bus stops to let people on and off. **2.** *n.* a building where workers in a particular service work. **3.** *n.* the specific location where a worker is assigned to work. **4.** *n.* the building or offices from which a television or radio broadcast is transmitted. **5.** *tv.* to place someone at a location for work; to assign someone to a location for work.

stationary ['ste ʃə ner i] *adj.* remaining in place; not moving; standing still. (Compare this with STATIONERY.)

stationery ['ste ʃə ner i] *n.* writing paper; writing supplies, including paper, pen, ink, envelopes, etc. (No pl. Compare this with STATIONARY.)

statue ['stæ tʃu] *n.* a sculpture of someone or an animal, made of stone, clay, wood, plaster, etc.

status ['stæt əs] *n.* someone's position within society or business; rank.

stay ['ste] **1.** *iv.* to remain in a place or position; to continue to be in a place or position. **2.** *iv.* to live in a place for a while, especially as a guest. **3.** *iv.* to continue being in a certain condition; to remain in a certain condition. **4.** *n.* a visit; a period of time when one visits someplace or when one is a guest someplace; a period of time that one lives someplace.

steadily ['stɛd ɪ li] *adv.* in a steady way; without wavering; without faltering.

steady ['stɛd i] **1.** *adj.* not changing in condition, place, or position; firm. (Adv: *steadily.* Comp: *steadier;* sup: *steadiest.*) **2.** *adj.* moving at an even, smooth pace; not moving in jerks and bursts. (Adv: *steadily.* Comp: *steadier;* sup: *steadiest.*) **3.** *adj.* calm; not excited; not upset. (Adv: *steadily.* Comp: *steadier;* sup: *steadiest.*) **4.** *tv.* to cause something to be stable and not changing.

steak ['stek] *n.* a slice or slab of a particular meat or fish, eaten as food. (A STEAK is beef unless stated otherwise.)

steal ['stil] **1.** *tv., irreg.* to take something that does not belong to one without paying for it or without permission. (Pt: STOLE; pp: STOLEN.) **2.** *tv., irreg.* [in baseball] to reach the next base before the pitcher throws the ball to the batter.

steam ['stim] **1.** *n.* the gas that water is changed into when it is boiled. (No pl.) **2.** *adj.* powered by ①; containing or using ①. **3.** *tv.* to cook something in ①. **4.** *tv.* to subject someone or something to ① or very hot water vapor. **5.** *iv.* to give off ①. **6.** *iv.* [for food] to cook in ①.

steamer ['stim ɚ] **1.** *n.* a ship that is powered by a steam engine. **2.** *n.* an enclosed pot or pan that uses steam to cook food.

steed ['stid] *n.* a horse that is to be ridden.

steel ['stil] **1.** *n.* a very hard substance made of iron, carbon, and other metals, used in constructing tools, machines, and buildings. (No pl.) **2.** *adj.* made of ①.

steep ['stip] **1.** *adj.* slanted at a sharp angle, one that is almost straight up and down. (Adv: *steeply.* Comp: *steeper;* sup: *steepest.*) **2.** *iv.* [for something, such as tea] to soak in hot liquid for a period of time. **3.** *tv.* to soak something in liquid; to immerse something.

steeple ['stip əl] *n.* a tower on the roof of a church or other building, especially a tower that ends in a point.

steer ['stɪr] **1.** *tv.* to cause something to go in a certain direction; to guide someone or something to go in a certain direction. **2.** *tv.* to guide someone toward or away from a course of action. (Fig. on ①.) **3.** *iv.* to aim in a certain direction.

stem ['stɛm] **1.** *n.* the main part of a plant above the ground, which is connected to the roots below the ground, and from which leaves or flowers grow. **2.** *n.* the part of a word that suffixes and prefixes are added to.

step ['stɛp] **1.** *n.* the movement made by putting one foot in front of the other while walking. **2.** *n.* the distance traveled by a single ①. **3.** *n.* a flat surface that one places one's foot on when going up or down stairs or a ladder. **4.** *n.* an action in a series of actions in a particular order. **5.** *iv.* to move as in ① in a certain direction.

stereo ['stɛr i o] **1.** *adj.* [of sound or electronic equipment making sound] coming from two or more speakers in a way that gives realistic effect. **2.** *n.* an electronic device that produces sound coming from two or more sources, providing realistic sound reproduction. (Pl ends in -s.)

stern ['stɚn] **1.** *adj.* strict; rigid in discipline. (Adv: *sternly.* Comp: *sterner;* sup: *sternest.*) **2.** *n.* the rear part of a boat or ship.

stew ['stu] **1.** *n.* a thick soup of vegetables and often meat cooked slowly in their own juices. (Pl only for types and instances.) **2.** *tv.* to cook something slowly in water and its own juices. **3.** *iv.* [for food] to cook slowly in water and its own juices.

stick ['stɪk] **1.** *n.* a small branch; a thin length of wood from a tree. **2.** *n.* a thin piece of wood used for a special purpose. **3.** *tv., irreg.* to attach something to something else with glue, tape, or something else adhesive. (Pt/pp: STUCK.) **4.** *tv., irreg.* to put something in a certain position. (Informal.) **5.** *iv., irreg.* to remain attached to something with glue, tape, or something else adhesive.

sticky ['stɪk i] **1.** *adj.* adhesive. (Comp: *stickier;* sup: *stickiest.*) **2.** *adj.* hot and humid; causing one to sweat. (Comp: *stickier;* sup: *stickiest.*) **3.** *adj.* awkward. (Comp: *stickier;* sup: *stickiest.*)

stiff ['stɪf] **1.** *adj.* rigid; not flexible; hard to bend. (Adv: *stiffly.* Comp: *stiffer;* sup: *stiffest.*) **2.** *adj.* firm; almost solid; not fluid. (Adv: *stiffly.* Comp: *stiffer;* sup: *stiffest.*) **3.** *adj.* harsh; severe. (Informal. Comp: *stiffer;* sup: *stiffest.*) **4.** *adj.* very formal; not relaxed. (Adv: *stiffly.* Comp: *stiffer;* sup: *stiffest.*)

stiffen ['stɪf ən] *iv.* to become stiff.

still ['stɪl] **1.** *adj.* not moving; at rest. (Comp: *stiller;* sup: *stillest.*) **2.** *adj.* quiet; not talking; not making noise. (Not prenominal.) **3.** *adv.* at a time past what was expected. **4.** *adv.* EVEN ④; yet [more]. (Comes after the adjective. Used with comparisons to make them stronger.)

stimulant ['stɪm jə lənt] *n.* something, especially a drug or chemical, that keeps someone awake or causes someone to be more active.

stimulate ['stɪm jə let] *tv.* to excite someone or something; to cause someone or something to be active or excited.

sting ['stɪŋ] **1.** *tv., irreg.* to pierce the skin of someone or something with something sharp; [for a bee, wasp, hornet, etc.] to pierce the skin with a stinger and inject a substance that causes a burning pain. (Pt/pp: STUNG.) **2.** *tv., irreg.* to cause someone to feel a tingling or burning pain. **3.** *iv., irreg.* to be able to pierce skin as with ①. **4.** *iv., irreg.* [for something] to hurt sharply. **5.** *n.* the piercing of the skin as with ① and the pain that accompanies it. **6.** *n.* a tingling or burning pain.

stinger ['stɪŋ ɚ] *n.* the stinging organ of bees, hornets, etc.

stink ['stɪŋk] **1.** *n.* a terrible smell; a very bad smell. **2.** *iv., irreg.* to smell bad. (Pt: STANK or STUNK; pp: STUNK.)

stir ['stɚ] **1.** *tv.* to mix something with one's hand or with an object. **2.** *tv.* to excite someone or an emotion; to cause someone to feel emotion or passion. **3.** *iv.* to change position; to move about. **4.** *n.* an exciting event; something that disturbs the usual order of things.

stitch ['stɪtʃ] **1.** *n.* one movement of a threaded needle through a fabric while sewing. **2.** *n.* the thread that is seen after one movement of a threaded needle through a fabric while sewing. **3.** *n.* a small amount of clothing. (No pl. Usually in negative constructions.) **4.** *n.* a sharp pain. **5.** *tv.* to sew something; to sew things together.

stock ['stɑk] **1.** *n.* a supply of something to be used or sold. (Pl only for types and instances.) **2.** *n.* a heavy broth made by cooking meats, usually with vegetables, for a long time—used to prepare sauce or soup. (Pl only for types and instances.) **3.** *n.* the total assets of a company divided into equal shares that are usually sold to the public. (No pl.) **4.** *n.* [a group of] shares of ③ of a specific company. **5.** *tv.* [for a store] to arrange to have ① of a product available for sale. **6.** *adj.* [of a response that seems] trite, rehearsed, and not sincere.

stocking ['stɑk ɪŋ] *n.* a long, knitted or woven sock.

stockpile ['stɑk paɪl] **1.** *n.* a large amount of something that is stored for future use or in case of an emergency. **2.** *tv.* to store a large amount of something for future use or in case of an emergency.

stole ['stol] pt of STEAL.

stolen ['stol ən] **1.** pp of STEAL. **2.** *adj.* taken without the owner's permission or knowledge.

stomach ['stʌm ək] **1.** *n.* the organ of the body in which food is digested. **2.** *n.* the front of the body below the chest and above the waist.

stone ['ston] **1.** *n.* the hard material of which rocks are made. (Pl only for types and instances.) **2.** *n.* a rock; a chunk of ①. **3.** *n.* a jewel; a gem. **4.** *n.* a small, hard object that forms in parts of the body, such as the kidney, and causes a lot of pain as it passes through the organ. **5.** *adj.* made of ①. **6.** *tv.* to throw STONES ② at someone or something, often as punishment or torment.

stood ['stʊd] pt/pp of STAND.

stool ['stul] **1.** *n.* a tall seat that usually has no support for one's back or arms. **2.** *n.* feces; waste matter that is expelled from the body. (Pl only for types and instances.)

stoop ['stup] **1.** *n.* a small porch at the door of a house. **2.** *n.* a bent posture, as if one is carrying a heavy weight on one's shoulders. **3.** *iv.* to bend down; to bend forward; to hold one's head and shoulders downward in front of one's body.

stop ['stɑp] **1.** *tv.* to end movement, progress, an activity, or an existence. **2.** *iv.* to move, progress, act, or function no longer; to cease. **3.** *iv.* to stay for a period of time. **4.** *n.* a short visit; a short stay. **5.** *n.* a place where a bus, train, or other vehicle STOPS as in ③ to let passengers get on and off the vehicle. **6.** *n.* a consonant that is made by ending the flow of the breath and suddenly releasing it.

stoplight ['stɑp laɪt] *n.* a traffic signal that has colored lights that indicate whether drivers should stop or go.

stopover ['stɑp ov ɚ] *n.* a place where one stops briefly during a journey, especially a stop at an airport between the city where one took off and the city that one is going to.

stoppage ['stɑp ɪdʒ] *n.* an organized strike; the organized stopping of work, such as during a disagreement between labor and management.

stopwatch ['stɑp wɑtʃ] *n.* a watch that can be started or stopped at any moment, used to determine how long something lasts.

storage ['stor ɪdʒ] **1.** *n.* keeping or storing [things]. (No pl.) **2.** *n.* a place for storing things. (No pl.)

store ['stor] **1.** *n.* a shop where goods or products are sold. **2.** *n.* a supply of something. **3.** *tv.* to keep something someplace so that it can be used later.

storekeeper ['stor kip ɚ] *n.* someone who owns or manages a store.

storeroom ['stor rum] *n.* a room where things are stored.

stork ['stork] *n.* a large bird with a long, sharp beak and a long neck.

storm ['storm] **1.** *n.* a period of severe weather with very strong winds, heavy rain or snow, and sometimes thunder and lightning. **2.** *n.* a violent attack or burst of anger. (Fig. on ①.) **3.** *tv.* to attack something with force. **4.** *iv.* [for the weather] to be severe, with strong winds, heavy rain or snow, and sometimes thunder and lightning.

story ['stor i] **1.** *n.* an account of something that has happened. **2.** *n.* a tale; an account that is fiction, told or written for entertainment or amusement. **3.** *n.* a lie. **4.** *n.* a news report; an article of news. **5.** *n.* one level of a building; one layer from floor to ceiling in a building. (In the United States, the floor on ground level is the first story.)

stout ['staut] *adj.* wide; fat; weighing too much. (Adv: *stoutly.* Comp: *stouter;* sup: *stoutest.*)

stove ['stov] *n.* an appliance that usually contains an oven and has burners on the top, used for cooking.

straight ['stret] **1.** *adj.* not bent; not curved; direct; continuing in the same direction. (Adv: *straightly.* Comp: *straighter;* sup: *straightest.*) **2.** *adj.* honest; sincere; telling the truth. (Adv: *straightly.* Comp: *straighter;* sup: *straightest.*) **3.** *adj.* without an interruption; continuous. (E.g., *five straight hours; five hours straight.*) **4.** *adv.* [going] directly [to a place without making a detour]. **5.** *adv.* [moving] in a line that is ①; without turning. **6.** *adv.* upright.

straighten ['stret n] **1.** *tv.* to cause something to be straight. **2.** ~ **out** to solve a problem; to resolve a conflict. **3.** ~ **up** to make something neat or orderly. **4.** ~ **(out)** to become STRAIGHT ①. **5.** ~ **up** [for someone] to begin to behave as desired or planned.

strain ['stren] **1.** *tv.* to stretch or pull something, especially as much as possible or in a way that causes injury. **2.** *tv.* to separate liquid from something solid by pouring it through a filter. **3.** *tv.* to place something under a burden; to place tension on something. (Fig. on ①.) **4.** *iv.* to stretch tightly; to work hard and carry a heavy load. **5.** *iv.* to use a lot of effort to do something. **6.** *n.* a burden or problem that causes someone distress. **7.** *n.* an injury to a muscle caused by stretching it or pulling it too hard. **8.** *n.* a variety of plant, bacterium, or virus.

strand ['strænd] **1.** *n.* one thread of a rope; one wire of a cable; a thread; a fiber. **2.** *tv.* to cause someone or something to be stuck or held at a location.

strange ['strendʒ] **1.** *adj.* unusual; odd; peculiar; not normal or usual. (Adv: *strangely*. Comp: *stranger*; sup: *strangest*.) **2.** *adj.* not familiar; not usually experienced. (Adv: *strangely*. Comp: *stranger*; sup: *strangest*.)

stranger ['strendʒ ɚ] *n.* someone who is not known to oneself; someone who is not familiar to oneself.

strap ['stræp] **1.** *n.* a strong, narrow strip of material used to secure something. **2.** *tv.* to secure someone or something with a strong, narrow strip of leather or other material.

straw ['strɔ] **1.** *n.* dried stalks of the plants on which grain grows. (No pl. Number is expressed with *piece(s) of straw*.) **2.** *n.* a plastic or paper tube used for drinking a liquid by sucking. **3.** *adj.* made of ①; containing ①.

strawberry ['strɔ bɛr i] **1.** *n.* a small, soft, red fruit that has tiny seeds on its surface. **2.** *adj.* made with or flavored with ①.

stray ['stre] **1.** *adj.* wandering. **2.** *adj.* occurring or arriving by chance. **3.** *iv.* to wander; to become lost; to leave the main path or topic. **4.** *n.* an animal that is lost; an animal that wanders around and has no home.

streak ['strik] **1.** *n.* a long, thin line or stripe. **2.** *n.* a period of time during which something is constant; a period of time during which something is not interrupted. **3.** *tv.* to mark something with long, thin lines or stripes. **4.** *iv.* to flow or race along in long, thin lines or stripes. **5.** *iv.* to run or move somewhere very fast.

stream ['strim] **1.** *n.* a small river. **2.** *n.* a steady flow of something, especially something liquid. **3.** *iv.* to flow somewhere steadily and in large amounts.

streamer ['strim ɚ] *n.* a very long, thin strip of paper or ribbon used as a decoration during a ceremony, parade, or celebration.

street ['strit] *n.* a road, usually one in a city or a town that has buildings or parks beside it. (Abbreviated *St.* in addresses.)

streetlight ['strit laɪt] *n.* a light, usually on a pole, that lights a street when it is dark outside.

strength ['strɛŋkθ] **1.** *n.* the quality of being strong. (No pl.) **2.** *n.* a virtue; a good feature of someone or something. (Fig. on ①.)

stress ['strɛs] **1.** *n.* the pressure caused by something that is heavy; strain. (No pl.) **2.** *n.* the mental pressure caused by something that is difficult or demanding; mental tension. (Fig. on ①.) **3.** *n.* emphasis

490

placed on a syllable when speaking by saying it louder or in a different tone. (Pl only for types and instances.) **4.** *n.* emphasis. (No pl.) **5.** *tv.* to place ③ on a syllable when speaking. **6.** *tv.* to place emphasis or focus on something. (The object can be a clause with THAT ⑦.)

stretch ['stretʃ] **1.** *tv.* to extend something. **2.** *iv.* to be elastic; to be able to be pulled without breaking. **3.** *n.* a continuous area of land. **4.** *n.* a continuous period of time.

stretcher ['stretʃɚ] *n.* a device like a light bed or cot, used to carry someone who is sick or dead.

strict ['strɪkt] **1.** *adj.* [of rules or discipline] severe, harsh, or demanding. (Adv: *strictly.* Comp: *stricter;* sup: *strictest.*) **2.** *adj.* absolute; exact. (Adv: *strictly.* Comp: *stricter;* sup: *strictest.*)

stridden ['strɪd n] pp of STRIDE.

stride ['strɑɪd] **1.** *n.* the length of one's step while walking. **2.** *n.* a long step made while walking. **3.** *iv., irreg.* to walk by taking long steps. (Pt: STRODE; pp: STRIDDEN. The pp is rarely used.)

strife ['strɑɪf] *n.* fighting; a bitter struggle; a heated argument or battle. (No pl.)

strike ['strɑɪk] **1.** *tv., irreg.* to hit someone or something; to hit something against something; to crash into something. (Pt/pp: STRUCK.) **2.** *tv., irreg.* to attack someone or something. **3.** *tv., irreg.* to light a match; to cause something to burn with fire. **4.** *tv., irreg.* to discover something underneath the ground by digging or drilling. **5.** *iv., irreg.* [for a group of workers] to refuse to work until their demands are met. **6.** *iv., irreg.* to attack. **7.** *iv., irreg.* to make contact; to have a negative effect [on someone or something]. **8.** *iv., irreg.* [for a clock] to make a sound like a bell to tell what time it is. **9.** *n.* the state that exists when workers refuse to work during a labor dispute. **10.** *n.* [in baseball] a penalty given to a player who swings the bat and misses the ball, who hits the ball foul, or who does not swing the bat when the umpire thinks that the ball went by the batter in a location that the batter could have hit it. **11.** *n.* [in bowling] an instance of knocking over all the pins at once. **12.** ~ **as** [for a thought or behavior] to affect someone a certain way.

string ['strɪŋ] **1.** *n.* a thin rope or a thick thread, especially used for tying something, binding something, or suspending something in the air. (No pl.) **2.** *n.* a length of ① or thread. **3.** *n.* a wire or cord that is stretched tight and is used to produce sound in certain musical instruments. **4.** *n.* a cord used to form the tightly pulled "net" found in a tennis racket and similar sports equipment. **5.** *n.* a number of people or things in a row. **6.** *tv., irreg.* to put ③ or ④ on a guitar, violin, tennis racket, etc. (Pt/pp: STRUNG.) **7.** *tv., irreg.* to place something on ②. (E.g., *to string beads.*) **8.** *tv., irreg.* to stretch something that is like ① from one place to another.

strings *n.* the musical instruments whose sounds are made by rubbing a bow across STRINGS as in STRING ③; the people who play the instruments having STRINGS as in STRING ③. (Treated as pl.)

strip ['strɪp] **1.** *n.* a long, flat piece of something. **2.** *tv.* to undress someone; to remove someone's clothes; to remove something's covering. **3.** *tv.* to make something empty or bare. **4.** *iv.* to take off one's clothes; to undress.

stripe ['straɪp] **1.** *n.* a long band of color or texture; a wide line; a wide line of something that is different from what is around it. **2.** *tv.* to mark something with ①; to put ① on something.

strive ['straɪv] *iv., irreg.* to work very hard for something; to struggle against something. (Pt: STROVE or *strived;* pp: STRIVEN or *strived.*)

striven ['strɪv ən] a pp of STRIVE.

strode ['strod] pt of STRIDE.

stroll ['strol] **1.** *n.* a pleasant walk. **2.** *iv.* to go for a pleasant walk.

strong ['strɔŋ] **1.** *adj.* having strength in the mind or body; having power in the mind or the body; using strength. (Adv: *strongly.* Comp: *stronger;* sup: *strongest.*) **2.** *adj.* able to last; able to withstand something; not easily broken; sturdy. (Adv: *strongly.* Comp: *stronger;* sup: *strongest.*) **3.** *adj.* [of a taste, smell, or color] intense. (Adv: *strongly.* Comp: *stronger;* sup: *strongest.*) **4.** *adj.* having a certain number [of people]. (Follows a specific number.)

strove ['strov] a pt of STRIVE.

struck ['strʌk] pt/pp of STRIKE.

structure ['strʌk tʃɚ] **1.** *n.* the way that something is put together; the way that something is built; the way that something or some creature is arranged. (No pl.) **2.** *n.* a building. **3.** *n.* something that is made from different parts. **4.** *tv.* to arrange something so that it has a certain form; to form something in a certain way; to make something from different parts.

struggle ['strʌg əl] **1.** *iv.* to work hard for or against something; to fight for or against something, using a lot of effort or energy. **2.** *n.* a hard fight for or against something; a difficult effort for or against something.

492

strung ['strʌŋ] pt/pp of STRING.

strut ['strʌt] *iv.* to walk somewhere arrogantly; to walk somewhere as though one were more important than one is.

stub ['stʌb] **1.** *tv.* to hurt a toe by hitting it against something. **2.** *n.* a short end of something that remains after the rest of it is taken or used.

stubborn ['stʌb ɚn] *adj.* not willing to do something that someone else wants; not yielding; not giving in. (Adv: *stubbornly*.)

stuck ['stʌk] pt/pp of STICK.

student ['stud nt] *n.* someone who studies or learns, especially at a school; a pupil.

study ['stʌd i] **1.** *tv.* to spend time learning information about something by reading, researching, observing, or experimenting. **2.** *tv.* to examine something closely; to scrutinize something; to observe something closely. **3.** *iv.* to be a student; to read, research, observe, or experiment in order to learn about something. **4.** *n.* the work or effort involved in learning. (The same meaning in sg and pl, but not countable.) **5.** *n.* an examination of something, as with ②. **6.** *n.* a room where someone works as in ③.

stuff ['stʌf] **1.** *n.* any substance that things are made of; the material that anything is made of. (No pl.) **2.** *n.* things; unnamed objects; belongings; possessions. (No pl.) **3.** *tv.* to fill something with a substance; to pack something into a space or container until there is no room left. **4.** *tv.* to fill the inside of a dead animal with a material that preserves it and maintains its shape so that it can be displayed.

stumble ['stʌm bəl] **1.** *iv.* to trip; to fall over something; to almost fall while one is moving; to walk in a clumsy way. **2.** *iv.* to speak in a clumsy way; to make mistakes while speaking; to trip on one's words. (Fig. on ①.)

stump ['stʌmp] **1.** *n.* the part of something that remains when the other part has been cut off, broken off, removed, or used. **2.** *tv.* to puzzle someone; to confuse someone.

stun ['stʌn] **1.** *tv.* to surprise someone completely; to amaze someone; to shock someone. **2.** *tv.* to cause something or someone to become unconscious, by a blow or by electrical shock.

stung ['stʌŋ] pt/pp of STING.

stunk ['stʌŋk] a pt of STINK; pp of STINK.

stupid ['stu pɪd] **1.** *adj.* not intelligent; not smart. (Adv: *stupidly.* Comp: *stupider;* sup: *stupidest.*) **2.** *adj.* silly; foolish. (Adv: *stupidly.* Comp: *stupider;* sup: *stupidest.*) **3.** *adj.* [of something] annoying; [of something] causing anger or irritation. (Comp: *stupider;* sup: *stupidest.*)

stupidity [stu 'pɪd ɪ ti] **1.** *n.* a lack of intelligence. (No pl.) **2.** *n.* the condition of being stupid, incorrect, or not appropriate. (No pl.)

sturdy ['stɚ di] *adj.* strong; firm; not easily knocked over. (Adv: *sturdily.* Comp: *sturdier;* sup: *sturdiest.*)

style ['staɪl] **1.** *n.* a way in which something is made, designed, done, said, or written. **2.** *n.* a particular design or theme in clothing or products at a particular period of time. **3.** *n.* the manner in which someone behaves. **4.** *tv.* to design or form something in a certain way.

stylish ['staɪ lɪʃ] *adj.* in the current fashion; in style; current; up-to-date. (Adv: *stylishly.*)

sub ['sʌb] **1.** *n.* a sealed boat that can remain still or travel underwater. (Short for SUBMARINE.) **2.** *n.* someone or something serving in the place of someone or something else. (Short for SUBSTITUTE.)

subdivision ['sʌb dɪ vɪ ʒən] **1.** *n.* a smaller part of a larger thing. **2.** *n.* a group of homes that are built on lots that were originally part of one tract of land.

subdue [səb 'du] **1.** *tv.* to bring someone or something under one's control. **2.** *tv.* to make someone or something less noticeable; to soften the strength or intensity of something.

subject ['sʌb dʒɪkt] **1.** *n.* a topic; something that is discussed, examined, or researched. **2.** *n.* a course; something that is studied; a particular field of knowledge. **3.** *n.* someone or something used in an experiment. **4.** *n.* someone who is ruled by a government or a ruler. **5.** *n.* a person, object, or scene that is painted or photographed. **6.** *n.* the noun or noun phrase representing the person or thing that performs the action in an active sentence, or that is the receiver of an action in a passive sentence.

subjective [səb 'dʒɛk tɪv] *adj.* of or about what someone thinks about something, instead of the actual facts about something. (Adv: *subjectively.*)

sublime [sə 'blaɪm] *adj.* supreme; wonderful; grand; inspiring. (Adv: *sublimely.*)

submarine ['sʌb mə rin] **1.** *n.* a ship that can travel completely underwater, used especially in war and for research. (Can be shortened to

SUB.) **2.** *n.* a large sandwich; a sandwich made with two long pieces of bread. (Usually SUB.)

submerge [səb 'mɚdʒ] **1.** *tv.* to put something under the surface of a liquid; to immerse something in water. **2.** *iv.* to go underwater; to go under the surface of a liquid.

subscription [səb 'skrɪp ʃən] *n.* an order for a series of issues of a magazine or newspaper.

subsoil ['sʌb sɔɪl] *n.* the layer of soil that lies below the surface soil of the earth. (No pl.)

substance ['sʌb stəns] **1.** *n.* the material that something is made of; matter. **2.** *n.* the essence; the important part of something. (No pl.)

substitute ['sʌb stɪ tut] **1.** *iv.* to be put in someone or something else's place as a replacement. **2.** *n.* a replacement; someone or something that is put in someone or something else's place. (Can be shortened to SUB.)

substitution [səb stɪ 'tu ʃən] **1.** *n.* the replacement of someone or something with someone or something else. (Pl only for types and instances.) **2.** *n.* someone or something that has been substituted as in ①.

subtract [səb 'trækt] **1.** *tv.* to take a part of something away; to take a quantity away [from another quantity]; to reduce something by a certain amount. (See also MINUS.) **2.** *iv.* to lessen or reduce [something] as in ①.

subtraction [səb 'træk ʃən] *n.* the reduction of something by a certain amount; the reduction of a quantity by another quantity. (Pl only for types and instances.)

suburb ['sʌ bɚb] *adj.* a city, town, or village that is next to or near a large city.

suburban [sə 'bɚ bən] *adj.* of or about the suburbs.

subway ['sʌb we] *n.* an underground electric train that provides transportation in large cities.

succeed [sək 'sid] **1.** *iv.* to be successful; to reach a goal. **2.** *tv.* to follow someone or something into a job or office.

success [sək 'sɛs] **1.** *n.* accomplishment; achievement. (Pl only for types and instances.) **2.** *n.* someone or something that is successful, especially someone or something that has become famous, important, or rich.

successful [sək 'sɛs fʊl] *adj.* showing evidence of having accomplished something or having reached a high status. (Adv: *successfully.*)

succumb [sə 'kəm] *iv.* to yield to something, especially a temptation, fatal disease, a human weakness, etc.

such ['sʌtʃ] *adj.* so great; so much.

suck ['sʌk] *tv.* to pull liquid into one's mouth by putting one's lips around something and drawing the liquid in; to pull something into one's mouth with one's lips.

sudden ['sʌd n] *adj.* unexpected; happening without warning. (Adv: *suddenly.*)

suddenly ['sʌd n li] *adv.* unexpectedly; without warning.

suds ['sʌdz] *n.* bubbles formed by soap mixing with water; lather; froth. (Treated as pl, but not countable.)

sue ['su] **1.** *iv.* to start a lawsuit; to file a claim against someone or something in court. **2.** *tv.* to bring a lawsuit against someone or something; to file a claim against someone or something in court.

suffer ['sʌf ɚ] **1.** *tv.* to experience physical or emotional pain because of illness or emotional loss. **2.** *iv.* to feel physical or emotional pain. **3.** *iv.* to worsen; to decline in quality.

sufficient [sə 'fɪʃ ənt] *adj.* enough; adequate; meeting a need or requirement. (Adv: *sufficiently.*)

suffix ['sʌf ɪks] *n.* a form added to the end of a word that changes or modifies the meaning or function of the word.

suffocate ['sʌf ə ket] **1.** *tv.* to kill someone or a creature by preventing it from getting the oxygen that is needed. **2.** *iv.* to die because one is unable to get the oxygen that is needed.

sugar ['ʃʊg ɚ] **1.** *n.* a sweet substance, usually in crystal form, that is made from certain plants and used to sweeten food and drinks. (No pl.) **2.** *n.* a sweet substance that is found naturally in many foods. (Pl only for types and instances.)

suggest [səg 'dʒɛst] **1.** *tv.* to propose something that will be considered; to express something that one thinks should be considered; to offer something as an option. (The object can be a clause with THAT ⑦.) **2.** *tv.* to bring something to one's mind; to cause something to be thought of in a certain way; to cause something to be a reminder to someone. (The object can be a clause with THAT ⑦.)

suggestion [səg 'dʒɛs tʃən] **1.** *n.* a hint; a trace; something that reminds someone of someone or something. (No pl.) **2.** *n.* a proposal

496

to be considered; an expression of something that one thinks should be considered; the offering of an option; something that is suggested.

suicide ['su ə saɪd] **1.** *n.* killing oneself on purpose. (No pl.) **2.** *n.* someone who has committed ①.

suit ['sut] **1.** *n.* a set of formal clothes, consisting of a jacket, pants, and sometimes a vest, made from the same material. **2.** *n.* a set of things, such as clothing or armor, that are worn together. **3.** *n.* a statement of claims against someone or a business, brought to a court of law. (Short for LAWSUIT.) **4.** *n.* one of the four different sets of cards found in a deck of playing cards: clubs, hearts, spades, and diamonds. **5.** *tv.* to meet the requirements of someone or something. **6.** *tv.* to look good with something; to look good on someone; to match someone.

suitable ['su tə bəl] *adj.* right or proper for the situation. (Adv: *suitably.*)

suitcase ['sut kes] *n.* a piece of luggage used for carrying clothing and other personal items while traveling.

suite ['swit] **1.** *n.* two or more rooms that are connected, especially as found in a hotel or office building. **2.** *n.* a set of furniture. **3.** *n.* a piece of music made of two or more related movements in the same key or in related keys.

sulk ['sʌlk] *iv.* to look forlorn and sit without speaking because one is in a bad mood.

sullen ['sʌl ən] *adj.* being silent and looking angry and irritated because one is in a bad mood. (Adv: *sullenly.*)

sum ['sʌm] **1.** *n.* the total of two or more amounts. **2.** *n.* an amount of money.

summarize ['sʌm ə raɪz] *tv.* to express the main ideas of something.

summary ['sʌm ə ri] *n.* the main ideas of something; a short statement about the important points of a longer speech or text.

summer ['sʌm ɚ] **1.** *n.* one of the seasons of the year, after spring and before autumn. **2.** *the adj.* use of ①.

summertime ['sʌm ɚ taɪm] *n.* summer; the season of summer. (No pl.)

summit ['sʌm ət] **1.** *n.* the highest point of something, especially a mountain. **2.** *n.* a meeting involving very important people, especially leaders of governments. (Fig. on ①.)

497

summon ['sʌm ən] **1.** *tv.* to order someone officially to do something. **2.** ~**s** *tv.* to SUMMON ① someone to court using ③. **3.** ~**s** *n.* an official order to appear in court. (Treated as sg.)

sun ['sʌn] **1.** *n.* a star; a star that gives light and warmth to a planet; a star that is orbited by a planet. **2.** *n.* the star at the center of our solar system; the star that shines on the earth. (Usually preceded by *the*. Sometimes capitalized.) **3.** *tv.* to expose oneself to the light of ②; to "bathe" oneself in sunlight. (Takes a reflexive object.) **4.** *iv.* to absorb the rays of ②; to "bathe" in the light of ②.

sunbeam ['sʌn bim] *n.* a ray of sunlight; a beam of sunlight.

sunblock Go to SUNSCREEN.

sunburn ['sʌn bən] **1.** *n.* redness and soreness of skin that has been exposed too long to sunlight. (Pl only for types and instances.) **2.** *iv.* [for one's skin] to acquire ①.

sundae ['sʌn de] *n.* a dessert made with ice cream and flavored sauces or toppings.

Sunday ['sʌn de] Go to DAY.

sung ['sʌŋ] pp of SING.

sunglasses ['sʌn glæs ɪz] *n.* glasses with dark lenses that are worn to protect the eyes from bright sunlight. (Treated as pl. Number is expressed with *pair(s) of sunglasses*.)

sunk ['sʌŋk] a pt of SINK; pp of SINK.

sunlight ['sʌn laɪt] *n.* the light that is given off by the sun. (No pl.)

sunny ['sʌn i] *adj.* with bright sunshine. (Comp: *sunnier;* sup: *sunniest.*)

sunrise ['sʌn rɑɪz] *n.* the time of day when the sun appears to be moving above the horizon in the east.

sunscreen AND **sunblock** ['sʌn skrin, 'sʌn blɑk] *n.* lotion or cream containing a chemical substance that helps prevent sun damage to the skin. (Pl only for types and instances.)

sunset ['sʌn set] *n.* the time of day when the sun appears to be moving below the horizon in the west.

sunshine ['sʌn ʃɑɪn] *n.* sunlight; light from the sun. (No pl.)

super ['sup ɚ] **1.** *adj.* excellent; wonderful; great; marvelous; fabulous. **2.** *adj.* extra large.

superb [sə 'pəb] *adj.* very good; excellent; of the best quality. (Adv: *superbly.*)

superior [sə 'pɪr i ɚ] **1.** *n.* someone who has a higher rank or position in relationship to someone else. **2.** *adj.* very good; above average; better than something else. (Adv: *superiorly.*)

superiority [sə pɪr i 'or ɪ ti] *n.* the condition of being superior to someone or something else. (No pl.)

superlative [sə 'pɚl ə tɪv] **1.** *n.* the form of an adjective or adverb, usually created with *most* or *-est*, that indicates the highest degree of comparison of that adjective or adverb. **2.** *adj.* best; having the highest quality. (Adv: *superlatively.*)

supermarket ['su pɚ mɑr kɪt] *n.* a large food store that stocks several kinds of each item, allowing customers a wide choice.

superstition [su pɚ 'stɪ ʃən] *n.* a belief that is based on tradition or legend instead of reason.

supervise ['su pɚ vaɪz] *tv.* to direct a worker or a group of workers; to direct something; to oversee someone or something.

supervision [su pɚ 'vɪ ʒən] *n.* paying attention to or watching over [someone or something]. (No pl.)

supervisor ['su pɚ vaɪz ɚ] *n.* someone who supervises other workers; a manager; an overseer.

supper ['sʌp ɚ] *n.* the meal eaten in the evening. (See also DINNER.)

suppertime ['sʌp ɚ taɪm] *n.* the time when supper is eaten. (No pl.)

supply [sə 'plaɪ] **1.** *tv.* to give someone something that is needed or wanted; to give something to someone who needs or wants it. **2.** *n.* an amount of something that is available. (Sometimes pl.)

support [sə 'port] **1.** *tv.* to provide someone with money, shelter, clothing, and food. **2.** *tv.* to bear the weight of something; to keep something vertical or in place so that it doesn't fall. **3.** *tv.* to give someone or something one's encouragement or favor; to show someone or something approval or favor. **4.** *n.* providing someone with money, shelter, food, and clothing. (No pl.) **5.** *n.* the strength and structure needed to bear the weight of someone or something. (No pl.) **6.** *n.* something that carries the weight of something; a beam; a prop. **7.** *n.* encouragement. (No pl.)

suppose [sə 'poz] **1.** *tv.* to consider or imagine that something is or will be true. (The object is a clause with THAT ⑦.) **2.** ~**d to** expected or intended to do something; obliged or allowed to do something.

499

supreme [sə 'prim] **1.** *adj.* having total authority; having total power; having the highest rank; being the most important. (Adv: *supremely.*) **2.** *adj.* of the highest degree of quality. (Adv: *supremely.*)

sure ['ʃʊr] **1.** *adj.* certain; confident or knowing that something is the case. (Adv: *surely.* Comp: *surer*; sup: *surest.*) **2.** *adv.* certainly. (Informal.) **3.** *adv.* [in response to a yes-or-no question] yes. (Informal.)

surely ['ʃʊr li] *adv.* certainly; without doubt; definitely.

surf ['sɚf] *n.* waves of water hitting the beach. (No pl.)

surface ['sɚ fəs] **1.** *n.* the outside of something; the outside layer of something. **2.** *n.* the top of a liquid. **3.** *iv.* [for something underwater] to go up to or above the ② of the water.

surge ['sɚdʒ] **1.** *n.* a sudden, powerful burst of electricity. **2.** *n.* a strong forward movement.

surgeon ['sɚ dʒən] *n.* a physician who performs surgery.

surgery ['sɚ dʒə ri] **1.** *n.* the science and practice of curing sickness and treating injury by performing an OPERATION ①. (No pl.) **2.** *n.* using ① in treating illness and disease.

surly ['sɚ li] *adj.* angry and rude; having bad manners; impolite and mean. (Comp: *surlier*; sup: *surliest.*)

surname ['sɚ nem] *n.* the family name; [in the United States] the last name.

surpass [sɚ 'pæs] **1.** *tv.* to do better than someone or something; to be better than someone or something. **2.** *tv.* to be larger or greater than something.

surplus ['sɚ pləs] **1.** *n.* an amount of something that is more than what is needed; an extra amount; an excess. **2.** the *adj.* use of ①.

surprise [sɚ 'praɪz] **1.** *n.* something that is not expected; something that happens without warning. **2.** *n.* the feeling that is caused by something unexpected happening. (No pl.) **3.** *tv.* to cause someone to feel ② by doing something or saying something unexpected. **4.** *tv.* to attack someone or something without warning. **5.** *adj.* unexpected; without warning.

surrender [sə 'ren dɚ] **1.** *iv.* to give up, especially when one has lost a battle, argument, or fight; to yield to a force that one has fought against. **2.** *tv.* to give someone or something up to someone; to yield someone or something to someone else. **3.** *n.* giving up as in ①. (No pl.)

500

surround [sə 'raʊnd] *tv.* to enclose someone or something on all sides; to be on all sides of someone or something.

survey 1. ['sɚ ve] *n.* a set of questions used to collect people's opinions and evidence of their attitudes. **2.** ['sɚ ve] *n.* a document containing ①. **3.** ['sɚ ve] *n.* an examination or study of the condition, contents, or details of something. **4.** ['sɚ ve] *n.* a description or analysis of a subject of study. **5.** ['sɚ ve] *n.* the measurement of land so that accurate maps can be made or so that the legal description of property boundaries is exact. **6.** ['sɚ ve] *tv.* to collect people's opinions on an issue; to ask people for their opinions on an issue. **7.** [sɚ 've] *tv.* to examine or study the condition, contents, or details of something. **8.** [sɚ 've] *tv.* to measure part of the surface of the earth—or a similar area—exactly, so that accurate maps or legal descriptions can be made.

survive [sɚ 'vaɪv] **1.** *iv.* to remain alive even after a threat to one's life; to live a very long life. **2.** *tv.* to endure someone or something and remain alive or functioning. **3.** *tv.* to outlive someone; to live longer than someone.

survivor [sɚ 'vaɪv ɚ] *n.* someone who remains alive; someone who did not die while others died.

susceptible [sə 'sɛp tə bəl] **1.** *adj.* easily persuaded by something; easily influenced by something. **2.** *adj.* likely to contract a sickness; likely to become sick.

suspect 1. ['sʌs pɛkt] *n.* someone who is thought to have committed a crime. **2.** ['sʌs pɛkt] *adj.* causing questioning or doubt. (Adv: *suspectly.*) **3.** [sə 'spɛkt] *tv.* to consider something to be likely or true. (The object can be a clause with THAT ⑦.)

suspend [sə 'spɛnd] **1.** *tv.* to hang something from something else; to cause something to hang down from something else above it. **2.** *tv.* to delay something; to stop something for a period of time. **3.** *tv.* to prevent someone from working at a job, attending classes, etc., for a period of time, as a punishment. **4.** *tv.* to cause something to float in the air or in a liquid.

suspenders [sə 'spɛn dɚz] *n.* a pair of elastic bands or adjustable straps—to hold up trousers—connected to the front and back of the trousers at the waistline. (Treated as pl.)

suspense [sə 'spɛns] *n.* an anxious, scary, or uncertain feeling that is caused by not knowing what is going to happen next. (No pl.)

suspicion [sə ˈspɪ ʃən] **1.** *n.* an uneasy feeling in which one suspects something. (No pl form.) **2.** *n.* a suspicious idea, as in ①, about someone or something.

sustain [sə ˈsten] **1.** *tv.* to nourish and care for living plants and creatures. **2.** *tv.* to keep something moving, going, or working; to prolong something. **3.** *tv.* to suffer an injury; to have an injury.

swallow [ˈswɑl o] **1.** *tv.* to cause food or drink to go down one's throat and into the stomach. **2.** *tv.* to believe something without question; to believe something that one is told, even if it is a lie; to accept something that one is told. (Fig. on ①. Informal.) **3.** *iv.* to take [something] into the body by way of the throat. **4.** *n.* the amount of something that can be taken into the mouth and sent down the throat. **5.** *n.* a kind of small songbird.

swam [ˈswæm] pt of SWIM.

swamp [ˈswɑmp] **1.** *n.* an area of very wet, muddy ground, sometimes covered with water. **2.** *tv.* to flood something, especially a boat.

swan [ˈswɑn] *n.* a large, white bird that lives near the water and has a long, curving neck.

swap [ˈswɑp] **1.** *iv.* to exchange; to trade. **2.** *n.* an exchange; a trade.

swarm [ˈsworm] *n.* a large number of people or animals, especially bees or other insects, that move together in a densely packed group.

swat [ˈswɑt] **1.** *tv.* to hit someone or something hard. **2.** *n.* a hard hit; a sharp blow.

sway [ˈswe] **1.** *iv.* to bend or swing back and forth; to bend to one side and then the other; to move back and forth. **2.** *tv.* to cause someone or something to bend or move back and forth; to bend or move someone or something back and forth. **3.** *tv.* to change someone's opinion or judgment; to influence someone. (Fig. on ②.)

swear [ˈswer] **1.** *iv., irreg.* to curse; to say bad words angrily. (Pt: SWORE; pp: SWORN.) **2.** *tv.* to promise or vow something.

sweat [ˈswɛt] **1.** *n.* the moisture that comes out of the body through pores in the skin. (No pl.) **2.** *n.* hard work; labor; something that causes ①. (No pl.) **3.** *iv., irreg.* [for moisture] to come out of the body through pores in the skin. (Pt/pp: *sweat* or *sweated*.) **4.** *iv.* to work very hard; to labor.

sweater [ˈswɛt ɚ] *n.* a warm piece of clothing worn above the waist, usually woven or knitted from wool or cotton.

502

sweatpants ['swɛt pænts] *n.* warm pants, usually with a soft or fluffy inside layer. (Treated as pl. Number is expressed with *pair(s) of sweatpants*.)

sweatshirt ['swɛt ʃɚt] *n.* a warm, long-sleeved shirt, usually with a soft or fluffy inside layer.

sweaty ['swɛt i] **1.** *adj.* covered with sweat. (Adv: *sweatily*. Comp: *sweatier*; sup: *sweatiest*.) **2.** *adj.* causing sweat, especially because of hot, humid weather or hard work. (Comp: *sweatier*; sup: *sweatiest*.)

sweep ['swip] **1.** *tv., irreg.* to clean a floor by passing a broom over it; to clean a surface by moving a broom or brush over it to push the dirt away. (Pt/pp: SWEPT.) **2.** *iv., irreg.* to clean as in ①. **3.** *n.* a smooth, flowing motion, especially in a curve; a swinging movement.

sweet ['swit] **1.** *adj.* tasting like sugar; like sugar or honey. (Adv: *sweetly*. Comp: *sweeter*; sup: *sweetest*.) **2.** *adj.* pleasant; pleasing; having personal charm. (Adv: *sweetly*. Comp: *sweeter*; sup: *sweetest*.)

sweeten ['swit n] *tv.* to cause something to become sweet; to add sugar to something.

sweets *n.* candy; pieces of something made with sugar or honey. (Treated as pl.)

swell ['swɛl] **1.** *iv., irreg.* to grow larger; to grow fuller; to rise or grow past the regular amount. (Pt: *swelled*; pp: *swelled* or SWOLLEN.) **2.** *iv., irreg.* to increase in size, amount, or intensity. **3.** *tv., irreg.* to cause someone or something to grow larger or fuller; to increase something in size, amount, or intensity. **4.** *n.* the rise and fall of waves.

swelter ['swɛl tɚ] *iv.* to suffer in very hot weather.

swept ['swɛpt] pt/pp of SWEEP.

swift ['swɪft] *adj.* rapid; quick; moving or passing fast. (Adv: *swiftly*. Comp: *swifter*; sup: *swiftest*.)

swim ['swɪm] **1.** *iv., irreg.* [for someone] to travel through water by moving arms and legs; [for an animal] to travel through water by moving paws, legs, fins, tail, etc. (Pt: SWAM; pp: SWUM.) **2.** *iv., irreg.* [for something] to seem to spin or revolve, owing to one's illness or the loss of one's ability to properly perceive. **3.** *n.* an instance of traveling through the water by moving one's arms and legs.

swimsuit ['swɪm sut] *n.* a piece of clothing worn for sunning or swimming; the clothing worn by someone who swims.

swindle ['swɪn dəl] **1.** *tv.* to cheat someone, especially to cheat someone out of money. **2.** *n.* cheating; cheating people out of their money.

503

swine ['swaɪn] **1.** *n., irreg.* a hog or a pig. (Pl: *swine.*) **2.** *n., irreg.* someone who is disgusting, unpleasant, or contemptible. (Fig. on ①.)

swing ['swɪŋ] **1.** *tv., irreg.* to move something in a sweeping or curved pattern. (Pt/pp: SWUNG.) **2.** *tv., irreg.* to move something in a sweeping or circular movement. **3.** *iv., irreg.* to move in a sweeping or curved pattern. **4.** *iv., irreg.* to move while hanging from a fixed point. **5.** *iv., irreg.* to turn suddenly or quickly. **6.** *iv., irreg.* to play on ⑧; to move one's body through the air on ⑧. **7.** *n.* a change; a variation. **8.** *n.* a seat that hangs on ropes or chains, which moves people, usually children, back and forth.

swipe ['swaɪp] **1.** *tv.* to steal something. (Informal.) **2.** *tv.* to move the magnetic strip of a plastic card through a slot that reads the information off the magnetic strip. **3.** ~ **at** to hit at someone or something; to strike at someone or something; to unsuccessfully attempt to hit someone or something.

switch ['swɪtʃ] **1.** *n.* a lever that turns electricity on and off. **2.** *n.* a change from one thing to another. **3.** *n.* a thin, flexible stick that is cut from a tree. **4.** *tv.* to change something; to swap or exchange things.

switchboard ['swɪtʃ bord] *n.* a control panel that an operator uses to connect telephone calls to the proper person.

swollen ['swol ən] **1.** pp of SWELL. **2.** *adj.* puffed up; having gotten bigger; growing in size. (Adv: *swollenly.*)

swoop ['swup] *n.* a dive through the air.

sword ['sord] *n.* a heavy metal weapon with a long, usually sharp blade attached to a handle.

swore ['swor] pt of SWEAR.

sworn ['sworn] pp of SWEAR.

swum ['swʌm] pp of SWIM.

swung ['swʌŋ] pt/pp of SWING.

syllable ['sɪl ə bəl] *n.* an uninterrupted segment of speech consisting of a vowel possibly with consonants on one or both sides.

symbol ['sɪm bəl] **1.** *n.* something that represents something else; something that stands for something else. **2.** *n.* a letter, number, or shape that represents a quantity, chemical element, mathematical operation, or other function.

symmetry ['sɪm ə tri] *n.* the arrangement of the opposite sides of something so that they look exactly alike. (No pl.)

sympathy ['sɪm pə θi] *n.* kind feelings for someone having problems and sorrows.

symphony ['sɪm fə ni] *n.* a long piece of music written for an orchestra.

symptom ['sɪmp təm] *n.* a sign, feeling, or problem that is evidence of the existence of something, especially of an illness.

synagogue AND **synagog** ['sɪn ə gɑg] *n.* a building for worship in the Jewish religion.

synonym ['sɪ nə nɪm] *n.* a word that has the same or almost the same meaning as another word.

syphon Go to SIPHON.

syringe [sə 'rɪndʒ] *n.* a device from which liquids are pushed out or into which liquids are pulled, usually through a long, thin needle.

syrup ['sɪr əp] *n.* a thick, sweet liquid eaten as food or used to deliver medication. (Pl only for types and instances.)

system ['sɪs təm] **1.** *n.* a group of things that work together to form a network; a group of things arranged in a particular way that function as one thing. **2.** *n.* a method of arrangement; a plan.

systematic [sɪs tə 'mæt ɪk] *adj.* organized and structured; based on a system or plan. (Adv: *systematically* [...ɪk li].)

T

tab ['tæb] **1.** *n.* a small flap that sticks out from the edge of a sheet of paper, cardboard, or something similar. **2.** *n.* a bill that is presented to a customer for payment.

table ['teb əl] **1.** *n.* an item of furniture whose top is a raised, flat surface supported by legs. **2.** *n.* a chart of numbers, facts, or data presented in columns or rows.

tablecloth ['teb əl klɔθ] *n.* a piece of fabric that covers the top of a table and hangs over the sides, for decoration or protection of the table's surface.

tablet ['tæb lət] **1.** *n.* a pad of paper; blank sheets of paper that are bound together along the top or side. **2.** *n.* a pill; a small, hard piece of medicine, drugs, or vitamins that a person swallows.

tack ['tæk] **1.** *n.* a small, thin nail with a large head. (See also THUMB-TACK.) **2.** *n.* a course of action that is different from an earlier one; an attempt to do something after earlier attempts have not worked. **3.** *n.* the direction that a ship travels as the result of the wind and the way that its sails are arranged.

tackle ['tæk əl] **1.** *tv.* to run after, dive onto, and throw a person to the ground, especially in the game of football. **2.** *tv.* to undertake a duty or a problem; to start working on something difficult. (Fig. on ①.) **3.** *n.* equipment used for fishing. (No pl.)

tact ['tækt] *n.* the ability to deal with people without offending them. (No pl.)

tactful ['tækt ful] *adj.* showing or having tact. (Adv: *tactfully.*)

tactic ['tæk tɪk] *n.* a skillful way of doing something in order to reach a goal. (Often pl.)

tadpole ['tæd pol] *n.* a small, round water creature that has a long tail and develops into a frog or a toad.

tag ['tæg] **1.** *n.* a small label that has information about the object that it is attached to. **2.** *n.* a game in which a player runs around trying to touch someone else, who then runs to touch another person. (No pl.) **3.** *tv.* to put ① on something or some creature. **4.** *tv.* to touch someone, especially in ②.

506

tail ['tel] **1.** *n.* the part of an animal that hangs off from its back, as an extension of the spine. **2.** *n.* the rear part of something; the last part of something. (Fig. on ①.)

tailor ['te lɚ] **1.** *n.* someone who makes or repairs clothes. **2.** *tv.* to make or repair an item of clothing so that it fits a certain person.

tailspin *n.* a sudden spinning or period of confusion.

take ['tek] **1.** *tv., irreg.* to get or obtain something by one's own action. (Pt: TOOK; pp: TAKEN.) **2.** *tv., irreg.* to accept something that is offered. **3.** *tv., irreg.* to capture something; to win something. **4.** *tv., irreg.* to eat or swallow something, such as medicine. **5.** *tv., irreg.* to use something on a regular basis; to require something as a habit. **6.** *tv., irreg.* to transport someone or something somewhere. **7.** *tv., irreg.* to use a form of transportation, especially public transportation. **8.** *tv., irreg.* to lead someone or something; to guide someone or something. **9.** *tv., irreg.* to record something; to make a picture with a camera. **10.** *tv., irreg.* to interpret something in a certain way. **11.** *tv., irreg.* to observe the measurement of something. **12.** *tv., irreg.* to suffer something; to endure something; to accept something. **13.** *tv., irreg.* to use up time; to consume time; to require that an amount of time be spent [doing something]. **14.** ~ **over** to gain control of someone or something. **15.** ~ **out** to remove someone or something as one exits. **16.** ~ **on** to accept a responsibility. **17.** ~ **off** [for an airplane] to lift into the air. **18.** ~ **up** to collect or receive something by hand **19.** ~ **up** to begin dealing with a matter.

taken ['tek ən] pp of TAKE.

takeoff ['tek ɔf] *n.* [an airplane's] leaving the ground and flying.

tale ['tel] **1.** *n.* a story. **2.** *n.* a lie.

talent ['tæl ənt] **1.** *n.* a special skill; a natural ability. **2.** *n.* people who have a special skill or a natural ability, especially singers or actors; people employed or seeking employment in the entertainment industry. (No pl. Treated as sg.)

talk ['tɔk] **1.** *iv.* to communicate by speaking; to speak; to say words. **2.** *iv.* to speak with someone; to have a conversation with someone. **3.** *n.* the production of words; speech. (No pl.) **4.** *n.* a conversation; a chat with someone. **5.** *n.* a speech; a lecture. **6.** *n.* gossip; rumors. (No pl.) **7.** ~ **back** to challenge verbally a parent, an older person, or one's superior.

talks *n.* conversations held for the purpose of negotiating something.

tall ['tɔl] **1.** *adj.* great in height; of a greater height than average; not short. (E.g., *the tree is tall; the tall tree.* Comp: *taller;* sup: *tallest.*) **2.** *adj.* extending a certain distance upward; reaching a certain distance above the ground. (E.g., *the tree is 30 feet tall.* Comp: *taller;* sup: *tallest.*)

tally ['tæl i] *n.* a score; a mark used to keep track of the number of something being counted; the number of points or votes someone or something has received.

tame ['tem] **1.** *adj.* not in a natural, wild state; living with people; being gentle rather than fierce. (Adv: *tamely.* Comp: *tamer;* sup: *tamest.*) **2.** *adj.* not shocking; not wild; not exciting; dull. (Fig. on ①. Adv: *tamely.* Comp: *tamer;* sup: *tamest.*)

tamper with ['tæm pɚ wɪθ] to alter something secretly, especially without permission; to fiddle around with something.

tan ['tæn] **1.** *iv.* [especially of people with fair skin] to permit one's skin to darken by being outdoors in sunlight or by exposing oneself to artificial sunlight. **2.** *tv.* to change the skin of an animal into leather by soaking it in a special chemical. **3.** *n.* darkness of the skin from exposure to sunlight as in ①. **4.** *n.* a light brown color. **5.** *adj.* light brown in color. (Comp: *tanner;* sup: *tannest.*)

tandem ['tæn dəm] *adj.* [of two or more people or things] in sequence, one behind another. (Adv: *tandemly.*)

tangent ['tæn dʒənt] *n.* a line that touches a circle at only one point.

tangerine [tæn dʒə 'rin] **1.** *n.* a small, orange citrus fruit; a kind of orange whose peel is easy to remove. **2.** the *adj.* use of ①.

tangle ['tæŋ gəl] **1.** *n.* a twisted clump of hair, string, chain, rope, limbs, etc. **2.** *n.* an argument; a disagreement. **3.** *iv.* [for strands] to become twisted together. **4.** *tv.* to twist strands together; to snarl something.

tank ['tæŋk] **1.** *n.* a container for storing air or liquid. **2.** *n.* a large vehicle, used by the military, that moves on heavy belts wrapped around a set of wheels.

tantrum ['tæn trəm] *n.* a bad display of temper and emotion. (Short for *temper tantrum.*)

tap ['tæp] **1.** *n.* a slight pressure or a very light blow made by something. **2.** *n.* a device that controls the flow of a gas or a liquid from a pipe or a barrel; a faucet. **3.** *tv.* to touch someone or something gently a number of times, especially with the tip of one's finger. **4.** *tv.* to cut something open so that liquid will flow out; to pierce something, such as a barrel, so that liquid will flow out.

tape ['tep] **1.** *n.* a paper or plastic strip with one side that is sticky, used to stick something to something else. (Pl only for types and instances.) **2.** *n.* a magnetic strip of plastic onto which sound or images can be recorded. (No pl.) **3.** *n.* a reel or cassette of (2); something recorded on a reel or cassette of (2). **4.** *tv.* to stick something to something else with (1); to seal something with (1). **5.** *tv.* to fix something that is torn by placing (1) over the tear. **6.** *tv.* to record sound or images onto (2). **7.** *iv.* to make a sound or video recording; to record.

tapestry ['tæp ə stri] *n.* a large cloth that has a design or decoration woven into it.

tar ['tɑr] **1.** *n.* a black substance similar to very thick oil, used to preserve or waterproof objects. (No pl.) **2.** *tv.* to cover something with (1); to preserve or waterproof something with (1).

tardy ['tɑr di] *adj.* late; not prompt; not on time. (Adv: *tardily.* Comp: *tardier;* sup: *tardiest.*)

target ['tɑr gət] **1.** *n.* someone or something that someone tries to hit or shoot when using a weapon. **2.** *n.* someone who is ridiculed, blamed, or made fun of. (Fig. on (1).) **3.** *n.* a goal that one would like to reach; an aim. (Fig. on (1).) **4.** *tv.* to establish something as a goal. **5.** *tv.* to focus on someone, something, or someplace; to give something, someone, or someplace the greatest amount of thought or effort.

tariff ['tɛr ɪf] **1.** *n.* a tax that a government charges on products entering or leaving a country. **2.** *n.* the cost of a service, such as the service provided by a utility.

tarnish ['tɑr nɪʃ] **1.** *n.* a coating found especially on metals that makes them less shiny. **2.** *iv.* to acquire (1). **3.** *tv.* to dull the shiny metal surface of something. **4.** *tv.* to taint or spoil something. (Fig. on (3).)

task ['tæsk] *n.* a duty; an errand; a responsibility; a chore; an item of work that someone must do, especially a difficult one.

taste ['test] **1.** *n.* the ability to sense or experience sweetness, saltiness, bitterness, or sourness with one's tongue. (No pl.) **2.** *n.* a particular flavor as experienced through (1). **3.** *n.* a small sample of food or drink. **4.** *n.* the quality of one's choice or selection in beauty, fashion, or art; the ability to judge what is suitable or fitting. (Pl only for types and instances.) **5.** *tv.* to sense or experience flavor with one's tongue. **6.** *tv.* to put something in one's mouth or on one's tongue so that one can know its flavor; to eat a very small amount of something so one can know its flavor. **7.** *tv.* to experience something for a short while. **8.** *iv.* [for a food] to have a particular flavor.

tasteless ['test ləs] **1.** *adj.* having no TASTE ②; having no flavor; bland. (Adv: *tastelessly.*) **2.** *adj.* showing poor TASTE ④; offensive; rude. (Adv: *tastelessly.*)

tasty ['tes ti] *adj.* full of flavor; delicious. (Adv: *tastily.* Comp: *tastier;* sup: *tastiest.*)

tatter ['tæt ɚ] *tv.* to tear a piece of cloth; to fray something.

taught ['tɔt] pt/pp of TEACH.

taunt ['tɔnt] **1.** *tv.* to tease someone; to make fun of someone; to ridicule someone; to provoke someone by saying something unkind. **2.** *n.* an unkind remark that is made to tease or ridicule someone.

taut ['tɔt] *adj.* pulled tight; having no slack; stretched. (Adv: *tautly.* Comp: *tauter;* sup: *tautest.*)

tavern ['tæv ɚn] *n.* a bar; a place where alcohol is sold and drunk.

tax ['tæks] **1.** *n.* money charged by a government to pay for the cost of the government and its services. **2.** *tv.* to make someone pay ①. **3.** *tv.* to charge ① on something; to burden something with ①. **4.** *tv.* to burden someone or something; to place a strain on someone or something. (Fig. on ③.)

taxi ['tæk si] **1.** *n.* a CAB, a TAXICAB. (Short for TAXICAB.) **2.** *iv.* [for an airplane] to move on the ground.

taxicab ['tæk si kæb] *n.* a car that, along with its driver, can be hired for short trips. (Can be shortened to TAXI or CAB.)

tea ['ti] **1.** *n.* the leaves of a bush grown in Asia that are dried and then soaked in boiling water to make a refreshing drink. (Pl only for types and instances.) **2.** *n.* a drink made from ①. (No pl.) **3.** *n.* a drink, like ②, made by soaking dried herbs or other plants in boiling water. (No pl.)

teach ['titʃ] **1.** *tv., irreg.* to provide instruction in a particular subject. (Pt/pp: TAUGHT.) **2.** *tv., irreg.* to instruct someone in how to do something. **3.** *iv., irreg.* to work as a teacher.

teacher ['titʃ ɚ] *n.* someone who teaches people something; someone who instructs people in a subject.

team ['tim] **1.** *n.* a group of players who form one side in a game or sport. **2.** *n.* a group of people who work together. **3.** *n.* two or more animals that work together to pull a vehicle or piece of farming equipment. **4.** ~ **up** to join with one or more persons; to collaborate with two or more persons.

teammate ['tim met] *n.* a member of a team that one is a part of; another person on one's team.

teamwork ['tim wɚk] *n.* the action of working together as a team. (No pl.)

teapot ['ti pɑt] *n.* a container with a handle and a spout, used to hold and pour tea.

tear 1. ['tɪr] *n.* a drop of liquid that falls from one's eye when one cries. **2.** ['tɛr] *n.* a rip; a place in a piece of cloth or paper that is ripped. **3.** ['tɛr] *tv., irreg.* to make a hole or a rip in something, especially by pulling it; to pull something into pieces. (Pt: TORE; pp: TORN.) **4.** ['tɛr] *iv., irreg.* to be ripped apart. **5.** ['tɛr] *iv., irreg.* to move somewhere very quickly. **6.** ['tɪr] *iv.* to cry; to begin to cry; to have tears form in one's eyes. (Pt/pp: *teared* ['tird].) **7.** ~ **away;** ~ **off** to leave someone or something, running or moving very fast.

teardrop ['tɪr drɑp] *n.* one tear; one drop of liquid that falls from one's eye.

tease ['tiz] **1.** *tv.* to taunt someone; to make fun of someone. **2.** *tv.* to flirt with someone, especially with sexual hints. **3.** *tv.* to separate strands of hair; to comb strands of hair apart. **4.** *iv.* to taunt [someone or something]; to annoy on purpose. **5.** *n.* someone who flirts with someone else as in ②.

technician [tɛk 'nɪ ʃən] *n.* someone who works in the field of industrial or mechanical sciences; someone who works in a laboratory, performing tests.

technique [tɛk 'nik] **1.** *n.* a special method of doing something. **2.** *n.* the skill involved in creating or performing art; the way that art is performed, displayed, or exhibited—showing the artist's skill. (No pl.)

technology [tɛk 'nɑl ə dʒi] *n.* the science and study of the mechanical and industrial sciences. (Pl only for types and instances.)

tedious ['tid i əs] *adj.* boring; dull; not exciting; not stimulating. (Adv: *tediously.*)

teem with ['tim wɪθ] to have an abundance of something.

teen ['tin] **1.** *n.* a teenager. **2.** the *adj.* use of ①.

teenage ['tin edʒ] *adj.* of, for, or about teenagers; of the ages from 13 through 19.

511

teenager ['tin edʒ ɚ] *n.* someone whose age is between 13 and 19.

teens *n.* the numbers 13–19 or 10–19. (When referring to age, it refers to the period of someone's life from the age of 13 through the age of 19.)

teeth ['tiθ] pl of TOOTH.

telegram ['tɛl ə græm] *n.* a message sent by telegraph.

telegraph ['tɛl ə græf] **1.** *n.* a machine that sends messages in electrical code over electrical wires. **2.** *tv.* to send a message by using ①. (E.g., *telegraphed his response.*) **3.** *tv.* to send [a message] to someone by ①. (E.g., *telegraphed John with his response.*)

telephone ['tɛl ə fon] **1.** *n.* a device that transmits sound by converting it into electrical signals; a PHONE. **2.** *tv.* to call someone by using ①. **3.** *iv.* to make a call with ①.

telescope ['tɛl ə skop] **1.** *n.* a device that makes distant objects, especially objects that are in the sky, look larger so that one can see them better. **2.** *iv.* to become shorter or longer by having one part slide over another as with ①. **3.** *tv.* to make something shorter or longer by sliding one part of it over another.

television ['tɛl ə vɪʒ ən] **1.** *n.* the transmission of an electronic signal containing sounds and images. (No pl. Can be shortened to TV.) **2.** *n.* the business of producing ① or the programs that are transmitted on ①. (No pl. Can be shortened to TV.) **3.** *n.* an electronic device that converts electronic signals into sounds and images. (Short for *television set.*) **4.** the *adj.* use of ①, ②, or ③.

tell ['tɛl] **1.** *tv., irreg.* to express something in words. (Pt/pp: TOLD.) **2.** *tv., irreg.* to inform someone [of something]. **3.** *tv., irreg.* to signal information [to someone]. **4.** *tv., irreg.* to reveal a secret. **5.** *iv., irreg.* to reveal [a secret]. **6.** *iv., irreg.* to try to make trouble for a person by saying (to an authority) what that person has done.

teller ['tɛl ɚ] *n.* someone who works at a bank, receiving and giving out money.

temper ['tɛm pɚ] **1.** *n.* mood; the condition of one's mind, especially in regard to anger. (No pl.) **2.** *n.* an angry mood; the potential of being angry. (No pl.) **3.** *tv.* to soften something; to lessen the force or impact of something; to make something more moderate.

temperament ['tɛm pɚ mənt] **1.** *n.* a person's mood; the way a person is or acts. **2.** *n.* the adjustment of musical pitches on a keyboard instrument by making slight changes in the pitch of the individual notes.

512

temperate ['tɛm pɚ ɪt] **1.** *n.* [of a climate] not hot and not cold. **2.** *adj.* controlled; moderate. (Adv: *temperately.*)

temperature ['tɛm pɚ ə tʃɚ] **1.** *n.* the degree of how cold or hot something is. **2.** *n.* the degree of the heat of one's blood, especially when it is above average; a fever.

tempest ['tɛmp əst] *n.* a violent storm.

temple ['tɛm pəl] **1.** *n.* a building used for worship and ceremonies. **2.** *n.* a Jewish house of worship. **3.** *n.* the flat part on the side of the head between the eye and the ear and above the cheekbone.

temporary ['tɛm pə rer i] *adj.* for a limited time; not permanent. (Adv: *temporarily* [tɛm pə 'rɛr ə li].)

tempt ['tɛmpt] *tv.* to arouse someone's desire; to make someone want something.

temptation [tɛmp 'te ʃən] **1.** *n.* desire; an instance of being tempted. (No pl.) **2.** *n.* someone or something that tempts a person.

ten ['tɛn] **1.** 10. Go to FOUR. **2.** *n.* a $10 bill.

tend ['tɛnd] *tv.* to take care of something.

tendency ['tɛn dən si] *n.* the likelihood that someone or something will do something naturally.

tender ['tɛn dɚ] **1.** *adj.* soft; not tough; easy to chew. (Adv: *tenderly.*) **2.** *adj.* sore; sore when touched; painful. (Adv: *tenderly.*) **3.** *adj.* kind; gentle; showing love or affection. (Adv: *tenderly.*) **4.** *tv.* to offer something formally or legally, such as to offer money in payment of a debt.

tennis ['tɛn ɪs] *n.* a sport played by two people or two pairs of people who use rackets to hit a small ball from one side of the playing area, over a net, to the other side of the playing area. (No pl.)

tense ['tɛns] **1.** *adj.* taut; not loose; not relaxed. (Adv: *tensely.* Comp: *tenser;* sup: *tensest.*) **2.** *adj.* nervous; not relaxed. (Adv: *tensely.* Comp: *tenser;* sup: *tensest.*) **3.** *tv.* to tighten something, such as a muscle; to stiffen something; to make something taut. **4.** *n.* a quality of a verb that indicates the time that the action or state it expresses takes place.

tension ['tɛn ʃən] **1.** *n.* the degree of tightness of something that is stretched. (Pl only for types and instances.) **2.** *n.* an anxious or nervous feeling; hidden anxiety or anger.

tent ['tɛnt] *n.* a temporary shelter made of fabric supported by poles and ropes.

tenth ['tɛnθ] 10th. Go to FOURTH.

term ['tɚm] **1.** *n.* the length of time that something lasts; a particular period of time. **2.** *n.* a division of a school year; a quarter or semester. **3.** *n.* an expression used in a particular field; a word.

terminal ['tɚ mə nəl] **1.** *adj.* happening at the end of something; at the end; last. (Adv: *terminally.*) **2.** *adj.* resulting in death; causing death; not able to be cured. (Adv: *terminally.*) **3.** *n.* a building that passengers enter and leave from, especially at an airport, bus station, or train station. **4.** *n.* something that makes an electrical connection; the place where current enters or leaves a battery or a circuit. **5.** *n.* a computer device consisting of a keyboard and a screen that displays the information sent to and from a computer.

terminate ['tɚ mə net] **1.** *tv.* to end something; to cause something to no longer exist. **2.** *tv.* to fire someone from a job. **3.** *iv.* to end; to come to an end; to no longer exist.

termite ['tɚ maɪt] *n.* an insect, similar to an ant, that eats wood, causing great damage to wooden objects and structures.

terms **1.** *n.* requirements; details; provisions. **2.** *n.* charges; fees and requirements.

terrace ['tɛr əs] **1.** *n.* a flat area connected to or next to the side of a house or apartment; a balcony or patio. **2.** *n.* a flat area of land that has been cut into the side of a hill or mountain.

terrain [tə 'ren] *n.* the physical features of an area of land.

terrible ['tɛr ə bəl] *adj.* awful; horrible; extremely bad. (Adv: *terribly.*)

terribly ['tɛr ə bli] **1.** *adv.* badly; horribly; awfully. **2.** *adv.* very; extremely.

terrier ['tɛr i ɚ] *n.* one of a group of breeds of small dogs, originally bred to be used in hunting.

terrific [tə 'rɪf ɪk] **1.** *adj.* great; wonderful; super; excellent. (Adv: *terrifically* [...ɪk li].) **2.** *adj.* extreme[ly bad]. (Adv: *terrifically* [...ɪk li].)

terrify ['tɛr ə faɪ] *tv.* to scare someone or something greatly.

territory ['tɛr ə tor i] **1.** *n.* land; area. (No pl.) **2.** *n.* an area of land controlled by a specific government, especially a government that is far away. **3.** *n.* an area of land that is dominated by an animal or group of animals.

terror ['tɛr ɚ] **1.** *n.* extreme fear. (Pl only for types and instances.) **2.** *n.* someone or something that causes extreme fear.

terrorism ['tɛr ɚ ɪz əm] *n.* the use of violence and terror to achieve political goals. (No pl.)

terrorist ['tɛr ə ɪst] *n.* someone who practices terrorism.

test ['tɛst] **1.** *n.* a series of questions or activities that determine someone's knowledge or skill; a school examination. **2.** *n.* an experiment; an action that is done to see how something works. **3.** *tv.* to determine someone's knowledge or skill by evaluating answers to questions or performance of activities. **4.** *tv.* to subject something to ② in order to measure its condition or see how it works.

testimony ['tɛs tə mo ni] *n.* the statements of a witness, especially in a court of law. (Not usually pl. Treated as sg.)

text ['tɛkst] **1.** *n.* the main words in a book or article, not the pictures, tables, graphs, indexes, etc. (No pl.) **2.** *n.* the words of a speech in written form. **3.** *n.* a book used by students in school or college. (Short for TEXTBOOK.)

textbook ['tɛkst bʊk] **1.** *n.* a book, designed for student use, that is used as a standard source of information about a specific subject. (Can be shortened to TEXT.) **2.** *adj.* [of possible examples] the best and most typical.

textile ['tɛks taɪl] **1.** *n.* cloth; something that is made by weaving. **2.** the *adj.* use of ①.

texture ['tɛks tʃɚ] **1.** *n.* the evenness or smoothness—or unevenness or roughness—of something. **2.** *n.* the appearance of having ①, such as with a design on paper or in art.

than ['ðæn] *conj.* as compared with someone or something; in comparison with someone or something. (Used before the second item of a comparison.)

thank ['θæŋk] *tv.* to show someone gratitude by saying "thank you"; to express gratitude for something that has been given or done.

thankful ['θæŋk fʊl] *adj.* grateful; showing thanks; expressing thanks. (Adv: *thankfully.*)

thanks **1.** *interj.* a polite expression that is used by the receiver of an action or gift, along with "yes" or "no" in response to a question, or to show gratitude. (Less formal than *Thank you.*) **2.** *n.* gratitude. (Treated as pl, but not countable.)

Thanksgiving [θæŋks 'gɪv ɪŋ] *n.* a holiday celebrated in the United States and Canada as an expression of individual and national gratitude. (THANKSGIVING is held on the fourth Thursday in November in the United States.)

that ['ðæt] **1.** *adj.* a form referring to someone or something already mentioned or someone or something of which both the speaker and hearer are aware. (Prenominal only. With pl nouns, use THOSE.) **2.** *adj.* a form referring to someone or something further away or the furthest away from the speaker. (Used in contrast with THIS. Prenominal only. With pl nouns, use THOSE.) **3.** *pron.* a form standing for someone or something already referred to or someone or something of which both the speaker and hearer are aware. (Pl: THOSE.) **4.** *pron.* a form standing for someone or something that is further away or the furthest away from the speaker. (Used in contrast with THIS. Pl: THOSE.) **5.** *pron.* which. (Used to connect sentences, clauses, and phrases with noun phrases. Only used with *restrictive clauses*. See WHICH for an explanation. Sometimes means "when" or "where" if it follows a noun phrase referring to a time or place.) **6.** *pron.* who; whom. (Used to connect sentences, phrases, or clauses with noun phrases. Only where WHO or WHOM would be appropriate.) **7.** *pron.* a form used to connect a verb with a clause that is the object of the verb. (Only certain verbs use THAT in this way. This THAT can be omitted.) **8.** *adv.* so; to such a degree. (E.g., [gesturing] *he is that big.*)

that's ['ðæts] **1.** *cont.* that is. **2.** *cont.* that has, where HAS is an auxiliary.

thaw ['θɔ] **1.** *iv.* [for ice] to melt; [for something frozen] to no longer be frozen; [for the weather] to be warm enough to melt ice or snow. **2.** *iv.* to become less formal; to relax. (Fig. on ①.) **3.** *tv.* to melt something; to cause something to no longer be frozen. **4.** *n.* a condition in which the weather has become warm enough to melt ice or snow.

the [ðə, ði] **1.** *article* a certain one; certain ones. (The definite article. Used before nouns or noun phrases to show that a definite thing, person, or group of people or things is being referred to. Pronounced ['ði] when emphasized or before vowel sounds.) **2.** *article* a form showing a general category. (Used before a noun that is used in a general sense.) **3.** *article* a form indicating the special or specific one, the one that is being talked about. (Used before some names and titles.)

theater AND **theatre** ['θi ə tæ] **1.** *n.* a building where movies are shown or where plays are performed. (The spelling *theatre* is used especially for buildings where plays are performed, and much less often for buildings where movies are shown.) **2.** *n.* the business of producing plays for the stage; the study of drama, performance, and acting. (No pl.)

theft ['θɛft] *n.* stealing; taking someone else's property without permission. (Pl only for types and instances.)

their ['ðɛɚ] **1.** *pron.* the possessive form of THEY; belonging to people, animals, or things that have already been mentioned. (Used as a modifier before a noun.) **2.** *pron.* ① standing for HIS ③; belonging to a person who has already been mentioned. (Used to refer to a preceding noun or pronoun, the sexual reference of which is unimportant, indeterminate, undetermined, or irrelevant. Adopted as a replacement for HIS ③ by those who see HIS ③ as referring to males only. Objected to by some as an unnecessary violation of grammatical number when used for sg nouns.)

theirs *pron.* the possessive form of THEY; belonging to people, animals, or things that have already been mentioned.

them ['ðɛm] **1.** *pron.* the objective form of THEY. (Used to refer to people, animals, and things. Used after prepositions and as the object of verbs.) **2.** *pron.* a form standing for HIM ②, referring to a person already mentioned. (Used to refer to a noun or pronoun, the sexual reference of which is unimportant, indeterminate, undetermined, or irrelevant. Adopted as a replacement for HIM ② by those who see HIM ② as referring to males only. Objected to by some as an unnecessary violation of grammatical number when used for sg nouns.)

theme ['θim] **1.** *n.* a subject of a speech or a text; a topic. **2.** *n.* a melody that is used to identify a certain program, movie, character, or emotion. **3.** *n.* the main melody of a piece of music. **4.** *n.* a visual or decorative concept that connects several parts of something. **5.** *adj.* of or about a piece of music that is readily identified with someone or something.

themselves [ðɛm 'sɛlvz] **1.** *pron.* the reflexive form of THEY, used after a verb or a preposition when the subject of the sentence refers to the same people, animals, or things that the pronoun refers to. **2.** *pron.* the reflexive form of THEY used after THEY or a pl noun phrase as an intensifier.

then ['ðɛn] **1.** *adv.* at that time. **2.** *adv.* next; following; after that. **3.** *adv.* therefore; in that case; so.

theology [θi 'ɑl ə dʒi] *n.* the study and science of religion. (Pl only for types and instances.)

theory ['θɪr i] *n.* knowledge of a science or an art, as opposed to the actual practice of a science or an art; the principles on which a science or an art are based. (Pl only for types and instances.)

there ['ðɛɚ] **1.** *adv.* to or toward that place; at that place; in that place; in that respect; at that point in time; at that point during a process. (Compare this with THEY'RE and THEIR.) **2.** *adv.* a form that begins a sentence or clause and is followed by a verb, which is then followed by the subject of the sentence. (The verb is usually BE—for example, *there is, there are*—but it can also be *go, come, stand, rest,* or another verb. In questions, the verb is placed before *there.*) **3.** *pron.* a particular place or location.

therefore [ˈðɛr fɔr] *adv.* for that reason; for those reasons; as a result; so; consequently.

there's [ˈðɛɚz] **1.** *cont.* there has, where HAS is an auxiliary. **2.** *cont.* there is.

thermometer [θɚ ˈmɑm ə tɚ] *n.* a device that measures the temperature of someone or something.

thermostat [ˈθɚm ə stæt] *n.* a device that maintats the temperature of a room or a machine.

these [ˈðiz] pl of THIS.

theses [ˈθi siz] pl of THESIS.

thesis [ˈθi sɪs] **1.** *n., irreg.* the premise of an argument; a statement that will be proved and defended in an argument. (Pl: THESES.) **2.** *n., irreg.* a research paper written by someone in order to obtain a degree from a school, college, or university.

they [ˈðe] **1.** *pron.* the third-person pl subject pronoun; the pl of HE, SHE, or IT. **2.** *pron.* the third-person pl subject pronoun used as a sg. (Used to refer to a preceding noun or pronoun, the sexual reference of which is unimportant, indeterminate, undetermined, or irrelevant. Adopted as a replacement for HE ② by those who see HE ② as referring to males only. Objected to by some as an unnecessary violation of grammatical number when used for sg nouns.) **3.** *pron.* people in general; a group of people.

they'd [ˈðed] **1.** *cont.* they would. **2.** *cont.* they had, where HAD is an auxiliary.

they'll [ˈðel] *cont.* they will.

they're [ˈðɛɚ] *cont.* they are. (Compare this with THERE, THEIR.)

they've [ˈðev] *cont.* they have, where HAVE is an auxiliary.

thick [ˈθɪk] **1.** *adj.* not thin; having a greater than average distance between two opposite sides; having a lot of space between two opposite sides. (E.g., *a thick board.* Adv: *thickly.* Comp: *thicker;* sup: *thickest.*) **2.** *adj.* measuring a certain distance between two opposite sides; having a certain depth or width. (E.g., *two feet thick.* Comp: *thicker.* No sup.) **3.** *adj.* dense; with very little space between things. (Adv: *thickly.* Comp: *thicker;* sup: *thickest.*) **4.** *adj.* not pouring easily, like glue or molasses; being liquid but not flowing easily. (Adv: *thickly.* Comp: *thicker;* sup: *thickest.*) **5.** *adj.* [of air] not clear; [of air] full of water vapor, smoke, or fog. (Comp: *thicker;* sup: *thickest.*) **6.** *adj.* [of an accent or manner of speaking] showing where the speaker is from.

thicken ['θɪk ən] **1.** *tv.* to cause something to become thicker. **2.** *iv.* [for a liquid] to become thicker.

thicket ['θɪk ət] *n.* an area of dense shrubs and trees.

thick-skinned *adj.* not easily upset or hurt; insensitive to offense.

thief ['θif] *n., irreg.* someone who steals things. (Pl: THIEVES.)

thieves ['θivz] pl of THIEF.

thigh ['θaɪ] *n.* [in humans and many animals] the part of the leg between the hip and the knee.

thimble ['θɪm bəl] *n.* a small metal or plastic cap, which is worn over one's finger while sewing so the finger is not injured when pushing the needle through material.

thin ['θɪn] **1.** *adj.* not thick; having less than the average distance between two opposite sides; having very little space between two opposite sides. (Adv: *thinly.* Comp: *thinner;* sup: *thinnest.*) **2.** *adj.* not fat; slender; slim; not having much fat on one's body. (Adv: *thinly.* Comp: *thinner;* sup: *thinnest.*) **3.** *adj.* not dense; spread out. (Adv: *thinly.* Comp: *thinner;* sup: *thinnest.*) **4.** *adj.* not thick; [of a liquid] containing a lot of water; flowing easily. (Adv: *thinly.* Comp: *thinner;* sup: *thinnest.*) **5.** *tv.* to make something runnier or ④.

thing ['θɪŋ] **1.** *n.* any object; an object whose name is not known; an object whose name is not important. **2.** *n.* an event; an action; a deed; a statement; an idea.

think ['θɪŋk] **1.** *iv., irreg.* to use one's mind; to have thoughts or opinions; to form ideas in the mind. (Pt/pp: THOUGHT.) **2.** *iv., irreg.* to be able to use one's mind; to have the ability to use one's mind. **3.** *tv., irreg.* to have a certain belief or opinion; to believe something. (The object can be a clause with THAT ⑦.)

thin-skinned *adj.* easily upset or hurt; sensitive.

third ['θɚd] 3rd. Go to FOURTH.

thirdly ['θɚd li] *adv.* in the third place; as a third point of discussion.

thirst ['θɚst] *n.* the feeling caused by having nothing to drink; the need to drink. (No pl.)

thirsty ['θɚs ti] *adj.* needing to drink; having had nothing to drink; having thirst. (Adv: *thirstily.* Comp: *thirstier;* sup: *thirstiest.*)

thirteen [ˈθɚˈtin] 13. Go to FOUR.

thirteenth [ˈθɚtˈtinθ] 13th. Go to FOURTH.

thirtieth [ˈθɚt i əθ] 30th. Go to FOURTH.

thirty [ˈθɚt i] 30. Go to FORTY.

this [ˈðɪs] **1.** *adj.* a form referring to a thing or person that has already been referred to or is obvious and present; a form referring to an object that one is pointing to or otherwise indicating. (Prenominal only. Use THESE with pl nouns.) **2.** *adj.* a form introducing a thing or person new to the conversation. (Colloquial. Prenominal only. Use THESE with pl nouns.) **3.** *adj.* a form referring to the thing, person, or point in time that is closer or the closest to the speaker. (Used in contrast with THAT. Prenominal only. Use THESE with pl nouns.) **4.** *pron.* a form standing for a thing or person that has already been mentioned or is obvious and present. (Pl: THESE.) **5.** *pron.* a form standing for the thing, person, or point in time that is closer or the closest to the speaker. (Used in contrast with THAT. Pl: THESE.) **6.** *adv.* to the indicated degree. (E.g., [gesturing] *he is this big*.)

thistle [ˈθɪs əl] *n.* any of several types of perennial plants with spiny leaves and large, usually purple, flowers.

thorn [ˈθorn] *n.* a sharp, pointed growth on a plant.

thorough [ˈθɚ o] *adj.* complete; done with great attention and in great detail. (Adv: *thoroughly*.)

those [ˈðoz] **1.** pl of THAT. **2.** *pron.* the people [who do something]. **3.** *adj.* a form referring to people or things already mentioned or people or things of which both the speaker and hearer are aware. (Prenominal only. With sg nouns, use THAT.) **4.** *adj.* a form referring to people or things farther away or the farthest away from the speaker. (Used in contrast with THESE. Prenominal only. With sg nouns, use THAT.)

though [ˈðo] **1.** *conj.* in spite of something; in spite of the fact that; although. **2.** *adv.* however.

thought [ˈθɔt] **1.** pt/pp of THINK. **2.** *n.* thinking; attention; time taken to think about an idea. (No pl.) **3.** *n.* an idea; an opinion; something that one thinks.

thoughtful [ˈθɔt fʊl] **1.** *adj.* considerate; caring about someone's feelings; kind. (Adv: *thoughtfully*.) **2.** *adj.* [of something] showing thought and consideration. (Adv: *thoughtfully*.)

520

thousand ['θaʊ zənd] **1.** *n.* 1,000; the number between 999 and 1,001. (Additional numbers formed as with *two thousand, three thousand, four thousand,* etc.) **2.** *n.* a group of 1,000 people or things.

thousandth ['θaʊ zəndθ] 1,000th. Go to FOURTH.

thread ['θrɛd] **1.** *n.* fine string, made of twisted strands of cotton, silk, or other fiber, that is used to sew pieces of cloth together or is woven to make cloth. (Pl only for types and instances.) **2.** *n.* a very thin strand of something; a length of ①. **3.** *n.* a theme or idea that links parts of an argument or a story. (Fig. on ②.) **4.** *n.* the raised ridge that wraps around the length of a screw or a bolt. (Usually pl, but not countable.) **5.** *tv.* to pass ① through something, usually a needle. **6.** *tv.* to place something on ① or on string, wire, etc.

threat ['θrɛt] **1.** *n.* a warning; a statement or action that indicates that someone is going to hurt or punish someone in a certain way. **2.** *n.* a sign of danger; a sign that something harmful or dangerous is going to happen.

threaten ['θrɛt n] **1.** *tv.* to express a threat against someone. (The object can be a clause with THAT ⑦.) **2.** *iv.* to be a threat; to be an indication of danger.

three ['θri] 3. Go to FOUR.

threshold ['θrɛʃ hold] **1.** *n.* the piece of wood, metal, or stone across the bottom of a door frame; the entrance to a building, house, or room. **2.** *n.* the beginning point of something. (Fig. on ①.)

threw ['θru] pt of THROW.

thrift ['θrɪft] *n.* the careful use of money and things; the habit of not wasting money or things. (No pl.)

thrifty ['θrɪf ti] the *adj.* form of THRIFT.

thrill ['θrɪl] **1.** *n.* an intense feeling of emotion, especially excitement, enjoyment, or fear. **2.** *tv.* to cause someone to feel full of emotion, especially excitement, enjoyment, or fear.

thrive ['θraɪv] **1.** *iv., irreg.* to grow and survive; to develop in a very healthy way. (Pt: THROVE or *thrived;* pp: *thrived* or THRIVEN.) **2.** *iv., irreg.* to be successful; to become very rich.

thriven ['θrɪv ən] a pp of THRIVE.

throat ['θrot] **1.** *n.* the front of the neck. **2.** *n.* the inside of the neck, where food and air pass.

521

throb ['θrɑb] **1.** *iv.* to beat strongly and quickly, as with the beating of the heart or some other pulse. **2.** *iv.* to have a pain that occurs with each heartbeat. **3.** *n.* one beat in a series of strong, quick beats.

throne ['θron] **1.** *n.* the chair that a king, queen, or other ruler or important person sits on. **2.** *n.* the position held by a king, queen, or other ruler or important person.

through ['θru] **1.** *prep.* from the outside of one end of something, into it, to the other end of it, and out of the other side of it. **2.** *prep.* because of something; on account of something. **3.** *prep.* moving throughout or within something. **4.** *prep.* during the entire time from beginning to end; during the entire way from start to finish. **5.** *adv.* in one side and out the other. **6.** *adv.* from beginning to end; from start to finish. **7.** *adj.* finished; done.

throughout [θru 'aʊt] *prep.* in every part of something; during every moment of something.

throve ['θrov] a pt of THRIVE.

throw ['θro] **1.** *tv., irreg.* to send something through the air; to hurl something; to cause something to move through the air. (Pt: THREW; pp: THROWN.) **2.** *tv., irreg.* to put someone or something someplace carelessly, with force, or in a hurry. **3.** *tv., irreg.* [for an animal] to cause a rider to fall off. **4.** *tv., irreg.* to move a switch in order to start or stop the flow of electricity. **5.** *tv., irreg.* to cause someone to be in a certain condition, especially a confused one.

thrown ['θron] pp of THROW.

thrust ['θrʌst] **1.** *tv., irreg.* to push someone or something forward with force; to push someone or something in a certain direction with force. (Pt/pp: *thrust.*) **2.** *tv., irreg.* to drive a sharp object at or into someone or something. **3.** *iv., irreg.* to move forward with force; to lunge, especially with a sharp object. **4.** *n.* a forceful movement in a certain direction; a lunge; a stab.

thud ['θʌd] *n.* the dull sound of something heavy falling onto, or hitting, something firm but unbreakable.

thumb ['θʌm] **1.** *n.* the first and shortest finger on the hand, separate from the other four, having two knuckles instead of three. **2.** *n.* the part of a glove or mitten that covers ①.

thumbnail ['θʌm nel] *n.* the nail on one's thumb.

thumbtack ['θʌm tæk] **1.** *n.* a tack with a large, flat head that is pressed with one's thumb to drive the pointed part into a surface. (See also TACK.) **2.** *tv.* to attach something to a surface with ①.

522

thump ['θʌmp] **1.** *n.* the sound made by hitting someone or something with something hard or against something hard. **2.** *tv.* to hit someone or something with something hard; to hit someone or something against something hard.

thunder ['θʌn dɚ] **1.** *n.* the loud noise that follows lightning. (No pl.) **2.** *n.* any loud noise or explosion that sounds like ①. **3.** *iv.* [for weather conditions] to make ①. **4.** *iv.* to make a noise like ①; to walk or move, making noise like ①.

thundershower ['θʌn dɚ ʃaʊ ɚ] *n.* rain with thunder and lightning.

thunderstorm ['θʌn dɚ storm] *n.* a storm with thunder and lightning.

Thursday ['θɚz de] Go to DAY.

thus ['ðʌs] *adv.* therefore; for this reason; for these reasons; as a result.

tick ['tɪk] **1.** *n.* the short, quiet sound made by a watch or a clock. **2.** *n.* a small, flat insect that attaches to the skin of animals and sucks their blood. **3.** *n.* a mark that is made when counting something or checking something. **4.** *iv.* [for a clock, watch, or other timepiece] to make a short, quiet sound each second.

ticket ['tɪk ɪt] **1.** *n.* a piece of paper that shows that its owner has paid for transportation or for entrance into a place. **2.** *n.* a piece of paper that is given as a receipt when one leaves something at a repair shop, cleaners, or other business so that one can get the item back. **3.** *n.* a piece of paper that is given to someone who has broken a traffic or parking law, requiring that person to pay a fine or appear in court.

tickle ['tɪk əl] **1.** *tv.* to touch a person's body in a way that causes him or her to laugh. **2.** *tv.* to amuse someone. (Fig. on ①.) **3.** *iv.* to cause a feeling that causes someone to laugh. **4.** *n.* an itchy feeling; a feeling that one needs to scratch, cough, or sneeze.

ticklish ['tɪk lɪʃ] **1.** *adj.* sensitive to tickling; likely to laugh when tickled. (Adv: *ticklishly.*) **2.** *adj.* difficult; hard to answer; delicate; requiring careful thought or action. (Fig. on ①. Adv: *ticklishly.*)

tide ['taɪd] *n.* the rise and fall of the ocean, caused by the pull of the sun and the moon.

tidy ['taɪ di] **1.** *adj.* very neat; orderly; not messy. (Adv: *tidily.* Comp: *tidier;* sup: *tidiest.*) **2.** *tv.* to make something ①.

tie ['taɪ] **1.** *tv.* to form string, rope, cord, or thread into a knot or bow, often as a way to connect it to something or to join two pieces or ends together. (Pres. part.: *tying.*) **2.** *tv.* to join someone in occupying the same position in a list that ranks a group of things; to have the same score as the opposite player or team. **3.** *iv.* [for two teams] to have the same score; to occupy the same position as someone else in a list that ranks a group of things. **4.** *n.* a NECKTIE; a strip of cloth that is looped around the neck and TIED as in ① so there is a knot at the neck and the two ends hang down in front of one's shirt. **5.** *n.* a result of a game where both teams or players have the same score; a ranking where two or more people or things have the same rank.

tiger ['taɪ gɚ] *n.* a large, fierce animal that is a member of the cat family and has orange or yellow fur with black stripes.

tight ['taɪt] **1.** *adj.* not loose; having no extra room on the sides or around the edges; fitting closely. (Adv: *tightly.* Comp: *tighter;* sup: *tightest.*) **2.** *adj.* [of a schedule] having no extra time; having no appointments available. (Fig. on ①. Adv: *tightly.* Comp: *tighter;* sup: *tightest.*) **3.** *adj.* closely held; firmly fastened; fixed. (Adv: *tightly.* Comp: *tighter;* sup: *tightest.*) **4.** *adj.* stretched; taut. (Adv: *tightly.* Comp: *tighter;* sup: *tightest.*) **5.** *adv.* in a manner that is ①; firmly; closely. (Comp: *tighter;* sup: *tightest.*)

tighten ['taɪt n] **1.** *tv.* to make something tight; to make something tighter. **2.** *iv.* to become tight; to become tighter.

tightrope ['taɪt rop] *n.* a rope or cable that is stretched tight, high above the ground, and on which acrobats perform.

tights *n.* a garment that is worn below the waist and fits closely against one's body, generally worn by women and dancers; pantyhose. (Treated as pl. Number is expressed with *pair(s) of tights.*)

tile ['taɪl] **1.** *n.* baked clay or ceramic material formed into useful shapes for construction and decoration. (Pl only for types and instances.) **2.** *n.* a thin, formed piece of ① used for covering floors, walls, roofs, and other surfaces in buildings and houses. **3.** *n.* a square of soft material that absorbs sound and provides decoration, used in the construction of ceilings. **4.** *tv.* to cover a surface with ② or a similar substance. **5.** *iv.* to work by covering surfaces with ②.

till ['tɪl] **1.** *tv.* to plow land; to prepare soil for planting. **2.** *n.* the drawer in a cash register or counter where money is kept in a place of business. **3.** *prep.* UNTIL; up to a certain time; during a period of time up to a certain time. **4.** *conj.* UNTIL; up to a certain time. **5.** *conj.* UNTIL; before.

tilt ['tɪlt] **1.** *tv.* to turn something to its side; to slant something. **2.** *iv.* to be turned to the side; to be tipped; to slant; to slope.

timber ['tɪm bɚ] **1.** *n.* trees that are growing; a forest; woods. (No pl.) **2.** *n.* a thick length of wood.

524

time ['taɪm] **1.** *n.* every moment that ever was, is now, and ever will be; a continuous state of being from the past, through now, and into the future. (No pl.) **2.** *n.* a period of ①; a period of ① between two events. (No pl.) **3.** *n.* the amount of ① that it takes to do something. (No pl.) **4.** *n.* an exact moment in the passage of ①; some moment in the passage of ①. **5.** *n.* the appropriate moment, day, week, etc., to do something. (No pl.) **6.** *n.* an occasion of doing something; an instance of something being done. **7.** *tv.* to measure the existence of something that is happening; to measure how long or how fast it takes someone to do something. **8.** *tv.* to determine the best ④ for doing something, and do it then. **9.** *tv.* to set or arrange something so that it does something at a certain TIME as in ④.

timepiece ['taɪm pis] *n.* a device, especially a clock or a watch, that keeps track of time.

timer ['taɪm ɚ] *n.* someone or something that records time, especially a device that can be set to indicate when a certain amount of time has passed.

times ['taɪmz] **1.** *n.* periods of time and the events that occurred during them. **2.** *prep.* multiplied by a number. (Represented by the symbol "×".)

timid ['tɪm ɪd] *adj.* full of fear; easily scared. (Adv: *timidly.* Comp: *timider;* sup: *timidest.*)

tin ['tɪn] **1.** *n.* a metal that is mixed with other metals to make bronze and is used as a coating for steel so that the steel doesn't rust. (No pl.) **2.** *n.* a can or a container made of ① or plated with ①, or a modern steel can containing no ①. (Usually limited to containers that hold cookies, crackers, and sardines. CAN is used more frequently.) **3.** *adj.* made of or coated with ①.

tinge ['tɪndʒ] **1.** *n.* a very small amount of something, such as a color or an emotion. **2.** *tv.* to add to or improve something with a small amount of something.

tingle ['tɪŋ gəl] **1.** *n.* a light prickly or stinging feeling, as though one received a small shock or thrill. **2.** *iv.* to experience a light stinging feeling, as though one has received a small shock or thrill.

tinkle ['tɪŋ kəl] **1.** *n.* a short, quiet, high-pitched ring or clinking sound something like a soft jingle. **2.** *iv.* to ring in a short, quiet, high-pitched way.

tint ['tɪnt] **1.** *n.* a color; a weakened shade of a color. **2.** *tv.* to color something slightly; to give a small amount of color to something; to dye hair with ①.

tinted ['tɪn təd] *adj.* slightly colored.

tiny ['taɪ ni] *adj.* very small. (Adv: *tinily.* Comp: *tinier;* sup: *tiniest.*)

tip ['tɪp] **1.** *n.* the very end part of an object; the top of an object. **2.** *n.* money that is given to someone for a service. **3.** *n.* a hint; a suggestion; a piece of advice. **4.** *tv.* to lean something to the side; to cause something to slant. **5.** *tv.* to give someone money for a service; to leave someone ②. (E.g., *tip the porter.*) **6.** *tv.* to give a certain sum or percentage of money in gratitude for service. (E.g., *tip 15 percent for good service.*) **7.** *iv.* to lean to the side; to slant. **8.** *iv.* to give people money for their services.

tiptoe ['tɪp to] **1.** *n.* the tips of the toes, referring to walking on the toes. **2.** *iv.* to walk on the tips of one's toes; to walk very quietly or lightly.

tire ['taɪɚ] *n.* a circular structure of rubber that surrounds a wheel and is filled with air.

tired ['taɪɚd] **1.** *adj.* sleepy; wanting to sleep; exhausted. (Adv: *tiredly.*) **2.** *adj.* impatient with someone or something; annoyed with someone or something. (Adv: *tiredly.*)

tiring ['taɪr ɪŋ] *adj.* causing one to become tired, especially because it requires a lot of energy, patience, or attention; exhausting. (Adv: *tiringly.*)

tissue ['tɪʃ ju] **1.** *n.* a very soft piece of paper that is used to wipe the skin or for blowing the nose. **2.** *n.* a part of a plant or an animal that is made of many cells having the same function; the group of cells in a plant or animal that form a particular organ. (Pl only for types and instances.)

title ['taɪt əl] **1.** *n.* the name of a book, movie, song, play, picture, or poem. **2.** *n.* a word, often abbreviated, that is placed before a person's name, indicating rank, profession, or social position. **3.** *n.* the official name of a job or position. **4.** *n.* an official document showing that someone owns something. (Compare this with DEED ②.) **5.** *tv.* to give something ①.

tizzy ['tɪz i] *n.* an excited and confused condition; a fuss.

to [tu, tə] **1.** *prep.* in the direction of someone or something; toward someone or something; in the direction of a place, position, or condition; toward and reaching a place. **2.** *prep.* as far as some time, place, thing, or person; until; through. (Often indicated with a hyphen or short dash, as in "1997–1999.") **3.** *prep.* a form that marks the indirect object of a verb, showing the action of a verb toward someone or something. **4.** *prep.* for each; in each; included in each. **5.** *prep.* as far as someone or something; against someone or something. **6.** *prep.* before a certain time. **7.** the marker of the infinitive form of verbs. (This use of TO is often considered to be a preposition, but it has none of the qualities of a preposition.)

toad ['tod] *n.* a small animal similar to a frog, but which lives mostly on land.

toast ['tost] **1.** *n.* sliced bread that has been browned by heat. (No pl. Number is expressed with *piece(s)* or *slice(s) of toast.*) **2.** *n.* a statement made before an invitation for everyone present to take a drink in approval or agreement. **3.** *tv.* to brown a slice of bread by heating it; to brown something by heating it. **4.** *tv.* to warm something, especially marshmallows, over a fire. **5.** *tv.* to honor someone or something by taking a drink; to drink to the honor of someone or something.

toaster ['tos tɚ] *n.* an electrical appliance that toasts bread.

tobacco [tə 'bæk o] *n.* a plant whose leaves are dried to be smoked in cigars, cigarettes, or pipes or to be chewed. (Pl only for types and instances.)

toboggan [tə 'bɑg ən] **1.** *n.* a long sled without blades. **2.** *iv.* to ride on ①; to go down hills on ①.

today [tə 'de] **1.** *n.* this day; the current day. **2.** *n.* in this period of time. **3.** *adv.* in the current age or general time period. **4.** *adv.* on this day.

toe ['to] **1.** *n.* one of the fingerlike projections on the front of the foot; one of the digits on one's foot. **2.** *n.* the part of a shoe, boot, sock, or other piece of footwear that covers or encloses one or more ①.

toenail ['to nel] *n.* the thin, hard plate that covers the front part of the end of the toe.

together [tə 'gɛ ðɚ] **1.** *adv.* as one group of people or things. **2.** *adv.* at the same time; simultaneously.

toil ['tɔɪl] **1.** *n.* hard work; hard labor; work that requires a lot of physical energy or effort. (Pl only for types and instances.) **2.** *iv.* to work hard; to labor; to do work that requires a lot of physical energy or effort.

toilet ['tɔɪ lət] **1.** *n.* a bathroom; a room that has ②; a restroom. **2.** *n.* a strong, ceramic bowl, connected to a drain and having a seat attached to it, into which one expels urine or feces.

token ['tok ən] **1.** *n.* a sign of something; a reminder of something; visible proof of something; evidence of something. **2.** *n.* a small piece of metal, similar to a coin, that is used instead of money. **3.** *adj.* only serving as a symbol of something; done solely for the way it will appear to others.

told ['told] pt/pp of TELL.

tolerance ['tɑl ə rəns] **1.** *n.* the ability to endure pain, difficulty, or annoying behavior. (No pl form in this sense.) **2.** *n.* a resistance to the effects of a chemical, drug, or medicine built up over a long time. (No pl form in this sense.)

tolerant ['tɑl ə rənt] *adj.* willing to allow others to do something or to live the way they want to. (Adv: *tolerantly.*)

tolerate ['tɑl ə ret] *tv.* to endure someone or something; to manage to accept someone or something.

toll ['tol] **1.** *n.* a fee paid for the privilege of doing something, especially traveling on certain routes. **2.** *n.* the extra charge for certain telephone calls that are not local. **3.** *iv.* [for a bell] to ring slowly and repeatedly. **4.** *tv.* to ring a bell slowly and repeatedly.

tomato [tə 'me to] **1.** *n.* a round, soft, red fruit that grows on a vine and is eaten as food. (Pl ends in -*es.*) **2.** *adj.* made or flavored with ①.

tomb ['tum] *n.* an enclosure in which someone is buried, especially a structure that is above ground level.

tombstone ['tum ston] *n.* a grave marker; a large slab of stone at a grave that shows who is buried at that place and when that person was alive.

tomorrow [tə 'mɑr o] **1.** *n.* the day after today. (Usually sg.) **2.** *n.* the future. (No pl.) **3.** *adv.* during ①; at some time during ①.

ton ['tʌn] *n.* a unit of measure of weight equal to 2,000 pounds. (Also called a *short ton;* used in the United States and Canada.)

tone ['ton] **1.** *n.* a sound as it relates to its quality, intensity, or pitch. **2.** *n.* a quality of one's voice that reveals one's feelings or attitude. **3.** *n.* a style, character, or mood of an event or circumstance. **4.** *n.* firmness of the muscles. (No pl.)

tongs ['tɔŋz] *n.* a tool or utensil that has two arms joined by a hinge or spring and is used for holding or moving something. (Treated as pl. Number is expressed with *pair(s) of tongs.*)

tongue ['tʌŋ] **1.** *n.* the long, typically pink, movable organ in the mouth, used for tasting, managing food, and, in humans, speaking.

2. *n.* the ① of an animal, eaten as food. (No pl.) **3.** *n.* a language. **4.** *n.* the flap of material that is part of a shoe and fits under the laces. **5.** *n.* a flame; a pointed section of fire.

tongue-in-cheek insincere; joking.

tonic ['tɑn ɪk] **1.** *n.* a remedy; something that is good for one's health; something that provides strength. **2.** *n.* a kind of flavored soda water that is somewhat bitter.

tonight [tə 'naɪt] **1.** *n.* this evening; this night. **2.** *adv.* during ①; at some time during ①.

tonsil ['tɑn səl] *n.* one of two small organs in the very back of the mouth at the side of the throat.

too ['tu] **1.** *adv.* as well; also; in addition. **2.** *adv.* more than enough; more than is desired; beyond what is desired. **3.** *adv.* very; extremely. **4.** *adv.* a form used after BE, WILL, DO, HAVE, CAN, SHOULD, WOULD, and COULD to strengthen them in response to a negative statement.

took ['tʊk] pt of TAKE.

tool ['tul] **1.** *n.* anything that helps someone work; an instrument that is used to help someone do work. **2.** *n.* someone who is used by someone else, especially in an unfair way. (Fig. on ①.)

toolshed ['tul ʃed] *n.* a small building where gardening tools are stored.

toot ['tut] **1.** *n.* a short blast of a horn or a whistle. **2.** *tv.* to cause a horn or whistle to make a short noise.

tooth ['tuθ] **1.** *n., irreg.* one of the hard, usually white, bony objects in the mouth, used for biting and chewing while eating. (Pl: TEETH.) **2.** *n., irreg.* something shaped like ①, especially a small pointed object on a wheel that is part of a machine, the "fingers" of a rake, or the points along the length of a comb or saw.

toothache ['tuθ ek] *n.* a pain in or around a tooth.

toothbrush ['tuθ brəʃ] *n.* a small brush that is used for cleaning the teeth.

toothpaste ['tuθ pest] *n.* a paste that is placed on a toothbrush and is used for cleaning the teeth. (Pl only for types and instances.)

toothpick ['tuθ pɪk] *n.* a small, thin piece of wood that is used to remove pieces of food from between one's teeth.

top ['tɑp] **1.** *n.* the highest part of something; the upper part of something; the peak of something; the upper surface of something. **2.** *n.* the highest position; the highest rank; the most successful position;

the most important position. **3.** *n.* a cover; a cap; a lid. **4.** *n.* a piece of clothing worn above the waist, especially on women. **5.** *adj.* on or at the highest part of something. **6.** *adj.* first; best; most important. **7.** *adj.* greatest; strongest; at the highest intensity. **8.** *tv.* to place something on the highest part of something; to place something on something else.

topic ['tɑp ɪk] *n.* the subject of something that is being written or talked about.

topple ['tɑp əl] **1.** *iv.* to fall over; to fall down; to collapse. **2.** *tv.* to knock something over; to knock something down; to cause something to collapse.

torch ['tortʃ] **1.** *n.* a large stick or club whose upper end is on fire. **2.** *n.* a machine that makes a very hot flame, used to cut or join together pieces of metal by melting them. **3.** *tv.* to set something on fire; to destroy something with fire.

tore ['tor] a pt of TEAR.

torment 1. ['tor ment] *n.* a severe emotional or physical pain; agony. (Pl only for types and instances.) **2.** [tor 'ment] *tv.* to cause someone severe pain or agony; to cause someone to suffer.

torn ['torn] **1.** a pp of TEAR. **2.** *adj.* having a tear; ripped.

tornado [tor 'ne do] *n.* a violent wind that spins in circles very fast and can cause a great amount of damage. (Pl ends in -s or -es.)

torpedo [tor 'pi do] **1.** *n.* an explosive device that is fired underwater from a submarine or ship toward another submarine or ship. (Pl ends in -es.) **2.** *tv.* to attack something with ①; to explode something by firing ① at it.

torrent ['tor ənt] **1.** *n.* a swift, dangerous current of water. **2.** *n.* a heavy rainstorm. **3.** *n.* a violent flowing of a fluid other than water. **4.** *n.* a stream or flow of something. (Fig. on ③.)

tortoise ['tor təs] *n.* a turtle, especially one that lives only on land.

torture ['tor tʃɚ] **1.** *n.* the inflicting of pain in a cruel way. (No pl.) **2.** *tv.* to cause someone to suffer pain in a cruel way.

toss ['tɔs] **1.** *tv.* to throw something lightly or gently; to throw something carelessly. **2.** *tv.* to lift and throw something upward; to cause something to move as if it had been thrown. **3.** *tv.* to flip a coin into the air in order to decide a choice based on which side of the coin appears when it falls; to roll dice. **4.** *iv.* to turn; to move restlessly. **5.** *iv.* to be thrown, especially by water; to be moved with force. **6.** *n.* an instance of throwing something.

total ['tot əl] **1.** *n.* the whole amount; the sum; the number obtained by adding other numbers together. **2.** *adj.* whole; complete; entire. (Adv: *totally*.) **3.** *tv.* to calculate ①. **4.** *tv.* to come to a certain amount; to reach a certain amount.

totally ['tot ə li] *adv.* completely; entirely.

tote ['tot] *tv.* to carry something.

touch ['tʌtʃ] **1.** *tv.* to place one's finger, hand, or some other body part on someone or something. **2.** *tv.* to place one object against another; to place one object on another. **3.** *tv.* to border something; to share a border with something. **4.** *tv.* to make contact with something; to have no space between two or more objects. (No actual movement is involved.) **5.** *tv.* to handle something; to use something. (Especially in negative constructions.) **6.** *iv.* [for people or things] to make contact or be in contact. **7.** *tv.* to affect someone, especially in a sad way. **8.** *n.* an instance of placing one's finger or hand on someone or something. **9.** *n.* someone's handling or gentle pressure as sensed by the person being TOUCHED as in ①. (No pl.) **10.** *n.* a detail that improves something or adds to something. **11.** *n.* a small amount of something; a little bit of something. **12.** *n.* a special or unique skill or style; evidence of one's skill or style.

touchy ['tʌtʃ i] *adj.* easily angered; easily upset; irritable; too sensitive. (Adv: *touchily*. Comp: *touchier*; sup: *touchiest*.)

tough ['tʌf] **1.** *adj.* not tender; difficult to chew. (Comp: *tougher*; sup: *toughest*.) **2.** *adj.* hard to do; difficult; not easy. (Comp: *tougher*; sup: *toughest*.) **3.** *adj.* strong and determined; not weak. (Adv: *toughly*. Comp: *tougher*; sup: *toughest*.) **4.** *adj.* stubborn; not likely to have a change of mind. (Adv: *toughly*. Comp: *tougher*; sup: *toughest*.) **5.** *adj.* rough; violent; dangerous. (Adv: *toughly*. Comp: *tougher*; sup: *toughest*.) **6.** *adj.* unfortunate; unlucky. (Informal. Comp: *tougher*; sup: *toughest*.) **7.** *n.* a criminal; someone who is violent or dangerous.

tour ['tʊ ɚ] **1.** *n.* a trip in which several places of interest are visited; a trip in which one visits an interesting place. **2.** *tv.* to travel through a place; to move through a place for entertainment. **3.** *tv.* [for a performance and its performers] to visit or travel to many places in order to be seen. **4.** *iv.* to travel around from place to place in order to be seen.

tourism ['tʊɚ ɪz əm] **1.** *n.* travel; visiting interesting places, especially for a vacation. (No pl.) **2.** *n.* the business of attracting and serving tourists. (No pl.)

tourist ['tʊɚ ɪst] **1.** *n.* someone who travels for pleasure. **2.** the *adj.* use of ①.

tournament ['tʊɚ nə mənt] *n.* a contest involving several people or teams who play several games in such a way that the winner of one game plays the winner of another game until there is only one champion remaining.

tow ['to] **1.** *tv.* to pull something with a rope or chain. **2.** *n.* an instance of pulling something with a rope or chain.

toward(s) ['tord(z)] **1.** *prep.* [facing] in a certain direction; facing someone. **2.** *prep.* about or in relation to someone or something. **3.** *prep.* just before a certain time. **4.** *prep.* as a payment to someone or something.

towel ['taʊ əl] *n.* a piece of cloth or paper that is used to take away moisture from a surface.

tower ['taʊ ɚ] *n.* a tall building or structure; a tall part of a building or structure.

town ['taʊn] **1.** *n.* an area where people live that is smaller than a city but larger than a village. **2.** *n.* the part of a city where businesses, stores, and markets are found. (No pl.) **3.** *n.* a city. **4.** *n.* all the people who live in ①. **5.** the *adj.* use of ①, ②, or ③.

toy ['tɔɪ] **1.** *n.* something that is made to amuse a child. **2.** *adj.* made to be played with.

trace ['tres] **1.** *n.* a very small amount of something. **2.** *tv.* to draw or copy the outline of something by putting a thin piece of paper on top of it and then drawing over the lines one sees through the thin paper. **3.** *tv.* to follow the path of something's growth, development, or history. **4.** *tv.* to seek the origin of something.

track ['træk] **1.** *n.* the marks made by a vehicle, person, or animal traveling from place to place. **2.** *n.* a pair of parallel metal rails that trains travel on. **3.** *n.* a trail; a path; a rough road. **4.** *n.* a circular pathway used for running or racing. **5.** *n.* a group of sports activities including running, jumping, and other tests of individual endurance and strength. (No pl.) **6.** *tv.* to follow the trail of a person or other creature.

traction ['træk ʃən] *n.* the grip of a wheel or shoe on a surface that allows the wheel or shoe to apply energy to the surface in order to move ahead. (No pl.)

tractor ['træk tɚ] *n.* a motor vehicle with large, thick tires, used for pulling farm equipment in fields.

532

trade ['tred] **1.** *n.* the business of buying and selling products. (No pl.) **2.** *n.* a particular business. **3.** *n.* a job that utilizes a skill. **4.** *n.* the exchange of someone or something for someone or something else. **5.** *tv.* to exchange someone or something for someone or something else. **6.** *iv.* to exchange; to swap. **7.** ~ **in** to return something (such as a car, to a place where that item is sold) as partial payment on a new item.

trademark ['tred mɑrk] **1.** *n.* a word, name, or symbol—used and owned by a manufacturer—that identifies a product. **2.** *n.* a mark or feature that is associated with a certain person or thing. (Fig. on ①.) **3.** *tv.* [for a manufacturer] to protect ① by registering it with the government.

trader ['tred ɚ] *n.* a merchant; someone who buys and sells things as a business.

tradition [trə 'dɪ ʃən] *n.* the way that something has been done from generation to generation. (Pl only for types and instances.)

traditional [trə 'dɪʃ ə nəl] *adj.* relating to tradition. (Adv: *traditionally*.)

traffic ['træf ɪk] **1.** *n.* vehicles and their movement—or slowness of movement—on land, on water, or in the air. (No pl.) **2.** *n.* the process of buying and selling. (No pl.)

tragedy ['træ dʒə di] **1.** *n.* a serious play that has a sad ending. **2.** *n.* a disaster; a sad, unfortunate, or terrible event.

tragic ['træ dʒɪk] **1.** *adj.* of or about serious plays with sad endings. (Adv: *tragically* [...ɪk li].) **2.** *adj.* sad; terrible; unfortunate. (Adv: *tragically* [...ɪk li].)

trail ['trel] **1.** *n.* the marks made by a vehicle, person, or animal as it travels from place to place; the scent left by a person or animal as it travels from place to place. (See also TRACK.) **2.** *n.* a path through an area that a car cannot travel over; a path for walking, biking, etc. **3.** *tv.* to follow someone or an animal by its scent, footprints, or other clues that the person or animal leaves behind. **4.** *tv.* to leave something dirty on a surface by walking or dragging something across it.

trailer ['tre lɚ] **1.** *n.* a vehicle that is pulled by another vehicle. **2.** *n.* a small, prefabricated house on wheels that is towed to a place and set on the ground; a mobile home. **3.** *n.* an advertisement for a movie.

train ['tren] **1.** *n.* a line of railroad cars pulled by an engine. **2.** *tv.* to teach someone a skill; to give someone the knowledge needed to do a job. **3.** *iv.* to prepare [oneself] for a job, contest, or a performance.

traitor ['tret ɚ] *n.* one who betrays one's country or leader.

tramp ['træmp] **1.** *n.* someone who lives by begging; a male who lives on the streets and does not have a home. **2.** *n.* the sound of someone marching. (No pl.) **3.** *iv.* to walk heavily and steadily.

transaction [træn 'zæk ʃən] *n.* a business deal; an agreement or negotiation that has been completed.

transfer ['træns fɚ] **1.** *n.* the movement of something from one place to another place. (No pl.) **2.** *n.* a ticket that allows someone to get off one vehicle, usually a bus, and get on another one without paying a second fare. **3.** *iv.* to move from one vehicle to another; to get off one vehicle and get on another one. **4.** *iv.* to move from one site to another site. **5.** *tv.* to move something from one place to another place. **6.** *tv.* to cause someone to move from one job site to another job site.

transform [træns 'form] *tv.* to change something's or someone's shape, form, nature, or appearance.

transfusion [træns 'fju ʒən] *n.* the process of transferring blood from one person to another.

transistor [træn 'zɪs tɚ] *n.* a small electrical device that controls the flow of current in electronic circuits.

transit ['træn zɪt] *n.* transportation; movement of people or goods. (No pl.)

translate ['træn slet] **1.** *tv.* to change something written or spoken from one language to another. **2.** *iv.* to change [something written or spoken in one language] to another language.

translation [trænz 'le ʃən] *n.* changing a message in one language into an equivalent message in another language; changing a sequence of symbols in one code into another code. (Pl only for types and instances.)

translator ['trænz le tɚ] *n.* someone who translates sentences of one language into another.

transmit [trænz 'mɪt] *tv.* to send information by way of electricity or radio waves.

transmitter ['trænz mɪt ɚ] *n.* a piece of electronic equipment that transmits electromagnetic waves, as for radio or television.

transparent [trænz 'per ənt] **1.** *adj.* clear and able to be seen through. (Adv: *transparently.*) **2.** *adj.* obvious; easily recognized; [of something meant to deceive] easy to figure out. (Fig. on ①. Adv: *transparently.*)

transport ['trænz port] **1.** *n.* carrying people or things from one place to another. (No pl.) **2.** *tv.* to carry someone or something from one place to another.

transportation [trænz pɚ 'te ʃən] **1.** *n.* the system of moving people and goods from one place to another. (No pl.) **2.** *n.* moving people or goods from one place to another. (No pl.)

trap ['træp] **1.** *n.* a device used to catch animals or people. **2.** *n.* a bend in a drainpipe in which water rests in order to prevent harmful gases from the sewer from going into a building. **3.** *tv.* to catch someone or something in ①. **4.** *tv.* to prevent someone or something from escaping, leaving, or getting out.

trapper ['træp ɚ] *n.* someone who traps animals, skins them, and sells the fur.

trash ['træʃ] **1.** *n.* things that are thrown away; rubbish; refuse. (No pl.) **2.** *tv.* to throw something away. (Slang.)

trauma ['trɔ mə] **1.** *n.* an emotional shock; an emotional response to a shock. **2.** *n.* an injury; a wound; damage to the body.

travel ['træv əl] **1.** *iv.* to visit [places other than where one lives]; to journey. **2.** *iv.* to move through space; to move across a distance. **3.** *tv.* to move on a path or route as one makes a journey. **4.** *tv.* to move over a specific distance as one makes a journey. **5.** *n.* going to and visiting places other than where one lives. (No pl.) **6.** the *adj.* use of ⑤.

traveler ['træv lɚ] *n.* someone who travels; someone who goes on trips or journeys.

tray ['tre] *n.* a flat panel with a slightly raised rim, used to carry things, especially food.

treacherous ['tretʃ ə rəs] **1.** *adj.* dangerous; unstable. (Adv: *treacherously.*) **2.** *adj.* not loyal; not trustworthy; not faithful. (Adv: *treacherously.*)

treason ['tri zən] *n.* the betrayal of one's country; the betrayal of the leader of one's country. (No pl form in this sense.)

treasure ['trɛ ʒɚ] **1.** *n.* valuable objects, especially ones that are stored; someone or something that is highly valued. **2.** *tv.* to value someone or something highly.

treasurer ['trɛ ʒɚ ɚ] *n.* someone who is in charge of the money of an organization or unit of government.

treasury ['trɛ ʒə ri] **1.** *n.* the money that is owned by an organization or unit of government. **2.** *n.* the department of a government in charge of spending and saving public money.

treat ['trit] **1.** *n.* a bit of tasty food, such as candy or ice cream. **2.** *n.* something that is pleasing. **3.** *tv.* to handle or consider someone or something in a certain way. **4.** *tv.* to try to cure something.

treatment ['trit mənt] **1.** *n.* the way someone or something is dealt with. (No pl.) **2.** *n.* the method by which someone tries to cure someone. **3.** *n.* the way in which a story or script is presented.

treaty ['trit i] *n.* a formal agreement between two or more nations.

tree ['tri] **1.** *n.* a tall plant whose stem and branches are made of wood, and that often has leaves growing from the branches. **2.** *n.* a diagram that represents the relationship between different levels or positions of power by expressing them as branches at different levels.

treetop ['tri tɑp] *n.* the top of a tree.

trek ['trɛk] **1.** *n.* a long journey, often done walking. **2.** *iv.* to travel on a long journey, often on foot.

tremble ['trɛm bəl] **1.** *iv.* to shake, especially because of fear, excitement, sickness, or cold. **2.** *n.* a shaking movement.

tremendous [trɪ 'mɛn dəs] **1.** *adj.* huge; enormous; very large; immense. (Adv: *tremendously.*) **2.** *adj.* wonderful; excellent; superb. (Adv: *tremendously.*)

tremor ['trɛm ɚ] *n.* a shaking movement, especially one caused by an earthquake, fear, or disease.

trespass ['trɛs pæs] **1.** ~ **on** to go on someone's property without permission. **2.** ~ **against** to sin against someone or something; to do something against someone or something. **3.** *n.* going on someone's property without permission. (No pl form in this sense.) **4.** ~s *n.* sins; transgressions.

trestle ['trɛs əl] *n.* a braced structure that supports a road or railroad across a gap.

trial ['trɑɪl] **1.** *n.* the examination of evidence in a court of law by a judge or jury to settle a legal question, such as guilt or innocence. **2.** *n.* an experiment; a test to see if something works; a test to see if something provides a benefit. **3.** *n.* a difficult ordeal; a problem; a disease and the problems it causes. **4.** *adj.* concerning the first test or an early attempt to get results. **5.** the *adj.* use of ①, ②, or ③.

triangle ['trɑɪ æŋ gəl] **1.** *n.* a figure that has three sides and three angles. **2.** *n.* a flat, three-sided object with three sides, used for drawing lines and angles. **3.** *n.* a metallic musical instrument in the shape of ①, that is struck with a small rod to make a ringing noise.

536

tribe ['traɪb] *n.* a group of people having the same customs, religion, language, and culture; a local division of a larger ethnic group.

tribute ['trɪb jut] *n.* a show of respect or honor.

trick ['trɪk] **1.** *n.* something that is done to deceive someone. **2.** *adj.* made to be used in ①; intended to deceive.

tricky ['trɪk i] **1.** *adj.* difficult to do; puzzling; hard to deal with. (Adv: *trickily*. Comp: *trickier*; sup: *trickiest*.) **2.** *adj.* full of tricks; clever and good at deceiving people. (Adv: *trickily*. Comp: *trickier*; sup: *trickiest*.)

tricycle ['traɪ sɪk əl] *n.* a small vehicle with three wheels, two in back and one in front, made for young children to ride on.

trifle ['traɪ fəl] **1.** *n.* a small amount of something; a small amount of money. **2.** *n.* something that is very inexpensive; something that is not valuable. **3.** ~ **with** to toy with someone; to tease, annoy, or fiddle with someone.

trigger ['trɪg ɚ] **1.** *n.* the small lever on a gun, used to fire the gun. **2.** *n.* something that causes something else to happen. (Fig. on ①.) **3.** *tv.* to cause something to happen; to cause something that starts a sequence of events.

trillion ['trɪl jən] **1.** *n.* the number 1,000,000,000,000. (Additional numbers formed as with *two trillion, three trillion, four trillion*, etc.) **2.** *n.* a group of 1,000,000,000,000 people or things. **3.** *adj.* consisting of 1,000,000,000,000 things.

trillionth ['trɪl jənθ] 1,000,000,000,000th. Go to FOURTH.

trilogy ['trɪl ə dʒi] *n.* a set of three books, plays, movies, etc., that share a common theme or characters and events.

trim ['trɪm] **1.** *tv.* to make something neat by cutting; to cut something neatly. **2.** *tv.* to reduce something; to decrease something. **3.** *tv.* to decorate something. **4.** *adj.* [of someone] thin and of the proper weight. (Adv: *trimly*. Comp: *trimmer*; sup: *trimmest*.) **5.** *n.* the wood around a door or window or along the floor.

trio ['tri o] **1.** *n.* a group of three, especially a group of three performers. (Pl ends in *-s*.) **2.** *n.* a piece of music written for three instruments or three voices. (Pl ends in *-s*.)

trip ['trɪp] **1.** *n.* a journey between two places; a journey from one place to another. **2.** *iv.* to stumble; to fall over something; to hit one's foot against someone or something, causing a loss of balance. **3.** *tv.* to cause someone to fall; to cause someone to stumble and lose balance.

4. *tv.* to release a lever or a switch, thus causing something to function.

tripod ['traɪ pɑd] *n.* a support or stand that has three legs, especially one that supports a camera.

trite ['traɪt] *adj.* [of an expression] shallow and simpleminded. (Adv: *tritely.* Comp: *triter;* sup: *tritest.*)

triumph ['traɪ əmf] **1.** *n.* celebration; the glory of victory; a victory. (Pl only for types and instances.) **2.** *iv.* to win; to be very successful.

trivial ['trɪv i əl] *adj.* not important; not significant. (Adv: *trivially.*)

trolley ['trɑ li] *n.* a vehicle that is operated by electricity and runs along a track in the street.

trombone [trɑm 'bon] *n.* a brass musical instrument, played by blowing air into one end with tensed lips, while moving a long sliding part into different positions.

troop ['trup] **1.** *n.* a group of people or animals, especially a group of soldiers. **2.** *iv.* to walk or move as a group.

trooper ['trup ɚ] *n.* an officer in the state police, usually the highway patrol. (Short for *state trooper.*)

troops *n.* soldiers. (Treated as pl, but not countable.)

trophy ['tro fi] **1.** *n.* something that is taken from a battle or a hunt as a symbol of one's success. **2.** *n.* a small statue or prize that is given to the winner of an event or contest.

tropic ['trɑp ɪk] **1.** *n.* one of two imaginary circles around the earth, 23.45 degrees north and south of the equator. **2.** *adj.* TROPICAL; hot and humid.

tropical ['trɑp ɪ kəl] *adj.* of or about the tropics; of or about the weather conditions of the tropics; found in the tropics. (Adv: *tropically* [...ɪk li].)

trot ['trɑt] **1.** *n.* the movement of a horse between a walk and a gallop; the movement of a human between a walk and a run. **2.** *iv.* to move faster than walking, but not as fast as running.

trouble ['trʌb əl] **1.** *n.* worry; difficulty; anxiety. **2.** *n.* annoyance; bother. **3.** *n.* a sickness; a health problem. **4.** *n.* someone or something that causes worry, difficulty, anxiety, irritation, bother, or problems. **5.** *tv.* to worry someone; to cause someone difficulty or anxiety. **6.** *tv.* to bother or delay someone with an inquiry. **7.** *tv.* to cause someone to feel pain.

troublesome ['trʌb əl səm] *adj.* causing trouble; causing problems. (Adv: *troublesomely.*)

trousers ['trɑʊ zɚz] *n.* pants; a piece of clothing worn below the waist, having a separate tube, hole, or compartment for each leg and extending to the ankles. (Treated as pl. Number is expressed with *pair(s) of trousers.* Rarely sg.)

trout ['trɑʊt] **1.** *n., irreg.* a freshwater fish commonly eaten as food. (Pl: *trout.*) **2.** *n.* the flesh of ①, eaten as food. (No pl.)

trowel ['trɑʊ əl] **1.** *n.* a tool used to apply and smooth mortar or plaster. **2.** *n.* a tool used in gardening for digging small holes and planting individual plants.

truant ['tru ənt] **1.** *adj.* absent from school without permission. (Adv: *truantly.*) **2.** *n.* someone who is absent from school without permission.

truce ['trus] *n.* an agreement to stop fighting.

truck ['trʌk] **1.** *n.* a large motor vehicle designed to carry objects or cargo rather than people. **2.** the *adj.* use of ①. **3.** *tv.* to transport something by ①.

trudge ['trʌdʒ] *iv.* to walk slowly and heavily, as though one were very tired; to plod.

true ['tru] **1.** *adj.* being a fact; actual; real; not false. (Adv: *truly.* Comp: *truer*; sup: *truest.*) **2.** *adj.* sincere; genuine; not fake; not artificial. (Adv: *truly.* Comp: *truer*; sup: *truest.*) **3.** *adj.* properly fitted; at the proper angle. (Adv: *truly.* Comp: *truer*; sup: *truest.*)

truly ['tru li] *adv.* really; honestly; genuinely.

trumpet ['trʌmp ɪt] **1.** *n.* a brass musical instrument on which different notes are produced by blowing air into one end while pressing different combinations of three valves. **2.** *iv.* [for an elephant] to make a characteristic elephant noise.

trunk ['trʌŋk] **1.** *n.* the main stem of a tree. **2.** *n.* the body of a human without its head, arms, or legs. **3.** *n.* a large, sturdy box for transporting or storing clothes or other objects. **4.** *n.* the long, tube-shaped nose of an elephant.

trunks *n.* a swimming suit for men. (Treated as pl. Number is expressed with *pair(s) of trunks.*)

trust ['trʌst] **1.** *n.* a strong belief in the honesty of someone or something. (No pl.) **2.** *tv.* to believe in the honesty of someone or something. **3.** *tv.* to hope something. (The object is a clause with THAT ⑦.)

539

trustworthy ['trʌst wɚ ði] *adj.* deserving to be trusted; reliable. (Adv: *trustworthily.*)

truth ['truθ] **1.** *n.* the quality of being true or a fact. (No pl.) **2.** *n.* a fact; a true state.

truthful ['truθ fʊl] **1.** *adj.* [of a statement] able to be proven as true. (Adv: *truthfully.*) **2.** *adj.* regularly telling the truth; honest. (Adv: *truthfully.*)

try ['traɪ] **1.** *iv.* to make an attempt. **2.** *tv.* to use something to see if one likes it; to test something to see if it works well. **3.** *tv.* [for a judge or jury] to hear a [legal] case in a court of law. (E.g., *try a case.*) **4.** *tv.* [for a judge or jury] to subject an accused person to a trial in a court of law. (E.g., *try someone for a crime.*) **5.** *n.* an attempt; an effort to do something.

trying ['traɪ ɪŋ] *adj.* burdensome; straining someone's patience; annoying; upsetting. (Adv: *tryingly.*)

tsar Go to CZAR.

T-shirt ['ti ʃɚt] *n.* a light, cotton shirt with short sleeves and no collar.

tub ['tʌb] **1.** *n.* a large, round or oval container with a flat bottom. **2.** *n.* a BATHTUB.

tuba ['tub ə] *n.* a large brass instrument that makes very low notes. (TUBAS are also sometimes made of lighter-weight material.)

tube ['tub] **1.** *n.* a hollow pipe used for holding or conveying something. **2.** *n.* a soft container that holds paste, such as toothpaste, icing, or medicine.

tuck ['tʌk] *n.* a fold that is sewn shut to make an item of clothing shorter or fit tighter.

Tuesday ['tjuz de] Go to DAY.

tug ['tʌg] *n.* a hard pull; a yank.

tulip ['tu ləp] *n.* a flower with a bright, colorful, cup-shaped bloom.

tumble ['tʌm bəl] **1.** *n.* a fall. **2.** *iv.* to fall over; to fall accidentally; to fall helplessly.

tummy ['tʌm i] *n.* the stomach or belly. (Informal; used especially with children.)

tumor ['tu mɚ] *n.* a group or cluster of diseased cells in a body that grow independently of the surrounding tissue or structure.

tuna ['tu nə (fɪʃ)] **1.** *n., irreg.* a large ocean fish, commonly used for food. (Pl: *tuna* or *tunas.*) **2.** ~ **(fish)** *n.* the flesh of ①, eaten as food.

540

(No pl form in this sense.) **3.** ~ **(-fish)** *adj.* made with or flavored with ②.

tune ['tun] **1.** *n.* a melody; a piece of music or a song. **2.** *tv.* to adjust a musical instrument so that its tones are at the proper intervals from each other. **3.** *tv.* to adjust something so that it works properly.

tunnel ['tʌn əl] **1.** *n.* a passage that is underground, underwater, or through a mountain. **2.** *iv.* to make a passage that goes underground, underwater, or through a mountain.

turbine ['tɚ bɪn] *n.* a large engine or motor that is powered by pressure from wind, water, or some other liquid or gas.

turd ['tɚd] *n.* a lump of fecal material. (Potentially offensive. Use only with care. Colloquial.)

turf ['tɚf] **1.** *n.* the surface of soil with plants or grass growing on it. (No pl.) **2.** *n.* the area that is controlled by a person or group of people. (Usually sg.)

turkey ['tɚ ki] **1.** *n.* a large fowl that is often raised for its meat. **2.** *n.* the meat of ① used as food. (No pl.) **3.** *adj.* made with ②.

turn ['tɚn] **1.** *tv.* to move something around in a circle or an arc; to cause something to move in a circle or an arc. **2.** *tv.* to aim a moving object or vehicle in a different direction. **3.** *tv.* to change the position of something, such as an electrical switch, lever, or handle. **4.** *tv.* to reach a certain age. **5.** *iv.* to go in a different direction; to change direction. **6.** *iv.* to change position by moving in a circle or an arc; to change position to face a different direction. **7.** *iv.* to change, especially in form, state, color, or quality; to become some form, state, color, or quality. **8.** *n.* the movement of something that is going in a circle. **9.** *n.* a change in direction. **10.** *n.* a change in a situation; a change in circumstances. **11.** *n.* a chance to do something, especially when two or more people alternate an action. **12.** ~ **back** to stop one's journey and return. **13.** ~ **into** to change to a particular condition or state; to become something. **14.** ~ **up** [for someone or something] to appear in a place.

turtle ['tɚt əl] *n.* a reptile with a round body that is protected by a thick, hard, rounded shell.

tusk ['tʌsk] *n.* a very long, pointed tooth that projects from the face of some kinds of animals.

tutor ['tut ɚ] **1.** *n.* someone who is employed as a private teacher; a teacher who gives private lessons. **2.** *tv.* to teach someone privately. **3.** *iv.* to work as ①.

tuxedo [tək 'si do] *n.* a man's outfit for very formal occasions, including a black jacket, a white shirt, a black bow tie, and pants. (Pl ends in -*s*.)

tv. an abbreviation of *transitive verb.*

TV ['ti 'vi] an abbreviation of TELEVISION or *television set.*

tweed ['twid] **1.** *n.* a rough wool fabric. **2.** *adj.* made of ①.

twelfth ['twɛlfθ] 12th. Go to FOURTH.

twelve ['twɛlv] 12. Go to FOUR.

twentieth ['twɛn ti əθ] 20th. Go to FOURTH.

twenty ['twɛn ti] 20. Go to FORTY.

twice ['twaɪs] **1.** *adv.* two times; on two occasions. **2.** *adv.* two times as much; double.

twig ['twɪg] *n.* a small branch.

twilight ['twaɪ laɪt] **1.** *n.* the time of day after the sun sets and before the sky is completely dark. (No pl.) **2.** *n.* the dim light at ①.

twin ['twɪn] **1.** *n.* one of two children born at the same time from the same mother; one of two offspring born at the same time from the same mother. **2.** *n.* one of two things that are part of a matched set. **3.** *adj.* [of two offspring] born at the same time from the same mother. **4.** *adj.* forming a pair of two things that are similar or matching.

twine ['twaɪn] *n.* strong string made of two or more strands that are twisted together. (Pl only for types and instances.)

twinkle ['twɪŋ kəl] **1.** *iv.* to alternate between shining brightly and not so brightly; to flicker; to sparkle. **2.** *n.* a light that alternates between shining brightly and dimly; a flicker.

twirl ['twəl] **1.** *tv.* to spin something; to move something in circles. **2.** *iv.* to spin; to turn in circles. **3.** *n.* a spin; a circular movement.

twist ['twɪst] **1.** *tv.* to turn something; to rotate something in an arc. **2.** *tv.* to injure a body part by turning it sharply. **3.** *tv.* to bend and turn part of something to change its shape. **4.** *iv.* to curve; to bend; to change shape or direction; to turn one part of a length of something while keeping the other part in place. **5.** *n.* a curve; a state resulting when one part of a length has been turned while the other part stays in one space. **6.** *n.* the movement of TWISTING as in ①.

two ['tu] 2. Go to FOUR.

type ['taɪp] **1.** *n.* a kind, sort, or category; a group of related people or things. **2.** *n.* a block of wood or metal, with the raised shape of a letter or number on it, used in printing. (No pl.) **3.** *n.* a style or kind of print, especially the shape or darkness that printed letters have. (No pl.) **4.** *tv.* to write something using a keyboard. **5.** *iv.* to use a keyboard.

typewriter ['taɪp raɪ tɚ] *n.* a machine for printing letters onto paper.

typical ['tɪp ɪ kəl] *adj.* average; usual; ordinary; regular; having the main qualities of a type of something. (Adv: *typically* [...ɪk li].)

typo ['taɪp o] *n.* an error made in printing or typing. (Pl ends in *-s*. Short for *typographical error*.)

tyranny ['tɪr ə ni] *n.* the cruel and unfair use of government power. (No pl.)

tyrant ['taɪ rənt] *n.* a ruler who is cruel and unfair.

U

ugly [ˈʌg li] **1.** *adj.* not pleasant to look at; not attractive. (Comp: *uglier;* sup: *ugliest.*) **2.** *adj.* not pleasant; menacing. (Comp: *uglier;* sup: *ugliest.*)

ulcer [ˈʌl sɚ] *n.* a sore on a part of the body that may bleed and become infected.

ultimate [ˈʌl tə mət] *adj.* final. (Adv: *ultimately.*)

ultimately [ˈʌl tə mət li] *adv.* in the end; at the final decision about an issue.

umbrella [əm ˈbrɛl ə] *n.* a dome-shaped wire frame connected to a handle and covered with waterproof fabric, used as protection against the rain.

umpire [ˈʌm pɑɪɚ] **1.** *n.* a referee; someone who enforces the rules of certain sports; someone who judges the plays in certain sports. **2.** *iv.* to act as ①. **3.** *tv.* to referee a game; to judge the plays in certain sports.

unaccustomed [ən ə ˈkəs təmd] *adj.* not used to someone or something.

unafraid [ən ə ˈfred] *adj.* not afraid; brave; without fear.

unanimous [ju ˈnæn ə məs] *adj.* in complete agreement; agreed to by everyone; with everyone saying "yes." (Adv: *unanimously.*)

unarmed [ən ˈɑrmd] *adj.* not armed; not carrying any weapons; without any weapons.

unassisted [ən ə ˈsɪs tɪd] *adj.* without assistance; without help.

unattractive [ən ə ˈtræk tɪv] *adj.* not attractive; plain; not pretty. (Adv: *unattractively.*)

unaware [ən ə ˈwɛr] *adj.* not aware; not conscious of someone or something; not knowing of someone or something.

unbelievable [ən bə ˈliv ə bəl] *adj.* extreme and not able to be believed. (Adv: *unbelievably.*)

unbiased [ən ˈbɑɪ əst] *adj.* not biased; fair; not favoring one side over another. (Adv: *unbiasedly.*)

unbreakable [ən ˈbrek ə bəl] *adj.* not able to be broken. (Adv: *unbreakably.*)

544

uncertain [ən 'sɚt n] **1.** *adj.* [of a decision] able to change or be changed; not sure. (Adv: *uncertainly*.) **2.** *adj.* not known for sure; not yet decided. **3.** *adj.* changeable; not reliable. (Adv: *uncertainly*.)

uncle ['ʌŋ kəl] *n.* the brother of one's father or mother; the husband of one's aunt. (Also a term of address. Capitalized when written as a proper noun.)

unclear [ən 'klɪr] *adj.* not clear; not understood well. (Adv: *unclearly*.)

uncomfortable [ən 'kʌmf tə bəl] **1.** *adj.* not comfortable; feeling uneasy. (Adv: *uncomfortably*.) **2.** *adj.* causing discomfort. (Adv: *uncomfortably*.)

uncommon [ən 'kɑm ən] *adj.* not common; rare; unusual. (Adv: *uncommonly*.)

unconscious [ən 'kɑn ʃəs] **1.** *adj.* not conscious; no longer conscious. (Adv: *unconsciously*.) **2.** *adj.* done without thinking. (Adv: *unconsciously*.) **3.** *n.* the part of one's mind of which one is not aware. (No pl.)

undecided [ən dɪ 'saɪd ɪd] **1.** *adj.* unsure of how one will decide; not having made a decision. (Adv: *undecidedly*.) **2.** *adj.* [of a matter that has] not yet been determined. (Adv: *undecidedly*.)

under ['ʌn dɚ] **1.** *prep.* in or at a place below or beneath someone or something; to or into a place below or beneath someone or something. **2.** *prep.* less than something. **3.** *prep.* affected by the control or influence of someone or something; ranked beneath someone or something. **4.** *adv.* below; below the surface; beneath.

underclothes ['ʌn dɚ kloʊ(ð)z] *n.* underwear; underpants and undershirts; the clothing worn next to the skin, usually under other pieces of clothing. (Treated as pl, but not countable.)

underclothing ['ʌn dɚ kloʊ ðɪŋ] *n.* underwear; underclothes. (No pl. Treated as sg.)

undergo [ən dɚ 'goʊ] *tv., irreg.* to experience something, especially something that is difficult. (Pt: UNDERWENT; pp: UNDERGONE.)

undergone [ən dɚ 'gɔn] pp of UNDERGO.

undergraduate [ən dɚ 'græ dʒu ət] **1.** *n.* a college student who has not yet received a bachelor's degree. **2.** the *adj.* use of ①.

underground ['ʌn dɚ graʊnd] **1.** *adj.* below the surface of the ground; in the earth. **2.** *adj.* secret. (Fig. on ①.) **3.** *adv.* below the surface of the ground; in the earth. **4.** *adv.* in secret. (Fig. on ③.)

underline ['ʌn dɚ laɪn] **1.** *tv.* to draw a line under a word to give the word emphasis; to emphasize a word by drawing a line under it. **2.** *n.* a line that is drawn under a word to give the word emphasis.

undermine [ən dɚ 'maɪn] *tv.* to weaken something by wearing away support; to weaken someone or something gradually.

underneath [ən dɚ 'niθ] **1.** *prep.* beneath someone or something; below someone or something; under someone or something. **2.** *adv.* under someone or something that is on top; under someone or something.

underpaid [ən dɚ 'ped] *adj.* not paid as well as one should be; not given enough money for one's work.

underpants ['ʌn dɚ pænts] *n.* an article of clothing worn next to the skin below the waist, usually under other clothing. (Treated as pl. Number is expressed with *pair(s) of underpants.* Also countable.)

undershirt ['ʌn dɚ ʃɚt] *n.* a piece of clothing worn above the waist next to the skin, usually under other clothing.

undershorts ['ʌn dɚ ʃɔrts] *n.* underpants; a piece of clothing worn below the waist next to the skin, usually under other clothing. (Treated as pl. Number is expressed with *pair(s) of undershorts.*)

underside ['ʌn dɚ saɪd] *n.* the surface of the bottom part of someone or something.

understand [ən dɚ 'stænd] **1.** *iv., irreg.* to know; to be aware of the meaning of something; to know about something; to be familiar with something. (Pt/pp: UNDERSTOOD.) **2.** *tv., irreg.* to know something; to know the meaning of something. **3.** *tv., irreg.* to assume something; to believe something. (The object is a clause with THAT ⑦.)

understanding [ən dɚ 'stænd ɪŋ] **1.** *n.* the ability to understand. (No pl.) **2.** *n.* an informal agreement. **3.** *adj.* able to understand; sympathetic.

understood [ən dɚ 'stʊd] pt/pp of UNDERSTAND.

undertake [ən dɚ 'tek] *tv., irreg.* to begin work on something; to begin an action; to start something. (Pt: UNDERTOOK; pp: UNDERTAKEN.)

undertaken [ən dɚ 'tek ən] pp of UNDERTAKE.

undertaker ['ʌn dɚ te kɚ] *n.* someone who arranges funerals.

undertook [ən dɚ 'tʊk] pt of UNDERTAKE.

underwater [ən dɚ 'wɑ tɚ] **1.** *adj.* under the surface of water. **2.** *adj.* made for use under the water. **3.** *adv.* under the surface of water.

underwear [ˈʌn dɚ wɛr] *n.* underclothing, especially underpants; clothing worn next to the skin, usually under other clothing. (No pl. When this refers to underpants, number is expressed with *pair(s) of underwear.*)

underweight [ˈʌn dɚ wet] *adj.* not weighing as much as one should; weighing too little.

underwent [ən dɚ ˈwɛnt] pt of UNDERGO.

underworld [ˈʌn dɚ wɚld] *n.* the world of crime; criminals and their society.

undid [ən ˈdɪd] pt of UNDO.

undo [ən ˈdu] **1.** *tv., irreg.* to cancel the effects of something; to cause something to be as though nothing had ever been done to it. (Pt: UNDID; pp: UNDONE.) **2.** *tv., irreg.* to untie something; to unfasten something.

undoing [ən ˈdu ɪŋ] *n.* something that causes failure or ruin. (No pl.)

undone [ən ˈdʌn] pp of UNDO.

undoubtedly [ən ˈdaʊ tɪd li] *adv.* without doubt; certainly; obviously; surely.

undress [ən ˈdrɛs] **1.** *tv.* to remove someone's clothes. **2.** *iv.* to take off one's own clothes.

undue [ən ˈdu] *adj.* not deserved. (Adv: *unduly.*)

unduly [ən ˈdu li] *adv.* in an excessive way; in an excessively negative way.

unearth [ən ˈɚθ] **1.** *tv.* to remove something from the ground; to dig something up from the earth. **2.** *tv.* to discover and reveal something; to disclose something; to expose something. (Fig. on ①.)

uneasy [ən ˈi zi] *adj.* not comfortable; upset; anxious; worried. (Adv: *uneasily.*)

uneducated [ən ˈɛdʒ ə ket ɪd] *adj.* not educated; not having attended school; not having been taught.

unemployed [ən ɛm ˈplɔɪd] *adj.* not employed; not having a job; out of work.

unemployment [ən ɛm ˈplɔɪ mənt] *n.* the lack of a job or the lack of jobs in general. (No pl form in this sense.)

unequal [ən ˈi kwəl] *adj.* not equal in size, amount, degree, importance, or worth. (Adv: *unequally.*)

547

uneven [ən 'i vən] **1.** *adj.* [of a surface] not even; not smooth; rough; bumpy. (Adv: *unevenly.*) **2.** *adj.* [of a process or flow] not constant; varying; irregular. (Adv: *unevenly.*) **3.** *adj.* not equal; unequal. (Adv: *unevenly.*)

unexpected [ən ɛk 'spɛk tɪd] *adj.* not expected; surprising; [of something that happens] not known about before it happens. (Adv: *unexpectedly.*)

unfair [ən 'fɛr] *adj.* not fair; unjust; not right; unequal. (Adv: *unfairly.*)

unfasten [ən 'fæ sən] **1.** *tv.* to open something by removing a fastener; to make something loose by adjusting a fastener. **2.** *iv.* to become loose or open.

unfold [ən 'fold] **1.** *tv.* to spread something out; to open something that is folded. **2.** *iv.* to develop; to become known; to be revealed.

unforeseen [ən for 'sin] *adj.* not anticipated; not foreseen; not known in advance.

unforgettable [ən for 'gɛt ə bəl] *adj.* unable to be forgotten; always remembered. (Adv: *unforgettably.*)

unfortunate [ən 'for tʃə nət] *adj.* not fortunate; not lucky. (Adv: *unfortunately.*)

unfriendly [ən 'frɛnd li] *adj.* not friendly; hostile. (Comp: *unfriendlier;* sup: *unfriendliest.*)

unguarded [ən 'gɑr dɪd] **1.** *adj.* not guarded; not protected; open to attack. **2.** *adj.* careless, especially in trying to keep secrets. (Adv: *unguardedly.*)

unhappy [ən 'hæp i] *adj.* not happy; sad; not pleased. (Adv: *unhappily.* Comp: *unhappier;* sup: *unhappiest.*)

unhealthy [ən 'hɛl θi] **1.** *adj.* bad for one's health. (Adv: *unhealthily.* Comp: *unhealthier;* sup: *unhealthiest.*) **2.** *adj.* sick; having bad health. (Adv: *unhealthily.* Comp: *unhealthier;* sup: *unhealthiest.*)

unicorn ['ju nə korn] *n.* a mythical creature resembling a horse with a single horn on its forehead.

uniform ['ju nə form] **1.** *n.* the clothes that are worn by all the members of a certain group. **2.** *adj.* identical; alike; not varying; having no variation. (Adv: *uniformly.*)

unify ['ju nə faɪ] **1.** *tv.* to unite something or a group; to bring many parts together to make one whole thing. **2.** *iv.* to become united; to be brought together to make one whole thing.

unimportant [ən ɪm ˈport nt] *adj.* not important; not significant. (Adv: *unimportantly.*)

uninteresting [ən ˈɪn trɛs tɪŋ] *adj.* not interesting; not causing interest; boring. (Adv: *uninterestingly.*)

union [ˈjun jən] **1.** *n.* the joining together of two or more people or things. **2.** *n.* the bond between two or more people or things that are joined together. **3.** *n.* an organization whose members work together in support of a common interest, especially an organization of workers in a particular trade. **4.** the *adj.* use of ② or ③.

unique [ju ˈnik] *adj.* unlike anything else; having no equal; being the only one of its kind. (No comp. or sup. Adv: *uniquely.*)

unison [ˈju nə sən] *adj.* making one sound; [all] sounding the same note.

unit [ˈju nɪt] **1.** *n.* a single thing or person; one part of a group of people or things. **2.** *n.* a group of things thought of as being one thing. **3.** *n.* an amount of a standard measurement.

unite [ju ˈnaɪt] **1.** *tv.* to join two or more people or things together; to bring two or more people or things together. **2.** *iv.* to join together; to come together.

united [ju ˈnaɪt ɪd] *adj.* brought together; joined together, especially because of a common purpose. (Adv: *unitedly.*)

unity [ˈju nə ti] *n.* the condition of being together; the condition of being united. (No pl.)

universal [ju nə ˈvɚ səl] **1.** *adj.* shared by every member of a group; of or about everyone; understood by everyone. (Adv: *universally.*) **2.** *n.* a concept that is ①.

universe [ˈju nə vɚs] *n.* everything that exists in space; all of space and everything that exists in it.

university [ju nə ˈvɚ sə ti] *n.* a school for higher education, usually consisting of one or more colleges for undergraduates and usually one or more schools for graduate students.

unjust [ən ˈdʒʌst] *adj.* not just; unfair; not right. (Adv: *unjustly.*)

unkind [ən ˈkaɪnd] *adj.* not kind; mean; without concern for others. (Adv: *unkindly.* Comp: *unkinder;* sup: *unkindest.*)

unknown [ən ˈnon] **1.** *adj.* not known; unfamiliar. **2.** *adj.* not famous; not recognized. **3.** *n.* someone who is not (widely) known; something that is not known.

unlawful [ən 'lɔ fʊl] *adj.* not legal; illegal; against the law. (Adv: *unlawfully.*)

unless [ən 'lɛs] *conj.* except under the circumstances that something specific happens. (Followed by a clause.)

unlike [ən 'laɪk] **1.** *adj.* not like someone or something else; not equal; not similar; different. (Prenominal only.) **2.** *prep.* not similar to someone or something; different from someone or something. **3.** *prep.* not characteristic or typical of someone or something.

unlikely [ən 'laɪk li] *adj.* not probable; not likely; likely to fail; not likely to succeed.

unlimited [ən 'lɪm ə tɪd] *adj.* not limited; without limits; not restricted. (Adv: *unlimitedly.*)

unlock [ən 'lak] *tv.* to open a lock.

unlucky [ən 'lʌk i] **1.** *adj.* not lucky; not having good luck; unfortunate. (Adv: *unluckily.* Comp: *unluckier;* sup: *unluckiest.*) **2.** *adj.* causing bad luck; causing misfortune. (Adv: *unluckily.* Comp: *unluckier;* sup: *unluckiest.*)

unmentionable [ən 'mɛn ʃə nə bəl] *adj.* not able to be mentioned; not to be mentioned, especially because it would not be polite to do so. (Adv: *unmentionably.*)

unmistakable [ən mɪ 'stɛk ə bəl] *adj.* not able to be mistaken; able to be recognized easily. (Adv: *unmistakably.*)

unnecessary [ən 'nɛs ɪ sɛr i] *adj.* not necessary; not needed; not essential; extra; beyond what is needed. (Adv: *unnecessarily.*)

unpack [ən 'pæk] **1.** *tv.* to remove objects that have been packed; to remove objects that are in a box or suitcase. **2.** *iv.* to remove objects that have been packed.

unpleasant [ən 'plɛz ənt] *adj.* not pleasant; not pleasing; not nice; not enjoyable. (Adv: *unpleasantly.*)

unpopular [ən 'pap jə lɚ] *adj.* not popular; not preferred by many people. (Adv: *unpopularly.*)

unreal [ən 'ril] *adj.* not real; incredible; unbelievable.

unrealistic [ən ri ə 'lɪs tɪk] **1.** *adj.* not realistic; not seeming real; seeming fake. (Adv: *unrealistically* […ɪk li].) **2.** *adj.* not practical. (Adv: *unrealistically* […ɪk li].)

unreasonable [ən 'ri zə nə bəl] **1.** *adj.* not reasonable; not sensible; not rational. (Adv: *unreasonably.*) **2.** *adj.* too much; excessive. (Adv: *unreasonably.*)

unrest [ən 'rɛst] *n.* a feeling of not being satisfied; a troubled or uneasy feeling. (No pl.)

unruly [ən 'ru li] **1.** *adj.* badly behaved; not obedient; not paying attention to authority. **2.** *adj.* [of hair] not orderly; [of hair] hard to control.

unsafe [ən 'sef] *adj.* not safe from danger; providing risk. (Adv: *unsafely.*)

unsatisfactory [ən sæt ɪs 'fæk tə ri] *adj.* not satisfactory; not good enough; not adequate. (Adv: *unsatisfactorily.*)

unscientific [ən saɪ ən 'tɪf ɪk] *adj.* not scientific; not using principles of science. (Adv: *unscientifically* […ɪk li].)

unscrew [ən 'skru] **1.** *tv.* to remove something, such as a screw or a lid, by turning it. **2.** *iv.* [for a screw, lid, bolt, etc.] to rotate and become loose.

unseen [ən 'sin] *adj.* not seen; hidden; out of sight.

unstable [ən 'ste bəl] **1.** *adj.* not secure; not having proper balance. (Adv: *unstably.*) **2.** *adj.* not steady; likely to change. (Adv: *unstably.*) **3.** *adj.* [of someone] mentally disturbed or troubled. (Adv: *unstably.*)

unsteady [ən 'stɛd i] **1.** *adj.* shaky; not secure. (Adv: *unsteadily.*) **2.** *adj.* not dependable; likely to change. (Adv: *unsteadily.*)

unsuccessful [ən sək 'sɛs fʊl] *adj.* not successful; without success. (Adv: *unsuccessfully.*)

unsure [ən 'ʃʊr] *adj.* not sure; uncertain. (Adv: *unsurely.*)

untidy [ən 'taɪ di] *adj.* not tidy; not clean; messy. (Adv: *untidily.* Comp: *untidier;* sup: *untidiest.*)

untie [ən 'taɪ] **1.** *tv.* to loosen something that is tied; to undo something that is tied. (The pres. part. is *untying* in both senses of the verb.) **2.** *iv.* to become undone as in ①.

until [ən 'tɪl] **1.** *prep.* up to a certain time; during a period of time up to a certain time; continuing during a period of time and then stopping at a certain time. (See also TILL.) **2.** *conj.* up to a time when something happens; up to a time when a certain condition is met. (Followed by a clause.) **3.** *conj.* before. (Used with a negative construction in the main clause.)

untimely [ən 'taɪm li] **1.** *adj.* not timely; happening too soon; happening too early. **2.** *adj.* not suitable; not appropriate; at the wrong time.

unto [ən tu] *prep.* to someone or something. (Formal or old.)

551

untold [ən 'told] **1.** *adj.* not told; not expressed; not revealed. **2.** *adj.* countless; too great to be counted.

untrue [ən 'tru] *adj.* not true; false; incorrect. (Adv: *untruly.*)

unusual [ən 'ju ʒu əl] *adj.* not usual; strange; different; not ordinary. (Adv: *unusually.*)

unwanted [ən 'wɑn tɪd] *adj.* not wanted. (Adv: *unwantedly.*)

unwelcome [ən 'wɛl kəm] *adj.* not welcome; not wanted. (Adv: *unwelcomely.*)

unwell [ən 'wɛl] *adj.* not well; sick; ill.

unwholesome [ən 'hol səm] *adj.* not good for one's morals or one's health. (Adv: *unwholesomely.*)

unwind [ən 'wɑɪnd] **1.** *tv., irreg.* to remove something that is wound around an object. (Pt/pp: UNWOUND.) **2.** *iv., irreg.* to relax. **3.** *iv., irreg.* [for something] to become loose and to pull away from an object that it is wound around.

unwise [ən 'wɑɪz] *adj.* not wise; foolish; silly. (Adv: *unwisely.*)

unwound [ən 'wɑund] pt/pp of UNWIND.

up [ʌp] **1.** *adv.* from a lower level toward a higher level. **2.** *adv.* toward the north; northward; in the north. **3.** *adv.* into a vertical or almost vertical position; in a vertical or almost vertical position. **4.** *adv.* completely; totally. (Used especially with verbs such as *eat, drink, use,* and *finish.*) **5.** *adv.* tightly; into a tight condition; firmly. (Used especially with verbs such as *roll, curl, fold,* and *wind.*) **6.** *adv.* together; into a condition in which things are together. (Used especially with verbs such as *add, total, count, link, connect,* and *gather.*) **7.** *adj.* over; finished. (Not prenominal.) **8.** *prep.* on or along something to a higher level or position.

update ['ʌp det] **1.** *n.* something that has new information, especially a news report that has more information. **2.** *tv.* to make something more modern; to make something up-to-date. **3.** *tv.* to provide the latest information; to inform someone of the latest news.

updated [əp 'det ɪd] *adj.* made modern; changed or made to be modern or current.

upheld [əp 'hɛld] pt/pp of UPHOLD.

uphold [əp 'hold] **1.** *tv., irreg.* to confirm something, especially for a court to confirm or approve a lower court's ruling. (Pt/pp: UPHELD.) **2.** *tv., irreg.* to support something; to defend something against criticism.

upkeep [ˈʌp kip] **1.** *n.* maintenance; the work required to maintain something. (No pl.) **2.** *n.* the cost of ①. (No pl.)

upon [ə ˈpɑn] **1.** *prep.* on the surface of someone or something. **2.** *prep.* at the instant of doing something; on the occasion of something happening; immediately or very soon after something has happened.

upper [ˈʌp ɚ] *adj.* the higher of two things; closer to the top of something than to the bottom.

uppercase [ˈʌp ɚ ˈkes] *adj.* [of a letter or letters] in the larger size as with *B* in *Bill*; capitalized. (Compare this with LOWERCASE.)

upright [ˈʌp rɑɪt] **1.** *adj.* standing straight up; erect; perpendicular to a flat surface. **2.** *adj.* [of someone] honest, moral, following the law. **3.** *adv.* to an UPRIGHT ① position.

uproar [ˈʌp ror] *n.* a loud, noisy, confused activity.

uproot [əp ˈrut] **1.** *tv.* to pull up a plant, including its roots. **2.** *tv.* to cause someone to move from where one lives. (Fig. on ①.)

upset 1. [əp ˈsɛt] *adj.* worried about something. **2.** [əp ˈsɛt] *adj.* [of someone's stomach] feeling bad or sick. **3.** [əp ˈsɛt] *tv., irreg.* to knock something over; to tip something over; to turn something over. (Pt/pp: *upset.*) **4.** [əp ˈsɛt] *tv., irreg.* to defeat someone or something that was expected to win. **5.** [əp ˈsɛt] *tv., irreg.* to disturb someone; to bother someone; to make someone worried. **6.** [əp ˈsɛt] *tv., irreg.* to make someone's stomach feel bad. **7.** [ˈəp sɛt] *n.* a surprise victory; the defeat of someone or something by someone or something else that was not expected to win.

upside down [əp sɑɪd ˈdɑun] *adj.* having the top part at the bottom; having the wrong end or side up. (Hyphenated before a nominal.)

upstairs 1. [ˈʌp ˈstɛrz] *adj.* located on an upper floor; located on a higher floor. **2.** [əp ˈstɛrz] *adv.* on or toward the next floor of a building; on or toward an upper floor of a building. **3.** [ˈʌp ˈstɛrz] *n.* the top floor of a building; the upper floor of a building. (Treated as sg.)

upstream [ˈʌp ˈstrim] *adv.* against the current of a river.

up-to-date [ˈʌp tə ˈdet] *adj.* current; including or based on the latest facts or information.

upward [ˈʌp wɚd] *adj.* moving UP; climbing; rising; advancing. (Adv: *upwardly.*)

upward(s) *adv.* to or toward a higher position; to or toward a higher level; to or toward the top part of something.

uranium [jə 'ren i əm] *n.* a chemical element used mainly as fuel for nuclear reactors. (No pl.)

urban ['ɚ bən] *adj.* of or about a city or cities in general; not suburban or rural.

urge ['ɚdʒ] **1.** *n.* a strong feeling, desire, or need to do something. **2.** *tv.* to force or encourage someone or something to go forward. (The object can be a clause with THAT ⑦.)

urgent ['ɚ dʒənt] *adj.* very important; [of something] needing attention before anything else. (Adv: *urgently.*)

urinate ['jʊr ə net] *iv.* to cause or allow urine to flow from the body.

urine ['jʊr ɪn] *n.* a liquid waste product removed by the kidneys and discharged from the body. (No pl.)

urn ['ɚn] **1.** *n.* a large vase or pot, often used for plants or for ashes from a dead person's remains. **2.** *n.* a large container for holding hot liquids, especially coffee.

us ['ʌs] *pron.* the objective form of WE, referring to a group of people including the speaker or writer.

U.S. Go to U.S.A.

U.S.A. AND **U.S.** ['ju 'ɛs ('e)] *n.* the United States of America.

usage ['ju sɪdʒ] *n.* the way words in a language typically occur in speech. (No pl.)

use 1. ['jus] *n.* consuming or operating something; the intended function of something; the purpose of something, especially the purpose of meeting people's needs. (Pl only for types and instances.) **2.** ['juz] *tv.* to employ someone or something for a certain purpose; to put something into service. **3.** ['juz] *tv.* to treat someone badly or to one's own advantage.

used 1. ['juzd] *adj.* already owned; not new; secondhand. **2.** ~**d to** ['jus tə] accustomed to [doing something]; [to be] comfortable with [doing something].

useful ['jus fʊl] *adj.* helpful; able to be used. (Adv: *usefully.*)

useless ['jus ləs] *adj.* not helpful; not able to be used; having no effect; having no purpose. (Adv: *uselessly.*)

usher ['ʌʃ ɚ] **1.** *n.* someone who shows people to their seats in a church, auditorium, theater, or other place where people gather. **2.** *tv.* to guide someone to a seat; to escort someone to a seat.

usual ['ju ʒu wəl] *adj.* ordinary; typical; customary; common; regular. (Adv: *usually.*)

usually ['ju ʒə li] *adv.* typically and customarily.

utensil [ju 'tɛn səl] *n.* a tool that helps someone do something, especially a tool that helps someone cook or eat.

utility [ju 'tɪl ə ti] **1.** *n.* a service providing products such as electricity, water, gas, and waste removal to homes and businesses. **2.** *n.* a company that provides a public service. **3.** *adj.* having a basic function; providing for basic service. (Prenominal only.)

utilize ['jut ə laɪz] *tv.* to use something practically; to make use of something; to employ something for a purpose.

utmost ['ʌt most] *adj.* greatest possible; maximum.

utter ['ʌt ɚ] **1.** *tv.* to say something; to express something aloud. **2.** *adj.* complete; total. (Adv: *utterly.*)

utterance ['ʌt ə rəns] *n.* speaking; uttering words. (Pl only for types and instances.)

V

vacancy ['ve kən si] **1.** *n.* a job or position that is not filled; an opening in employment; a job opening. **2.** *n.* an empty room or building that is available for rent.

vacant ['ve kənt] **1.** *adj.* not occupied; not being used; empty; not filled. **2.** *adj.* [of a look on someone's face] blank, showing no thought or intelligence. (Fig. on ①. Adv: *vacantly.*)

vacation [ve 'ke ʃən] *n.* time when one does not have to work or go to school. (Pl only for types and instances.)

vaccination [væk sə 'ne ʃən] *n.* the use of a vaccine to protect people against disease. (Pl only for types and instances.)

vaccine [væk 'sin] *n.* a substance that is given to people in order to protect them from a certain disease.

vacuum ['væk jum] **1.** *n.* a space that is completely empty and does not have any air in it. **2.** *n.* a machine used to suck up dirt from carpets and other floor coverings. (Short for *vacuum cleaner.*) **3.** *adj.* creating or causing ①. **4.** *tv.* to clean a surface by sucking up dirt with ②. **5.** *iv.* to clean by sucking up dirt with ②.

vague ['veg] **1.** *adj.* not precise; not exact. (Adv: *vaguely.* Comp: *vaguer;* sup: *vaguest.*) **2.** *adj.* having no expression on one's face. (Fig. on ①. Adv: *vaguely.* Comp: *vaguer;* sup: *vaguest.*)

vain ['ven] *adj.* having too much pride about how one looks or about what one has done. (Adv: *vainly.* Comp: *vainer;* sup: *vainest.*)

valiant ['væl jənt] *adj.* very brave; very courageous; heroic. (Adv: *valiantly.*)

valid ['væl ɪd] **1.** *adj.* effective; legally usable or acceptable. (Adv: *validly.*) **2.** *adj.* true; able to be defended or proved; based on facts. (Adv: *validly.*)

valley ['væl i] *n.* a low area of land between two high areas of land; a low area of land that is drained by a large river and the smaller rivers that flow into the larger river.

valor ['væl ɚ] *n.* courage. (No pl.)

valuable ['væl jə bəl] **1.** *adj.* worth a lot of money; having a great value. (Adv: *valuably.*) **2.** *adj.* helpful; useful; important. (Adv: *valuably.*)

556

valuables *n.* items that are VALUABLE ①. (No sg.)

value ['væl ju] **1.** *n.* the amount of money that something is worth. (No pl.) **2.** *n.* something that is actually worth more than the amount one paid for it; a bargain. **3.** *n.* something of great use; benefit. (No pl.) **4.** *n.* an amount that is represented by a sign or symbol. **5.** *tv.* to believe that something is worth a certain amount of money. **6.** *tv.* to think someone or something is valuable; to regard someone or something as useful or worthy; to regard someone or something highly.

valve ['vælv] *n.* a flap or other device in a tube that controls the amount of something that passes through the tube.

van ['væn] *n.* a covered motor vehicle that has a large amount of space behind the driver's seat for carrying large objects or extra people.

vandal ['væn dəl] *n.* someone who damages other people's property or public property on purpose.

vandalism ['væn də lɪz əm] *n.* the damaging of other people's property or public property on purpose. (No pl form in this sense.)

vandalize ['væn də laɪz] *tv.* to damage other people's property or public property on purpose.

vanilla [və 'nɪl ə] **1.** *n.* a flavoring made from the bean of a certain tropical plant. (No pl.) **2.** *adj.* flavored with ①; tasting like ①.

vanish ['væn ɪʃ] *iv.* to disappear; to be seen no longer.

vanity ['væn ə ti] **1.** *n.* the condition of being vain; the condition of having too much pride about how one looks or what one has done. (No pl.) **2.** *n.* a cabinet with drawers, especially such a unit in a bathroom, with a sink included in the top surface.

vanquish ['væŋ kwɪʃ] *tv.* to defeat someone in a battle, sporting contest, argument, or other conflict.

vapor ['ve pɚ] *n.* a liquid or solid in the form of a gas.

variable ['vɛr i ə bəl] **1.** *adj.* able to be changed; flexible. (Adv: *variably.*) **2.** *adj.* likely to change; not staying the same. (Adv: *variably.*) **3.** *n.* something that changes, especially an amount that changes depending on other factors.

variant ['vɛr i ənt] **1.** *adj.* different; having a particular difference as compared with something standard or the norm. **2.** *n.* a different form of something, especially a different way of spelling a word.

variation [vɛr i 'e ʃən] *n.* (minor) differences; a minor difference. (Pl only for types and instances.)

557

variety [və 'raɪ ə ti] *n.* differences of choice; diversity. (Pl only for types and instances.)

various ['ver i əs] *adj.* different; several; having several kinds of something; having many kinds of something. (Adv: *variously*.)

varnish ['vɑr nɪʃ] **1.** *n.* a clear liquid that is painted onto the surface of objects made from wood to protect the wood and give it a hard, shiny appearance. (Pl only for types and instances.) **2.** *tv.* to paint a surface with ①.

vary ['ver i] **1.** *iv.* to change; to be different; to appear or be used in different forms. **2.** *tv.* to change something; to cause something to be different; to make something different.

vase ['ves] *n.* a decorative container, often used for holding flowers.

vast ['væst] *adj.* very large in size or amount; of an immense size or amount. (Adv: *vastly*. Comp: *vaster*; sup: *vastest*.)

vat ['væt] *n.* a large container, used for storing liquid, especially liquor while it is being made.

vault ['vɔlt] **1.** *n.* a secure, locked room where valuable things are kept and protected. **2.** *n.* a leap; a jump made with the help of a pole or one's hands. **3.** *tv.* to jump a certain distance.

veal ['vil] *n.* the meat of a young cow used as food. (No pl.)

vegetable ['vedʒ tə bəl] **1.** *n.* a plant that is eaten as food; a part of a plant that is eaten as food. **2.** *adj.* made with or including ①.

vegetarian [vedʒ ɪ 'ter i ən] **1.** *n.* someone who does not eat the flesh of animals. **2.** *adj.* [of food] made without the flesh of a once-living creature. **3.** *adj.* serving or eating food other than animal tissue.

vegetation [vedʒ ɪ 'te ʃən] *n.* plant life; plants in general. (No pl. Treated as sg.)

vehicle ['vi ɪ kəl] *n.* a machine that is used to carry people or things, especially on roads, including cars, buses, trucks, vans, motorcycles, bicycles, sleds, sleighs, and carriages. (But not trains or airplanes.)

vehicular [vɪ 'hɪk jə lɚ] *adj.* of or about vehicles. (Adv: *vehicularly*.)

veil ['vel] *n.* a piece of cloth used to hide something.

vein ['ven] **1.** *n.* a vessel that carries blood from parts of the body back to the heart. **2.** *n.* a line that forms part of the framework of a leaf or the wing of an insect. **3.** *n.* a layer of coal or metal within a mass of rock.

velocity [və 'lɑs ə ti] *n.* speed, especially the speed of an object moving in a specific direction. (Pl only for types and instances.)

velvet ['vɛl vɪt] **1.** *n.* a soft fabric whose threads are short and close together and stick up on one side of the fabric. (Pl only for types and instances.) **2.** *adj.* made of ①.

vengeance ['vɛn dʒəns] *n.* hurting someone or damaging someone's property as a form of revenge. (No pl form.)

venom ['vɛn əm] **1.** *n.* the poison in the bite or sting of a snake, spider, and other similar creatures. (No pl.) **2.** *n.* extreme hatred. (Fig. on ①. No pl.)

venomous ['vɛn ə məs] **1.** *adj.* full of venom; containing venom. (Adv: *venomously.*) **2.** *adj.* full of extreme hatred. (Fig. on ①. Adv: *venomously.*)

vent ['vɛnt] **1.** *n.* an opening to a passage through which air or other gases can move. **2.** *tv.* to express one's feelings; to make one's feelings known.

ventilate ['vɛn tɪ let] *tv.* to bring fresh air into a room or an enclosed space; to expose something or someplace to fresh air.

ventilation [vɛn tɪ 'le ʃən] *n.* the movement of fresh air into or out of a place. (No pl form in this sense.)

ventilator ['vɛn tɪ le tɚ] **1.** *n.* a fan that moves air into or out of a room or enclosed space. **2.** *n.* a device that supplies air or oxygen to someone who cannot breathe without help.

venture ['vɛn tʃɚ] **1.** *n.* a risky thing to do, especially an action taken in business where one risks one's money in order to gain more money. **2.** *tv.* to risk something; to expose something to danger; to place something in danger. **3.** *iv.* to go into a place that could be dangerous.

verb ['vɚb] *n.* a word that describes what someone or something is or does; a word that expresses being, action, or occurrence.

verbal ['vɚb əl] **1.** *adj.* expressed in words; oral; spoken, not written. (Adv: *verbally.*) **2.** *adj.* of or about a verb; formed from a verb. (Adv: *verbally.*)

verbal auxiliary Go to AUXILIARY VERB.

verdict ['vɚ dɪkt] **1.** *n.* the decision of a judge or a jury at the end of a trial. **2.** *n.* a conclusion; a judgment; an opinion.

verse ['vɚs] **1.** *n.* poetry; language as it is used in poetry. (No pl.) **2.** *n.* a group of lines in a poem or song. **3.** *n.* a portion of a chapter of a book of the Bible.

version ['vɚ ʒən] **1.** *n.* one person's account or description of something that has happened. **2.** *n.* a form of something that is different from another form of it, such as being in a different language or medium.

vertical ['vɚ tɪ kəl] *adj.* straight up and down. (Adv: *vertically* [...ɪk li].)

very ['vɛr i] **1.** *adv.* especially; quite; extremely; greatly; to a large degree. (Used to strengthen the meaning of an adjective or another adverb. *Very* is not used with the comp. forms, but is used with sup. forms, following *the*, to strengthen meaning.) **2.** *adj.* same; actual; identical. (Prenominal only.) **3.** *adj.* mere; simple. (Prenominal only.)

vessel ['vɛs əl] **1.** *n.* a container used to hold liquids. **2.** *n.* a large ship or boat.

vest ['vɛst] *n.* a piece of clothing that has no sleeves and is worn above the waist on top of a shirt and usually under a suit coat or jacket.

vet ['vɛt] **1.** *n.* someone who has served in the military, especially during a war. (Short for VETERAN.) **2.** *n.* a doctor who treats only animals. (Short for VETERINARIAN.)

veteran ['vɛt (ə) rən] **1.** *n.* someone who has served in the military, especially during a war. (Can be shortened to VET.) **2.** *n.* someone who has a lot of experience with something. (Fig. on ①.) **3.** *adj.* experienced; having a lot of experience with something.

veterinarian [vɛt (ə) rə 'nɛr i ən] *n.* a doctor who treats only animals. (Can be shortened to VET.)

veto ['vi to] **1.** *n.* an instance of using one's authority to stop a proposed bill from becoming law. (Pl ends in *-es.*) **2.** *tv.* to stop a bill from becoming law; not to allow something to happen.

vibrate ['vaɪ bret] **1.** *iv.* to move back and forth very quickly; to shake; to quiver. **2.** *tv.* to move something back and forth very quickly; to shake something.

vibration [vaɪ 'bre ʃən] *n.* the motions of moving back and forth very quickly.

vice ['vaɪs] *n.* a bad or immoral habit.

vicinity [vɪ 'sɪn ə ti] *n.* a neighborhood; the location around someone or something; the surrounding area.

vicious ['vɪʃ əs] **1.** *adj.* fierce; cruel; likely to cause pain; dangerous. (Adv: *viciously.*) **2.** *adj.* evil; cruel. (Adv: *viciously.*)

560

victim ['vɪk təm] *n.* a person or an animal that dies, suffers, or loses something because of someone else's actions, a sickness, an accident, or a natural disaster.

victimize ['vɪk tə maɪz] *tv.* to cause someone to be a victim; to cause someone to suffer.

victor ['vɪk tɚ] *n.* a winner; someone who wins a fight, game, contest, race, etc.

victory ['vɪk tə ri] *n.* winning; achieving success: the success of defeating an enemy or opponent. (Pl only for types and instances.)

video ['vɪd i o] **1.** *n.* moving visible images, such as what is recorded on videotape; the visible part of a television program; the display seen on a computer monitor. (No pl.) **2.** *n.* a movie that is available on videotape; motion or action that is recorded on videotape. (Pl ends in -s.) **3.** *n.* a short film or taped version of a song. (Pl ends in -s.) **4.** the *adj.* use of ①, ②, or ③.

videocassette ['vɪd i o kə 'sɛt] *n.* a device that holds videotape, which is put into a video camera or a videocassette recorder to record or play back images.

videotape ['vɪd i o tep] **1.** *n.* a length of plastic tape on which images can be recorded and played back. (No pl.) **2.** *n.* a reel or cassette of ①; a copy of a movie or a television show that is recorded on ①.

view ['vju] **1.** *n.* the way something looks from a place; a scene. **2.** *n.* an opinion; the way someone thinks about something. **3.** *tv.* to examine someone or something; to look at someone or something closely.

viewpoint ['vju pɔɪnt] *n.* an opinion; the way someone thinks about something.

vigil ['vɪdʒ əl] *n.* an act or instance of staying awake during the night to watch something, to pray, or to take care of someone who is sick.

vigilant ['vɪdʒ ə lənt] *adj.* on guard; watchful; watching over someone or something. (Adv: *vigilantly.*)

vigor ['vɪg ɚ] *n.* strength; energy; DRIVE ⑥. (No pl.)

vile ['vaɪl] **1.** *adj.* very bad; very unpleasant; disgusting. (Adv: *vilely.* Comp: *viler;* sup: *vilest.*) **2.** *adj.* evil; wicked; immoral. (Adv: *vilely.* Comp: *viler;* sup: *vilest.*)

village ['vɪl ɪdʒ] **1.** *n.* a small town; a group of houses and businesses in the country or suburbs. **2.** *n.* all the people who live in a particular ①. **3.** the *adj.* use of ① or ②.

villager ['vɪl ɪdʒ ɚ] *n.* someone who lives in a village.

villain ['vɪl ən] *n.* someone who is wicked or evil, especially someone who is the bad person in a story or movie.

vine ['vɑɪn] *n.* a plant that has long, thin stems that crawl along the ground or the sides of an object.

vinegar ['vɪn ɪ gɚ] *n.* a sour liquid made from wine or apple juice, used to flavor or preserve food. (No pl.)

vinyl ['vɑɪ nəl] **1.** *n.* a kind of common plastic. (No pl.) **2.** *adj.* made of ①.

viola [vi 'o lə] *n.* a stringed musical instrument that is similar to, but larger than, a violin.

violence ['vɑɪ ə ləns] *n.* rough force; actions that hurt or damage people or things. (No pl. Number is expressed with *act(s) of violence.*)

violent ['vɑɪ ə lənt] **1.** *adj.* using rough force that can hurt or damage people or things. (Adv: *violently.*) **2.** *adj.* showing violence. (Adv: *violently.*)

violet ['vɑɪ ə lɪt] *n.* a small plant that has dark purple flowers with a delicate smell.

violin [vɑɪ ə 'lɪn] *n.* a four-stringed musical instrument played with a bow.

violinist [vɑɪ ə 'lɪn ɪst] *n.* someone who plays a violin.

viper ['vɑɪ pɚ] *n.* a venomous snake, especially one with fangs.

virtual ['vɚ tʃu əl] **1.** *adj.* having an effect as though someone or something were the real person or thing. (Adv: *virtually.*) **2.** *adj.* of or about interaction on the Internet; of or about interaction with other people through computers. (Adv: *virtually.*)

virtue ['vɚ tʃu] **1.** *n.* goodness, especially in behavior or morals. (No pl.) **2.** *n.* a good moral behavior or trait; a trait that is valued by society. **3.** *n.* an advantage; a benefit.

virus ['vɑɪ rəs] *n.* a living thing so small it can only be seen under a microscope. (Viruses cause infections and diseases in humans, animals, and plants, including chicken pox, rabies, and the common cold.)

visa ['vi zə] *n.* an official stamp, signature, or attachment put in a passport, which allows its owner to enter a certain country.

vise [vɑɪs] *n.* a machine made of metal jaws that can be pushed tightly together, used for clamping something tightly so that it doesn't move while someone works on it.

562

visibility [vɪz ə 'bɪl ə ti] **1.** *n.* the condition of being visible; the degree to which someone or something is noticed or causes someone or something to be seen. (No pl form in this sense.) **2.** *n.* the degree to which the sky is clear; the distance that one can see because of weather conditions. (No pl form in this sense.)

visible ['vɪz ə bəl] *adj.* able to be seen; not hidden. (Adv: *visibly.*)

vision ['vɪ ʒən] **1.** *n.* the ability to see; the power of sight. (No pl.) **2.** *n.* something that is seen or experienced in a dream, in one's imagination, or in one's memory. **3.** *n.* insight; the ability to understand what something means and how it will affect the future. (No pl.)

visit ['vɪz ɪt] **1.** *tv.* to go to a person or a place for a period of time; to be with a person as a visitor; to be at a place as a visitor. **2.** *tv.* to examine or inspect something as part of one's job. **3.** *iv.* to be someone's guest; to stay at someone's house or at a place as a guest or tourist. **4.** *n.* an act or instance of someone going or coming to a place for a period of time in order to see someone or something, experience something, or talk with someone.

visitor ['vɪz ɪ tɚ] *n.* someone who visits someone or someplace as a guest or tourist.

visual ['vɪ ʒu əl] *adj.* of or about vision or seeing. (Adv: *visually.*)

vital ['vaɪt əl] **1.** *adj.* very important; absolutely necessary; essential. (Adv: *vitally.*) **2.** *adj.* of or about life; necessary for life. **3.** *adj.* active; full of life. (Adv: *vitally.*)

vitamin ['vaɪ tə mɪn] *n.* a chemical compound that is important for a person's health and cannot be made by the body.

vivid ['vɪv ɪd] **1.** *adj.* clear; distinct. (Adv: *vividly.*) **2.** *adj.* strongly or brightly colored; deeply colored. (Adv: *vividly.*)

vocabulary [vo 'kæb jə lɛr i] **1.** *n.* the words that someone knows; the words that are part of someone's language. (No pl.) **2.** *n.* the words used in a certain business, profession, or activity. (No pl.) **3.** *n.* a list of words with brief meanings, like those found in foreign-language dictionaries; a glossary of words and their meanings. **4.** *n.* all the words of a language. (No pl.)

vocation [vo 'ke ʃən] *n.* an occupation; a trade; a profession.

voice ['vɔɪs] **1.** *n.* the sounds made by a person who is speaking or singing; the sounds made when speaking or singing. **2.** *n.* a medium or channel for representing someone's opinions. **3.** *n.* a grammar term that describes the relation of the subject of a sentence to the verb. **4.** *tv.* to express an opinion by speaking. **5.** *tv.* [in phonetics] to give a certain quality to a sound by vibrating the vocal folds and making the sound of ①.

void ['vɔɪd] **1.** *adj.* not binding according to the law; having no legal authority; having no legal effect; no longer valid. **2.** *tv.* to cause a law to stop being a law. **3.** *n.* an area that is empty; an empty space; a gap.

volcano [vɑl 'ke no] *n.* a mountain with an opening at the top or on the sides from which steam, gas, molten rock, and ash sometimes are ejected by pressure or force from inside the earth. (Pl ends in *-s* or *-es*.)

volleyball ['vɑl i bɔl] **1.** *n.* a sport where two teams on opposite sides of a net try to hit a large, light ball back and forth over the net without letting the ball touch the ground. (No pl.) **2.** *n.* the ball used to play ①.

volt ['volt] *n.* a unit of measurement of electrical force.

voltage ['vol tɪdʒ] *n.* an amount of an electrical force, measured in volts.

volume ['vɑl jəm] **1.** *n.* a book, especially one book in a series of books. **2.** *n.* the loudness of sound. (Pl only for types and instances.) **3.** *n.* an amount of something. **4.** *n.* the expression of space in three dimensions, determined by multiplying an object's length, width, and depth.

voluntary ['vɑl ən ter i] **1.** *adj.* [done] by one's own choice. (Adv: *voluntarily* [vɑl ən 'ter ə li].) **2.** *adj.* supported by volunteers or gifts.

volunteer [vɑl ən 'tɪr] **1.** *n.* someone who does work for free; someone who agrees to take on a job or task. **2.** *tv.* to offer one's time, help, or energy at no cost; to give one's services for free. **3.** *tv.* to say something without being forced to talk; to say something by one's own choice. **4.** the *adj.* use of ①. **5.** ~ **for** to submit oneself for some task.

vomit ['vɑm ɪt] **1.** *tv.* to throw food up after one has eaten it; to bring something up from the stomach. **2.** *iv.* to throw [something] up from the stomach through the mouth. **3.** *n.* something that has been thrown up from the stomach through the mouth. (No pl.)

vote ['vot] **1.** *n.* a formal or legal expression of one's opinion on an issue, especially on political issues. **2.** *n.* the ①, viewed collectively, of a large number of people who share a certain characteristic or background. (No pl. Treated as sg.) **3.** *iv.* to express one's opinion on an issue by raising one's hand or marking one's choice on a ballot.

voter ['vot ɚ] *n.* someone who has the right to vote in an election.

vow ['vaʊ] **1.** *n.* an oath; a sincere promise. **2.** *tv.* to make ①; to swear that one will do something. (The object can be a clause with THAT ⑦.)

vowel ['vaʊ əl] **1.** *n.* a speech sound that is made without completely closing any parts of the mouth while air passes through it. **2.** *n.* a letter of the alphabet that represents a speech sound that is not a CONSONANT; [in English] the letters *a, e, i, o,* and *u*. **3.** the *adj.* use of ① or ②.

voyage ['vɔɪ ədʒ] *n.* a journey, especially one made over water, through the air, or in space; a journey made on a ship, airplane, or spacecraft.

vulture ['vʌl tʃɚ] *n.* a large bird that lives on the meat of dead animals.

W

waddle ['wɑd l] *iv.* to walk with slow, short steps while moving the body from side to side, as a duck walks.

wade ['wed] **1.** *iv.* to walk through shallow water or mud. **2.** *tv.* to cross a shallow body of water by walking through it.

waffle ['wɑf əl] **1.** *n.* a thick round or square pancake with depressed squares that form a grid. **2.** *iv.* to change one's mind on an issue many times.

wag ['wæg] **1.** *tv.* to move something up and down or from side to side many times. **2.** *iv.* to move up and down or from side to side many times.

wage ['wedʒ] **1.** *tv.* to begin and continue a war, battle, or struggle against someone or something. **2.** *n.* payment for work, especially when a certain amount is paid for each hour worked. (Often pl with the same meaning. Compare this with SALARY.)

wager ['we dʒɚ] **1.** *n.* a bet. **2.** *tv.* to risk an amount of money on the outcome of an event. **3.** *tv.* to bet that something will happen; to bet that something is or will be the case. (The object is a clause with THAT ⑦.)

wagon ['wæg ən] **1.** *n.* a strong four-wheeled vehicle (with a flat bottom) that is pulled by horses, mules, or oxen. **2.** *n.* a small, light four-wheeled cart with a flat bottom that is pulled as a children's toy.

wail ['wel] **1.** *n.* a long, loud cry, especially one of pain or sadness. **2.** *iv.* to cry out with a long, loud sound because of pain or sadness. **3.** *tv.* to utter something with a long, loud cry of pain or sadness. (The object can be a clause with THAT ⑦.)

waist ['west] **1.** *n.* the part of the body below the bottom of the ribs and above the hips. **2.** *n.* the part of a piece of clothing that covers ①; the part of a piece of clothing that hangs from ①.

waistline ['west lɑɪn] *n.* an imaginary line around the body at the smallest part of one's waist, usually where the top hem of a pair of pants or a skirt rests on the body.

wait ['wet] **1.** *iv.* to stay in a place until someone or something else arrives or returns; to stay in a place until something happens. **2.** *n.* a period of time that one WAITS as in ① for someone or something.

566

3. ~ **on** to serve someone as a waiter or waitress or as a clerk behind a counter.

waiter ['we tɚ] *n.* a man who serves customers at a restaurant.

waitress ['we trɪs] *n.* a woman who serves customers at a restaurant.

waive ['wev] **1.** *tv.* to give up something, especially a right or a privilege. (Compare this to WAVE.) **2.** *tv.* to allow someone not to have to do something that is usually required; to excuse someone from fulfilling a requirement.

wake ['wek] **1.** *n.* a gathering, shortly before a funeral, of the friends and relatives of someone who has recently died. **2.** *n.* the path on the surface of a body of water caused by a boat or ship traveling through the water. **3.** ~ **up** to cause someone or some creature to stop sleeping; to awaken.

waken ['wek ən] **1.** *iv.* to wake from sleep; to stop sleeping. **2.** *tv.* to wake someone or something from sleep.

walk ['wɔk] **1.** *iv.* to move on foot at a normal speed and in a way that only one foot at a time is on the ground. **2.** *tv.* to move in, on, or through a space as in ①. **3.** *tv.* to exercise an animal, usually a dog, by taking it for ⑤. **4.** *tv.* to go with someone to a certain place. **5.** *n.* an act of WALKING as in ①, especially as exercise or for pleasure; a journey on foot. **6.** *n.* a path; a place where one can WALK ①. **7.** ~ **out** to exit something or someplace.

wall ['wɔl] **1.** *n.* the side of a room from the floor to the ceiling; the side of a building from the ground to the roof. **2.** *n.* a large, flat side of anything; anything that looks like ①. **3.** *n.* a thin tissue that encloses a part of the body of a human, plant, or animal.

wallet ['wɑl ət] *n.* a small, flat case that is used for carrying money, identification, credit cards, etc. (Often made of leather.)

wallpaper ['wɔl pe pɚ] **1.** *n.* paper, usually with a design on it, that is used to cover and decorate walls. (No pl.) **2.** *tv.* to cover a wall with ①. **3.** *iv.* to apply ① to a wall; to put up ①.

walnut ['wɔl nət] **1.** *n.* the tree that produces a delicious, edible nut. **2.** *n.* the nut of ①; the nut of ① and its shell. **3.** *n.* wood from ①. (Pl only for types and instances.) **4.** *adj.* made with ② or from ③.

waltz ['wɔlts] **1.** *n.* a dance, with three beats to every measure of music, in which couples turn in a circle as they dance around the dance floor. **2.** *n.* music that has three beats to every measure and is written for ① or suitable for ①. **3.** *iv.* to dance ①.

wander ['wɑn dɚ] *iv.* to travel in no specific direction; to roam somewhere.

wane ['wen] **1.** *iv.* to become less important, less strong, less intense, or smaller. **2.** *iv.* [for the moon] to gradually appear to be smaller after a full moon. (Compare this with WAX ④.)

want ['wɑnt] **1.** *tv.* to desire to have someone or something. **2.** *n.* a desire; a need; something that someone would like to have. **3.** *n.* a lack. (No pl.)

war ['wɔr] *n.* fighting or conflict between two or more nations, especially involving a military force of one country attacking another country. (Pl only for types and instances.)

ward ['wɔrd] **1.** *n.* someone, especially a child, who is under the protection of the state, the government, a judge, or someone chosen by a court. **2.** *n.* a political division of a city, especially one that is represented by someone in a city council. **3.** *n.* a section of a hospital, usually containing the beds for patients having similar medical conditions.

warden ['wɔrd n] *n.* someone who is in charge of a prison or jail.

wardrobe ['wɔr drob] **1.** *n.* a collection of clothes. **2.** *n.* a piece of furniture that looks like a large box with a door, and is used to store clothing.

warehouse ['wer hɑʊs] **1.** *n., irreg.* a place where large amounts of goods are stored before they are sold or used. (Pl: [...hɑʊ zəz].) **2.** *tv.* to store something in ①.

wares ['werz] *n.* goods or products that are made or manufactured for sale. (Treated as pl.)

warm ['wɔrm] **1.** *adj.* somewhat hot; not too hot but not cold. (Adv: *warmly.* Comp: *warmer;* sup: *warmest.*) **2.** *adj.* capable of retaining heat. (Adv: *warmly.* Comp: *warmer;* sup: *warmest.*) **3.** *adj.* pleasant; friendly; indicating that one is pleasant or friendly. (Adv: *warmly.* Comp: *warmer;* sup: *warmest.*)

warmth ['wɔrmθ] **1.** *n.* a small amount of heat. (No pl.) **2.** *n.* kindness; pleasantness; friendliness. (No pl.)

warn ['wɔrn] **1.** *tv.* to alert someone to danger; to inform someone about something dangerous or risky. **2.** *tv.* to tell someone not to do something, implying that punishment will follow repeated violations.

warning ['wɔr nɪŋ] *n.* something that warns; a statement, sign, or threat of danger.

warrant ['wɔr ənt] **1.** *n.* a written order that gives an authority the right to do something such as search someone, search a place, arrest someone, or carry out other legal orders. **2.** *tv.* to justify something; to cause something to seem reasonable.

warranty ['wɔr ən ti] *n.* an official guarantee; a written promise from a manufacturer that something will function in the way that it is supposed to.

warrior ['wɔr jɚ] *n.* someone who is trained to fight; a soldier; a fighter.

warship ['wɔr ʃɪp] *n.* a ship equipped with weapons for making war.

wart ['wɔrt] *n.* a hard, ugly bump that swells from the skin, especially on the face, neck, and hands.

wary ['wɛr i] *adj.* aware; on guard against harm or danger; careful. (Adv: *warily*. Comp: *warier*; sup: *wariest*.)

was ['wʌz, 'wɑz, wəz] *iv.* a pt of BE used with the first and third persons sg.

wash ['wɑʃ] **1.** *tv.* to clean someone or something with water or some other liquid. **2.** *tv.* to remove dirt through the use of water or some other liquid. **3.** *tv.* [for water] to carry or move something. **4.** *iv.* to clean [oneself or some part of oneself] with water or some other liquid. **5.** *iv.* to be carried or moved by water. **6.** *n.* laundry; clothes that need to be, are being, or have been cleaned as in ①; clothes that are cleaned as in ① together at one time. (No pl.) **7.** *n.* an act or instance of cleaning or being cleaned as in ①, ②, or ④.

washcloth ['wɑʃ klɔθ] *n., irreg.* a small cloth used for washing one's body, especially the face. (Pl: ['wɑʃ klɔðz].)

washer ['wɑʃ ɚ] **1.** *n.* a washing machine; a machine that washes clothing. **2.** *n.* a small, flat circle of metal or rubber, with a hole in the center, that is put under the head of a bolt or screw or between a nut and a bolt to make a tighter seal.

washroom ['wɑʃ rum] *n.* a bathroom; a restroom; a room with a toilet.

wasn't ['wʌz ənt] *cont.* was not.

wasp ['wɑsp] *n.* a large stinging insect that is similar to a bee but is able to sting again and again.

waste ['west] **1.** *tv.* to use something foolishly or wrongly; to use too much of something. **2.** *n.* garbage; trash; something that is not used and is thrown away. (No pl.) **3.** *n.* a poor or foolish use of something; the failure to use all of the parts of something that are able to be used.

(No pl.) **4.** *n.* material that is sent out from the body; urine and feces. (Sometimes pl with the same meaning, but not countable.)

wastebasket ['west bæs kɪt] *n.* a container that is used to hold trash.

wastepaper ['west pe pɚ] *n.* paper that is not needed and is thrown away or reused. (No pl.)

watch ['wɑtʃ] **1.** *tv.* to observe something as it happens; to pay someone or something attention; to look at someone or something to see what happens. **2.** *tv.* to guard someone or something; to protect someone or something. **3.** *iv.* to pay attention to someone or something; to look at someone or something carefully and attentively. **4.** *n.* a device, typically worn on one's wrist, that displays the time.

water ['wɔt ɚ] **1.** *n.* the liquid that forms oceans, lakes, and rivers; the liquid that falls from the sky as rain and is drunk by humans and animals. (No pl.) **2.** *n.* the surface of a body of ①. (E.g., *the water reflected the image of the clouds.* No pl.) **3.** *tv.* to provide a plant with ①; to put ① on the soil around a plant. **4.** *iv.* [for one's eyes] to fill with tears. **5.** *iv.* [for one's mouth] to fill with moisture, especially when one is about to eat or is thinking about eating food.

waterfall ['wɔt ɚ fɔl] *n.* a flow of water off the side of a mountain, rock, or dam.

watermelon ['wɔt ɚ mel ən] **1.** *n.* a large, round or oval fruit that grows on the ground on a vine and has a thick green rind and a juicy, pink inside containing a lot of black seeds. **2.** *adj.* tasting like ①.

waterproof ['wɔt ɚ pruf] **1.** *adj.* not allowing water to pass through; able to keep water inside or outside; not leaking water. **2.** *tv.* to cause something to resist water as in ①.

waters *n.* vast amounts of water as found in rivers, oceans, or large lakes.

watertight ['wɔt ɚ taɪt] **1.** *adj.* not allowing water to pass through; able to keep water inside or outside; not leaking eating. **2.** *adj.* perfect; [of an agreement or argument] having no mistakes or defects. (Fig. on ①.)

wave ['wev] **1.** *n.* a moving ridge of water made by wind, the tide, or the movement of something through water. **2.** *n.* a ridge in the surface of something. **3.** *n.* a movement of the hand as in ⑥. **4.** *n.* an increase in crime, heat, or cold. **5.** *tv.* to move something, especially one's hand, when greeting someone, trying to get someone's attention, or calling attention to oneself. **6.** *iv.* to greet someone, to get someone's attention, or to call attention to oneself by moving one's hand. **7.** *iv.* to move up and down or back and forth in the air.

wax ['wæks] **1.** *n.* an oily or fatty substance that melts easily when it is warmed but hardens when it is cool, used to make candles, floor polish, and other substances. (Pl only for types and instances.) **2.** *n.* an oily substance that is produced in the ears. (No pl.) **3.** *tv.* to coat or polish a floor with ①. **4.** *tv.* [for the moon] to gradually appear to be brighter and fuller before a full moon. (Compare this with WANE.)

way ['we] **1.** *n.* a manner; the manner in which something is done; a method. **2.** *n.* a habit; a custom; a regular manner in which something is done. (Usually pl.) **3.** *n.* the route to a certain place. (No pl.) **4.** *adv.* far; far away in time or space.

wayside ['we sɑɪd] *adj.* along the way, road, or highway.

we ['wi] **1.** *pron.* the first-person pl subjective pronoun, referring to the speaker or writer—"I"—together with at least one other person. **2.** *pron.* a special use of ① as a first-person sg subjective pronoun, meaning "I, the speaker or writer." (Used by writers and sometimes by royalty.) **3.** *pron.* everyone; all humans.

weak ['wik] **1.** *adj.* lacking power or strength; not strong or powerful. (Adv: *weakly.* Comp: *weaker;* sup: *weakest.*) **2.** *adj.* lacking strong morals; lacking a moral character. (Adv: *weakly.* Comp: *weaker;* sup: *weakest.*) **3.** *adj.* having too much water; diluted. (Adv: *weakly.* Comp: *weaker;* sup: *weakest.*)

weaken ['wik ən] **1.** *iv.* to become weak. **2.** *tv.* to cause someone or something to become weak.

weakness ['wik nəs] **1.** *n.* the condition of being weak, especially concerning the health of someone's mind or body. (No pl form.) **2.** *n.* a fault; a flaw; something that weakens someone or something.

wealth ['wɛlθ] *n.* riches; a large amount of money or property. (No pl.)

wealthy ['wɛl θi] *adj.* rich; having a large amount of money or property. (Adv: *wealthily.* Comp: *wealthier;* sup: *wealthiest.*)

wean ['win] *tv.* to cause a child or young animal to begin to eat food other than milk from the mother.

weapon ['wɛp ən] *n.* any object or machine used to hurt someone, to kill someone, or to defend oneself during a fight or an attack.

wear ['wɛr] **1.** *tv., irreg.* to have something on the body, including clothes, glasses, jewelry, perfume, makeup, and similar things. (Pt: WORE; pp: WORN.) **2.** *tv., irreg.* to have something on or related to the body kept or held in a particular way. **3.** *tv., irreg.* to damage something gradually because of continued use. **4.** *iv., irreg.* to damage or worsen gradually. **5.** *n.* gradual damage that is caused because of continued use. (No pl.) **6.** *n.* clothing, especially a collection of clothing available for sale at a store. (Used in combinations such as *resort wear, business wear,* etc. No pl. Treated as sg.)

weary ['wɪr i] **1.** *adj.* tired; exhausted; fatigued. (Adv: *wearily.* Comp: *wearier;* sup: *weariest.*) **2.** *iv.* to become tired, exhausted, or fatigued.

weather ['wɛð ɚ] **1.** *n.* the condition of the outside air, including the temperature, the amount of moisture in the air, and the presence or absence of rain, snow, wind, clouds, and sunshine. (No pl.) **2.** *tv.* to withstand something (especially bad WEATHER ①) without damage. **3.** *tv.* [for kinds of ①] to damage something. **4.** *iv.* to change because of exposure to ①.

weave ['wiv] **1.** *tv., irreg.* to make something by crossing threads or strips of material from side to side so that they go over and under threads or strips of material that are stretched up and down. (Pt: WOVE; pp: WOVEN.) **2.** *tv., irreg.* to cross threads or strips of material from side to side so that they go over and under threads or strips of material that are stretched up and down. **3.** *tv., irreg.* to make something by combining different things into a whole. (Fig. on ①.) **4.** *iv., irreg.* to move so that one is always changing direction. (Pt: sometimes *weaved.*)

web ['wɛb] **1.** *n.* a net of thin, silky threads made by spiders in order to trap other insects for food. **2.** *n.* a network; a detailed arrangement of things that cross and connect with each other. (Fig. on ①.) **3.** *n.* the piece of thin skin between the toes of ducks and other animals that live in or near the water.

we'd ['wid] **1.** *cont.* we had, where HAD is an auxiliary. **2.** *cont.* we would.

wed ['wɛd] **1.** *tv., irreg.* to marry someone; to take someone as a husband or wife. (Pt/pp: *wedded* or *wed.*) **2.** *tv., irreg.* to cause two people to become married by performing a marriage ceremony. **3.** *iv., irreg.* to become married.

wedding ['wɛd ɪŋ] **1.** *n.* the ceremony where two people become married to each other; a marriage ceremony. **2.** *n.* a merger or formation of a close association. (Fig. on ①.)

wedge ['wɛdʒ] **1.** *n.* a piece of wood, metal, or other material that is thick at one end and narrows to an edge at the other end. **2.** *n.* any object shaped like ①. **3.** *tv.* to stick someone or something in a tight space between two people or things, especially so that nothing or no one can move.

Wednesday ['wɛnz de] Go to DAY.

weed ['wid] **1.** *n.* a rough plant that grows in a place where it is not wanted. **2.** *tv.* to remove ① from an area of ground, such as a lawn or garden. **3.** *tv.* to remove a specific kind of ①. **4.** *iv.* to clean or improve [a garden or lawn] by removing ①.

week ['wik] **1.** *n.* a period of seven days. (See a list of days of the week at DAY.) **2.** *n.* a period of seven days beginning on a Sunday and ending on a Saturday. (According to the calendar.) **3.** *n.* the five or six days during which most workers work, especially Monday through Friday.

weekday ['wik de] **1.** *n.* Monday, Tuesday, Wednesday, Thursday, or Friday. **2.** *adj.* happening on ①; of ①. (Prenominal only.)

weekend ['wik ɛnd] **1.** *n.* the period of time from Friday evening to Sunday night. **2.** *adj.* happening at some time between Friday evening and Sunday night. (Prenominal only.)

weekly ['wik li] **1.** *adj.* happening every week; happening once a week. **2.** *adj.* payable every week. **3.** *adv.* every week; once a week. **4.** *n.* a magazine or newspaper that is issued once a week.

weep ['wip] **1.** *iv., irreg.* to cry. (Pt/pp: WEPT.) **2.** *tv., irreg.* to shed tears; to cry and make tears.

weigh ['we] **1.** *tv.* to use a scale to determine the weight of someone or something. **2.** *tv.* to think carefully and compare different options or alternatives when making a choice or decision. **3.** *iv.* to have a certain weight. **4.** *iv.* to have a particular kind of influence on someone or something.

weight ['wet] **1.** *n.* the degree of heaviness of someone or something or how heavy someone or something is, as measured according to a specific system. (No pl.) **2.** *n.* a heavy object, used for exercising. **3.** *n.* a heavy object, especially one that keeps something in place, holds something down, or balances something. **4.** *n.* a mental burden; something that occupies one's thoughts. (No pl.) **5.** *n.* influence; important factors.

weird ['wɪrd] *adj.* very strange; very odd; very unusual. (Adv: *weirdly.* Comp: *weirder;* sup: *weirdest.*)

welcome ['wɛl kəm] **1.** *tv.* to greet someone in a friendly way. **2.** *tv.* to be happy to receive or experience something. (Fig. on ①.) **3.** *n.*

the act of greeting or receiving someone or something with pleasure. **4.** *adj.* accepted with pleasure; wanted.

weld ['wɛld] **1.** *tv.* to join two pieces of metal together with high heat, sometimes using additional metal. **2.** *n.* the joint where two metals have been welded together.

welfare ['wɛl fɛr] **1.** *n.* a state of having good health, comfort, and enough money to live satisfactorily. (No pl.) **2.** *n.* money provided by the government for poor people to live on; the system of providing money for poor people to live on. (No pl.)

we'll ['wil] *cont.* we will.

well ['wɛl] **1.** *adv., irreg.* in a good way. (Comp: BETTER; sup: BEST.) **2.** *adv.* enough; sufficiently; to a good degree. **3.** *adv.* completely; thoroughly; fully. **4.** *adj., irreg.* healthy; in good health. (Comp: BETTER.) **5.** *n.* a deep hole that is dug in the ground to reach water, gas, or oil.

well- *adv.* WELL ①, ②, or ③ used in compounds.

well-fed ['wɛl 'fɛd] *adj.* eating enough good food to be healthy. (Hyphenated only before a nominal.)

well-fixed Go to WELL-HEELED.

well-heeled AND **well-fixed; well-off** *adj.* wealthy; having a sufficient amount of money.

well-known ['wɛl 'non] *adj.* usually known by many people; [of people] famous. (Hyphenated only before a nominal.)

well-made ['wɛl 'med] *adj.* properly constructed; sturdy; made with skill. (Hyphenated only before a nominal.)

well-off Go to WELL-HEELED.

well-to-do *adj.* wealthy and of good social position.

went ['wɛnt] pt of GO.

wept ['wɛpt] pt/pp of WEEP.

we're ['wɪr] *cont.* we are.

were ['wɚ] **1.** *iv.* pt of BE used with pl forms and YOU sg. **2.** *iv.* the form of BE used with all nouns and pronouns to indicate something that is contrary to fact.

weren't ['wɚnt] *cont.* were not.

west ['wɛst] **1.** *n.* the direction to the left of someone or something facing north; the direction in which the sun sets. (No pl.) **2.** *n.* the western part of a region or country. (No pl. Capitalized when referring to a region of the United States.) **3.** *adj.* to ①; on the side that is toward ①; facing ①. (Not prenominal.) **4.** *adj.* from ①. (Especially used to describe wind. Not prenominal.) **5.** *adv.* toward ①; into the western part of something.

western ['wɛs tɚn] **1.** *adj.* in the west; toward the west; facing the west. **2.** *adj.* from the west. (Especially used to describe wind.) **3.** *n.* a movie, book, or television show about the development of the part of the United States that is in the West during the 1800s. (Sometimes capitalized.)

wet ['wɛt] **1.** *adj.* not dry; covered with or soaked with liquid. (Adv: *wetly.* Comp: *wetter;* sup: *wettest.*) **2.** *adj.* [of weather] rainy. (Adv: *wetly.* Comp: *wetter;* sup: *wettest.*) **3.** *adj.* allowing liquor to be sold [legally]. **4.** *tv., irreg.* to make someone or something ①; to cause someone or something to be ①. (Pt/pp: *wet, wetted.*) **5.** *tv., irreg.* to urinate on oneself, on something, or in one's own clothes. (Pt/pp: usually *wet.*)

wetness ['wɛt nəs] *n.* moisture; liquid that can be felt or seen. (No pl.)

we've ['wiv] *cont.* we have, where HAVE is an auxiliary.

whale ['ʍel] *n.* a very large mammal that lives in the ocean and breathes through an opening on top of its head.

wharf ['wɔrf] *n., irreg.* a platform where ships can dock in order to load or unload people or cargo; a pier. (Pl: WHARVES.)

wharves ['wɔrvz] pl of WHARF.

what ['ʍʌt] **1.** *interrog.* a form used as the subject or object of a sentence or clause when asking questions to get more information about someone or something. **2.** *interrog.* a form used before nominals when asking questions to get more information about that noun or nominal. **3.** *pron.* that which; the thing that; the things that. **4.** *interj.* a form showing great surprise.

whatever [ʍət 'ɛv ɚ] **1.** *pron.* anything that; everything that. **2.** *pron.* no matter what. **3.** *interrog.* an emphatic form of WHAT ①, similar to *What possibly?* **4.** *adj.* any; no matter what.

what's ['ʍʌts] **1.** *cont.* what is. **2.** *cont.* what has, where HAS is an auxiliary.

wheat ['ʍit] **1.** *n.* a kind of cereal grain grown for its seeds. (No pl.) **2.** *n.* the seed of ①, ground to make flour. (No pl. Number is expressed with *grain(s) of wheat.*) **3.** *adj.* made from ②.

wheel [ˈʍil] **1.** *n.* a sturdy circular object that turns around a central point and is connected to an axle. **2.** *n.* the round object used to steer a vehicle. (Short for *steering wheel.*)

wheelbarrow [ˈʍil bɛr o] *n.* an open container attached to a frame with one wheel in front and handles behind to steer it.

wheelchair [ˈʍil tʃɛr] *n.* a chair that has wheels instead of legs, usually two large wheels in back and two small ones in front, for people who are unable to walk.

when [ˈʍɛn] **1.** *interrog.* at what time? **2.** *conj.* at the time that; at that certain time. **3.** *conj.* considering [the fact that]; as.

whenever [ʍɛn ˈɛv ɚ] **1.** *conj.* at any time; at whatever time. **2.** *conj.* every time; each time. **3.** *interrog.* when?; at what time? (Used for emphasis.)

where [ˈʍɛr] **1.** *interrog.* in what place?; at what place?; in which location? **2.** *conj.* in that place; at that place; in that location. **3.** *conj.* in the case; such that; wherever.

whereas [ʍɛr ˈæz] **1.** *conj.* but; however; on the other hand; on the contrary. **2.** *conj.* since; because. (Used to introduce legal documents.)

where's [ˈʍɛrz] **1.** *cont.* where has, where HAS is an auxiliary. **2.** *cont.* where is.

whether [ˈʍɛð ɚ] *conj.* a form used with some kinds of questions when more than one answer is possible; if.

which [ˈʍɪtʃ] **1.** *interrog.* a form used in questions to ask about or distinguish among specific people or things; what one or ones? (E.g., *Which students were late?* Used before a noun.) **2.** *adj.* a form used to distinguish among people or things mentioned or known from the context; what [one or ones]; the [one or ones]. (Prenominal only.) **3.** *pron.* a form used to show the differences among people or things already mentioned or known from the context; what one or ones; the one or ones. (Treated as sg or pl.) **4.** *pron.* a form used after a word, phrase, or clause and serving to introduce extra, incidental, or descriptive information about the word, phrase, or clause rather than information needed to identify it; the one or ones that. (Treated as sg or pl.) **5.** *pron.* a form used after a word or a phrase and serving to introduce special, contrastive, or distinctive information about the word or phrase; the one or ones that. (Treated as sg or pl.)

whiff [ˈʍɪf] **1.** *n.* an odor. **2.** *n.* a bit of an odor sensed by the nose.

while ['ʍɑɪl] **1.** *conj.* during that time; during a certain time that; at the same time as that. **2.** *conj.* and, in contrast; although; on the other hand; and; whereas. **3.** *n.* a length of time. (No pl.)

whim ['ʍɪm] *n.* a sudden wish to do something, especially an unreasonable wish.

whimper ['ʍɪm pɚ] **1.** *n.* a small, quiet moan or cry, especially from someone or something that is afraid. **2.** *iv.* to moan quietly, as though one were afraid. **3.** *tv.* to say something while whimpering, as in ②. (The object can be a clause with THAT ⑦.)

whine ['ʍɑɪn] **1.** *n.* a cry not made with the mouth open very much; a soft, high-pitched cry. **2.** *iv.* to complain in a sad, annoying, childish voice. **3.** *tv.* to make a complaint in a sad, annoying, childish voice. (The object can be a clause with THAT ⑦.)

whip ['ʍɪp] **1.** *n.* a long strip of leather, usually attached to a handle, used for hitting people or animals. **2.** *n.* a member of a political party who organizes and manages members of the party serving in a legislative body. **3.** *tv.* to hit or strike someone or an animal with ①. **4.** *tv.* to beat eggs or cream until the mixture bubbles into a froth. **5.** *tv.* to beat an opponent in a contest or game by a wide margin. (Fig. on ③.)

whirl ['ʍɚl] **1.** *tv.* to move something around quickly in a circle; to spin something quickly. **2.** *iv.* to move around quickly in a circle; to spin quickly. **3.** *n.* an act of spinning around quickly. **4.** *n.* very busy movement or activity. (Fig. on ③.)

whisk ['ʍɪsk] **1.** *n.* a wire tool for whipping eggs, cream, and other mixtures. **2.** *tv.* to whip eggs, cream, and other mixtures into a froth.

whisker ['ʍɪs kɚ] *n.* a hair that grows from near the mouth of a cat and certain other animals; a hair that is part of a beard.

whiskey ['ʍɪs ki] **1.** *n.* a strong alcohol for drinking made from corn, rye, or other grains. (Pl only for types and instances.) **2.** *n.* a glass of ①; a drink of ①.

whisper ['ʍɪs pɚ] **1.** *tv.* to say something with the breath only, not using the full voice. (The object can be a clause with THAT ⑦.) **2.** *iv.* to speak as in ①. **3.** *n.* speaking done with the breath only, not using the voice.

whistle ['ʍɪs əl] **1.** *n.* a small metal or plastic instrument that makes a shrill, high-pitched sound when one blows air into it. **2.** *n.* a shrill, high-pitched sound made by passing air through a small opening between one's lips or through ①. **3.** *tv.* to make a melody with a

577

shrill, high-pitched sound made by passing air through one's lips.
4. *iv.* to make a shrill, high-pitched sound by passing air through ①
or through one's lips.

white ['ʍaɪt] **1.** *n.* the color of salt or milk. (Pl only for types and
instances.) **2.** *n.* someone who has light-colored skin, usually persons
of European descent. **3.** *n.* the clear part of an egg, which turns ①
when it is cooked. **4.** *adj.* having the color of salt or milk. (Adv:
whitely. Comp: *whiter;* sup: *whitest.*) **5.** *adj.* pale. (Comp: *whiter;* sup:
whitest.) **6.** *adj.* [of people, usually of European descent or their skin]
light-colored. (See also CAUCASIAN. Comp: *whiter;* sup: *whitest.*)

whiten ['ʍaɪt n] **1.** *tv.* to cause something to become white; to make
something white. **2.** *iv.* to turn pale.

whittle ['ʍɪt əl] **1.** *tv.* to cut pieces of wood away a little bit at a time
with a knife; to shave off small strips from a piece of wood. **2.** *tv.* to
carve an object from wood, cutting away small pieces.

whiz ['ʍɪz] **1.** *iv.* [for something] to move very quickly through the
air while making a sound as it passes by someone or something. **2.** *n.*
an expert; someone who is very skilled at something; someone who
can do something quickly and very well. (Fig. on ①.)

who ['hu] **1.** *interrog.* what or which person or people? (The possessive form is WHOSE. The objective form is WHOM.) **2.** *pron.* a person or
the people mentioned. (Standard English requires WHOM instead of
WHO as the object of a verb or preposition. WHO can be used in *restrictive* and *nonrestrictive clauses.*)

who'd ['hud] **1.** *cont.* who had, where HAD is an auxiliary. **2.** *cont.* who
would.

whoever [hu 'ɛv ɚ] **1.** *pron.* anyone; any person who. **2.** *interrog.* who?

whole ['hol] **1.** *adj.* made of the entire amount; consisting of all parts;
not divided; not separated; complete. (Adv: *wholly.*) **2.** *adj.* healthy
or the feeling of good health, in the mind or body. **3.** *adj.* not
expressed as a fraction or a decimal number. **4.** *n.* something that is
complete; something that has all of its parts; the entire amount.

wholesale ['hol sel] **1.** *adj.* [of products] sold in large numbers to
people who will sell the products one at a time to customers. (Compare this with RETAIL.) **2.** *adj.* done on a large scale; in large amounts.
(Fig. on ①.) **3.** *adv.* in large quantities as in ① and at a favorable
price.

wholesaler ['hol sel ɚ] *n.* someone who buys products from a manufacturer and sells them to store owners.

who'll [ˈhul] *cont.* who will.

wholly [ˈho li] *adv.* completely; entirely; totally.

whom [ˈhum] *pron.* the objective form of WHO. (Not common in informal English. See the comments at WHO.)

whomever [hum ˈɛv ɚ] the objective case of WHOEVER.

who's [ˈhuz] **1.** *cont.* who has, where HAS is an auxiliary. **2.** *cont.* who is.

whose [ˈhuz] **1.** *pron.* the possessive form of WHO and WHICH; of whom or of which. (WHOSE can be used in *restrictive* and *nonrestrictive clauses.*) **2.** *interrog.* a form used to determine the identity of the person who owns, possesses, or is associated with something; of or belonging to whom?

why [ˈmaɪ] **1.** *interrog.* for what reason? **2.** [ˈmaɪ] *conj.* the reason that; the reason for which. **3.** [ˈwaɪ] *interj.* a form used to express surprise, dismay, disgust, or some other emotion.

wicked [ˈwɪk əd] *adj.* evil; very bad; vile. (Adv: *wickedly.*)

wide [ˈwaɪd] **1.** *adj.* not narrow; broad. (Adv: *widely.* Comp: *wider*; sup: *widest.*) **2.** *adj.* being a certain distance from side to side; measured from side to side. (E.g., *a yard wide.* Follows the measurement of width. Comp: *wider.*) **3.** *adj.* large in size, range, or scope. (Adv: *widely.* Comp: *wider*; sup: *widest.*) **4.** *adv.* as far as possible; to the greatest amount or extent.

widow [ˈwɪd o] *n.* a woman whose husband has died, and who has not married again.

widower [ˈwɪd o ɚ] *n.* a man whose wife has died, and who has not married again.

width [ˈwɪdθ] *n.* distance, from side to side. (No pl.)

wield [ˈwild] **1.** *tv.* to hold and use something, especially a weapon. **2.** *tv.* to have and use power, especially as though it were a weapon. (Fig. on ①.)

wiener [ˈwin ɚ] *n.* a beef or pork sausage, often eaten on a long bun.

wife [ˈwaɪf] *n., irreg.* the woman a man is married to. (Pl: WIVES.)

wig [ˈwɪg] *n.* a head covering simulating one's own hair; a head covering made of real or artificial hair.

wiggle [ˈwɪg əl] **1.** *iv.* to move back and forth in quick, little movements. **2.** *tv.* to cause something to move back and forth in quick, little movements.

wiggly [ˈwɪg li] *adj.* shaking or squirming.

wild ['waɪld] **1.** *adj.* growing or living in nature; not tame; not grown or kept by a human. (Adv: *wildly.* Comp: *wilder;* sup: *wildest.*) **2.** *adj.* not in control; out of control; lacking control; reckless. (Adv: *wildly.* Comp: *wilder;* sup: *wildest.*)

wilderness ['wɪl dɚ nəs] *n.* a large area of land with no human residents. (No pl. Number is expressed with *wilderness area(s).*)

wildfire ['waɪld faɪr] *n.* an uncontrollable fire or flame in the outdoors.

wildflower ['waɪld flaʊ ɚ] *n.* a flower that is not grown by a person; a flower that grows in nature.

wildlife ['waɪld laɪf] *n.* wild animals as a group, especially as they live in their natural condition; wild plants and animals as a group. (No pl form in this sense.)

will ['wɪl] **1.** *interrog.* a form used with a verb to indicate politeness by turning a command into a question. (See also WOULD ③.) **2.** *aux.* a form used with a verb to indicate the future tense. (See also SHALL. See WOULD ① for the past-tense form. Reduced to *'ll* in contractions.) **3.** *aux.* a form used with a verb to command someone to do something. **4.** *aux.* can; be able to. **5.** *aux.* a form used to express something that is always true or something that always happens. **6.** *n.* the power one has in one's mind to do what one wants to do; an intention to do something. **7.** *n.* a legal document that details how one's assets will be distributed after one's death. **8.** *tv.* to leave something to someone in one's ⑦.

willful ['wɪl fʊl] **1.** *adj.* intended; meant; done on purpose. (Adv: *willfully.*) **2.** *adj.* stubborn. (Adv: *willfully.*)

willing ['wɪl ɪŋ] *adj.* eagerly ready to do something; happily prepared to do something or to be of service. (Adv: *willingly.*)

willow ['wɪl o] **1.** *n.* a tree that has many long, thin, drooping branches with long, thin leaves. **2.** *n.* wood from ①. (No pl.) **3.** *adj.* made of or from ②.

willpower ['wɪl paʊ ɚ] *n.* the ability to control one's will. (No pl.)

wilt ['wɪlt] **1.** *iv.* to wither; [for the leaves or branches of a plant] to lose their strength and sag downward. **2.** *iv.* [for someone] to lose energy. (Fig. on ①.) **3.** *tv.* to cause something to wither or sag as in ①.

wily ['waɪ li] *adj.* crafty; shrewd; sly; cunning. (Comp: *wilier;* sup: *wiliest.*)

win ['wɪn] **1.** *tv., irreg.* to receive or achieve first place in a contest or competition. (Pt/pp: WON.) **2.** *tv., irreg.* to achieve or earn something

580

through hard work or effort. **3.** *iv., irreg.* to be in first place in a contest or competition; to be the best in a contest. **4.** *n.* a victory; a triumph.

wind 1. ['wɪnd] *n.* the movement of air; moving air. (Pl with the same meaning, but not countable.) **2.** ['wɪnd] *n.* breath or the ability to breathe. (No pl.) **3.** ['wɪnd] *tv.* to cause someone to be out of breath; to cause someone to have a hard time breathing. **4.** ['waɪnd] *tv., irreg.* to tighten the spring of a device such as a watch or a clock. (Pt/pp: WOUND.) **5.** ['waɪnd] *iv., irreg.* to move in one direction and then another; to move in twists and turns.

winded ['wɪn dɪd] **1.** *adj.* out of breath; gasping for breath. **2.** pt/pp of WIND ③.

windmill ['wɪnd mɪl] *n.* a structure that uses metal or wooden blades to capture the power of the wind.

window ['wɪn do] **1.** *n.* an opening in a wall or door, usually covered with a sheet of glass, that allows light and air into a place. **2.** *n.* the sheet of glass that covers an opening in a wall or door.

windowpane ['wɪn do pen] *n.* the sheet of glass that covers an opening in a wall or door.

window-shopping *iv.* the habit or practice of looking at goods in shop windows or in stores without actually buying anything.

windowsill ['wɪn do sɪl] *n.* the flat ledge at the bottom of a window.

windpipe ['wɪnd paɪp] *n.* the tube in the body that allows air to travel between the mouth and the lungs.

windshield ['wɪnd ʃild] *n.* the large, curved piece of glass in the front of a car, truck, or bus.

windy ['wɪn di] *adj.* having a lot of wind; with a lot of wind. (Comp: *windier;* sup: *windiest.*)

wine ['waɪn] *n.* a drink that contains alcohol and is made from fruit juice, especially the juice of grapes. (Pl only for types and instances.)

wing ['wɪŋ] **1.** *n.* one of the upper limbs of a bird, or a flying mammal, used for flight. **2.** *n.* an extension on the side of an insect's body, used for flight. **3.** *n.* a structure on an airplane that stands out from its body, which allows the airplane to stay in the air during flight. **4.** *n.* a part of a building that is built out from the central or main part of the building. **5.** *tv.* to shoot a bird in the ① without killing it.

wink ['wɪŋk] **1.** *iv.* to shut and open one eye quickly, especially either as a signal or to show amusement or interest. (Compare this with

BLINK.) **2.** *n.* an act of shutting and opening one eye quickly, especially either as a signal or to show amusement or interest.

winner ['wɪn ɚ] *n.* someone or something that wins.

winter ['wɪn tɚ] **1.** *n.* one of the four seasons of the year; the season between fall and spring. **2.** *adj.* concerning or associated with ①. **3.** *iv.* to live in a certain place during ①.

wipe ['waɪp] **1.** *tv.* to rub the surface of someone or something with something in order to clean or dry it. **2.** *tv.* to remove something liquid from a surface, using something absorbent. **3.** ~ **off** to remove something from someone or something by wiping.

wire ['waɪɚ] **1.** *n.* a thin metal strand; a thread of metal, especially one used to transmit electricity. (No pl.) **2.** *n.* a length or segment of ①. **3.** *n.* a message that is sent by telegram. **4.** *tv.* to send a message or money by telegraph. (The object can be a clause with THAT ⑦.) **5.** *tv.* to install ① in a building for electricity; to install or adjust any kind of ①. **6.** *tv.* to fasten or secure something with ①. **7.** *tv.* to install hidden microphones in a place so that one can record what is said there.

wisdom ['wɪz dəm] *n.* intelligence, especially intelligence that is a result of experience; the knowledge required to make good decisions; the quality of being wise. (No pl.)

wise ['waɪz] *adj.* able to make good decisions; showing good judgment; intelligent. (Adv: *wisely.* Comp: *wiser*; sup: *wisest*.)

wish ['wɪʃ] **1.** *n.* a desire for something. **2.** *tv.* to express ①; to hope that something happens. (The object is a clause with THAT ⑦.) **3.** *iv.* to have a desire to do something.

wit ['wɪt] **1.** *n.* the ability to understand ideas quickly and make intelligent, clever, and funny comments about them. (No pl.) **2.** *n.* someone who has the ability to understand ideas quickly and make intelligent, clever, and funny comments about them.

witch ['wɪtʃ] **1.** *n.* someone, usually a woman, who has or claims to have magical powers or who practices a pagan religion. **2.** *n.* a mean or ugly woman. (Derogatory.)

with ['wɪθ] **1.** *prep.* among someone or something; including someone or something; in the company of someone or something; in addition to someone or something. **2.** *prep.* by means of something; by using something. **3.** *prep.* showing a quality or characteristic; showing a state or emotion.

582

withdraw [wɪθ 'drɔ] **1.** *tv., irreg.* to remove someone or something from someplace; to take someone or something away or back from someplace. (Pt: WITHDREW; pp: WITHDRAWN.) **2.** *iv., irreg.* to move away from someplace; to step back; to step away; to leave; to go away. **3.** *iv., irreg.* to no longer be a participant in a race; to drop out of a race.

withdrawn [wɪθ 'drɔn] **1.** pp of WITHDRAW. **2.** *adj.* quiet, reserved, and unemotional; not likely to talk to others about one's feelings.

withdrew [wɪθ 'dru] pt of WITHDRAW.

wither ['wɪð ɚ] **1.** *iv.* to shrivel; to wilt; [for a plant] to turn brown, sag, and dry out. **2.** *tv.* to cause a plant to shrivel, droop, or wilt; to cause a plant to turn brown and dry out.

withheld [wɪθ 'hɛld] pt/pp of WITHHOLD.

withhold [wɪθ 'hold] *tv., irreg.* to hold or keep something back [from someone or something]. (Pt/pp: WITHHELD.)

within [wɪθ 'ɪn] **1.** *prep.* inside someone or something; in or into the inside part of someone or something. **2.** *prep.* not beyond a specific boundary; between certain limits. **3.** *adv.* into the inside of someone or something.

without [wɪθ 'ɑʊt] *prep.* not including someone or something; lacking someone or something.

withstand [wɪθ 'stænd] *tv., irreg.* to resist someone or something; to oppose someone or something; not to yield to someone or something. (Pt/pp: WITHSTOOD.)

withstood [wɪθ 'stʊd] pt/pp of WITHSTAND.

witness ['wɪt nəs] **1.** *n.* someone who sees something happen; someone who is in the same place where something happens; a spectator. **2.** *n.* someone who sees the signing of a legal document. **3.** *tv.* to see something happen; to be in the same place where something happens. **4.** *tv.* to sign a legal document as a way of swearing that one has watched another person, who is directly affected by the document, sign it, and thus show that the other person's signature is real.

witty ['wɪt i] *adj.* full of wit; cleverly comical. (Adv: *wittily.* Comp: *wittier*; sup: *wittiest.*)

wives ['wɑɪvz] pl of WIFE.

wizard ['wɪz ɚd] **1.** *n.* someone, usually a male, who has or claims to have magical powers. **2.** *n.* an expert; someone who is very skilled at something. (Fig. on ①.)

woe ['wo] *n.* sorrow; sad trouble; grief. (No pl form in this sense.)

woke ['wok] a pt of WAKE.

woken ['wok ən] a pp of WAKE.

wolf ['wʊlf] *n.*, *irreg.* a wild animal (related to the dog) that eats meat and travels in groups. (Pl: WOLVES.)

wolves ['wʊlvz] pl of WOLF.

woman ['wʊm ən] **1.** *n.*, *irreg.* an adult female person; an adult female human being. (Pl: WOMEN.) **2.** the *adj.* use of ①.

womb ['wum] *n.* the organ in women and certain other mammals where the developing baby is protected and fed until birth.

women ['wɪm ən] pl of WOMAN.

won ['wʌn] pt/pp of WIN.

wonder ['wʌn dɚ] **1.** *n.* someone or something that is amazing, surprising, or like a miracle. **2.** *tv.* to wish to know something; to want to know something. **3.** *adj.* very good, helpful, or of great benefit.

wonderful ['wʌn dɚ fʊl] *adj.* very good; amazing; remarkable; marvelous. (Adv: *wonderfully.*)

wonderland ['wʌn dɚ lænd] *n.* an area or place that is wonderful.

won't ['wont] *cont.* will not.

woo ['wu] **1.** *tv.* to court someone with the intention of marrying. **2.** *tv.* to encourage someone or a group to cooperate, join something, or buy something.

wood ['wʊd] **1.** *n.* the hard substance that trees make as they grow. (Pl only for types and instances.) **2.** *n.* a kind or type of ①. **3.** *n.* a small forest; an area where there are many trees. (Usually pl, but not countable. The meaning is the same for the sg and the pl.) **4.** the *adj.* use of ①, ②, or ③.

wooden ['wʊd n] **1.** *adj.* made of wood. **2.** *adj.* stiff; not easily moved; not moving easily; not flexible. (Fig. on ①. Adv: *woodenly.*)

woodland ['wʊd lænd] *n.* an area of land that is covered with trees. (Sg or pl with the same meaning, but not countable.)

woodpecker ['wʊd pɛk ɚ] *n.* a bird that has a long, sharp beak for piercing holes in trees and a long tongue to catch insects inside the tree.

woodwind ['wʊd wɪnd] *n.* a group of musical instruments, many of which are made of wood or used to be made of wood, and many of which are played by blowing air across a reed.

woodwork ['wʊd wɚk] *n.* something that is made of wood, especially the trim on the inside of a house or building. (No pl.)

woody ['wʊd i] **1.** *adj.* covered with woods; covered with trees. (Comp: *woodier;* sup: *woodiest.*) **2.** *adj.* [of a plant] containing wood. (Comp: *woodier;* sup: *woodiest.*)

wool ['wʊl] **1.** *n.* the soft, curly hair of sheep and goats. (Pl only for types and instances.) **2.** *n.* thread, yarn, or fabric made from ①. (No pl.) **3.** *adj.* made from ②; WOOLEN.

woolen ['wʊl ən] *adj.* made of wool.

word ['wɚd] **1.** *n.* a speech sound or group of speech sounds that has a particular meaning; a written symbol or a group of written symbols that represent a speech sound or group of speech sounds that has a particular meaning. **2.** *tv.* to express something by choosing ① carefully.

wordy ['wɚd i] *adj.* having too many words; using more words than necessary to express something. (Adv: *wordily.* Comp: *wordier;* sup: *wordiest.*)

wore ['wor] pt of WEAR.

work ['wɚk] **1.** *n.* an activity that requires effort. (No pl.) **2.** *n.* the effort required to do an activity. (No pl.) **3.** *n.* something that is a result of effort or energy; a piece of music or art. **4.** *n.* a job; an occupation; a career; what one does for a living; what a person does to make money. (No pl.) **5.** *n.* the place where one's job is located; the job site. (No pl.) **6.** *iv.* to be employed; to have a job; to labor; to earn money at a job. **7.** *iv.* to function properly; to operate properly. **8.** *tv.* to cause something to function as intended. **9.** *tv.* to cause someone or something to operate or function; to cause someone or something to be active; to cause something to use energy. **10.** *tv.* to plow or farm land. **11.** ~ **on** [for a physician] to treat someone; [for a surgeon] to operate on someone. **12.** ~ **on** to repair or tinker with something.

workbook ['wɚk bʊk] *n.* a textbook for students, often including pages that assignments can be written on.

worker ['wɚk ɚ] *n.* someone who works; someone who is employed.

workout ['wɚk aʊt] *n.* a period of physical exercise.

world ['wɚld] **1.** *n.* the planet earth. **2.** *n.* the people who live on the planet earth; the human race. **3.** *n.* a planet other than earth, especially as the source of other life forms. **4.** *n.* an area of human activity, thought, or interest.

worldwide [ˈwɚld ˈwaɪd] *adj.* found or occurring throughout the world; involving everyone in the world.

worm [ˈwɚm] *n.* any of numerous small, soft, tube-shaped animals having no legs or head, including some that crawl underground and others that live as parasites in animals or people.

worn [ˈworn] **1.** pp of WEAR. **2.** *adj.* reduced in value or usefulness owing to wear.

worn-out [ˈworn ˈaʊt] **1.** *adj.* completely reduced in value or usefulness because of wear. **2.** *adj.* very tired; exhausted.

worry [ˈwɚ i] **1.** *n.* a feeling of anxiety; a fear of trouble. (Pl only for types and instances.) **2.** *n.* someone or something that causes ①. **3.** *tv.* to be anxious that something bad might happen; to suspect that something bad might happen. (The object is a clause with THAT ⑦.) **4.** *tv.* to cause someone to feel anxiety or to fear trouble.

worse [ˈwɚs] **1.** *adj.* more bad; less good; inferior. (The comp. form of BAD.) **2.** *adv.* in a way that is ① than some other way. (The comp. form of *badly*.)

worsen [ˈwɚs ən] **1.** *tv.* to make something worse. **2.** *iv.* to become worse. **3.** *iv.* to become more sick.

worship [ˈwɚ ʃɪp] **1.** *tv.* to honor someone or something greatly; to adore someone or something. (Pt/pp: *worshiped*. Pres. part.: *worshiping*.) **2.** *iv.* to attend a church service. (Pt/pp: *worshiped*. Pres. part.: *worshiping*.) **3.** *n.* what is done at a church service; the praise and honor of a spirit, ancestor, god, object, or person. (No pl.)

worst [ˈwɚst] *adj.* most bad; least good; most inferior. (The sup. of BAD.)

worth [ˈwɚθ] **1.** *n.* the value of something; the amount of money that something could sell for. (No pl.) **2.** *n.* the importance of someone or something; the degree to which something is able to be used. (No pl.) **3.** *n.* the amount of something that can be bought for a specific amount of money. (No pl.)

worthless [ˈwɚθ ləs] *adj.* having no value or importance; useless. (Adv: *worthlessly*.)

worthy [ˈwɚ ði] *adj.* deserving one's time, energy, or attention; deserving; useful; having value or importance. (Adv: *worthily*. Comp: *worthier*; sup: *worthiest*.)

would [ˈwʊd] **1.** *aux.* a form used as the pt of WILL to express the future from a time in the past, especially in indirect quotations or in constructions where other past-tense verbs are used. (Contraction: -'d.)

2. *aux.* a form used to express something that happened many times in the past. **3.** *aux.* a form used instead of WILL ① to make commands more polite by turning them into questions. (Contraction: -'d. See also WILL ①; using *would* is usually more polite than using *will.*)

wouldn't ['wʊd nt] *cont.* would not.

would've ['wʊd əv] *cont.* would have, where HAVE is an auxiliary.

wound 1. ['waʊnd] pt/pp of WIND ④ and ⑤. **2.** ['wund] *n.* an injury where the skin is torn or punctured. **3.** ['wund] *n.* an injury to one's feelings. (Fig. on ②.) **4.** ['wund] *tv.* to injure someone; to cause someone to have ② or ③.

wove ['woʊv] pt of WEAVE.

woven ['woʊ vən] pp of WEAVE.

wrath ['ræθ] *n.* severe anger, especially from someone with a lot of power. (No pl.)

wreath ['riθ] *n., irreg.* a decoration of flowers and leaves arranged in a certain shape, especially a circle. (Pl: ['riθs] or ['riðz].)

wreathe ['rið] *tv.* to make a circle around something.

wreck ['rɛk] **1.** *n.* a serious accident, especially where something is destroyed. **2.** *n.* a ruined vehicle that remains after a serious accident. **3.** *n.* someone or something that is a mess. (Fig. on ②.) **4.** *tv.* to destroy something.

wreckage ['rɛk ɪdʒ] *n.* whatever remains after a serious accident or disaster. (No pl. Treated as sg.)

wrench ['rɛntʃ] **1.** *n.* a tool that turns nuts, bolts, pipes, and other objects into or out of position. **2.** *tv.* to twist or pull something with force. **3.** *tv.* to injure a part of the body by twisting it or pulling it.

wrestle ['rɛs əl] **1.** *tv.* to force someone or something loose, down, away, etc., with force. **2.** *iv.* to participate in a sport in which one WRESTLES one's opponent down as in ①.

wring ['rɪŋ] **1.** *tv., irreg.* to squeeze or twist something very forcefully. (Pt/pp: WRUNG.) **2.** ~ **out** to squeeze and twist something to remove liquid. **3.** ~ **out of** to remove water from something by twisting and squeezing it very forcefully.

wringer ['rɪŋ ɚ] *n.* an old-fashioned washing machine that removes water from clothes by pressing them as the clothes are passed between two rollers.

wrinkle ['rɪŋ kəl] **1.** *n.* a crease; a small fold or line, such as in clothing that has not been ironed or on the skin of an old person. **2.** *iv.* to become creased; to get small lines in one's skin or on the surface of something. **3.** *tv.* to cause someone's skin or the surface of something to have ①; to cause creases, folds, or lines to form on the surface of someone or something.

wrist ['rɪst] *n.* the part of the body where the hand joins the lower part of the arm.

write ['raɪt] **1.** *tv., irreg.* to make words or symbols on a surface with a pen, pencil, chalk, etc. (Pt: WROTE; pp: WRITTEN.) **2.** *tv., irreg.* to put thoughts or ideas into writing; to organize words or symbols into meaningful prose. **3.** *iv., irreg.* to mark on a surface with a pen, pencil, chalk, etc., as with ②. **4.** *iv., irreg.* to work by creating the content for books, articles, movies, plays, or other texts; to be an author; to be a writer. **5.** *iv., irreg.* to prepare and send [a letter or note to someone]. (E.g., *Please write when you can.*)

writer ['raɪt ɚ] *n.* an author who writes for a living; someone who has written something.

writhe ['raɪð] *iv.* to twist and turn in pain or as though in pain.

writing ['raɪt ɪŋ] **1.** *n.* making sentences, words, or letters with a pen, a pencil, chalk, or other writing instrument. (No pl.) **2.** *n.* sentences, words, or letters made with a pen, a pencil, chalk, or other writing instrument. (No pl.) **3.** *n.* something that is written; a book, poem, or other document. (Sometimes pl with the same meaning.)

written ['rɪt n] **1.** pp of WRITE. **2.** *adj.* placed in writing; printed or spelled out in writing.

wrong ['rɔŋ] **1.** *adj.* not correct; not true; mistaken; in error. (Adv: *wrongly.*) **2.** *adj.* bad; evil; illegal; immoral; not lawful. (Adv: *wrongly.*) **3.** *adj.* not desired; not wanted; incorrect. (Adv: *wrongly.*) **4.** *adj.* out of order; not working properly; faulty. **5.** *adv.* in a way that is ③. **6.** *n.* a bad, illegal, improper, or immoral action. **7.** *tv.* to treat someone badly or unfairly.

wrote ['rot] pt of WRITE.

wrung ['rʌŋ] pt/pp of WRING.

X

Xerox™ [ˈzɪr ɑks] *n.* a copy of a document, especially one made on a copier manufactured by Xerox™. (A protected trade name for a process used to make copies of documents.)

X-ray [ˈɛks re] **1.** *n.* a ray of energy that can pass through solid or nearly solid matter, such as the body. (Used especially to take pictures of the insides of people or objects.) **2.** *n.* a picture of the inside of a person or an object, made by passing ① through the person or object onto film. **3.** *tv.* to take a picture of the inside of a person or an object using ①.

xylophone [ˈzaɪ lə fon] *n.* a musical instrument made of a series of wooden bars of different sizes, each of which makes a different note when struck with a small wooden hammer.

Y

yacht ['jɑt] **1.** *n.* a large boat or ship used for pleasure or racing. (Powered by sails, engines, or both.) **2.** *iv.* to travel somewhere on water in ①.

yam ['jæm] **1.** *n.* a vegetable similar to the potato, grown in tropical areas. **2.** *n.* a sweet potato, which is orange and does not taste like a potato.

yank ['jæŋk] **1.** *tv.* to pull someone or something quickly, with force. **2.** *n.* a quick pull; a sharp tug.

yard ['jɑrd] **1.** *n.* a unit of measurement of length equal to 36 inches, 3 feet, or about 91.44 centimeters. **2.** *n.* the land that surrounds a house or other dwelling.

yardstick ['jɑrd stɪk] **1.** *n.* a ruler that is 36 inches—that is, one yard—long. **2.** *n.* something that other things are compared with; a standard. (Fig. on ①.)

yarn ['jɑrn] **1.** *n.* thick, soft thread that is used for things like knitting or weaving. (Number is expressed with *ball(s)* or *skein(s) of yarn.*) **2.** *n.* a tale; a story that is not completely true.

yawn ['jɔn] **1.** *iv.* to stretch one's mouth open and breathe in and out slowly and deeply, especially when one is tired or bored. **2.** *iv.* [for something like a hole] to have a very wide opening. (Fig. on ①.) **3.** *n.* an act of opening one's mouth, as in ①.

year ['jɪr] **1.** *n.* 12 months; 365.25 days; the time it takes for earth to revolve around the sun. **2.** *n.* a full or partial ① spent doing a certain activity. **3.** *n.* a particular level of study in a school, college, or university.

yearly ['jɪr li] **1.** *adj.* happening once a year; occurring each year. **2.** *adv.* once a year; each year; every year.

yeast ['jist] *n.* a very small fungus that causes bread to rise and is also used to make alcohol. (Pl only for types and instances.)

yell ['jɛl] **1.** *tv.* to say something loudly; to scream something; to shout something. **2.** *iv.* to speak loudly; to scream; to shout. **3.** *n.* a loud cry; a shout.

yellow ['jɛl o] **1.** *n.* the color of a ripe lemon or of the yolk of an egg. (Pl only for types and instances.) **2.** the *adj.* use of ①. (Comp: yel-

590

lower; sup: *yellowest.*) **3.** *adj.* timid; scared to do something. (Informal. Comp: *yellower;* sup: *yellowest.*)

yelp ['jɛlp] **1.** *n.* a short, high-pitched bark; a short, high-pitched shout of pain or emotion. **2.** *iv.* to make ①.

yen ['jɛn] **1.** *n.* a strong desire; a strong feeling of wanting something. (No pl.) **2.** *n., irreg.* the basic unit of money in Japan. (Also ¥. Pl: *yen.*)

yes ['jɛs] **1.** *n.* a statement showing that someone agrees with something or gives permission to do something. **2.** *n.* an act of voting showing that one agrees with the proposal. **3.** *adv.* a word showing approval, consent, or willingness. **4.** *adv.* a word emphasizing a positive statement, especially when denying a negative one. (E.g., *Yes, it is!*)

yesterday ['jɛs tɚ de] **1.** *n.* the day before today. **2.** *adv.* on the day before today.

yet ['jɛt] **1.** *adv.* up to a certain point in time; by a certain point in time; as of a certain point in time. **2.** *adv.* eventually, even with barriers and delays. **3.** *adv.* still; even; even more. **4.** *adv.* and in spite of that; however; nevertheless. **5.** *conj.* but; however; nevertheless; although.

yield ['jild] **1.** *iv.* to bend, break, or move out of the way because of someone or something that is stronger or more powerful. **2.** *iv.* to surrender to someone or something, especially someone or something that is stronger or more powerful; to submit to someone or something. **3.** *iv.* to allow other traffic or people to have the right of way; to allow another vehicle or person to move first. **4.** *tv.* [for plants or animals] to supply or produce something such as food. **5.** *n.* the amount of something that is produced.

yoke ['jok] **1.** *n.* a frame of wood that fits around the necks of animals so they can pull something heavy that is attached to the frame. (Compare this with YOLK.) **2.** *tv.* to put ① on oxen or other strong animals.

yolk ['jok] **1.** *n.* the round, yellow part inside an egg. (Compare this with YOKE. E.g., *use four egg yolks.*) **2.** *n.* the substance of ①. (No pl. E.g., *spilled some egg yolk.*)

yonder ['jɑn dɚ] *adv.* over there.

you ['ju] *pron.* the second-person pronoun, sg and pl.

you'd ['jud] **1.** *cont.* you would. **2.** *cont.* you had, where HAD is an auxiliary.

you'll ['jul] *cont.* you will.

591

young [ˈjʌŋ] **1.** *adj.* in the early part of life; not old; having been alive for a short period of time as compared with an average age. (Comp: *younger;* sup: *youngest.*) **2.** *adj.* new; in an early stage of development; recently formed or started. (Comp: *younger;* sup: *youngest.*) **3.** *n.* the offspring of an animal or a human. (No pl. Treated as pl. Countable, but not usually used for one offspring.)

youngster [ˈjʌŋ stɚ] *n.* a young person; a child.

your [ˈjʊɚ] *pron.* the possessive form of YOU, the second-person sg and pl pronoun; belonging to the person(s) being spoken or written to. (Used as a modifier before a noun. Compare this with YOU'RE.)

you're [ˈjʊɚ] *cont.* you are. (Compare this with YOUR.)

yours [ˈjʊɚz] *pron.* the possessive form of YOU, the second-person sg and pl pronoun; the one or ones belonging to the person(s) being spoken or written to. (Used in place of a noun.)

yourself [jʊɚ ˈsɛlf] **1.** *pron.* the reflexive form of the sg form of YOU. **2.** *pron.* a strong form of YOU [sg].

yourselves [jʊɚ ˈsɛlvz] **1.** *pron.* the reflexive form of the pl of YOU. **2.** *pron.* a strong form of YOU [pl].

youth [ˈjuθ] **1.** *n.* the quality of being young. (No pl.) **2.** *n.* the period of time when one is a child or teenager. (No pl.) **3.** *n.* children or teenagers, as a group. (No pl. Treated as pl, but not countable.) **4.** *n.* someone who is young, especially a male; a child or teenager.

you've [ˈjuv] *cont.* you have, where HAVE is an auxiliary.

yummy [ˈjʌm i] *adj.* having a good taste; delicious. (Informal. Comp: *yummier;* sup: *yummiest.*)

Z

zeal ['zil] *n.* a strong passion for a belief or cause; excitement. (No pl.)

zebra ['zi brə] *n., irreg.* a horselike mammal that has a whitish hide with dark brown or black stripes. (Pl: *zebra* or *zebras*.)

zenith ['zi nəθ] *n.* the highest possible point.

zephyr ['zɛf ɚ] *n.* a gentle wind; a breeze.

zero ['zi ro] **1.** *n.* the number 0. (Pl ends in *-s* or *-es*.) **2.** *n.* nothing. (No pl.) **3.** ~ **in** to aim directly at someone or something.

zest ['zɛst] *n.* enjoyment, especially for life; excitement. (No pl.)

zinc ['zɪŋk] *n.* a metallic element. (No pl.)

zip ['zɪp] **1.** *tv.* to open or close something, using a zipper. **2.** *iv.* to move somewhere very quickly. **3.** *n.* energy; vigor. (Informal. No pl.)

zip code ['zɪp kod] *n.* one of the five-digit or nine-digit numbers that is part of the United States Postal Service's postal coding system. (An acronym for *Zoning Improvement Plan*.)

zipper ['zɪp ɚ] **1.** *n.* a fastener made of two strips of tiny teeth that lock together when a sliding piece is moved over them. **2.** *tv.* to zip something; to open or close something using ①.

zone ['zon] **1.** *n.* an area, especially one that is different in some way from nearby areas. **2.** *tv.* to divide a city into different areas limited only to certain uses; to limit an area to certain uses.

zoo ['zu] *n.* a place where wild animals are kept so that they can be seen by people.

zookeeper ['zu kip ɚ] *n.* someone who takes care of animals at a zoo.

Important Lists of Words

These are important lists of words that can be consulted quickly. For further information or definitions, each word should be looked up in this dictionary.

List A

Nouns defined in this dictionary that never take the plural *s*. See the entry heads listed for details.

admiration	chess	elegance	health
advice	citizenship	employment	hockey
anybody	clothing	endurance	homework
anyone	confusion	equipment	housework
anything	consent	esteem	hypnotism
applause	conservation	estimation	importance
appreciation	contempt	evidence	independence
arctic	courage	excellence	indigestion
arrogance	cowardice	Fahrenheit	information
assistance	dark	fame	insurance
attendance	darkness	few	intelligence
aviation	daybreak	filth	interference
awe	daylight	flesh	isolation
baggage	decay	former	jazz
bathwater	destruction	freight	jewelry
blackness	devout	frostbite	knowledge
bliss	digestion	fun	laughter
bloodshed	diplomacy	furniture	leakage
bookkeeping	dirt	fuzz	left
bowling	disgust	glamour	legislation
bulk	dishwater	gloom	leisure
carelessness	distress	golf	lighting
cash	distrust	gratitude	lightning
Catholicism	drainage	greed	likelihood
cattle	dust	grief	lint
Centigrade	ease	grime	literacy
chaos	east	guilt	livestock
chatter	electricity	happiness	logic

595

loot	offspring	psychology	secrecy
luck	ooze	publicity	segregation
luggage	opposition	punctuation	self-confidence
machinery	overkill	quickness	self-control
magic	overtime	quiet	self-discipline
magnetism	ownership	racism	self-esteem
maintenance	oxygen	ransom	self-respect
malice	ozone	rapidity	self-service
mankind	pantyhose	readiness	selfishness
math	paradise	realism	senility
mayonnaise	parsley	reasoning	seniority
menstruation	participation	recklessness	serenity
merchandise	patience	recognition	seriousness
Midwest	peace	recreation	several
might	pep	redness	severity
mirth	perfection	refuse	sewage
misconduct	perjury	rejoicing	shame
mistrust	personnel	relief	shelving
moderation	persuasion	research	shipping
moisture	petroleum	revenge	shopping
molasses	photography	ridicule	shrewdness
moonlight	pity	rot	shrubbery
morale	plenty	rubbish	shyness
morality	plumbing	rudeness	sightseeing
more	poetry	running	significance
most	police	rust	silence
motherhood	poor	sadness	silver
much	pork	safekeeping	silverware
mucus	postage	safety	simplicity
nausea	poultry	sameness	sincerity
needlework	poverty	sanitation	sizzle
neglect	precision	sanity	skepticism
nightlife	preservation	sarcasm	skiing
nonsense	prevention	say	slander
north	prey	scenery	slavery
northeast	produce	schoolwork	sleep
northwest	progress	science	sleet
nothing	propaganda	scrutiny	slime
now	prose	scuba	slush
nutrition	prosperity	seafood	smuggling
obedience	prudence	seaside	soccer
occult	psychiatry	seclusion	software

596

some	supervision	unrest	west
something	surf	upkeep	wetness
sorcery	suspense	uranium	wilderness
south	tact	valor	willpower
southeast	teamwork	vanilla	wisdom
southwest	tennis	veal	woodwork
spaghetti	terrorism	vegetation	worship
spinach	thunder	vigor	worth
starvation	tourism	violence	wrath
static	traction	vomit	wreckage
stationery	traffic	warmth	young
storage	transportation	wastepaper	zeal
strife	trash	wealth	zest
stuff	twilight	wealthy	zinc
stupidity	underclothing	wear	
sunlight	underwear	weather	
sunshine	undoing	welfare	

List B

Nouns defined in this dictionary that can take the plural *s* resulting in the meaning "kinds, types, instances, or varieties of." See the entry heads listed for details.

action	blue	change	conquest
addition	brass	charcoal	contraction
adhesive	bronze	charm	conversation
adoption	broth	cheese	copulation
adventure	brown	cherry	cord
agony	butter	chocolate	cork
alcohol	buzz	choice	cost
amputation	cake	cider	cotton
appointment	cancer	clay	court
architecture	candy	cleaner	crime
ash	canvas	cloth	cruelty
bacon	caramel	coal	crystal
bait	cardboard	coffee	debt
ballet	cargo	combination	defense
bark	cement	comparison	denial
beer	cereal	concern	depth
behavior	chalk	confession	destiny
bleach	champagne	conflict	detention

597

dew	frosting	length	pastry
difference	fruit	liquor	payment
difficulty	fur	lotion	pecan
dip	future	loyalty	pepper
disagreement	gas	lubrication	performance
discipline	gasoline	luxury	perfume
discomfort	gauze	marble	philosophy
disgrace	glass	margarine	pick
division	glue	meal	pie
divorce	gold	meat	pigment
dough	grain	meatloaf	pine
duck	grammar	medicine	pink
dynamite	grass	membership	pitch
elm	gravel	mesh	pizza
enjoyment	gravy	metal	plaster
escape	gray	meter	plastic
evaluation	green	mileage	pleasure
evil	gum	misfortune	poison
examination	ham	mold	polish
explanation	harmony	mortar	pollen
exposure	honey	moss	popcorn
fabric	horror	motion	poplar
failure	hurt	mousse	posture
fantasy	identification	movement	powder
fashion	immersion	mulch	power
fat	increase	mustard	prejudice
fate	indentation	mystery	primer
fear	infection	mythology	privilege
feed	influence	noise	prohibition
felt	injection	notepaper	promotion
fiber	ink	novelty	pronunciation
fiction	inspection	number	prophecy
film	intensity	oak	protection
fire	irritation	oil	pudding
flight	ivy	opinion	purple
flour	jam	orange	quarantine
foam	jelly	pain	race
foil	juice	paint	reality
food	ketchup	pardon	rebellion
force	landscape	passion	red
friendship	language	pasta	redwood
frost	leather	paste	regularity

regulation	silk	sunscreen	utterance
religion	sin	syrup	vacation
repetition	skin	tape	vaccination
resignation	smell	tea	variation
responsibility	soap	technology	variety
rhythm	soil	tension	varnish
rice	soup	terror	velocity
rope	speculation	theft	velvet
routine	speed	theology	victory
sacrifice	stain	theory	volume
salt	starch	thread	walnut
sand	stew	tile	war
sandpaper	stock	tissue	wax
satin	stone	tobacco	whiskey
satisfaction	stool	toil	white
sauce	stress	toothpaste	wine
scripture	substitution	torment	wood
seaweed	subtraction	tradition	wool
separation	success	translation	worry
shampoo	sugar	triumph	yeast
sherbet	sunblock	twine	yellow
shortening	sunburn	use	

List C

Nouns defined in this dictionary that have irregular or variable plurals. Plural variants are separated by "/". The asterisk "*" means there is a unique feature of pronunciation. See the entry heads listed for details.

aircraft, aircraft	calf, calves	elf, elves
antenna, antennas/ antennae	chairman, chairmen	elk
	child, children	emphasis, emphases
aquarium, aquaria/ aquariums	cloth*	fish
	cod	fisherman, fishermen
basis, bases	courthouse*	focus, focuses/foci
bath*	craftsman, craftsmen	foot, feet
beaver		footpath*
bookshelf, bookshelves	crisis, crises	formula, formulae/ formulas
	deer	
	die, dice	fowl
booth*	doghouse*	fungus, funguses/ fungi
buffalo	dwarf, dwarves	
cactus, cactuses/cacti		

599

gentleman, gentlemen
goldfish*
goose, geese
grandchild, grandchildren
greenhouse*
half, halves
hippopotamus, hippopotamuses/ hippopotami
hoof, hooves
house*
index, indexes/indices
knife, knives
leaf, leaves
life, lives
lighthouse*
loaf, loaves
man, men
medium, mediums/ media
mink
moose
moth*
mouse, mice

mouth*
nucleus, nuclei
oasis, oases
oath*
octopus, octopuses/ octopi
ox, oxen
parenthesis, parentheses
path*
penthouse*
perch
policeman, policemen
policewoman, policewomen
radius, radiuses/radii
rhinoceros, rhinoceros/ rhinoceroses
salesman, salesmen
salesperson, salespeople/ salespersons
saleswoman, saleswomen
salmon

scarf, scarves
schoolchild, schoolchildren
sheath*
sheep
shelf, shelves
shellfish
shrimp
snowman, snowmen
sole
sportsman, sportsmen
thief, thieves
tooth, teeth
trout
tuna, tuna/tunas
warehouse*
washcloth*
wharf, wharves
wife, wives
wolf, wolves
woman, women
wreath*
yen
zebra, zebra/zebras

List D

Transitive verbs defined in this dictionary that can take a clause beginning with *that* as an object. [As with *I know that you can do it!*] These verbs can also take other forms of direct objects. See the entry heads listed for details.

accept
admit
advertise
advise
announce
answer
anticipate

appreciate
argue
ask
assume
believe
calculate
claim

confess
confirm
consider
decide
declare
demand
deny

determine
detest
discover
dream
establish
estimate
expect

600

explain	notice	realize	shout
feel	observe	recognize	show
find	ordain	recommend	signal
foresee	parrot	regret	signify
forget	petition	relate	state
guarantee	plead	remark	stress
guess	pledge	remember	suggest
hear	preach	report	suspect
imagine	predict	request	think
indicate	prefer	require	threaten
know	prescribe	resent	urge
learn	proclaim	reveal	vow
legislate	profess	say	wail
maintain	prophesy	scream	whimper
mention	propose	scribble	whine
murmur	protest	see	whisper
note	prove	sense	wire

List E

Transitive verbs defined in this dictionary that have a clause beginning with *that* as an object. [As with *I agree that you should go.*] See the entry heads listed for details.

agree	figure	judge	reply
believe	grant	move	respond
bet	guess	note	rule
brag	hint	observe	suppose
comment	hope	pray	trust
conclude	imagine	pretend	understand
exclaim	imply	promise	wager
fear	indicate	provide	wish
feel	joke	reason	worry